23/12

7/22

12/17/62

XII

J. Guy Graham
from H.A.L. 1945

JOHN BUNYAN

HIS LIFE, TIMES, and WORK.

JOHN BUNYAN.

From Robert White's Pencil Drawing.]
(Cracherode Collection, British Museum.)

JOHN BUNYAN

(1628—1688)

HIS LIFE, TIMES, AND WORK

BY

JOHN BROWN, B.A., D.D.

(MINISTER of the CHURCH at BUNYAN MEETING, BEDFORD, FROM 1864 TO 1903)

THE TERCENTENARY EDITION

REVISED BY

FRANK MOTT HARRISON

With Marginal Notes, Addenda, and Appendices.

PROFUSELY ILLUSTRATED.

LONDON: *GLASGOW*: *BIRMINGHAM*:

THE HULBERT PUBLISHING COMPANY (LIMITED)

1928.

PRICE ONE GUINEA.

(Limited Edition.)

First Edition, 1885. *Second Edition,* 1886. *Third Edition,* 1887.
Re-printed, 1888 : 1890 : 1900.
Fourth Edition, Two Volumes (*Abridged*), 1902.
Re-printed, 1918.
New and Revised Edition (*Tercentenary*), 1928.

EDITOR'S PREFACE.

John Bunyan is a personality still dear to the English-speaking people throughout the world, although three hundred years have elapsed since he first saw the light of day at Elstow. No one would be more surprised than he to know the fame he has attained. That a despised and persecuted tinker from an obscure village should rise to such eminence in the realm of English literature is almost beyond credibility; and yet, in the approaching commemoration of his birth, Bunyan's name will be acclaimed throughout the whole earth by means of written or spoken eulogy. The printing-press is already at work, and anon the aerial will take up the theme. The pens of the great and mighty have been wielded for two and a half centuries in his honour, and they will continue to be wielded so long as the English language exists.

Few authors have indeed had such attention paid to them, and the tributes to Bunyan have oft been quoted; but least frequently, perhaps, what "Arnold of Rugby" has written: "I have left off reading our Divines. . . . But if I could find a great man amongst them I would read him thankfully and earnestly. As it is, I hold John Bunyan to have been a man of incomparably greater genius than any of them. . . ." Of *The Pilgrim's Progress,* Dr. Arnold says: "I have always been struck by its piety: I am now struck equally, or even more by its profound wisdom."

The record of Bunyan's life is remarkable; it is unique; especially when it is considered what he might have been (but for the interposition of God) had he simply obeyed the law and so evaded long years of imprisonment. The hand of Divine Providence was in it all; and unwittingly—but not unwillingly—the Dreamer was led on step by step. It would be difficult to say, when reviewing his career three centuries later, which stage of his life could have been omitted without marring the whole.

Dr. Brown's work is of such paramount value to the bibliophile that its revision has been deemed not only advisable but imperative; for there are few copies of the original editions now available, and yet the interest in "JOHN BUNYAN, his life, times, and work," is as keen as it ever has been.

The occasional appearance of a rare item in the auction-room has added zest to the public appreciation of Bunyan; but to the sincere student of his writings there is a larger and greater value in such a book as this by Dr. Brown.

In the new edition attention has been given to details biographical, bibliographical, and topographical, as well as to historical and antiquarian. The research involved in such an undertaking has been considerable; yet, when compared with the indefatigable labours of the late Dr. Brown, it sinks into insignificance. Perhaps there could be no better memorial to the esteemed author, JOHN BROWN, B.A., D.D., than the re-issue of this great work.

Questions which still remain unsettled are left to a future reviser: for, as one lays down the pen another takes it up: only thus can history be carried on from one generation to another.

The revision consists chiefly of marginal notes and editorial comments bracketed thus [].

An addendum to some of the chapters is unavoidable; for, in deference to the wishes of the family of the late Dr. Brown that his work should be left intact, this method has been adopted to obviate the otherwise necessary re-writing of those chapters.

The editor acknowledges with gratitude the kind fellowship of the late Richard Henry Poynter, for many years curator of the Bunyan Museum at Bedford.

Sincere thanks are accorded to the minister, the Rev. C. Bernard Cockett, M.A., the Trustees, and the honorary curator and librarian, Mr. Joseph Whiting, of the Bunyan Meeting, Bedford, for access to books and relics in the Bunyan Museum; to Mr. Arundell Esdaile, M.A., and other officials at the British Museum; to Dr. Guppy and his staff at the John Rylands Library, Manchester; to the Chief Librarian and his assistants at the Bodleian, Oxford; and to the librarians at Cambridge and other

Universities and Colleges at home, and in the Colonies, the United States of America, and the Continent; also to Professor Sir Charles H. Firth, M.A., LL.D., for his invaluable criticism of the Addendum to Chapter III.; to Sir Leicester Harmsworth, Bart., and to Mr. C. K. Robjohns for the use of their valuable libraries; to Mr. John Beagarie of Hitchin; Mr. W. Henman of Bedford; to publishers and editors, public officials, and others, for assistance in researches; and to Mr Frederick Harrison, M.A., F.S.A., for reading the proof-sheets.

FRANK MOTT HARRISON.

December, 1927.

CONTENTS.

CHAPTER VI.

CHAPTER VII.

CHAPTER VIII.

CHAPTER IX.

CHAPTER X.

CHAPTER XI.

CHAPTER XII.

CHAPTER XIII.

CHAPTER XIV.

CHAPTER XV.

CHAPTER XVI.

CHAPTER XVII.

CHAPTER XVIII.

CHAPTER XIX.

ILLUSTRATIONS.

Rev. JOHN BROWN, B.A., D.D.

Photo: J. Russell & Sons, 51 Baker St., W.]

APPRECIATION

OF THE

Late Rev. JOHN BROWN,

B.A. (Lond.), D.D. (Yale),

BY THE

Rev. J. D. JONES, C.H., D.D.

SINCE the last issue of this authoritative "LIFE OF JOHN BUNYAN" the revered author of it has passed away. It is therefore fitting that by way of foreword to this new edition of what is undoubtedly his *magnum opus* some brief account should be given of Dr. Brown himself.

The chief events of his life can be set forth in a few sentences, for it was not a life marked by much adventure or striking incident. John Brown was essentially the faithful pastor and patient student, and the course of life led him, for the most part, into green pastures and by still waters. He was born in Bolton, in Lancashire, in the year 1830. He was fortunate in his parents, both of them being earnest Christian people—his father being a deacon of Mawdesley Street Congregational Church and superintendent of the Sunday School for no less a space than fifty years. He was educated in such schools as Bolton then possessed, and at the end of his school years was apprenticed to a bookseller and printer in the town, who was a friend of his father's. The business was congenial to young John Brown, and in it he found opportunities for widening his acquaintance with literature and deepening his love for it. It was not long, however, before the call to the ministry came to him, and after a year of preparation—during which he matriculated in the University of London—John Brown entered the Lancashire Independent College in the autumn of 1851. The College had for its Principal, Dr. Robert Vaughan, a man of fine historical instinct, and of commanding oratorical power, and amongst its professors was Dr. Samuel Davidson, a pioneer amongst the critics—who had subsequently to resign his professorship because of the panic created by his advanced views. Both of these men had their influence upon the young student. During the five years of his ministerial training John Brown also attended lectures at the Owens' College, and before his course was finished took his degree of B.A. (Lond.).

His first settlement was at the Park Chapel, Cheetham, Manchester. He laboured there for nine happy and successful years. It was during this pastorate that he married Miss Ada Haydon Ford—herself a daughter of a minister—who throughout his long career was his devoted and able helpmeet, and who still survives. But Manchester was almost an episode in his ministerial life. His real life work began when in 1864 he was called to the pastorate of Bunyan Meeting, Bedford. There, for the rest of his ministerial life, he remained, exercising a gracious and fruitful ministry over the long space of thirty-nine years. Bunyan Meeting is a historic church and boasts of a great line of distinguished pastors. In that shining list the name of John Brown will always occupy an honoured place. He was a forceful and inspiring preacher, retaining his freshness to the finish by assiduous study: he had the pastoral heart: he was himself a gracious, kindly, lovable personality. He left his impress deeply graven on the lives and characters of his people. Nor did Bunyan Meeting exhaust his activities. He interested himself in the country churches of Bedfordshire, and to their ministers he was a true "father in God." In Bedford itself he won for himself a sure and ultimately unshared place in the affection and esteem of the people, so that, when he came to leave, it is not too much to say all Bedford bewailed the loss of its most distinguished and best beloved citizen.

During the busy years of his Bedford pastorate, John Brown found time to pursue his historical studies. He had given evidence of his love of historical research while still a student. But it was during the long years at Bedford he found himself able to follow his bent. I have been with him when he was busy searching dusty old church registers. It seemed dull work to me. But it was not dull to him. "Fox-hunting is nothing to it," he said, while that sunny smile of his spread over his face. John Brown was a man of the Puritan breed—a Puritan with the grace of culture and the charm of geniality—but a Puritan nevertheless. It is not surprising therefore that the Puritan period should have been his chosen field. To his love of the Puritans the list of his books bears ample witness. In 1895 he published the book entitled *The Pilgrim Fathers and their Puritan Successors,* a charming book, lit up by characteristic flashes of humour. In the same year he contributed to H. D. Traill's *Social England* chapters on "Puritanism and Nonconformity in the Reign of Elizabeth"; "The Religious Struggle": "Puritans and Nonconformists in 1603." In 1900 he delivered the Yale Lecture in America on Puritan Preaching. In 1910 he returned again to his favourite theme with a volume on *The English Puritans.* But the dearest of all the Puritans to him was John Bunyan, the dreamer of the immortal dream. I daresay it was the fact that he found himself as minister of Bunyan Meeting in the line of succession to the inspired tinker that gave him his special and peculiar interest in his life and work. Anyhow, in the course of the years John Brown became *the* authority on Bunyan. He did a vast amount of original research in his resolve to search out the facts about Bunyan. The result of his labours was the publication of his *John Bunyan* in 1885, a book whose merits were so quickly recognised that it was reprinted in 1886; a second edition was issued in 1887, this edition was reprinted in 1888, 1890, and 1900; and finally a third edition was issued in 1902. This biography is not likely ever to be superseded; it is the authoritative and final word about the author of the 'Pilgrim.' It is on this book that Dr. Brown's literary fame will mainly rest, as it is with John Bunyan's name that his own remains inseparably associated. Indeed the association sometimes went the length of identification. He himself used to delight to tell—with that infectious laugh of his—how he saw himself announced in America as the author of *The Pilgrim's Progress.*

His work as minister and author bore his name and fame far beyond the bounds of Bedford. Yale University conferred the D.D. upon him in 1887. In 1899 the same great University invited him to deliver the Lyman Beecher Lectures on Preaching. Nor was he without honour in his own country. He had become a national figure, so far as Congregationalism was concerned, and in 1891 his brethren recognised his outstanding position by electing him Chairman of the Congregational Union of England and Wales.

Nothing has been said here of his more personal characteristics—of his tact and wisdom, of his skill in affairs, of his kindly spirit. Suffice it to say that the man was bigger than his work. Those of us who were his friends owed him much. The writer of this brief tribute cannot forget the benediction of Dr. Brown's presence and words when he came to commend him to the people of his present charge. He was a Puritan, I have said, and very quickly one came to the granite of the Puritan conviction, but there was nothing grim or severe about him; his piety was shot through with sunshine. He left Bedford in 1903, but he was spared for well nigh a score of years after that, and in retirement he still served the Churches as strength permitted and opportunity offered. When he came to his end at last it was in fulness of honour and fulness of peace. Those of us who knew him are not likely to forget him—but long after those who knew him have also passed, this monumental work will keep his memory green and will win him the gratitude of generations yet to come.

J. D. JONES.

September, 1927.

BIBLIOGRAPHY OF THE WRITINGS

OF THE

Late Dr. BROWN.

COMPILED BY

GEOFFREY LANGDON KEYNES, M.A., M.D. (CANTAB.).

F.R.C.S. (ENG.).

[Note.—All the works recorded in this list have been examined, with the exception of a few pamphlets which are marked with an asterisk.]

A. WRITINGS.

1866.

LECTURES ON THE BOOK OF REVELATION.
18 cms. London: F. Pitman, 1866.
Fourteen lectures delivered at Bunyan Meeting, Bedford. Also issued by Hodder and Stoughton under the title: "The Book of Revelation: A Series of Expositons, 1866."

1874.

THE BOOK OF THE BUNYAN FESTIVAL. Ed. W. H. Wylie.
18 cms. London: James Clarke & Co. Bedford: Rowland Hill & Sons, 1874.
pp. 1-21.—"An Historical Sketch of Bunyan Meeting, Bedford." By the Rev. John Brown, 9th July, 1874.
pp. 75-78.—"The Statue and the Time." Speech by the Rev. John Brown at the unveiling of the statue of Bunyan, presented to Bedford by the Duke of Bedford, June 10th, 1874.

1876.

THE DISESTABLISHMENT AND DISENDOWMENT OF THE CHURCH OF ENGLAND.
21-5 cms. Bedford: W. P. Robertson. London: Society for the Liberation of Religion from State Patronage and Control. [1876.]
A lecture delivered at Bedford, April 4th, 1876, in reply to the Rev. Dr. Thornton, of the Church Defence Institution.

1881.

GOD'S BOOK FOR MAN'S LIFE: A Series of Lectures.
18 cms. London: Hodder and Stoughton. Edinburgh: Macniven and Wallace, 1881.
Twelve lectures delivered at Bedford, printed in a revised form.

1885.

JOHN BUNYAN: His Life, Times, and Work. With illustrations by Edward Whymper.
22-5 cms. London: Wm. Isbister, Limited. 1885.
With an appendix containing a bibliography of "The Pilgrim's Progress." Also published at Boston, U.S.A., by Houghton, Mifflin & Co. The preface is dated October 14th, 1885.

1886.

JOHN BUNYAN: His Life, Times, and Work. With illustrations by Edward Whymper.
[Second Edition.]
22-5 cms. London: Wm. Isbister, Limited. 1886.
A chronological list of Bunyan's works is added. The preface is dated April 13th, 1886.

1887.

JOHN BUNYAN: His Life, Times, and Work. With illustrations by Whymper.
[Third Edition. Fifth Thousand.]
22 cms. London: Wm. Isbister, Limited.
The preface is dated October 10th, 1887. Reprinted in February, 1888; September, 1890; February, 1900. Fourth edition, 1902, q.v.

1887.

*CONGREGATIONAL REVIEW. Edited by Dr. G. Rogers.
1. Historical manuscripts and their fortunes.
2. The Prior of Dunstable and the Burgesses.
3. The Abbess and Nuns of Elstow.
4. Bishop Williams of Lincoln: The Holy Table.
5. An English Ancestor of R. W. Emerson.

1888.

*THE REVOLUTION OF 1688. Reasons for its celebration.
London: Congregational Union of England and Wales. 1888.

1891.

BUNYAN'S HOME. By John Brown, D.D. Illustrated by Allan Barraud.
10 by 25 cms. London: Ernest Nister. New York: E. P. Dutton & Co. 1891.

THE HISTORIC CHRISTIAN PEOPLE: A Re-assertion of their Duties and Rights.
21 cms. London: Congregational Union of England and Wales. 1891.
An address delivered from the Chair of the Congregational Union of England and Wales in the Cambridge Hall, Southport, October 13th, 1891.

THE HISTORIC EPISCOPATE: A Re-examination of its Claims.
21 cms. London: Congregational Union of England and Wales. 1891.
An address delivered from the Chair of the Congregational Union of England and Wales, in the City Temple, London, May 12th, 1891. Second and third editions printed in London. Calcutta Press edition printed by Saptahik Samband, Bhowamipore. 1891.

1892.

IN THE FOOTSTEPS OF THE POETS. By Prof. David Masson, LL.D., and others.
18 cms. London: Isbister and Company, Ltd.
pp. 105-124.—"Herbert." By John Brown, D.D. First printed in the "Sunday Magazine," 1892.

1893.

*THE CLAIMS OF APOSTOLIC SUCCESSION.
London: The Free Church Council. 1893.
Free Church Tracts, No. 2.

*CONGREGATIONALISM: Old and New.
London: Congregational Union of England and Wales. 1893.
Tercentenary Tracts, No. vi.

THE STUNDISTS: The Story of a Great Religious Revolt. With photographs of typical Stundists and a map of Southern Russia, showing distribution of the body.
23-5 cms. London: James Clarke & Co. 1893.
pp. v.-viii.—Preface by John Brown.

1895.

SOCIAL ENGLAND: A Record of the Progress of the People. By various writers. Edited by H. D. Traill, D.C.L.
[In Six Volumes.]
22 cms. London: Cassell & Company, Limited. 1895-1897.
Contributions by the Rev. John Brown, D.D.:
Vol. iii., pp. 424-431.—"Puritanism and Nonconformity [in the reign of Elizabeth]."
Vol. iv., pp. 36-42.—"The Religious Struggle: Puritanism and Nonconformity (1603)."
pp. 254-260.—"The Religious Struggle: Presbyterians, Independents, Nonconformists."
Vol. v., pp. 229-240.—"Nonconformity, 1689-1815."
Vol. vi., pp. 141-150.—"The Free Churches, 1815-1885."

THE PILGRIM FATHERS OF NEW ENGLAND and Their Puritan Successors. With Illustrations by Charles Whymper.
21-5 cms. London: The Religious Tract Society. 1895.
The preface is dated July 25th, 1895. Also published by Fleming H. Revell Company, New York, with an introduction by the Rev. E. Dunning, D.D.

1896.

CENTENARY CELEBRATION OF THE BEDFORDSHIRE UNION OF CHRISTIANS: The Story of a Hundred Years.
18 cms. London: Congregational Union of England and Wales. 1896.

1897.

THE PILGRIM FATHERS OF NEW ENGLAND and Their Puritan Successors. With illustrations by Charles Whymper.
[New and Cheaper Edition.]
20-5 cms. London: The Religious Tract Society. 1897.

1898.

*THE SPIRITUAL MEANING OF THE LORD'S SUPPER.
London: Congregational Union of England and Wales. 1898.
A paper read at the Halifax Assembly of the Congregational Union.

THE TIMES OF OLD.
18-5 cms. London: 1898.
Sermon preached at Carr's Lane Chapel on the occasion of the 150th anniversary.

APOSTOLIC SUCCESSION IN THE LIGHT OF HISTORY AND FACT: The Congregational Union Lecture for 1897.
22 cms. London: Congregational Union of Engalnd and Wales. 1898.
Eleven lectures delivered in the Memorial Hall, Farringdon Street, in 1897.

1899.

*FELLOWSHIP AND INDIVIDUALISM.
London: Congregational Union of England and Wales. 1899.
A paper read at the International Congregational Council, Boston, U.S.A.

THE PRESENT CRISIS IN THE CHURCH OF ENGLAND: Eight Lectures on the Principles of Protestantism delivered in Bunyan Meeting, Bedford.
21-5 cms. London: Congregational Union of England and Wales. Bedford: W. T. Robinson. 1899.
Reprinted from the "Bedfordshire Times." Preface dated March, 1899.

1900.

PURITAN PREACHING IN ENGLAND: A Study of Past and Present.
19 cms. London: Hodder and Stoughton. 1900.
The Lyman Beecher Lectures on Preaching, delivered at Yale University, October, 1899. Copyright in the U.S.A. by Charles Scribner's Sons.

1902.

JOHN BUNYAN: His Life, Times, and Work. In Two Volumes.
[Fourth Revised Edition.]
16-5 cms. London: Isbister & Co., Ltd. 1902.

1904.

COMMONWEALTH OF ENGLAND.
17-5 cms. London: National Council of Evangelical Free Churches. 1904.
Eras of Nonconformity, ed. Rev. C. Silvester Horne, M.A. No. vi.

FROM THE RESTORATION OF 1660 TO THE REVOLUTION OF 1688.
17-5 cms. London: National Council of Evangelical Free Churches. 1904.
Eras of Nonconformity, ed. Rev. C. Silvester Horne, M.A. No. vii.

1906.

THE PILGRIM FATHERS OF NEW ENGLAND and Their Puritan Successors. With Illustrations by Charles Whymper.
[Third Edition.]
18 cms. London: The Religious Tract Society, 1906.

1908.

THE COLONIAL MISSIONS OF CONGREGATIONALISM: The Story of Seventy Years.
18 cms. London: The Congregational Union of England and Wales. 1908.

PROCEEDINGS OF THE THIRD INTERNATIONAL CONGREGATIONAL COUNCIL, Held in Edinburgh, June 30-July 9, 1908. Edited by Rev. John Brown, B.A., D.D.
23-5 cms. London: Congregational Union of England and Wales. 1908.
Contributions by the Rev. John Brown.
pp. iii.-iv.—Preface.
pp. 195-6.—Response to Dr. Whyte's Address.
pp. 588-591.—Closing address.
Facing pp. 544.—Portrait of Dr. Brown.

1910.

THE ENGLISH PURITANS.
16-5 cms. Cambridge: At the University Press. 1910.
The Cambridge Manuals of Science and Literature. Preface dated June 20th, 1910.

1911.

THE CAMBRIDGE HISTORY OF ENGLISH LITERATURE. Edited by A. W. Ward, Litt.D., and A. R. Waller, M.A. Vol. vii. Cavalier and Puritan.
23 cms. Cambridge: At the University Press. 1911.
Chap. vii., pp. 166-185.—"John Bunyan. Andrew Marvell." By the Rev. John Brown, D.D.

THE HISTORY OF THE ENGLISH BIBLE.
16-5 cms. Cambridge: At the University Press. 1911.
The Cambridge Manuals of Science and Literature. Preface dated March 11th, 1911.

1920.

THE PILGRIM FATHERS OF NEW ENGLAND and Their Puritan Successors. With illustrations by Charles Whymper.
[Fourth Edition.]
18 cms. London: The Religious Tract Society, 1920.

B. BOOKS EDITED.

1887.

THE HOLY WAR. By John Bunyan. Edited with introduction and notes by the Rev. John Brown.
18 cms. London: Hodder and Stoughton. 1887.

THE PILGRIM'S PROGRESS. By John Bunyan. Edited with introduction and notes by the Rev. John Brown.
18 cms. London: Hodder and Stoughton. 1887.

1888.

GRACE ABOUNDING TO THE CHIEF OF SINNERS. By John Bunyan. Edited with introduction and notes by the Rev. John Brown.
18 cms. London: Hodder and Stoughton. 1888.

THE PILGRIM'S PROGRESS and THE HOLY WAR. By John Bunyan.
28 cms. London: Cassell & Co., Ltd. 1888.
pp. ix.-xxviii.—Life of Bunyan. By John Brown.
Issued in 27 parts. Re-issued in 27 parts in 1892, and again in 6 parts in 1896.

1889.

A BOOK FOR BOYS AND GIRLS: or, Country Rhymes for Children. By John Bunyan. Being a facsimile of the unique first edition with an introduction by the Rev. John Brown, D.D.
18 cms. London: Elliot Stock. 1889.

1895.

THE PILGRIM'S PROGRESS AS JOHN BUNYAN WROTE IT: Being a facsimile reproduction of the First Edition, published in 1678. With an introduction by Dr. John Brown.
17 cms. London: Elliot Stock. 1895.

1898.

THE PILGRIM'S PROGRESS. By John Bunyan. With Index and Prefatory Memoir by the Rev. John Brown, D.D.
18 cms. London and Edinburgh: W. R. Chambers, Ltd. 1898.

1905.

JOHN BUNYAN: Life and Death of Mr. Badman and The Holy War. The text edited by John Brown, D.D.
19-5 cms. Cambridge: At the University Press. 1905.
Cambridge English Classics.

JOHN BUNYAN: Grace Abounding and The Pilgrim's Progress. The text edited by John Brown, D.D.
19-5 cms. Cambridge: At the University Press. 1907.
Cambridge English Classics.

THE SERMONS OF HENRY SMITH, The Silver-Tongued Preacher. A selection edited by John Brown, D.D.
14 cms. Cambridge: At the University Press. 1908.

1909.

THE SERMONS OF THOMAS ADAMS, the Shakespeare of Puritan Theologians. A selection edited by John Brown, D.D.
14 cms. Cambridge: At the University Press. 1909.

1911.

THE PILGRIM'S PROGRESS. By John Bunyan. With a Life of the Author by the Rev. John Brown, D.D.
25 cms. London: Cassell & Co., Ltd., 1911.

EXCERPTS

From Dr. Brown's Prefaces to the First and Third Editions (1885 and 1887).

EVERY author has, of course, a more or less sufficient reason for sending forth his book to the world. If I honestly gave mine I should say that in the first instance I drifted into its production by force of circumstances rather than set it before myself of deliberate choice.

As the minister for more than twenty years of the Church of which Bunyan also was minister, and as the official guardian of such personal relics and memorials of him as remain to us, I have necessarily been brought into intercourse with the yearly increasing stream of visitors who, from all parts of the world, come to Bedford and Elstow to see for themselves the scenes and associations of Bunyan's life. I have found from a somewhat wide observation that, more than most writers, he has not only secured the intellectual interest of his readers, but also their personal affection; and that everything relating to him that can be reliably told is matter of unfailing interest to minds the most diverse. Innumerable questions from others, therefore, first sent me forth on researches of my own, and, as a relaxation from the more serious duties of my ministry, this work became to me one of the pleasures of my life.

. . . .

My long residence among the scenes and surroundings of Bunyan's life has given me some advantage over previous biographers, who were only able to make occasional visits to the neighbourhood. I have had, however, still greater advantage in the fact that recent years have made available, for purposes of local and personal history, resources till lately quite unknown or inaccessible to the historical student. For the purpose of this biography researches have been made among the stores brought to light by the Royal Commission on Historical Manuscripts. Through the labours of the gentlemen who have acted as inspectors under that Commission, there have been found, among the MSS. of the House of Lords and in the numerous private collections scattered through the country, documents which have supplied missing links in our history, and made more vivid to us the story of the past. The papers relating to the diocese of Lincoln, in the Archbishop's Library at Lambeth, I have also found to be of considerable interest and value. I have, of course, availed myself of the priceless stores garnered up among the State Papers at the Record Office, and among the steadily accumulating materials in the manuscript and printed departments of the British Museum. I have also found great help from the collections in the Bodleian, in the University Library at Cambridge, and in Dr. Williams' Library in London. Among resources of a more local kind I have found the most valuable assistance from the Transcript Registers and Act Books of the Archdeaconry of Bedford, the Minute Books and other documents in the archives of the Bedford Corporation, and the Bedfordshire wills preserved in the district registry of the Court of Probate at Northampton.

In addition to these materials of a more public and national character, the records of the Church at Bedford, with which Bunyan was so long associated, have for the first time been woven into the story of his life; and for the first time, also, his general works have been placed in due order and chronological relation to his personal history. On this latter point it may be well to say, that as during the sixty years of Bunyan's life he wrote something like sixty books, the account of most of these had necessarily to come within limited space. I have, therefore, sought to give not so much an abstract or general estimate as to bring together whatever was most characteristic of his special genius and cast of mind.

. . . .

It has been gratifying, indeed, to receive from many, both in this country and in the United States, the assurance that this, the latest biography of the great dreamer, has met and supplied a want felt in our literature.

. . . .

It may be interesting to mention a reference to Bunyan's maternal grandfather, William Bentley, recently met with. In the month of November, 1886, Mr. G. A. Aitken, of Kensington, purchased at Sotheby's a number of old deeds principally relating to property in Elstow, and in looking them through I found

William Bentley's signature as that of a witness attesting a deed of sale between two inhabitants of Elstow, bearing date 12th of July, 1611. This signature of the father of Bunyan's mother is written in a superior manner, and indicates an amount of education not common in those days even among persons of good social position. There was also another deed by which Thomas Purney sold to Thomas Hoddle, late of Elstowe, "All that messuage, tenement, or Inne called The Bell in Elstowe. between a tenement in the tenure of William Bentley on the south side and a tenement in the tenure of Widdowe Braye on the north." This deed is dated 1st November, 1612, and indicates the spot which was the home of Bunyan's mother in the days of her childhood.

In conclusion, I would fain express the hope that this life of a brave and godly Englishman may further those principles of civil and religious freedom to which he bore such faithful testimony, and on behalf of which he suffered so much. Above all, it is pleasant to me to think that renewed intercourse with the spirit of Bunyan in these pages may deepen the religious life in the hearts of some of my readers, bringing them into a closer, diviner fellowship with his Lord and theirs.

JOHN BROWN.

JOHN BUNYAN:
(1628-1688)
HIS LIFE, TIMES AND WORK.

I.

EARLY CHURCH LIFE IN BEDFORDSHIRE.

JOHN BUNYAN, born in the English Midlands, may be taken as in some sense a characteristic representative of the region that gave him birth. For the tract of country between the Trent and the Bedfordshire Ouse, which from its northern half gave the Pilgrim Fathers to New England, furnished from its fens and fields in the south a succession of men of his own sturdy independence of thought, and in strong sympathy with his own Puritan faith. In the development of even the most original genius, the environment counts for much; it may help us, therefore, to a truer estimate of the man if we first briefly recall the spiritual antecedents of the county in which he was born and in which his life was spent.

When the Reformation broke in upon the old ecclesiastical system of England, Bedfordshire seems to have been more than usually receptive of the new ideas then rising over Europe. Not that the whole county, any more than other counties, was prepared to become Protestant at a stroke. Here, as elsewhere, many Englishmen, after their manner, were inclined to "stand in the ways, and see and ask for the old paths." Leading families, like the Mordaunts of Turvey, remained firm in their allegiance to the ancient faith, and turned their houses into hiding-places for its bishops and priests during the hard days of Elizabeth and James. Not a few of the yeomen also held tenaciously to the old well-worn modes of religious thought, even while diligently attending the services of a Reformed Church. As late as 1579, or more than forty years after England had broken with the See of Rome, farmers like Robert Bonyon,* of Wingfield, in the parish of Chalgrave, in the wills they made, still commended their souls not only to Almighty God, but also "to our blessed Ladie St. Mary and to all the holy company of heaven."[1] No wonder, therefore, that Protestant vicars did not always find it easy to carry their slowly moving parishioners with them. It was far on in the reign of Elizabeth, for example, when Peter White, the Minister of Eaton Socon, having reconstructed the rood-loft of his parish church, where anciently stood the rood called Mary and John, had in 1581 to preach and publish a "Godlye and fruitefull sermon against Idolatrie," to quiet "the conscience of the simple." He found it needful to assure troubled souls among his parishioners that the changes he had made were really very slight. "The Rood-lofte wanteth nothing of his former state, but only the images and uppermost front." The loft itself, "being nine foot in bredth, yet standeth with the beame," only instead of having "the Roode or Idoll," "the Tabernacle that sometimes stood upon the Altar is placed from the beame aforesaid." The rest "remaineth as it did in the time of popery." Even yet they were not altogether reassured, and another pamphlet issued by the vicar the following year, shows that the feeling roused by his Protestant innovations was neither slight nor soon allayed.[2] Possibly similar clashings of opinion disturbed other parishes in the county; and it is tolerably certain that in the hearts of many there was still, from old association, a strong attachment to the religious usages and superstitions of the Church, now no longer the Church of the State.

* The Editor possesses a deed dated 1583, referring to land which once belonged to Robert Bonyon, yeoman, of Tebworth, Chalgrave, Bedfordshire.

Still, these instances were exceptional. The tradespeople in the towns, as well as a majority of the gentry in the country-houses, were staunchly Protestant, as were also the two great noblemen, the natural chieftains of the county, the Earls of Kent and Bedford. The county, indeed, became a recognised asylum of religious liberty for many from across the sea.

[1] *Bedfordshire Wills,* 1576-9, No. 126.

[2] *A Godlye and fruitefull Sermon against Idolatrie.* Preached the xv daye of Ianuarie 1581, in the Parrishe Church of Eaton Sooken, within the Countie of Bedforde, by P. W., Minister and preacher in that place. London: Imprinted by Frauncis Coldocke, 1581, 8vo. [black letter].

An Ansvveare vnto certaine crabbed Questions, pretending a real presence of Christ in the Sacramente. Gathered & set foorth by Peter Whyte. London, Imprinted by John Wolfe and Henry Kirkham, 1582.

Refugees for conscience' sake came from Alençon and Valenciennes, and settled at Cranfield in 1568, bringing with them their lace pillows, and establishing the lace trade of the district. And while many Protestants from the Netherlands, fleeing from Philip of Spain and the Duke of Alva, thus found a home in the villages of Bedfordshire, introducing names still to be recognised in the parish registers, collections were also made in the churches of the county for others still in their own land, and still suffering cruel hardships on account of their faith.

Both before the Reformation and for a century after we get what is probably the most realistic view possible to us now of the ecclesiastical life of the people of England, from a source hitherto comparatively neglected, the Act Books of the Archdeacons' Courts. From the middle of the fifteenth century certainly, and probably much earlier, with the exception of the brief reign of Edward VI., down to the year 1640, when the procedure known as *ex officio* was abolished, there was kept up a close surveillance of the lives of the people in each parish of each of the deaneries of which the archdeaconry was composed. These Courts, which were regularly held, took cognisance of every conceivable offence against morals as well as against ecclesiastical discipline. The form of procedure was either by *Inquisition,* when the judge was the accuser; by *Accusation,* when some other person made the charge; or by *Denunciation,* which was simple presentment. The most frequent penalty on conviction was a money fine, but in many cases the culprit had to do penance in a white sheet, or make public confession before a congregation of his neighbours. More serious offences were followed by excommunication, a penalty carrying with it social consequences of the gravest kind. For example, from the Act Books of the Bedford Archdeaconry, we find that in 1617 William Worrall of Kempston was cited before the Court at Ampthill for buying and selling with Thomas Crawley, which he ought not to have done because Thomas Crawley was an excommunicate person. The same year John Glidall, fuller, of Cranfield, and Francis Crashop, were cited and fined, "for setting Richard Barrett, an excommunicate person, a work." Even love must be crossed and courtship forbidden till the Church was reconciled. In 1616 Roger Perriam, of St. Cuthberts, Bedford, was cited, "for that there is a report that he doth frequent and keep company with Margaret Bennett, who standeth excommunicate." If an excommunicated person ventured to appear among his neighbours in the parish church, the minister was compelled to call public attention to his presence, and absolutely stop the service till the proscribed person had left the building. Indeed, the consequences which followed a man through life did not cease even with his death. Robert Baker, the parish clerk of Potton, was punished for burying the body of an excommunicate person in the churchyard; and some years later Anne Skevington of Turvey was herself excommunicated because that, in widowed grief, she had been present at the burial of her own husband, who for his nonconformity had died under the ban of the Church.

It lies outside the range of our present purpose, of course, but it would be interesting to show what curious light the records of the various Archdeacons' Courts throw on the morals and manners of our forefathers. A large proportion were cases of intemperance and impurity. Among the ecclesiastical offences were such as refusing to follow the cross in procession, hanging down the head at the elevation of the host, throwing the pax-bread on the ground, separating the holy oil, washing hands in the baptismal font, singing the Litany derisively, refusing to pay dues and keep feast days, reading heretical and English books during the mass, not receiving ashes on Ash Wednesday, and not confessing at Easter. Among offences of a more miscellaneous character, we find one man bringing judgment upon himself for "marieing his wife in their parish church in her mask"; another "for being married to his wife under a bush"; and yet a third, "for that the day he was marryed he dyd blowe oute the lightes about the altar and wolde suffer no lightes to bourne." One unloving spirit was dealt with "for not treating his wife with affection"; another, yet more unloving, "for cheening his wife to a post and slandering his neighbours." People offended by "exercising the magic art," by consulting cunning women, by using private conventicles, and by "hiring foreigners to work at their art." It was an offence also not to "make two torches and keep the drynkynge in the parish, according to the laudable use and custom"; and a shoemaker was punished, for that he "kepeth his bedd upon the Sundaies and other holy days at time of mattens and mass, as it were a hownde that shuld kepe his kenell." One man came into trouble for "folding some sheep in the church during a snow storm";

and another, for "living in the church-porch, and suffering his wife to travail in childbirth there and to continue there her whole moneth." Women fell under the judgment of the Court for "coming to be churched without kercher, midwife or wyves"; or not "as other honest women, but comygne in her hatt, and a quarter about her neck"; or for "not coming in a vaile"; and one brisk housewife, striking out a bright idea on a rainy day, found to her cost that she had offended by "hanginge her lynnen in the church to dry."

The law was administered with even-handed justice against the officials of the parish as well as against the common people. The clergy were cited for "not sprinkling holy water on the parishioners," for "letting divers die without howsill or shrifte throw his defaute"; for "refusing to reply to the archdeacon in the Roman tongue"; for refusing to hear confessions, "because it grieves him to heare the confessions made." One rector went quite wrong by "taking upon himself to the scandal of his calling, to be lord of misrule at Christmas among certein yongelinges," and another by leaving some ecclesiastical ceremony to be present at the more exciting spectacle of an execution. The churchwardens incurred penalty by "suffering unrulie persons to ring and jingle the bells out of due season," by permitting a minstrel to play in church at a wedding, and because the white sheet used for penance was missing. The schoolmaster was fined for teaching children above sixteen years of age without licence, or for "being negligent in his place, his schollers not profiting under him." And, finally, that chartered libertine, the parish clerk, was dealt with summarily, and surely most righteously, "for that he singeth the psalmes in the church with such a jesticulous tone and altitonant voyce, viz. squeaking like a pigg, which doth not only interrupt the other voyces, but is altogether dissonant and disagreeing unto any musicall harmonie."[1]

Some of the citations in the Act Books of the Court of the Archdeaconry of Bedford relate to Puritan scruples on the part of several of the clergy of the county. For example, in 1601, Cæsar Walpole, curate of Woburn, and in 1617, William Moore, minister of Sharnbrook, Oliver Roberts, vicar of Goldington, and Christopher Watson, curate of Pertenhall, were cited for

[1] Hale's *Precedents and Proceedings in Criminal Causes*, 1457—1640.

"not wearing the surplisse usuallie," or for "wanting a hoode," or for not making the sign of the cross in baptism, or for not reading prayers on Wednesdays and Fridays. It is usually assumed that the Puritan party were the only strict Sabbatarians in the country; but in Bedfordshire, as a matter of fact, the same court and the same commissary dealing with the ministers just named for Puritanism, enforced also upon the laity the strictest observance of the Sabbath. Within the years 1610—1617, Oliver Lenton and Walter Lewin of Barford were punished for looking on football players on Sunday; John Hawkes of Renhold, for playing at nineholes; and William Shellie, of Bedford, for playing at tables on that day. Roger White of Risely also was cited for travelling his horses on the Sabbath day; Robert Kinge of Shelton, "for going towards London on the Sabbath day in winter," and William Dennys of Bedford, "for going out of St. John's Church to Elstowe in sermon tyme." The following persons were also cited: John Tirold of Bedford, for "bringing in his wares on the Sabbath day in praier time"; John Sharman, for killing meat; Thomas Styles, for dressing a calf in the open Butcher-rowe, and Peter Lord, the barber of Woburn, for "trimming men" on that day. Saints' days were to be as rigorously observed as Sundays. Three parishioners of Milton Ernys came under the lash of the court: Leonard Willimot for carting on St. Luke's day; James Hailey, for winnowing corn on Easter Tuesday; and Walter Griffin, "for putting upp netts and catching larks on a holliday." John Neele of Luton also found to his cost that he had done wrong in "stocking a fruit tree on All Saints' day," so did Thomas Bigrave of Pavenham, and John West of Stevington, who were "at a foote-ball plaie on Ascension Day, and absent from praiers"; and Henry Waters of Litlington had to answer at Ampthill "for carrying a burthen of woode home from Beckring Park on Easter day last." Among others presented before the court were five parishioners of Poddington, for not receiving the communion thrice a year; Anna Chandler of Studham for being "a Brownist"; the wife of John Wheeler of Cranfield, with others of his neighbours, for not frequenting church; Richard Reade of Keysoe, for so far anticipating the Quaker, George Fox, by some thirty years as to sit "with his hatt on usually at the reading of the Epistle and Gospell," and William Shackspeare of Odell, for not communicating.

It is curious to see the uses to which the churches were sometimes put in the days to which the Act Books refer. Indeed we are almost startled to find Harman Sheppard, the curate of the parish, presented in 1612, for baiting a bear in the church at Woburn.[1] Some years later, also, the churchwardens of Knotting were cited because that on three successive Shrove Tuesdays they and their sons and Mr. Alvey, the rector of the parish, "permitted and were present at cockfightings in the chancell of the said church in or about the sacred place where the communion table stands, many persons being there assembled and wagers laid."[2] In still later years the rector of Carlton was presented because "immediately before service he did lead his horse in at the south doore into the chancell of Carlton church, where he sett him and there continued all the time of the said service and sermon." Patrons of benefices also, as well as clergy and churchwardens, sometimes dealt with the sacred edifice in remarkably free and easy fashion. An instance of this may be found in a village between Bedford and Northampton, of which in 1641, it was certified that the vicarage had been pulled down, the glebe lost, and the tithes detained, and that the lord of the manor, Jasper Hartnell, after dismantling the body of the church, selling the lead and the bells, had turned the chancel into a kennel for his greyhounds, and the steeple into a dove-house for his pigeons.[3]

The country squires who could so rudely handle the churches would not be over nice in their treatment of the clergy. Jasper Fisher, the rector of Wilden, in his visitation sermon preached at Ampthill in 1635, complained that "the great men do send God's messengers upon their base errands, place them below their serving-men, esteem them below their parasites; nay, deride and abuse, persecute and destroy them for their message."[4] In the same strain speaks out that Shakespeare of the Puritans, as he was called, Thomas Adams, the vicar of Willington. In a Visitation Sermon preached at St. Paul's, in Bedford, in 1612, he asks, "Shall the Papists twit us that our *Our Father* hath taken from the Church what their *Paternoster* bestowed upon it? Were the goods of the Church for this intrusted to gentlemen and lords of the manors, that they should set them to sale and turn their benefits into their own purses? . . . We are

[1] *Lambeth MSS.* Miscell., 952; 43.
[2] *State Papers, Dom.,* Chas. I., 1637, vol. ccclxx., 90.
[3] *A Certificate from Northamptonshire,* 4to. London, 1641.
[4] *The Priest's Duty and Dignity,* by Jasper Fisher, Presbyter and Rector of Wilden in Bedfordshire. London, 1636.

well freed from the Bonners and butchers of Christ's lambs; but we have still fleecers enough—too many—that love to see learning follow Homer with a staff and a wallet. Every gentleman thinks the priest mean, but the priest's means hath made many a gentleman."[1]

The Puritan movement, like the Protestant before it, found a congenial home in Bedfordshire. Thomas Brightman, the vicar of Hawnes, a celebrated preacher and writer in his time, was one of several ministers who, in 1603, waited upon King James, at that time the guest of the Cromwells at Hinchinbrook, near Huntingdon. Speaking for the people from whom they came they "had some good conference with his Majesty and gave him a book of reasons." They pleaded against the use of the sign of the cross in baptism, against baptism by women, and against the use of the cap and surplice. They urged that there ought to be examination into the life of such persons as came to the communion, and that ministers ought not to be called priests. They petitioned against "longsomeness of service, and the abuse of church songes and music," against profanation of the Lord's Day, and against excommunication by such lay persons as the Archdeacon's commissary, or for trifles, and without the consent of pastors.[2]

It need not be repeated here how the Puritans got nothing from King James but this "good conference" at Hinchinbrook. But though disappointed in their hopes from him they held on their way, their opinions obtaining wider and firmer hold among the people. In 1633, the Bishop of Lincoln, reporting the condition of his diocese to Archbishop Laud, observes, "Some in Bedfordshire use to wander from their own parish churches to follow preachers affected by themselves, of which the officers are caused to take special care." The following year Laud himself reports to the King: "As for Lincolne, it being the greatest diocese in the kingdom, I have now reduced that under Metropolitical Visitation, and visited it this preceding year. My visitors there found Bedfordshire most tainted of any part of the diocese, and in particular Mr. Bulkeley is sent to the High Commission for Nonconformity."[3] The first of the two visitors

[1] *Heaven and Earth reconciled*: a sermon preached at St. Paul's Church in Bedford, Oct. 3rd, 1612. Adams' Practical Works, 1862, I., 448, *et seq.*

[2] Petition to King James, Nov. 30th. 1604. *Addl. MSS.* 8978.

[3] Laud's Annual Reports of his Province to the King. 1633. 1634. *Lambeth MSS.* 943, p. 251.

here referred to by the Archbishop was Dr. Farmery, chancellor of the diocese of Lincoln, who in July, 1634, reported to him as follows: "That sort of people that run from their own parishes after affected preachers are the most troublesome part of the ecclesiastical inquisition in Buckingham and Bedfordshires, where they found great abettors in this their disorder. The new recorder of Bedford questioned at a sessions one of my apparitors for troubling, as he said, these godly men, and then delivered publicly that if men were thus troubled for going to hear a sermon when their minister at home did not preach, it would breed a scab in the kingdom."[1]

It was at this time that Archbishop Laud revived the long disused claim to Metropolitical Visitation, sending his Vicar-General, Sir Nathaniel Brent, to report upon the ecclesiastical condition of the whole of the diocese of Lincoln. The month after Dr. Farmery's report had been received, Sir Nathaniel set forth, beginning at Lincoln and working his way southward. He unearthed strange doings and met with curious experiences. Ale-houses, hounds, and swine were kept in churchyards; copes and vestments had been embezzled; clandestine marriages were celebrated by the clergy; and both clergy and laity were much given to drunkenness. At Saxby, Lord Castleton's bailiff was found melting in the middle aisle of the church the lead he had stripped from the roof. At Brigstock, the Court had to deal with a clergyman who was charged with ensuring an audience to the end of his discourses by the simple expedient of locking the church door upon his congregation, keeping them there till it was quite dark. After this we come upon a different class of offenders. "At Huntingdon, divers ministers in that division were suspected for Puritanisme, but being questioned they professed absolute conformitie." Brent reached Bedford on the 26th of August, of which he reports: "Mr. Peter Bulkeley, rector of Odell, suspected for Puritanisme, was suspended for absence. He came to me to Aylesburie, where he confessed he never used the surplisse or the crosse in baptisme. He is to appear in the High Commission Court the first court day in November if he reform not before. Divers ministers in Bedford, especially Mr. Smith, are suspected for Nonconformitie."[2]

[1] *State Papers, Dom.*, Chas. I., 1634, July 14th.
[2] *Ibid.*, 1634, vol. cclxxiv., 12.

This Peter Bulkeley, thus singled out by the Vicar-General, had succeeded his father, Dr. Edward Bulkeley, as rector of Odell, in 1620. His sister was the wife of Sir Oliver St. John, of Keysoe, and therefore the mother of that Oliver St. John, who was afterwards Cromwell's Lord Chief Justice. Educated at St. John's College, Cambridge, Peter Bulkeley was fellow of his college at an early age, and is spoken of by those who knew him as eminent for scholarship. He was equally eminent for his godly life. Cotton Mather says of him that he was "full of those devotions which accompany a conversation in heaven," and no neighbour could talk with him, but "he would let fall some holy, serious, divine, and useful sentences ere they parted." He was in the full career of his usefulness when silenced by Brent. The summons to the Vicar-General's court reached him, says Mather, "at the time his ministry had a notable success in the conversion of many unto God." Finding after his appearance at Aylesbury he could not, with a good conscience, retain his ministry, he took sorrowful leave of the good people of Odell, and accompanied by Zachary Symmes, minister of the Priory Church of Dunstable, sailed for New England, where he joined the Pilgrim Fathers in 1635. Resting for a time at Boston, he subsequently pursued his way "thro' unknowne woods" to the banks of the Musketaquid river, where he founded the town of Concord, the first inland plantation of the Massachusetts colony. It may be interesting to mention that Ralph Waldo Emerson, Concord's best known citizen, sprang from Peter Bulkeley, whose granddaughter was married to the Rev. John Emerson in 1665.[1]

While thus dealing with the two Pilgrim Fathers who went from Bedfordshire, Sir Nathaniel Brent still went on his tour of search. From Ampthill, where he was on the 30th of August, he reports to Laud that "great complainte was made of the inconformitie of Mr. Shirley, the vicar of Hawnes, Mr. Holmes, the vicar of Whipsnade, and many others whom I questioned for inconformitie." Of Bow Brickhill, where he was on the 2nd of September, he says: "The people thereabouts, and indeed in all the south part of this diocese, are much addicted to leave their parish churches to go to hear affected preachers elsewhere. The country much complayneth of the Court at Leyton and those

[1] *The Bulkeley Family, or the Descendants of the Rev. Peter Bulkeley*, by F. W. Chapman. Hartford, Conn., 1875.

of the Court, of Puritanisme. Much complayning, but no proving." With which words Sir Nathaniel took his leave.

When the Vicar-General was gone the officers of the local Ecclesiastical Courts still zealously carried out the policy of driving conscientious men into those ways of conformity so dear to the ecclesiastical mind. Among the MSS. in the House of Lords, calendared in recent years by the Historical Manuscripts Commission, there are numerous petitions, interesting to the local historian, which throw light on the course steadily pursued. In one petition, for example, John James of Olney complains that, though nothing had been proved against him, he had been compelled to pay a fine of £10 towards the building of St. Paul's, in London, the ordinary fees, and £16 to the Court. He had also, he says, to give a beaver to Sir John Lambe, Dean of Arches, "which cost your petitioner £4 more." His own minister being suspended, and no preaching going on in his own parish church, he went to hear a sermon elsewhere, and, though this sermon was preached in a parish church, and not in a conventicle, he was for this offence excommunicated. To obtain absolution from this sentence cost him the ordinary fees and a fine of £24 more. John James has further sorrows to recount, "all which unjust proceedings have caused your petitioner to sell his inheritance, and to spend above £100, and tend greatly to his undoing."[1]

It would seem that many of the clergy fared no better than the laity. Another petition is from Daniel Clarke, vicar of Steventon, and others, and complains that Walter Walker, the commissary of the Court at Bedford, "hath, by virtue of his office, tyrranized over the clergy of sett purpose to ingratiate himself with the Archbishop of Canterburie." In apportioning the tax laid upon the clergy for the King's expedition to Scotland, he had made excessive assessments, "threatening to suspend them, and to return their names if they did not comply." From Clarke he had demanded £5 instead of forty-six shillings, and from Thomas Wells, the rector of Carlton, £6. "This was greatly too much, and because he did not pay he cited Mr. Wells (though a hundred years olde) to Bedford Courte, being five miles from his living; and because he did not appear he suspended

[1] *House of Lords MSS.*, Feb. 9th, 1640, 1641. Petition of John James.

him, and called him an old owle, and would not dismiss him till he paid the £6." The petition, which was evidently a combined expression of grievances, goes on to describe how "the said commissarie did suspend the curate of Bromham for referring to the Government in his sermon," and did "exhibit articles against the rector of Stondon for reading divine service once without a surplice, though it was proved by witnesses that at that time his surplice was at the washers"; how "he suspended the vicar of Cardington for once omitting to weare the surplice in the afternoon, though he had worne it in the morning"; and how he declared he would make Richard Kifford, the churchwarden of Cockayne Hatley, stand in three market towns barefooted and bareheaded, or pay a fine of £13 6s. 8d., for not presenting that the font was in decay.[1]

In another section the same petition complains of a change of procedure forced upon the parishioners of St. Paul's, in Bedford, in the manner of observing the Communion of the Lord's Supper. From the time of the Reformation and the abolition of the mass there had been no rails round the communion-table. As to whether it was a table or an altar, whether its right place was in the body of the church or chancel, or altarwise at the east end, controversy had been briskly waged. But, practically, a compromise, favourable to the Puritans, had been come to in Elizabeth's time, which was substantially adopted in the canons of 1603. According to this the table should stand in the church where the altar stood before the Reformation, *except at the celebration of the Communion,* at which time it was to be brought out and placed where the communicants could most conveniently see and hear the minister, and then to be returned to its former place when the service was over. The Eighty-Second Canon distinctly enjoins a moveable Communion-table, so that a fixed altar with altar-rails and kneeling communicants thereat were unlawful innovations introduced into the Church of England by Archbishop Laud.

In his endeavour to change the practice thus established Laud was met by stout resistance. In 1636 he reported to the King that in Bedfordshire there was great opposition both to the erection of altar-rails and to the kneeling before them. He

[1] *House of Lords MSS.*, August 5th, 1641. Petition of Daniel Clarke, vicar of Steventon, &c.

says, "The people in some places refuse to do so. His lordship [the Bishop of Lincoln] desires direction, as this is not regulated by any canon of the Church." On the margin of this report there is, in the well-known handwriting of the King, the following note: "C. R. Try your way for some time."[1] Immediately after, as the petition referred to complains, the commissary "ordered steppes to be raised at the upper end of the chancel of St. Paul's in Bedford, and gave strict orders that the communion-table be sett there north and south." This was done, yet, in spite thereof, both minister and people still retained the mode of administration to which they had been long accustomed. The petition then relates, that in 1639 Walter Walker "gave orders to John Bradshaw, vicar of St. Paul's in Bedford, to keep within the railes at the administration of the communion, and because he did not, but came down to the communicants, he complained against him. He gave orders to the communicants of St. Paul's to come up to the railes about the communion-table, and first went up thither himself to show them how. Those that failed he cited, and threatened to make them make public confession in the church."[2]

The commissary was a resolute man, but the men with whom he had to deal were resolute also. A year later, in October, 1640, the vicar of St. Paul's was cited before the High Commission Court, and asked plain questions as to his mode of administering the communion. He replied that he knew of no canon forbidding him to administer the sacrament to them that did not come up to the rails.[3] In this attitude he was sustained by his leading parishioners, among whom were John Eston, his churchwarden of the previous year, John Grewe, and Anthony Harrington, three men whom we shall meet with again as the founders of the church to which Bunyan afterwards belonged.

What the Court of High Commission did with John Bradshaw there remain no records to show. For before long both that court and those who inspired its proceedings had more urgent duty on their hands than that of looking after him. A storm was gathering, before the fury of which great heads were soon to bend low, and within a few months there was summoned that Long Parliament which was to change so many things before

[1] Laud's Reports to the King, 1636. *Lambeth MSS.*, 943, p. 267.
[2] *House of Lords MSS.*, Aug. 5th, 1641.
[3] *State Papers, Dom.*, Charles I., Oct. 7th, 1640, vol. cccclxix., 52.

its work was done. To this ever-memorable assembly Bedfordshire sent up three parliamentarians, Sir Beauchamp St. John of Bletsoe, Sir Oliver Luke, and his son, Sir Samuel of Cople Wood End, and the royalist Lord Wentworth of Todyngton. Within a month Lord Wentworth was raised to the Upper House in his own right, and Sir John Burgoyne, a parliamentarian, took his place. By this change the county in its representation came to be wholly on the side of Pym and Hampden in the impending struggle. The feeling of the time was electric, both as to hopes and fears. Parliament met in November, and in January those of "the nobility, knights, gentrie, ministers, freeholders, and inhabitants of the county of Bedford" who were for Laud and the King sent up a petition desiring to "manifest their affection to the Book of Common Prayer, which was with such care and sinceritie refined from the dross of Romish intermixture, with so much pietie reduced to its present purity"; and they pray that the present form of Church government may be continued, and the statutes concerning offenders against the same be put into execution.[1]

Parliament received this petition, but not with the same sympathetic attention they bestowed upon another document sent up from Bedfordshire on the 13th of the same month. This was a petition and articles from John Harvey of Cardington against Dr. Pocklington, rector of Yelden, "as a chiefe author and ringleader in all those innovations which have of late flowed into the Church of England." Hugh Reeve also, of Ampthill, another Bedfordshire clergyman of like proclivities, was ordered to be arrested by the Sergeant-at-Arms for his popish practices, and in the early months of 1641 petitions from aggrieved parishioners went up from all sides, like leaves before the storm. Nor did the men of Bedfordshire content themselves with seeking redress of local and private wrongs. On Tuesday, the 16th of March, a petition was presented to Parliament by Sir John Burgoyne, who was accompanied by some two thousand persons, "the high sheriff, knights, esquires, gentlemen, ministers, freeholders, and others, inhabitants of the county of Bedford." They first express their gratitude to Parliament for what in so short a space had already been accomplished; for the pious care which had removed scandalous and superstitious innovations in religion; for the reassembling of Parliament, the removal of illegal taxes;

[1] *State Papers, Dom.*, Charles I., 1640, 1641 [Jan.], No. 110.

for the abolition of the Star Chamber and the Court of High Commission, and for the taking away of bishops' votes in Parliament. With an obvious reference to Strafford and Laud, who were then in the Tower awaiting their trial, the petition asks for the displacement of all evil councillors and the punishment of all delinquents, and for the complete removal of all burdensome and scandalous ceremonies, and of all corrupt and scandalous ministers. They desire also that a learned, pious, and conscientious ministry may be provided for and maintained, especially in market towns and populous places; that the pious and painful divines, who for unjust and frivolous causes had been deprived by the bishops and their officers, might receive ample reparation, and that there might be "a faithfull magistracie as well as a painfull ministrie."[1]

Such was the tenor of the petition subscribed so numerously and presented to Parliament so impressively by the people of Bedfordshire. In the then prevailing temper of the House of Commons, both the petition and the demonstration were right welcome at Westminster. It was ordered that Mr. Speaker, in the name of the House, shall take particular notice, and give the gentlemen of Bedfordshire thanks for their petition. It was no ordinary occasion, no common display of the feeling of the country, and even London was stirred at the sight. For these men from the Midlands rode four abreast through the city on their way to Westminster. "I myself," says Nehemiah Wallington, "did see above two thousand of these men come riding from Finsbury Fields, four in a rank, with their protestations in their hats."[2]

[1] Broadside, Printed by a true copy with the petitioners' approbation, at the charge of John Chambers, 1641.

[2] *Historical Notices*, II. 31.

II.

ELSTOW AND THE BUNYANS OF ELSTOW.

If, as is not improbable, any considerable portion of the two thousand petitioners from Bedfordshire started from the county town, Bunyan, who was then a lad of twelve, may have stood and with wistful eyes watched this significant cavalcade as it passed through his native village, along the main street of which then lay the high road to London.

Elstow, a little more than a mile to the south-west of Bedford, is a quaint, quietly nestling place, with an old-world look upon it, scarcely touched by the movements of our modern life. Fronting the road-side, with overhanging storeys and gabled dormers, are half-timbered cottages, some of which, judging from the oaken rafters and staircases of their interiors, have seen better days. The long building in the centre of the village, and now turned into cottages, with projecting upper chambers and central overhanging gateway, still retains much of the external appearance it presented as a hostelry for pilgrims in pre-Reformation times.* Opposite to the gate of this hostelry is the opening to the village green, on the north side of which stands what we may call the Moot Hall of the parish, a picturesque building of timber and brick, which, with its oaken beams bearing traces of Perpendicular carving and its ruddy tiles touched here and there with many-tinted lichen, presents to the eye in the summer sun-light a pleasant combination of colour and form. This curious structure of fifteenth century work, furnishing a somewhat fine example of the domestic architecture of the period, was probably originally erected to serve as the *hospitium* for travellers, and while not far from the road was yet within the *ballium* or outer court of Elstow Abbey.[1] At a later time, when the manorial rights passed from the Abbess to the Crown, there were held in the upper chamber those courts

* It has been suggested that this was The Bell Inn mentioned in Dr. Brown's Preface in this volume.

[1] *Architectural Notes*, by M. J. C. Buckley, 1885.

Photo: G. A. Gearey, Bedford.]

THE MOOT HALL: ELSTOW GREEN.

of the lord of the manor with View of Frankpledge, of which Bunyan's ancestors had some experience in the century before his birth. It was the scene, also, of village festivities, statute hirings, and all public occasions of village life.

To the west of this building, on what was probably once the centre of a much larger green, rises the pedestal and broken stem of the ancient market cross round which were held those famous fairs of Elstow, possible suggestions of Vanity Fair, which had been a great village institution ever since the days of Henry II. It was on the green sward stretching this way and that round the cross that Bunyan played his Sunday games and heard those mysterious voices which changed for him the current of his life.

The elm-trees by the churchyard wall have, for safety's sake, been shorn of their upper branches, and the Church, of stern necessity, but with loving, heedful care, has been extensively restored; but the church tower, standing apart and, like the towers of Blyth, Shrewsbury, and Christchurch, of later date than the main building, remains the same as when Bunyan leaned against its doorway and delighted to ring the bells in the chamber overhead. The massive buttresses, the time-worn oaken door, "the roughly paved floor trodden with the hob-nailed boots of generations of ringers," the very bells themselves are unchanged by the two hundred and eighty years which have come and gone since he was there.

Passing through the church, or round it, on the south side we come upon a park-like meadow, with its handsome trees and colony of rooks, once part of the monastic enclosure; upon the delightful little chamber, with its groined roof and central pillar of Purbeck marble, sometimes, though erroneously, called the chapter house, sometimes the nuns' choir, but the actual use of which, standing as it does west of the church, it is not so easy to determine. We come also upon the fish ponds of the abbey, now choked with weeds, and upon the old mansion of the Hillersdons, whose stately doorway, and ruined walls, and mullioned windows strong shoots of ivy have covered with a mantle of green.

Elstow, or Helenstow, the *stow* or stockaded place of St. Helen, a name cognate to such forms as Bridestow and Morwenstow, was so called because of the dedication of the old Saxon church to Helena, the mother of Constantine the Great. In 1078 there was founded in the place, by Judith, the niece of the Conqueror, a Benedictine nunnery, which remained the central feature of Elstow life till the surrender of the monasteries at the Reformation. In 1553 a grant was made by the Crown to Sir Humphrey Radcliffe, of "the whole demesne and site of the late Monastery or Abbey of Elenstowe, in our County of Bedford, dissolved." And while the abbey with its surroundings was thus handed over to the grantee, the church was dismantled, the materials being probably used in the construction of the mansion-house hard by; the nave was shortened by two bays; the central tower beyond, and the transepts, chancel, and Lady Chapel were taken down; a beautiful Norman doorway was removed from the east end, to form the present north-west entrance; and the church tower now standing by itself was constructed to hold the bells, which had been removed from the central tower.

Sir Humphrey Radcliffe died in 1566, his widow surviving him at Elstow till 1594. In 1616 his son, Sir Edward, sold the Elstow estate to Sir Thomas Hillersdon, who, in the days of James I., built at least a part of the house now in ruins to the south-west of the church. The Hillersdon arms are to be seen over the very graceful porch, which is in the best style of the English Renaissance. Of this part of the building Mr Buckley says:—"The harmony of its proportions and the grace of its details show this little edifice to have been the work of a master hand; in the masques and arabesques which decorate the *intrados* of the arch, as well as the panels in the pediments of the pilasters, are traces of Italian taste; and from the general style of the work there seems every reason to believe that Inigo Jones planned and added this elegant porch to the old manor-house."[1] Standing back a little way from the high road, its carriage-drive leading up to this finely sculptured entrance, the manor-house was at its best in Bunyan's Elstow days, and may have suggested to him the conception of that "very stately palace* the name of which was Beautiful, which stood just by the highway side."

* Or, more probably, Houghton House, on Ampthill Heights.

Turning now from the surroundings of Bunyan's native village to his family antecedents, we find that his ancestors were in

[1] *Architectural Notes*, p. 205. In support of the opinion here expressed, it may be mentioned that Inigo Jones is known to have been on a visit to Bedfordshire about the time this porch was built.

Bedfordshire as early at least as 1199. From the fact that in 1219 the form of the name was Buignon, really an old French word equivalent to the modern *beignet*,[1] it is more than probable that the Bunyans sprang from those Northmen who came to us through Normandy. At all events, the name was found on the other side of the Channel as well as on this, for in the time of Henry VIII. the authorities of Dieppe complained to the deputy of Calais that the Flemings had taken prisoners Jehan Bunon and Collin Allais.[2]

The earliest settlement of the Bunyans in Bedfordshire seems to have been at Pulloxhill (*Polochessele*), a village about nine miles from Elstow. When Norman nobles quartered themselves upon English lands they gathered round them retainers and domestics from across the sea. In this way probably the Bunyans came to be the feudal tenants of Nigel de Albini, the ancestor of the Earls of Arundel, whose son Henry established himself at Cainhoe Castle, and to whom Pulloxhill, and eleven other neighbouring manors, belonged. In the Dunstable Chronicle we find the following record made by prior Richard de Morin in 1219: "In this year the aforesaid Justiciaries were at Bedford in presence of whom we obtained our return against Henry Bunyan for the land of John Travayle."[3] The Assize Roll of Bedfordshire for that year has preserved no record of this case, which may, however, have been on a missing membrane, but it shows that at the same Assize there were presentments made by commissioners of Henry Buignon by Simon son of Robert, and of John Buingnon by Roger son of Walter.[4] In

[1] Godefrey gives this quotation from an early Soissons MS.: "Et bone char et granz buignons." *Dictionnaire de l'Ancienne Langue Française et de tous ses Dialectes du* IXe *Siècle*. The word signifies a little raised pattie with fruit in the middle, and came to be applied to any round knob or bunch (*Ital.* bugnon); any small elevation or convexity (*Icelandic* bunga). Thus we get *bun* and *bunch* and curiously enough the ordinary *bunion*, a raised swelling on the feet. *Vide* Skeat's *Etymol. Dict.*

It may be mentioned that as the surname of the Bedfordshire family the word has been spelt in no fewer than thirty-four different ways, thus: In the *Assize Rolls* of 1 John and 3 Henry III. it was spelt Bingnon, Buingnon, and Buniun; in the *Dunstable Chronicle* of the same century: Boinun, Boynun, and Bunyun; in the *Subsidy Rolls* of a century later: Bonionn, Boynon, Boynonn and Boynun: in the *Book of the Luton Guild* of 1518: Bonean and Boynyon; in the *Court-Roll* of the manor of Elstow (1542—1550), and in the Chalgrave *Register* (1539—1628): Bonyon; in the *Transcript Registers* from Elstow (1603—1640): Bonion, Bonionn, Boniun, Bonnion, Bonnionn, Bonniun, Bonoyon, Bonyon, Bonyonn, Boonyon, Bunen, Bunian, Bunion, Bunnion, Bunnionn, Bunyin, Bunyan, Bunyon, Bynyon; and finally in the record of Bedfordshire *Administrations* it is twice spelt Binyan and once Binnyan. Bunyan's grandfather signed himself Bonyon; his father seems to have been the first to give the name the form it has since retained. [*Vide* Addendum.]

[2] *Letters and Papers*, Henry VIII., vol. iii. part 3, 1521.

[3] *Annales Monastici*, edited by H. R. Luard, M.A., 1866, vol. iii., 54.

[4] *Assize Rolls*, Bedfordshire, 3 Henry III.

the Dunstable Chronicle[1] there are three other references by a subsequent prior, showing the relation of the family to Almaric St. Amand, the descendant of de Albini. They are as follows: "In the same year (1257), after the feast of St. Martin, we bought of Almaric St. Amand land which he had of John Boynun at Pullokeshille for forty-three marks and a half." Three pages later the entry is repeated, with the addition that the purchase made from St. Amand was land which he had "of the gift of John Boinun." It would appear that this John Boynun or Boinun was a freeman of St. Amand's, for on the death of the latter in 1286 the then prior of Dunstable tells us that scutage was paid to St. Amand's executors, and that "for the fee of John Boynun who made service for half a knight," a certain payment was made. This is some clue to his social position, for the prior had previously said that a knight's service was for five hides of land, so that Boynun held some two hundred and twenty acres on condition of furnishing military service to the extent of half a knight. This scutage fee paid on the death of his chief amounted to about £80 of present value.

From Pulloxhill the family of the Bunyans moved, one part of them to the south, in the direction of Chalgrave and Dunstable, the other branch to the north in the direction of Elstow. Of those who moved to the south there sprang one concerning whom there remains this dark and evil record in the Assize Roll of 1219: "In the half-hundred of Stanburgh. A certain clerk unknown was found killed in the fields of Toternhoe. William Turviter was the first person who found him, but he is not suspected; Ralph Buingnon of Dunstable, who was hanged for that death, acknowledged that he killed him, and on account of that death was arrested. Let enquiry be made at Dunstable for his chattels. The Englishry was not presented, therefore the crime was murder."[2] The meaning of this being, of course, the Normans, living in the midst of the hostile population they had conquered, for their own defence enacted and kept in force till 1340, the law known as the Presentment of Englishry, in accordance with which an unknown man found slain was presumed to be a Norman, unless the hundred in which he was found could prove that he was an Englishman. If they could not a fine was levied on the hundred, and in this case towards the

[1] *Annales Monastici*, vol iii., pp. 43, 204, 207.
[2] *Assize Rolls*, Bedfordshire, 3 Henry III., memb. 14.

payment of the fine for the murder of this unknown priest the murderer's own chattels were to be inquired for.

Leaving this Ralph Buingnon, who came to an end so tragic in the south of the county, we turn now to that portion of the Bunyan family with whom we are more immediately concerned, and who, at least twenty years earlier, had moved in the direction of Elstow. The earliest reference we have to the name relates to these. In 1199 William Buniun pleaded against the abbess of Elstow in the Court of King's Bench that William of Wilsamstede had sued him in respect of half a virgate of land which he held in that place.[1] The meaning of the plea probably being that this was a friendly suit to determine the title to the land—to settle, in fact, whether Buniun was the tenant of the abbess or of the aforesaid William. The point of interest for us in the case, of course, is that as early as 1199 there was a Buniun holding land at Wilstead, only a mile away from Elstow.

The next document is even more interesting still, inasmuch as it shows that not only had the Bunyans come to Wilstead, but that a William Boynon, probably a descendant of the William of 1199, was living in 1327 on the very spot in the fields by Harrowden and Elstow, on which, three hundred years later, John Bunyan was born. This document, again, relates to an agreement made at Westminster, on the morrow of All Souls, in which Simon, son of Robert atte Felde, of Elnestowe, and William de Maydenbury Peleter were the plaintiffs, and Wm. Boynon, of Harewedon, and Matilda his wife were deforciants of a messuage and an acre of land with the appurtenances in Elnestowe. A certain covenant was made; " and for this acknowledgment, warranty, fine, and agreement the said Simon and William gave to the aforesaid William Boynon and Matilda one hundred shillings of silver."[2]

It is a long interval between this document of 1327 and the year 1542, yet between these two dates no references to the Bunyan family of any kind have reached us. There has been preserved in the Augmentation Office the Court Roll of the manor of Elstow, embracing the years between 1542 and 1550, which presents several points of interest. The earlier records of the manor appear to have been lost with the rest of the

[1] *Rot. Cur. Reg.*, 1 John (20th June, 1199). I., 417.

[2] *Fines*, Bedford, 20 Edward II. (1327). No. 2.

documents in the possession of the Abbess of Elstow. During these years, which were those between the surrender of the monastery and the grant to Sir Humphrey Radcliffe, the manor was vested in the Crown, and there was held each spring and autumn a Court of the Manor, with view of Frankpledge. That is to say, at these Courts the socmen, or juratores, or homagers, as they were variously termed, the men who held lands under the manor did fealty for those lands, or paid fines on renewal or relief in socage, which was a kind of succession duty to the lord of the manor. Besides transacting such business as this, these Courts also exercised jurisdiction over the general affairs of the village, marking delinquencies, settling disputes, redressing grievances, and punishing offenders. The first Court of which the Roll makes mention was held on the 13th of April, 1542, and among the homagers present was Thomas Bonyon. After the record of other business transacted, there is the following entry:

"At this Court it is witnessed by the homage that William Bonyon who held freely of the lord the King as of his manor of Elnestow a messuage and a pightell with the appurtenances in Elnestow. And nine acres of land particularly and severally lying in the fields of Elnestow by fealty, suit of court, and rent by the year of three shillings and one halfpenny from which last Court he died. And that Thomas Bonyon is the son and next heir of the aforesaid William Bonyon and is of the age of forty years and more, whereupon there falls to the lord the king of relief in socage—iij^{s} 0½^{d}—which said Thomas Bonyon acknowledges that he holds the aforesaid messuage, pightell, and nine acres of land by the rent and service aforesaid. And that the aforesaid messuage and pightell are situate together and lie in Elnestow aforesaid between the messuage and close of Thomas Whytebred on the west part and the highway there on the east part."

In the record of the Court held six years later, on 30th of April, 1548, there is the following entry, which is interesting as describing yet more accurately the identical spot, with its surroundings, on which, eighty years afterwards, Bunyan was born. It relates to the sale of three roods of the land which had belonged to the Bonyons, and the subsequent readjustment of the small quit rent payable to the lord of the manor:

"Elnestow — View of Frankpledge with Court, 30th April, 38 Henry VIII. Fealty. To this court came Robert Corteys and acknowledged that he held freely of the said lord the king as of the manor aforesaid by fealty suit of court and rent of a penny and a halfpenny by the year three roods of arable land together lying in the east field of Elnestow

ELSTOW CHURCH AND BELFRY.

upon the furlong called Pesselynton, between the land of John Gascoign, knight, on either side, and abuts on the north head upon Cardyngton broke and the south head upon the close called Bonyon's End. which he had of the gift of Thomas Bonyon of Elnestowe, in the county of Bedford, labourer, as by the charter of the said Thomas bearing date the 18th day of the month of April in the 37th year of the said lord the king is fully clear, which said three roods were late parcel of a messuage and certain lands late of William Bonyon, father of the aforesaid Thomas Bunyon, and which said messuage and lands were charged to the said lord the king with one whole yearly rent of three shillings and fourpence. And the aforesaid three roods were apportioned at the aforesaid rent of a penny and a halfpenny by the year. And the aforesaid Thomas Bonyon is discharged of the same yearly rent of a penny and a halfpenny."[1]

Thomas Bonyon was evidently going down in the world, and selling piece by piece his ancestral land. For a year later came John Lynwood to the Court, acknowledging "that he held freely of the lord the king as of his manor there by fealty, suit of Court and rent of 2d. by the year, three acres and a rood of land particularly and severally lying in Harodon Sharpe-fold, in the parish of Cardyngton, which were formerly of Thomas Bonyon."

There were sixteen Courts of the manor of Elstow of which we have knowledge at the end of the reign of Henry VIII. and the beginning of that of Edward VI., and at all of them but one Thomas Bonyon appears among the dozen or so of juratores or homagers. Besides the sale, first of three roods and then of three acres and a rood of his land, there are signs that either he or his wife was in trouble at twelve out of the sixteen of these Courts. She is described in one place as "a common brewer of beer"; and in another as "a common baker of human bread"—human bread, we may presume, as distinguished from horse-bread; and eleven times over she was fined for breaking the assize of beer and bread—that is, for asking higher prices than those fixed by the Court of the manor. In the days of the Abbess she would have been sent to the cucking-stool for her repeated offences; but in the more lenient days on which she had fallen, she was simply amerced seven times at a penny and four times at twopence. In 1547 Thomas Bonyon himself and not his wife appeared before the Court as the offending brewer of beer, and was fined a penny. This, however, did not

[1] Exchequer Court of Augmentations, *Court Rolls*, portfolio xi., No. 22.

prevent his being chosen, in the autumn of the same year, along with Thomas Crowley, as parish constable, to which office he was duly sworn. Seven years later this ancestor of Bunyan, who seems to have been the keeper of a small roadside inn on the way to Medbury, was called before a much more august tribunal than that of the Court of the manor. In 1554, for some reason not given, he was summoned to appear before the Privy Council at Westminster. In the register of the Council there is a minute under date November 18th, ordering "certain persons to attende upon the lorde Cobham at Rochester at the commyng in of the lorde Cardynall Pole, and from thence to Gravesend." Two days later another meeting of Council was held, when letters of appearance were addressed from their lordships to "baylief Williams, George Walton, gent., Bunyon, victualler, all of Ellstowe, in the Countie of Bedford," with seven other persons from the same parish, whose names were also given.[1] The mention of Cardinal Pole at this time is suggestive of the returning tide of Papal power in England. Was it for his Protestantism that Bunyon the victualler was summoned before the Privy Council of Queen Mary?

The Court Roll of the manor, interesting as it is in itself, is interesting also as furnishing incidental confirmation of the tradition among the people of Elstow as to the exact spot which was Bunyan's birthplace. There is a cottage shown in the village street as Bunyan's cottage, in which there is no doubt he lived for some time after his marriage; but the ancients of the place have always maintained that he was born in the eastern fields of the parish, and close to the hamlet of Harrowden. That extremity of the parish they called Bunyan's End—the name by which, as we have seen, it was known eighty years before Bunyan was born, and probably for centuries earlier. A pathway in the fields was spoken of as Bunyan's Walk; two fields on the slope beyond the southern stream still go by the name of "Bunyans" and "farther Bunyans" among the labourers on the farm; and finally, with the persistence of English village names, the piece of land between the two streams is still known as "the furlong called Pesselynton," as the Roll shows it was in the days of Henry VIII. When, in addition, we remember that a small farmer named John Rogers, who died in the village of Elstow in 1859, at the advanced age of ninety-two, and whose

[1] *Privy Council Register,* 1553—1558, p. 189.

great-grandfather, living in the next house to the Bunyans, was John Bunyan's playfellow, frequently pointed out to his neighbours as the dreamer's birthplace the piece of land south of "Cardyngton broke" described by the Roll of the manor as Bonyon's End, we feel at once that State document and popular tradition combine to give us certainty as to the site.

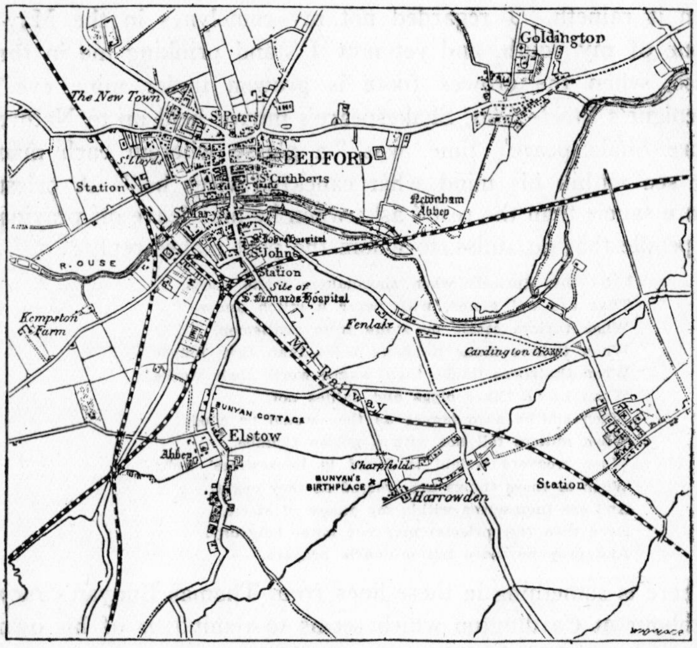

Map of Bedford and Elstow, showing Bunyan's Birthplace.
Scale—One inch to a mile.

Before passing from the sixteenth century to the seventeenth, there is one point of literary interest on which for a moment we are tempted to linger. The Court Roll, it will be remembered, describes Bonyon's End as having on both sides of it the land of John Gascoign, knight. Sir John was at that time living at Cardington, the adjacent parish, where his son George was born about 1525. So that George Gascoigne, our earliest English satirist, and John Bunyan, our greatest religious allegorist, were born within half a mile of each other, and on ancestral lands which interlaced. Gascoigne, with not a little original genius and freshness of thought, was one of the earliest of our strictly vernacular poets. It is said that Shakespeare's *Winter's Tale* was partly suggested by the joint version of the *Phenissae* by

Gascoigne and Kinwelmersh.[1] He had certainly not a few quaint touches and homely thrusts such as Bunyan himself might have written; as when he says that "he who will throw a stone at everie dogge which barketh had neede of a great satchell or pocket"; or when, in after years, regretting his wanton, wasted youth, he says: "I have loytred, I confesse, when the sunne did shine, and now I strive al in vaine to loade the cart when it raineth. I regarded not my comelynes in the May-moone of my youth, and yet now I stand prinking me in the glasse, when the crowes foote is growen under mine eye." Gascoigne's *Steele Glas,* Shakespeare's mirror held up to Nature before Shakespeare's time, was "a glasse wherein each man may see within his mind what canckred vices be." A priest "more saucie than the rest" asks when he may leave off praying for people that do amiss, to whom the poet makes reply:

"I tel thee (priest) when shoomakers make shoes,
That are wel sowed, with never a stitch amisse,
When taylors steale no stuffe from gentlemen,
When tinkers make no more holes than they founde,
When thatchers thinke their wages worth their worke,
When Davie Diker diggs and dallies not,
When smiths shoo horses as they would be shod,
When millers toll not with a golden thumbe,
When weavers weight is found in housewives' web:
When al these things are ordered as they ought,
And see themselves within my glasse of steele,
Even then (my priests) may you make holy day,
And pray no more but ordinarie prayers."

There is something in these lines from Thomas Bunyan's racy neighbour at Cardington which seems to remind us of his own descendant, and having thus connected the two for a moment in our minds, we may now return once more to the Bunyans themselves. Of them, after the Court Roll, of 1550, and the Privy Council minute of 1554, we know nothing more till 1603, when the Transcript Registers commence. The Parish Register of Elstow for the period earlier than 1641 has long been lost, but fortunately the returns sent year by year to the Registry, in accordance with the canon of 1603, come to our assistance. Almost the first entry we find in the first return from Elstow is that of the baptism of John Bunyan's father, which is recorded thus:

1602-3: "Thomas the Sonne of Thomas Bunyon the xxiiijth daye of ffebr."

[1] The *Complete Poems* of George Gascoigne: Collected and edited for the Roxburghe Library, by W. C. Hazlitt, 1869. Two vols. 4to.

Fac-Similes from the Elstow Transcript Registers.

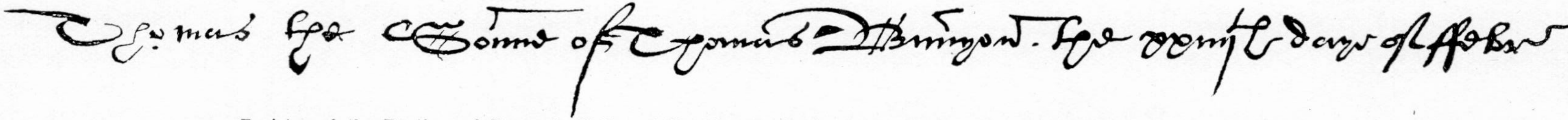

Register of the Baptism of Bunyan's Father, 1603—*Thomas the Sonne of Thomas Bunyon the* xxiiijth *daye of February.*

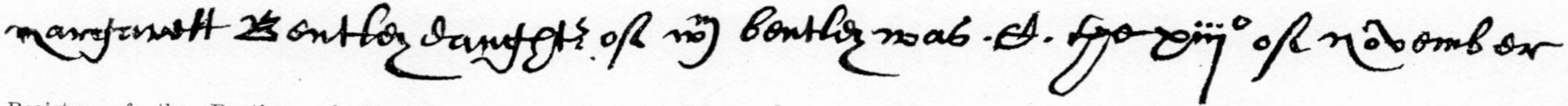

Register of the Baptism of Bunyan's Mother, 1603—*Margaret Bentley daughter of Wm. Bentley was C[hristened] the* xiijth *of November.*

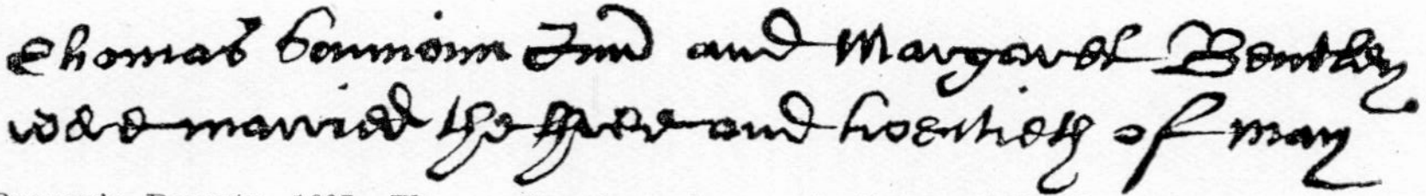

Register of the Marriage of Bunyan's Parents, 1627—*Thomas Bonnionn Junr and Margaret Bentley were married the three and twentieth of May.*

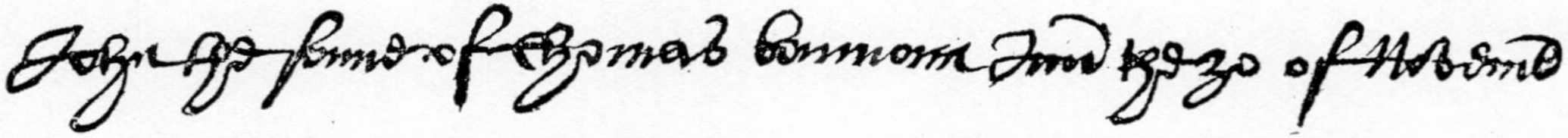

Register of Bunyan's Baptism, 1628—*John the Sonne of Thomas Bonnionn Junr the* 30 *of Novembr.*

The mother of the child then baptized may have died in giving him birth, for towards the end of the same year Thomas Bunyon, the father, was again married at Elstow Church to Elizabeth Leigh. This Thomas, the elder, the grandfather of John, lived on till 1641, and describes himself in his will as a "pettie chapman," or small village trader. Like his grandson after him he appears not to have been quite so submissive to the authorities of the time as they could have desired. Two, and only two time-worn Act Books of the Archdeaconry of Bedford relating to the times of James I. have been preserved. From one of these we find that at the Court held at Ampthill, October 21st, 1617, two of the Elstow parishioners were presented by the churchwardens before the commissary. One of these was Thomas Cranfield, who was charged with "refusing to sit in a seat of the church where the churchwardens placed him"; the other was Thomas Bonion, who was presented for telling the churchwardens they were "forsworne men." Feeling was evidently running high just then, and indeed that year matters ecclesiastical were altogether in a bad way in Elstow, for three months later the vicar of the parish himself, Henry Bird, was presented at the same court for neglecting his cure; "on Sonday was a fortnight there was noe service," and on another occasion "Rose Ravens of Elstowe was cited for churching herself, the minister being at home."

Seven other children were born to the elder Thomas Bonion after the birth of Bunyan's father, four of whom died in infancy. He himself surviving till 1641, made his will on the 25th of November in that year, in which he describes himself as, "I Thomas Bonyon of the parish of Elstowe in the countie of Bedford, Pettie Chapman, being sicke of bodie but of perfect remembrance, thanks be given to Almightie God, doe make and ordayne this my last Will and Testament in manner and forme following That is to say First I give and bequeathe my soule into the handes of Almightie God my Creator assuringe myselfe by the death and passion of my blessed Saviour Jesus Christ to receive pardon and remission for all my sinnes and that my soule shall be received into his heavenly kingdome ther to rest with him for ever And my bodie to the earth whereof it is made to be buried in Christian buriall at the discreson of my executrix hereafter named And for the worldly goods that God hath blessed me withall I doe dispose of as followeth Item I give and bequeath to Anne Bonyon my wife [his third wife] after my decease the Cottage or Tenement wherein I doe now dwell with the appurtenances during the tearme of her naturall life And after the decease of Anne Bonyon my said wife I give and bequeath the said Cottage or Tenement with the appurtenances unto my Two Sonnes Thomas Bonyon and Edward Bonyon and their Heires for ever to be equally parted and devided between them after the decease of my said wiffe." He further leaves the sum of £5 to his daughter, Elizabeth Watson, the wife of Thomas Watson, and to his grandchildren, of whom, of course John Bunyan was one, "sixe pence a peece toe bee paied them when they accomplish their several ages of one and twentie yeares." Everything else he leaves to Anne Bonyon, his 'loveing' wife, whom he makes whole and sole executrix, concluding thus: "I doe further make and ordayne Thomas Carter of Kempston in the said countie of Bedford, gentleman, my loveinge and Kind Friend, overseer of this my last Will and Testament And do give him Twelve pence in remembrance for his paines to be taken in seeinge this my last Will and Testament duly and truly executed."[1] The document was signed with a cross in the presence of Henry Latham and Walter Cooper, and was proved before Walter Walker on the 14th of December, 1641.

Thomas Bonyon, the son of this man and the father of John, was first married to Anne Pinney, at Elstow Church, on the 10th of January, 1623, when he was in his twentieth year. In 1627 Anne died, and so far as the register shows, died childless. The same year he came again to Elstow Church to be married, this time to the wife who was to be the mother of his illustrious son. As we did not, till the recent search among the Transcript Registers, know the maiden name of the mother of the Dreamer, it may be well to give the entry in full, which is as follows:

1627. "Thomas Bonnionn, Junr., and Margaret Bentley were married the three and twentieth of May."

We who, in the course of modern thought, have come to attach so much importance to hereditary transmission, would have been glad to know more than we do of the character and personality of the parents of one who occupies so prominent a place in English literature, and who was unmistakably a child

[1] *Bedfordshire Wills*, 1641. No. 202.

of genius. Unfortunately, their son, while telling so much about his own inward experiences, tells us but little concerning his father and mother. Even the little he does tell seems as if it ought to be qualified. When we remember that the wills of his father and grandfather, and of his maternal grandmother have been preserved in the Registry of the District Court of Probate from a time when the poorest of the poor never made any wills at all, and that the house in which he was born had been the property of his ancestors from time immemorial, it would seem as if Bunyan in his humility had depreciated the social position of his family more than he had need. He says, "For my descent then, it was, as is well known by many, of a low and inconsiderable generation, my father's house being of that rank that is meanest and most despised of all the families in the land." That these expressions ought not to carry the full force they carry to-day is shown by the fact he proceeds to state. "But yet, notwithstanding the meanness and inconsiderableness of my parents, it pleased God to put it into their hearts to put me to school to learn both to read and write, the which I also attained according to the rate of other poor men's children." Still, when all fair deductions are made, Bunyan's parents were poor enough no doubt, and the struggle of life with them keen enough. It need scarcely be said, however, that he was not the man to give forth unmanly wailings about the lowliness of his position or the hardships of his lot. In his own hearty religious fashion he sums up the question by saying: "Though I have not here, as others, to boast of noble blood or of a high-born state according to the flesh, all things considered I magnify the heavenly Majesty for that by this door he brought me into this world, to partake of the grace and life that is in Christ by the Gospel."

Thomas Bunyan, his father, usually spoken of as a tinker, described himself in his will as a "braseyer."[1] Working at his forge by the cottage in the fields, repairing the tools and utensils of his neighbours at Elstow or Harrowden, or wandering for the purposes of his trade from one lonely farmhouse to another, he would be neither better nor worse than the rest of the craftsmen of the hammer and the forge. We may perhaps regard this tinker of Elstow as the counterpart of the tinker of Turvey, a well-known character of those times, who lived some half-dozen

[1] In the books of the Norwich Freemen the "brasyers" included pewterers, plomers and belyaters, or bell-founders.—Rye's *History of Norfolk*. 1885. [*Vide* Addendum.]

miles away across the fields, and who is supposed, in the year of grace 1630, to have "hammered out an epistle to all strolling Tinckers and all brave mettle-men that travel on the Hoofe." In this production of his he boasts of the country he has bestridden, the towns he has traversed, and of the fairs in which he has been drunk. He claims that "all music first came from the hammer," that "the tincker is a rare fellow," for that "he is a scholler and was of Brazen-nose Colledge in Oxford, an excellent carpenter, for he builded Coppersmith's Hall."[1] Thomas Bunyan may not have been to the full the roystering blade this brother "mettle-man" was, but in the course of his rounds he would meet with him and the like of him, and under the trees of the village green or on the settle of the village inn could probably tell as good a story and perhaps drink as deep.

Margaret Bunyan, the tinker's wife, and the Dreamer's mother, like her husband, was a native of Elstow, being born there in the same year in which he was born, as the following entry from the Transcript Register shows:

1603. "Margarett Bentley, daughter of Wm. Bentley, was C. [christened] the xiij° of November."

Though her parents, William Bentley and Mary Goodwin were married, in 1601, at St. Paul's Church, in Bedford, we may infer that since Mary Bentley, her grandmother, died in Elstow, as a widow, in 1613, the Bentleys, like the Bunyans, had been long resident in the parish. Their names do not occur in the Court Roll of Elstow between 1542 and 1550, but are found in the earliest Transcript Register. In any case, as they were both born in Elstow in the same year, Margaret Bentley had known Thomas Bunyan all her life, when in 1627, at the age of twenty-four, she was married to him in Elstow Church, her sister Rose being also married to his brother Edward the following year. Her mother died as a widow in 1632, though in what year her father died the register omits to state. Her mother's will, drawn up in the neat, scholarly handwriting of John Kellie, the vicar of Elstow, giving as it does some idea of the social condition of John Bunyan's mother before her marriage, as well as a Dutch-like picture of an Elstow cottage interior of two hundred and ninety-five years ago, may in part at least be worth recording.

[1] *The Tinker of Turvey, or Canterbury Tales*, London, 1630. Edited by J. O. Halliwell, F.R.S.

It was on the 27th of June, 1632, that "Mary Bentley, of Elnestoe in the countie of Bedford, widow," after bequeathing her soul to Almighty God her Maker in whom she hopes to be saved through Jesus Christ her Saviour, and her body to be buried in the churchyard at Elnestoe, goes on to say: "Item I give and bequeath to John Bentley my sonne one brasse pott, one little table and all the painted cloaths about the house and the standing Bed in the loft. Item I give to my daughter Margaret the joined stoole in the chamber and my little case. Item I give to my daughter Rosse the Joined forme in the chamber and a Hogshead and the dumbe flake. Item I give to my daughter Elizabeth the lesser kettle and the biggest plater, a flaxen sheet and a flaxen pillowbere, a trumell bed and a coffer in the chamber and the table sheet. Item I give to my daughter Anie my best hatt, my best cuffe, my gowne, my best petticoate, the presse in the chamber, the best boulster and blankett, the coffe above, the skillet and a pewter platter, and the other trummle bed, a harder sheet and a pillowbere." All else she gives and bequeaths to her daughter Mary, whom she makes sole executrix, and whom she charges to see her "honestly buried" and "her buriall discharged." The will was attested by John Kellie, the vicar of Elstow, and Margerie Jaques, a widow, and was proved in the October following. The cottage equipments, and the way they are described, seem to indicate that Margaret Bunyan came not of the very squalid poor, but of people who, though humble in station, were yet decent and worthy in their ways, and took an honourable pride in the simple belongings of their village home.

Scanty as are the references which Bunyan makes to his father, those to his mother are scantier still. This may arise partly from the fact that she died before he reached the age of sixteen, and his remembrance of her may have been dim and distant when two and twenty years later he wrote that story of his life which we find in the *Grace Abounding.* It is of course useless to speculate much where we know so little, yet we are tempted to think that the mother of a child so much above the common kind must herself have been a woman of more than common power. We should not be surprised to be told that she was one of those strongly-marked personalities sometimes met with in English village life—a woman of racy, ready wit, and of picturesque power of expression, who, Mrs. Poyser-like, had a very distinct individuality of her own, and the capacity of making a very distinct impression upon those around her. Unfortunately to us she is little more than a name, and we recall her for a moment from the nameless crowd and from the midst of her "homely joys and destiny obscure" because of the one great event of her life, the birth of her distinguished son, her first-born. The record of that event quietly takes its place in the list of the nineteen christenings of that year, at Elstow Church, in the following form:

1628. "John the sonne of Thomas Bonnionn, Junr. the 30th of Novemb."

The return is signed by John Kellie, minister, and Anthony Manley and William Allerson, churchwardens. The entry is commonplace enough, and made in the same routine fashion as were hundreds more, yet as we read, the record becomes more than usually suggestive of the simple beginnings of a great strong life. Once again we seem to see the wondrous babe carried on that last of the chill days of November of 1628 to Elstow Church. Rude was the little cradle out of which he was lifted, and common-place the cottage, with its grimy forge, out of which he was carried. Looking at all his unpromising surroundings, there comes into our minds a rustic story told about the father of this child by quaint old Thomas Archer, the rector of Houghton Conquest, parish next neighbour to Elstow itself. The delightful old man kept a sort of *chronicon mirabile* of the little rural world in which, king's chaplain as he was, his tranquil days were spent, and in his record, as a curiosity of natural history, he sets down this: "Memorandum.—That in Anno 1625 one Bonion of Elsto clyminge of Rookes neasts in the Bery wood ffound 3 Rookes in a nest, all white as milke and not a blacke feather on them."

Vividly the whole scene comes back to us. This "Bonion of Elsto," the father of the Dreamer, wandering in vacant mood in the Ellensbury Wood, looks and wonders at the three milk-white birds in the black rook's nest. And as we watch him, the surprise on his face becomes symbol and presage of a wider world's wonder than his, the wonder with which men find in the rude nest of his own tinker's cottage a child all lustrous with

ELSTOW VILLAGE

the gifts of genius, a life memorable in the literature of the great world stretching far away beyond Elstow Green, and memorable, too, in the spiritual history and experience of many souls in many nations through the centuries to come.

ADDENDA—Chapter II.

(Footnote, p. 19.)

In *English Surnames: Their Sources and Significations,* by C. W. Bardsley, M.A., 1875, is an interesting account of name derivations. The author says: "If John were doughty, he became 'Prujean,' that is, preuxjean; if fat, 'Grosjean'; if young, 'Youngjohn'; if clownish, 'Hobjohn'; if big, 'Micklejohn'; if small, 'Littlejohn' or 'Petitjean.' Lastly, we have the estimable 'Bonjohn,' the origin, I doubt not, of 'Bonyon' and 'Bunyan,' the familiar bearer of the latter form of which we shall doubtless admit to be worthy of his name. . . . It is a happy chance that when we speak, as we often do, of 'good John Bunyan,' we simply give him a reduplication of that very title which none more richly merits than he. In 1310 there was a 'Jon Bonjon' in London, and still earlier than this a 'Durand le Bon John' figures in the Hundred Rolls."

(Footnote, p. 29.)

The writer of *John Bunyan: A Study,* in the Elstow Edition (1881) of *The Pilgrim's Progress,* says (p. xx.): "The inhabitants of villages in the seventeenth century depended more upon the tradesmen of their own place than is the case now, and the brazier, who made and mended household cooking utensils, occupied the same position in the trading community as an ironmonger does now. They sent out workmen to do repairs, as is the custom still, and John Bunyan would, in the ordinary course, be expected and would be glad to take journeys as his father's representative."

Elstow Village.

Elstow in 1670 consisted of sixty-one houses, of which, according to the Hearth Tax Rolls, twenty-five had one hearth each, eighteen two, and eight three. The other ten houses had from four to seventeen hearths each. Thomas Bunyan, the father of John Bunyan, dwelt in a cottage with one hearth; Robert Crumpton (mentioned in Chapters VII. and X.) lived in an eight-hearth house; and Robert Holstock in one with two hearths. (Chapter IX.)

III.

THE CIVIL WARS.

[*NOTE.*—The curtailment or revision of this chapter would have debarred the reader from following the close, accurate reasoning of the author of this biography, although he, in the last edition, 1902 (in two volumes) did abbreviate and amend it. The present editor, however, feels that Dr. Brown's original argument should be retained intact, so comment and supplementary detail are given in the addenda.]

THE cottage at Bunyan's End in which Bunyan was born has long since disappeared. Portions of it were still remaining at the close of the eighteenth century, when the site was ploughed up, and, with the nine acres of land once belonging to it, was added to the neighbouring farm. It stood at the foot of a gently sloping hill, and between two streams which, after enclosing "the furlong called Pesselynton," met a little farther on in the hamlet of Harrowden. One of these streams flowed close past the cottage, and after heavy rains turned the field behind, as the land still shows, into a veritable Slough of Despond, into which whosoever wandered stuck fast in miry perplexity.

Thomas Bunyan's family, living only a few yards within the Elstow parish boundary, were almost as near to Bedford town as to Elstow Church, the spire of St. Paul's seen through the elm-trees from the top of the grassy slope to the south, being only about a mile away. A bridle-road from Wilstead through Medbury, passing near the front of the cottage, took the line of the willow-trees still to be seen in the hedgerow and joining the main road at the leper house of St. Leonard, went into the town by the ancient hospital of St. John. If Bunyan was sent to Bedford to school rather than to Elstow village, this would be the path he took. In the *Scriptural Poems,* published as his in the collected works,[1] there are these lines:

"For I'm no poet, nor a poet's son,
But a mechanic guided by no rule
But what I gained in a grammar school,
In my minority."

[1] Offor's Edition, 1862, II., 390.

If these lines were really Bunyan's own, they would settle the point that he was educated at Bedford on the foundation of Sir William Harpur;* but, to say the least, their genuineness is very doubtful. No one seems to have heard of these poems till twelve years after Bunyan's death. Charles Doe, who saw in the possession of his eldest son John, all the unprinted MSS. Bunyan left behind him, makes no mention of them either in the catalogue of 1692, or in the one still more carefully drawn up in 1698. And when we look at the poems themselves there is certainly but little to remind us of Bunyan's special vein. It may readily be granted that his attempts at poetry do not show him at his best, that his muse "is clad in russet, wears shoes and stockings, has a country accent, and walks along the level Bedfordshire roads,"† yet even in his rudest rhymes there is pith and power, occasionally a dash of genius, and a certain sparkle of soul nowhere to be found in these *Scriptural Poems* set forth under his name for the first time in 1700.[1]

* The Rev. C. F. Farrar, M.A., in his interesting work, *Old Bedford* (p. 151), maintains — and gives conclusive proof— that the name should be spelt Harper.

† Quoted from Alexander Smith, the Scottish poet (1830-1867). *Vide* preface to *Divine Emblems.* London: Bickers and Son. N.D.

The line about the grammar school, therefore, must be counted for little. That he did go to school, however, Bunyan tells us himself. Poor as his parents were, "it pleased God to put it into their hearts to put me to school to learn both to read and write." The scholarship thus acquired was of course of the slenderest, "according to the rate of other poor men's children," and the little he learned was soon lost, "even almost utterly." If he went to Elstow, school inspectors had not yet risen above the village horizon, and even the endowed foundations in the neighbourhood had fallen upon evil days. The Free School of Sir Francis Clarke, in the neighbouring parish of Houghton Conquest, had its master, Christopher Hills, displaced by the master and fellows of Sidney Sussex College, in 1645, "for his wilful neglect and forsaking of the school contrary to our trust

[1] *Scriptural Poems*, &c., by John Bunyan. London, printed for J. Blare, at the Looking Glass on London Bridge, 1700. The doubtfulness of this work is increased by the name of the publisher. As early as 1688, Blare had published in Bunyan's name a spurious book entitled *The Saints' Triumph.* In 1705 also he issued a shameless book under the title of *The Progress of the Christian Pilgrim,* which was *The Pilgrim's Progress* merely latinized, but on the title page of which there was no mention of Bunyan's name. The veil under which the book was disguised was the most transparent possible: Christian became Christianus; Pliable, Easie; Worldly Wiseman, Politick Worldly; and so on. This man who carried on the business at the "Looking Glass" on London Bridge, was a repeated offender against the laws of honest dealing, and he is almost certainly one of the men to whom Nathaniel Ponder referred in 1688, when on the reverse of the title of Bunyan's *One Thing is Needful,* he printed the following: "Advertisement—This author having published many books which have gone off very well: there are certain ballad-sellers about Newgate and *on London Bridge,* who have put the two first letters of this author's name and his effigies to their rimes and ridiculous books, suggesting to the world as if they were his."

reposed in him."[1] And the then modest foundation of Sir William Harpur at Bedford in those days fared no better. A petition referring to the time when Bunyan was between nine and twelve years of age complains that William Varney, the schoolmaster, had not only charged fees which he had no right to do, but had also "grossly neglected the school by frequent absence from it, by night-walking and mis-spending his time in taverns and ale-houses, and is also very cruel when present to the boys."[2]

* Dr. H. Stebbing ventures to assert that Thomas Bunyan took his son from school to save the boy's morals. *Life of Bunyan*, vol. i. p. viii.

In any case, school-days were few, if not evil, for the tinker's son.* The education he received was mainly that given in the great school of human life where so many other sturdy natures have received such effective training. "I never went to school to Aristotle or Plato," says he, "but was brought up at my father's house in a very mean condition, among a company of poor countrymen." In the cottage by the stream bread-eaters must as soon as possible become bread-winners, and Bunyan passed quickly enough from the bench of his master to the forge of his father, necessity, if not choice, indicating that he must be a "braseyer" too.

† The grave cannot now be identified.

The growing lad had been at work some time when there came to him, in his sixteenth year, the first great sorrow of his life; for in the June days of 1644 his mother sickened and died, and within another month his sister Margaret also, the playmate of his childhood, was carried across the fields to the same quiet grave in Elstow Churchyard.† Nor was this all. Before yet another month had gone by over this twice-opened grave, his father had brought home another wife to take the vacant place. This indignity to his mother's memory, which the lad was old enough to understand and affectionate enough keenly to resent, must have estranged him from his father and his home. The removal of the gentler influence of mother and sister at the formative period of his life, and the revulsion of feeling created by the indecent haste with which his father married again, may have had not a little to do with those wild and wilful ways of the next few years, which he lived to describe so vividly and to repent so bitterly.

[1] *Harl. MSS.*, 4115, 79.
[2] *House of Lords MSS.*

It was probably about six or eight months after his mother's death that Bunyan entered the Army, and had those experiences of a soldier's life to which he makes brief reference in the *Grace Abounding*. Earlier it could not have been, for it was not till November, 1644, that he had reached the then Army regulation age of sixteen. And it is not probable that his military life was prolonged beyond a few months; for in the month of June, 1645, the battle of Naseby practically ended the first Civil War, leaving only the fag end to wear itself out in the West. The side on which Bunyan was arrayed in the great civil conflict of the seventeenth century, Parliamentarian or Royalist, has long been matter of dispute. Lord Macaulay says that "he enlisted in the Parliamentary army, and served during the decisive campaign of 1645." The reason for this opinion is probably given in the further statement that "his Greatheart, his Captain Boanerges, and his Captain Credence are evidently portraits, of which originals were among those martial saints who fought and expounded in Fairfax's army."[1] On the other hand, Mr. Froude says that "probability is on the side of his having been with the Royalists," giving as the reason for this opinion that his father was of "the national religion," and that John Gifford, the minister at Bedford, had been a Royalist.[2] Whatever weight may be attached to his father's sympathies—and there is no doubt about these, for he had a son christened Charles on the 30th of May, 1645—the reference to Gifford is out of all historical perspective. Certainly his opinions can have had very little to do with the side Bunyan took in the Civil Wars, seeing that Gifford did not become minister at Bedford till 1650, and that these two men did not even know of each other's existence till years after the Civil Wars were over. Perhaps a brief consideration of the course of events in Bedfordshire during those days of storm and stress may help us to a probable conclusion on the point at issue, and at the same time serve to make more vivid the surroundings of Bunyan's life.

There is no doubt as to the side which Bedfordshire took as a county. With the shires of Huntingdon, Cambridge, Herts, Essex, Suffolk, and Norfolk, it formed the Associated Counties from which Parliament drew its main strength and supplies.

[1] *Biographies*, pp. 30, 31.
[2] *English Men of Letters*. Bunyan, p. 12.

Clarendon says that the king had not in Bedfordshire "any visible party, nor one fixed quarter." There were several Royalists in the county, of course, but they do not seem to have been sufficiently numerous to organize themselves into anything like effective shape. The Earl of Cleveland, of Toddington, spent life and fortune in the King's service, but chiefly with the Royal forces at a distance. William Gery of Bushmeade raised a troop of horse in the county of Huntingdon, and his brother George was with the King, and was taken prisoner at the battle of Naseby; the two brothers, William and Richard Taylor of Clapham, also were in active service, and surrendered as prisoners of war, the one at Nantwich and the other at Truro. Among those who joined the king at Oxford and surrendered under the Articles when the city was taken, were Henry, Earl of Peterborough, of Turvey, who was a minor and who afterwards withdrew to France; Spencer Potts of Chalgrave; Thomas Joyce, the vicar of Hawnes; Sir Francis Crawley of Luton; Edward Russell, the brother of the Earl of Bedford; Sir William Palmer of Warden; and the widow and son of John Wingate of Harlington. Besides those who surrendered at Oxford, other Bedfordshire Royalists took up arms, though it is not known in what engagements, if any, they took part. Of these, Sir Peter Osborne of Chicksand went beyond seas to escape the consequences of his delinquency; Richard Conquest of Houghton Conquest was a prisoner in the King's Bench; Robert Spencer, also, of Eaton Socon, was for some time a prisoner of war. Besides these, there were Robert Audley of Northill, a youth of seventeen; Michael Grigg of Dunstable; John Russell, a younger brother of the Earl of Bedford; Thomas Foster, a yeoman of Elstow, and Richard Cooke of Cranfield.

With the exception of those who were excused under the Articles of Oxford, the Royalists who remained in the county made their submission to Parliament, took the Solemn League and Covenant and the Negative Oath, and compounded for their estates at Goldsmiths' Hall. Among those thus compounded were several who, though they did not take up arms, in some way or other declared their sympathies. These were Lord Capelle of Warden; Sir George Bynnion of Eaton Socon; Sir Edward Ashton of Wymington; Sir Thomas Leigh of Leighton; Sir Robert Napier of Luton; Charles Ventriss of Shefford; Sir

John Huet of Thurley; Sir Ludovick Dier of Colmworth; Charles Upton of Tempsford; Humphrey Freemonger of Stanbridge; Mr. Simley of Wootton; Mr. Watson of Ampthill; Mr. Yarway, and Mr. Browne of Kempston; and Owen Brett of Southill. Some of these compounded at one-tenth of the value of their estates, and others at one-sixth. The annual value of the sequestrations in houses, lands, and woods in the town and county of Bedford was £11,700. The entire amount sent up by the sequestrators of the county to the public treasurer at Guildhall between 1644 and 1647 was £9,659 3s. 8d. Of this a very small portion indeed came from the town of Bedford, which appears to have gone almost entirely one way. In 1648, Francis Bannister, the mayor, writes officially: "We have not had any sequestered in our Towne but a Barber, and little could be had from him; and two little prebends, yielding £13 6s. 0d."[1] By far the most resolute and conspicuous Royalist in Bedfordshire was Sir Lewis Dyve of Bromham. Whatever organization there may have been, centred in him; but in July, 1642, he had to flee for his life, narrowly escaping arrest by swimming the Ouse where it flows past Bromham Hall. The following year he was defeated at Newport Pagnel, after which he appears to have abandoned all farther hope of success in Bedfordshire, and proceeded to active service with the main body of the Royal forces in the west.

The great military leader in the county on the other side, against Sir Lewis Dyve, was Sir Samuel Luke of Cople Wood End, who was a tower of strength for what he called "the good old cause." He was one of the Members for Bedford in the Long Parliament, scout-master to the Army, and governor of the garrison of Newport Pagnel. He is said to have been the original of Butler's *Hudibras* and the special object of his satire. If this be so, the picture there given of Sir Samuel will scarcely be accepted as a picture from the life by those who have gathered

[1] The authorities for the details here given are (1) *The Royalist Composition Papers*—Bedfordshire, in the Record Office, and (2) *The Original Accounts of Estates of Delinquents seized by Parliament*, in the British Museum—*Addl. MSS.*, 5494, Beds., Nos. 1—27. It may be well to say that the *Royalist Composition Papers* are in two series. The First Series consists of 7,300 sets of papers bound in 113 vols. folio, arranged in counties and comprising the correspondence and order of the commissioners for sequestration and sale. The Second Series contains 3,034 sets of papers, and is bound in 54 vols. folio. The series not being arranged in counties is more difficult to search, but for purposes of local history is especially valuable as containing original particulars given in on oath of the estates and personal property of those Royalists who were permitted to compound on payment of fine, with the amount of fine. Cf. Selby's *Lancashire and Cheshire Records*, Record Society, 1882.

their impressions of this knight of Cople from his own Letter Book during the three years he was governor of Newport. This consists of four MS. volumes[1] and contains letters to him from Cromwell, Fairfax, and other great leaders and officials of the Government, and from him to them and also to his father, Sir Oliver Luke, to his son and his son's tutor, to his neighbours in the county, to his brother officers and others. In all these he leaves the impression upon us of a man of shrewd observation, of unquestionable valour, of godly life, and, what we should not have gathered from Butler's caricature, of considerable breadth of humour and humanness. He is certainly far from conforming to the conventional idea of a narrow and ascetic Puritan. We find him writing to his son at Geneva, where he is travelling with his tutor, and while urging him to keep the fear of God before his eyes, he wishes him to "strive to perfect his Italian hand, to follow his mathematics, ffencing, vaulting and exercise both of Picke and musket." Writing to Pelham Moore, one of the Secretaries of State, he is not too much concerned about war supplies to forget to ask, "If there bee any new wynes come over y^t^ are excellent good pray send mee down a Teirce or two half hogsheads upon ye lees of best Claritt." The wine was sent, but not the war supplies, and Sir Samuel rallies "fforgetful Mr. Moore" upon the long time he is in sending him the needful "shovells, spades, mattockes, Iron Crowes, Drums, Cullors and Halberds," and thinks he must be "a kinn or some greate acquaintance of that Sir Thomas Bayers who wore his Cloaths five yeare in his head before hee putt them to the making." He adds: "Your Claritt wine is starke naught both in the eye and mouth." Therefore Mr. Moore, who has just come away from the presence of Cromwell, whom he has left "well and merry," tells his friend: "Coming thence by Boate I saw a Salmon taken in the Tames which I present to y^r^ Honour hoping the tast thereof will meliorate my wine." That Sir Samuel could appreciate the good things of life as well as the best cavalier is seen in the message he sent to his father, Sir Oliver, who is in Parliament, where "wee satt in the House till six at night and fought the Babbell stoutly." Sir Samuel, to fortify his stout-hearted father for battle with the Parliamentary obstructives of his day sends him a "Red Deer Pie, with which

[1] *Egerton MSS.*, 785, 786, 787. *Ashburnham MSS.* Stowe Collection, 229.

you shall receive three brace of Phesants, two Couple of Tayle, six Cockes, two brace of Partridges and two dozen of Snipes." That he had some regard also to the pomps and vanities is seen from the order he gives to his father's confidential servant, Edward Bynion, who, there is reason to believe, was John Bunyan's uncle—his father's brother Edward, who also married his mother's sister Rose. Bynion has found "in Mr. Cubberd's shop French Scarlett" for Sir Samuel's cloake at two guineas a yard, as good as any in London. "To tryme the Cloake will require eight and a half dozens of Buttons and Loopes which, if they be rich will cost forty shillings a dozen," so that "cloake and tryming will come to £30." Remembering how much this sum meant in those days, it would not seem that the Presbyterian soldier, whom Butler styles Sir Hudibras, erred on the side of parsimony or Puritan sadness.

As this is probably the man under whom John Bunyan served his brief soldier life, we are interested in catching these few glimpses of him. He appears to have been a man of keen insight and strong common sense; his personal valour was as unquestioned as his military skill, and it was probably easier for Butler, after living under his roof, to lampoon him at a safe distance in his *Hudibras* than it was for the enemy to meet him in the fair encounter of an open field. Royalist ridicule of men who had grave and anxious duties to discharge in defending the ancient constitutional liberties of England may be very amusing to read, but it is not history, and must not be mistaken for it.[1]

Bedfordshire, through its representatives in Parliament as well as by its military action, pronounced strongly against the unconstitutional policy of Charles. There were only three counties in England all of whose members for county and borough alike were on the side of Hampden and Pym, and Bedfordshire was one of the three. In the Upper House the Earl of Bedford was, at the beginning of the struggle, on the same side, as was the Earl of Bolingbroke and also Lord St. John of Bletsoe, who lost his life at the battle of Edgehill. Henry, Earl of Kent, who succeeded his father at Wrest Park in 1643, was also a Parlia-

[1] It would seem that Oliver Cromwell's eldest and most promising son served under Sir Samuel Luke, and died in Newport garrison, while he was governor. In the *Parliament Scout* for March 15th—22nd, 1643—4, there is the following entry: "Cromwell hath lost his eldest son, who is dead of the small pox in Newport [Pagnel], a civil young gentleman and the joy of his father."

mentarian, as was the Earl of Manchester, whose seat was only a mile or two over the county border, and who, as Lord Kimbolton, had resisted the King in Parliament, as he did afterwards in the field. In addition to the leaders there were resolute men in all parts of the county, and in all ranks of life, whose sympathies were actively on the same side.

The stream being thus mainly one way, Bedfordshire did not suffer within its own borders from the consequences of civil war, to the same extent as some other counties. There were hardships endured from the free quartering of the soldiery, and there were occasional raids and skirmishes, of course. In the autumn of 1643 Sir Lewis Dyve rode into Ampthill with a party of horse, and carried off as prisoners to Oxford "divers of the well-affected gentry and freeholders, who were met as a committee appointed by Parliament."[1] In the following June the King, passing through Hockliffe, on a Sunday, towards Bedford, plundered Leighton by the way, and also sent another party to Dunstable, who, finding the people at church, began to cut and wound right and left, "and shot a case of pistols at the minister, but missed him, yet afterwards abused him almost as bad as death."[2] Rushworth also tells us that in October, 1643, Colonel Urrey and Sir Lewis Dyve, with a great party of horse, entered Bedford, took Sir John Norris and others prisoners there, and routed three hundred of their horse, and sufficiently plundered the town and other parts of that country."[3] On the other hand, the Royalists also used to tell how they had suffered from the quartering of soldiers upon them, and from the loss of cattle and sheep for the army; how that Mrs. Orlebar's coachman at Harrold lost his life from refusing to deliver up his horses to Cromwell's party without the leave of his mistress; and how, while Mr. Gery was away with the King at Oxford, the Parliamentary forces fired into the windows at Bushmead Priory, his wife fleeing from room to room with her children till she was able to take refuge with a tenant, as the soldiers plundered the house. There is, too, a touch of human pathos, and a vivid glimpse into the sorrows of those days, in a petition found among the Royalist Composition Papers, from a youth of seventeen, the son of Sir Henry Cayson of Dungey Wood.

[1] Wallington's *Historical Notices*, II., 73.
[2] *Perfect Diurnall*, No. 48.
[3] *Historical Collections*, VI., 61.

Photo: G. A. Geary, Bedford.]

ELSTOW CHURCH
Before Restoration in 1880.

The lad asks that his father's estate may not be altogether taken away for his delinquency, for that while Sir Henry and his lady had left "his own house in the Parliamentary quarters, and gone to visit his wife's friends in Bristol, while it was the King's garrison, they both dyed there, one shortly after the other, leaving nine children, all infants of tender yeares, fatherlesse and motherlesse." We can easily conceive also that Bedford town was all astir as one Sunday evening in August Lord St. John's troopers rode up to St. Cuthbert's Church and arrested the rector, Giles Thorne, at the close of the service, because he was in the habit of praying publicly for the King, and defying from his pulpit the authoritiy of Parliament.[1] Naturally enough, incidents like these occurred here and there, but they were few and inconsiderable when contrasted with the sufferings which were endured nearer to the scenes of conflict. They were only incidental consequences of a war which, as civil wars always do, roused the bitterest passions of the human breast.

Having regard, then, to all the local circumstances of the case, to the fact that there was a strong set of the stream in the Parliamentary direction; that Bunyan was a mere lad of sixteen; that he listened at Elstow church to the preaching of Christopher Hall, a vicar who so far went with the prevailing current as to preach against Sunday sports, and to christen his son with Cromwell's name of Oliver; it seems scarcely likely that he would think his way to independent conclusions so wide apart from those of his neighbours, break through all the carefully kept lines of the Parliamentary forces west of the county, and join the Royalist army with the King. It is much more probable that as soon as he had reached the regulation age of sixteen he was included in one of the levies made by Parliament upon the villages of Bedfordshire, and without any choice of his own in the matter was sent with others of his neighbours to the important garrison of Newport, "geometrically situate," as a Parliamentary ordinance describes it, between the associated counties on the east and the Royalist district to the west.

The same ordinance of Parliament, which constituted Newport garrison, provided also "that the county of Bedford, within fourteen days, shall send into it 225 able and armed men for souldiers." And if we come to the few months during which

[1] *Mercurius Rusticus*, Ed. 1685, p. 45.

alone Bunyan could have served, we find, from entries in the governor's letter-book, that these and subsequent orders were complied with. Bunyan was sixteen, and therefore old enough to serve in the early part of November, 1644. On the 28th of that month the governor writes: "Wee have now about 800 in the Towne, and noe pay. . . . Bedfordshire men make a fayre show, and tell them strange things." Again, on the 17th January, there is the following letter to the committee at Bedford from Richard Cockayne: "Since my last unto you yesterday I have received order from Sir S. Luke concerning the sending out of the 300 men, which he desires may be done with all expedition that may be." Once more, under date April 13th, the governor, writing to the Earl of Northumberland, says, "Bedfordshire has sent in some prest men"; and we happen to know, from other letters, that two of these "prest men" came, the one from Wootton and the other from Cotten End, villages close to Elstow. It is not unlikely, therefore, under these circumstances, that Bunyan also was one of the men drafted to Newport for service.*

* *Vide* Addendum.

He says, "When I was a soldier I with others were drawn out to go to such a place to besiege it." This would very well accord with the experience of the men under Sir Samuel Luke, who were often called out for service elsewhere. The day before the Christmas of 1643, for example, a large siege party left the garrison, and stormed and took Grafton House, in Northamptonshire. The following month Captain Abercrombie set out from Newport with a hundred men of the new levies and took Hillesdon House; later in the same year Captain Ennis, sent out by Sir S. Luke, surprised and captured a party of Royalists near Bicester. In 1645 also, at the time Bunyan was in the army, Captain Bladwell received orders to march, with three hundred of the men of the Newport garrison, to Aylesbury, and thence to Farnham, there to await farther instructions. Probably as one of some such party Bunyan had been sent on some military operation on the occasion when, as he tells us, "once I fell into a creek of the sea, and hardly escaped drowning." The nearest creek of the sea to a midland county like Bedfordshire was a long way off, and it is probable that this deliverance from the sea, like that from the musketball, was one of the experiences of his soldier life.

It has been frequently stated, though Bunyan himself does

not mention the fact, that he was at the siege of Leicester in the summer of 1645. The statement rests upon the authority of two writers, each of whom published a short sketch of Bunyan's life after his death. The first of these is simply worthless. It is entitled "An Account of the Life and Actions of Mr. John Bunyan, from his Cradle to his Grave." It was first printed at the end of the spurious third part of *The Pilgrim's Progress,* and is evidently a mere piece of literary hack-work, made up from the *Grace Abounding.* Where the writer is original he is manifestly wrong. He tells us, for example, that at the siege of Leicester the town was "vigorously defended by the King's forces against the Parliamentarians," the case, of course, being precisely the reverse. Then, by way of explaining how Bunyan came to be in the army, he says, "When the unnatural civil war came on, finding little or nothing to do to support himself *and small family,* he, as many thousands did, betook himself to arms." As at the time of the siege of Leicester Bunyan was sixteen and seven months old, it is clear the writer knew very little either of Bunyan's "small family" or of Bunyan himself. Eventually this sketch was, for some reason, withdrawn, and another account of Bunyan's life, to which reference has been made, took its place in 1700. It professes to be written by a personal friend. The writer says that Bunyan, "being a soldier in the Parliament's army at the siege of Leicester in 1645, he was drawn out to stand centinel, but another soldier voluntarily desiring to go in his room," was shot dead. He has evidently confused two separate stories, as he might easily do, writing some fifty years after the event. Bunyan himself says, "When I was a soldier I with others were drawn out to go to such a place to besiege it; but when I was just ready to go one of the company desired to go in my room, to which, when I had consented, he took my place; and coming to the siege, as he stood sentinel he was shot into the head with a musket-bullet, and died." Either, therefore, this account does not refer to the siege of Leicester, or Bunyan was not at that siege, for, wherever it was, he distinctly says that, though he was drawn to go, he did not actually go, because another man went in his place. Yet, though this personal friend of Bunyan's has thus confused two separate things, he was evidently quite sure in his own mind that Bunyan was at the siege of Leicester, and probably had it from his own lips. It is certain that there were soldiers from Newport garrison present at that siege, defending the town against the assault of the Royal forces. We know that these men from Newport, under Major Ennis, were placed in charge of that portion of the fortifications of Leicester called "the Newarke" or "new worke," on the south side of the town, near an old stone wall, against which Prince Rupert had directed the King's artillery to be planted. In this wall a large breach had been made, but was repaired and defended by Ennis, who twice drove back the enemy with great loss. For three hours after the rest of the town was taken Major Ennis and his Newport men maintained their position, and obtained good terms of capitulation, when they were surrounded, and had at last to surrender.

The stirring scenes and incidents of these soldier days, the many-phased aspects of life and contrasts of character presented on every side, would, of course, do much to widen the mind of the impressible lad from Elstow. It must have been a curious school of experience to be among these fighting, preaching, praying majors and captains, who could one day storm and take Grafton or Hillesdon House, and the next preach to edification in Newport Church. Eagerly taking in this new world, all so vivid to him, he marches, it may be, with Captain Bladwell to Aylesbury and the Surrey Downs, or stands with the men in Lathbury Field to hear Captain Hobson preach, or give military salute in Newport garrison to Sir Samuel Luke, or along with Major Ennis fights amidst the rain of death on Leicester walls. The memories of these days came back in after years, making more intensely real to him the fight with Apollyon, the expedition of Greatheart, or the winning back of Mansoul for Emmanuel.

ADDENDA—Chapter III.

[The Editor acknowledges with gratitude his indebtedness to Sir Charles H. Firth, M.A., LL.D., Regius Professor of History, Oxford (1904—1925), for the kind revision and criticism which have considerably enhanced the value of this Addendum.]

Dr. Brown's conjectures were sound, and the side on which Bunyan served is no longer speculation: it is fact. In March, 1898, Mr. Ernest G. Atkinson, one of the keepers of the records at the Record Office, wrote to *The Presbyterian,* stating that

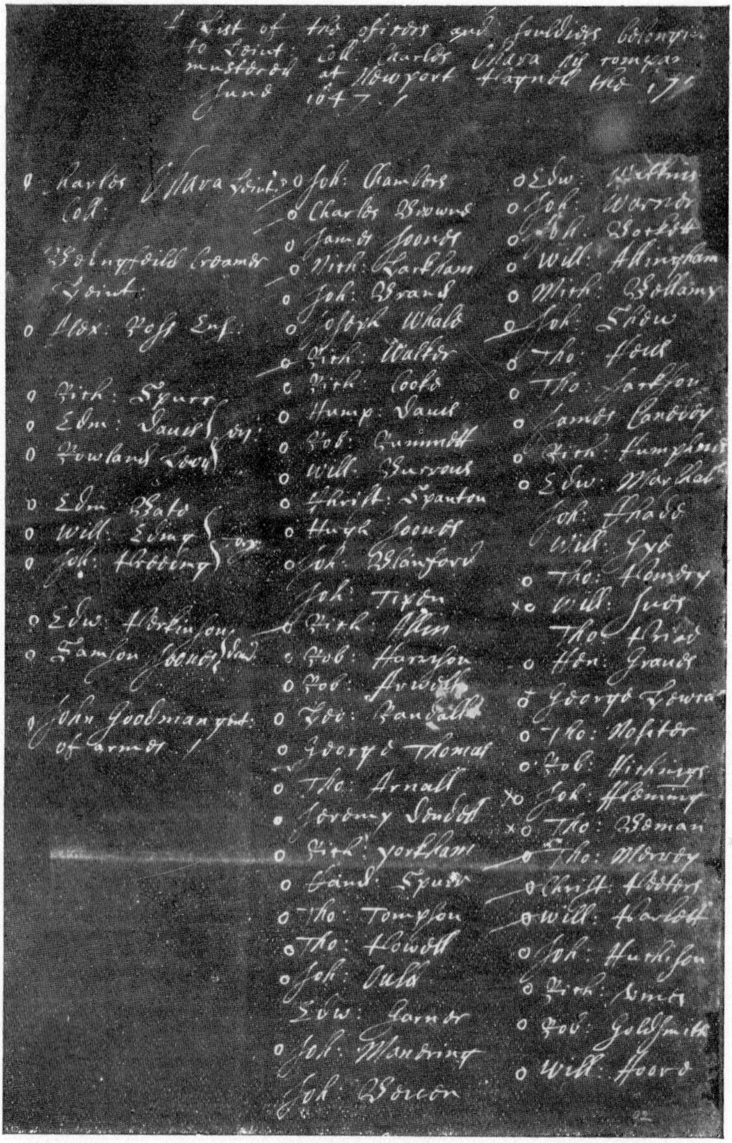

A List of the officers and souldiers belonginge to Lieut: Coll: Charles O'Hara his company mustered at Newport Pagnell the 17 June 1647.

o Charles O'Hara Lieut: Coll:
Bellingfeild Creamer Lieut:
o Alex: Ross Ens:
o Rich: Spurr
o Edm: Davis } Serj:
o Rowland Lord
o Edm: Bate
o Will: Edmg } Corp:
o Joh: Hebbing
o Edw: Atkinson
o Samson Joones Drum:
o John Goodman gent: of armes.

o Joh: Chambers
o Charles Browne
o James Joones
o Nich: Larkham
o Joh: Brand
o Joseph Whale
o Rich: Walter
o Rich: Cooke
o Hump: Davis
o Rob: Cummett
o Will: Burrous
o Christ: Spanton
o Hugh Joones
o Joh: Blanford
Joh: Tixon
o Rich: Allin
o Rob: Harryson
o Rob: Arwick
o Rob: Randall
o George Thomas
o Tho: Arnall
o Jeremy Sandell
o Rich: Yorkham
o Sam: Spurr
o Tho: Tompson
o Tho: Howell
o Joh: Ould
Edw: Jarnes
o Joh: Mandring
Joh: Bowen

o Edw: Watkins
o Joh: Warner
o Joh: Bosket
o Will: Allingham
o Nich: Bellamy
o Joh: Snow
o Tho: Houll
o Tho: Jackson
o James Cantrey
o Rich: Humpheries
o Edw: Marshall
Joh: Shade
Will: Gyb
o Tho: Flowdry
xo Will: Judd
Tho: Friad
o Hen: Grande
o George Lowran
o Tho: Webster
o Rob: Hitchings
xo Joh: Fleming
xo Tho: Bowman
o Tho: Mowby
o Christ: Abbots
o Will: Harlott
o Joh: Hutchison
o Rich: Amey
o Rob: Goldsmith
o Will: Hoord

MUSTER ROLL.
Newport Pagnell, 1647.

Public Record Office, London.]

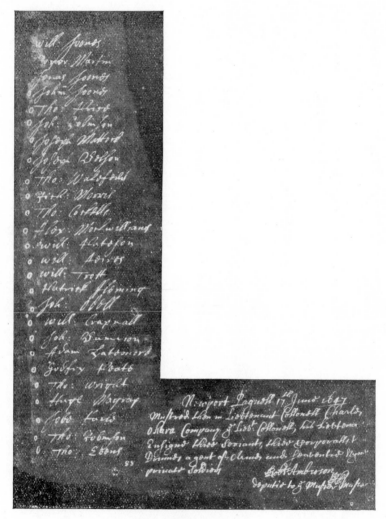

MUSTER ROLL.
Newport Pagnell, 1647.

(Signed by Robert Amberson, deputy Muster-Master.)

Public Record Office, London.]

in 1896 he discovered amongst some unsorted Commonwealth Papers, 1644-5, two pages of the Muster Rolls of the Newport Pagnell garrison. On these Bunyan's name appears, and shows that he was in the Parliamentarian Army for over two and a half years. During the greater part of this period, Sir Samuel Luke had command,[1] and Bunyan served in two of his regiment's companies; first under Lieut.-Col. Richard Cokayn, and afterwards under Major Boulton. In the roll of Col. Cokayn's company, and amongst the 'centinels' (*i.e.*, privates) mustered there on November 30th, 1644, is the name of John Bunion (also spelt Bunnion).[2] Bunyan was born in 1628, and christened on November 30th of that year, so, being sixteen years of age, he was eligible for service. On March 22nd, 1645, his name disappears from Col. Cokayn's company, and appears in that of Major Boulton, where it remains until May 27th, four days before the siege of Leicester by King Charles. In the lists given of the parties by Major Boulton's men "commanded out by the Committee of Both Kingdoms," one on January 18th, 1645, and the other on May 6th of the same year, Bunyan's name does not appear. So there is no evidence that he left Newport Pagnell for Leicester. The detachment from Newport Pagnell which served there consisted of dragoons, and, apparently, no foot soldiers went from that garrison. It is also now known how long he served. Mr. Atkinson in his further researches found a folio sheet of paper, giving a list of the officers and soldiers belonging to Lieut.-Col. Charles O'Hara, "his company, mustered at Newport Pagnell, the 17th of June, 1647," and the name of John Bunnion is amongst the seventy-nine privates in it. The roll is attested by the deputy muster-master, Robert Amberson.

O'Hara's company was not part of the garrison of Newport Pagnell. Charles O'Hara had been a captain in Col. Robert Hammond's regiment of foot in the New Model Army ever since its formation in April, 1645. In April, 1647, he volunteered to serve in Ireland, and half-a-dozen officers with about four hundred men of the regiment followed his example. The volunteers included O'Hara's whole company. The rest of the regiment refused to go. These volunteers were formed into a

[1] Sir Samuel Luke, being a Member of Parliament, had to give up the command of the foot-regiment there on account of the Self-Denying Ordinance. Cokayn succeeded him.

[2] His service must have begun about a month earlier for him to get mustered in November as entitled to a month's pay.

new regiment under Col. Owen O'Conolly, of which O'Hara became lieutenant-colonel, and were drawn off from the rest of the army, and quartered at Newport Pagnell or near it, till the time came for them to march to their place of embarkation.[1] But they never went to Ireland, because Parliament on July 21st, 1647, ordered them to be disbanded.[2]

Bunyan's appearance in the list of O'Hara's company on June 17th can probably be explained as follows: On August 6th, 1646, Parliament ordered that the works of Newport and other towns should be demolished, and the garrisons employed in Ireland.[3] Men willing to serve in Ireland were to receive a month's pay, those who refused were to be disbanded. Bunyan apparently was willing to serve in Ireland, and was therefore put into Hammond's regiment, which was to be sent in advance of the rest to secure Dublin, and was actually marched to Chester for the purpose.[4] Bunyan's escape from drowning in "a creek of the sea" may have taken place near Chester.[5]

As it is seen, the regiment did not go to Ireland; it marched back to the headquarters of the army in April, 1647, and then broke into two sections, one refusing to serve in Ireland, the other willing to do so. Bunyan, who stuck to his company commander, belonged to the minority, marched under O'Hara to Newport Pagnell, was mustered there June 17th, and was disbanded about the end of July, 1647.

Although Bunyan's military service was not arduous, it was prolonged. It began about October, 1644, and ended about July, 1647. Possibly it may have been intermitted for a few months between August, 1646, and March, 1647.

As Bunyan writes in *Grace Abounding*—"When I was a soldier I with others were drawn out to go to such a place to besiege it"—it was presumed for at least two centuries and a quarter that he referred to Leicester, and, as Dr. Brown points out, two writers of Bunyan's own time (one professing to be his personal friend) state that he was at that siege; but as

[1] Rushworth, vi. 463, 466, 468, 493.
[2] *Lords' Journals*, ix. 343.
[3] *Acts and Ordinances*, i. 862.
[4] *Commons' Journals*, March 9th, 1647.
[5] Dr. Brown (in his edition of *Grace Abounding*, Hodder and Stoughton, 1888) says: "As the nearest creek of the sea to the midland town of Bedford was very far distant, this may be a reminiscence of his [Bunyan's] soldier days." Bunyan's words are: "But God did not utterly leave me, but followed me still, not now with Convictions, but with Judgment; yet such as were mixed with Mercy. For once I fell into a Creek of the Sea, and hardly escaped drowning." (*Grace Abounding*, par. 12 of sixth (1688) and later editions.

one of these is unreliable in other details, his statement is of little value.

Though Newport Pagnell was a place of strategic importance, it was never the scene of siege or skirmish;[1] yet many commentators have contended that Bunyan must have seen some active service, or have witnessed some actual warfare, to have depicted so graphically his scenes in *The Holy War.* But Professor Sir Charles Firth, the eminent authority on the Cromwellian period, says: "It has been suggested that realistic details of the great Civil War may be gleaned from Bunyan's pages, but the fighting in *The Holy War* is a curious mixture of realism and literary reminiscence. . . . Bunyan combines the weapons of different ages in his sieges and battles. . . . On the other hand," the writer continues, "some of the officers of Emmanuel's army might have been drawn from the well-known commanders of the New Model. 'They marched through the regions and countries of many people, not hurting or abusing any. . . . They also lived upon the King's cost in all the way they went,' instead of living upon the country. One scene described seems like a reminiscence of a review in which Bunyan himself had taken part. After the capture of Mansoul the Prince orders his army to show 'some feats of its war' to its citizens. . . . Even so, Private Bunyan and his regiment may have delighted the eyes of the citizens of Newport Pagnell before he laid down his musket and returned to the trade of mending pots and pans."[2]

In response to an enquiry, Sir Charles Firth further says: "It is clear to me that Bunyan saw no active service. There was no fighting of any importance near Newport Pagnell during the period of his service. The duties of a soldier there would be learning his drill, standing on guard, police duties in the town and neighbourhood, an occasional march out on a field day, and perhaps occupying an outpost in some neighbouring house. To prove that he did more you will have to prove that the regiment in which he was saw service (of which I have found no trace). The assumption that Leicester was the mysterious place referred to by Bunyan is unsupported by any evidence. All he tells us is that he might have lost his life if he had formed a part of a detachment in which one of his

[1] The town was first fortified and garrisoned in October, 1643.
[2] John Bunyan (*Journal of English Studies,* vol. 1., No 3). London: Horace Marshall and Son. 1913.

comrades served. If he had actually risked his life in battle or skirmish, I think he would have mentioned the experience." Such an emphatic statement by the author of *Cromwell's Army* (Methuen)—the classic work on the subject, must silence conjecture. Before Dr. Brown penned his biography writers of "lives" had successively followed their predecessors, but Dr. Brown searched farther afield, and delved deeper to discover the truth, and so, perhaps, some future biographer may find an unexplored region wherein is information that may yet link Bunyan with Leicester in his soldiering days.[1] That he visited the city in after years is known beyond doubt.

[1] Even Thomas Carlyle was beguiled into writing—"John Bunyan, I believe, is this night [14th June, 1645] in Leicester—not yet writing his *Pilgrim's Progress* on paper, but acting it on the face of the earth, with a brown matchlock on his shoulder. Or, rather without the matchlock, just at present; Leicester and he having been taken the other day."—(Comment "On Oliver Cromwell's Letter XIII., written from Harborough, 14th June, 1645.")

(Page 44).

Probably a similar warrant as that issued by Sir Samuel Luke, addressed to the constable and inhabitants of Salford, a village in south Bedfordshire, in July, 1643,[2] was sent to Elstow in the following year. It read as follows:

"These are to signify that it is Sir Samuel Luke's desire that it be published in your parish with all speed, that he will no longer dally with, or by more fair ways and means claw his countrymen, seeing that it is altogether vain and fruitless; but he is resolved that if all persons in every parish between sixteen and sixty, being able to carry arms, shall not severally appear at Leighton on Monday morning next, by seven of the clock, with all provisions with them, and arms and weapons for the service of the State and their own safety, he will proceed against such cold and insensible persons and parishes of this county with that vigour and severity as is done in other places, that the good may not always remain scoffed and derided at, but that they may receive such care and comfort by such his proceedings as is agreeable to all manner of equity and good conscience; and to let them know that all such as do come are to march away presently, and therefore desire them to come provided for that purpose. Fail you not therefore, and to bring a list of every man at your peril."—*The Ouse*, by A. J. Foster, M.A. (p. 44). London: Published by the S.P.C.K.

[2] Sir Samuel Luke, as one of the Parliamentary Committee for Bedfordshire, was authorised to impress men for service by the Ordinance of August 10th, 1643. However, he apparently anticipated his prerogative.

(Page 46).

As Dr. Brown hints, Bunyan may have come under the ministry of Captain Hobson at Newport Pagnell. He may also have been subconsciously influenced by the Baptist quasi-chaplain, whose book, *The Fallacy of Infants Baptisme*, seems to have aroused the ire of the Presbyterian governor of the garrison, Sir Samuel Luke. One sermon Hobson preached brought about a riot in the town, so that martial law was resorted to, and, for "setting up a conventicle," and absenting himself from "the public thanksgiving service for the victory at Naseby," he was plunged into prison by Sir Samuel Luke.[1] The delinquent subsequently retaliated by writing '*A Garden Inclosed and*

Wisdom justified only by her Children: Being two Exercises delivered at Newport Pagnell, for declaration whereof the Author was then imprisoned and since accused of Blasphemie. Paul Hobson. 1647.' He was soon released, however, for Fairfax, although possibly not approving his preaching methods, recognised in Hobson an officer that could ill be spared at such a time. Bunyan in his soldiering days was also ministered to by the Presbyterian divine, Thomas Ford, of Magdalen College, Oxford. Ford had been hunted from this country by Archbishop Laud, and on returning to England held a living in Northamptonshire; he was a member of the Westminster Assembly of Divines, and was subsequently appointed chaplain of the Newport Pagnell garrison.

[1] *Vide* p. 336, Cromwell's Army. By Sir Charles H. Firth, M.A., LL.D. London: Methuen & Co.

IV.

SPIRITUAL CONFLICT.*

* *Vide* Addendum.

On the disbanding of the army in 1646-7, Bunyan returned to his tinkering life at Elstow, and two or three years later took to himself a wife. Who she was and where he found her we have now no means of knowing. There is no entry of the marriage in the register at Elstow, which may arise from the fact that he found her at a distance, or that they were, according to the custom of the Commonwealth, married before some justice of the peace whose registers are lost. Apparently she was an orphan and a native of some other place than Elstow, for she used to talk to Bunyan about her father as though they were unknown to each other, telling him "what a godly man he was and how he would reprove and correct vice both in his House and amongst his neighbours; what a strict and holy life he lived in his Days both in Word and Deed." We know not who she was, we do not even know her Christian name, but we do know that her advent brought to Bunyan what he had not had since his mother's death, a real home brightened by the presence of love. It was not brightened by much else. "This woman and I," says he, "came together as poor as poor might be, not having so much household stuff as a dish or spoon betwixt us both." It was an unpromising beginning, but many that are more promising turn out worse. It may be that where there are health and hope and honest industry, mutual love and trust can better supply the lack of dish and spoon than an abundance of dishes and spoons can supply the lack of love.

Though the young wife brought no dower of wealth to her husband, she brought to him that which wealth cannot buy—saintly memories of a godly home and trained instincts for good; and, as we have seen, she would beguile their summer evening walks and their fireside winter talks by memories of the good man, her father, who had gone to heaven. She brought with her

THE 'BUNYAN' COTTAGE, ELSTOW.

also two books which had been his, the one, *The Plain Man's Pathway to Heaven,* by Arthur Dent,* the parish minister of Shoebury in Essex, and the other, *The Practice of Piety,* by Lewis Bayly, a bishop of Bangor, in King James' time. "In these," says Bunyan, "I should sometimes read with her, wherein I also found some things that were somewhat pleasing to me."

* In the catalogue of the sale of George Offor's library (mostly destroyed by fire) in 1865, a copy is described as being partly in "black letter," and dated 1625. It had on the bottom of its title-page the name M. BUNYAN, and was probably the actual volume here referred to. It unfortunately perished with many other interesting relics.

These two books which he thus thought worthy of special mention had, both of them, an unusual run of popularity. *The Plain Man's Pathway to Heaven*[1] was a little square, vellum-bound, black-letter book of about four hundred pages, which was first published in 1601, and in 1637 had reached the twenty-fourth edition. It is in the form of a dialogue between four persons, who appear as a divine, a plain honest man, an ignorant man, and a caviller, and who, having a long May day on their hands, repair by common consent "to yonder oke-tree, where there is a goodly arbour and handsome seats, and where they may all sit in the shadow and conferre of heavenly matters." The book seems to have filtered into Bunyan's mind and to have remained with him. In *The Life and Death of Mr. Badman,* which he published more than thirty years later, we shall see hereafter the traces of its influence. Dent's book is long, and for the most part wearisomely heavy and theologically narrow, but there are in it racy sayings and intensely English forms of expression, some of which remind us even of Bunyan himself. We come, for instance, upon such proverbial sayings as, "Who is so bold as blinde Baynard?" "He that never doubted never believed"; "Soft fire maketh sweet mault"; "A fool's bolt is soon shot"; and "Sweet meat will have sour sauce." Speaking of pride, the writer is satirical upon those who spend "a good part of the day in tricking and trimming, pricking and pinning, pranking and pouncing, girding and lacing and braving up themselves in most exquisite manner"; he likes not "these doubled and redoubled ruffes, these strouting fardingales, long locks, and foretufts"; and he thinks "it was never a good world since starching and steeling, buskes and whalebones, supporters and rebatoes, full moones and hobby horses came into use." "Even plain country folk," he says, "will flaunt it like

[1] *The Plaine Man's Pathway to Heaven*: Wherein euery man may clearly see whether he shall be saued or damned. Set foorth Dialogue-wise, for the better understanding of the simple. By ARTHUR DENT, Preacher of the word of God at South Shoobury in Essex. The 11th impression. London: Printed by *Melchisedeck Bradwood* for *Edw. Bishop,* and are to bee solde in Paul's Churchyard, at the syne of the Brasen Serpent. 1609.

courtiers, and the old proverb is verified, 'Everie Jacke will be a gentleman, and Joane is as good as my lady.'" The divine of the dialogue, speaking of oaths, objects even to men swearing by Cocke or Pie, or Mousefoot; whereupon the caviller says, "It seemeth you are an Anabaptist, you condemn all swearing"; from which we may infer that the Baptists of England were specially conspicuous for their simple yea, yea, and nay, nay, even before George Fox and the Quakers were born. It is further said that drunkenness is the "metropolitane Citie of all the Province of vices," and that the many "lazy lozels and luskish youths which doe nothing all the day long," forget that we must one day "give an account of our Baily-wicke." At the close of the dialogue the ignorant man of the party comes under deep concern about his moral state; whereupon the caviller asks him to go home with him and he can give him "a speedy remedy, for he has many pleasant and merry books, *Bevis of Southampton; Ellen of Rummin; The Merry Jest of the Fryer and the Boy; The Pleasant Story of Clem of the Clough; Adam Ball, and William of Cloudesly; The old tale of William Richard, and Humphry; The pretty conceit of John Splinter's last Will and Testament;* which all are excellent and singular books against heart-qualms."

The other book in which Bunyan read with his wife, was *The Practice of Piety.* It was first published in 1612 by Lewis Bayly of Evesham, afterwards bishop of Bangor, and by 1673 had been printed above fifty times in English, besides many times in Welsh, French, Hungarian, Polish, and other Continental languages. Notwithstanding its distinctly ecclesiastical tone, the book was a great favourite with the Puritans. The mother of Symon Patrick was brought up by its rules, Joseph Alleine received from it consolation on his deathbed, and James Frazer, of Brea, the minister of Culross, one of the Scottish confessors, tells us that he came to a Christian life after reading it one Sunday afternoon. So wide was its renown that it became the subject of satire on the part of men not much given to reading it. It was to be found on the desk of the Justice of the Peace along with his Dalton's *Duties of a Magistrate.* Peter Hansted, in 1644, satirizes a—

"Justice Parler on whose cushion ly
A Dalton and 'Practice of Piety.'"

The book was introduced into Congreve's *Old Bachelor,* and

in 1788, Peter Pindar makes George III. say to Mr. Whitbread, who was the member for Bedford at that time—

> "I'm told that you send Bibles to your votes,
> Pray'r books instead of cash to buy them coats—
> Bunyans and 'Practices of Piety.'"

Reading the book now, it is difficult to account for its widespread popularity. Men used to read it, however, because in the language of the times it struck home at the central verities of the religious life on which all Christians are agreed; it was, as the writer said, "an endeavour to extract out of the chaos of endless controversies the old practice of true piety which flourished before these controversies were hatched." It was a book to be read when men read books, not many but much.[1]

The effect of these books upon Bunyan's mind and heart was pleasing—pleasing only as yet—not convincing, not striking right home and giving him that despairing sense of sin through which he more than most men had to make his way to the better life. There was no cry from the depths as yet, but there were good desires coming up, and under their influence he went "to church twice a day, and that with the foremost." When there the natural reverence of his soul took forms not always elevating. The vine without trellis work to lift it up trails on the ground, and Bunyan's deeply religious nature not yet having found its healthful nutriment in eternal verities, expended itself in superstitious awe over sacred places and ecclesiastical persons. The high place in Elstow Church seemed to his vivid imagination like a piece of heaven brought down to earth, and the vicar, as he stood in the rude pulpit of former days, like a being of some supernal sphere; even that not very sublime personage the parish clerk, came in for a share of adoration. "So overcome was I with the spirit of superstition that I adored, and that with great devotion, even all things (both the high place, priest, clerk, vestment-service, and what else) belonging to the church." It has been assumed that the form of service at Elstow Church during the Commonwealth was Presbyterian, but this description of the worship that Bunyan attended there between 1649 and 1652, does not seem much like it. A Presbyterianism that had "high place, priest, clerk, vestment-service, and what else," must have had services strangely like those of Episcopacy. More-

[1] *Practice of Piety*, with biographical preface by Grace Webster, London, 1842. *Bishop Lewis Bayly and his Practice of Piety*, by J. E. Bailey, F.S.A., *Manchester Quarterly Review*, July, 1883.

over, Christopher Hall, the vicar, was certainly an Episcopalian, for he entered upon the living in 1639, when Archbishop Laud was supreme; he remained there all through the Commonwealth period, and he certainly continued vicar of Elstow for four years after the Restoration, and therefore two years after the Act of Uniformity, signing the returns from the register in 1664. Either, therefore, Bunyan's spiritual guide in his Elstow days was a wonderfully pliant man, a veritable 'vicar of Bray,' or, there was considerably more tolerance for Nonconforming Episcopalians under Cromwell than there was for Nonconforming Quakers and Presbyterians under Charles. The services and officials familiar to Bunyan in Elstow Church, and his Sunday tipcat experiences on Elstow Green would seem to suggest that neither the law of 1645 against liturgical forms, nor the law of 1644 against Sunday sports was very rigidly enforced in the remoter rural parishes of the land.

The four years of Bunyan's life which followed his marriage were those in which he went through the intense spiritual experiences he has described for us as with pen of fire in the *Grace Abounding*. It was an awful time, yet it had its compensations. It gave him that mighty hold of men's hearts which more than most writers and preachers he has always had. He knew it himself. "For this reason I lay so long at Sinai, to see the fire and the cloud and the darkness, that I might fear the Lord all the days of my life upon earth, and tell of His wondrous works to my children." As he entered into the struggle of those fearful years he was overwhelmed with a sense of his own evil; he paints his moral condition in the darkest colours. Many writers think the colours too dark, the shadows more sombre than the truth required. Lord Macaulay, for example, may be taken as the type of a class who have undertaken to vindicate Bunyan's character against the charges of Bunyan himself. We must not, he thinks, lay too much stress on the man's description of himself. He merely caught up the language of his time, and the worst that can be laid to his charge is, "that he had a great liking for some diversions quite harmless in themselves, but condemned by the rigid precisians among whom he lived and for whom he had a great respect." Indeed, some men would not have hesitated to commend rather than condemn. "A rector of the school of Laud would have held such a young man up to the whole parish as a model."[1] We cannot read these easy-going utterances alongside Bunyan's burning words without feeling that these two men had gone through incommensurable experiences. Probably Macaulay's natural temperament and his career of unruffled prosperity led him to take a somewhat complacent view both of this world and the next. Bunyan, on the contrary, had battled with the storm. He had looked down shudderingly into yawning depths and yearningly up to lofty heights, which when a man has once seen he can be complacent no more.

There are those who would probably consider any passionate agitation concerning the spiritual world as somewhat unreal and affected. They may be estimable neighbours and useful citizens, but, as Froude says of them, "be their talents what they may, they could not write a *Pilgrim's Progress,* or ever reach the delectable mountains, or even be conscious that such mountains exist." There are two ways of looking at sin; an easy-going way and a way that is more earnest. The more earnest way, which was Bunyan's, is that which looks upon sin in the light of the supreme anguish endured on Calvary for its expiation, and which sees in the sinner one of whom it is always true that he knows not what he does. This intenser way may seem to some to be overstrained, but it is in harmony with the whole literature of penitence from the Book of *Psalms* down to the latest utterance of the Christian ages; it is the outcome of a living spirit which cannot be destroyed without destroying also all that is noblest in aspiration and most glorious in achievement in the moral history of the race.

In estimating the sinfulness of Bunyan's early life it must be remembered that sin may take a spiritual as well as a sensual form. The sins for which he reproached himself were not specially those of the flesh. He was never a drunkard, and in after years, when the occasion called for it, he passionately denied that he had ever been unchaste. But a man's weakness is often the reaction from his strength; and he who of all men afterwards sought for reality and stood with worshipping awe before the sanctities of spiritual things was guilty of violent outrage against reverence and truth. The marvellous force which in after years displayed itself in vividness of spiritual vision and burning power of expression ran riot in weird blasphemies which made even blasphemers tremble. "Even as a child," he says, "I had few equals in cursing, swearing, lying, and blas-

[1] Macaulay's *Biographies.* John Bunyan p. 30.

pheming the holy name of God." The wickedness begun thus early lasted long. He was a grown man, when one who was "herself a loose and ungodly wretch," and therefore not over-nice, "protested that it made her tremble to hear him, that he was the ungodliest fellow for swearing ever she heard in all her life, and that it was enough to spoil all the youth in the whole town." Sins like these will be variously estimated. There is no ready gauge of outward consequence to measure their inward evil as in the case of drunkenness and impurity. Yet spiritual sins may be even more deadly than sensual in their moral recoil, laying waste the powers of the soul. It is not improbable that the spiritual condition induced by persistent lying and profane blasphemy had much to do with the prolonged and terrible struggles of Bunyan's after years.

The intensity of these struggles was, of course, largely due to the intensity of the spiritual nature in which they took place. As the storm sweeps most wildly and makes its dolefullest moaning through the tops of the tallest trees, the greatness of the man contributed to the greatness of his sufferings. They were intensified also by his ignorance and lack of spiritual guidance. Many of the shapes with which he wrestled in deepest anguish were the phantoms of his own heated imagination, the result of his own misinterpretation of the book of God. The battle which he was fighting was, of course, no phantom; it is the one battle of the ages for all who in a world of sin are seeking for the life of God; yet it might have been shortened and simplified by enlightened friendly aid. But it was Bunyan's misfortune to be surrounded by men who, either from want of sympathy or lack of light, could help him very little till his fiercest battle was fought out and ended. As in the case of his great contemporary, George Fox, men "spake not to his condition," but, and it was perhaps well, he was all the more thrown back upon God, and in the end, as always, God was faithful to His own.

In following this story of spiritual struggle as he has recorded it for us with his own burning pen, we seem at first to be looking upon shifting masses of cloud driven now east, now west, by opposing winds, mere movement without progress. But closer observation reveals a spiritual order under the seeming spiritual chaos. The swimmer battling for the shore is driven back again

STUMP OF THE OLD MARKET CROSS
ON ELSTOW GREEN.

and again till our very hearts ache for him, but he gains a little each time, and reaches land at last.

There are some natures to whom the great spiritual world of the unseen is always present as the background of life. It was so with Shakespeare. It was so also with Bunyan, though in a different way. Even when he was a child, the wrong things of the day were followed by the remorse and fears, and dread dreams of the night. But the real struggle began later, when after his marriage and the reading of his wife's books, he was seen "going to church twice a day, and that with the foremost." He had not done this long before there arose a fight with his conscience about Sunday sports, in the course of which there came the weird voices that seemed to be shouted into his ear on Elstow Green. Somewhere on the sward round the broken pillar of the old Market Cross he was one Sunday in the midst of a game of cat.* He had struck it one blow from the hole and was about to strike it the second time, when, as he says, "A voice did suddenly dart from heaven into my soul, which said, Wilt thou leave thy sins and go to heaven, or have thy sins and go to hell? At this I was put to an exceeding maze. Wherefore, leaving my cat upon the ground, I looked up to heaven, and was as if I had with the eyes of my understanding, seen the Lord Jesus looking down upon me, as being very hotly displeased with me." Thus conscience-stricken he afterwards made a desperate fling to be rid of conscience altogether, only to find, as other men have, that its grip was tighter than he thought. Then he swung round again and fell to some outward reformation, gave up swearing, took to reading the historical parts of the Bible, and set about keeping the commandments, which he flattered himself he did pretty well; so that in those days he thought he pleased God as well as any man in England. His neighbours were struck with the change, and wondered much to see Mad Tom of Bethlem become a sober man. Their exclamations of surprise flattered his vanity, he became proud of his godliness, and laid himself out for more and more of this kind of incense for about a twelvemonth or more.

* *Vide* Strutt's Sports and Pastimes.

When a man comes under the dominion of conscience, and is a stranger to love, conscience is apt to become somewhat of a tyrant; a false standard is set up, and things right enough in themselves seem to become wrong to the man. Bunyan had hitherto taken pleasure in the somewhat laborious diversion of ringing the bells in the tower of Elstow Church.* He began to think this was wrong, one does not quite see why; still, having this misgiving about it, he gave up his bell-ringing. But not the love of it. This seems to have lingered with him through life. Years afterwards, when he brings his pilgrims near to the Celestial City, he makes all the bells therein give them a peal of welcome, and when they pass within, leaving him without, he heard in his dream that "all the bells in the city rang again for joy." One can easily understand that in these Elstow days it was with many a pang and with reluctant step he turned from the belfry. He would come and lean against the old doorway, and look longingly while some neighbour pulled the bell-rope which he half-felt to be his. Then he was afraid even to do this. How if the bells should fall? How if even the steeple itself should come down? About that very time a flash of lightning had struck one of the village churches of Bedfordshire, and "passing through the porch into the belfry, tripped up his heels that was tolling the bell, and struck him stark dead." What if this should happen again? So the bell-ringing went.* Then there was the dancing with his neighbours in the old Moot Hall, or on the village green. If it was hard to give up the ringing, it was harder still to give up the dancing. It was a full year before he could quite leave that, but at last he did, and then thought to himself, "God cannot choose but be pleased with me now."

* *Vide* Addendum.

* It is recorded that Bunyan's bell did actually fall in after years, whilst a peal was being rung in honour of the coming-of-age of Lord Tavistock, son of the Duke of Bedford.

But if it is distressing to feel discontent with one's self, it is dangerous to feel content; aspiration and not self-complacency is the law of healthful life; and He, who was leading Bunyan by a way that he knew not, mercifully shook him out of this unwholesome self-satisfaction. It came about in this way. Going one day into Bedford, to work at his trade as a tinker, he saw, as everybody has heard, three or four poor women holding godly talk together as they sat at a door in the sunshine. He had by this time become somewhat of a brisk talker on religion himself; he therefore drew near and listened. He soon found, however, that their talk was above him, and he had to remain silent. They moved in a world of which he knew nothing; they spoke of a holy discontent with themselves and of a New Birth from above; they told how God had visited their

BELFRY DOOR, ELSTOW.

souls with His love in the Lord Jesus, and with what words and promises they had been refreshed, comforted, and strengthened; they "spake as if joy did make them speak," with such "pleasantness of Scripture language, and with such appearance of grace in all they said," that they seemed to him to have found a new world to which he was altogether a stranger. He was humbled yet fascinated, drawn again and again into their company, and the more he went the more did he question his condition, the more there came over him a "great softness and tenderness of Heart, and a great Bending in his mind" towards godly meditation.

So free from self-consciousness is true life that he in whom faith was beginning to work mightily, now began to wonder whether he had any faith at all. How can he find out? Shall he put it to the test of miracle on the rain pools in the Elstow road? If they should dry up at his word then there would be no doubt. But if not! would not that be proof positive that he "had no Faith but was a castaway and lost?" It is a great risk to run, too great, "nay, thought I, if it be so, I will never try yet, but will stay a little longer."

Then blossomed into shape his wonderful power of dreaming waking dreams. There were these good people at Bedford sitting on the sunny side of a mountain, while he was separated from them by a wall all about, and shivering in the cold. Round and round that wall he goes to see if there be no opening, be it ever so narrow, and at last he finds one. But it is narrow, indeed so narrow that none can get through but those who are in downright earnest, and who leave the wicked world behind them. There is just room for body and soul, but not for body and soul and sin. It must be a strait gate through which a man gets rid of self; but by dint of sidling and striving he first gets in his head, then his shoulders, and then his whole body, at which he is exceeding glad, for now too he is in the sunshine and is comforted. But as yet this is only in a dream, and dreams tarry not. Before long he is out of sunshine into storm again. This man who was an elect soul, if ever there was one —elect through suffering to help other souls—begins to torment himself as to whether he is elect or not. Perhaps he is not. How if the day of grace be past and gone, and he has overstood the time of mercy? Oh, would that he had turned sooner!

would he had turned seven years ago! Words cannot tell with what longings and breakings of soul he cried to heaven to call him, little thinking that the longings and breakings themselves were the very call for which he cried. Gold! could this blessing be gotten for gold, what would he have not given for it? For this the whole world would have gone ten thousand times over, if he had only had it. Meantime that very world went on its old way. How strange that it should; how strange that people should go hunting after perishable things with eternal things before them, that even Christian people should make so much of mere outward losses! If his soul were only right with God, and he could but he sure that it was, he should count himself rich with nothing but bread and water.

Strange alterations of gloom and glory came over him. Sometimes his soul was visited with such visions of light and hope that he could have spoken of God's love and mercy to the very crows on the ploughed land before him. He thought then that he should never forget that joy even in forty years' time. But alas! in less than forty days the vision was all faded and gone. Worse than gone, for there now came down upon him a great storm of conflict which handled him twenty times worse than before. Star after star died out of the firmament of his hope; darkness seized upon him, and to his amazement and confusion a whole flood of doubts and blasphemies poured in upon his spirit. They seemed to be coming in from morning to night, and to be carrying him away as with a mighty whirlwind.

Yet even in that dark time of despair there was this redeeming gleam of hope, that while dreadful things were pouring into his soul, there was something within him that refused to tolerate them. If he is borne along, he goes struggling and crying for deliverance, like the child some gipsy is carrying off by force and fraud from friend and country. A man is safe so long as the citadel of his own will is kept. There is the turning point of destiny—the centre of life's mystery. And all was right there. Floods of temptation came dashing against the outworks, but within he had, he says, great yearnings after God, and heart-affecting apprehensions of Him and His truth. So that he really was making way, getting out of himself more and on to the solid ground of divine fact. There began to come to him such words as these, "If God be for us, who can be against us?" and these, "He hath made peace by the blood of His cross." Fortunately too for him, some time before this the good people at Bedford had taken him to hear Mr. Gifford, their minister. Under his teaching how was his soul led on from truth to truth by the Spirit of Truth! Even from the birth and cradle of the Son of God to His ascension and second coming, he was "orderly led" into the gospel story; and so vivid was everything that it seemed to him as if he had actually seen Christ born and grow up, seen Him walk through the world from the cradle to the cross, had actually leaped at the grave's mouth for joy that Christ was risen again, had actually, in spirit, seen Him at the right hand of the Father, and that on his behalf.

At this stage of his experience also it was his hap to light upon an old book, a book so old that it was ready to fall to pieces in his hand if he did but turn it over. Yet never was gold more precious. For he found his own condition so largely and profoundly handled in it, as if it had been written out of his own heart. It was a copy of the *Commentary on the Galatians*, by Martin Luther, perhaps the one man of all the centuries most fitted to walk with Bunyan along that part of his journey which lay through the valley of the shadow of death. Bunyan, like his own Christian, "thought he heard the voice of a man as going before him." Grateful indeed was he for that. "This, methinks, I must let fall before all men, I do prefer this book of Martin Luther (excepting the Holy Bible) before all the books that ever I had seen as most fit for a wounded conscience."

One temptation loomed large in his experience. He was urged, as he thought, by the tempter "to sell and part with the blessed Christ, to exchange Him for the things of this life—for anything." Day and night almost for a whole year it was with him, so that he could not so much as "stoop for a pin, chop a stick, or cast his eye to look on anything," without the whisper coming into his soul, "Sell Christ for this, or sell Christ for that; sell Him—sell Him." His mental agitation would show itself in bodily movement. He would thrust forth his hands or his elbows in deprecation, and as fast as the destroyer said, "Sell Him," he would say back to him, "I will not, I will not; no, not for thousands, thousands, thousands of worlds." So he held out and held on, but at length one morning, as he lay in his bed under unusually fierce temptation, he felt the thought pass through his mind, "'Let Him go if He will!' Now was the battle won and down fell I, as a bird that is shot from the top of a tree, into great guilt and fearful despair." The great guilt was of course a great delusion, the mere outcome of a vivid brain giving concrete shape to its own creations. But though the sin of which he accused himself was imaginary, very far from imaginary was the inward misery it occasioned. No sin, thought he, was like his; it was point-blank against his Saviour. With all his picturesque power he puts his case in imagery the most varied. He is, he says, like a broken vessel, driven as with the winds; as those that jostle against the rocks, more broken, scattered, and rent; he is as a house whose foundations are destroyed; as a drowning child in a mill-pond; or he seems to himself to be standing at the gate of the City of Refuge, trembling for deliverance and with the avenger of blood close at his heels.

He remembered long years afterwards how at this dark time he went one day into Bedford, and, spent and weary, sat down upon a settle in the street. It seemed to him then as if the very sun in the heavens did grudge to give him light, as if the very stones in the street and the tiles upon the houses did bend themselves against him. "O how happy now was every creature over I was! for they stood and kept fast their station, but I was gone and lost." The worst, however, was now past, and daylight was near. As if in echo to his own self-reproaches a voice seemed to say to him, "This sin is not unto death." He wondered at the fitness and the unexpectedness of the sentence thus shot into his soul. The "power and sweetness and light and glory that came with it also were marvellous." Then again one night as he retired to rest there came to him the quieting assurance: "I have loved thee with an everlasting love," and next morning it was still fresh upon his soul. Again when doubts came as to whether the blood of Christ was sufficient to save him, there came also the words, "He is able." "Methought this word *able* was spoke loud unto me—it showed a great word, it seemed to be writ in great letters." One day as he was passing into the field, still with some fears in his heart, suddenly this sentence fell into his soul, "'Thy righteousness is in heaven'; and methought withal I saw with the eye of my soul,

BUNYAN'S BELL,
Elstow Church.

(By kind permission of Messrs Oliphant Ltd.)

Jesus Christ at God's right hand. I saw, moreover, that it was not my good frame of heart that made my righteousness better, nor yet my bad frame that made my righteousness worse; for my righteousness was Jesus Christ Himself, the same yesterday, to-day, and for ever. Now did my chains fall from my legs indeed; I was loosed from my afflictions and irons. Oh, methought, Christ! Christ! there was nothing but Christ that was before my eyes! I could look from myself to Him and should reckon that all those graces of God that now were green on me, were yet but like those crack-groats and fourpence halfpennies that rich men carry in their purses, when their gold is in their trunks at home! Oh, I saw my gold was in my trunk at home! In Christ my Lord and Saviour! Now Christ was all; all my wisdom, all my righteousness, all my sanctification, and all my redemption!"

ADDENDA—Chapter IV.

(Page 52.)

It has been suggested that Dr. Brown passes over too lightly the years between Bunyan being demobilised and getting married. Dr. Brown says: "On leaving the army Bunyan returned to his tinkering at Elstow . . ." If the anvil (described in App. iv.) be considered, there is proof at once that this statement is correct. There seems no valid reason why Bunyan should have delayed his return to his native village, after an absence of two and a half years, to resume the trade he had followed from a child. There is no clue whatsoever as to where he was married nor to whom he was married. That he lived in two cottages in Elstow, after his soldiering and before he moved into Bedford, in 1655, is quite probable.

(Page 60.)

The bells in Elstow's Tower bore the inscriptions:

Treble—"Christopher Grace made me. 1655."
Second—"Praise the Lord. 1602."
Third—"God save the King. 1631."
*Fourth—"A B C D E F A B C D E F."
Tenor—"Be y[t] knowne to all that doth me see
That Newcombe of Leicester made me. 1604."

* The Fourth Bell is said to be the one that John Bunyan pulled.

NOTE.—The Rev. S. V. Hartley, M.A., Vicar of Elstow, in *An Illustrated Guide Book to the Abbey Church of Elstow* (1927), gives the present *six* bells, the first of which is inscribed "Alfred Bowell made me, 1908. Voco Benedicat." This therefore, makes Bunyan's the *fifth*, or Alphabet Bell. Mr. Hartley's inscription stands thus: "ABCDEꟻG ⱯBCDE ᴚSꓕⱯM"

V.

THE CHURCH AT BEDFORD.

THE three or four godly women whom Bunyan heard talking together in the summer sunshine about their experiences of a diviner life, introduced him, he tells us, to their minister, Mr. Gifford, and to the little Christian community of which they were members. This simple brotherhood of believers is interesting to us for its own sake, as furnishing one of the phases of religious life during the English Commonwealth; and interesting also for the sake of Bunyan himself, who for the next five-and-thirty years of his life was closely associated with its history, first as a private member, and afterwards as its pastor. It may be worth while, therefore, to go back over the years between 1640 and 1650, and see how this Church at Bedford came to be founded, and how it took the shape it did.

The Long Parliament having, in the early part of 1641, received the address of the two thousand petitioners from Bedfordshire, of which we have spoken, and similar addresses from other parts of the country, set forth in earnest on the work of ecclesiastical reform. Commissioners were ordered to be sent into the various counties for "the defacing, demolishing, and quite taking away of all images, altars, or tables turned altarwise, crucifixes, superstitious pictures, monuments, and relics of idolatry out of all churches and chapels." This raid upon what was regarded as popery in disguise, though determined on then, was not actually carried out till a year or two later, and was simply intended as preliminary to a still more searching reform of the entire constitution of the Church of England. As to what that reform should be, the House was by no means as yet agreed. Some were for retaining Episcopacy, first purifying it of its evils. Others, known as the Root-and-Branch party, were for its abolition, for the annihilation of all dignities in the Church above that of simple presbyter or parish minister, and for the appropriation of ecclesiastical revenues to the uses of the State. Without having arrived at any very definite or open agreement on the matter, this party more and more aimed at the establishment in England of a Church after the Scottish Presbyterian fashion. Increasingly it began to be felt and to be said that the Churches of England and Scotland were "embarked in the same bottom, to sink or swim together."

In February, 1642, a Bill was passed for the exclusion of bishops from Parliament; and in June of the following year an ordinance was enacted and entered on the Journals of the House of Lords, to the effect that as "the present Church government by archbishops, bishops, their chancellors, commissaries, deans and chapters, archdeacons, and other ecclesiastical officers depending on the hierarchy is evil, and justly offensive and burdensome to the kingdom . . . the same shall be taken away, and such government settled in the Church as may be agreeable to God's Holy Word." By the same ordinance, the ecclesiastical committee known as the Westminster Assembly of Divines was appointed to confer upon such matters affecting the liturgy, discipline, and government of the Church as Parliament should propose. This body consisted of one hundred and forty-nine persons named in the ordinance, one hundred and nineteen of these being divines fixed upon a year before. To this assembly Thomas Dillingham, the minister of Deane, and Oliver Bowles, the rector of Sutton, were called from Bedfordshire. Dillingham was too old and infirm to take his seat, and Bowles died the following year.

In 1643 the Committees for dealing with Scandalous Ministers were followed by a Committee for Plundered Ministers—these being men who, under Laud or by the Royalist army, had been ejected from their livings. As the plundered were in many cases put in the place of the scandalous, the latter committee dealt with both. There was a central committee in London, and smaller committees in the counties, the latter subordinate to the former, and both to Parliament; and under these the work of judging ministers who were scandalous in life, or erroneous in doctrine, who deserted their cures, or assisted the forces raised against Parliament, proceeded in the most orderly and business-like fashion.

How far the clergy of Bedfordshire were affected by these

proceedings may be very fairly gathered from the minutes of the central committee in London which have been preserved. Walker, writing of the sufferings of the clergy during the Civil Wars, when speaking of this county is both inaccurate and incomplete. He mentions the following ministers of parishes as being sequestered from their livings: In the *town* of Bedford: Giles Thorne of St. Mary's and St. Cuthbert's; John Bradshaw of St. Paul's; and Theodore Crowley of St. John's. In the *county* of Bedford: Dr. Pocklington of Yelden; Robert Payne of Little Barford; Edward Martin of Houghton Conquest; Francis Walsall of Sandy; the Vicar of Chalgrave, name unknown; John Warren of Melchbourne; and John Gwin of Cople.[1] In three cases out of these ten Walker is certainly wrong. He relates a pathetic story about John Bradshaw, to the effect that, in consequence of his sequestration, his wife and four small children were left at his death in such extreme straits as to be under the necessity of begging from a public charity. But, first, State Papers already quoted (p. 13) show that Bradshaw was persecuted, not by Parliament for being a Royalist, but by Laud for being a Puritan. The court before which he had to appear was that Court of High Commission which Parliament abolished and of which Laud was the controller and instigator. Then, too, the story of the destitution of his widow and children as arising from his sequestration is seen to be apocryphal from the following entry in the register of his own parish church: "John Bradshaw did again become vicar of St. Paul's parish May, 1666, and continued till 1670"; that is, of course, till ten years after the Restoration. Walker is incorrect also about Dr. Francis Walsall, the rector of Sandy. It is certain that Walsall went so far in his Royalist sympathies as to be with the king's army at Oxford; it is equally certain that he was not removed from his living. The register and transcript registers of the parish show beyond doubt that he was rector of Sandy all through the Commonwealth period, and at the Restoration sent, in his own handwriting, the return of the previous ten years to the Registry of the Archdeaconry. And as for John Gwin, the vicar of Cople, whom Walker classes among his clerical sufferers, we know that he was set aside from his living by his Majesty's Commission for causes ecclesiastical

[1] *Sufferings of the Clergy,* by John Walker, 1714, Bedfordshire, pp. 189, 214, 303, 326, 374, 390, 417.

before the Civil War began, therefore before the Committee for Scandalous Ministers was even thought of. And if the miserable story of debauchery told about him in a pamphlet of 1641 be true, or at all near the truth, the pity is, not that he was set aside from the ministry, but that he was not set aside sooner.

But if Walker is thus inaccurate on the one hand, on the other hand he is incomplete; and there were sequestrations among the Bedfordshire clergy of which he seems not to have heard. The case of Hugh Reeve, vicar of Ampthill, who was arrested by the sergeant-at-arms for popish practices as early as 1641, has been already mentioned. There were also sequestered —John Goodwin of Leighton Buzzard, the vicar of Luton; Edward Marten of Houghton Conquest; Dr. Archer of Mepershall; Mr. Carr, the curate of Millbrook; Edward Savage of Tilbrook; John Bird of Hawnes; William Parreter of Carlton; Francis Kines of Tilsworth; Anthony Waters and Oliver Thorowgood, the vicar and curate of Bromham; William Ramsay of Flitton; William Witton of Tingrith; William Lake of Little Staughton; Nathaniel Hill of Renhold; Giles Kinge of Tempsford; and George Speeres of Potton.[1] In addition to these cases, Dr. Hammond, and Gilbert Sheldon, afterwards Archbishop of Canterbury, were detained in a kind of honourable captivity at Clapham, near Bedford, in the house of Sir Philip Warwick, Dr. Hammond often preaching in the parish church, "the poverty of the place protecting the minister in his reading the Common Prayer."

The sequestrations which took effect among the parish clergy of Bedfordshire, as elsewhere, were issued of course on various grounds. Some incumbents were set aside simply because they were pluralists, John Bird, the vicar of Hawnes, for example, being proceeded against for holding also the rectory of Bayleham, county Suffolk. Others were removed for graver reasons. Old Thomas Fuller, no prejudiced witness, says plainly that not a few of the clergy first ejected were really men of scandalous lives. John Ailmer, the vicar of Melchbourne, is described as "a comon frequenter of Ale-houses, and tipler there, as well on the Lord's dayes as on other dayes, and a common drunkard." Oliver Thorowgood is spoken of as a scandalous curate; and

[1] *Minutes of Committee of Plundered Ministers*: *Addl. MSS.* 15669, 15670, 15671. These minutes are in three vols. MS., and were purchased from the executors of the Dean of Lincoln for the British Museum in 1846.

similar charges were made against William Ramsey, the vicar of Flitton-cum-Silsoe. Edward Marten of Houghton Conquest, like Pocklington and Reeve, was charged with papistical innovations, openly praying for those in purgatory, and bowing five times before the altar each time he went up and came down the steps. He admitted also, before the committee, that he had lent money to the king for purposes of war; and his parishioners charged him with not having preached more than five times all the five years he had been parson of Houghton. Others of the clergy came under the strong hand of Parliament for assailing its authority and actively joining the Royalists. Nathaniel Hill of Renhold was sequestered for long absence and being in the king's army. It was charged against Savage of Tilbrook, that he had expressed "great malignancy against Parliament, calling them rogues and rascals, and inveighing against them with fearful curses"; while Witton of Tingrith "published the king's proclamation from his pulpit," at the same time "proclaiming the Earl of Essex and all his adherents traytors, refusing to publish the declarations of Parliament, and otherwise expressing great malignancy."

These clerical partisans of the Royalist cause, who were at no pains to conceal their convictions, suffered of course, as men expect to suffer who actively espouse the unsuccessful side in the bitterest of all conflicts, that of civil war. But the Committees for Ministers certainly professed care and leniency in determining who should be set aside. The mere existence of adverse opinions, apart from active hostility, was not sufficient to procure sequestration. William Lindall, for instance, was described by Bunyan in 1660 as that "old enemy to the truth, Dr. Lindall"; yet all through the Commonwealth time he remained vicar of Harlington. Two-thirds of the Episcopal clergy of the county remained undisturbed in their livings, while in the case of the sequestrated, one-fifth of the income of every ejected minister of a parish church was reserved for the maintenance of his family. In some cases, as in the village of Clapham, the Book of Common Prayer continued to be used in public worship; and it would seem as if there was some kind of official position still retained by archdeacons of the Episcopal Church. The following extract from the parish register of Sundon is interesting as bearing on this point, and as relating to people of whom we shall hear again in the course of this narrative: "1653.

William ffoster, of Bedford, gent., and Anne Wingate, the daughter of John Wingate, Esq., deceased, of Harlington, gent., were married Septemb. 22 by John [qy. William?] Lindall, Doctr. of Divinity, by vertue of a license from the Archdeacon."[1]

Perhaps next to Dr. Pocklington, Giles Thorne, Rector of St. Mary's and St. Cuthbert's, in Bedford, was the most conspicuous sufferer on the Episcopal side. Both these men, as officials of the Commissary's Court, had been prominent in enforcing the exactions made upon the clergy by the king for the purposes of the Scottish expedition, and they had also supported up to the hilt the reactionary policy of Laud. Naturally, therefore, they were marked for reprisals when the fortunes of the king were eclipsed. Thorne was a high-handed ecclesiastic, against whose proceedings there was earnest protest on the part of his parishioners even before the day of the Long Parliament had dawned. There is among the State Papers a petition to Archbishop Laud against him from Thomas and Dinah Margetts, who lived in his parish of St. Mary's, and whom he had harassed and all but ruined in the Commissary's Court and the Court of Arches for saying that "he maintained ill vices or unlawful recreations, as Whitsun ales, maypoles, and dancings." They plead with the Archbishop that they have "nyne small children and nothing but their daily labour to sustain them, and they humbly beseech His Grace (of his godly inclinacon to love and peace) to call the said Mr. Thorne before him." This petition of theirs had annexed to it a petition in support of its prayer from eighty or ninety of the leading inhabitants of the town, including the mayor, in which Thorne was further charged with harassing a gentlewoman of his parish for going to a christening in another parish, and a poor old woman of eighty for "going out of the parish on Saboth daies to take her dynner and supper of her owne children by charity."[2]

All this was before the turn of the tide; and when the turn had come Thorne was naturally one of the first to feel the change. In the month of August, 1642, articles were lodged against him in the House of Lords, in which he was charged with saying in St. Mary's church, "that Confession to a priest was as ancient as Religion, as the Scriptures, yea, as ancient as

[1] Bedfordshire *Notes and Queries*. Extracts from the *Parish Registers* of Sundon, p. 233.
[2] *State Papers, Dom.*, 1640 (?). Vol. ccccIxxiv. 40.

God Himselfe "—" a high blasphemy," says the petitioners, " and point-blank papistery." With sublime unconsciousness of the reflexive application of his words to himself, he also said in his sermon that, " though delivered by the mouth of Balaam's Asse, and though the minister have as little witt as Balaam's Asse, yet the Word is the Word, and the King's Proclamation is his proclamation, though delivered by the mouth of a Traitor." He was further charged with preaching against Parliament, and in reproof and discouragement of the raising of volunteers for the defence of the kingdom. It was, however, mainly upon political grounds that he was, as already stated, arrested by Lord St. John's troopers as he left the pulpit of St. Cuthbert's church one Sunday evening, and carried prisoner to the Swan. Summoned afterwards to the bar of the House of Lords, he was remanded first to the Fleet and then to Ely House, being detained about five years, and released in 1647.

In some few cases the clergy resisted their displacement by means of physical force. Giles King of Tempsford, for example, refused to yield his rectory to his successor, and was summoned for contempt. As he would neither yield nor appear, it was ordered (July 20th, 1647), " that the Serjeant-at-Arms of the House of Commons or his deputie doe bring the said Mr. King in safe custodie before this Committee to answer his said contempt." George Speeres also, who was succeeded by another Mr. Kinge, " intruded himself into the Vicarage house, being violent upon the said Mr. Kinge, his wife and servant."[1]

When the recalcitrant clergy had been subdued, and the old system of government by bishops set aside, then came the anxious question as to what form the new State Church should take. In London and Lancashire Presbyterianism, duly organized and established, had taken the place of Episcopalianism. It was not altogether a new thing in the country; for as early as 1572 a Presbytery had been set up at Wandsworth, in Surrey, and under the direction of the celebrated Thomas Cartwright, Presbyterianism attained such dimensions that between 1580 and 1590 there were no fewer than five hundred beneficed clergy of the Church of England, most of them Cambridge men, who were pledged to the revised form of the Wandsworth Directory of Discipline. The movement was especially strong in the counties of Essex, Cambridge, Northampton, Leicester, Rutland and

[1] *Minutes*, vol. iii.

Warwick. "Classes" were held secretly at the Bull, at Northampton, under the presidency of Edward Snape, curate of St. Peter's in that town, and attended by the clergy of Higham Ferrars, Wellingborough, and eight or nine other neighbouring towns. This movement was not without significance, and though it was put down by Archbishop Whitgift, it still lingered, a silent thought, in the hearts of many all through the reigns of James and Charles. As soon, therefore, as the Long Parliament had dispensed with bishops there was once more a Presbyterian movement in England. For about two years it seemed as if it were about to carry all before it. In 1643 the Solemn League and Covenant, which, by the way, must not be confounded with the Scottish National Covenant of 1638, was ordered to be subscribed and sworn to by the whole English realm. The Houses of Parliament set the example in St. Margaret's Church, and in the country the signing went on for months, the Covenant becoming the watchward of party and the test paramount of the citizen. In every parish church it was read aloud to the congregation, who were called up to swear to it with uplifted hands, and afterwards to sign it with name or mark, all refusals being duly reported. Governors of towns and garrisons were required to impose it upon their soldiers. No subject could practise in the courts of law, or become a common council-man, or hold office of trust till he had pledged himself. Copies of the Covenant, having attached to them the names of all parishioners above the age of eighteen, are still to be found among corporation records and in parish archives. In the library of Trinity College, Cambridge, there is a copy which was found a few years ago in the roof of the old rectory of Swyneshed, to the north of Bedfordshire, and bearing the signatures of Thomas Whitehand, the minister, and fifty of his parishioners. He had evidently not liked to destroy it, even after the Restoration came in. He had seen Episcopacy displaced by Presbyterianism, and then again Presbyterianism by Episcopacy; and in this uncertain world who could say what might happen again? The coil of parchment, therefore, was not shrivelled in flame, but hidden away in the old rectory roof, where it came to light in the nineteenth century, bearing the names of the parishioners who had signed it in the summer months of 1644.

The following January saw the climax of Presbyterianism in England, for on the 4th of that month an Ordinance of the

Commons passed the Lords, abolishing the use of the Prayer Book and adopting the New Westminster Directory, a subsequent Act of Parliament decreeing that England as well as Scotland should be Presbyterianised. But it is one thing to pass an Act of Parliament and quite another to secure the religious assent of a nation. From various causes the work hung fire. Even in London and Lancashire the system was not organized till the following year, and the rest of the country was less eager still. The Episcopalians were naturally averse, and at the opposite pole of thought were many who were favourable to a Congregational form of polity, and held that the early churches were separate brotherhoods of believers. Ever since the days of Elizabeth there had been voluntary associations based on this principle in Norfolk, Suffolk, Essex, and London. Some of their leaders perished on the scaffold, but their convictions did not perish with them. The principle they laid down was that "the magistrate is not to meddle with religion or matter of conscience, nor compel men to this or that form of religion, because Christ is King and Lawgiver of the Church and Conscience." These convictions lived on, obtaining wider lodgment in the hearts of Christian men, and, through the lips of Philip Nye, the vicar of Kimbolton, and four others, found expression even in the Westminster Assembly itself. Many were beginning to think that the Presbyterianism of that time was not as wide and tolerant as it might be, and that there was little use in merely exchanging one form of yoke for another.

These opinions found strong support in Bedfordshire at a very early stage in the national conflict. It so happened that there was in the county at that time, as rector of one of its parishes, a man of considerable intellectual force and strong individuality of character, with whom we shall find Bunyan in close personal relations at a later period, and who did more than most men in furthering these views both in the army and in the nation. This was William Dell, the rector of Yelden. He was a native of Bedfordshire, having been born near Maulden or Westoning, was a Fellow of Emmanuel College, Cambridge, and had been episcopally ordained. When Dr. Pocklington was sequestrated in 1642, Dell succeeded him in the rectory of Yelden, and as his parish was near to Melchbourne Park, he was brought into frequent intercourse with the Earl of Bolingbroke, who with the Countess attended his ministry, which they seem greatly to have valued. Through this connection Dell was brought into intimate relation with all the great Commonwealth leaders. In 1645-6 he was chaplain to the army under General Fairfax, and was the person appointed to bring the articles of the surrender of Oxford to Parliament. In 1649, on the sequestration of Thomas Batchcroft, he was made master of Gonville and Caius College, still retaining his Bedfordshire rectory, and was one of the commissioners sent to attend Charles I. before his execution. His position while with the army gave him great influence and many opportunities of spreading his opinions among the leaders of the time, and his sermons both before the House of Commons and in the country were matter of frequent debate in Parliament and of entries in the Journals of both Houses. He strenuously resisted the establishment of any national form of religion. He held strong views on the spirituality of the Church of Christ, and was averse to all stereotyped uniformity in its organization and worship.

"In nature," says he, "is no external uniformity; variety of form in the world is the beauty of the world. Even in earthly governments there is no sameness: York is not governed as Hull, nor Hull as Halifax. In Godmanchester the youngest son inherits, and across the bridge at Huntingdon the eldest. And what tyranny it would be to compel a man every day in the week to a uniformity of life, using the same positions, speaking the same words, or sitting, standing, or walking at the same set times. But how much more evil is it to insist upon uniformity in the life of a Christian, and of the Churches of Christ, taking away all freedom of the Spirit of God, who, being one with God, works in the freedom of God." "God hath not set up any company of men or synod in the world to shine to a whole nation so that all people shall be constrained to follow their judgment and to walk in their light. If two or three Christians in the country, being met in the name of Christ, have Christ Himself with His Word and Spirit among them, they need not ride many miles to London to know what to do." "What wild and woful work do men make when they will have the Church of God thus and thus, and get the power of the magistrate to back theirs, as if the new heavens wherein the Lord will dwell must be the work of their own fingers, or as if the New Jerusalem must of necessity come out of the Assembly of Divines at Westminster." "It is a great dishonour done to God and His Word when we cannot trust His Word to do its work, but must be calling in the power of the world. But if the power of the Word will not reform men, all the power of the world will never do it. Luther said well when he said, 'I will preach, and teach, and write, but I will constrain nobody.'"

Dell plainly said he did not see what was gained by knocking down an establishment of Episcopacy only to set up an establishment of Presbyterianism. "For what," asks he, "is a National Assembly but an Archbishop multiplied, and what a Provincial Assembly but a Bishop multiplied? and a Classical but a Dean and Archdeacon multiplied? Thus, the former lords being removed, the Church would swarm with other lords, and Christ's own kingdom would never be suffered to return to Christ's own lordship and dominion." In the true Church of Christ, Dell goes on to say, there are no distinctions nor differences of persons, no clergy or laity, all are as Peter says, "A chosen generation, a royal priesthood." Presbyters and bishops differ only in office, not in character, from the rest of the Church, and that office they receive from the Church, as an alderman or common council-man differs from the rest of the citizens, not in themselves, but only by the city's choice. "And all Churches are equal as well as all Christians, all being sisters of one mother, beams of one sun, branches of one vine, streams of one fountain, members of one body, branches of one golden candlestick, and so equal in all things."[1]

Such were the opinions of William Dell of Yelden, opinions which greatly influenced the course of Free Church life in the neighbouring town of Bedford. There would seem to have been a separate congregation founded about 1643, which, however, appears to have been of no long continuance. All that we know of it is that its minister was Benjamin Coxe. He was the son of a bishop, was himself a graduate of one of the Universities, and a man of learning. Formerly a beneficed clergyman in the county of Devon, he had been a zealous upholder of Laud's opinions. But in the conflicts of the time a change came over his views; he was led to embrace Congregational principles, and published a little quarto volume setting forth "the unlawfulness of giving the name of church to a house made of lime and stone, and the name of churches to parochiall congregations." How he found his way into Bedfordshire we have no means of knowing. He is described as "for some time minister of Bedford," and as being "an antient minister and of good reputation both for piety and learning." Richard Baxter tells us that in 1643 Coxe was sent for from Bedford to conduct a controversy in Coventry, which ended in his being sent to Coventry gaol. He appears not to have returned to Bedford,

[1] *Select Works of William Dell*, London, 1773.

for three years later we find him in prison in London, for distributing to the members of Parliament a Confession of the Faith held by himself and his brethren on the questions of the time.

Seven years after the brief ministry of Benjamin Coxe had ended, a Free Church was founded in Bedford in 1650, which was destined to be more permanent, to last, indeed, down to our own times. This was the Church with which for five-and-thirty years Bunyan's religious life was so closely identified. The records of this church have fortunately been preserved, presenting a vivid picture of the reality and earnestness of the majority of those who first composed its fellowship. The earliest of these records, those embracing the years between 1656 and 1672, appear to have been copied from an earlier book by a professional scrivener, presenting an unusually beautiful example of the writing of the period.

Prefixed to the minutes of the acts of the church there is a short historical sketch, commencing thus:

"In this Towne of Bedford and the places adjacent, there hath of a long time bene persons godly, who in former times (even while they remained without all forme and order as to visible Church Communion according to ye Testament of Christ) were very zealous according to their light, not onely to edify themselves but also to propagate the Gospell and help it forward, both by purse and presence, keeping alwayes a door open and a table furnished, and free for all such ministers and Christians who shewed their zeale for and love to the Gospell of Christ. Among these that reverend man, Mr. John Grew, was chief, also Mr. John Eston, sen., and brother Anthony Harrington, with others; Men that in those times were enabled of God to adventure farre in shewing their detestation of ye bishops and their superstitions. But as I saide, these persons with many more neither were, nor yet desired to be, embodied into fellowship according to ye order of the Gospell; onely they had in some measure separated themselves from the prelaticall superstitions, and had agreed to search after the non-conforming men, such as in those dayes did beare the name of Puritanes. But when it pleased God (who had before appointed that holy ordinance of the Communion of Saintes) to shew His mercy to this people, He placed Mr. John Gifford among them for their minister in Christ Jesus, and to be their pastor and bishop, and the steward of God to communicate unto them the knowledge of His will in the holy misteryes of the Gospell."

This man who is thus introduced to us as the founder of the Bedford Church, and who left upon it so powerfully the impress of his own individuality, was as little likely at one time to do this kind of work as was Saul of Tarsus to become Paul the Apostle. He was a Kentish man, and at the outbreak of the Civil War a Royalist and a major in the King's army. In 1648 there was made in that county one more desperate struggle to win back the country for the king. The rising was begun by the Kentish people themselves, but the Earl of Norwich came down to place himself at their head, and was joined by the well-known Bedfordshire Royalist, Lord Cleveland, of Toddington. Canterbury, Dover, Sandwich, and the castles of Walmer and Deal had been already won back from the Parliament when, towards the end of May, some ten or twelve thousand of the men of Kent were marching for London, with drums and banners. At Rochester they were met by the Parliamentary forces under the Lord General Fairfax; but it was at Maidstone there came on the fiercest of the fight. The struggle first began about a mile from the town, at seven o'clock in the evening, the forces of Fairfax driving the Royalists from thicket to fence, from hedge to hedge, till the town was reached. There, too, the battle was waged as hotly as ever. Street by street, turning by turning, house by house, Maidstone was fought for to the death. That Thursday night was long remembered as one of the most awful times in the whole history of the war. All the time the fight was raging the rain came down in torrents while eight pieces of cannon, mingling with the storm, were fired at close range upon the mass of struggling men fighting with each other, in the streets, for life and death. It was not till between twelve and one o'clock in the morning that victory declared for Fairfax, the insurgents leaving 300 of their number dead in the street. In addition to these, 1,400 Royalists surrendered as prisoners, some of them being taken in the early morning as they were hiding in the woods, hop-gardens, and fields round the town. Among these prisoners was John Gifford. From the leading part he had taken and the resolute spirit he had shown he was marked out for signal punishment, for while the great body of the prisoners were afterwards released this man and eleven others were adjudged to the gallows.[1]

"But," continues the Church record, "ye night before he was to

[1] *Letter from Lord General Fairfax to Speaker Lenthall,* dated Rochester, June 6th, 1648. *Newes from Bowe,* Rochester, June 4th, 1648. *Narrative of the Great Victory in Kent.* London: Robert Ibbitson in Smithfield, 1648. *Bloody Newes from Kent,* June, 1648. *King's Pamphlets,* British Museum.

dye, his sister coming to visit him and finding the sentinells that kept the doore asleep, and those also his companions within heavy through drinke, she told him of the doore and the watch that stood before it, and intreated him to take the opportunity to escape and save his life, which also he did and passed through them all, there being, as it were, a deep sleep from the Lord upon them, and made his escape into ye field, and, creeping into the bottom of a ditch, lay there about three dayes, till the great search for him was over, and then by the help of his friends he came disguised to London, where he abode not long, but was convayed downe into this country, where he also lay hid from his enemyes in ye houses of certaine great persons who were of like mind with himself. And after a while he came to Bedford and there, being utterly a stranger, he professed and practised physicke, but abode still very vile and debauched in life, being a great drinker, gamester, swearer, &c. But in his gaming, so it was that he usually came off by the losse, which would sometimes put him into some dumpish and discontented fitts and resolutions to leave ye practise: but these resolutions were but like the chaines on the man mentioned in the Gospell which would not hold when the fit to be vile was upon him, wherefore he went on and broke them still. But one night having lost, as I take it, about 15li., it put him into a rage and he thought many desperate thoughts against God. But while he was looking into one of Mr. Bolton's bookes† something therein took hold upon him and brought him into a great sense of sin, wherein he continued for ye space of a moneth or above. But at last God did so plentifully discover to him by His word the forgiveness of his sins for the sake of Christ, that (as he hath by severall of the brethren bene heard to say) all his life after, which was about ye space of five yeares, he lost not the light of God's countenance—no, not for an houre, save only about two dayes before he dyed."

† Possibly *Mr. Bolton's Last and Learned Worke of the Foure Last Things: Death, Judgement, Hell, and Heaven.* London: Printed by George Miller, dwelling in the Black Friers. 1633.

This man, thus brought through strange experiences, no sooner found the new life stirring within him than he sought the companionship of those who were in Christ before him. But, as in the case of the convert more illustrious than he, the brethren were afraid of him and "would not at first believe that he was a disciple." Yet, "being naturally bold," he minded not their shyness but "would inquire after their meetings, and would thrust himself againe and againe into their company both together and apart." Still they held themselves aloof; they were doubtful of a convert who "had indeed been a very vile man, who had done wild things in the town of public notoriety, and who often had thought to kill bro: Harrington, meerly from that great antipathy that was in his heart against the people of God and the holynes of the Gospell."

"But so it was that in little time he was much in his heart put upon it to preach, but yet would not without he advised first with the godly; but they being at a stand in the case he first offered his gift before them in private, and afterwards in an open way before the world; whose word God so blessed that even at the first he was made through grace a father to some through the Gospell, ffor instance, sister Cooper, a woman whose memory is yet precious among us, was converted by the first sermon he preached in publicke.

"Now, having continued preaching awhile and receiving some light in the Congregationall way, after some acquaintance also with other ministers, he attempted to gather into Gospell fellowship the saintes and brethren in and about the towne; but the more antient professors being used to live, as some other good men of those times, without regard to such separate and close communion, were not at first so ready to fall into that godly order.

"Wherefore many dayes were by him and them set apart for prayer to seeke of God light and counsaile therein; they also conferred with members of other societyes; and at last by the mercy and goodness of God they began to come to some blessed resolution therein. And first they consulted after they had determined to walke together in the fellowship of the Gospell, and so to build an house for the name of our God, who were most expedient to begin to be laide in this building as foundation stones. And at length twelve of the holy brethren and sisters began this holy worke, viz.: Mr. John Grew and his wife, Mr. John Eston, the elder, Anthony Harrington and his wife, Mr. John Gifford, sister Coventon, sister Bosworth, sister Munnes, sister ffenne, and sister Norton, and sister Spencer; all antient and grave Christians well knowne one to another, sister Norton being the youngest.

"The manner of their putting themselves into the state of a Church of Christ was: After much prayer and waiting upon God and consulting one with another by the word, they upon the day appointed for this solemne worke, being met after prayer and seeking God as before with one consent they joyntly first gave themselves to the Lord and one to another by the will of God.

"This done, they with one mouth made choyce of brother Gifford to be their pastor, or Elder, to minister to them the things of the kingdome of Christ, to whom they had given themselves before; wherefore brother Gifford accepted of the charge and gave himselfe up to the Lord and to His people, to walke with them, watch over them, and dispense the misteryes of the Gospell among them under that consideration by which he was chosen of them.

"Now the principle upon which they thus entered into fellowship one with another, and upon which they did afterwards receive those that were added to their body and fellowship, was ffaith in Christ and Holiness of life, without respect to this or that circumstance or opinion in outward and circumstantiall things. By which meanes grace and faith was incouraged, Love and Amity maintained, disputings and occasion to janglings and unprofitable questions avoyded, and many that were weake in the faith confirmed in the blessing of eternall life."

The Bedford Church thus founded upon this large and catholic basis was apostolic in numbers as well as in simplicity of spirit, consisting at first of twelve believing souls. We have already met with some of them; for among these twelve were the three or four poor women whose talk at some door in a Bedford street made a new era in the life of the listening tinker from Elstow. The brethren who were among the "foundation stones" of this new spiritual house were men of character and influence. Gifford, formerly a major, was now practising as a physician in the town, for which he may have been prepared before the wars came on. That there was room just then for a new medical practitioner in Bedford there is the following entry in the corporation records to show: "Request was made by Mr. Dr. Banister, Dr. of Physic, to the Council, for an Act of Ease to be passed for him in regard of his great age and debilitie of bodie." The request was granted, and the doctor freed from all liability to public office or appearance "at anie Councell Court or other Assemblie of this town." There was, therefore, clearly room for a successor in the healing art, and, qualified or unqualified, John Gifford took the place. Then next we come upon the name of "that reverend man, John Grew." He had been mayor of the town in 1646; he was again mayor in 1655; he was one of the churchwardens of St. Paul's Church in 1635; his namē appears in the list of Justices of the Peace for Michaelmas term 1650; and by an order of the Council of State of December 2nd of the same year he was made one of the Commissioners of Militia for the county of Bedford. In his will, executed in 1661, he is described as a gentleman, and he appoints as his executors his "beloved friends Wm. Whitbread, of Cardington, Esq., and John Whitman, of the same place, yeoman." Anthony Harrington again, though only a tradesman of the town, a cooper, seems to have been a man in fair position and repute, as we judge from the fact that he was one of the Common Councilmen in 1659; and his prominent standing among the Christian men of the town had singled him out for the especial hatred of John Gifford in the old bad days of his ungodly life. In the after days of persecution of 1669, when the flame waxed fiercest, Harrington in his old age was forced to flee from his home to a place of hiding. Thither a letter was addressed to him by the Church, in which they speak to him in much affection and say: "We are comforted in the remembrance of thee, brother, while we consider that notwithstanding thy natural infirmity yet thou prizest good conscience above thine own enjoyments; and since thou couldest not with quiet injoy it at home thou hast left thy concerns in this world (though in much hazzard and danger) that thou mayest keep it abroad."

But of the first members of the Church perhaps John Eston was locally the most eminent. He was an elderly man in 1650, when the Church was formed; for, as the register of St. Paul's shows, he had a son born to him in 1611, and his wife, Susanna Eston, had died, leaving him a widower in 1640. He was one of the Estons of Holme, in Bedfordshire, and his grandfather appears in the Visitation of the county in 1566. He himself was thrice mayor of Bedford, being mayor the year the Church was formed; he was also in the commission of the peace. His son after him was high sheriff of the county and a justice of the peace, both for the county and borough. It will be remembered, also, that John Eston was one of the churchwardens of St. Paul's in 1629, and again in 1639, the latter being the year in which Laud's agent in Bedford, Walter Walker, was compelling John Bradshaw, the vicar, and the parishioners of St. Paul's to erect altar-rails and to celebrate the communion kneeling, a mode which they regarded as superstitious and papistical.

Two of these early members of the Bedford Church seem to have striven for that Puritan simplicity in the council chamber of the town, which they preferred in their religion, as the following entry in the corporation records remains to show: "At a common council held in the Guildhall Chamber by Robert Bell, mayor, on Monday, the 15th day of March, 1651, Mr. Francis Banister, Doctor of Physic, Mr. John Eston the elder, Mr. John Grew, and Mr. John Hancock, Aldermen, appeared at this Councill without their Gownes, contrary to the ordinance made in that behalf, wherefore each of them hath forfeited, according to that ordinance, two shillings." The following Monday Banister and Eston again appeared without their gowns, and in September it is noted that Aldermen Eston and Grew repeated the offence. Their persistence was successful in the end, and in 1652 it was "ordained that an Act of the 16th August,

OLD BAPTIZING PLACE, BEDFORD.

"If Elstow was the natural birthplace of Bunyan, he himself would certainly have named as his spiritual birthplace the meeting-house at Bedford, and the stream of the Ouse, near the corner of Duck Mill Lane, where he was in middle life re-baptized."—Rev. A. P. Stanley, D.D., Dean of Westminster. (1874.)

INTERIOR OF THE MOOT HALL, ELSTOW.

1650, enjoining appearance at the town assemblies in a certain garb shall (as touching appearance in gownes at the Common Council) be henceforth voyd, and all forfeitures in that respect be discharged."[1]

These particulars, trifling enough in themselves, have yet a sort of interest for us as descriptive of the men with whom Bunyan came into closest relations of brotherhood in the Christian Church at a formative period of his life. The records of this Church were not formally kept till 1656, or six years after its formation. We have no means now of knowing where was their place of meeting during the first three years of their church-life. It appears, however, from the town records and the register of St. John's church that in 1653 the little community, while continuing in all other respects to conduct its affairs on Congregational principles, became part of the State Church of the Commonwealth. The fact is interesting as an illustration of the comprehensive character of the Cromwellian settlement of religion; and it came about in the following way.

In 1280 one Robert Parys, or De Parys, founded on the south side of the town of Bedford what was called the Hospital of St. John the Baptist. It was provided by the foundation that one master and one chaplain should "pray for the souls of the said Robert and Henry Saynt John and John his son, his nephews, and all of those who should give lands for the Hospitall," and that relief should be given to "such poor folk as chance to be dwellers in the town of Bedford." Even before the Reformation the church of the hospital had become the church of the parish, and the master its rector, the parish being but small, and containing, in 1546, no more than "87 houselinge people." At what time the right of presentation to the living was vested in the mayor and corporation of the town is uncertain; but it had been in their hands for centuries when, in 1653, Theodore Crowley, the then master and rector, for some cause unknown to us, was sequestered. It so happened that at that time Puritan and Parliamentarian influence was predominant in the council, and the corporation presented John Gifford to the living, in the place of Theodore Crowley.

To us, whose conception of a State Church has grown up after the establishment for more than two centuries of one

[1] *Minutes of Bedford Corporation.*

exclusive form of ecclesiastical polity, the Episcopal, it is strange to see a Congregational community in possession of the parish church, and its pastor installed there as rector. This could not, of course, have happened at any other time than between the years 1653 and 1660. During these seven years Cromwell's Broad Church was really broad—broader than anything ever known in this country either before or since, for it recognised and comprised the various forms of religious conviction to be found in the nation.

Abstractly considered, of course, there is no substantial reason why only one form of Church polity, and that confessedly not the earliest, should have place in a national settlement. There are grave objections to any State system of religion; but if there is to be one at all, Cromwell certainly hit upon the fairest that has yet been tried. Even that was not altogether fair—no State Church can keep quite clear of injustice — for Roman Catholics were disabled from voting and disqualified for election, and all such infidels and heretics as attacked the Christian faith were deprived of the electoral franchise. But taking into account simply the various sections of Protestant Christians in the country, there was literally no Act of Uniformity. The rights of patrons were not to be interfered with by the Commissioners. These remained as before, and we find, for example in Bedfordshire, Thomas Power admitted to the vicarage of Southill, upon the presentation of Thomas Snagg, Esq., patron; John Wigfall, and subsequently James Mabbison, to the vicarage of Roxton, upon the certificate of the patrons, the Master, Fellows, and Scholars of Trinity College, Cambridge; and John Power, to the vicarage of Thurleigh, on the presentation of the patron, Oliver, Earl of Bolingbroke, just as in the old Episcopal days.[1] A certificate was required from some responsible persons to whom the presented minister was known, simply testifying that he was a worthy man and a fit person to take the cure of souls. This was all. No articles of faith were prescribed, no subscription was enforced, and no mention made by name either of Episcopacy, Presbyterianism, Congregationalism, or of the question of baptism. If the Commissioners conserved the rights of patrons, they were not limited by any other statutory conditions, and were guided by no creed, statute, canon, or established usage.

[1] *Lambeth MSS.*—Augmentations, 1657, 1658.

Those appointed for Bedfordshire in 1657 were called the "Commissioners for the publique ffaith," and included the two leading members of the Bedford Church. The entire list for the county was as follows: John Hervy; John Cockayne of Cardington; Richard Wagstaffe of Ravensden; Samuel Bedford of Henlow; Edward Cater of Kempston; and John Grew and John Eston, described as aldermen of Bedford. It may be noted by the way that the day when they were appointed by the Council of the Commonwealth was the day also when Richard Cromwell emerged into public life. At the same meeting at Whitehall, "the Lord President reports his Highness' consent to the Order that Lord Richard Cromwell be one of his Highness' Counsell. Ordered that a Letter be written to ye Lord Richard Cromwell to attend his Highness and ye Counsell in order thereunto."[1]

Taking the country through, the commission for the different counties was variously composed. Upon it were Presbyterians, Independents, and Baptists. Access to benefices, therefore, was permitted to ministers of all three denominations. Episcopalians, also, were eligible, provided they would consent not to use the Book of Common Prayer, and as a matter of fact many of them were admitted.

Cromwell's Establishment, therefore, recognised no one form of ecclesiastical organization; it had no Church courts, no Church assemblies, no Church laws, no Church ordinances. Nothing was said about rites and ceremonies, nothing even about sacraments. The mode of administering the Lord's Supper and Baptism was left an open question to be determined by each congregation for itself. All that the Commissioners dealt with was the personal piety and intellectual fitness of the man presented to the living. If, in these respects, he were shown to be worthy he was at once installed. The church buildings were regarded as the property of the parish, and in one there was to be found a Presbyterian community, in another an Independent, and in a third a Baptist church. So complete was the freedom accorded that we find such an Order in Council as this: "On petition of several inhabitants of Abbot's Leigh parish, co. Hunts: That any godly persons whom the inhabitants may procure, have liberty to preach in the public meeting-place of the town on week-days, whereunto they may be summoned by a bell, and the incumbent and others concerned are not to inter-

[1] *S. P. Interregnum; Council Book*, i., 78, Thursday, December 10th, 1657.

fere."[1] If there were churches that preferred to worship outside the national system altogether they were at liberty to do so. The Articles of Government declare that such persons "shall not be restrained, but shall be protected in the profession of the faith and exercise of their religion, so as they abuse not their liberty to the civil injury of others, and to the actual disturbance of the public peace on their part." This liberty, however, was "not to extend to Popery or Prelacy, nor to such as, under the profession of Christ, held forth and practised licentiousness."[2]

Under this elastic system of church-life, introduced into England in 1653, there was, of course, nothing to prevent the Bedford Corporation from presenting, or the local Commissioners from admitting, John Gifford to the mastership and rectory of the hospital and church of St. John. For, though he had not before been a parish minister, he was the recognised pastor of the Church formed under his care; his blameless life during the past three years had secured for him the name of "holy Mr. Gifford"; and the consciences of his hearers had testified to the reality of his call as a teacher of the truth of God. Presented he was, therefore, and in the summer of 1653 he took possession of the ancient hall of the rectory; and his people of the parish church of St. John the Baptist close by.

This church has not greatly changed since those days; but, judging from Speed's sketch map of 1610, the hospital building has changed considerably from its former self. Standing to the north of the churchyard it had a lofty and imposing gateway to the street, the building itself retreating somewhat, and extending farther into the grounds on the east than the present rectory does. The kitchen buildings close to the street on the west, and the drawing-room and library on the east, are modern erections; but the old hall and dining-room, midway between, and with windows looking out upon the churchyard to the south, are part of the original hospital. The dining-room, which was the ancient refectory, was entered from the south, and as late as 1760, when Cole, the antiquary, saw it, was connected with the church by a cloister running under its north wall to the chancel door."[3] This room, with its oaken beams, is interesting, not merely as being a portion of perhaps the oldest dwelling-house

[1] *S. P. Dom. Interreg.*; 1657, vol. clvii., 155, 7.
[2] Articles xxxvi., xxxvii.: *Parl. Hist.*, iii., 1425.
[3] *Cole's MSS.*, 5832, f. 85.

ST. JOHN'S CHURCH, BEDFORD.

in the town, and as the living-room of the master and his co-brethren of the hospital for centuries, but also as the place where Bunyan and Gifford were often in conference together, as the seeking Pilgrim and the guiding Evangelist of the time.

The year that Gifford entered into residence at St. John's was the year that Bunyan joined the Church. The Record of the Acts of the Church was not commenced till 1656, or three years later; but the Roll of members was kept from the foundation of the Church in 1650, and Bunyan's name appears on the list, the next above those of William Whitbread of Cardington, and Lettice his wife, from whom is descended the present Mr. Samuel Howard Whitbread, C.B., M.A., J.P., of Southill, Lord-Lieutenant of Bedfordshire.

Gifford was Bunyan's guide and helper only for two years after this, for he died in the early part of September, 1655. But little is known of him beyond the facts already given. He came to Bedford, as we have seen, a lonely fugitive in the summer of 1648, and afterwards married there, gathering his family about him. In the register of St. Paul's church there is the record of a burial on the 30th of June, 1651, of John, son of John Gifford. His other three children were daughters. He died in the prime of life, and appears to have known, some weeks before, that he was fatally stricken; for under exceptional circumstances he made a will on the 2nd of August, 1655, which is still in existence in the District Registry. By this will he constitutes his "loving wife" sole executrix, leaving to his eldest daughter, Mary, £55, payable on the day of her marriage or on her attaining the age of twenty-one; to his daughter Elizabeth, £50; and also to a child yet unborn the sum of £50. This child, born early the following year, was named Martha, and was married in 1675 to William Hawkes, who was a deacon of the Church during Bunyan's pastorate, was one of the four witnesses who attested Bunyan's will, and was the person who entered in the Church Book the sorrowful record of Bunyan's death. Gifford's second daughter, Elizabeth, as we find from the register, was buried in St. Paul's churchyard on the 4th of September, 1665. His eldest daughter, Mary, was married to a person of the name of Negus, and was in the fellowship of the Church in 1696, her son, Gifford Negus, being a tradesman of the town in 1730. The only other references* we possess to John Gifford himself are in the "Book of Fines and Agree-

* There is an entry in *A Perfect Diurnall of some Passages in Parliament* (under date of May 13th, 1646), respecting the surrender of Dudley Castle, signed by the Commissioners for the King, one of whom is (Major) John Gifford.

ments of the Court of Pleas" belonging to the Corporation, one of which sets forth that, on the 25th of October, 1654, one message with appurtenances in the town of Bedford was sold by Robert Risely to John Gifford, gentleman, on the payment of a fine of £10 sterling. His death the following year brought changes, and on the 24th of September, 1656, Margaret Gifford, widow, came to the same Court of Pleas, "craving the enrollment of a fine of £10 between Thos. Gibbs, gentleman, and her the said Margaret, touching one message with appurtenances in the parish of St. Paull."

John Gifford was pastor of the church at Bedford not quite five years, yet he left his mark broad and deep, and his work remains. He was a man of sufficient force of character to be capable of impressing powerfully men who were themselves of strong individuality. The "great extravagancy of minde and wildenes of heart," said to have been in his nature when he was the Royalist Saul, were turned into chastened fervour and force when he became the Puritan Paul. Bunyan tells us how real the man was, and how real he himself felt his teaching to be. Others, too, who came under his influence, showed in the deepest experience of their lives how vital that influence was. The three or four poor women who looked up to him as their pastor, and whom Bunyan heard talking together of the things of God, were evidently well-instructed in the lore of the kingdom. The roots of their spiritual life went down deep into the eternal verities, and its boughs and branches shot up high into the sunlight of heaven. "They spake as if Joy did make them speak: they spake with such pleasantness of Scripture Language and with such appearance of grace in all they said, that they were to me as if they had found a new World." Gifford, therefore, could say with Paul, "Need we epistles of commendation? Ye are our epistle written in our hearts, known and read of all men." Bunyan, drawn by them under the same influence, bore testimony in his turn to the soul-subduing power of this converted Royalist major. "These people," says he, "told Mr. Gifford of me, who himself also took occasion to talk with me, and was willing to be well-persuaded of me, though I think but from little grounds." Evangelist was clearly a man of insight. "He invited me to his House, where I should hear him confer with others about the dealings of God with their Souls, from all which I received

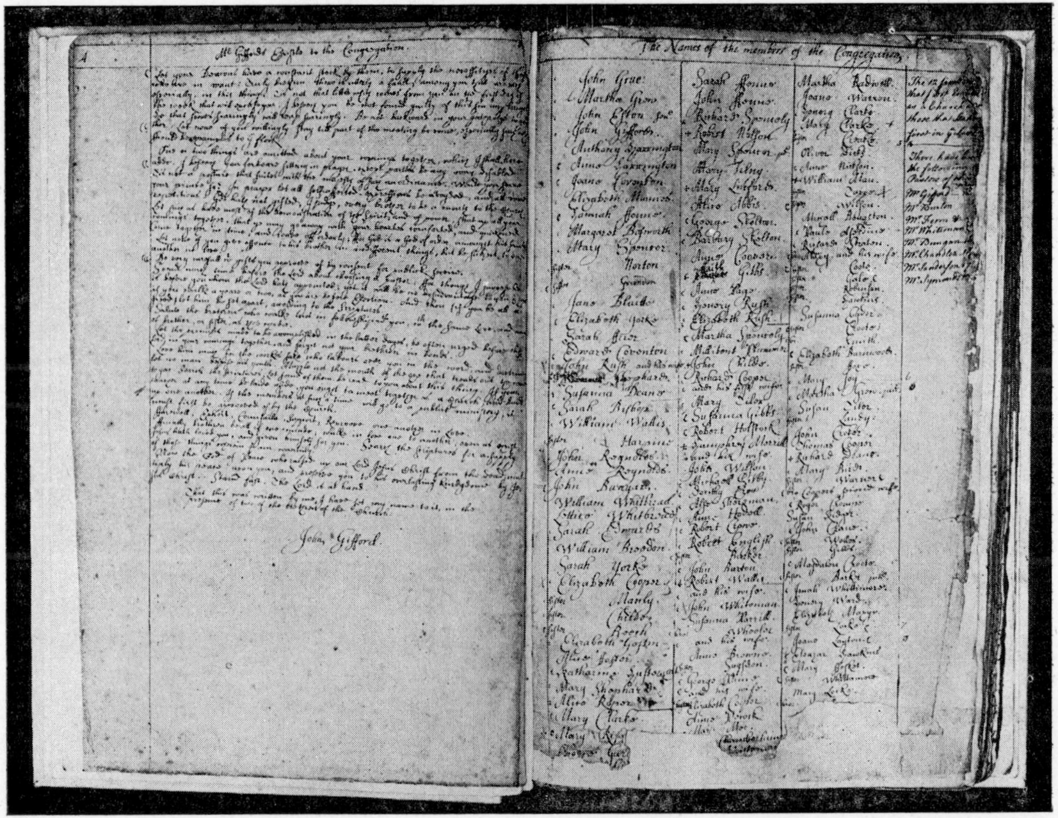

ACT BOOK: BEDFORD CHURCH.
LIST OF MEMBERS.
(The name of John Bunyan appears in first column.)

(Preserved at the Bunyan Meeting, Bedford.)
Photo: C. A. Cleavey, Bedford.]

more conviction." Farther on also in that stern story of spiritual conflict told in the *Grace Abounding,* he says, "At this time I sat under the ministry of holy Mr. Gifford, whose Doctrine, by God's Grace, was much for my stability. This man made it much his business to deliver the People of God from all those false and unsound rests that, by nature, we are prone to take and make to our souls. He would bid us take special heed that we took not up any truth upon trust, as from this or that, or any other man or men, but to cry mightily to God that He would convince us of the reality thereof and set us down therein, by His own Spirit, in the Holy Word."

Gifford left no writings behind him save one solitary letter written from his death-bed, a letter which Southey has described as "wise, tolerant, and truly Christian," and which was addressed, "To the Church over which God made me an Overseer, when I was in the world." In the opening sentence, "I beseech you," he says, "brethren beloved, let these words (wrote in my love to you and care over you, when our heavenly Father was removing me to the Kingdom of his dear Son) be read in your church-gatherings together." In this letter, which was read on New Year's Day at the meeting of the Bedford Church,* Gifford urges them affectionately to walk together in all love and in the ordinances of Jesus Christ their Lord, and to keep together when he their pastor shall be no more with them, for they "were not joined to the ministry but to Christ and the Church." He would have them refrain from divisions about minor things and keep to central verities: "Concerning separation from the Church about baptism, laying on of hands, anointing with oil, psalms, or any externals, I charge every one of you respectively, as you will give an account of it to our Lord Jesus Christ, who shall judge both quick and dead at his coming, that none of you be found guilty of this great evil." Worldly distinctions should have no place in the Church of God: "Let no respect of persons be in your comings-together. When you are met as a Church there's neither rich nor poor, bond nor free, in Christ Jesus. 'Tis not a good practice to be offering places or seats when those who are rich come in; especially it is a great evil to take notice of such in time of prayer, or the word; then are bowings and civil observances at such times not of God." He urges those who are most eminent in profession to let their faith,

* This custom continued through Dr. Brown's ministry, but it was subsequently discontinued.

love, and zeal be very eminent; he that casts a dim light harms the Church. "Let there," says he, "be kept up among you solemn days of prayer and thanksgiving, and let some time be set apart to seek God for your seeds." Charging them to be careful and prayerful in the choice of his successor, to be all of one mind, and walk in love one to another even as Christ Jesus hath loved them, he commends them to the peace of God, charging them to "Stand fast; the Lord is at hand."

After signing this letter in the presence of two of the brethren, Gifford went home to be with God. No stone marks the spot where he was buried in the churchyard of St. John's, but there his dust lies—mingling with that of the long line of masters and rectors, of bedesmen and brethren, stretching through more than six hundred years, and of whom he was one.

VI.

FIVE YEARS OF BEDFORD LIFE: 1655—1660.

It has been already mentioned that Bunyan was formerly received to the Church at Bedford, in 1653, at which time he was still living on at Elstow. In his account of himself he is provokingly reticent in the matter of dates, but it was probably in 1651 or 1652, that he began to come into Bedford to listen to the preaching of John Gifford. His doing so created an unusual stir among his neighbours, and brought unexpected fame to the preacher. That a "town-sinner" so notorious should become so changed, brought over the people of Elstow to hear for themselves. "When I went out," says he, "to seek the Bread of Life, some of them would follow me and the rest be put into a muse at home. Yea, almost all the town at first at times would go out to hear at the place where I found good. Yea, young and old for a while had some reformation on them; also, some of them perceiving that God had mercy on me, came crying to Him for mercy too." So that Gifford soon found that this was no ordinary convert who had come under his influence.

As we know from the parish register, Bunyan continued to live at Elstow for about two years after his reception into the Bedford Church. Mary, his blind child, and Elizabeth, his second daughter, were both born there, as these entries in the register show:

"Mary, the daughter of John Bonion, was baptized the 20th day of July, 1650."

"Elizabeth, the daughter of John Bonyon, was born 14th day of April, 1654."

The birthplace of these two children was the little roadside dwelling in the village of Elstow, still pointed out as Bunyan's cottage. Within living memory it was a thatched building with a lean-to forge at the south end, but there is now little of the original structure left beyond the walls and the oak beam of the interior.

It was, therefore, after the birth of his second daughter, in 1654, and probably in the year 1655, that Bunyan removed altogether from Elstow and went to live in Bedford. The town into which he thus removed his household, the implements of his craft, and his few simple belongings, was even then one of the most ancient boroughs in the kingdom. Its earliest existing charter, of the reign of Henry II., is simply confirmatory of charters earlier still by which there were secured to its burgesses the same custom, law, and liberty as those possessed by the citizens of Oxford. They were to be "quit of toll and pontage, of stallage, lastage and passage, and of assorts, and of all other customs throughout England and Normandy, by earth and by water, by sea-beach, biland, and bistrand." The corporation of the town consisted of the customary mayor, aldermen, and councillors, with recorder, deputy-recorder, town-clerk, bailiffs, and chamberlains, with minor and less dignified, but perhaps not less necessary officers, in the shape of beadle, field-drivers, bucket-keepers, ale-tasters, fish and flesh searchers, and wood and chimney searchers.

In Bunyan's time, Bedford consisted of the same five parishes as at present, but the houses were widely scattered. There were large enclosures of field and orchard within the borough boundaries; and the population was only between one and two thousand. In the previous century there were 800 "houseling people" in the parish of St. Paul, and as another return in Elizabeth's time states the number of families in the whole town at 191, 135 of these being in the parish of St. Paul, the entire population would be then a little over a thousand.[1] A century later, according to the Hearth Tax list of 1673, there were 446 householders in the town, and therefore a population a little over two thousand.[2]

It goes without saying that the general appearance of the town has greatly changed since Bunyan was a dweller within its borders. Till within quite recent times some of the buildings in the High Street were roofed with thatch, and their windows sheltered by primitive shutters which were lowered downwards upon

[1] *Harleian MSS.*, 618.

[2] *S. P. Subsidies*—Hearth Tax, 25 Car. II. The 446 householders were thus distributed: Parish of *St. Paul*, 256; *St. Cuthbert*, 47; *St. Peter*, 23; *St. Mary*, 73; *St. John*, 47. These numbers include those who were too poor to pay chimney-money and were exempted by legal certificate.

hinges. Few, indeed, of the old buildings of his time remain to ours. Some of the churches are substantially the same, though enlarged. The interesting gateway of the pre-Reformation hostelry, known as the Old George, still lingers among more modern erections. But the ancient bridge with its picturesque gateways and its prison chamber midway over the stream; the Old Swan inn at the foot of the bridge; the Guildhall Chamber which, with the pillory and maypole, stood in the High Street; the county gaol at the corner of the Silver Street, so memorable to Bunyan and to us; the old buildings with butcher-row and fish-shops, which, as so often in the olden-time, were crowded close to the churchyard wall and seemed almost to hustle the dead with the needs of the living—all are gone. With them also have disappeared the old abbey of Caldwell, the leper-house of St. Leonard, the gateway of St. John, and the manor-house in St. Cuthbert's.

Bedford, in the days to which we are now looking back, was rigidly exclusive. Foreigners, by which were meant natives of English towns elsewhere, were not admitted to the merchant-guild; no townsman was permitted to let his house to a foreigner without the consent of the mayor; and no innholder or victualler could receive a stranger into his house for more than eight days and nights without reporting him to the mayor. After ten o'clock at night till five next morning the traffic over the bridge was stopped. Indeed, personal safety almost necessitated the keeping within doors after nightfall; for the streets were badly paved where paved at all; and, judging by an ordinance of 1656, they were even worse lighted than paved. In these days of gas and the electric-light there is a delightful old-world simplicity about a minute to be found in the Act Book of the Corporation, under date October 10th, 1656. By that minute it was "Ordayned: That on St. Luke's Day next comyng until Candlemas following, and soe yearlie for ever, lights shall be sett forth in the High Streete of this town all along on both sides of the River of Ouze from the house called the Peacock in St. Peter's parish to the Bridge in St. John's parish on the way to Ampthill. And they shall be sett up at the Shutting in of the Evening and be continued until eight o'clock following. Each occupier of Shops and other Edifices next the Streete shall each of them according to the turne of the side set out a Candle-light of the bigness at least of Sixteen in the pound." One night, one side of the street was to be lit up, and the next, the opposite; the Bridge-house and all public-houses to be always lit. Further, "the Bedell of Beggars, for the time being, shall upon St. Luke's day next comyng, and Every Evening after at the Shutting in of the Evening, make public call in the Streete for setting forth of lights; and shall give notice to the Mayor next day of defaulters."

Almost from the time of his removal from Elstow to Bedford, Bunyan's life seems to have been darkened by sorrow. His own health appeared to be seriously failing. He says: "I was somewhat inclining to a consumption, wherewith about the Spring, I was suddenly and violently seized with much weakness in my outward man, insomuch that I thought I could not live." Elsewhere also he says: "I was at another time very ill and weak, all that time also the Tempter did beset me strongly, for I find he is much for assaulting the Soul when it begins to approach towards the grave, then is his opportunity." This sickness did not, however, prove so serious as he feared. It was simply weakness of body, resulting from intense overstrain of mind and heart; and subsequently he tells us, "My sickness did presently vanish, and I walked comfortably in my work for God again." But though these fears vanished, a dark shadow came over his home and clouded his heart and life. He was spared, but the wife of his youth was taken. It adds to the pathos of the first years of his Bedford life, to remember that they were spent under the shadow of this great bereavement, and that, while he was still battling with inward conflict, he had at the same time to be both father and mother to his poor blind child and to the other three children whom his wife had, in dying, left to his care.

Mr. Offor supposes that by the time Bunyan joined the Church at Bedford, in 1653, he had risen considerably in social position. He infers this from the fact that, on the 13th of May in that year, an important document went up to Cromwell from Bedfordshire, containing, among other names, that of a John Bunyan. This document was the formal return of two Members to Parliament for the county. It will be remembered that in that year Cromwell set aside the ordinary constitutional usage, and sent to the godly of the nation to return him a Parliament on which he could rely. The assembly thus returned was called the Little Parliament, or the Parliament of Saints, and had but a brief existence. It was in response to this call there was sent the "Letter from the people of Bedfordshire to the Lord General Cromwell and the Councell of the Army," which came into the possession of John Milton as Latin Secretary, and is preserved among the Milton Papers belonging to the Society of Antiquaries. It is to this effect:

"We (we trust) servants of Jesus Christ, inhabitants in the County of Bedford, haveinge fresh upon our hearts the sadde oppressions we have (a longe while) groan'd under from the late parlyament, and now Eyeing and owneing (through grace) the good hand of God in this great turne of Providence, being persuaded that it is from the Lord that you should be the instrument in his hand at such a time as this, for the Electing of such persons whoe may goe in and out before his people in righteousness, and governe these nations in judgment, we haveinge sought the Lord for you, and hopeing that God will still doe greate things by you, understanding that it is in your hearte through the Lord's assistance, to establish an authority consisting of men able, loveing truth, feareing God, and hateing covetousness; and we haveing had some experience of men with us, we have judged it our duty to God, to you and to the rest of his people, humbly to present two men, viz.: Nathaniell Taylor and John Croke, now Justices of the Peace in our County, whom we judge in the Lord qualified to manage a trust in the ensuing government."

There were thirty-six names appended to this document, one of which was a John Bunyan whom Mr. Offor very naturally concluded to be the writer of *The Pilgrim's Progress*. This conclusion, however, though natural, was mistaken. In 1653, it is scarcely likely that John Bunyan, the working tinker of Elstow, would be asked to join in a return of Members of Parliament for the County. He had only that year joined the Bedford Church, if indeed he had joined it so early as the month of May. He was, as yet, altogether unknown to fame, and was simply an ordinary labouring man from a village. On the other hand, the rest of the names upon the document in question were those of men in the rank of magistrates, rectors of parishes, gentlemen, and yeomen. It was signed by John Eston, John Grewe, John Gifford, and Thomas Gibbs; by William Dell, the rector of Yelden, John Donne, the rector of Pertenhall, William Wheeler, the vicar of Cranfield, and John Gibbs, the vicar of Newport Pagnel; the rest of the signatories, too, so far as we know them, being men of influence and position. It will be said, of course, but there is the name—John Bunyan. To which it may be replied: (1) That there were in Bedfordshire at that time no fewer than three other John Bunyans, each of whom would be more likely to be asked to sign the return than the tinker of Elstow. One of these was a farmer at Streatley, the other two, father and son, were yeomen at Cranfield. The Court Book of the Manor of the Earls of Middlesex, who were Barons of Cranfield, mentions a Johannes Bonyon in 1642, and in 1655 and 1656, a John Bunion, the elder, yeoman, holding land under the manor in Cranfield parish.[1] Then (2) the signature is altogether unlike that known certainly to be Bunyan's, the one appended to his Will and attested by four witnesses. A comparison of the fac-similes* will show that the signature to the Cromwellian document of 1653, which was earlier by thirty-two years than the one appended to the deed of 1685, is yet very much the more educated signature of the two.

* *Vide* Addendum.

It was shortly after Bunyan came to reside in the town of Bedford that his pastor and friend John Gifford was called away by death. In the minute-book of the Common Council there is the following entry under date September 19th, 1655: "Whereas the Rectorie and Hospitall of St. John Baptist in this Town (the patronage whereof belongs to ye Corporacon) is fallen void by the death of Mr. John Gifford: It is agreed that Mr. Hayes, of Papworth, bee presented thereto, and Mr. Maior is hereby authorized to set the Town Seale to an Instrument to that purpose." To the Church itself, however, this appointment was unwelcome, and was resisted. A minute of the 15th October states that "certaine persons, members of the Corporation and others, to weaken the presentation, submitted to His Highness that it was surreptitiously and suddenly contrived and carryed on." This allegation the friends of Mr. Hayes denied, whereupon Cromwell determined to hear both sides for himself. The minute goes on to say: "And whereas also on Wednesday next His Highness hath appointed to heare the difference of allegation of both parties, this Councell doe agree that appearance bee made in defence of the said Act and Petition, And that Mr. John Baxter and two Aldermen or other members of the Corporation appear as Agents for y^e^ Corporation." The

[1] *Addl. MSS.*, 18458, ff. 113, 114, 149, 232.

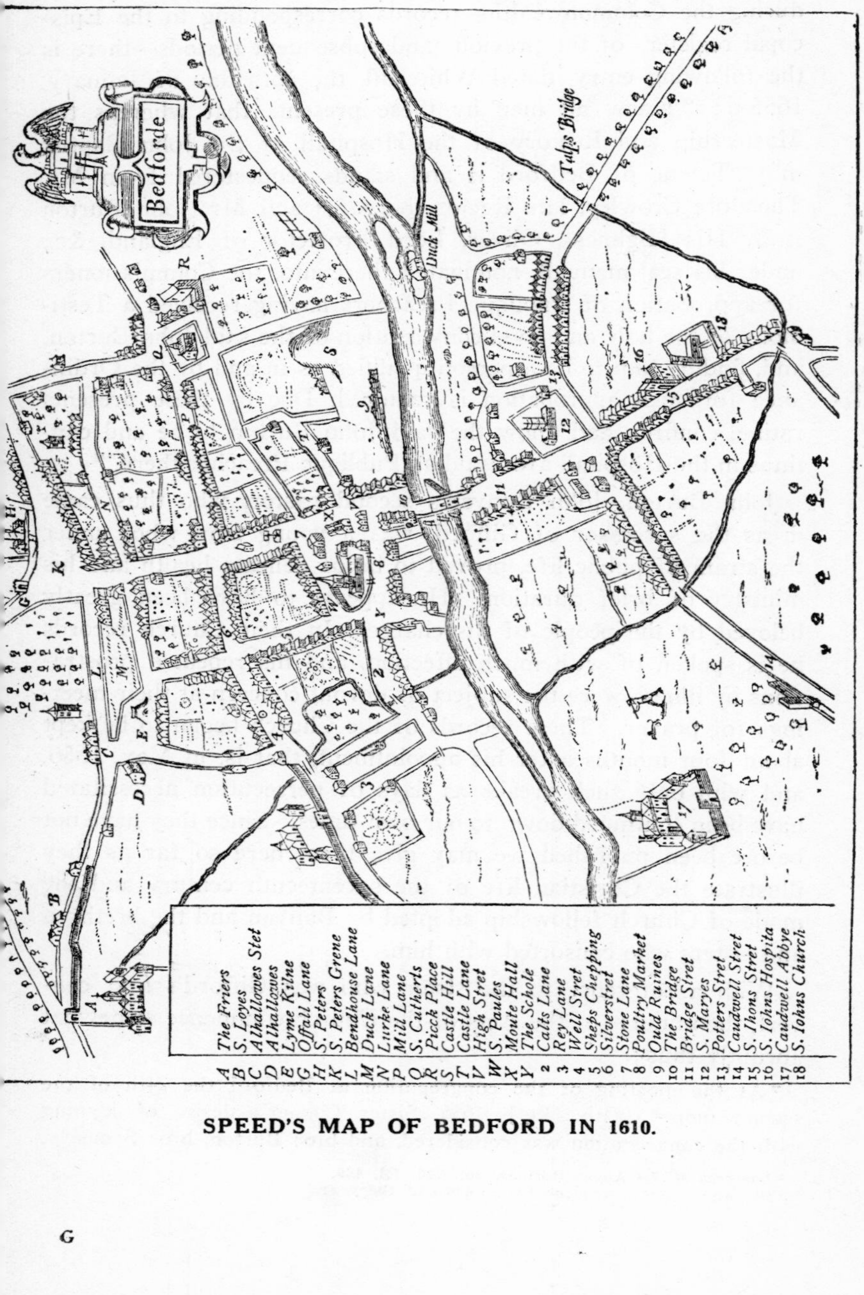
Bedforde
Duck Mill
A The Friers
B S. Loyes
C Alhallowes Stet
D Alhallowes
E Lyme Kilne
G Offall Lane
H S. Peters
K S. Peters Grene
L Bendhouse Lane
M Duck Lane
N Lurke Lane
P Mill Lane
Q S. Cuthberts
R Pecck Place
S Castle Hill
T Castle Lane
V High Stret
W S. Paules
X Moute Hall
Y The Schole
2 Calts Lane
3 Rey Lane
4 Well Stret
5 Sheps Chepping
6 Silverstret
7 Stone Lane
8 Poultry Market
9 Ould Ruines
10 The Bridge
11 Bridge Stret
12 S. Maryes
13 Potters Stret
14 Caudwell Stret
15 S. Ihons Stret
16 S. Iohns Hospita
17 Caudwell Abbye
18 S. Iohns Church

SPEED'S MAP OF BEDFORD IN 1610.

appeal resulted as the Church desired, Cromwell deciding that the appointment should be in favour of John Burton. In the carefully kept registers of ecclesiastical appointments made during the Commonwealth—records corresponding to the Episcopal registers of the previous and subsequent periods—there is the following entry, dated Whitehall, the 16th day of January, 1655-6: "Know all men by these presents that whereas the Mastership and Rectory of the Hospitall of St. John Baptist in ye Towne of Bedford is and stands sequestered from Mr. Theodore Crowley, late Rector thereof;* and Mr. John Burton is by His Highness, Oliver, Lord Protector of England, &c., under his seal manuall, nominated thereunto, the Commissioners for approbation of Publique Preachers having received a Testimony of the holy and good conversation of the said John Burton, and, finding him to be a person qualified as in and by the Ordinance for such approbation is required, Doe by these presents ratifie, confirm, and allow the said John Burton to be and continue in the Hospitall aforesaid as Publique Preacher there."[1]

* According to *Bedfordshire Notes and Queries*, 1893, edited by F. A. Blaydes (p. 153), Theodore Crowley was restored as Master and Rector of St. John's in 1660.

John Burton, John Bunyan's second pastor, who thus came in as the successor of Gifford, was a young man who, under the strain of public life, proved to be of delicate health and his ministry of brief duration. He appears to have been greatly beloved by the people of his charge. In their Church records he is spoken of with much affection, and his repeated prostrations by illness were the subject of devout concern at their meetings for prayer. These records of the Church began to be kept about four months after his appointment, that is, in May, 1656, and with only such breaks as days of persecution necessitated have been continued down to our own times. Since they have not before been published we may give them here so far as they illustrate the Christian life of the seventeenth century and the mode of Church fellowship adopted by Bunyan and the brethren and sisters who consorted with him.

With a reference to the sister who was Gifford's first convert, the minutes of the Acts of the Church commence somewhat abruptly thus:

"At the meeting of the congregation at Bedford the 24th of the second mon:[2] [24th May], 1656, Sister Cooper's desire of joyning with the congregation was considered, and bro: Burton, bro: Spensely,

[1] *Lambeth MSS.*—Augmentations, vol. 996, fol. 469.
[2] Old style: April was the first month of the year.

and bro: Harrington were appointed to go to her, for the further satisfaction of the Church.

"26th of the 4th moneth [26th July], John Wilson's desire of joyning with the congregation was mentioned, and it was agreed that he should give an account of the worke of grace in his soul, next meeting.[1] Some brethren at Woollaston desiring to joyne in ffellowship with us it was agreed that before the next meeting a day should be set apart to seek the Lord concerning it. It was concluded likewise that the members of the Church of Christ in and about Steventon may breake bread with us and we with them as the Lord shall give opportunity.

"28th of the 6th moneth [28th Sept.]. It is agreed that a speedy course be taken either by publick petition or some private way to gather a sume of money for the release of our Sister Deane. It is agreed also that next fourth day of the weeke come fortnight be set apart to seeke God by prayer.

"1st day of the 8th moneth [1st Nov.]. It was agreed that two brethren should be made choyce of every monethly meeting to go abroad to visit our brethren and sisters; and to certify us how they doe body and soule; and to stirre them up to come (especially at our monethly meetings) to us to Bedford; and to let them know if they come not, the Church will expect an account of the reason of their absence. It was desired that bro: Burton would spend one houre in the weeke, in exhorting the prisoners in the County Goale, and he consented to enter upon that worke the next weeke following.

"The latter part of the 9th moneth [Dec.]. It was agreed that the 5th day of the next weeke be kept as a day of prayer to God upon the account of God's hand upon many of the members, and others in the places where we dwell. In respecte of the present distresse of many of our friends, upon whom God's hand of visitation lyes, it is thought fit and agreed that our brethren doe according to their severall abilityes deposite something in the hands of our bro: Spencely: who is desired to spend the same to and for our severall distressed friends use.

"25th of the 10th moneth [25th January]: Upon friend Allen's desire of joyning with us bro: Whitbread and bro: Grew were appointed to commune with him. We do also agree that such persons as desire to joyne in fellowship, if upon the conference of our friends with them, who shall be sent for that purpose, our saide friends be satisfyed of the truth of the worke of grace in their heartes; then they shall desire them to come to the next Church Meeting, and to waite neare the place assigned for the Meeting, that they may be called in: And if notwthstanding that first satisfaction, it be afterwards thought fitt that any persons so appearing be yet delayed; that then some of the brethren go forth and have conference with them, and labour in the Wisdome and Spirit of the Gospell to incourage them to farther

[1] John Wilson was afterwards the first minister of the Nonconformist Church at Hitchin, and one of the editors of the first collected edition of Bunyan's works, published in 1692.

waitinge; and indeavour the prevention of any Temptation that by the denyall of admittance they may be exposed to. It was appointed that the 15th day of the next moneth be set apart to seek God and return praises to him. Information was also given to the Church of the miscarriage of bro: Oliver Dicks of Milton which was very great: ffor he (as he saide) having lost a sheep and a sheep being staide in another field, he was sent to owne it if it were his: and he came and owned it; and tho' by the way (as himself expressed) he judged in his Conscience that it was not his; yet did not carry it back againe, but tooke it away and kept it, and sold the fleece and would have sold the sheep, there being not above 4d. or 8d. difference in bargaining: But the sheep being owned he was brought before a Justice where he restored the sheep and 20d. for the fleece to the party whose owne it was. And all this to the great dishonour of God, the wounding of his owne soule and great scandall to the Church of Christ, of which he is a member. Upon consideration thereof, being sent for by the Congregation; after a full debate had and things aforesaide prooved to him, besides some confession of his owne; his evill also being opened and charged home upon him, he was by generall consent withdrawne from for the present.

"25th day of the 12th moneth [25th March]: Whereas bro: Thomas Allen desireth to walk in fellowship with us and we are satisfyed of the work of grace in his soule, onely do require that he should submit his gift (formerly exercised) to the judgement of the Church; and he not being at present willing thereto was desired to consider of it till the next Meeting.

"1657, 6th day of the 1st moneth [6th April]. Whereas bro: Thomas Allen yet refuseth it is agreed that his receiving be stayed for the present. It was agreed that the 13th day of the next moneth be set apart to seek God about the affaires of the Church; the affaires of the Nation and the worke of God in ye world.

"At the Meeting of the Church the 30th of the 2nd moneth [30th May]. Many of the Friends were absent upon a publick occasion so that nothing was then acted.

"28th of the 3rd moneth [June 28th]: It was agreed that bro: John Crane be admitted a member of this Congregation upon his profession that he joyneth with us, as we are in union with Christ though differing in judgement about some outward things. Bro: Bunyan, bro: Childe and bro: John Fenn were appointed to go to friend Stratton, junr., of Stoughton.

"It is agreed that next 2nd day of the week come seven-night be set apart to praise God for his goodness in delivering us out of our late troubles, and to seeke God for direction in discoursing with any of our dissenting friends."

The last three entries point to some grave cause of anxiety, of more than merely local concern, which was agitating the Bedford Church in the spring and summer of 1657. We find them anxious unto prayer "about the affaires of the nation"; friends among them are absent from a church-gathering "upon a publick occasion"; and, finally, when the strain is over, they set apart a day to praise God for delivering them out of their "late troubles," and to seek for direction in discoursing with their "dissenting friends," who are evidently not in thankful mood with the rest of their brethren.

The occasion was memorable enough both for them and for the nation. About midnight of January 8th a determined attempt had been made, by setting fire to Whitehall Palace, to take away Cromwell's life. Fortunately, it failed. Parliament appointed a day of thanksgiving for the Protector's deliverance, and waited on him in a body to congratulate him upon his escape. But that escape had been narrow, and some began seriously to consider whether the nation would not be more settled if Oliver were to become king, with succession of his heirs male to the crown. A Humble Address and Remonstrance was read in the House of Commons, asking the Protector to concur with Parliament in a total recasting of the existing constitution. The first article after the preamble ran thus: "That your Highness will be pleased to assume the name, style, title, dignity, and office of King of England, Scotland, and Ireland." The rest of the address was in accordance with this first clause. There was to be an end to arbitrary power, and once more government under a limited monarchy. On the 25th of March, by a majority of 123 to 62, or, as nearly as possible, two to one, the kingship clause was carried, in a somewhat amended form, and the title, Address and Remonstrance changed into that of Petition and Advice.

The rumour of this gradually got abroad in the country, creating great division of opinion. There was a strong party in Bedfordshire adverse to the proposed change. William Dell of Yeldon, with John Donne of Pertenhall, and others, drew up a document, a copy of which, dated April 14th, 1657, is among the broadsides in the King's Library,[1] and is entitled "The Humble and Serious Testimony of many hundreds of godly and well-affected people in the county of Bedford and parts adjacent, constant adherers to the cause of God and the Nation." This document states that the object of the late war was to "recover

[1] *British Museum*, 190. g. 12/223

our civill and religious rights and liberties," and that this good cause "is now in danger of being brought into a particular Quarrell between Person and Person, Family and Family touching the administration of Government in these Nations." The subscribers state they have neither heart nor hand in these late "Declinings from the cause of Christ nor in the change of Government from a Commonwealth." They think that the proposed change will "lay the foundation for a new, most bloody and desolating war"; they apprehend "the forme of a Commonwealth as opposed to Monarchy to be more expedient, yea, necessary, seeing the interest of no single person will probably be able long to stand against the interest and Family of the Stuarts, which the Commonwealth wisely managed may better doe. Wherefore we declare that we still remaine faithfull to the first good cause."

The signing of this testimony was evidently regarded in Bedford as involving peril and demanding secrecy. Those who have looked most closely into the evidence think it by no means certain that Cromwell himself knew anything beforehand, or had anything to do with originating the proposal for a kingship; but there can be little doubt that the officials of the Government were actively promoting it. It is tolerably clear that Secretary Thurloe had written down to Robert Fitzhugh, the Mayor of Bedford, ordering the arrest of all who had taken part in the "Humble and Serious Testimony." For on the 24th of April the Mayor and John Barber, one of the magistrates, wrote to Thurloe, asking for the release of their fellow-townsmen, and enclosing all the evidence they could obtain. They express the opinion that the information obtained from Mr. Pare is the most important; they had sent for Robert Grew (John Grew's son), but he was out of the town, and they should, they said, keep their eyes and ears open. "In the meantime we await your commands, and humbly crave that you put a speedy period to the restraint of our neighbours." In the evidence forwarded by the Mayor, Richard Cooper, a member of the Bedford Church, deposed that "he had signed the paper afterwards taken from Nich. Hawkins, but is not free to discover the persons' names who brought it to him, and further saith not." John Fenn, haberdasher, another member of the Church, admitted that "he did set his hand to the paper, but will not acknowledge what it concerned, nor when nor where he did sign it; nor is free to answer any question concerning it." The evidence of John Pare, which the Mayor described as the most material, was as follows:

"This informant saith that the last Lord's day, in the morning, he being walking abroad did meet with Robt. Grew, who asked him what the news was last night at the Free School, being the time and place when Nich. Hawkins and others were first examined in order to the paper stiled 'The Humble and Serious Testimony.' He answered that he might rather ask him. The said Grew replied 'that he thought long to know, for his father being late there, and he being in bed before his return, could hear nothing of it.' Whereupon this informant said again, 'What is this business which is called a plot?' The said Robt. Grew answered and told him several particulars which this informant hath forgot. Then he asked Grew what hands were to it? The said Robert answered, ' . . . that some of the persons that subscribed were his father and himself, Mr. John Eston the elder and younger, Colonel Okey, Thos. Gibbs, Mr. Cater of Kempston, and divers others, gentlemen in Bedford and Bedfordshire and about Olney and St. Neots to the number of 100; and further said to the informant that Mr. Dell and Mr. Donne were the contrivers of the said paper, or at least had a hand in forming of it, and further saith not.'"[1]

There is other evidence to the same purpose, but it is sufficiently clear that in Bedford, as in the army, and, indeed, in the Protector's own council, there were "contrariants" who inclined more to the left, in the direction of a real republic, than to the right, in the direction of monarchy. On the 3rd of April Cromwell, in effect, though not in form, refused the offer of kingship; on the 4th, Parliament by a majority of seventy-eight to sixty-five, again pressed upon him their "Petition and Advice." The matter was kept pending for a whole month, but on the 8th of May Cromwell said positively enough, "I cannot undertake this Government with the title of King: and that is mine Answer to this great and weighty business." A new Protectorial Constitution was thereupon settled, and amidst public rejoicings his Highness was solemnly installed in his second Protectorate. This took place in Westminster Hall on Friday, June 26th, and the following Sunday the Church at Bedford set apart a day of praise to God for His goodness in delivering them out of their late troubles, and to ask for direction in dealing with their "dissenting friends," that is, those members of the Church who would have nothing to do with the "Humble and Serious Testimony" against Oliver's kingship.

[1] Thurloe's *State Papers*, vol. vi., pp. 228—230.

There is only brief reference in the minutes of the following year to the death of Cromwell and the succession of his son Richard; but an address was sent up from the county magistrates in Quarter Sessions and from the Corporation of Bedford, offering submission to his Highness, the new Lord Protector, and presenting congratulations "touching his happie comyng to the Government of the Commonwealth." A copy of the one from the county was sent up to Thurloe, the Secretary of State, by Samuel Bedford of Henloe, accompanied by a letter under date October 12th, 1658, asking to "bee put in the list of mourners at the funeral of his late Highness," and saying that he finds the country generally very well satisfied with the new Government, and "no regrett towards the old family. The Cavaleeres with us very quiett and much dasht att his highnesse's peacable entrance, and does not seem to have the least hopes."[1]

There is no evidence to show what was Bunyan's feeling concerning the "Humble and Serious Testimony" against the Lord Protector's assumption of the kingship of the nation. The Testimony itself has been preserved on a printed broadside, but the original document, with the names appended to it, is not in existence; we cannot say, therefore, whether his name was among them or not. In 1657, when it was presented, he was already earnestly engaged in that exercise of preaching which was to be to life's end his great life-work. On a comparison of dates it appears that about two years after he joined the Church, that is in 1655, he was asked by the brethren to speak a word of exhortation in their gatherings. Like all true souls, he was modest in his self-estimate, and this request of theirs, he says, did much "dash and abash" his spirit. Nevertheless he rose to the call, and though with much weakness and infirmity, "did discover his gift among them." Those fortunate first listeners felt at once that no common seer had risen up among them. "They did solemnly protest, as in the sight of the great God, that they were both affected and comforted, and gave thanks to the Father of Mercies for the grace bestowed on me." Then he began to go out with the brethren, who went into the country to teach, and would sometimes add a word to what had been said by them. These added words were words of power, and more and more the call of God became plain to himself

[1] Thurloe's *State Papers*, vol. vii., p. 438.

and to others. So plain that, on the earnest desire of the Church, and after some solemn prayer to the Lord, with fasting, he was more particularly called forth and appointed to a more ordinary and public preaching of the Word. His very success surprised and humbled him. "Though of myself of all the Saints the the most unworthy, yet I but with great fear and trembling at the sight of my own weakness did set forth upon the work and did according to my gift and the proportion of my Faith preach that blessed Gospel that God had shewed me." The work grew marvellously. When the country understood that he, the tinker, had turned preacher, "they came to hear the word by hundreds, and that from all parts, though upon sundry and divers accounts."

He had been preaching about a year when he became entangled in a controversy with the Quakers, which led to his first appearance as an author. In 1654 William Dewsbury, who has been described as the Quaker Apostle of Bedfordshire, came for the first time into the county, and made that year a notable convert in the person of John Crook, who had been sent up, as we have seen, the previous year to the Little Parliament of 1653. He was a county magistrate, living at Beckring's Park, an estate off the high road between Ampthill and Woburn. Dewsbury came to this old manor-house and preached to a company of Bedfordshire people gathered there, when his words went home with great power to the heart of John Crook and his neighbour at the next farm, James Nagill. Speaking of this visit of Dewsbury's, Crook said in after years, "Had I known he was a Friend I would have avoided hearing him. His words, like spears, pierced and wounded my very heart, yet so as they seemed unto me as balm also; and I came to see what it was that had so long cried in me on every occasion of serious inward retiring of my own spirit." From that time these convinced neighbours cast in their lot with the rising sect, William Dewsbury reporting "that many Friends witnessed in much boldness for the truth, among whom were Justice Crutt [Crook] and James Nagill, who were great in the outward, and whose dwellings were at Beckring's Park, Beds." From that time Crook laboured almost as zealously, and suffered almost as grievously as George Fox. One of his pamphlets is dated from Reading Gaol, another from Ipswich Town Gaol, two from the gaol at Huntingdon, and yet three others from Aylesbury Common Gaol.[1] The year after William Dewsbury's visit George Fox himself came to John Crook's house, where there was a great meeting, and people generally convinced in the Lord's truth. He was told that the next day several of those that were called the gentlemen of the country would come to dine with him, and discourse with him.

From that time Beckring's Park became in the Midlands what Swarthmoor Hall was in the North Country—a place of munificent hospitality and social rendezvous for the Society of Friends. In 1658 the old manor-house, with its great square hall, its wide staircase, and balustraded open galleries, took its place in history as the place of the first of the general or circular yearly meetings of the Quakers still observed. "The meeting lasted for three days, and many Friends from most parts of the nation came to it, so that the inns and towns round about were filled, for many thousands of people were at it. And although there was some disturbance by some rude people, yet the Lord's power came over all, and a glorious meeting it was."[2] The descendants of Raven, who succeeded Nagill in the farm near by, and the long resident family of the Hows, at Aspley Guise, kept up the tradition of the great gathering of 1658, and described occurrences at inns, farms, and private houses in the neighbouring villages where Friends were hospitably entertained.

Two years before this first great yearly meeting at Beckring's Park individual Quakers had found their way into the town of Bedford, and there delivered their testimony on the inward light in terms which, to Bunyan and other members of the Church, seemed to come perilously near to a disparagement of the written word. From casual glimpses in the writings both of Edward Burrough and of Bunyan himself, we find controversies going on in public between the latter and some of the Friends. Danson speaks of a conflict between Bunyan and some Quakers at the market cross in Bedford; Burrough tells us of certain words spoken by Bunyan on the 12th of April at Patnam [Pavenham]; of what John Burton and John Bunyan said in Paul's Steeple-house in Bedford town on the 23rd of May, 1656; and of what John Bunion and one Fenn and John Child laid down on the 23rd of the 8th month [23rd November], 1656. On one of these occasions a zealous Quaker sister took part in

[1] *The Design of Christianity*, Testified in the Books, Epistles, and Manuscripts of that Ancient, Faithful Servant of Christ Jesus, JOHN CROOK. London, 1701.
[2] *Journal of George Fox*, I., 463, Ed. 1836.

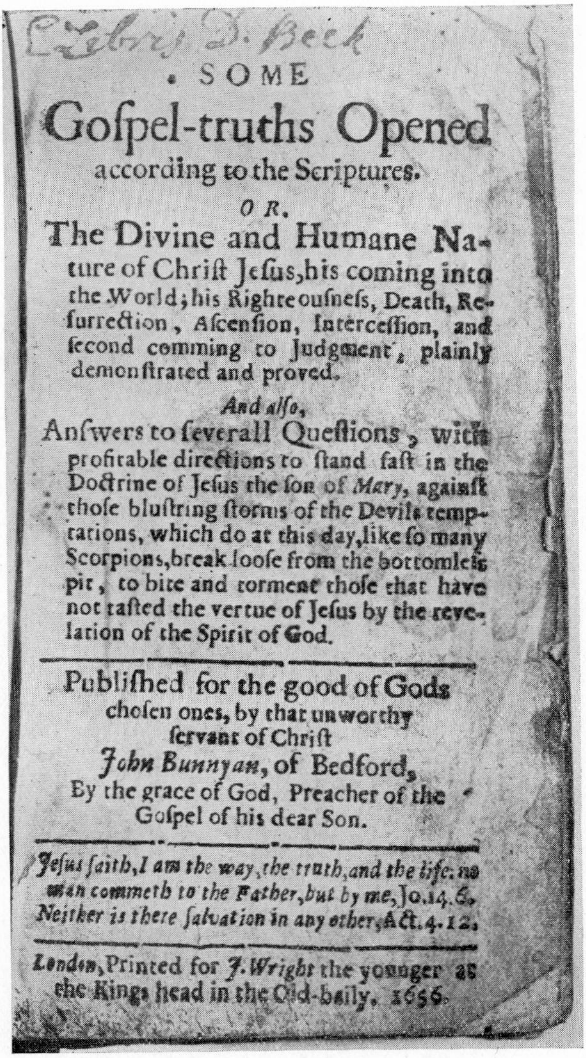

Libris D. Beck

SOME

Goſpel-truths Opened
according to the Scriptures.

OR,

The Divine and Humane Nature of Chriſt Jeſus, his coming into the World; his Righteouſneſs, Death, Reſurrection, Aſcenſion, Interceſſion, and ſecond comming to Judgment, plainly demonſtrated and proved.

And alſo,

Anſwers to ſeverall Queſtions, with profitable directions to ſtand faſt in the Doctrine of Jeſus the ſon of *Mary*, againſt thoſe bluſtring ſtorms of the Devils temptations, which do at this day, like ſo many Scorpions, break looſe from the bottomleſs pit, to bite and torment thoſe that have not taſted the vertue of Jeſus by the revelation of the Spirit of God.

Publiſhed for the good of Gods choſen ones, by that unworthy ſervant of Chriſt
John Bunnyan, of Bedford,
By the grace of God, Preacher of the Goſpel of his dear Son.

Jeſus ſaith, I am the way, the truth, and the life: no man commeth to the Father, but by me, Jo.14.6.
Neither is there ſalvation in any other, Act.4.12.

London, Printed for *J. Wright* the younger at the Kings head in the Old-baily, 1656.

TITLE-PAGE OF JOHN BUNYAN'S FIRST BOOK.
'SOME GOSPEL TRUTHS OPENED'
1656.

the discussions, for Bunyan says to Burrough: "I shall tell you of your sister, Anne Blackley, who did bid me in the audience of many to throw away the Scriptures; to which I answered, No! for then the devil would be too hard for me." Burrough complains farther "that John Bunion said the 30th of the 10th month [30th January] that the Spirit of Christ doth nothing (mark!) within man as to justification—O horrid blindness; not to be parrelelled."

Into this controversy Bunyan entered with so much interest that, as we have hinted already, it led to his first venture in the way of authorship. Evidently thrown off at a heat, and in the midst of the steeple-house disputations of that same year, there appeared a little volume in duodecimo of about two hundred pages, entitled '*Some Gospel Truths Opened,* by that unworthy servant of Christ, John Bunnyan of Bedford, by the Grace of God, preacher of the Gospel of his dear Son.' Possibly there was no bookseller in Bedford then; or he may, for reasons of friendship, have resorted to one whose acquaintance he made in his soldiering days;* for the imprint runs thus: "London, printed for J. W., and are to be sold by Mathias Cowley, Bookseller in Newport Pagnell, 1656."[1] There was an epistle prefatory by John Burton, in which he says of Bunyan: "This man is not chosen out of an earthly but out of the heavenly university, the Church of Christ. . . . He hath through grace taken these three heavenly degrees, to wit, union with Christ, the anointing of the Spirit, and experiences of the temptations of Satan, which do more fit a man for that mighty work of preaching the Gospel than all university learning and degrees that can be had." He adds that he himself has had "experience with many others of this man's soundnesse in the faith, of his godly conversation and his ability to preach the Gospel."

* *Vide* Addendum.

The drift of the book was a protest against what he thought the dangerous mysticism of Quaker teachings. There was really an historic Christ, Son of Mary and Son of God, as well as a spiritual Christ revealed in the soul. He will plant his feet firmly on the facts of revelation, and has too much common sense to allow everything to be explained away into mere trans-

[1] The only known copy of the first edition of this, Bunyan's first book, is in the possession of Mr. William Tarbutt of Cranbrook. [Mr. Tarbutt's copy, with the Newport Pagnell imprint, is now in the John Rylands Library, Manchester. Two other copies exist: one at the British Museum Library, and the other in the possession of the Editor. These bear the London imprint.]

cendentalism. Spiritual he is to his heart's core, but vainly mystical he will not be. This was his controversy with the Quakers. He will have no spiritualising away into thin air of the facts of our Lord's life. Here Jesus lived in a body like our own, and here he literally died. He was no mere shadow, but "the very substance of all things that did in any way type out Christ." He was truly born into the world, truly died, and was buried, and in true and real sense, and not in any merely spiritual signification ascended into heaven. "I was told to my face," says he, "that I preached up an idol because I said that the Son of Mary was in heaven with the same body that was crucified on the Cross." And His second coming will be as literal as His first. "The day shall burn as an oven, and the evil shall be as stubble. Ah, friends, put a red hot oven and stubble together and what work there will be!" He takes his farewell, warning his readers against those who are for a Christ within, a cross within, a resurrection and intercession within, and not for a Christ without, a resurrection of Christ without, an intercession of Christ without. He will have them receive a Son of Man and Son of God in truth, and they will do more work for God in one hour than mere visionaries can do in a lifetime.

This little book of Bunyan's fell into the hands of Edward Burrough, a young man of three-and-twenty, a fervent, earnest soul among the Quakers, who, six years later, sealed his testimony with his life in the gaol of Newgate. There quickly appeared a reply entitled, '*The True Faith of the Gospel of Peace,* contended for in the spirit of meekness . . . against the secret opposition of John Bunyan, a professed minister in Bedfordshire.' One wishes that these two good men could have had a little free and friendly talk face to face. There would probably have been better understanding and fewer hard words, for they were really not so far apart as they thought. Bunyan believed in the inward light, and Burrough surely accepted an objective Christ. But failing to see each other's exact point of view, Burrough thunders at Bunyan, and Bunyan swiftly returns the shot. Within a few weeks there appears from the pen of the latter *A Vindication of Gospel Truths Opened,** in which he tells Friend Burrough that he is very censorious, and utters many words without knowledge. These mystical doctrines of

* The only two copies known to exist of *A Vindication of Gospel Truths Opened* (1657) are in the Library of Trinity College, Cambridge. One bears the London publisher's name, John Wright; and the other that of Mathias Cowley, Newport Pagnell. *Vide* Addendum.

his, he says, are not new; "the very opinions that are held at this day by Quakers are the same that long ago were held by the Ranters, only the Ranters had made them threadbare at an alehouse, and the Quakers have set a new gloss upon them again by an outward legal holiness." "Other lame arguments thou tumblest over like a blind man in a thicket of bushes," which Bunyan passes by, following him up closely as to the difference between the light of conscience and the light of the Spirit, for on this point Burrough has given "but a glavering answer." "Surely if salvation comes by our conscience, or by the convictions or commands thereof, Christ Jesus died for nothing. He that doth think to be born again by following his conscience or any other light that is in an unregenerate man, will be deceived, and shall one day know that there is a difference between conscience and Christ; between the light of nature and the Spirit of God." Burrough had said that, as a preacher, Bunyan had run before he was sent, and did not profit the people. To which Bunyan replies, that he is willing to leave that to the judgment of the people of God in the country where he dwells, who will testify the contrary for him, "setting aside the carnal ministry, with their retinue, who are as mad against me as thyself."†

† To this came a *Reply unto his* (Bunyan's) *second book called* 'A Vindication,' &c., &c. *And this to clear the Truth from above* 100 of John Bunion's *foule dirty lyes and slanders*: *By a friend of the Truth; and not as it is in mens carnall apprehensions.* Edward Burrough. *London*: Printed for *Giles Calvers*, at the Black-spread-Eagle, near the West end of Paules. 1657.

But though Bunyan's first appearance as an author was in the region of controversy, it was not along this line his best work was to be done. He was to win the homage of men's hearts by holding up those central verities on which Christians are mainly agreed, and by unfolding the fairer aspects of that life from God which makes them one. Preaching became the passion, as it had become the work, of his life. He gave himself wholly to it, in the sense that he was a whole man in it. At a later time, as he lay a prisoner in Bedford Gaol, he went back in thought over the five years between 1655 and 1660, when he was at large, and laid bare for us the heart-experiences to which he was no stranger as he pleaded with men. More than most, he compassed the range, ascended the heights, and sounded the depths of the preacher's life. Sometimes, he says, he would start with clearness, evidence, and liberty of speech, and before long become so straitened before the people that it seemed to him as if his "head had been in a bag all the time of the exercise." Sometimes he would be seized with a strange faintness and strengthlessness of body on his way to the place of meeting, and afterwards be "tempted to pride and liftings up of heart" at his hold over the people. With the instinct of a real prophet of God, he wished to see the truth, not through other men's eyes, but through his own. He could not use other men's lines, finding "by experience that what was taught him by the Word and Spirit of Christ could be spoken to, maintained, and stood to by the soundest and best established conscience." No preacher of doubts was he, but of assured verities. He felt, he says, "as if an Angel were at his back"; that which he spoke lay with such power and heavenly evidence upon his soul that he could "not be contented with saying I believe and am sure; methought I was more than sure (if it be lawful so to express myself) that those things which then I asserted were true."

With the true preacher's passionate longing, he strove to get firm grip of the souls of his hearers. "In my preaching I have really been in pain, I have, as it were, travailed to bring forth Children to God." If his work were fruitless it mattered little who praised, or if it were fruitful, who condemned. He often noticed that "when he had a work to do for God in a place, there was a great going of God upon his spirit, leading him to desire to go there." He also observed that such and such souls in particular were strongly set upon his heart, and these very souls afterwards given him as the fruits of his ministry. It was not always his best preparation he found to be most effective. "A word cast in by the by hath done more execution in a Sermon than all that was spoken besides." Sometimes, when he thought he had done no good he did most, and at other times, when he though he should catch men, he has fished for nothing. Occasionally he has been about to take up some smart and searching portion of the Word, when up starts the Tempter and asks him if he really is going to preach a Truth which so plainly condemns himself; but he thanks God, who helped him to put down these horrid suggestions, and to bow himself with all his might to condemn Sin and Transgression wherever found, even upon his own conscience. "Let me die, thought I, with the Philistines, rather than deal corruptly with the blessed Word of God."

When tempted to vanity over his success, "the Lord of his precious mercy hath so carried it towards me that for the most part I have had but small joy to give way to such a thing. For it hath been my every day's portion to be let into the evil of my own heart, and still made to see such a multitude of corruptions and infirmities therein that it hath caused hanging down of the head under all my Gifts and Attainments. I have felt this thorn in the Flesh the very God of mercy to me." He saw that, if he had gifts, but wanted saving grace, he was but as a tinkling cymbal. "This consideration was as a maul on the head of Pride and desire of vain glory. What, thought I, shall I be proud because I am a sounding brass? Is it so much to be a Fiddle?" Love will never die, but gifts will cease and vanish; gifts are not our own, but the Church's, and to be accounted for in stewardship. Gifts, indeed, are desirable, but yet great grace and small gifts are better than great gifts and no grace. At sight of this the snare was broken and he escaped. The enemy not being able to overthrow him by inward temptations set about outward opposition. Bunyan noticed, and could "instance particulars" to show, that "where the Lord was most at work Satan was busiest, hath there begun to roar in the hearts, and by the mouths of his servants; where the world has raged most there souls have been most awakened."

In his teachings he proceeds to tell us that he cared not to meddle with things that were controverted and in dispute amongst the saints, especially things of the lowest nature. His work, he felt, lay in another channel, to contend with great earnestness for the word of faith and remission of sins by the death and sufferings of Jesus; to carry an awakening word; and to that, therefore, did he stick and adhere. He took special notice that the Lord led him to begin where His word begins with the sinner—at the condemnation of the law, because of sin. This part of his work he "fulfilled with great sense," for in those earlier days the terrors lay heavy on his own conscience. He preached what he felt, what he "smartingly did feel." He seemed to go in chains to preach to them in chains, and carried that fire in his own conscience that he persuaded them to beware of.

It was at this time in his life-experience, when as yet love had not cast out fear, that he sent forth his work on the parable of the rich man and Lazarus, entitled *Sighs from Hell.*[1] Taking the parable as descriptive of the literal facts of the unseen world, Bunyan gives play to a vivid but weird imagination. "Consider," says he, "how terrible it will be to have all the ten commandments condemn thee one after another, more terrible than to have ten of the biggest pieces of ordnance in England to be discharged against thy body, thunder, thunder, one after another!" While the drift of the book is serious, there are such strokes of the writer's special humour as these: The careless man lies like the smith's dog at the foot of the anvil, though the fire-sparks flee in his face. Some men despise the Lazaruses of our Lord Jesus Christ because they are not gentlemen, because they cannot with Pontius Pilate speak Hebrew, Greek, and Latin. The rich man remembers how he slighted the Scriptures: "The Scriptures, thought I, what are they? A dead letter, a little ink and paper of three or four shillings price! Alas! what is the Scripture? Give me a ballad, a newsbook, *George on horseback* or *Bevis of Southampton;* give me some book that teaches curious arts, that tells of old fables." Speaking of Christ's condescension he says, "He became poorer than they that go with flail and rake." In Him death has no fear for us. "Death can do thee no harm. It is only a passage out of a prison into a palace, out of a sea of troubles into a haven of rest, out of a crowd of enemies to an innumerable company of true, loving, and faithful friends." There is infinite comfort for us in Christ. "I tell thee, friend, there are some promises that the Lord hath helped me to lay hold of Jesus Christ through and by, that I would not have out of the Bible for as much gold and silver as can lie between York and London piled up to the stars."

There is prefixed to this book a lengthy address to the reader, signed with the initials "J. G.," which are probably those of John Gibbs, the minister of Newport Pagnel,* certainly not of John Gifford, as Mr. Offor takes for granted, for, as we now

* Mr. F. W. Bull, F.S.A., says that the Rev. J. Gibbs granted Bunyan licence to preach at Newport Pagnell.

[1] *A Few Sighs from Hell,* or the Groans of a Damned Soul, &c., by that poor and contemptible servant of Jesus Christ, John Bunyan. London: printed by Ralph Wood for M. Wright, at the King's Head in the Old Bailey, 1658. This book was published a few days before Cromwell's death. The *Commonwealth Mercury* of the week, Sept. 2-9, 1658, came out with a deep black border, and immediately after the announcement of the Protector's death came this advertisement: "There is lately published *A few Sighs from Hell,* or the Groans of a Damned Soul, by John Bunyan." A writer in *Notes and Queries* (Third Series, iii., 325), asks whether the placing of this advertisement after the announcement was a mere accident, or a piece of malicious suggestion on the part of some royalist? This third book of Bunyan's has been translated into Welsh (*Ocheneidiau o Uffern*: Caerfyrddin, 1829), and into Gaelic (*Osnachean bho Ifrinn*: Edinburgh, 1846). [In Welsh as early as 1781.]

know, Gifford had been dead three years when the book appeared. In this address the writer says that Bunyan, because of his fidelity, had been sorely shot at by the archers. He himself tells us the same thing. Slanders were heaped upon him, the grossest immoralities were charged against him; it was rumoured that he was a wizard, a Jesuit, a highwayman, and the like. "What shall I say," asks he, "to those who have bespattered me? Shall I threaten them? Shall I chide them? Shall I flatter them? Shall I entreat them to hold their tongues? No, not I. It belongs to my Christian profession to be vilified, slandered, reproached, and reviled. I rejoice in reproaches for Christ's sake."

Known as a tinker, his orders and his right to preach were always of course being questioned. "When I went first to preach the word abroad, the doctors and priests of the country did open wide against me." Yet if ever man were God-ordained this was he. He had all the signs of apostleship. The inward call from above, a "secret pricking forward to the work" in his own soul, the solemn setting apart of the Church and the response of the souls to whom he spoke; "they would bless God for me, and count me God's instrument that shewed to them the way of salvation." Having this three-fold seal from on high, he was comparatively indifferent to the challenge of the world around him. Once, at least, even in Commonwealth days, the arm of the law was invoked against what was regarded as this irregular ministry of his. In the month of March, 1658, we find the Church at Bedford praying "for counsaile what to doe with respect to the indictment against brother Bunyan at the Assizes for preaching at Eaton." As we hear nothing more of this, probably nothing more came of it. Indeed, he seems about this time to have preached in several of the national church buildings without molestation. There is a tradition that he did so in the old and now disused parish church of Ridgmount. The author of the little sketch of his life published in 1700, also tells us that he, "being to preach in a country village in Cambridgeshire"—probably Melbourn—"and the people being gathered together in the churchyard, a Cambridge scholar, and none of the soberest of them neither, enquired what was the meaning of that concourse of people (it being upon a weekday), and being told that one Bunyan, a tinker, was to preach there, he gave a boy twopence to hold his horse, saying, 'He was resolved to hear the tinker prate,' and so he went into the church to hear him." The writer goes on to say that he had this story from the man himself, who out of that service also became a preacher of the truth—possibly referring to William Bedford, the founder in after days of Congregationalism in Royston. To these years before the Restoration belongs also the story of Bunyan's encounter on the road near Cambridge with the university man, who asked him how he, not having the original Scriptures, dared to preach. To this he gave answer by asking this scholar, in turn, if he himself had the originals, the actual copies written by prophets and apostles. No, but he had what he knew to be true copies of the originals. "And I," said Bunyan, "believe the English Bible to be a true copy also," upon which the university man went his way.

In addition to this small passage of arms with the gownsman, there was yet a more formal encounter between the tinker and the university librarian. One Daniel Angier, of Toft, in Cambridgeshire, occasionally invited Bunyan to come over and preach in his barn.* In the month of May, 1659, Bunyan was holding a service in Angier's barn, when towards the end of the sermon in walked Thomas Smith, of Cambridge, who was at once rector of Gawcat, professor of Arabic, reader in rhetoric, lecturer at Christ's College, and keeper of the university library. Bunyan was preaching from 1 Tim. 4, 16, and in the course of his sermon told his audience that he knew most of them to be unbelievers. At the close of the service, and in the midst of some confusion, Smith went up to Bunyan and asked him what right he had to say that of men half of whose faces he had never seen before. St. Paul called the people to whom he wrote saints and beloved of God, and all the Protestant preachers beyond seas addressed their auditors as *Fideles;* what right had he, then, to call a company of baptized people unbelievers? Clearly he was uncharitable, and being uncharitable, was unfit to preach. To all this Bunyan replied that when Christ preached from a ship to his hearers on the shore, He taught that there were four kinds of ground into which the good seed of the sower fell, and that only one of the four brought forth fruit. "Now," says Bunyan, "your position is that he that in effect condemneth the greater part of his hearers hath no charity,

* The Rev. Frank M. Smith of Catford, a native of the near village, says: "I do not think any verification of the barn is possible. The tradition is that 'C. H. S'[purgeon] preached in the same barn, and that, I believe, is (or a part of it) standing to-day."

and is therefore not fit to preach the gospel. But here the Lord Jesus did so; then your conclusion is the Lord Jesus Christ wanted charity, and was therefore not fit to preach the gospel."[1] Bunyan having thus defended himself, his friend, Daniel Angier, also rose up to defend him and to rebuke his assailant; but Smith denied the layman's right to preach, and asked Bunyan what he had to say to the apostle's question: "How shall they preach except they be sent?" To this, of course, Bunyan replied that the Church at Bedford had sent him, to which, equally of course, Smith rejoined that the Church at Bedford, being only lay people, could not give the tinker that which they had not themselves. So ended the parley in the barn.

The learned professor was not satisfied, however, with this encounter with the unlearned tinker, and in the course of a few weeks he published '*A Letter to Mr. E. of Taft, four miles from Cambridge.*' Since Mr. E. would not hear him in the barn, nor suffer his daughters to stay, he will now write part of what he meant to say then. Hoping he "will not believe him whom his friends generally call the tinker upon his bare word, I shall," he says, "follow that method which the tinker commanded me, shewing first his false doctrine, and then prove 'tis a dangerous sin in him to preach (as he did so publickly), and in the people to hear him." Starting by saying that "if any man among you (though he be a wandering preaching tinker, for you must give me leave to call him so till I know what other name he hath) seemeth to be religious, and bridleth not his tongue, that man's religion is vain." He goes over again the question of a layman's right to preach, and concludes that such preaching is a piece of presumption. "All this your tinker hath been guilty of and much more, for he hath not only intruded into the pulpits in these parts, and caused the people of your town to hate their lawful minister [Mr. John Ellis, sen.], but (as he told me) encouraged them to proceed so far as to cudgel him and break open the church doors by violence." We may reasonably suppose that there is some misunderstanding here, or that this professor of rhetoric was drawing upon a rhetorical imagination. With the usual arguments, often advanced and as often refuted, Smith having tried to prove his case, thus concludes: "And now, sir, let me beseech you for God's sake, for Christ's sake, for the

[1] Charles Doe's account, Folio of 1692.

JOHN BUNYAN PREACHING IN FRONT OF THE MOTE HALL, BEDFORD, OCTOBER 18, 1659.

Printed for S. Cleaver, Bedford.

[Reduced fac-simile of an old unique Etching in the Bunyan Collection, formerly in the possession of Count Moriz von Fries, Vienna.]

Church's sake, for your reputation's sake, for your children's sake, for your country's sake, for your own immortal soul's sake to consider these things sadly and seriously, not to think a tinker more infallible than the pure Spouse of Christ, and to foresee what will be the sad consequences both to the souls, and bodies, and estates of you and your children in following such strangers."[1]

It does not appear that Bunyan made any reply to this letter from Thomas Smith. A reply was, however, made on his behalf by Henry Denne,[2] himself a Cambridge man, and an old friend of the university librarian. Appealing to Smith, he says:—

"You seem to be angry with the tinker because he strives to mend souls as well as kettles and pans. The main drift of your letter is to prove that none may preach except they be sent. Sir, I think him unworthy the name of a tinker that affirms that any one is sufficient to preach the gospel without sending. By your confession the tinker thinks otherwise, and doth not deny what you labour to prove, and so you contend with a shadow. He proves his mission and commission from the Church at Bedford, you should also have proved that Mr. Thomas Smith hath a better commission from some other Church than the tinker either hath or can have from the Church at Bedford. You must give me leave to propound something for your consideration: Some shipwrackt men, swimming to an island, find there many inhabitants, to whom they preach; the heathen hearing are converted, and walk together in love, praising the Lord: whether the preaching of these shipwrackt men were a sin? Secondly, whether it be not lawful for this congregation to chuse to themselves pastors, governours, teachers, &c.? Thirdly, whether this congregation may not find some fitting men full of faith and the Holy Ghost to preach to other unbelieving heathen?"

Besides Henry Denne another university man not only thought that Bunyan had a right to preach, but set him up in the pulpit of his own church to do so. This was William Dell, the rector of Yelden, who was also master of Gonville and Caius. When in 1660 the tide of the Commonwealth had turned and the King come back, some of Dell's Royalist parishioners sent up a petition to the House of Lords against him. It is dated June 20th, 1660, and endorsed as dismissed on July 25th. Among other complaints brought against him it is alleged that he had "declared

[1] *The Quaker Disarmed.* With a Letter in Defence of the Ministry and against Lay-Preachers. London: Printed by J. C., and are sold neer the Little North-Door of *St. Paul's* Church, 1659.

[2] *The Quaker no Papist.* London: Francis Smith, 1659.

in the public congregation that he had rather hear a plain countryman speak in the church that came from the plough than the best orthodox minister that was in the country. Upon Christmas Day last one Bunyan, of Bedford, a tinker, was countenanced and suffered to speak in his pulpit to the congregation, and no orthodox minister did officiate in the church that day."[1] Let us hope that these discontented parishioners of Yelden whose petition was dismissed, recovered in time from the indignity of having had to listen to a tinker in their parish church, especially considering how memorable a tinker he became; and let us thank them for giving us this glimpse of the friendship existing between two men so interesting to us as John Bunyan and William Dell.*

* William Dell was a Bedfordshire man. He served in Fairfax's army (1645-7). At the Restoration he lost his mastership at Gonville and Caius College, Cambridge, also his rectory. He died in 1664 and was by his own wish buried in unconsecrated ground.

It was in the year in which he preached in Yelden church, the last before his imprisonment, that Bunyan made his fourth appearance as an author. The book was entitled *The Doctrine of the Law and Grace unfolded.*[2] The well-known bookseller, Thomason, who made the collection of books and pamphlets now in the King's Library, marked this work as coming out in May, 1659. It was the outcome of Bunyan's experience and of his preaching in the second stage of his life as a teacher, of which he says that, after he had gone forth, for the space of two years, crying out against men's sins, the Lord came in upon his soul with some staid peace and comfort through Christ: "Wherefore now I altered in my preaching (for still I preached what I saw and felt); now, therefore, I did much labour to hold forth Jesus Christ in all His Offices, Relations, and Benefits unto the World." This is really the substance of this work of his on Law and Grace, the last of his books before his prison life. It is marked by firm grasp of faith and a strong, clear view of the reality of Christ's person and work as the one Priest and Mediator for a sinful world. There are in it, as in some other of his writings, telling references to his own experience, showing how he had himself gone through all the struggles of doubt right up to the daylight of faith, in which, as he says, "I saw through grace that it was the blood shed on Mount Calvary

[1] *House of Lords MSS.* June 20th, 1660.

[2] *The Doctrine of the Law and Grace unfolded.* Published by that Poor and Contemptible Creature *John Bunyan* of *Bedford.* London: Printed for M. Wright, at the sign of the King's Head in the old Bailey, 1659. [It was also published by Matthias Cowley, at Newport Pagnell, in 1659. A copy of this edition is in the library of Sir Leicester Harmsworth, Bart. *Vide* Addendum.]

Agoriad i athrawiaeth y ddau Gyfammod. Caerfyrddin, 1767, 12º *Yr ail argraphiad,* &c. Trefecca, 1781, 12º.

that did save and redeem sinners as clearly and as really with the eyes of my soul as ever methought I had seen a penny loaf bought with a penny." Laden with sin he had found that "when tears would not do, prayers would not do, repenting and all other things would not reach my heart, then the blood let out with the spear hath in a very blessed manner delivered me." And while he thus speaks of Christ with boldness, he still speaks of himself with that deep humility which marked him to the end of his life. Almost with pathos he pleads for his readers' prayers. "Christians," says he in the epistle which was prefixed as a foreword, "pray for me to our God, with much earnestness, fervency, and frequently, in all your knockings at our Father's door, because I do very much stand in need thereof, for my work is great, my heart is vile, the devil lieth at watch, the world would fain be saying, Aha, aha, thus would we have it! and of myself, keep myself I cannot, trust myself I dare not; if God do not help me I am sure it will not be long before my heart deceive, and the world have their advantage of me."

It may be well now to close the story of the first five years of Bunyan's life in Bedford by returning to the Records of the Church in 1657, when we left the brethren concerned about Cromwell's Kingship, and continuing them to 1660, when the Restoration brought back a king of quite other sort to the Lord Protector.

"1657. At a meeting of the Church the 27th of ye 6th moneth: [27th Sept.] our bro: John Whiteman was received into full comunion with this congregation. Whereas there hath heretofore bene time spent in seeking God to direct us in the choyce of officers necessary for the Congregation, according to the order of the Gospell; and whereas heretofore there were nominated, and appointed for tryall our bro: Spensely, bro: Bunyan, bro: Coventon, and bro: Robert Wallis; to exercise the office of deacons; and bro: Bunyan being taken off by the preaching of the Gospell: We are agreed: That bro: Bunyan being otherwise imployed, our other three brethren before-named be continued: and upon farther debate and good consideration, have also made free choyce of our bro: John ffenne to be joyned with them: and that at the next meeting God be sought to by the Church upon his behalfe, that he with the other may be directed in their worke.

"It is agreed that next 5th day of the week be set apart to joyne in prayer with the rest of our brethren in ye three nations; according to the motion made by bro: Jesse and others with him.

"13th of the 9th moneth [13th Dec.]. This day fortnight was set apart to seek the Lord in by prayer; and to returne praise to him for his appearances with our brethren in their preaching of the Gospell.

"Latter part of the 10th moneth [Jan.]. It was agreed that the 14th of the next moneth be set apart to seek the Lord for the carrying on of his worke in the nation; and for the bringing forth of many soules that seeme to be brought to the birth; and for our friends that are ill.

"25th of the 12th moneth [25th March]: Upon the relation of the brethren sent to bro: Skelton, the Church still remaining dissatisfyed, did appoint bro: Bunyan and bro: Childe farther to speak with him. And bro: Bunyan and bro: Samuell ffenne were appointed to go againe to Sister Chamberlaine. It is also agreed that the 3rd day of the next moneth be set apart to seeke God in the behalf of our bro: Wheeler who hath bene long ill in body, whereby his ministery hath bene hindered, and also about ye Church affairs, and the affaires of the Nation, and for our bro: Whitbread, who hath been long ill: and also for counsaile what to doe with respect to the indictment against bro: Bunyan at ye Assizes for preaching at Eaton.

"1658. 29th of the 2nd moneth [29th May]: It was agreed that bro: Burton and bro: Harrington do speake with Sister Wit about her withdrawing from the ordinances of Christ in ye church. Bro: Bunyan and bro: Childe having neglected to speake with Sister Chamberlaine and bro: Skelton; were againe reminded of it and required to take care of it against next meeting.

"It was agreed that the 10th of the next moneth be set apart to seeke the Lord in regard of his hand both at home and abroad which is stretched out in visiting many with sickness.

"It was agreed that letters be written to those friends related to us now walking (with our consent) with other congregations for their farther edification.

"30th of the 7th moneth [30th Oct.]: For the continuing of unity, and preventing of differences among the congregations walking with Mr. Donne, Mr. Wheeler, and Mr. Gibbes and ourselves: it was agreed that bro: Burton, bro: Grew, bro: Harrington, bro: Whiteman, and bro: Bunyan should w^th^in few dayes meet together to consider of some things that may conduce to Love and unity amongst us all.

"27th of ye 11th moneth [27th Feb.]: By the brethren now assembled and by the papers containing the Votes of those absent our bro: Grew and bro: Whiteman were chosen elders.

"Whereas our bro: Bunyan hath spoken with bro: Childe to come and render a reason of his withdrawing to some of the brethren and he refuseth to do it unless he may come before the whole congregation; we are agreed he have notice given him to come to the next Church meeting. There having bene some meetings of the friends of the severall adjacent Congregations to conferre of some things for the furthering of unity and love amongst us, and another meeting being appointed for the finishing of some conclusions to that end; we do agree that bro: Bunyan, bro: Grew, bro: Harrington do meet with the brethren of the other Churches about this matter.

"1659. 30th of the 4th moneth [30th July]: We are agreed to meet next 2nd day of the weeke to seek the Lord for our bro: Burton in respect of that weakenes which the Lord hath for some time exercised him with.

"27th of the 7th moneth [27th Oct.]: We are agreed to set apart the 5th of the next moneth to seeke the Lord in prayer for the giving in assistance to our bro: Burton, for the teaching of the Word, as also to blesse God for our late deliverance, &c.

"Latter part of the 8th moneth [Nov.]: The 4th day of the next moneth was appointed to be kept as a day of thanksgiving: but it was ordered that the last day of this moneth should be first spent in solemne seeking God for the nation, &c.

"Latter part of the 9th moneth [Dec.]: Whereas in regard of the weakenes of our bro: Burton and the great burthen of preaching and caring for the Church that lyes upon him, the Lord hath put into our heartes to seeke to him for direction, to leade us to some fitt person to be an assistant to him in this great worke: In order thereunto we are agreed that the Elders and Deacons, upon the next day of prayer, to be the 7th of the 10th moneth [7th Jan.] do consider thereof; that letters be sent (according to the advice of our brethren of the adjacent churches) to Mr. Simson, Mr. Jesse and Mr. Cockin; for their assistance and furtherance in our inquiring out such an able godly man as may be suitable for our help.

"29th of the 10th moneth [29th Jan.]: It was appointed that every monethly meeting some of our brethren: viz. one at a time, to whom the Lord may have given a gift, be called forth and incouraged to speake a word in the Church for our mutuall edification; And that one of the brethren be desired to begin next meeting. And that every 3rd monethly meeting especially all our brethren and sisters be desired to come together without any delay or excuse. We are agreed to set apart the 5th day of the next weeke to seeke the Lord especially upon the account of the distractions of the nation.

"1660. 29th of the 1st moneth [29th April]: We are agreed considering our bro: Burton's weakenes to entreat our bro: Wheeler, Bro: Donne, Bro: Gibbes and bro: Breeden to give their assistance in the work of God in preaching and breaking of bread once every moneth or 3 weekes one after another on the Lord's dayes during the time of his weakenes.

"The 16th day of the next mon: was appointed to be spent in seeking God with reference to the affaires of the nation, and the weakenes of our bro: Burton.

"25th of the 2nd moneth [25th May]: We are agreed that our meetings on the 2nd day of the week begin henceforth at noone and that the time be spent in prayer.

"It was ordered according to our agreement that our bro: Bunyan be prepared to speake a word to us at the next Church meeting and that our bro: Whiteman faile not to speake to him of it.

"At a meeting of the Church the latter part of the 6th moneth [Sept.]: Whereas the Lord hath taken to himself our teacher bro: Burton, we are agreed to set apart the 17th of the next moneth to seek to the Lord for direction in our advising and considering of a Pastor or Teacher suitable for us, and that our friends be very earnest with the rest of our brethren and sisters to give their assistance in this worke according to our duty.

"We desire our bro: Harrington, bro: Coventon, bro: John ffenne to take care to informe themselves of a convenient place for our meeting so soone as they can (we being now deprived of our former place) and reporte it to ye Church."

. . . .

Thus dark and gloomy was the outlook for the Church at Bedford in the autumn days of 1660. Their minister was taken away from them by death, and their church building by the Restoration of King Charles. They must now seek another pastor and another place of meeting. Their hearts were sore and sorrowful. They would have been sorer still, and yet more sorrowful, could these brethren have seen beforehand that long wilderness march through twelve years of persecution which lay between the farewell to St. John's and the then distant day when the Church should once more have a meeting place of its own.

ADDENDA—Chapter VI.

(Page 96.)

Bunyan's Signatures.

The fact that several of those who belonged to the Church at Bedford, and others whom he knew, signed the document, certainly suggests that the 'John Bunyan' on it is the subject of this biography. Mr. Offor's argument that Bunyan had risen socially is of little value to prove the genuineness of the signature; and Dr. Brown's surmise that the writing is that of another John Bunyan, although it should be taken into account, has no more foundation in fact than that of Mr. Offor. At all events, no other 'John Bunyan' figures in connection with John Eston, John Grew, and John Gifford—not to mention William Dell and John Gibbs—with all of whom THE John Bunyan was intimately linked up. This must therefore still remain an open

1653.
On a deed in the Possession of the Society of Antiquaries, London.

1672.
On the application for Licence to Preach.

1673.
On the Title-Page of Vavasour Powell's 'Concordance' in the Library of the Baptist College, Bristol.

1685.
On the Deed of Gift in the possession of the Bunyan Meeting, Bedford.

'BUNYAN' SIGNATURES.

question. Bunyan's known signatures are given here for comparison by those who are interested. It may be mentioned that Charles Doe in his Folio title-page speaks of the 'smallness' of Bunyan's writing; and, as Dr. Brown says, Bunyan had, as the Church Book shows, two styles of handwriting, "one bolder, and one exceedingly minute."

(Footnote, p. 107.)

Mathias Cowley.

The copy of *Some Gospel Truths Unfolded,* referred to by Dr. Brown as the property of Mr. William Tarbutt of Cranbrook, with the Newport Pagnell imprint, is now in the John Rylands Library at Manchester. It may be of interest to refer a little more to the bookseller of the Buckinghamshire town—Mathias Cowley. Dr. Brown suggests that there was no bookseller in Bedford. That may have been so, but his further suggestion is the more probable—that Bunyan and Cowley had been a few years earlier fellow comrades-in-arms. Mr. Frederick W. Bull, F.S.A., of Newport Pagnell, has kindly supplied some particulars of Cowley, whose name has been handed down through his connection with Bunyan. It appears that Mathias Cowley married, on April 24th, 1655, Mary Roberts of Olney. Their wedded life was, however, soon sundered, for the wife and child were buried in April, 1657. In 1659 Cowley's signature, as churchwarden, appears on a paper respecting a collection made in Newport Pagnell; and about this time he, apparently, married again, as in September, 1662, an entry tells that "An infant of Mathyas Cowley's (not baptized) was put into ye grave." Whether Cowley had left the Church with the "put out" Reverend John Gibbs is a matter for speculation; but it would account for his unbaptised child. In the year 1666 the plague caused two hundred and fifty-seven deaths in Newport Pagnell, and Mathias Cowley was amongst the victims of the terrible scourge.

That John Bunyan had kept up the acquaintance is evident, as both his second book, *A Vindication of . . . Some Gospel Truths* (1657), and his third book, *The Doctrine of the Law and Grace Unfolded* (1659) bear the imprint: "London, Printed for Matthias Cowley Bookseller in Newport Pagnell." The name of Cowley still subsists in the town.

VII.

HARLINGTON HOUSE AND THE CHAPEL OF HERNE.

THE removal of Cromwell by death was the removal of the one strong man alone capable of controlling the conflicting forces of the Commonwealth. Richard Cromwell succeeded to the position of Lord Protector, but not to the inheritance of his father's genius, and in eight months had vanished into private life again, glad, in his easygoing way, to be rid of the trouble of ruling a nation he was not strong enough to govern. The Army party having disposed of him, restored the Parliament his father had dismissed in 1653. It was not, however, the representative body it had been when elected in 1640. It had not been before its constituents for twenty years; many of its original members had been set aside by unconstitutional means, and when the House was called, forty-two Members were all that could be mustered; at no period, indeed, of its now renewed session were there ever more than one hundred and twenty-two belonging to it. Nothing could be said for it except that it was in power, and its continued existence naturally caused grave dissatisfaction in the nation.

Still there were some willing to hope good of it. Six weeks after it met, a petition was presented "from divers Freeholders and others well affected to the Commonwealth of England, within the county of Bedford," who desire as they say to stir up the flagging zeal of Parliament that it may set about the removal of Tithes, the reformation of Courts of Law, the securing of Religious Toleration, so that no man may be imprisoned, or his goods distrained without the breach of some known law. The petitioners further pray that the militia may be placed only in the hands of persons faithful to the good old cause, and finally express the opinion that if their petition be not granted the Parliament will find their places as slippery to them as they were to those who went before them.[1] This petition went up

[1] *Broadside*, British Museum, $\frac{669,\ f.\ 21}{51}$

on the 17th June, and on the 27th, Parliament practically declined to accede to its prayer so far as interference with Cromwell's State Church was concerned, voting that tithes shall continue to be paid as they now are, "unless this Parliament shall find out some other and more equal and comfortable maintenance." This Parliament had not much time to find out anything, for having taken the Army in hand it was in turn taken in hand by the Army and dismissed by a *coup d'état,* under Lambert, on the 13th October. Then, under the Wallingford House Government, the Army was supreme, but not for long. The Monday after the Christmas Day falling on that Sunday on which Bunyan was preaching in Yelden church, General Monk set up the Rump Parliament once more, the soldiers and the populace cheering them as, the mace being carried before them, they walked from Whitehall to Westminster.

But all this could not alter the fact that they did not fairly represent the nation, and that they had kept out of the Chamber men whom the nation had elected. Bedfordshire was naturally discontented, for not one of its representatives was there. Sir Samuel Luke had been excluded by the test of 1648 as a Presbyterian; Sir Beauchamp St. John was outside, so were Sir John Burgoyne and Sir Oliver Luke. In the month of February, 1659-60, a public meeting was called from which there went up a "Declaration of the Gentlemen Freeholders and Inhabitants of the county of Bedford," of no mild or measured sort. They say that being "truly sensible of the heavy pressure we lye under, having all our Civill and Religious Rights and Liberties daily invaded they cannot in this common day of calamity be silent, but with the rest of the nation make some enquiry after the way of Peace and Settlement." They ask for "the Assembly of a full and free Parliament without any Oaths or Engagements or qualifications whatsoever, saving what was in the year 1648 before the force put upon Parliament, or the readmitting of the secluded members to the execution of their trusts." In a very resolute spirit these people of Bedfordshire go on to say: "Until one of these be done we do declare we shall not hold ourselves engaged to pay the taxes imposed upon us without our consent so first had in Parliament."[1]

[1] *Broadside,* British Museum, $\frac{669.\ f.\ 23}{55}$

A month later the House was dissolved by its own consent and a new Parliament summoned. When that new Parliament met, on the 25th April, it was clear beyond all doubt that a great change had come over the feeling of the nation. All were weary of the perpetual see-saw which had been going on between the Army and the Parliament ever since Cromwell's death. The very Oliverians were becoming Royalist in their sympathies, and men of diversified opinion were beginning to think that it might be best after all to bring back the king and come to honourable terms if they could. Even in Bedfordshire, where at one time the Royal cause had been hopeless, a great change had come over the public mind. Of the four members who went up to this Convention Parliament two were Royalists. From county and borough alike the Members were one and one. For the county, Samuel Browne, who had been in the Cromwellian Parliament of 1658, had for his colleague Lord Bruce of Ampthill, a strong Royalist, who was afterwards among the peers and commoners who went over to the Hague to solicit the king's return; and Sir Samuel Luke, representing the borough, was accompanied by Sir Humphrey Winch, who, like Lord Bruce, was a Royalist, and who, on the elevation of the latter to the peerage, as the Earl of Ailesbury, in 1661, took his place as Member for the county. Lord Bruce long previous to his election had been carrying on negotiations with the king at the Hague. An inscription in Millbrook Church, over George Lawson, one of the rectors, which was set up by his lordship himself, tells how Lawson had been employed by him, "in several messages in order to the king's restoration."

It is not wonderful, therefore, that the new Parliament soon declared itself in favour of the king's return, and, as all the world knows, the next month the king came back, the pent-up feeling finding vent in a perfect delirium of loyalty. During the royal progress to London, the long highway of twenty-five miles from Rochester to Whitehall, was lined on both sides with acclaiming multitudes, so that it seemed "one continuous street wonderfully inhabited,"[1] while all the country through there were proclamations and reproclamations, peals of bell-ringing, bonfires and shouting mobs, public feasts, and conduits running with wine.

[1] Masson's *Milton*, vi. 9.

The king entered London on the 29th May, and, as early as the month of June, Parliament proceeded to deal with the regicides who had put his father to death. There were eleven of these for whom there was to be no mercy—those who had sat in judgment on the late king, and who had not delivered themselves up within the fourteen days allowed by the king's proclamation. Two of the eleven were Bedfordshire men, Colonel John Okey of Brogborough, and Sir Michael Livesey of Puddington. They had both been present when sentence against the king was declared, and they had both signed his death-warrant afterwards. For them, they themselves knew full well, there could be no hope of clemency or spared life, and they left the country. Of Sir Michael Livesey, nothing farther seems to be known. Colonel Okey fled to Delft, in Holland, where he was living under an assumed name, when, two years later, through the activity of Sir George Downing, the English ambassador, he was arrested along with two other regicide fugitives, Barkstead and Corbet, and in spite of some demur on the part of the Dutch was shipped to London in a frigate. Taken from the Tower on a sledge, all three were hanged, drawn and quartered at Tyburn on Saturday, the 19th April, 1662. Downing got not much credit for his part in this matter, for even round the gallows at Tyburn the people were telling how at one time he "owed his bread" to Okey, having begun life as a chaplain in Okey's dragoon regiment, and so, as old Pepys tells us "all the world takes notice of him for a most ungrateful villain for his pains."

When the question of the regicides had been dealt with in Parliament, and also the subject of Supply and Revenue, there came the more vast and momentous question of the Church. The great body of the members of the Convention Parliament of 1660, though Royalist in sympathy were Presbyterian in ecclesiastical opinion, and they had committed the great blunder of letting the king come back without imposing upon him any conditions whatever. At first the intention was to negotiate with him at the Hague on the basis of the conditions offered to his father in the Treaty of Newport, in 1648, by which the return of prelacy would have been prevented and a Presbyterian Church Establishment made permanent. While he was still in Holland, Charles might probably have consented to this, but once he was in England the tide of popular feeling swept on in full stream, and it was then too late. There was nothing left but the king's own voluntary declaration, at Breda, promising liberty to tender consciences, and giving assurance that no man should be disquieted or called in question for differences of opinion in matters of religion which do not disturb the peace of the kingdom. This, in the lips of a king like Charles II., might mean much or little according to circumstances, and there was one man with the king, who had shared his exile and had great ascendancy over him, who had resolved that it should mean very little indeed, and certainly should not be permitted to stand in the way of the restoration of Episcopacy along with the restoration of the monarchy. This was Hyde, afterwards Lord Clarendon. Whether Charles knew his own mind or not, this man knew his, and never for a moment did he waver or by so much as a hair's breadth swerve from the policy of reviving the Episcopal Church as it existed in England before the Civil War began.

It is true there was much talk in the air about the comprehension of Presbyterians in the National Church, but on the part of the king and Hyde it was never intended to be more than talk; there was even conference as to mutual concession, which from the first meant concession only on the side of the Presbyterians. Meantime, while meaningless talk went forward in one direction, decisive action was going forward in another. The old Episcopal clergy were coming forward by scores, claiming to be reinstated in the livings from which they had been sequestered; and before Parliament separated, on the 13th September, an Act was passed for the confirming and restoring of ministers, and providing that all "formerly ejected or sequestered ministers" still surviving should re-enter upon the possession of their benefices.

During the Parliamentary recess, which extended from September 13th to November 6th, matters moved on apace. In Bedfordshire the county magistrates, in Quarter Sessions at Bedford, issued an order "for the publick reading of the Liturgy of the Church of England," and the following Sunday William Annand, the minister of Leighton Buzzard, preached, and afterwards published two sermons to conciliate the minds of his parishioners in favour of the Book of Common Prayer.[1] These sermons he dedicates "To the Most Noble and Right Honourable Patriots, the Lords, Knights, and Gentlemen, Justices of the Peace for the County of Bedford," the writer hoping they will give protection to this tender plant, not yet ten days old, since their order was the sole and only cause of its production. Five days later, on the 17th October, for the first time for many years, a new Bishop of Lincoln was elected. Thomas Winniffe, who was elected in 1642, had only held the position for a few months, when Episcopacy was overthrown by the Long Parliament, and he retired to Lambourne, in Essex, where

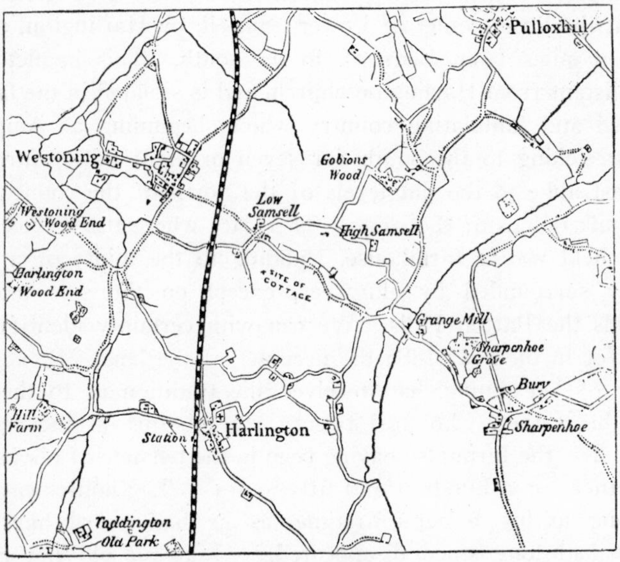

MAP OF THE DISTRICT. Scale—One inch to a mile.

he died in 1658, at the age of seventy-eight. The See of Lincoln had, therefore, been practically vacant for sixteen years, and actually vacant for two years more, when on the 17th October, 1660, Robert Sanderson was elected Bishop, and a week later consecrated. He was then an old man of seventy-three, but when some weeks afterwards he made public entry into the town of Bedford, which had almost forgotten what a bishop was like, it was more after the manner of a victorious general than

[1] *Panem Quotidianum*: or a Short Discourse to prove the Legality, Decency, and Expediency of Set Forms of Prayer. By William Annand, M.A., Minister of Leighton Beaudezort, in Com., Bedford. London, 1661.

that of a bishop of the Church, the trained bands, as he passed, "giving a handsome volley," and then "a second salute with their muskets."[1]

This "handsome volley," followed by this "second salute" of musketry in Bedford streets, came strangely upon the ears of another "bishop," who happened just then to have been recently lodged in Bedford gaol. John Bunyan had the honour of leading the van of those who suffered for conscience' sake in the reign of the second Charles. Within little more than a month of the passing of the Order of the Justices, at Bedford, for the restoration of the Book of Common Prayer, that is, on the 12th November, 1660, he went by agreement to hold a religious service at the little hamlet of Lower Samsell, by Harlington, about thirteen miles from Bedford, to the south. This hamlet is a mile distant from Harlington church, and is situated in the finely-wooded and undulating country which, beginning at Ampthill and stretching to the south for seven or eight miles, forms a contrast alike to the flat levels of the north of the county and the chalk downs of the south. The place where the service was to be held was a farmhouse, standing in the midst of a field thickly surrounded by elm-trees, except on the side looking towards the Barton Hills. We can with certainty identify the spot, for in the year 1885 the occupier of the land, Mr. George Smith of Westoning, had received the tradition as to the site from his father, who died twenty years before at the age of eighty-five, the farm also having been in the tenancy of his family altogether for a hundred and fifty years. The house was still standing in his father's lifetime, as he had heard him say, but it had long since disappeared. Like all old houses in the immediate neighbourhood that were in lonely situations, it was defended by a moat, the drawbridge of which could be lifted at night. The line of the foundations could be traced, and the moat round them, and near by also stood, though pollard and stunted, the elm-tree, which grew on the edge of the moat, and close to the house, when Bunyan was there. In the same field there was an old hawthorn-tree, beneath the shade of which Bunyan is said to have often stood and preached, and which was long known to the people of Samsell at Bunyan's thorn. An old man working on the farm remembered it well; but age and decay told upon it at last, and it slowly

[1] *Mercurius Publicus.*

disappeared. But it was November when Bunyan paid that visit to the place with which we are now concerned, and therefore the service was not this time to be under the hawthorn-tree, but in the house itself. When he reached the place of meeting, several of the friends who were to form his congregation were already gathered, but he felt at once that their usual glad reception was wanting. There were anxious looks and subdued whisperings, for they knew, what as yet he knew not, that the neighbouring magistrate, Mr. Francis Wingate, had issued a warrant against him, and that if he persisted in preaching he was to be arrested. The brother, at whose house the service was to be held, questioned the wisdom of proceeding. "As for my friend," says Bunyan, generously, "I think he was more afraid for me than for himself." But Bunyan had no fear for himself and, when the people suggested the desirability of setting aside the service for that day, he promptly exclaimed, "No, by no means; I will not stir, neither will I have the meeting dismissed for this. Come, be of good cheer, let us not be daunted. Our cause is good, we need not be ashamed of it; to preach God's word is so good a work that we shall be well rewarded even if we suffer for it."

The time previously fixed for the service not being yet come, Bunyan passed out of the house, and paced the field by which the house was surrounded. It is still fringed with elm-trees, which were more numerous then, and beneath the leafless branches he passed to and fro, the burden of grave responsibility strong upon him. His thoughts, he tells us, were these: He had hitherto showed himself hearty and courageous in his preaching, and through God's mercy had been able to encourage others. Were he now, therefore, to turn and run, it would have a very ill look in the country round. What would the new converts think but that he was not as strong in deed as he was in word? Besides, if he ran before a warrant, others would run before mere words and threats. If God in His mercy had chosen him to go upon a forlorn hope in the country, had honoured him to be the first that should be opposed for the gospel and he should fly, this would be a discouragement to the whole body that might follow after. Moreover, the outside world would certainly take occasion from such cowardliness to blaspheme the gospel, and to suspect worse of him and his profession than it deserved.

Back, therefore, to the house he came, with mind more resolute than before. There was still time to flee if to flee he wished, for it was yet a full hour before the constable would arrive; but flee he would not, being resolved to see the utmost of what they could say or do unto him.

Meantime his friends were gathering. Along the path by the elm-trees from Harlington, and across the fields from Higher Samsell and Pulloxhill on one side, and from Westoning and Flitwick on the other they came to the meeting, and Bunyan began. He began with prayer. Prayer was always a real thing to him, and probably never more real than then. Prayer being over and their Bibles opened, Bunyan was proceeding to speak to the people, when the constable, with Mr. Wingate's man, came in upon them, ordering him to stop and go with them. Bunyan turned to go, but as he did so he begged the people not to be discouraged, for it was a mercy to suffer upon so good an account. They might, he said, have been apprehended as thieves or murderers, or the like, but blessed be God it was not so; they were only suffering as Christians for well-doing; and, after all, it was better to be the persecuted than the persecutors. As Bunyan went on thus, the constable grew impatient, and would have him away; and so they left the house.

Mr. Wingate not being at home that day, a friend of Bunyan's, possibly some neighbouring farmer of substance, engaged to bring him to the constable next morning, "otherwise," says he, "constable must have charged a watch with me or have secured me some other ways, my crime was so great."*

* There is a tradition that Bunyan was shut up in a room at the top of Harlington House, which is still known as "Bunyan's cell."

The next day Bunyan and his friend went first to the constable, and then all three to the justice. Their path led through pleasant fields to the height on which stands Harlington church, from which a few minutes' walk brought them to Mr. Wingate's house. It is a quaint old building, with no pretension to size or stateliness, standing at the north-west angle of the four cross-roads. At that time it was entered, not on the south side as now, but through a heavy gateway at the front of the house, looking towards the old vicarage and the church. Portions of the buildings are of great antiquity. There used to be a plate on the oldest part bearing date 1396, at which time it was passed over by marriage from the Belverge family to a Wingate of the neighbouring village of Sharpenhoe. The Wingates of Harling-

HARLINGTON HOUSE.
Room in which John Bunyan appeared before Mr. Wingate, November 13, 1660.

Photo: G. A. Gearey, Bedford.]

ton were included in the list of the gentry of the county at the Visitation of the time of Henry VI., but they were not lords of the manor, and their estate was never more than of the most modest dimension. The old house had once the honour of receiving King Charles II. as guest on a flying visit, and the china bowl with blue dragons round it, out of which the king is said to have breakfasted, is still preserved as a family relic. In the roof of one of the gables there is a curious hiding-place, which may have done good service to fugitive Royalists in the stormy days of civil war.

Francis Wingate, with whom we are now concerned, succeeded to the estate as a minor, and while a mere boy in his teens had married Lettice Pierce, the daughter of the vicar of Hitchin; so that when Bunyan appeared before him, though both men were born in the same year, and neither of them many years over thirty, Wingate had nine children in his house ranging from Mistress Lettice, a young damsel of fifteen, down to the newly-born babe, just christened Charles in honour of the king. There is no portrait of Wingate himself, but there is a fine portrait of his son, Sir Francis, by Sir Peter Lely; and if father and son were at all alike, Francis Wingate's face showed strength of will and a dash of haughtiness rather than intellectual force, and indicated a considerable liking for the good things of this life.

The examination of his memorable prisoner would take place in the hall, wider then than now, or in the great parlour, as it was called—an apartment with panelled walls and low ceiling having oaken cross-beams centred by a carved rose boss. As soon as prisoner and magistrate stood face to face, Wingate asked the constable what the people were doing when he made the arrest, wishing, as Bunyan suggests, to throw out the suspicion that they had come together armed and for unlawful purposes. When, however, the constable quietly replied that there were only a few people met together to hear the preacher, and no sign of anything further, he knew not what to say. The truth was, he had acted in unnecessary haste and shown uncalled-for zeal. It cannot be said he had no alternative but to act as he did. No new law had been enacted and no overt act committed when he issued his warrant. He had to fall back on the old statute of 35 Elizabeth. It is true that the Parliament recently called to Westminster was Royalist in its sympathies, but it is equally true that it was largely Presbyterian. The elections of the following year, no doubt, changed all that; but in November, 1660, it was still unchanged. The king had made from Breda a declaration, promising liberty and consideration for tender consciences, and there was still some hope of religious comprehension in the nation. The order of the justices in Quarter Session made at Bedford the previous month did no more than provide for the restoration to the churches of the Book of Common Prayer; and the Act of Uniformity did not become law till a year and a half later. It may be doubted whether there was another Justice the country through in such eager haste as was Francis Wingate. Perhaps he had an ancient grudge to feed. At the outbreak of the Civil War, his father's death made him a ward of the Crown, and his mother took him to the King's Quarters at Oxford, where they remained with the Royalists from September to February, 1642. For this offence she had to compound with Parliament for such portion of her estate as she had by jointure, and to pay a fine of £100 to the Committee at Goldsmith's Hall. After her subsequent marriage with Richard Duncombe, she had also to take the negative oath and sign the Solemn League and Covenant.[1] Possibly her son did not forget this, and when his turn came he was eager to avenge the past. Indeed, he was more eager than wise. It turned out that he was singularly unfortunate in his very first victim, and in arresting his prisoner he for all time pilloried himself.

When he found from the constable that the gathering at Samsell was only a meeting of peaceable, harmless folk, Wingate turned to Bunyan and asked him what he was doing there, and why he did not mind his own business. To which Bunyan modestly replied that he had merely come to instruct the people, get them to forsake their sins, and close in with Christ; and he thought he could, without confusion, both follow his business and preach the word. Wingate lost his temper at this, and said he would break the neck of these meetings, to which Bunyan simply replied, "It might be so."

Upon this sureties were called, were immediately forthcoming, and the bond was drawn up, Wingate emphatically stating that

[1] *Royalist Composition Papers*, G. 53; No. 146, p. 163.

the prisoner must be kept from preaching till his appearance at the Sessions, otherwise the bond would be forfeited. Hearing this, Bunyan at once released his friends from all farther responsibility, saying that on these conditions the bond was useless: for he should certainly break it, he could not leave off speaking the word of God; in that there could be no harm, and it was a work to be rather commended than blamed. This decisive utterance put an end, of course, to all farther parley, and Wingate retired to draw up the mittimus for Bedford gaol.

While he was absent, in came one whom Bunyan describes as "that old enemy of the truth, Dr. Lindall." Lindall was vicar of Harlington, where he had been the last seventeen years. In 1635 he had been curate to Mrs. Wingate's father, Dr. Stephen Pierce, the vicar of Hitchin, and after Pierce's death had married his widow, so that he was Wingate's father-in-law. The old vicarage was only about two minutes' walk up the road towards the church, and probably having some knowledge of what was going forward at Wingate's house, Lindall came in to give this tinker-preacher a piece of his mind. He commenced taunting the prisoner with many reviling terms. Bunyan, with fitting self-respect, quietly told him in reply that he was not there to speak with him, but with the Justice. Lindall then angrily asked how he could prove that he had any right to preach? Bunyan replied that he had the right which the Apostle Peter gave when he said, "As every man hath received the gift, even so let him minister the same." A little nonplussed at this, Lindall fell into that abuse which is sometimes the refuge of men foiled in argument, and said tauntingly that he remembered reading of one Alexander, a coppersmith, who did much oppose and disturb the Apostles—"Aiming, 'tis like, at me," says Bunyan, "because I was a Tinker." Not to be behindhand, Bunyan replied that he too remembered something from his reading, to the effect that very many priests and pharisees had their hands in the blood of our Lord Jesus Christ. He was in the mood, he tells us, for going a little further still, but just at that moment there came into his mind the passage, "Answer not a fool according to his folly"; and after that he was, as he says, as sparing of his speech as he could be without prejudice to the truth.

By this time the mittimus was made out, and Bunyan started with the constable for Bedford gaol. As they were going down the road from the house, they were met by two friends, who thought that something might still be done for Bunyan's release. At all events, they would have him wait till they had been to Wingate and made the attempt. So he and the constable waited. Presently the two friends returned with the message that if Bunyan would only say certain words to the Justice he might be released. Turning to his friends with that earnest look of his, Bunyan replied that if the words asked for were such as could be spoken with a good conscience he would say them, not else—an utterance surely not unworthy to be placed by the side of that other of Luther's, "Here I stand; I can no other. God help me!"—an utterance, too, the resolute spirit of which has, in all ages, built up the rampart of liberty against the encroachments of tyranny.

The prospect was not hopeful, still all went back together to Wingate's house. "Wherefore as I went," says Bunyan, "I lift up my heart to God for light and strength, to be kept, that I might not do anything that might either dishonour Him or wrong my own soul, or be a grief or discouragement to any that were inclining after the Lord Jesus Christ." By this time the short November day was drawing in, and when they were once more in the house, there came out of another room, and holding up a candle, one William Foster, afterwards Dr. Foster, a lawyer of Bedford. He had married Wingate's sister Amy, some seven years before, but had lost her by death the previous year. Seeing by the light of his uplifted candle who it was, "What, John Bunyan!" cried he, "with such seeming affection as if he would have leaped on my neck and kissed me." But Bunyan held himself back, and did "somewhat wonder that such a man as he, with whom I had so little acquaintance, and besides, that had ever been a close opposer of the ways of God, should carry himself so full of love to me." He had not yielded to force, he would not now to flattery. "A right Judas," says he; and as in after years he saw what this man did, he remembered that it was somewhere written, "Their tongues are smoother than oil, but their words are drawn swords." We shall meet with this man Foster again and again during the next five-and-twenty years of our history. We shall find him as Chancellor of the Diocese of Lincoln and Commissary of the Court of the Bedford Archdeaconry, harassing the Noncomformists from parish to parish and from year to year. There was a sort of sinister significance in his appearance at this point, therefore. Coming in through the open door, with uplifted candle and inquiring look, he might be taken as the incarnate spirit fo that era of persecution which was now at the door. With a tongue smoother than oil, as Bunyan says, he tried to prevail upon him to leave off preaching. There was the usual argument on the one side, to the effect that no man ought to preach Christ's gospel but he who was sent forth by bishop and by Parliament; and the usual and sufficient reply on the other, that a call from God and a fire in the soul could not be kept within the bounds of bishop's licence or of the statutes at large. It was little use to argue further. The time for words had gone by, the time for deeds and suffering had come. "Thus," says Bunyan, "we parted. And verily, as I was going forth of the doors, I had much ado to forbear saying to them that I carried the peace of God along with me. But I held my peace, and, blessed be the Lord, went away to prison with God's comfort in my poor soul."

Before parting finally with Francis Wingate and Harlington House,* it may be well to anticipate a little the story of the years to come, and show how Bunyan may be said to have had, curiously enough, a sort of holy revenge upon the man who sent him to prison. There were, as we have seen, many bright-faced children in the old house on that November day of 1660. One wonders whether they gathered round the prisoner whom their father was sending to Bedford gaol, looked into his face, and remembered him again when they heard in after years of the marvellous book he had written. Of the eldest son, Francis, then a lad of eleven, we happen to know something definite. Eleven years later we find him the chosen friend of Lord Altham, the scapegrace son of the Earl of Anglesey. Through the influence of this Earl, who was of the Privy Council, young Francis was knighted in 1672, and therefore during the lifetime of his father, who died in 1675. Some years later Sir Francis married Lady Anne Annesley, the fourth daughter of Lord Anglesey. Her father was cousin to Dr. Samuel Annesley, the eminent Nonconformist minister, and therefore she was second cousin to Susannah Wesley, the mother of John. Lord Anglesey himself was on terms of friendship with John Milton, calling upon the poet at his house in Artillery Place; and though,

* The manor house remained in the possession of the Wingate family for several centuries. In recent times it was occupied by a connection of the family, but in 1925 the property passed into other hands.

as has been said, of the King's Privy Council, he had strong sympathy with the Nonconformists, had usually one of their ministers residing in his house as chaplain, knew much of their affairs, and interested himself greatly on their behalf. The countess, his wife, also was a member of Dr. Owen's church, and was so much attached to him and his ministry that, at her own request, she was buried in the same vault with him, "that dying as well as living she might testify her regard for him."[1]

On the marriage of the young Sir Francis Wingate with their daughter, Lady Anne, great preparations were made at poor Harlington for the reception of the bride. The hall and state bedchamber were newly fitted up for the occasion, the chamber being hung with tapestry "disfiguring and representing" the judgment of Paris and other classical stories, the bed being of damask, richly adorned with fringe and gilding. But, alas! the roads down into Bedfordshire in those days were atrociously bad, the house which was to be her future home, in spite of its attempts at grandeur, seemed to her poor and small, and Lady Anne, tired and weary with her journey and with some yearnings still for the home she had left behind her, sat down and burst into tears.[2] It was an unpromising beginning to her country life, but she had too much good sense to weep for long over a position which she had accepted for herself. With characteristic vigour she set about those duties of life, which are serious both in lowly and lofty places, and in after years was really the stay of the house, rescuing her husband's estate from the consequences of his spendthrift ways. As might be expected from her early associations, her sympathies were warmly on the side of the Nonconformists, her husband sometimes saying half jocularly, half bitterly, that when he was gone she would certainly turn his great hall into a conventicle. It is more than likely that she did, for he died in 1690 at the early age of forty-two, and we find that several of his children joined the Nonconformists. Three of his daughters, Frances, Anna Letitia, and Rachel Wingate became members of the Church at the Old Meeting in Bedford of which Bunyan had been minister. One of these, Anna Letitia, the fourth daughter, married the Rev. John Jennings, the son of an ejected minister, and himself the pastor

[1] Orme's *Life of John Owen*, p. 287.

[2] *Memories of Seventy Years.* By one of a Literary Family, 1883.

of the Congregational church at Kibworth, and tutor of the Dissenting Academy there.* It was therefore in the house of Sir Francis Wingate's daughter that Philip Doddridge lived in his student days, finding there that atmosphere of a refined and educated home life of which he speaks in his letters. Through this Mrs. Jennings we come also upon a strain of Nonconformist descendants of more than merely local fame. Her daughter married the Rev. John Aikin, and became the mother of that Dr. Aikin and Anna Letitia Barbauld, who gave us *Evenings at Home,* and the grandmother of Lucy Aikin, a lady of some reputation in the literary world, who died in 1864. Frances, another daughter of Sir Francis Wingate, married Thomas Woodward, one of the deacons of the Bedford church; and her two daughters, Frances and Ann, married, the first the Rev. Samuel Sanderson, one of Bunyan's successors at Bedford; and the second, the Rev. James Belsham, becoming thus the mother of Thomas and William Belsham, names well-known in the circles of liberal thought nearly a century ago.

* Doddridge's chair is still to be seen in Kibworth Chapel, Leicestershire,

The names of the Wingates have died out at Harlington, all three sons of Sir Francis passing away childless. In succession they each possessed the old house of their father, but the first dissipated more than his successors could retrieve and, at the death of the last of the brothers, the small remaining estate passed to their nephew, Arthur Jennings, the son of the pastor of Kibworth. Francis Jennings, the brother of Arthur, was an active member and trustee of the Bedford Church, and, as a tablet on the wall of the burial ground testifies, he and four of his children found resting place there. His youngest son David, who died at Ampthill at an advanced age in 1824, was by his own request brought to Bedford to be laid in the old burial place by the side of the rest, their dust mingling with that of Bunyan's own wife, his children, and grandchildren. The Wingates, the Woodwards, and the Jenningses, all sprung from Francis Wingate, lie sleeping at the very foot of the steps leading up to those bronze memorial doors given by the Duke of Bedford in honour of Bunyan himself. Could the veil of the future have that day been for a moment uplifted, Bunyan's soul would surely have been strengthened by the unexpected sight of so many Nonconformists sprung from the man who was trying to crush Nonconformity in him.

Returning now to that November scene of 1660 which sent us forth on these wanderings of ours, we come back once more to Bunyan and the constable whom we left closing the gate of Harlington House behind them. Foster's uplifted candle serves to remind us that it was growing dark as they left and that the night was near. Tarrying, therefore, somewhere in safe custody, they waited for the morning, when they started for Bedford gaol. This was thirteen miles away, the distance being probably travelled on foot either through Pulloxhill to the high road at Silsoe, and so through Wilstead and Elstow, or by way of Westoning and Ampthill. A strange world of experience seemed behind, and a new world was opening before as these two travellers, bemired with the November roads, made their way towards Bedford bridge and over it to the grim prison at the corner of Gaol Lane. The old gate, swung open to receive them, then swung back again to shut them in, and Bunyan left many pleasant things on the other side of it. But not everything; not those divine compensations God gives to faithful souls even here; not those visions of glory which for many a day were to gladden the gloom.

The news that Bunyan was in gaol soon spread through the town, carrying consternation to the hearts of his family and of his brethren in the Church. Could nothing be done? They would at least try to get bail till the sessions. Mr. Crompton, the Justice at Elstow, was waited upon. He knew Bunyan, and was not indisposed to accept the offered sureties, but he was perplexed; there had as yet been no other arrest for preaching, and thinking that there surely must be some more serious charge, and, on the ground that he was only a young man, he declined to act. Bunyan tells us that before going to meet the Justice he first committed the matter absolutely to the Lord and left it in His hands. If he might do more good by being set at liberty he asked that liberty might be granted. But if not, then God's will be done, for he was not altogether without hope his imprisonment might be the awakening of the saints in that country. Having thus in all simplicity committed the matter to God, there came into his heart that inward peace God ever gives to trustful souls. When he found from his gaoler that Mr. Crompton had refused the bail he was not at all daunted, but rather glad, and saw evidently that the Lord had heard him. "Verily, at

CHAPEL OF HERNE, BEDFORD,
where John Bunyan was tried.
January 1660-1.

my return," says he, "I did meet my God sweetly in prison again, comforting of me and satisfying of me that it was His will and mind that I should be there." He wrote these words immediately on returning to the prison chamber, and adds—"Here I lie waiting the good will of God to do with me as He pleaseth, knowing that not one hair of my head can fall to the ground without the will of my Father who is in heaven; that, let the rage and malice of men be what they may, they can do no more and go no farther than God permits them; and even when they have done their worst, we know that all things work together for good for them that love God."

Seven or eight weeks after Bunyan's arrest, the January Quarter Sessions came on at Bedford. There being then no shire hall in the county town the Sessions and Assizes were held in a curious old building known as the Chapel of Herne, and because it stood near to the Grammar School, sometimes called School-house chapel. The origin of the name Chapel of Herne is lost in antiquity. The building itself from its appearance may have served as a house for one of the ancient guilds or as a chantrey chapel, and at the east end there was an Early English window roughly bricked up, with a door inserted beneath. From the corporation minutes we find that this once ecclesiastical structure had to adapt itself to a variety of uses in the interval of Sessions and Assize. In 1647 it was let on lease to John Faldo,* with the understanding on his part that "he shall sweep and cleanse it against the Judges comying to sitt, and leave it open for their sitting, and so upon any other public occasion." Again in 1666 a lease was granted of "the Chapel of Herne, alias School-house Chappell," to Joseph How, he "to beare all taxes and allow the use of the house for the Justices of Assize and other public meetings of the countrie, and to that end upon warning to remove his goods and timber out of the house, and white the wall and repaire the floore of the house."

* A deed, in the possession of the Editor, dated 2 December, 1650, says: 'In consideracion of the sum of . . . Have granted aliened bargained and sold . . . to the said Maior Bayliffes . . . And all that Ancient building commonly called the Chappell Herne late used for one of the Courts of Judicature . . . and two tenements . . . to the said Chapell Herne adjoining and belonging.'

In this primitive Palace of Justice, Bunyan made his appearance for trial about the second week of January, 1660-1. The county magistrates upon the bench that day were Sir John Kelynge of Southill; Sir Henry Chester of Lidlington; Sir George Blundell of Cardington; Sir Wm. Beecher of Howbury; and Thomas Snagg of Millbrook, afterwards high sheriff. Their antecedents considered, they were not a promising bench for a Nonconformist culprit to appear before. Sir John Kelynge was chairman of the Sessions on the occasion. He had been long biding his time, and had therefore small inclination to be merciful. Called to the bar as early as 1632, there is yet from that time to the Restoration no mention made of him in the Reports. Clarendon described him to the king as "a person of eminent learning and eminent suffering, who never wore his gown after the Rebellion, but was always in gaol"; and he himself, on his being made a Judge in 1663, speaks of his "twenty years' silence." He was one of the first batch of new serjeants-at-law called in 1660; in October he acted as one of the counsel for the Crown in the trial of the Regicides; and two years later he also conducted the prosecution of Sir Harry Vane, towards whom his conduct was unfeelingly harsh and insulting. He was returned for Bedford to the Parliament of 1661, and in May prepared the Act of Uniformity which was passed the following year. He vacated his seat in 1663 on being made a Judge of the King's Bench, and two years later became Lord Chief Justice. An eminent authority has said that "he retained the place for the remainder of his life, with little reputation as a lawyer, and frequently incurring censure by his want of temper and discretion."[1] He has been described as fitter to charge Roundheads under Prince Rupert than a jury in Westminster Hall. In violent overbearing way he once fined a jury a hundred marks apiece for acquitting a few poor people who had met for worship with Bibles but without Prayer Books. Yet, as is often the case with blustering people, he could be cowardly enough when he himself was in peril. Arbitrary proceedings on the bench and contemptuous allusions to Magna Carta brought him before the notice of the House of Commons, which at first was disposed to treat him with severity, and it was only by an act of the most obsequious submission that Kelynge escaped the most serious consequences. Yet he soon forgot this stern reminder, for in 1670 he was compelled to humble himself at the bar of the House of Lords for his insolence to Lord Hollis on his trial in the Court of King's Bench. Such was the man who presided at Bunyan's examination in 1661, and the man whom Bunyan probably had in his mind when he drew the character of Lord Hategood in the trial of Faithful at Vanity Fair.

[1] *Judges of England*, by Edward Foss, F.S.A., of the Inner Temple, London, 1870.

Of the other magistrates on the occasion, Sir Henry Chester of Tilsworth and Lidlington, Francis Wingate's uncle, was created Knight of the Bath at the coronation of the King a few months later, and was the justice who with so much angry feeling tried to steel the heart of Sir Matthew Hale against the appeal of Bunyan's wife, in the Swan Chamber; Sir William Beecher of Howbury was knighted the same week that Bunyan was arrested, and Sir George Blundell of Cardington Manor somewhat later. Sir George was one of the delinquents whose estates had been decimated in Bedfordshire, in 1655, and who was therefore under some temptation to use the strong hand when his turn came. As late as 1670 we find him still vigorously persecuting Quakers and other Nonconformists, and on one occasion when property of theirs, which had been distrained, was put up for sale, and no one would buy, Sir George angrily declared that "he would sell a cow for a shilling rather than that the work should not go forward." The remaining magistrate, Thomas Snagg of Millbrook and Marston, was, according to old Thomas Archer, "disinherited by his father in his lyfe tyme," but appears to have recovered his position, and a few years later was sheriff of the county.

Such were the men before whom John Bunyan, of the town of Bedford, labourer, was indicted for "devilishly and perniciously abstaining from coming to church to hear divine service, and for being a common upholder of several unlawful meetings and conventicles to the great disturbance and distraction of the good subjects of this kingdom, contrary to the laws of our sovereign lord the King." Bunyan must have smiled to himself on hearing the little meeting at Samsell described in such ponderous and awful terms; and on being asked by the clerk of the court what he had to say to the charge, he quietly answered that he did go to the church of God, and by grace was a member with the people over whom Christ is the head. Kelynge, impatient at this, asked him straight out, "But do you come to church, you know what I mean, to the parish church, to hear divine service?" Bunyan replied that he did not, whereupon they fell to on the subject of the respective merits of praying with book and without. The discussion became somewhat entertaining, but at length Bunyan's direct utterances seemed to one of the magistrates to be assuming a form so dangerous that he was for stopping him;

but Kelynge said there was nothing to fear, the Prayer Book was in no danger, "having been ever since the Apostles' time," a fact apparently not known to any church historian previous to Kelynge. Be that as it might, and let all be said for the Prayer Book that could be said, Bunyan told them that he for his part could pray very well without it. This was too much for these champions of Episcopacy, and one of them asked him if Beelzebub was not his god, while some of the others told him more than once that he was possessed with the spirit of delusion and of the devil. "All which sayings," says he, "I passed over; the Lord forgive them." He contented himself with simply saying that in their meetings for prayer, "they had had the comfortable presence of God among them, blessed be His name!"

Kelynge called this pedlar's French, told him to leave off canting, and asked him to show his authority for preaching. To Kelynge as to Lindall, Bunyan produced the passage from the Epistle of Peter about every one ministering as he had received the gift. Whereupon Kelynge, having recovered his temper a little, was disposed to be facetious, and while descanting against irregular preaching turned irregular preacher himself. "Let me," says he, "a little open that Scripture to you. 'As every man hath received the gift'; that is, as every man hath received a trade, so let him follow it. If any man have received a gift of tinkering, as thou hast done, let him follow his tinkering; and so other men their trades and the preacher his." Bunyan was proceeding to show that this piece of exegesis from the bench would not hang together with the next verse where the reference was to the oracles of God, when Kelynge, finding that he himself had by this time got out of his depth, would have no more. As Bunyan was going on to say that if it was a sin to meet together to seek the face of God and exhort one another to follow Christ, he should be a sinner still, for so they should continue to do, Kelynge stopped him and asked him point-blank, did he confess to the indictment or did he not? To which the prisoner replied, that he and his friends had had many meetings together for mutual help and exhortations, when they had enjoyed the sweet comforting presence of the Lord among them, blessed be His name; in no otherwise was he guilty. Then said Kelynge, "Hear your judgment, you must be had back to prison and there lie for three months following, and if then you do not submit to go to church and leave off preaching, you must be banished the realm." If, after such banishment he was again found in the country without special licence from the King, he was told he should stretch by the neck for it. The gaoler was then ordered to remove his prisoner, who, as he went down, gave a parting look at his judge, and left these farewell words behind him, "I am at a point with you; for if I were out of prison to-day, I would preach the gospel again to-morrow, by the help of God!"

"So being again delivered up to the gaoler's hands, I was had home to prison again." In this unhomelike home he remained the next three months, during the last week of which he received a visit in a semi-official capacity from Mr. Cobb, the clerk of the peace. Cobb came, as he explained to Bunyan, on behalf of the justices, to admonish him, and to demand his submission to the Church of England. Partly by threats and partly by friendly persuasion, he tried to extort a promise from him that this preaching should come to an end. It would surely have been more regular to have set the prisoner free at the expiration of his sentence, and wait till he had committed some new offence against the law before dealing with him farther. But that was not justice's justice in those days, and as a matter of fact without any farther indictment or sentence, and therefore in defiance of Habeas Corpus, Bunyan was kept a prisoner for the next six years. Cobb came to demand his submission under the threat that if he did not give it at the next sessions it might go worse with him than at the last; he might have to be banished the realm, perhaps worse even than that. Three months' confinement had done nothing to subdue the spirit of this resolute prisoner. He still held to his purpose, and still defended their meetings, the object of which he said was simply to do each other as much good as they could according to their light, and not to disturb the peace of the nation.

Fortunately for Cobb's argument, and unfortunately for all peaceable Nonconformists, some three months before, a foolish riot had broken out in London under Thomas Venner and a few Fifth Monarchy men who had read themselves out of their senses by literal renderings of the Apocalypse. Cobb made use of this riot to discredit all conventicle gatherings. Bunyan would not concede that the cases were parallel. Thieves might sometimes come out of the wood, but all men coming out of the wood were not thieves. For himself he was a law-abiding subject, and held it to be his duty to behave himself under the King's government as became a man and a Christian, and if only opportunity were given him he would willingly manifest his loyalty to his prince both by word and deed. Finding that threats prevailed not and that in argument he was worsted, Cobb fell to persuasion. He would have neighbour Bunyan to consider the matter seriously and submit himself like a sensible man. Could he not come to the authorised gatherings of the Church and be content to hear like other folks? Had he received a gift so far above others that he could not hear other men preach? Bunyan modestly replied that he was as willing to be taught as to teach, and looked upon it as his duty to do both; and as for sitting still awhile, as he was advised, to see how things would go, he remembered that Wycliffe had said that he who left off preaching and hearing the word of God for fear of the excommunication of man was already excommunicated of God, and would in the day of judgment be counted a traitor to Christ. So they went on going the whole round of the argument by which officialism in all ages has tried to bind fast the free life of God; they went the same round as before and with the same result. Cobb, who seems to have been on the whole a fair-minded man, having to discharge an unwelcome and fruitless task, makes one more appeal to neighbour Bunyan, in which he is sustained in friendly manner by the gaoler. He would have him consider the matter seriously between now and Quarter Sessions and submit himself. "You may," says he, "do much good if you continue in the country, but what benefit will it be to your friends, or what good can you do to them if you should be sent away beyond the seas into Spain or Constantinople, or some other remote part of the world? Pray be ruled." Cobb's knowledge of English colonial geography was evidently rather vague for a clerk of the peace, but probably he only selected at random two countries which might have a nameless terror for a Protestant and Christian mind. It was all in vain "Sir," said Bunyan, "the law hath provided two ways of obeying: the one to do that which I in my conscience do believe that I am bound to do actively; and where I cannot obey actively then I am willing to lie down and suffer what they shall do unto me. At this he sate still, and said no more; which when he had done, I did thank him for his civil and meek discoursing with me; and so we parted. O! that we might meet in heaven."

Three weeks later, on the 23rd of April, came the King's coronation, when release of prisoners in honour of the event might be looked for from the royal clemency. Many did on that occasion receive their liberty, but Bunyan was not among them. The names to be recommended depended upon the local authorities, and these bore no goodwill to the resolute tinker-teacher. Barabbas was preferred to the Master, no wonder therefore that felons were preferred to the disciple. If it came to strict law, they had, as we have said, no right to keep Bunyan in prison at all, having preferred no charge openly and given no trial. But he had dared to think for himself, to think differently from the men who happened just then to be uppermost, and while they could forgive other crimes, they could not forgive this. Therefore while many gaol-bound men received enlargement at the King's coronation, Bunyan did not. That day, which ended in a portentous thunderstorm for the nation, ended in disappointment for him.

From April, therefore, till August he tarried on in prison. In the latter month was held what, though falling in August, was called the Midsummer Assize. Bunyan hoped something from this; he hoped he might now get a hearing in open court. Three several times, through his faithful wife, he presented a petition to the judge of assize, praying for this. The first time she presented it to Sir Matthew Hale,* who happened that year to come to Bedford, on circuit. He received both her and her petition kindly, telling her he would do what good he could, but feared he could do none. The next day, as the judge's carriage was passing through St. Paul's Square from the Swan to the chapel of Herne, the resolute woman threw a petition in at the window to Twisden, who was the other judge of assize. He caught it up snappishly, and told her angrily that it was of no use, that her husband could not be released till he would promise not to preach. Undaunted even by this, the brave woman resolved once more to try Sir Matthew Hale. There was something about him that gave her hope; he was a Christian man, he was generous-hearted, he would, she was sure, help her if he could. In some

* For a fair estimate of Hale, as both man and judge, see *Life and Death of Sir Matthew Hale, Kt.* Written by Gilbert Burnett, D.D., London, 1682.

pause of the business of the court, therefore, Elizabeth Bunyan made her way through the throng of lawyers, counsel, and witnesses to the judge on the bench. Again he received her kindly; but Sir Henry Chester, happening to be near Sir Matthew at the time, dashed her hopes by telling the judge that her husband had been duly convicted, and that he was a hot-spirited fellow, with more to the same purpose. At this, Sir Matthew took no further interest in his great contemporary, and with sorrow in her heart, and probably tears in her eyes, Elizabeth Bunyan fell back again into the crowd. Edmund Wylde of the Grove, Houghton Conquest, was high sheriff that year—let us remember his name with honour, for he was the only man who spoke a word of cheer to the weary-hearted woman in this her day of trial. He had probably seen her in conference with the judge, and noted her disappointed look as she left Sir Matthew and passed by him on her way to the street outside. He spoke kindly to her, and cheered her on to one more effort on behalf of her husband. There would be yet an opportunity in the Swan chamber when the assizes were over, and before the judges left the town.

Taking the high sheriff's advice, Bunyan's wife made her way to "the Swan chamber, where the two judges and many justices and gentry of the county were in company together." The scene which followed has become classic in the fair annals of Puritan womanhood. Making her way into the presence of all these great people, Elizabeth Bunyan, "with abashed face and trembling heart," turned to Sir Matthew Hale, saying, "My lord, I make bold to come once again to your lordship." She then pleaded for her husband as only a woman can; pleaded that he had not been lawfully convicted, and that he had never answered to the indictment. At this, Judge Twisden spoke angrily to her, and Chester was especially severe upon her, saying, petulantly, over and again, "It is recorded, woman, it is recorded." Turning from this hard-hearted country justice to the more hopeful pitifulness of Sir Matthew Hale, she told him how she had been to London—a serious journey for a peasant woman in those days—to see if she could obtain her husband's liberty; how she had there delivered a petition to Lord Barkwood, which he had showed to some other peers in the House of Lords, who said they could not release him, but had committed his releasement to the judges at the next assize; to the judges, therefore, she had come with the warrant of the peers to make her appeal. Sir Matthew seemed as if he did not hear her; but Chester, true to himself, kept on saying, "He is convicted" and "It is recorded," and assured the judges that this husband of hers was a pestilent fellow, the like of whom there was not in the country. At this point Twisden interposed, by asking her if Bunyan would leave off preaching. If he would, she might send for him. "My lord," said she, "he dares not leave off preaching as long as he can speak." What, then, was the use of talking about him? asked Twisden, to which she made reply that her husband simply desired to live peaceably and to follow his calling, and so maintain his family. "There is need for this, my lord," adds she, "for I have four small children that cannot help themselves, of which one is blind, and we have nothing to live upon but the charity of good people." "Hast thou four children?" asked Sir Matthew Hale, pitifully. "Thou art but a young woman to have four children." "My lord," replied she, "I am but mother-in-law to them, having not been married to him yet full two years. Indeed, I was with child when my husband was first apprehended; but being young and unaccustomed to such things, I being smayed at the news, fell into labour, and so continued for eight days, and then was delivered; but my child died." Sir Matthew, feeling the pathos of this touching story, exclaimed, "Alas, poor woman!" But Twisden, a man of quite another mould, rudely repelled her, and told her plainly that she made poverty her cloak, and that, as he understood, her husband had found it a much better thing to run up and down preaching than to follow his calling. "What is his calling?" asked Sir Matthew, to which a chorus of voices replied, "A tinker, my lord!" "Yes," said the dauntless woman, "and because he is a tinker and a poor man, therefore he is despised and cannot have justice." Sir Matthew, apparently still sympathizing, advised her either to apply herself to the King or sue out her husband's pardon, or obtain a writ of error. There was not much help for the anxious woman in all this jargon of the law; but there was more sympathy in it than the unrelenting Chester cared to hear. He grew more angry, and said, "My lord, he will preach and do what he lists"; but, replied she, "he preacheth nothing but the word of God!" Twisden, too, irritated both at the persistent woman and his more lenient colleague, went into a great rage. Elizabeth told her husband afterwards that she thought he would have struck her. "*He* preach the word of God!" cried he; "he runneth up and down and doeth harm." "No, my lord," said she, "it is not so; God hath owned him, and done much good by him." "God!" exclaimed the angry man; "his doctrine is the doctrine of the devil!" "My lord," said she, "when the righteous Judge shall appear, it will be known that his doctrine is not the doctrine of the devil!" Elizabeth Bunyan was simply an English peasant woman: could she have spoken with more dignity had she been a crowned queen?

But the days had then come in England when, for a generation, truth had fallen in the street and equity could not enter. Nothing came of her pitiful plea, and while she went back to her lonely cottage her husband tarried in his cheerless den. All through that winter Bunyan remained in Bedford gaol, and when, in 1662, the Spring Assizes came round again, he made the most strenuous efforts to get his case brought on in court. But the justices and the clerk of the peace did so work it about that, though his name was at first inserted into the calendar among the felons, it was again withdrawn. "Thus was I hindered and prevented at that time also from appearing before the judge, and left in prison. Farewell."

VIII.

TWELVE YEARS IN BEDFORD GAOL.

TILL recent years there was a rooted tradition and belief that the picturesque old gaol which had stood so long on Bedford bridge, and was taken down in 1765, was the place in which Bunyan spent the many years of his prison life. This was accepted without question till Mr. Blower of Bedford, in a letter to a local paper, first called attention to the difficulties in the way of an entire reception of the current belief. Subsequently, in the year 1868, Mr. Wyatt of the same town read a paper before the Archæological Society, sustaining the position taken by Mr. Blower. He pointed out, for example, that Bunyan's offence was committed, not in the borough, but within the county jurisdiction, and that the warrant by virtue of which he was apprehended was issued by a county magistrate, whereas the prison on the bridge was the town gaol and under the sole jurisdiction of the municipal authorities. A reference to the Corporation Records also showed that in the year 167¾, when Bunyan was a prisoner, the bridge dungeon was swept away by a great flood in the river. The entry is as follows: "Whereas, through a sodain inundãcon of ye waters of Ouse the ston house called ye Bridge house in this towne is p'talie fallen down and ye rest much shaken and like to fall, and ye foundãcon or pile whereon it stood, a great part washed away, &c." In this dismantled condition the Bridge Prison remained from 1671 till 1675, so that the last few months of Bunyan's imprisonment must have been spent elsewhere, even if the former part had not. But it is tolerably certain that the whole of the twelve years' imprisonment was spent in the County Gaol. Mr. Wyatt's position is supported by two or three considerations to which he himself does not refer. Not only was Bunyan arrested under the warrant of a county magistrate for a county offence, but, as we might expect, he was tried also at the Quarter Sessions for the county, and before county magistrates only; and when at length his imprisonment was over and the time of his release had come, the king's pardon, under the great seal, described him still as "a prisoner in the common gaol for our *county* of Bedford."

And then, again, even if the prison on the bridge were at the disposal of the county authorities, which it was not, it was only a small apartment capable of holding some six or eight prisoners at most; and we happen to know that Bunyan had very many more companions in gaol. His friend, who wrote the anonymous sketch of his life published in 1700, tells us that on the occasion of a visit he paid him in prison, "there was above three-score dissenters besides himself there, taken but a little before at a religious meeting at Kaistoe, in the county of Bedford; besides two eminent dissenting ministers, to wit, Mr. Wheeler and Mr. Dun (both very well known in Bedfordshire, though long since with God), by which means the prison was very much crouded." It is a simple impossibility that these sixty people could have been locked up in the prison on the bridge, which would have been crowded to suffocation by a fifth part of the sixty.

Yet while thus putting the case on that side even more strongly than Mr. Wyatt did, I do not feel called upon at the same time to give up with him the long-standing tradition that Bunyan was imprisoned in the dungeon overlooking Bedford river, and that it was there he dreamed his wonderful dream. This tradition goes back at least to the time when Bunyan's own grandchildren were living in the town, and is therefore not lightly to be set aside. I think it will be shown hereafter that there is no need to set it aside. It is part of the truth, though not the whole truth; and all the requirements of the case are met by the explanation that Bunyan was again in gaol after an interval of liberty, and that it is to this, the last of his imprisonments, that the old tradition refers. In this chapter we can only concern ourselves with his first imprisonment; but when, in a subsequent part of the narrative, we have the whole of the evidence before us, I think we shall be led to the conclusion that Bunyan was in both prisons at Bedford, that his long imprisonment of nearly twelve years was in the County Gaol for county offences, and that his shorter term of six months was passed in the prison on the bridge, for the offence of preaching within the boundaries of the borough. The tradition of the latter imprisonment probably survived that of the former, because it came three years later, and after he had risen into greater prominence as the minister of the Bedford Church.

The County Gaol, in which Bunyan spent twelve years of his life, from 1660 to 1672, was taken down in 1801. It stood on the site of what is now a cinema at the corner of High Street and Silver Street. This street was so named because it was the quarter where the Jews in early times trafficked in the precious metals. It was afterwards known as Gaol Lane, but, since the disappearance of the prison, has become Silver Street again. The only trace of the gaol itself subsequently left on the spot was a rough stone wall on the north side, which was the wall of the small courtyard used by the prisoners, but it is no longer visible. From the interior of the prison, a massive door made of three transverse layers of oak, fastened through with iron bolts, and having bars across an open centre, is preserved in the vestibule of Bunyan Meeting, Bedford, as a relic of Bunyan's imprisonment; but no sketch of the building itself of any kind has come down to us. There were iron-grated windows on the Gaol Lane, or Silver Street side, and the older people of the last generation used to tell how the prisoners hung purses out of these windows on Sunday mornings, asking the pitiful help of such passers-by as were on their way to church or chapel. John Howard, in his quiet matter-of-fact manner, describes the gaol as consisting mainly of a ground floor and first floor. The ground floor was appropriated to felons, and had two day rooms, besides sleeping rooms. There were also two dungeons underground, one in total darkness, and reached by a descent of eleven steps. The first floor, which was for debtors, consisted of four sleeping rooms and one common day room, which was also used for a chapel, all the rooms being eight-and-a-half feet high. There was also a small courtyard which was common to all the prisoners.[1]

Such, so far as we can reproduce it now, was the place which was to be John Bunyan's home during the next twelve years of his life. He took in with him two familiar friends. "There also," says his visitor, "I surveyed his library, the least and

[1] *State of the Prisons in England and Wales.* By John Howard. Third Edition, 1785, p. 283.

yet the best that ever I saw, consisting only of two books—a "Bible" and the "Book of Martyrs." A copy of Foxe's *Book of Martyrs,* the black letter edition of 1641, in three volumes folio, with the name, JOHN BUNYAN, written in large capitals at the foot of each of the three title-pages, was once in the library of the Literary and Scientific Institute at Bedford.* The third volume has both the name and the date, thus—John Bunyan, 1662. Southey saw the book in 1829, and describes it as having been purchased in the year 1780 by Mr. Wontner, of the Minories, from whom it descended to his daughter, Mrs. Parnell. In two of the three volumes there are scribblings of rhyme on the margin of various pages. These verses are the merest doggerel, and one of them may serve as a specimen of the rest. Under the story of John Huss in the first volume, there is the following:

* These interesting volumes were disposed of by the Literary Institute in 1911 for £2,000, to the late Mr. Pierpoint Morgan, of New York. For a full account of this "xxth Century Episode," see *Old Bedford,* by the Rev. C. F. Farrar, M.A. (Bedford: F. R. Hockliffe, 1926).

"Heare is John hus that you may see,
Uesed in deed with all crulity;
But now leet us follow and look one him,
Whear he is full field in deed to the brim."

One is somewhat staggered on reading this to find so consummate a judge as Southey, saying that it is "undoubtedly Bunyan's own composition." There are three reasons which seem to me conclusive against this opinion: (1) Nowhere in any document indisputably Bunyan's is there any approach to doggerel so miserably bad as this; (2) the handwriting is very different from that which we know to be his; (3) and, most conclusive of all, the handwriting is the same as that of another signature. This is on the verso of the frontispiece portrait in the first volume, and runs thus: "Simon Hancock his Book May 9 Day 1715." This seems to settle the point as to the authenticity of the lines without touching the question of the genuineness of the Bunyan signatures on the title-page, the ink of which is undoubtedly old; but, being in large printed capitals, not decisive.

The hardships of Bunyan's prison life during these twelve years have been variously described, being now exaggerated and now minimised, according to the writer's point of view. William Parry, then of Little Baddow, and afterwards of Wymondly College, wrote, in 1790, a pamphlet on *Religious Tests,* showing, from Bunyan's case, as he might fairly do, that as a rule disabilities thus created act most prejudicially against the worthiest men. But in describing Bunyan's sufferings he gave somewhat too free rein to his imagination. He pictured the damp and dreary cell, the narrow chink through which came scanty rays of light making visible the abode of woe, the prisoner, pale and emaciated, seated on the humid earth, the blind child in pensive sadness near. Summers' suns come round, but bring to him no reviving rays; seasons return, but not for him is the cheering light of day or smiling bloom of spring or sound of human joy. The writer asks, Who is this unfortunate captive? What is his guilt? What his crimes? Is he a traitor, or a parricide, or some vile incendiary? No, he is a Christian sufferer. It is honest John Bunyan who has been twelve years here for teaching plain country people the knowledge of the Scripture and the practice of virtue. Such was Parry's way of putting the case, perhaps a little sensationally; but it was merely adopted as illustrative to an argument, not as descriptive of the facts, and when some deduction is made on this account from the style, the argument is sound, the appeal is fair, and it is a righteous protest against unrighteous tyranny.

But upon this passage, writer after writer on the other side has made fierce onslaught, and by way of resisting exaggeration in one direction has gone to another extreme and extenuated everything. Mr. Froude is perhaps the most recent, as he is the most notable instance in point. He almost seems, in his Life of Bunyan,[1] to have accepted a brief on behalf of Bunyan's persecutors. To him they appear, on the whole, to be patient, estimable persons who, unfortunately for themselves, had to deal with an impracticable and wrong-headed man. There was, he thinks, every desire on their part to avoid extremities; and if Bunyan had only reflected, he would have seen in Venner's insurrection a real reason for the temporary enforcement of the Act against conventicles. As that insurrection, however, did not take place till Bunyan had been in prison six weeks it is not easy to see how it could account for his own arrest, and as this enforcement, which is described as temporary, lasted in Bunyan's case for twelve years, no amount of reflection could have enabled him to see the real reason of it, so clearly as Mr. Froude seems to have done. Bunyan, he says, was not asked to give up preaching, only public preaching, that is to say—though speaking to a few people in a cottage at Samsell was

[1] *English Men of Letters.* Bunyan. By J. A. Froude. 1880.

plainly illegal—these excellent magistrates would not have made it penal for him to speak to a neighbour whom he might chance to meet in the High Street. England was really free England still, and Bedfordshire justices went to the utmost limits of indulgence, only, unfortunately, Bunyan did not understand the law or appreciate their forbearance. They were really aiming at his good if he had only known it. They kept him in prison to save him from transportation across the seas, and the most real kindness they could show him was to leave him where he was.

Then, as to his imprisonment. Much eloquent declamation, Mr. Froude thinks, has been wasted upon it. That imprisonment might have ended at any time if only Bunyan, surrendering an Englishman's valued right of free speech, would have confined his addresses to private circles, how private and why private, Mr. Froude does not say. It did end after six years, and though he was arrested again, at the end of six years more he was again let go. It is certainly true that a third time he was again taken prisoner, but this third time he was detained only a few months, and that only as a matter of form. After this release the policy of the Government was changed, and he was then free for the rest of his life. What could be simpler or more satisfactory? We feel ourselves almost convinced by this kind of reasoning, were it not that as we listen the suspicion creeps upon us that it might be possible in this way to defend the most iniquitous law ever enacted, and to palliate the most grievous tyranny under which human life was ever degraded. Resistance to wrong is the very life-breath of freedom. If men tamely submitted to despotism, despotism would be a perpetual inheritance. Some brave soul must bleed if ever unrighteous laws are to die, some heroic spirit must gather the sheaf of spears into his own breast if ever the Fatherland is to be free. Surely Mr. Froude is writing in a nobler strain and worthier of his better self when he afterwards applauds the constancy of the prisoner in Bedford gaol, and says: "Be true to yourself whatever comes, even if damnation comes. Better Hell with an honest heart than Heaven with cowardice and insincerity!"

The gaol at Bedford was probably not one of the worst in those times. It certainly was not so hideous as some of those

—the one at Launceston, for example—in which George Fox sometimes found himself. But very few prisons in England in the seventeenth century were even decent, and there is no reason to suppose that the one at Bedford was an exception to the general rule. Even in John Howard's time the day rooms were without fire-places, and the prisoners slept on straw, £5 a year being allowed to the gaoler for the purpose. In his day, too, gaol fever broke out, carrying off several of the prisoners, William Daniel, the surgeon, and many of the townspeople outside.[1] A century earlier the state of things was probably still worse. There is contemporary evidence that it was not better. John Bubb, who was in Bedford gaol in 1666, and therefore at the same time as Bunyan, sent up a pitiful petition to the king, stating that he had been in this prison for a twelvemonth, in which time he says, "He hath suffered as much misery as soe dismall a place could be capable to inflict, and soe is likely to perish without His Majestie's further compassion and mercy towards him." Bubb sent also a petition to Sir William Morton, one of the judges of assize at Bedford, praying to be released from prison, "where he hath long remained in a calamitous condicon."[2]

But it may be said that though money cannot in these days purchase mitigations and comforts for prisoners, it could in those, and Mr. Froude is of opinion that the Church at Bedford would see to it that Bunyan had them. "To have abandoned to want their most distinguished pastor would have been intensely discreditable" to them, and, for his part, he will not "charge so reputable a community with a neglect so scandalous." This view of the case, however, appears less forcible when we remember that, as indeed Mr. Froude himself a few pages further on tells us, Bunyan was really not chosen pastor at Bedford till after his release. He was therefore not their minister at all till 1672, when his imprisonment was over, and he certainly could not be said to be distinguished till six years later still when, in 1678, his "Pilgrim" saw the light. The little community

[1] *State of Prisons*, 1785, p. 283.

[2] *State Papers, Dom.*, Chas. II., 1666. This man was ultimately released. He had been charged with killing George Edwards, in a drunken brawl at Leighton Buzzard, but the doctor at Eversholt, and Dorothy Sparks, a *gentlewoman surgeon* of good repute at Woburn, attested that Edwards lived a month after the wound given him by Bubb. A good deal of interest was taken in Bubb's case, and by request of Francis Wingate, of Harlington, a collection was made for him in Toddington Church, amounting to 11s. 7d. One wonders whether Mr. Wingate took any farther interest in Bubb's fellow-prisoner, Bunyan?

of which he was then simply a private member, would doubtless do all they could for a brother so greatly beloved, but they could not do all they would. For many of them were themselves at various times his fellow-prisoners in Bedford gaol; others had to flee from their homes, to avoid arrest; and many were stripped of their possessions, to pay the ruinous fines imposed upon them as Noncomformists.

That Bunyan had an amount of liberty which in the case of a prisoner nowadays would be simply impossible, is beyond all question. But considerable mistakes have been made in this matter by writers who have applied to the whole of his imprisonment a statement which Bunyan carefully confines to the six months between the Autumn Assizes of 1661 and the Spring Assizes of 1662, when he was doing his utmost to get his name inserted in the calendar of prisoners for trial. This, for obvious reasons, was an exceptional period, and he carefully notes that it was "between these two assizes I had by my Jailor, some liberty granted me, more than at the first, and how I followed my wonted course of preaching, taking all occasions that was put into my hand to visit the people of God, also having somewhat more liberty I did go to see Christians at London." But while he tells us this he tells us also that this unusual liberty soon came to an end, for "my enemies hearing of it were so angry that they had almost cast my Jailor out of his place, threatening to indite him, and to do what they could against him. . . . Whereupon my liberty was more straightened than it was before; so that I must not look out of the door."

This necessity for greater accuracy applies also to the statement often made, that during his imprisonment Bunyan was present at the meetings of the Church of which he was a member. This is true as applied to some portions of the time, but it is also true that from the 28th October, 1661, to the 9th October, 1668, or for the long period of seven years out of the twelve, his name does not once occur in the records of the Church. After that, for the next four years it occurs occasionally. The probability is that his experience of hardship varied as the gaol administration varied. A contemporary writer tells us that he was "sometimes under cruel and oppressive gaolers in an uncomfortable and close prison," and another says that on the commencement of his second term of imprisonment in 1666, "Even the jailor took such pity of his rigorous sufferings that he did as the Egyptian jailor did to Joseph, put all care and trust into his hands." The matter is very simple. Cynical pooh-poohing of painful facts on the one side is just as foolish and as needless as eloquent declamation on the other. Bunyan himself never whines over his sufferings; he was too manly for that. He deliberately made his choice, and as deliberately he accepted the consequences of his choice. He gave utterance to no bitter or foolish repinings on his own behalf; nor would he have wished anyone else to do this for him. At the same time we cannot forget that twelve years' imprisonment more or less rigorous was inflicted on a man of two-and-thirty with the fulness of life and love of action which that age brings; that with strong affection for wife and children, especially for his poor blind child, he was prevented from earning for them that which they needed; that from the very beginning he felt, as he says, like a man who at the bidding of conscience was pulling down his house upon the heads of those he loved best; and when we remember also that as a personal friend of his tells us, "When he came abroad" again after his imprisonment, "he found his temporal affairs were gone to wreck, and he had as to them to begin again as if he had newly come into the world"; I say when we remember all this as being inflicted on a man of genius and fine feeling like Bunyan, and for such offences as his, it is difficult to prevent surprise deepening into a stronger feeling when writers, who at other times seem to value human freedom and high-minded conscientiousness, thus in a covert way apologize for tyranny, and reduce conscientiousness to an obstinacy which is simply perverse.[1]

To a man confined in prison for so many years during the most vigorous period of life, the right occupation of his time must have been felt to be a somewhat serious question. But in those days prisoners had to provide their own maintenance for the most part, and this necessity would stand first. The anony-

[1] There is a well-known story told about Bunyan to the effect that when on one occasion his gaoler allowed him to go forth at large he was seized with a feeling of misgiving, and came back before the gaoler expected him. He had not returned long before one of the magistrates came to enquire if all the prisoners were in, and especially if John Bunyan was safe. The gaoler, immensely relieved, is reported to have told Bunyan he might now go out when he liked, for that he knew better when to come than he could tell him.

I do not know upon what authority this story rests; there is no contemporary mention of it, and a precisely similar story is told concerning himself by John Grattan, a Quaker, who was confined in Derby gaol in 1683.

mous friend who first made Bunyan's acquaintance in prison tells us that he did not, while shut up there, "spend his time in supine and careless manner, nor Eat the Bread of Idleness, for I have been witness that his own hands have ministered to his and his familie's necessities, making many hundred gross of long Tagg'd Laces to fill up the vacancies of his time, which he had learn'd for that purpose since he had been in Prison."

Besides this, and possibly other handicraft, which occupied the bulk of his time, Bunyan still held the position of spiritual counsellor to some who were permitted to bring their affairs to him in prison. In *The Life and Death of Mr. Badman* he says, "When I was in prison there came a woman to me that was under a great deal of trouble. So I asked her, she being a stranger to me, what she had to say to me." It turned out that she was in the service of a shopkeeper at Wellingborough, whose box she had robbed again and again, and smitten with remorse she came to ask Bunyan what she should do. Though in prison, therefore, he was the spiritual guide and confidant of some who were outside, and he had still upon mind and heart the spiritual care of those who had heard his sermons or heard of his fame like this conscience-stricken woman from Wellingborough.

Then again, though a prisoner, he was a preacher still. There were times during those twelve years when Bedford gaol was crowded almost beyond its capacity, and that too with saintly men and women who valued the truth of God—Samuel Fenn, John Fenn, and many more of his fellow-members in the Bedford Church were there as his companions in tribulation. John Donne, the recently ejected rector of Pertenhall, was there also, so were William Wheeler, the ejected rector of Cranfield, and John Wright, the pious saddler of Blunham. John Donne was in the habit, after his ejectment, of gathering his people for worship by night in Keysoe Wood. On one of these occasions, as we have seen, they were surprised by the officers of the law, and the whole body of them, some sixty in number, marched off to Bedford gaol. Thus there was a considerable congregation within the walls of the prison itself. The writer to whom we are indebted for the knowledge of these facts adds, "In the midst of the hurry which so many new comers occasioned, I have heard Mr. Bunyan both preach and pray with that mighty Spirit of Faith and Plerophory of Divine Assistance, that has made me stand and wonder." The day room on the first floor of the gaol which, as John Howard tells us, was used also as a chapel, was doubtless the scene of many heart-stirring times when the Lord was felt to be with them.

Some of the sermons there preached afterwards grew into books, and by means of friends found their way to Francis Smith, the publisher near Temple Bar, and through him to the world at large. In this way Bunyan's *Holy City,* published in 1665, came into shape as he tells us himself: "Upon a certain first day, I being together with my brethren in our prison chamber, they expected that according to our custom, something should be spoken out of the word for our mutual edification; but at that time I felt myself, it being my turn to speak, so empty, spiritless, and barren, that I thought I should not have been able to speak among them so much as five words of truth with life and evidence." There came, however, a sudden break in the clouds; he seemed to see in the chapter before him "something of that jasper in whose light you there find this holy city is said to come or descend"; with an inward cry "I did carry my meditations to the Lord Jesus for a blessing, which He did forthwith grant according to his grace; and helping me to set before my brethren, we did all eat and were well-refreshed, and behold also that while I was in the distributing of it, it so increased in my hand, that of the fragments that we left, after we had well dined, I gathered up this basketful." The subject grew yet further upon him afterwards, and "through frequent prayer to God, what first with doing and then with undoing, and after that with doing again I thus did finish it." In this vivid sketch we have doubtless the history of more than one of his prison books. For his good pen was his true friend during those tedious years, and we may gain some insight into the growth of his mind if we follow the order in which his books appeared during his prison life.

His first venture of a literary sort after his arrest was into the region of poetry in a work entitled *Profitable Meditations.*[1] This first of his prison books was lost till about seventy years ago, when Mr. J. Camden Hotten, of Piccadilly, found a copy bound up in a volume of pamphlets.* This copy, now in the British Museum, is in quarto, and for the time rather handsomely

* An interesting representation of this edition was published in 1860 by Mr. Hotten, for which Mr. George Offor wrote an introduction.

[1] *Profitable Meditations, Fitted to Man's Different Condition.* In a *Conference* between *Christ* and a *Sinner.* In nine *Particulars.* By John Bunyan, Servant to the Lord Jesus. London: Printed for *Francis Smith,* at the sign of the *Elephant and Castle,* without *Temple Bar.*

printed. After the publisher's name, Francis Smith, some person—who, judging from the colour of the ink and the form of the figures, was probably a contemporary—has added the date 1661; and at the foot of Bunyan's address to the reader, where he subscribes himself, "I am thine in Christ, John Bunyan of Bedford," the same hand with the same ink as that of the date has added the words, "A Brasher now in prison in Bedford, 1664." The book is in the form of poetical dialogue, has small literary merit of any sort, and is simply interesting as being his first prison production, and as giving, in a supposed conversation between Satan and the tempted soul, the first idea of the parley between Christian and Apollyon in *The Pilgrim's Progress*, the line of thought being somewhat similar.

His next book sent forth from gaol was one of stronger sort. It is entitled *Praying in the Spirit*,[1] and is a treatise on prayer by a man with whom prayer was a real grappling of soul with the Eternal, living commerce with the living God. "Much," says he, "of my own experience could I here discover." He has, he says, found prayer to be the opener of the heart to God, and a means by which the soul, though empty, is filled. It is a living thing done in sincerity—that sincerity which is the same in a corner alone, as it is before the face of the world. It knows not how to wear two vizards, one for an appearance before men, and another for a short snatch in a corner, but it must have God, and be with Him in the duty of prayer. It is not lip-labour that it doth regard, for it is the heart that God looketh at. Prayer carries with it a sense of sin when the soul is overpressed with grief and bitterness, a sweet sense of mercy received when the prayers of saints are turned into thanksgiving, and yet are prayers still; and a sense of mercy to be received when the man not by fits and starts, but mightily, fervently, and continually groans out his condition before the Lord.

Apart from the deep spiritual vein in the book it is interesting as a kind of prison manifesto of the reasons which made him

[1] *I will pray with the Spirit and with the Understanding also; or a Discourse Touching Prayer.* The earliest existing Edition of this is the Third. London: Printed for the Author [1685]. No publisher's name. [A copy of the *Second* Edition with two title pages, both bearing the imprint, *London*, Printed for the Author, 1663, is now in the British Museum Library. It was acquired in 1914. Another copy is in the Pierpoint Morgan Library, New York; and the Editor possesses a title-page *only* (1663) of this unique little volume. The First Edition is unknown. In the catalogue of Mr. Offor's library (destroyed by fire in 1865) mention is made —item 1806—of a "reproduction of the second edition, published in 1818."

Gweddiaf a'r Yspryd; neu, Draethawd ar weddi. Translated by T. Watson, 1790. 12º.

so resolute against using the forms found in the Book of Common Prayer. In his account of his imprisonment, when speaking of the period of six months' comparative freedom between the Autumn and Spring Assizes of 1661—2, he says he "took all occasions that were put into his hand to visit the people of God, exhorting them to be stedfast in the faith of Jesus Christ, and to take heed that they touched not the Common Prayer," the use of which was now being revived with so much vigour through the kingdom. This second prison book, written in 1662, and published the following year, is evidently the substance of the addresses thus delivered. He returns to this point again and again. Speaking of what prayer really is, he says, "A good sense of sin and the wrath of God, and some encouragement from God to come unto Him is a better common prayer book than that which is taken out of the papistical mass-book, being the scraps and fragments of the devices of some popes, some friars, and I know not what." The men who are so zealous in thrusting this book upon their neighbours, who are hot for the form and not for the power of praying, judging from their drunken debauched lives, know scarcely one in forty of them what it is to be born again. In somewhat satirical vein he reminds his readers that the Apostle Paul, in his humility, said he knew not what he should pray for as he ought, yet surely he was as capable as any pope or proud prelate in the Church of Rome. He was fain to come off with sighs and groans, sighs and groans too deep for utterance. "But here now the wise men of our days are so well skilled as that they have both the matter and manner of their prayers at their finger-ends; setting such a prayer for such a day, and that twenty years before it comes. One for Christmas, another for Easter, and six days after that. They have also bounded how many syllables must be said in every one of them at their public exercises. For each saint's day also they have them ready for the generations yet unborn to say. They can tell you also when you shall kneel, when you shall stand, when you should abide in your seats, when you should go up into the chancel, and what you should do when you come there. All which the apostles come short of, as not being able to compose so profound a manner." He is angry that men of the most dissolute lives should be counted the only honest men because they come to Church and say Our Father, while those of more sober principles who scruple vain traditions must be looked upon to be the only enemies of God and the nation. "Though a man be willing to live never so peaceably, yet because he cannot for conscience' sake own that for one of the most eminent parts of God's worship which He never commanded, must he be looked upon as factious, seditious, erroneous, heretical—a disparagement to the Church, a seducer of the people, and what not." "If," concludes he, "you desire the clearing of the minor,[1] look into the jails of England, and into the alehouses of the same; and I trow you will find those that plead for the spirit of prayer in the jail, and them that look after the form of men's inventions only in the alehouse."

Bunyan's third prison-book appeared the same year as his work on prayer. It was entitled *Christian Behaviour,*[2] and is a treatise upon a true life as the fitting outcome of a sound faith. Christian men should be living men; he would have them take heed of being painted fire, wherein there is no warmth; and painted flowers, which retain no fragrance; and painted trees, wherein there is no fruit. In the main the book is a plain common-sense utterance on the duties and relations of husbands and wives, parents and children, masters and servants; but there are not wanting Bunyanesque touches here and there which show the hand from which they came. He will be brief, for multitude of words drown the memory, and a thing may be put so that you may find that on one side of a sheet which some are forced to hunt for in a whole quire. Zeal without knowledge is like a mettled horse without eyes, or like a sword in a madman's hands, and there is no knowledge where there is not the Word. He would have parents take heed of filling their children's heads with whimsies and unprofitable notions, for this will sooner learn them to be malapert and proud than sober and humble. In the way of reproof speak not much nor often, but pertinent to them with all gravity. He is severe upon empty men whose tongue is tipt with a talk and tattle of religion. In the Second Part of *The Pilgrim's Progress* there is a charming illustration where Christiana, at the house of Interpreter, is

[1] *i.e.*, the minor premiss in his argument.
[2] *Christian Behaviour;* or The Fruits of true *Christianity*: Shewing the ground from whence they flow in their Godlike Order in the Duties of Relations. By John Bunyan, a Prisoner of *Hope*. London: Printed for *F. Smith,* at the *Elephant* and *Castle,* without *Temple-Bar.*

shown the diversity in unity of the flowers of the garden, where some are better than some, yet where the gardener has set them they stand, and quarrel not with one another. The thought was anticipated twenty years earlier in the little book before us—"When *Christians* stand every one in their places and do the work of their relations, then they are like the flowers in the garden that stand and grow where the gardener hath planted them, and then they shall both honour the garden in which they are planted and the gardener that hath so disposed of them. From the hyssop on the wall to the cedar in Lebanon their fruit is their glory." Few things in his writings are more beautiful than this other simile, found also in this little book—"Christians are like the several flowers in a garden, that have upon each of them the dew of heaven, which, being shaken with the wind, they let fall their dew at each other's roots, whereby they are jointly nourished, and become nourishers of each other."

Charles Doe, in his Catalogue of Bunyan's Writings, assigned *Christian Behaviour* to the year 1674. Both he and Mr. Offor were evidently unaware of this first edition of 1663, a copy* of which was found in 1864 by Mr. Tarbutt of Cranbrook, among the books of a Nonconformist farmer of Staplehurst. This edition differs from the later ones by having the words "By John Bunyan, a Prisoner of Hope," on the title-page, and on the last page these parting words, "Farewell, From my place of confinement in Bedford this 17th of the 4th month, 1663." This interesting addition gives new meaning and pathos to the closing sentences of the book, which seem to indicate that he sometimes expected that the door of his prison-cell might one day open upon the scaffold—"Thus have I, in few words, written to you before I die, a word to provoke you to faith and holiness, because I desire that you may have the life that is laid up for all them that believe in the Lord Jesus, and love one another, when I am deceased. Though then I shall rest from my labours, and be in paradise, as through grace I comfortably believe, yet it is not there, but here, I must do you good. Wherefore, I not knowing the shortness of my life, nor the hinderance that hereafter I may have of serving my God and you, I have taken this opportunity to present these few lines unto you for your edification."

* This copy is now in the Library of the British Museum. It was acquired in 1895.

Between 1663, the date of this publication, and the end of 1665 there appeared from Bunyan's pen *Serious Meditations on the Four Last Things* and *Ebal and Gerizim,*[1] two works in poetic form which call for no special remark; the *Holy City; The Resurrection of the Dead;* and *Prison Meditations.*

The *Holy City,*[2] which appeared in the fifth year of his imprisonment, had, as we have seen, its origin in a prison sermon. It is prefaced with a characteristic epistle to four sorts of readers, in which he anticipates that the learned reader will blame him because neither in line or margent has he a cloud of sentences from learned fathers. Learned sentences and words he gives not, because he has them not, nor has he read them. Had it not been for the Bible he had not only not done it thus, but not at all. The book itself is an exposition of the vision of the New Jerusalem given in the concluding chapters of the Book of Revelation. Treading on the perilous ground of apocalyptic interpretation his spiritual insight and strong common-sense guide Bunyan aright. To him the New Jerusalem is not the outward home of the Church of God in the life beyond. It is the symbol of the Church itself. The great community of redeemed men is set forth under the double similitude of the Bride the Lamb's wife, and of the City of Life, the figure of the Bride bringing into prominence the tender relations existing between Christ and His own, and that of the City, the vastness, the glory, the many-sidedness of the Church of the redeemed. Seeing the two symbols to be thus complemental, he steers clear of the vagaries into which too many have fallen. And musing on the vision he looks longingly for the hour of manifested glory. It is not yet. The saints are yet but as an army routed, and are apt, sometimes through fear, and sometimes through forgetfulness, to mistake the word of their Captain-General, the Son of God, and are also too prone to shoot and kill even their very right-hand man. But a better day is coming. "Never was fair weather after foul, nor warm weather after cold, nor sweet and

[1] The Earliest Edition of these works in existence is the Fourth: the Title-page runs thus: *One thing is Needful*: *or Serious Meditations upon the Four Last Things;* unto which is added *Ebal and Gerizim*: or the Blessing and the Curse, with *Prison Meditations.* By John Bunyan. London: Printed for and are to be sold by the Booksellers of *London* and Westminster (1700?). [The British Museum Library acquired, in 1888, a copy of the Third Edition—'Printed for *Nath. Ponder,* at the Peacock in the Poultry, 1683; but in a copy of *Sighs from Hell,* Fifth Edition, published by Francis Smith in 1675, is advertised—*One Thing Needful,* Third Edition. So, apparently, there was an earlier "third" edition, issued in 1675. *Vide* Collection at the Bodleian Library, Oxford.]

Myfyrdodau difrifol ar y pedwar peth diweddaf: sef, Angeu, Barn, Nef ac Uffern, Caerfyrddin, 1767.

[2] *The Holy City;* or the New Jerusalem. Wherein its goodly light, walls, gates, angels and the manner of their standing are expounded. London: Printed in the year 1665.

beautiful spring after a heavy and nipping and terrible winter, so comfortable, sweet, desirable, and welcome to the poor birds and beasts of the field as this day will be to the Church of God. Then will all the spiders and dragons and owls and foul spirits of Antichrist be brought to light, and all the pretty robins and little birds in the Lord's field most sweetly send forth their pleasant notes, and all the flowers and herbs of His garden spring."

The vision of the City of God was one specially suited to his peculiar genius, and full of suggestiveness. The city, he notes, has twelve gates, three to each point of the compass, to show that God hath a people in every corner of the world, and that from what quarter or part of the world soever men come for life, for those men there are the gates of life even right before their doors. On the foundations of the city are written the names of the twelve Apostles of the Lamb, because it is the doctrine of the Apostles that holds up the walls of the New Jerusalem, the doctrine upon which both Christ and grace and all happiness standeth firm and sure for ever. The right preacher is the man that can preach the doctrine of the twelve. In the end it shall not be as it is now, a Popish doctrine, a Quaker's doctrine, a Prelatical doctrine, and the Presbyter, Independent, and Anabaptist, thus distinguished, and thus confounded and destroying. Then the city is of pure gold, as showing how invincible and unconquerable is the spirit of the people of God. For gold is a metal invincible even by fire; the fire may burn it, and melt and consume its dross, but the gold remains and holds its ground; yea, it gets ground even of the furnace and fire itself; for the more it is burned and melted, the more it recovers its colour and shakes off its dross and dishonour. Just thus it is with the people of God, and hath been so from the beginning; the more they oppressed them the more they grew.

The gates of the city are each one several pearl, one entire pearl, as showing that as none can enter in but by Christ, so none can enter in but by a whole Christ. Christ must be helpful to thee every way, or He will be helpful to thee no way; thou must enter in by every whit of Christ, or by never a whit of Him. There is but one street in this city, for at last the saints shall walk in one way, and in one light. It is Antichrist that hath brought in all these crossings, bye-lanes, and odd nooks that to this day many an honest heart doth greatly lose itself in. Men must have pure hearts for that golden street, which is, as it were, transparent glass. It is not every clown with his clumping dirty shoes that is admitted into the King's privy chambers and private palaces; neither doth or will God at the day of the New Jerusalem suffer any to trace about this golden street but such as have golden feet, and that are beautified with golden shoes. The men who shall walk that street must be golden men with golden hearts, with graces that are much more precious than of gold that perisheth.

"Thus," says Bunyan, "have I showed you my present light into this portion of Holy Scripture. If any can give me further, I hope I shall not refuse it; but as yet, methinks, this is the genuine sense and the very track of John himself."

This book, the *Holy City,* was first issued without publisher's name in 1665, and again in 1669 with the name of Francis Smith as publisher. With the exception of the title-page, both editions are of the same impression, even to the "Errata and Corrections," and in both issues there is the following note: "Reader, By reason of the Author's distance from the Press some Faults have escaped (notwithstanding the Printer's care), which thou art desired to correct thus." The corrections which follow are the same in both editions.

The book entitled *The Resurrection of the Dead*[1] appeared the same year as the first issue of the *Holy City,* 1665. In that year, also, appeared a poetical production entitled *Prison Meditations: Dedicated to the Heart of Suffering Saints and Reigning Sinners:* By John Bunyan, in Prison, 1665.[2] It would appear that some friend had written to him in gaol, sending him words of cheer and encouraging him to keep his head above the flood. This poetical effusion was Bunyan's reply to his friend. He takes it kindly of him, he says, thus to write to him, and assures him that his heart is still undaunted, for his feet upon Mount Sion stand. He is in prison, it is true, but then his mind is free.

[1] *The Resurrection of the Dead, and Eternal Judgment.* By John Bunyan, a Servant of the Lord's Christ. London: Printed for Francis Smith [1665]. The only known copy of the First Edition was destroyed by fire with the rest of Mr. Offor's collection in 1865. [The British Museum Library acquired a copy as far back as 1838. It seems that Dr. Brown must have overlooked this]

[2] *Prison Meditations*: Dedicated to the Heart of Suffering Saints and Reigning Sinners. By John Bunyan, in Prison, 1665. *Carchar-fyfyrdodan.* J. B. Aberystwith, 1809. 12º.

GRACE
Abounding to the chief of Sinners:

OR,
A Brief and Faithful

RELATION

Of the Exceeding Mercy of God in Chriſt, to his poor Servant

JOHN BUNYAN.

Wherein is particularly ſhewed, The manner of his Converſion, his ſight and trouble for Sin, his Dreadful Temptations, alſo how he deſpaired of Gods mercy, and how the Lord at length thorow Chriſt did deliver him from all the guilt and terrour that lay upon him.

Whereunto is added,

A brief Relation of his Call to the Work of the Miniſtry, of his Temptations therein, as alſo what he hath met with in Priſon.

All which was written by his own hand there, and now publiſhed for the ſupport of the weak and tempted People of God.

Come and hear, all ye that fear God; and I will declare what he hath done for my ſoul, Pſal. *66.16.*

LONDON:
Printed by *George Larkin.* 1666.

TITLE-PAGE OF THE FIRST EDITION
OF
GRACE ABOUNDING,
BY
JOHN BUNYAN,
1666.

From the copy in the British Museum Library.]

"For though men keep my outward man
Within their bolts and bars,
Yet, by the faith of Christ, I can
Mount higher than the stars.

Here dwells good conscience, also peace,
Here be my garments white;
Here, though in bonds, I have release
From guilt, which else would bite.

The Truth and I, were both here cast
Together, and we do
Lie arm in arm, and so hold fast
Each other: this is true."

After sending forth this poetical epistle to his friend, Bunyan seems next to have set about the composition of a book, which, under the title of *Grace Abounding to the Chief of Sinners,* gives, as he only could give it, the story of his life.[1] This proved to be one of his most memorable compositions, and associates itself in one's mind with Augustine's confessions and the heart-utterances of Luther. In a preface, which is not the least powerful part of it, he dedicates the book to those whom God hath counted him worthy to beget to faith by his ministry in the Word. He is, he says, taken from them in presence, but his soul having fatherly care and desire after their welfare, now once again, as before, from the top of Shenir and Hermon, so now from the lions' dens and from the mountains of the leopards he looks after them all, greatly longing to see their safe arrival into the desired haven. He thanks God upon every remembrance of them, and even now, while he sticks between the teeth of the lions in the wilderness, he rejoices over the grace God has bestowed upon them. Their aspirations of soul, their tenderness of heart, their trembling at sin, their sober and holy deportment before both God and men is great refreshment to him, for they are his glory and joy. He sends them here enclosed a drop of that honey he has taken out of the carcase of the lion. He has eaten thereof himself, and been much refreshed thereby. In this discourse they may see much of the grace of God towards him. It was much indeed, for it was above his sins and above Satan's temptations too. His fears and doubts and sad months are now as the head of Goliah in his hand. The remembrance of his great sins, of his great temptations, and of his

[1] *Grace Abounding to the Chief of Sinners:* or a brief and faithful Relation of the exceeding mercy of God in Christ to his poor servant, John Bunyan. London: Printed by George Larkin, 1666. *De Genade Uytgebreyt tot de Grooste der Sondaren.* Amsterdam: Boekholt, 1689, 12°. Helaethrwydd o Ras, i'r pennaf o bechaduriaid. Dolgelleu, 1803. 8°. *Grâce de Dieu répandue abondamment.* Traduite par J. F. Nardin, Genève, 1824. 12°. *Gràs am paitteas do cheannfeadhna nam peacach.* Gael. Edinburgh, 1847. 12°. *Die überschwängliche Gnade an dem grössten der Sünder.* Hamburg: 1864. *Overvættes Naade mod den Störste blandt Syndere.* Bergen: 1874.

great fears of perishing for ever bring afresh to his mind the remembrance of his great help, of his great support from heaven, of the great grace that God extended to such a wretch as he. He would have them also search for the hid treasure of their first and second experience of the grace of God—to remember the word that first laid hold of them, their terrors of conscience, and fears of death and hell, their tears and prayers to God, and how they sighed under every hedge for mercy. Had they never a Hill Mizar to remember? Had they forgotten the close, the milk-house, the stable, the barn, and the like, where God did visit their souls? In writing this book he could have stepped into a style much higher than that in which he has discoursed, but he dare not. God did not play in convincing him, nor the devil in tempting him, neither did he himself play when he sank as into a bottomless pit, and the pangs of hell caught hold of him; whereupon he may not in telling the story but be plain and simple, and lay down the thing as it was. He that likes it may receive it, he that does not, let him produce a better.

This book, which in parts is weird and terrible as his own picture of the valley of the shadow of death, is yet in its alternations a faithful transcript of the writer's soul, and must be read in order to a right understanding of the man as he was, both in strength and weakness. It appeared in 1666, the year of his first but short release, and was published in London by George Larkin. Till 1883 no copy of the first edition was known to be in existence, but in July of that year one was purchased at a sale for the British Museum.* It is beautifully printed in duodecimo form, and is shorter than the subsequent editions by some fifty or sixty paragraphs. Some of the most interesting personal reminiscences and effective touches appear to have been added after the first publication. In this first edition there is no mention of his falling into a creek of the sea or into Bedford river, or of his plucking out the tongue of an adder, when he was a boy, or of his going to be a soldier afterwards. The whole of the characteristic account of his giving up bell-ringing in Elstow steeple, and of his dancing with the Elstow lasses was a later addition; so, too, was the eminently interesting passage about his meeting with Martin Luther's *Commentary on the Galatians*, and the long and earnest vindication of his character against the charges of inchastity, found

* Other copies are now in Henry E. Huntington and Pierpoint Morgan Libraries, U.S.A.

in sections 304—317 of the edition of 1688 is entirely wanting in the edition of 1666. The pathetic references to his blind child also were intensified in the later edition, and all the way through, little touches were added here and there which heighten the effect, and give finish to the picture. Whether they were all added in the second edition, we do not happen to know, since there are no remaining copies known of any edition between the first, of 1666, and the sixth, of 1688.† In the first edition he says, "I was had home to prison again, where I have now lain above five years and a quarter, waiting to see what God will suffer these men to do with me." In the sixth edition he says he has lain now complete twelve years, and as he still retains the words about waiting to see what yet may come, it seems probable that no additions were made to the *Grace Abounding* after his release from prison, and that the edition of 1688 is simply a reprint of one issued about 1672, of which no copy seems to be known.

† Since Dr. Brown wrote this, copies dated 1680 and 1685, were sold by auction in London. The Pierpoint Morgan Library possesses a copy of the third edition which bears no date.

It has been noticed that while all Bunyan's previous prison books were published by Francis Smith, the *Grace Abounding* was issued by George Larkin. The change may have been required because Smith himself was at that time in the furnace as well as Bunyan, for publisher and author were indeed companions in tribulation. Francis Smith's place of business was at the Elephant and Castle, near Temple Bar, and as "Anabaptist, *alias* Elephant Smith," he was known to his contemporaries as "a man of great sincerity and happy contentment in all circumstances of life." But according to his own account he went through experiences which must have strained his happy contentment to its utmost pitch of tension. As early as 1659, when the Restoration tide was beginning to turn, he was looked upon as "a disaffected Person and a Phanatick," and as such his house was frequently searched for arms, and all his windows broken. In 1660, for publishing a little book entitled *The Lord's Loud Call to England,* and similar productions, he was three times a prisoner in the hands of the King's Messengers at a noble a day, the whole costing him £50. At the time of Venner's insurrection he was ill in bed, but that did not prevent his house being searched ten times, his person being assaulted to the peril of his life, or his property plundered. The following August he and piles of books from his shop were seized by warrant, he being carried to the Gatehouse Prison, for "having a hand in printing and compileing dangerous Books," which surely were not so very dangerous, seeing that those who carried them off straightway sold the sheets to the trade again, and put the money into their own pockets. It was during this imprisonment that he says, "I was locked up in a room where I had neither chair nor stool to rest upon, and yet ten shillings per week must be the price, and before I had been there three nights £7 15s. was demanded for present fees. That is to say, £5 to excuse me for wearing irons, ten shillings for my entrance week lodging, five shillings for sheets, five shillings for garnish money, and the rest for Turnkey's fees."

Recounting some of his other troubles he mentions a fact of some interest to us when he says, "Immediately before that dreadful Fire that the Papists brought upon London in 1666 one Mr. Lillycrop, a Printer, and another, both servants to Mr. L'Estrange, as his assistance in surveying the Press, came to my shop and warehouse near Temple Bar, with their general warrant to seize unlicensed Books, and took of Mr. Allen's, *Mr. Bunnyan's,* and others, barely as unlicensed, though the prejudice the Licensers were pleased to take against the Authors, constrained my printing them without License, being Books neither against Church nor State: nevertheless they took as many as two Porters could stand under, and carried them to Mr. L'Estrange's Lodging, then at the King's Wardrobe, some of which, with much difficulty and charge, was obtained again: the rest it's supposed the Fire took."

Raids like this repeated would go far to account for the scarcity of Bunyan's earlier works, and may partly explain also the change of publisher. Francis Smith was clearly a marked man, and his warehouse not safe. We can scarcely wonder. Many of the other authors for whom he published were, like Bunyan, of a class unacceptable to Roger L'Estrange, the Censor of the Press, and those for whom he acted. Smith had a way, too, of getting a book licensed if he could, but if he could not, then, with sweet simplicity, he laid the blame of its irregular appearance upon the authorities who, by their refusal, constrained him, as he says, to print the book without licence. Still further, not merely as a publisher, but as a citizen, he was a man to be carefully watched, for he was painfully plain-spoken on subjects on which city gentlemen were naturally sensitive. He went so far as to lay his profane hand on the sacred institution of the Sheriff's Feast. In a pamphlet written by himself he pointed out that "the fifth part of the charge of the Shrievalty is for wine, the growth of another country, and that the Cheque and Spittle Feasts have become scandalous, the latter, after the pretended service of God in hearing a sermon, costing above £300 to each Sheriff." He points out also that while thirty years ago a lord or gentleman used to spend only £100 in wine when living at the rate of £10,000 or £12,000 a year, now out of every £3,000 spent in the city above £500 went in wine.[1]

About the time of the appearance of the *Grace Abounding*, Bunyan had a few weeks' brief release from his imprisonment. The friend, who wrote the continuation of this book in 1692, tells us that after six years' confinement, "by the intercession of some in trust and power that took pity upon his suffering, he obtained his freedom." Other events also at that time conspired to shake the resolution of the hard-handed men who were then in power. The Plague had desolated London in a way that was simply appalling, and in some instances had spread down into the country. It was even raging round Bedford gaol. Out of the small population then in the town no fewer than forty persons, as St. Paul's register informs us, died of the Plague, on the north side of the river, and were buried in a field, ever after known as Pesthouse Close. Then after the Plague came the great Fire of London, carrying terror through the country. And, what was even more to the purpose, Lord Clarendon, able but pitiless, the arch instigator of all repressive measures against Nonconformists, was beginning to totter, in his high place, towards that ruinous fall which was now so near. So there came a breathing space, of which Bunyan received the advantage, but not for long. Charles Doe tells us that "a little after his release they took him again at a meeting, and put him in the same gaol, where he lay six years more." Where this arrest took place, or for what offence, we are not told; but as he was again committed to the county gaol it must have been within the county jurisdiction. Speaking of the time when he was cast into prison, Bunyan says, "The subject I should have preached upon even then when the constable came was, 'Dost thou believe on the Son of God?'" This might apply to his first arrest at

[1] *Account of Injurious Proceedings against Francis Smith*, 1680. Folio, 20 pp.

Samsell; but the writer of the continuation, already referred to, tells us that this was his text on the occasion of his second arrest. In the biography of 1692 it is said that when the constable came to take him, Bunyan, with the open Bible in his hand, fixed his eyes upon the man, who turned pale, let go his hold, and stood back, Bunyan exclaiming, "See how this man trembles at the Word of God!"[1] The story may be true, but it is in a vein a little too melodramatic to be characteristic, and is without sufficient contemporary authority to rest upon.

But whatever the circumstances of his arrest, in 1666, and for six years more Bunyan was back in his old quarters in Bedford gaol. It is curious to notice that of this second period of six years' imprisonment we know very much less than we know of the first. In the first imprisonment he wrote and published no fewer than nine of his books, during the second he seems to have produced only two books, his *Confession of Faith,* and the work entitled *A Defence of the Doctrine of Justification by Faith,* the latter being written off rapidly in the space of six weeks shortly before his release in 1672. It is tolerably certain that his masterpiece, *The Pilgrim's Progress,* though written in prison as he himself tells us, was not written during his longer term of twelve years, but during that shorter term of six months' imprisonment, which fell in 1675. The reason for this opinion may be more conveniently given when we come to speak of the book itself and of that later time. After his frequent utterances from 1660 to 1666 his almost entire silence as an author from 1666 to 1672 is certainly remarkable. Was it because he was not able to get any of his writings licensed and Francis Smith was now too carefully watched to be able to publish them unlicensed? Was it that the claims of his family's maintenance made greater demands upon his time now that the long continuance of persecution had made friends fewer? Or was it that he was becoming more broken-spirited and for a time at least had lost something of his old elasticity of mind?

Be the reason what it may, our knowledge of those six years is a comparative blank. Two facts and two only stand out to view. His wife and children were at this time living in the parish of St. Cuthbert, and there is a fine stroke of irony in the fact that while Bunyan was still a prisoner, a collection

[1] Is not a similar story told of George Fox?

was made all through that parish in the month of October, 1670, "for the poor inslaved English Christians cap[tured] in Algiers; by virtue of a brief from the King's Most Excellent Majesty and his Most Honourable Privy Councill read and urged on the Lord's day, by exhortation and perswasion in the Parish Church thereof." Though the brief was read and urged in church, the collection, which amounted to seven shillings, appears to have been made from house to house, for the contributors' names are all given, fifteen in number. Among these the name of "John Bunnian" appears as that of a subscriber of sixpence to the fund, which, as he was a prisoner himself, was probably contributed by his family on his behalf.[1]

In the early part of 1671, Edward Fowler, rector of Northill, in Bedfordshire, afterwards Bishop of Gloucester, published a book entitled, *The Design of Christianity,* a copy of which found its way to Bunyan in Bedford gaol the following February. This book roused in him once more the spirit of controversy, and within six weeks he sent forth a lengthy reply to the work, dated "From Prison, the 27th of the 12th month, 1671," or according to new style March 27th, 1672.[2] The writer though living only a few miles from Bedford is personally a stranger to him. "I know you not by face, nor your personal practice." He cannot tell, therefore, whether he is one of the many ignorant Sir Johns* in the pulpits of the land; all he knows of him is that being first one of the ejected of 1662, and then one, who afterwards conformed, having shown an unstable weathercock spirit which could not but stumble the weak and give advantage to the adversary. It is his book, however, not himself, against which he protests, and this because it is alien to the Evangelic spirit of the Articles of the Church of England and therefore to the gospel itself. The writer seems to him to speak more of reformation than regeneration, more of the restoration of the merely natural qualities than of the impartation of the new nature of sonship in Christ. This is not enough; it is not enough for the old nature to go forth in holiday clothes, there must be a new creation in righteousness and true holiness. In Bunyan's judgment Fowler makes too light of Christ's great sacrifice

* A common name for a priest.

[1] *St. Cuthbert's Parish Register.*

[2] *A Defence of the Doctrine of Justification by Faith in Jesus Christ*: showing, true gospel Holiness flows from thence. London: Printed for Francis Smith, 1672. [In his *General Catalogue of Books* (1674), Robert Clavel mentions "Baxter's *Answer* to Fowler's *Design of Christianity*. Printed for Nevil Simons."]

in its character as an expiation for human guilt, making it to appear that Christ merely holds the point of the sword of justice, not that he received it into his own soul, that he suspended the curse from us, not that He Himself was made a curse for us, and in this way he steppeth over Christ's sacrifice as a spider straddleth over a wasp. A pale shadowy gospel like this the writer, he says, proves not from Scripture but from the Cambridge thinker John Smith, while John Smith goes in turn to Plato, and so they wrap the business up. Further, laying aside all fear of man and, as he says, "not regarding what you may procure to be inflicted upon me for this my plain dealing with you," he protests against Fowler's turning liberty to looseness by saying that in matters of worship we have leave to do whatsoever is commended by custom, or commanded by superiors, or made convenient by circumstances. For in this way you may hop from Presbyterianism to the prelatical mode, and if time and chance should serve you, backwards and forwards again and make use of several consciences. How then if God should cast you into Turkey, where Mahomet reigns as Lord? It is but reckoning that it is the religion and custom of the country and that it is authorised by the power that is there, and then, for peace' sake and to sleep in a whole skin, you may comply and do as your superior commands. So he leaves Fowler for the present, destined to hear from him before the year was out.

The time for Bunyan's release was now nearer than he knew. Before this book was well out of the printer's hands he was out of the gaoler's. Twelve days before he dated the preface from prison the King dated the Declaration of Religious Indulgence from Whitehall. This declaration suspended, not by due course of law but by royal prerogative, the execution of all and all manner of penal laws in matters ecclesiastical against whatsoever sort of Nonconformists or Recusants. On the 8th of May following, a petition was presented to the King in Council from John Fenn, John Bunyan, John Dunn, Thomas Haynes, Simon Haynes, and George Farr, prisoners in the gaol of Bedford, for being at Conventicles and Nonconformity. The petition was ordered to be referred to the Sheriff of the County who was forthwith to certify the Privy Council "whether the said parties are detained in prison for the offences therein mentioned or for what other crimes." Thomas Bromsall of Blunham was

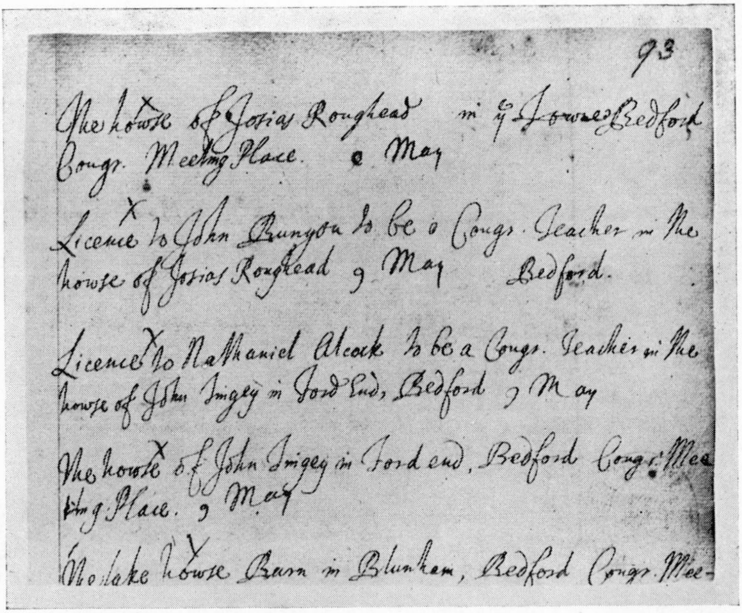

93

The howse of Josias Roughead in ye ~~Towne~~ Bedford
Congr. Meeting Place. 9 May

Licence to John Bunyon to be a Congr. Teacher in the
howse of Josias Roughead 9 May Bedford.

Licence to Nathaniel Alcock to be a Congr. Teacher in the
howse of John Ingey in Ford End, Bedford 9 May

The howse of John Ingey in Ford end, Bedford Congr. Mee
ting Place. 9 May

The lake howse Barn in Blunham, Bedford Congr. Mee-

LICENCE GRANTED TO JOHN BUNYAN TO PREACH: May 9, 1672.

(Public Record Office, London.)
Photo: G. A. Gearey, Bedford.]

sheriff that year and seems to have acted with promptitude in the matter, for his certificate that the prisoners in question were simply "Convicted upon several statutes for not conforming to the rights and ceremonyes of the Church of England, and for being at unlawful meetings," was dated the 11th of May, or only three days after the Order in Council. On the 17th, therefore, at the next meeting at Whitehall, it was "Ordered by his Ma[tie] in Council, That the said petition of the Bedford prisoners and certificate of the Sheriff, be (and are herewith) sent to his Ma[tie's] Attorney Generall, who is authorised and required to insert them into the Generall Pardon to be passed for the Quakers." This general pardon under the great seal was witnessed at Westminster on the 13th of September, 1672, and beginning with the gaol of Newgate within the City of London, specifies the names of the prisoners to be released from various gaols in the kingdom, and amongst them these: "John Fenn, John Bunnion, John Dunn, Thomas Haynes, George Farr, James Rogers, John Rush, Tabitha Rush, and John Curfe, Prisoners in our Common Gaol for our County of Bedford." In the previous lists James Rogers is described as being in the gaol at Cambridge. This pardon is extended, as required by the forms of laws, so that every name is repeated eleven times, Bunyan's being spelt four different ways, *Bunyan* five times, *Bunnyan* three times, *Bunnion* twice, and *Bunnyon* once.[1]

But though Bunyan's pardon under the great seal was finally issued only on the 13th September, it is not improbable that his actual release took place as early as May; for on the 9th of that month he was duly licensed as a teacher under the Declaration of Indulgence. In the volume marked "Indulgences, 1672," and under the head "Congregationall," there is the following document, a copy of which Bunyan carried with him as his passport:

Bedford Licence for John Bunnyon to be a teacher in the House of Josias Roughed, 9 May, 72.

CHARLES, &c. To all Mayors, Bailiffs, Constables, and others, Our Officers and Ministers, Civill and Military whom it may concerne, Greeting. In Pursuance of our Declaration of the 15th of March, 167½, Wee doe hereby permitt and licence John Bunyon to bee a Teacher of the Congregation allowed by Us in the House of Josias Roughed, Bedford, for the use of such as doe not conforme to the Church of England, who are of the Perswasion commonly called Congregationall. With further licence and permission to him the said John Bunyon

[1] *Offor*, I. xcviii. *The Christian Progress of George Whitehead*: 1725, pp. 359—366.

to teach in any other place licensed by Us according to our said Declaration. Given at our Court at Whitehall the 9th day of May in the 24th yeare of our Reigne, 1672,

By his Maties command,

ARLINGTON.

Thus constancy had conquered at last, and the right to teach was in the end conceded by the power which had spent twelve years in asserting that it did not exist. Those twelve years of memorable experience had been borne with a bravery and patience quite as memorable. Says his friend: "It was by making him a visit in prison that I first saw him and became acquainted with him; and I must confess, I could not but look upon him to be a man of an excellent spirit, zealous for his Master's honour and chearfully committing all his concernments unto God's disposal. He bore that tedious imprisonment in an incomfortable and close prison and sometimes under cruel and oppressive gaolers with that Christian patience and presence of mind as became a minister of Jesus Christ, and such a cause as he was engaged in and suffered for." He himself also, speaking of the fact that he was so long in bonds, quietly says: "In which condition I have continued with much content through grace." "I was made to see that if ever I would suffer rightly I must first pass a sentence of death upon everything which can properly be called a thing of this life, even to reckon myself, my Wife, my Children, my Health, my Enjoyments, and all, as dead to me and myself as dead to them. And second to live upon God that is invisible. I see the best way to go through suffering is to trust in God through Christ as touching the world to come; and as touching this world to count the grave my House, and to make my Bed in darkness. That is to familiarize these things to me."

Thus he found like many before and since that the way of earthly renunciation is the way of heavenly peace, that by giving up all, we gain all. Yet like the rest of us he found this path steep and arduous. "I found myself a man and compassed with infirmities. The parting with my Wife and poor Children hath often been to me in this place as the pulling of the Flesh from my Bones; and that not only because I am somewhat too fond of these great Mercies, but also because I should have often brought to my mind the many hardships, miseries and wants that my poor Family was like to meet with should I be taken from them, *especially my poor blind Child,* who lay nearer my heart than all I had besides; O the thoughts of the hardship I thought my Blind one might go under, would break my heart to pieces. . . . Yet recalling myself, thought I, *I must venture you all with God, though it goeth to the quick to leave you.* O, I saw in this condition I was as a man who was pulling down his house upon the head of his Wife and Children. Yet, thought I, I must do it, I must do it."

His earliest struggles of soul seem to have been his severest. "When but a young prisoner and not acquainted with the law this lay much upon my spirit. That my Imprisonment might end at the Gallows for aught I can tell." Yet it was not hanging he feared so much as that when the time came to die he might be left without savour of the things of God, without any evidence upon his soul that all was well. "I thought with myself, if I should make a scrabbling shift to clamber up the Ladder, yet I should either with quaking or other symptoms of faintings give occasion to the enemy to reproach the way of God and his People, for their timorousness. This, therefore, lay with great trouble upon me, for methought I was ashamed to die with a pale Face and tottering Knees for such a cause as this." Then came this gleam of hope and cheer that he might even upon the him die, "and thought I, if it must be so, if God will but convert one soul by my very last words, I shall not count my Life thrown away nor lost." And even should it be that in the supreme hour of departing life God should hide His face from him, "'Twas my duty to stand to his Word, whether he would ever look upon me or no, or save me at the last. Wherefore, thought I, the point being thus, I am for going on and venturing my eternal State with Christ, whether I have comfort here or no. If God doth not come in, thought I, I will leap off the Ladder even blindfold into Eternity, sink or swim, come heaven, come hell. Lord Jesus, if thou wilt, catch me, do; if not, I will venture for thy Name."

These days of storm were followed by years of calm, when his soul was kept as with the peace of God. It was of the years that slowly came and went in Bedford gaol he was speaking when he said: "I never had in all my life so great an inlet into the Word of God as now. The Scriptures that I saw nothing in before are made in this place to shine upon me. Jesus Christ also was never more real and apparent than now. Here I have seen him and felt him indeed. I have seen *that* here that I am persuaded I shall never while in this world be able to express. I never knew what it was for God to stand by me at all turns, and at every offer of Satan to afflict me, as I have found Him since I came in hither. As being very tender of me, he hath not suffered me to be molested, but would with one scripture and another strengthen me against all; insomuch that I have often said, were it lawful I could pray for greater trouble for the greater comfort's sake. Many more of the dealings of God towards me I might relate, but these out of the spoils won in battle have I dedicated to maintain the house of God."

IX.

THE CHURCH IN THE STORM.

In one of those quarto pamphlets, which were the newspapers of the seventeenth century, there is an account of a tempest that, in the year of Bunyan's release, swept with unusual violence over the town of Bedford. It began with a great darkness which was soon exchanged for such vivid flashes of lightning "that the people of the adjacent places did believe the whole town of Bedford to be on a light flame." In the half hour during which it raged, the storm lifted great gates from off their hinges, whirled the goods of the tradesmen out of their shops, and the stacks of the farmers out of their fields. "Twenty of Justice Barber's stoutest Elms were torn up by the roots, and one great Tree was carried from beyond the river over our Paul's steeple." Some of the churches were "much damnified," stone walls were hurled to the ground, and "two houses torne down in an instant to the dreadful amazement of the spectators." This stern visitation, the story of which was duly attested at the end of the pamphlet by Mithnal the mayor, Gardener the recorder, Christy the lawyer, and Rush the waggoner, would probably have been accepted by the Church at Bedford, as nature's own symbol of that other storm through which they themselves had been passing during the years between the Restoration of 1660 and the Declaration of Indulgence of 1672. We have followed Bunyan's personal fortunes during this period, it may be well now to go back and see what was happening to his brethren in the church while he was spending his time in gaol.

It was but a trifling matter, perhaps, but it was a significant sign of altered times when the Corporation of Bedford, in

1661, admitted into the Town Guild as burgesses, and as a special mark of distinction, four of the five justices who a few months before had sent Bunyan to Bedford gaol, Kelynge, Chester, Beecher, and Blundell. To the same honour, also, and at the same time they received Wingate's brother-in-law, Foster, whom Bunyan had described as "a right Judas," and of whose hard hand the Nonconformists of Bedfordshire were to have such stern experience for some years to come.

Nationally, too, as well as locally, there were omens of stormy weather. One Sunday evening, some seven weeks after Bunyan's arrest, a riot had broken out in the City of London among some Fifth Monarchy men, led by a wine-cooper named Venner. Phrenzied by literal interpretations of the book of Revelation, these fanatics rushed out into the streets in the neighbourhood of St. Paul's, intending at once to set about the destruction of the mystical Babylon, the overthrow of monarchy, and the setting up of the reign of King Jesus. In this mad venture many of them lost their lives, some being slain in the outbreak, and thirteen brought to the scaffold afterwards. But this was the least of the mischief. This escapade of theirs brought results of the most serious kind to many innocent people throughout the country. The men who had just grasped the reins of power were on the outlook for some plausible excuse for putting down the worship of Noncomformists, and here it was ready to their hand. They were not slow to use it. The very day after the riot was suppressed, a proclamation was issued from Whitehall "for restraining all seditious meetings and conventicles under pretence of religious worship, and forbidding any meetings for worship, except in parochial churches or chapels." The Quakers and Baptists were expressly named in the proclamation along with the Fifth Monarchy men, and though the Independents were not actually named they knew themselves to be involved in the consequences. Venner had himself protested that these people were no associates of his; twenty of the London ministers among the Independents published a manifesto, declaring their abhorrence of the rebellion, and their loyalty to the King and his government; thirty-five of the Baptist ministers did the same; and George Fox with others published "A declaration from the harmless and innocent people called Quakers, against all sedition, plotters, and fighters in the world."

It was all to no purpose. What small respect had hitherto been shown for the King's promise from Breda, ceased altogether, and soon the silenced and imprisoned were to be counted by scores over the country.

Exactly four months after the Venner insurrection, the new parliament met on the 8th of May, 1661. The great majority of its members were cavaliers, old and young, and Church of England men to the backbone. Their mettle was quickly shown by the way they began business. The first thing they did was to pass a resolution that every member of the House should receive the sacrament on a fixed day, according to the form prescribed in the liturgy, and scrutineers were to report defaulters. To this parliament there went up from Bedfordshire, Lord Bruce and Sir John Winch for the county, and Sir John Kelynge and Richard Taylor for the borough. The next month the House set about the Act of Uniformity, Sir John Kelynge being appointed with others to draw up the Bill, which was read for the first time on the 14th of January, 1662. The House was prepared for much, but a measure so drastic roused strong resistance even in such a parliament as that. It was opposed at every step, and important as its consequences have been for more than two centuries, it was only passed eventually by a majority of six, the numbers being 186 for and 180 against.

The difficulties in the way of the Bill in the House of Lords were even greater than those in the Commons, some of the peers wishing to exempt schoolmasters, and ministers acting as tutors. There was a conference of the two Houses, when the Lords, more liberal than the Commons, reminded the latter of the King's declarations from Breda in favour of tender consciences, the Commons replying that a schismatical conscience was not a tender conscience. But at length, after much delay, the Bill passed the Lords on the 8th of May. It was still hoped, however, that considering the narrow majority in the Commons, and the opposition in the Lords, the royal assent would be withheld. It was a time of much anxiety through the country. Good Philip Henry of Broad Oak wrote in his journal, "A severe Act has passed both Houses of Parliament, but it is not yet signed by the King. Lord, his heart is in Thy hand; if it be Thy will, turn it; if otherwise, fit Thy people to suffer, and cut short the work in righteousness." It was even so; hopes were vain and fears well-founded, for the King gave his assent on the 19th of May, when the Act of Uniformity became law.

While other matters were involved of merely temporary interest, the two provisions in the Act of vital moment were the one which required that every minister in the Church should before the 24th of August, openly, publicly, and solemnly read the morning and evening prayer, and after such reading, openly and publicly declare before the congregation his unfeigned assent and consent to everything contained in the Book of Common Prayer; and the other which made episcopal ordination indispensable to every minister in the Church, no matter whether previously ordained in any other way or not. The first of these provisions, as Hallam says, amounts in common use of language to a complete approbation of an entire volume, such as a man of sense hardly gives to any book; and the second at a stroke cut off the Anglican church from all the other Protestant churches of Europe. From the beginning of the Reformation it had not been unusual to admit ministers ordained in foreign Protestant churches to benefices in England, without requiring re-ordination. This no longer suited the passion and policy of the time, and was brought to an end.

These, then, were the terms of continuance about which there was to be no temporizing. Refusal of assent was to be followed by forfeiture of benefice; any person preaching after being disqualified should be subject to three months' imprisonment, and any person acting as a minister of the Church of England, without having received episcopal ordination, no matter what his previous ordination might have been, should be liable to a penalty of £100.

Upwards of two thousand ministers of the Church, devout and, as they showed by the sacrifices they made, conscientious men, felt that the conditions were such as they could not accept. On the ever-memorable 24th of August, 1662, the Black Bartholomew of the English Church, they went forth from their livings and their flocks, the greater part of them not knowing whither they went. Thirteen of these were from Bedfordshire. The ejected clergy from this county were William Millington of Cardington, William Wheeler of Cranfield, Robert Perrot of Deane, Samuel Fairclough of Houghton Conquest, John Hind of Milton, John Donne of Pertenhall, James Mabbison of Roxton, Edward Rolt of Tempsford, William Shepherd of Tilbrook, William Blagrave of Woburn, William Dell of Yelden, William Willows, and William Milburn. Edward Fowler of Northill was dissatisfied at first, but ultimately conformed, and was eventually made Bishop of Gloucester. John Thornton, the chaplain at Woburn Abbey, though losing no incumbency by the Act of Uniformity, yet was kept out of preferment by it, and lived and died a Nonconformist. During the life of the first Duke of Bedford he still remained at the Abbey, reading mathematics with Lord William Russell, and afterwards residing with Lady Rachel till he lost his sight and retired into private life.[1] It is pleasant to find that old Mr Ashurst, the vicar of Arlsey, though at heart a Nonconformist, was not disturbed. He was a kind, good man, revered by the whole parish for his piety and humility, and as he had been eposcopally ordained, and his eminent parishioner, Justice Brown, stood his friend, he was allowed to continue, and permitted to read and practise as much as he believed, and to leave the rest. Edward Stillingfleet, also, as rector of Sutton, sheltered in his own rectory one of the ejected ministers, and took a large house in the parish for another, his old friend, Richard Kennett, the ejected minister of East Hatley, starting him in a school there, which was supported by the neighbouring gentry. Kennett, who was related to the father of the Bishop of Peterborough of that name, lived on at Sutton till 1670, when he died of fever, and was buried in the chancel of the church. These evasions of the law were less difficult in the diocese of Lincoln, perhaps, than elsewhere, inasmuch as Bishop Laney was more tolerant than most bishops of his time. "Not I but the law," said he to his clergy, and to use his own expression, he could look through his fingers, as he evidently did.

The Church at Bedford, having lost its minister by death some three months after the Restoration, was deprived of its place of meeting two years before the Act of Uniformity came into force. Had John Burton lived longer, he would probably have added one more to the ejected clergy of Bedfordshire, in 1662, but, dying as he did at the very crisis of change, the living at St. John's fell vacant at a time when the Corporation were little likely to appoint a successor acceptable to the Church which had worshipped there for seven years past. The brethren there-

[1] *Letters of Rachael Lady Russell*, i., 114.

fore found themselves deprived of their place of meeting as early as the autumn of 1660. After this they met where they could, sometimes in each other's houses in the town, and sometimes in the barns and kitchens of farm-houses in the country round. In 1670, ten years later, we find them meeting for worship at John Fenn's house in the High Street; and from the records they kept it appears that they held their meetings also at Hawnes and Cotten End, villages about four miles distant, at Edworth on the Hertfordshire borders, and at Gamlingay in Cambridgeshire, some fifteen miles away. The following are the minutes of the church between 1660 and 1663:

"At a meeting of the Church ye latter part of ye 8th moneth [Nov. 7th]. It having been the agreement of the churches together that if the Lord should remove any pastors or teachers from any of us, that we should advise with our brethren in the other Congregations, with respect to our future choyce; we are agreed that letters be sent to our brother Wheeler, brother Donne and brother Gibbs, to meet with our brother Eston, brother Grew, brother Whitbread, brother Harrington, brother ffenne, the 8th day of the next moneth; these brethren being deputed by the Church to conferre with them, about our affaires in ye matter.

"We are agreed to set apart ye 12th of ye next moneth to seeke the Lord in ye behalfe of the congregation, that God would directe and keepe us in such a time as this; and also for all the churches of God and for ye nation, that he would direct our governors in their meeting together.

"ffor as much as some of our brethren and sisters have neglected to come to our Church meetings, and their withdrawing giveth very ill example to others, we are agreed to desire our brother Eston, brother Grew, brother Whiteman, and brother Harrington to take some time speedily to speake to them seriously concerning their withdrawing from us, and to mind them of their duty.

"At a meeting of ye Church the latter part of ye 9th moneth [Dec.]. We having according to our agreement last Church meeting sent to our brethren afore mentioned to meet with and advise with us about ye choyce of a Pastor; and before y^t^ meeting a considerable company of the brethren of our Society met together, and upon debate thought to make choyce of Mr. Wheeler, and when our saide brethren were come we imparted our thought to y^em^, and to our brother Wheeler, whose answer was That he would consider the thing and seek the Lord y^t^ he might see his hand leading him to us, and also that it might be mentioned to that congregation where he is a member, and to that end we have wrote a letter to Mr. Gibbs, teacher of that congregation. It is agreed that brother Whitbread be desired to speake a word to us the next Church Meeting.

"At a meeting of ye Church the latter part of ye 10th moneth [Jan.]. Whereas some of our brethren and sisters have absented themselves, and our visiting of them by certaine of our members hath for some time bene layde by; we desire our sister Cooper and sister Bishop to speake with sister Wheeler and sister Peacock fully about their withdrawing, and to give an account to the Church of the frame of their spirits. Our sister Warner being in affliction by the losse of her husband and streights also as to her outward state, we desire brother John Fenne and brother Harrington to go visit her and give an account to the Church of her condition.

"1661. Our meetings (viz. of this sort) having bene for some time neglected through the increase of trouble, the 28th of the 6th moneth [Sept. 28th], 1661, the Church through mercy againe met: agreed, That whereas certaine of our friends have not onely withdrawne themselves, but also otherwaies failed, some of our ffriends be sent to admonish them of the same, viz.: Our brother Samuell ffenne to Sister Pecock of Okely, and sister Phebe Gibbs; our brother Bunyan to brother Robert Nelson and Sister Manly, &c.

"26th of the 7th moneth [26th Oct.]: There was received into fellowship with this congregation Thomas Cooper. The next 6th day of the week was appointed to be spent in prayer. We desire brother Bunyan and brother John ffenne to go againe to Sister Pecock. And that brother Harrington to visit brother Wallis being sick: and brother John ffenne Sister Coote.

"Latter part of the 8th moneth [Nov.]. Our brother John Croker and Richard Deane were admitted to have comunion with us. We are agreed that next 2nd day of the week come sevennight be set apart to seek God. Brethren were also appointed to repaire to brother Nelson and in the name of the Church acquaint him with their sense of his disorder, and as much as in them lyeth indeavour his sense and reformation of his miscarriage.

"It is also agreed and desired that the severall members of the Church be all visited betwixt this and the next Church Meeting; and that the members intrusted with that worke and duty be all present at ye next meeting and give an account of their performance therein. ffor visiting the members inhabitinge at Bedford is appointed brother John ffenne, and brother Croker, and brother Harrington and brother Samuel ffenne; ffor Cardington, brother Whiteman and brother Whitbread; ffor Kempston, brother William Wallis and brother English; ffor Okely and ffensom, brother Paine; ffor Wilshamstead, Houghton, and Hanes, brother Aseldine and brother Man; ffor Elvestow, brother Holstock.* These deputed members may as they shall see occasion from what they heare or observe deale severally with them that they visit; and desire their generall appearance, if it may be, at the next Church meeting.

* *Vide* Appendix.

"1662. At ye meeting of the Church the 15th of the second moneth [15th May], 1662: It is agreed that brother Donne, brother Wheeler, brother Gibbs, and brother Holcroft be desired to spend their paines with us once in three weekes by turnes: Mr. Donne ye 4th day of the 3rd moneth [4th June]: brother Wheeler that day 3 weekes; brother Holcroft, the 3rd first day after, and Mr. Gibbs the 3rd day after.

"Also that it be inquired of the Pastors in London whether the pastor of one Congregation do administer the ordinance of the supper to another Congregation; and on what Scripture grounds they do it or refuse.

"1663. At a meeting of the Church in Bedford the beginning of the 10th moneth [Jan.], '63. The former intention and desire of the Church that Mr. Wheeler should minister unto them in the office of a pastor or elder, not being prosecuted; by reason partly of the unwillingness of the congregation whereof he was a member to give him up to us and also his owne unwillingness upon that account; and partly because the Church here afterwards thought it not convenient to presse it, least it might indeed proove a disadvantage to their brethren aforesaide: The Church (notwithstanding their sore persecutions now come upon them) having spent many dayes in prayer with fasting, to seeke a right way of the Lord in this matter; did joyntly make choyce of brother Samuell ffenne (now lately delivered out of prison) and brother John Whiteman for their pastors and elders, to minister the word and ordinances of Jesus Christ to them; and they at this meeting did solemnely before God and the Lord Jesus Christ, and the elect angells, give up themselves to serve, feed, and watch over this congregation, for Jesus' sake (according to the charge layde upon them and accepted by them) according to the measure of grace received.

"At a meeting of the Church the latter part of the 10th moneth [Jan.], Bedford. There was received into fellowship with this congregation our Sister Barker of Kempston.

"At a meeting of ye Church at Hanes the 22nd of the 11th moneth [22nd Feb.]: God appearing in his glory to build up his Zion, there was with joy received into fellowship with this congregation Jonah Whittimore, Henery Warde, Elizabeth Maxye, Sister Locke, and Joane Layton.

"At the meeting of the Church at Bedford ye 28th of the 11th moneth [28th Feb.], there was received into fellowship with us Eleazar Hawkins and Mary ffosket.

"At a meeting of the Church at Hanes, the 26th of the 12th moneth [26th March], the Church received to walke in fellowship with them, Sister Whittimore, Mary Locke, brother Foxe and Oliver Thody.

"At another Church meeting at Hanes were received to walke in fellowship with the congregation, brother Warren and Sister Warren, Sister Lee, and Sister Randall."

. . . .

This was the last entry for 1663, after which there comes a long and ominous gap of five years and a half, the next recorded meeting of the Church being held at Hawnes on the 9th of September, 1668. To understand the meaning of this break in the records we must briefly recall the policy of the nation in the interval.

The immediate effect of the Act of Uniformity was to drive through the nation that line of cleavage which has continued ever since. There had, of course, been varied phases of Nonconformity before, but never so distinctly defined and separated as after 1662. Henceforth there were on one side of the line those who accepted Episcopacy and conformed to its ritual and requirements, and on the other the Nonconformists, who, as they contended, on scriptural grounds declined to do this and preferred a simpler and freer worship. Between these two opposing parties there was to be for years no truce or parley. The Act of Uniformity having become law, Clarendon, as he himself says, "thought it absolutely necessary to see obedience paid to it without any connivance." The policy of the Church towards Nonconformity was therefore to be a policy of stamping out. It remained to be seen which side could hold out longest. As Beza said to the King of France, it is the part of the Church to suffer rather than to strike, but it is an anvil that has worn out a good many hammers. In the days of the second Charles it was destined to wear out one hammer more.

Not that the king himself had very much heart in the high-handed policy of the Chancellor and the House of Commons. If under his easy-going indolence he had any serious purpose at all, it was to obtain toleration for the Roman Catholics. He had a secret policy of his own with the Pope apart from Clarendon. At a private meeting of leading Roman Catholics, held at the house of the Earl of Bristol, it was agreed that the best policy for them to pursue would be to bestir themselves for a toleration of all Nonconformists. Burnet, who is probably right, says that though the Earl of Bristol was the one seen moving in the matter, the real designer out of sight was the king himself. Be that as it may, on the 26th of December, 1662, and therefore before the Act of Uniformity was more than a few months old, there went forth from the Court at Whitehall a declaration of a General Religious Toleration, stating that in the next Session of Parliament the king would ask the House to concur with himself in devising some means of freeing from the penalties of the Act those who living peaceably desired.

"through scruple or tenderness of misguided conscience," to worship in their own way. It was a distinct challenge of Clarendon's policy, and the House of Commons was not slow to take it up on his behalf. The only effect of this attempt to secure greater liberty for the Nonconformists was to stir up at once a more determined animosity against them. The passing of the Conventicle Act was the answer of Parliament to the appeal from the Crown. This Act provided that the first offence of being in a conventicle or meeting of more than five persons in addition to the members of a family, for any religious purpose not in conformity with the Church of England, should be punished with a fine of £5 or three months' imprisonment, the second with a fine of £10 or six months', and the third, after trial and conviction at the Assize or Quarter Sessions, by transportation for seven years, unless the person convicted redeemed himself by paying down £100. The Act was to come into operation on the 1st of July, 1664, and to be in force for three years.

This Act is the explanation of the long and ominous silence in the Bedford Church book. The members of that Church still kept up their meetings for worship, as is shown by the remonstrances afterwards addressed to those who stayed away from them; but their gatherings were in secret places, and they kept no minutes of their proceedings. In prison and out, fined and ruined by accumulated fines, they went on their way for five years. Some quailed before the storm, "breaking covenant with God, and fellowship with this congregation," or "recanting their profession at a General Quarter Sessions," or being "openly and profanely bishopt to the great profanation of God's order and the heartbreaking of their Christian brethren." But there was always a stouthearted remnant who stood firm and quailed not.

The Act of Uniformity fell mainly upon the ministers among the Nonconformists, the Conventicle Act upon the people. In October, 1665, the Five Mile Act followed the Conventicle Act, and was another blow aimed at the ministers, banishing them under a penalty of £40 to a distance of five miles from any city or town-corporate, or borough sending members to Parliament, or any parish or place where they had formerly preached or taught. The chief promoters of this heartless and cruel measure were Clarendon, Archbishop Sheldon, and Dr. Seth Ward, Bishop of Salisbury, and its immediate effect was to banish hundreds of blameless men, deprived of their livings and struggling for bread, to a distance from all their friends, into obscure places where there was no chance of earning a livelihood.

But if it was an ill time for the Nonconformists, it was by no means a good time for the nation. The great Plague cast its dark shadow, and the great Fire its lurid glare, not only over the city they devastated, but over the whole land of which that city was the capital. The profligates of the Court were appalled for the moment, and even the king "had been heard during that time to speak with great piety and devotion of the displeasure that God was provoked to." But with the king, as with some other people, pious reflections were not necessarily followed by pious behaviour. The old life of sensuality went its old vicious round. In the nation credit was sinking, money misspent, and the war with the Dutch taking bad ways. But the shock most startling and most humbling of all came when the Dutch actually sailed up the Thames and the Medway, and there was no one to stop them, "everybody flying, none knew why or whither." As the citizens were packing up their valuables and sending them into the country and there was talk of removing the Court to Windsor, the high-spirited English nation, more accustomed to invade than to be invaded, were led to reflect. Now, if never before, they began to think it would have been well, had it been possible, to have Cromwell back for awhile. "It is strange," says Pepys, "how everybody do nowadays reflect upon Oliver and commend him, what brave things he did and made all the neighbour princes fear him; while here a prince, come in with all the love and prayers and good liking of his people, hath lost all so soon, that it is a miracle what way a man could devise to lose so much in so little time."

In the crash of that evil time came down Clarendon, the ruling spirit of persecution, and with the fall of the minister the monarch assumed more direct control. With the ascendancy of Clarendon's successors there came relaxations of the severities against Nonconformists. The Parliament was unchanged. Even though it had spent a large part of the Session of 1667-8 in impeaching Clarendon and banishing him from the country, it was itself, as has been said, "in two-thirds of its bulk still an obdurate mass of unmitigated Clarendonianism in all matters ecclesiastical." The Conventicle Act expired on the 2nd of March, 1667-8, and Parliament set about renewing the Act;

indeed, the bill for that purpose had passed the Commons on the 28th of April by 144 votes to 78; but before it could pass the Lords, on the 9th of May the two Houses adjourned by the king's desire, and the Act was therefore not renewed.

It was seventeen months before Parliament met again, and, as there was now no Conventicle Act, during that brief breathing time the Nonconformists enjoyed more liberty than they had done since 1663. Both in London and the country they were connived at, and people went openly to their meetings, without fear. John Bradshaw, the vicar of St. Paul's in Bedford, thought indeed that this liberty, small as it was, would be the country's ruin. In a letter to the Dean of Lincoln, dated June 13th, 1668, he says, "The separatists increase daily. God amend all things in this nation." This accounts for the fact that in 1668 the Church at Bedford held its meetings again and commenced once more, after five years and a half, that record of its acts which has never been interrupted since. Forthwith we come upon the following entries, which must have been recorded with very mingled feetings:

"1668. At a meeting of the Church at Hanes, the 9th of the 7th moneth [9th Oct.], '68, We then received Sister Heath and Sister Halle, of Clophill, to walke in fellowship with us.

"At Bedford ye 25th of the 7th moneth [25th Oct.], There was received with gladness into comunion with this Church Thomas Hunilove, and Edward Isaac and his wife.

"Bedford, ye 30th day of the 8th moneth [30th Nov.]. Many of the friends having in these troublous times withdrawne themselves from close walking with the Church and not being reclaimed by those admonitions, that, as time would serve, had been sent to them formerly, some also being guilty of more grosse miscarriages, the Congregation having kept certaine days with fasting and prayer, bewailed their fall, did now agree in a solemne way to renew their admonitions; And did agree That brother Samuel ffenne and brother John ffenne and brother Bunyan should speake with brother Robert Nelson and admonish him for his withdrawing from the Church and other miscarriages. And that brother Samuell ffenne and brother John Croker go to our brother Richard Deane to admonish him and rebuke him for his withdrawing from the assemblyes of the saints, and to inquire into ye truth of those scandalous reports that we heare concerning him. It was desired also that brother Bunyan and brother Harrington send for brother Merrill and admonish him concerning his withdrawing from the Church and his conformity to ye world's way of worship. And brother Bunyan and brother Cooper were appointed to go to brother Coventon to admonish him and endeavour his conviction for his sin in withdrawing from the Church assemblyes.

"1669. Bedford, the 14th of y[e] 3rd moneth [14th June], '69: There was received into comunion with this congregation brother John Wileman and Nehemiah Coxe, and John Spencer was desired to waite a while longer.

"Bedford, the 10th day of y[e] 6th moneth [10th Sept.]. It was proposed to the Church to consider of some others to be chosen to the office of deacons for tryall, the worke lying too hard on brother John ffenne. It was farther agreed upon by the Church that brother George Skelton should be againe admonished either by word of mouth or by letter as soone as possible may be: for his inhumane carriage towards his wife and children, and other evills which he stands guilty of. The Church also having taken notice of the utter neglect of brother Coventon and brother Wallis in the executing of the office of a deacon, whereunto they had formerly bene appointed, did judge them unworthy of that honourable employment, and divest them of all authority and trust of that nature comitted to them formerly.

"Bedford, the 14th of the 7th moneth [14th Oct.]: William Man and John Crocker gave an account to the Church of their visiting and requiring Humphrey Merrill, Richard Deane, and Edward Coventon to come to their Church meeting, whose carriage was as followeth: As for brother Merrill, though their words and carriage were so winning and full of bowells that he could not well breake out into that impatiency as he had sometimes done; yet after some windings he began in an obscure way to charge the Church with rebellion and also with taking some portions of Scripture that made for their purpose and refusing the other. To which things, though he was fully answered, yet to their last entreaty of him to come before the Church he peremptorily, with great confidence, replyed That he knew them well enough already and would have no more to do with them, bidding them do their worst, saying, Their faire speeches should not flatter him, &c. Richard Deane seemed more yielding: These things considered, the Church thought good to send brother John Bunyan and brother John Whiteman once more to admonish them. They found not Robert Wallis at home, nor Robert Nelson, therefore brother Bunyan and brother John ffenne were again appointed to admonish him.

"Bedford, y[e] 14th of the 8th moneth: Our brethren appointed to go to brother Coventon, related that they had done their message, but he gave them no answer; but that brother Wallis did very Christianly receive them, acknowledging his owne guilt and sin in w[th]drawing, &c., promising in the strength of Christ to indeavour reformation for time to come; who also was at this meeting and gave consent to the choosing of brother Man and brother Crocker as deacons, at which our hearts were gladded.

"Bedford, the 16th of the 9th moneth [16th Dec.]: The brethren that were appointed to visit those under admonition, did relate their carriage as followeth: Brother Coventon is through mercy hopefully recovering from his backsliding. Richard Deane did acknowledge himself not sensible as yet, but desired the prayers and patience of the Church. It was agreed that brother Bunyan and brother Breeden should go to Humphrey Merrill, and brother Bunyan and brother Whiteman to Richard Deane.

"Bedford, the 14th of the 10th moneth [14th Jan.]: It was agreed that Humphrey Merrill (still refusing admonition) should, the next Church meeting, be cut off from this congregation of God if repentance prevent not. It was agreed that an admonition be prepared to be sent to brother William Whitbread, for withdrawing from the Church and ordinances of God. It was agreed also that brother Bunyan and brother Man should reason with Mr. Sewster about his desire of breaking bread with this congregation w^th^out sitting downe as a member with us. Also that brother Sam. ffenne and brother Bunyan should discourse with Sister Landy about those scruples that lye upon her conscience about breaking bread with this congregation. The congregation also having taken into consideration the desire of Gamlingay friends to joyne with us, did agree that next meeting they should come over and give in their experience.

"At a full assembly of this Congregation, the 21st day of the 10th moneth [21st Jan.]: Humphrey Merrill was cut off from, and cast out of this Church of Christ, ffor—

"1. Breaking covenant with God and fellowship with this congregation.

"2. ffor an open recanting his profession at a General Quarter Sessions.

"3. And rejecting and trampling upon the admonitions and intreaties, and all indeavours of the Church to recover him to amendment of life: disdainefully returning for their care and indeavours to reclaime him such ungodly railings as these: That they had their hands in the blood of the King: that they were disobedient to government, and that they were not a Church; despising also the gifts of and doctrines of God in the Congregation: together with severall other false and heinous accusations.

"Testified by these brethren:

Joh. Croker.	Joh. Bunyan.
Tho. Cooper.	Will. Man.
Sam. ffenne.	Joh. Whiteman.
	Will. Breeden.

"Received at the same time these brethren by name: Oliver Scott, Wm. Scott, Edward Dent, John Thornely, Ralph Underhand, Luke Astwood, Nicholas Malings, Samuell Smith, James Giddins. [The brethren from Gamlingay referred to at the previous meeting.]

"Bedford, 4th of the 11th moneth [4th Feb.]: There was received with gladness into this congregation brother Samuell Henceman, Joh. Henceman, and Susannah Cooper. The work of repentance goes hopefully on in brother Coventon, who now frequents our meetings.

"Bedford, 25th day of the 11th moneth [25th Feb.], 1669—70. Brother Samuell ffenne and brother Bunyan declared that according to the Church's desire they discoursed with Sister Landy and found her willing to receive instruction, and therefore were appointed againe by the Church as occasion served to endeavour her farther satisfaction. Our brother Bunyan and brother Samuell ffenne were ordered to write to yᵉ adjacent congregations to let them understand the Churches proceedings against Humphrey Merrill.

"1670. Bedford, the 25th day of the 2nd moneth [25th May]. Brother John ffenne certifyed the Church that he and brother Bunyan had indeavoured to speake with Richard Deane, but (he continually indeavouring to avoide their delivering their message by keeping out of the way) they could by no means accomplish it, whereupon the Church did agree shortly to proceed farther with him.

"Bedford, 8th day of the 3rd moneth [8th June]. The Church appointed brother Samuell ffenne and brother Bunyan farther to discourse with Sister Landy and to relate to them in what frame they find her.

"1671. Bedford, the 21st day of the 1st moneth [21st April]. Robert Nelson and Richard Deane were cut off from and cast out of this Congregation. Brother Whiteman and brother Neh. Coxe were appointed to declare to Rich. Deane the just and fearful sentence that in the name and power of the Lord Jesus had bene denounced against him. As for Rob. Nelson it is to be considered which way notice may be given him thereof also, because for the present he cannot be spoken with. It was agreed also that an Epistle should be sent to yᵉ churches of Christ in and about Keyshowe, Newport Pagnell, and Steventon, to acquaint them with the Churches proceedings in the case afore mentioned. The copy of the letter sent to each of them here followeth: Dearly beloved brethren: Grace be with you by Jesus Christ your Lord and oures. Amen. Blessed be God and the ffather of our Lord Jesus Christ for the grace bestowed upon you, brethren, and for the faith you have in the Lord Jesus and your love to all the Saints. We, your brethren, the Congregation of Christ in and about Bedford, give you to understand what troubles have come upon us by reason of Robert Nelson and Richard Deane, persons sometimes members of this congregation, but now cut off and cast out from the Church of God for these wickednesses following:

"Things laide to yᵉ charge of Richard Deane:

"1. ffor that he after a very ungodly manner separated himself from this congregation and the word and ordinances of Christ therein.

"2. He after this lived a loose and ungodly life accompanyed with defrauding in his calling; selling to severall persons deceitfull goodes, to the great scandall of our profession.

"3. ffor speaking contemptuously of the Church.

"4. He went in the name of the Church, particularly naming Joh.

Bunyan and Sam. ffenne, and yet wholly without their knowledge or consent, to beg the charity of ye good people of St. Neots; ffor all which things, and many others, he hath bene admonished, by the space of some years; yet could not be brought to repentance for the same.

"Robert Nelson's practices were as followeth:

"1. He forsooke the Church with the order of the Gospell therein.

"2. In a great assembly of the Church of England, he was openly and profanely bishopt after the Antichristian order of that Generation; to ye great profanation of God's order and heartbreaking of his Christian brethren.

"ffor these he hath bene often admonished, and that for the space of sixe or seven yeares, but hath contemned and slighted the same. And besides he hath so trampled upon our holy order and fellowship, that for the space of eight or nine yeares, he could not be gotten to be present at any of our Church Assemblyes.

"Wherefore we warne and beseech you in the name of our Lord Jesus Christ, that as occasion or opportunity offereth itself you carry it towards them in all things, as becometh a people that keep faithfull with the Lord.

"Written by the appointment of the congregation, and on their behalf signed by:

"Sam. ffenne. Joh. Whiteman.
Joh. Bunyan. Joh. ffenne."

If however there were thus in the little Bedford community those who, after running well, had been hindered and caused pain and heartbreak to their Christian brethren, there were others, as the following entries show, whose consistency and steadfastness were cause for gratitude.

"In the latter part of the yeare 1669 our brother Harrington being driven from his family to avoyde being taken with a writ De Excom. capiend., and other friends having of long time had their habitation at a distance from us, the Congregation did appoint the Elders in their names to write certaine letters to them for their comfort and edification, the copyes of some of them (which were sent with ye Churches full approbation) being now come to hand are here inserted.

"To our brother Harrington was sent this following" [from which, as being evidently from Bunyan's hand, some extracts may here be given]:

"Dearly beloved brother, Grace, mercy, and peace be with you alwayes. With length of dayes is understanding; your long progresse in the wayes of God and our ffather, hath given you rich experience. Wherefore, brother, make it manifest that you are one of those scribes we read of, not only instructed into but unto the Kingdome of God. Gravity becometh the ancients of the House of God: ffathers should be examples unto children. We are comforted in the remembrance of thee, brother, while we consider that, notwithstanding thy naturall infirmity yet thou prizest good conscience above thine owne injoyments: and since thou couldest not with quiet injoy it at home, thou hast left thy concernes in this world (though in much hazzard and danger) that thou mayest keep it abroad. But remember that good word of God: no man shall desire thy Land when thou shalt go up to appeare before the Lord thy God, thrice in ye yeare. Wherefore let neither the remembrance of what thou hast left, nor thought of its being subject to casualty either distract thee in thy comunion with God, or prevaile with thee to do aught against good conscience, or unworthy thy gray haires; which are then the glory of old men when found in the way of righteousnes.

"You, brother Harrington, have lived to see the slippery and unstable nature that is in earthly things; wherefore we beseech you to expect no more therefrom, then the word of God hath promised, which is as much in little as in much thereof, if not more in many respects. While Israell sate by the fleshpots in Egypt they had no manna from heaven, they dranke not the water out of the Rock. We hope it is because God loveth you that he hath driven you from your incumbrances, that you may have occasion before you dye to solace yourself with your God and the Lord Jesus Christ. We meane that you may doe it with more leisure and lesse distraction than when ye lowing of the oxen had continuall sound in your eares.

"God is wise, and doth all things for the best for them that love him. You know not but you shall know afterwards what sins and temptations God hath prevented by driving you thus from your habitation, and how hereby he made way for the exercise of some graces that could not so well discover themselves in their virtues when you was here. How subject we are to dote upon and to be intangled with the snares that lye couched and hid in the things of this present world, you have had great experience with us. When we are desolate then we trust in God, and make prayers and supplications to him night and day. God help you, therefore, that you spend your vacant houres not as they that wept for Tammuz, but as they who plainely confesse to all they are strangers and pilgrims in the earth. Arm yourself with y^t^ mind you read of, Heb. xii. 2, 3, 4, that you may have your garments alwayes white, and that your head may lack no oyntment. You cannot be there where no eyes are upon you. You are a spectacle to God, Angells, and Men; and being exalted to ye profession of Christianity, and also to the comunion of God and his saintes, you can neither stand nor fall by yourself, but the name and cause and people of God shall in some sense stand and fall with you. Yea, let us have joy in thee, brother, refresh our spirits in the Lord. And remember that God hath saide, Though there were of you cast out to the uttermost part of heaven, yet will I gather them from thence, and will bring them unto the place that I have chosen to set my name there.

"ffinally, brother, ffarewell. Grace be with thee. Amen.

"Written by the appointment of ye Congregation to which you stand related in ye faith of the Gospell, and subscribed with their consent by the hands of your brethren.

"John Whiteman.	Samuell ffenne.
John Bunyan.	Joh. ffenne, &c."

The next letter, "To our deare Sister Foxe," is not signed by Bunyan, and has nothing in it of his peculiar vein. The two following letters have his signature appended, and were evidently written by him. The first of these is "To our beloved Sister Katharine Hustwhat." After the usual greeting they go on to say:

"We heare (to our increase of joy) how our God supporteth thee in all temptations, and spirituall desertions, thou meetest with in ye world. The poor and afflicted people God will save. To be distressed and tempted while here is a manifestation of our predestination to the ease and peace of another world. Predestinated to be conformable, or (as in ye old translations) predestinate that we should be like fashioned unto the shape of his Son, a great part of which lyeth in our being distressed, tempted, afflicted as he. And therefore it is, when he was departing hence to the ffather, that he, as it were, looked back as over his shoulder to such, saying, You are they that have continued with me in my temptations; unto you I appoint a Kingdome, as my ffather hath appointed unto mee.

"Sister, thy keeping lowe and being emptied from vessell to vessell, is that thou mightest be kept sweet and more cleane in thy soule than thou wouldest or couldest otherwise be. The first wayes of David were his best, and yet those wayes were most accompanyed with affliction.

"They that are naked and lodge without clothing, that have no covering in the cold, and that are wet with the showres of the mountaines, these imbrace the Rock for want of a shelter. As outward distresses make us prize outward blessings, so temptations and affliction of soule make us prize Jesus Christ. He suffereth us to hunger and to wander in a bewildered condition, that we may tast and relish the words of God, and not live by bread alone. Temptations always provoke to spirituall appetite, and are therefore very necessary for us, yea, as needfull as worke and labour to the body, without which it would be overrun with diseases and unfit for any imployment. Therefore, our beloved Sister, stirre up the grace of God that is in thee, and lay hold by faith on eternall life; and count when thou art tempted much, yet the end of that temptation will come, the end and then effect. And remember that even our dearest Lord could not breake off the tempter in ye middle. But when Sathan had ended all the temptation, then he departed from him for a season.

"That Gospell which thou hast received is no cunningly devised fable, but the very truth and verity of God. Wherefore be not shaken in minde, or troubled with unbelief or Atheisme. Looke to the promise, looke to Jesus, looke to his blood, and what work it hath with the justice of God for sinners.

"Lastly, sister, ffarewell. Watch and be sober; have patience to the Coming of the Lord. And in the meane while looke to thy lamp. The Lord poure of his golden oyle into it, and also into the vessell of thy soule. Keepe thy worke before thee, and be renewed in the spirit of thy minde. Blessed are those servants whom the Lord when he cometh shall find so doing.

"Written by the appointment of this congregation, and subscribed by their consent by your dear brethren, who pray for you and intreat prayers for this despised handfull of the Lord's heritage.

"John Whiteman.
John Bunyan.
Will. Man, &c."

The last of the letters to the persecuted, preserved in the Church Book, was sent to John Wilson, afterwards the first pastor of the church at Hitchin. It is addressed:

"To our dear brother Joh. Wilson: We are comforted in thee, our dearely beloved, when we remember that from a childe thou hast knowne the Holy Scriptures, that in thy tender yeares thy faith was fruitfull, to the great comfort of us thy brethren. It is also joy to us to behold, that notwithstanding thy lot is cast in a place of high transgression, yet thou showest out of a good conversation thy works with meekness of wisdome. God help thee, brother, to remember the dayes of thy youth; the first wayes of David were best. There are but few can say as Caleb: As my strength was forty yeares since so it is now, both to go out and come in before the people of God. 'Tis also saide of Moses, to ye day of his death his naturall force was not abated, neither did his eye waxe dimme.

"Brother, be alwayes looking into the perfect Lawe of liberty and continue therein. The customes of the people are vaine; learne therefore of no man any of the deeds of darkenes. We must give an account of ourselves to God. It argueth not onely wisdome but great grace when the soul makes all lye levell to the word and Spirit of God; when he scorneth and counteth that unworthy of his affections that hath not on it a stamp of the things of heaven. It is saide of the children, especially the Elders of Israell, They saw God and did eat and drinke; that's the right eating and drinking indeed.

"Honoured brother, God hath not onely counted you worthy to believe in his Son, but also to professe him before ye world; weare his name in your forehead. They that Christ will owne for his Servants for ever, must say plainely, I love my Master; they must declare plainely they seek a country.

"'Tis saide of Hananiah he feared God above many. God continue our joy of thee, brother, our hope of thee is stedfast through grace. It is a strange sight to behold those who did feed delicately to be desolate in the street, and they that were brought up in scarlet to imbrace dunghills. We speake not these things to shame thee, but as our beloved brother we warne thee. O Timothy, keep that which is committed to thy trust; watch and be sober. And if thou incline to sleep, let that of Delilah rouze thee: the Philistines be upon thee, Sampson.

"Grace be with thee. The Lord is at hand. Behold, the judge stands at the doore; Amen. Even so come, Lord Jesus.

"Written by the appointment and subscribed in ye name and with the Consent of the Congregation, by

"Your brethren in the faith and patience of Christ, who also begge your prayers for this despised Congregation.

"Sam. ffenn.	Joh. Whiteman.	Joh. Bunyan.
Joh. ffenn.	Joh. Croker.	Will. Man, &c."

These letters, it will be remembered, were sent during the comparative lull in the storm which took place between the expiration of the Conventicle Act on the 2nd of March, 1668, and its re-enactment on the 11th of April, 1670. From the fact that letters were sent to those who had to flee from their homes, it will be evident that persecution continued all through the time the Act was in suspense. This is borne out by local evidence of the most indisputable kind, that of the Act Books of the Archdeacon's Court. The record of the proceedings of Dr. Foster as Commissary of that Court during the entire period the Conventicle Act was in force appears to have been lost from the Registry of the Archdeaconry. But, curiously enough, the minutes of proceedings relating to the very seventeen months when Parliament was not sitting, and when there was an abatement of the fury of the persecution, have been preserved, and show how little abatement there really was. Foster held eight Courts at the Visitations of the Archdeacon between May 6th, 1668, and October 8th, 1669—four at Bedford and four at Ampthill. Several of the cases that came before him related, of course, to the condition of the churches through the different deaneries of the county. At Pulloxhill, for example, it appears that the "Steeple is fallen down and the Vicarage house pulled down"; Stagsden chancel windows "want glasseing," and "Stevington Chancell is almost downe." So is the steeple at Arlsey, where they also want a vicar, from which we may conclude that good old Mr. Ashurst has by this time gone to Heaven. At Studham there is "neither surplice, communion cup, nor cushion for the pulpitt"; at Maulden they want "a Church Bible and a book of Homilyes"; at Farndish almost everything —"the Bible translated in King James his raigne, A hearse cloth, a book of homilies, a poore man's Box, a sufficient chest with Lock and Keyes for the Church Ornaments, and a Terriar of the Gleab Lands." Foster, therefore, at these Courts of his found work for the trowel as well as the sword. But the work of upbuilding was small in comparison with that of smiting down. The vast majority of the cases he dealt with, according to his own record, were those of Nonconformists, whom he fined, excommunicated, or imprisoned for refusing to pay church rates, dues, or tithes; for refusing to come to church for more than a month; for not having their children baptized; for being present at the buryall of an excommunicate person; for being at and keeping a conventicle; for refusing to receive the sacrament at Easter; for not being churched; for being absent from church six months; for teaching school without licence; and for standing excommunicate above forty days last past.

There were two or three special cases. John White, the undergaoler at Bedford, was presented for refusing to pay the church rate. He was at this time one of Bunyan's custodians, and may have been in some things of the same mind with his prisoner. If so, he lacked the constancy his prisoner showed, for he afterwards went to John Bradshaw at the Registry, and paid the rate. Henry Thurrowgood of Northill, was dealt with for burying his mother in a garden. Thomas Hawkins, of Dunstable, and Mary Herbert, for that they, "under pretence of a marriage after a phanatique manner, live together"; which means that they thought it sufficient to celebrate their marriage at the Quaker's Meeting. At Studham, George Seer, innholder, had been guilty of "keeping Conventicles on ye Lord's day, as the fame is"; so that for once the village inn was turned into the village place of prayer. But the great majority of the cases were those of persons refusing to come to church, or to pay rates, dues, or tithes.

Some idea may be formed of the vast amount of work Foster had to get through when we find that, during those two years, which were years of comparative exemption, more than fourteen hundred cases came before him for judgment from the towns, but chiefly from the villages of Bedfordshire. This includes great numbers of renewed cases of prosecution, as, for example, those of stout-hearted Quakers like Joshua Wheeler and Edward Franklyn of Cranfield, the Albrights and Colemans of Woodburne, the Laundrys of Bolnhurst, and the Rushes of Kempston, who were prosecuted at every one of the four Courts held for their respective deaneries. From all parts of the county, indeed, the most numerous and most persistent offenders were the Quakers, but there were also great numbers of Baptists and Independents, and a few Presbyterians. More than once we find the name of Lawrence Bunion, joiner, of Westoning, possibly a kinsman of the greater Bunyan then in Bedford gaol; and again and again there appear for judgment well-known members of the Bedford Church. The culprits who, in such continuous stream, were brought under the penalties of Foster's Court in 1668 and 1669, were from various grades of life. Some six or eight of them are styled esquire, from twenty to thirty, gentlemen, perhaps twenty are described as yeomen, and about as many more as farmers; but, as in all the persecutions which have fallen upon the Church of Christ through the ages, the vast majority were drawn from the ranks of artisans and the labouring poor. They were the great undistinguished crowd of cordwainers, hempdressers, husbandmen, weavers, warreners, plow-wrights, gardeners, fellmen, fullers, and the like. In deanery after deanery, and from village after village in Bedfordshire, their names stand recorded in the fading pages of Foster's Act Book, with his judgment and penalties written against them. But they make their appeal from his judgment to that of other tribunals—the tribunal of posterity and the tribunal of God, and they have not made their appeal in vain.

Dark and evil as had been the days from 1660 to the autumn of 1669, still darker and more evil days were preparing. Archbishop Sheldon had resolved that Nonconformity might be entirely uprooted and should be. He was convinced that its extent was greatly exaggerated, and that vigorously taken in hand it might soon be overcome. With intent to show this, and as the basis of future legislation, on the 8th of June he had written from Lambeth to the Commissary of the province of Canterbury, directing that inquiries should be made from the clergy in every parish as to all unlawful religious assemblies, what were the numbers attending them, of what sort of people they consisted, and who were their leaders and teachers? The returns are preserved among the *Tenison MSS.* at Lambeth, and are of considerable local interest. They are, of course, the returns of the enemies of Nonconformity, and contain inaccuracies, therefore, but are no doubt approximately true. Those for Bedfordshire are found among the papers relating to Lincoln Diocese.[1] They state that there is one Conventicle at Bedford, in the parish of St. Paul—number in attendance about 30; quality, the meanest sort; Heads and Teachers—"John Fenne, hatter; Thomas Honylove, cobbler; Samuel Fenne, hatter; and Thomas Cooper, heelemaker. The said Samuel Fenne and Thomas Cooper being lately apprehended at a Conventicle by a warrant from William Foster, Esq., one of his Majesty's Justices, and by him and John Gardner, Esq., one other Justice of the Peace, committed to gaol for six months, where they now remaine."

The next entry of interest is that relating to Bolnhurst, where there are two Conventicles reported, one for the Independents and one for the Quakers. The number attending at the former place is given at about 80; their quality "of meane condicion"; Head and Teacher—"John Donne, ejected out of the Rectory of Pertenhall. Upon the King's return he was apprehended teaching att a Conventicle by William Foster, Esq., J.P., and committed to the Gaol att Bedford where he should still remaine, have received his tryall upon the statute for Banishment of Conventiclers and convicted thereof. He usually preaches at his House at Keysoe." The number attending the Quaker Conventicle is not given, but their teachers are: "John Croot of Eversholt [probably John Crook], Richard Laundy, senr., a prisoner in Bedford Gaol upon a write *De Excom.* He is commonly att home and they doe preach att his house." The Independents, with the Quakers at Keysoe, are numbered at 100; quality, "the meanest," but their preachers numerous. There is a Presbyterian as well as a Quaker Congregation reported from Woburn, but the numbers are "not knowne," and a Society of "Freewillers" at Sundon, numbering 40. There were 40 Baptists at Pavenham, 50 at Stevington, 50 at Blunham, 20 at Edworth, 12 at Northill, 40 at Caddington, and 30 at Houghton Regis. The Quakers altogether are returned at 390; the Baptists at 277; and the Independents at 220, but the numbers in several villages besides are given as unknown or uncertain. The

[1] *Tenison MSS.*, 639. Acct. of Conventicles, 1669, Co. Bedford.

whole of the Nonconformists of the county are reported at about a thousand; which, after nine years of determined persecution and in a sparsely populated shire, was a remarkable result to have attained, and says much for the vitality of their convictions.

The Cavalier Parliament met again for its eighth Session, on October the 19th, 1669, and sat for only two months. But in those two months it fell again with fury upon the Nonconformists after their seventeen months' breathing time. Numerous informations and complaints were laid before the two Houses as to evasions of the Conformity Acts, and the increase of Conventicles and wooden "tabernacles" in London and elsewhere, and a Bill was again brought in for renewing the Conventicle Act. As Parliament was prorogued, however, on the 11th of December, there was no time to carry this Bill, which was deferred till the following Session.

On the 11th of April, 1670, the King gave his assent to the *New Conventicles Act.* It was more severe than the Act of 1664. Marvell calls it the "quintessence of arbitrary malice." It defined an Illegal Conventicle to be any meeting for worship otherwise than according to the practice of the Church of England which, if held in a house, should have present thereat more than four persons besides the family; or if in the fields or any uninhabited place, more than four persons in all. The penalty for the first offence of attending a Conventicle was five shillings, and for the second, ten shillings, for all persons over sixteen years of age; while the penalty for the preacher was to be £20 for the first offence, and £40 for every other; householders allowing such conventicles to be held on their premises were to forfeit £20 for each offence. To facilitate discovery and conviction one-third of the fine in every case was to go to the informer and his assistants. At every point the Act was made to breathe the resolute spirit of those who passed it into law. Justices of the Peace and constables were empowered to break open doors in carrying out its provisions, and Lieutenants and Deputy-lieutenants of Counties were to disperse assemblies with horse and foot, if necessary, and in any case of doubt, the Act was always to be interpreted in the way most favourable to the suppression of Conventicles.

This resolute spirit of oppression was met, as is usual in the case of Englishmen, with an equally resolute spirit of resistance.

The Act was passed on the 11th of April and, within a month, had come into active operation in the town of Bedford. "On Lord's day (*May* 15) at the dwelling-house of one *John Fen,* a haberdasher of Hatts, many persons being assembled for Religious Exercise: One *West* and *Fecknam* (two apparitors), by a warrant from one Mr. *Foster,* who is a Justice of Peace and the Commissaries' Deputy, did enter the House and force the Meeters to Mr. *Foster's* House,* who fined every one of them severally according to their reputed abilities, and committed the Preacher to Prison."[1] The following Friday, Thomas Battison,† a Churchwarden of St. Paul's, proceeded to levy the fines thus inflicted, beginning at the malt-house of John Bardolf. But John had been a little beforehand with the churchwarden and had sold his malt. The question arose, therefore, as the malt was no longer Bardolf's, whether it was legal to break open the malt-house door? While Battison and the other officers were debating this point in the open yard, "a great number of all sorts of persons were gathered about them, expressing (by turns) their indignation against him for attempting this against *Bardolf,* whom the whole Town knew to be a just and harmless man; and the common sort of people covertly fixing a Calves tayl to Battison's back, and deriding him with shouts and hollows, he departed without taking any distress there." This was not a good beginning; and, somewhat discomfited, the party made their way to the shop of Edward Covington, a grocer, to levy a fine of five shillings for his wife being at the meeting. Covington refusing to pay, Battison took a brass kettle for the fine, but when he had brought it to the street-door, the officers, probably afraid of the chaff of the crowd, refused to carry it away, and at last he had to pay a boy sixpence to carry it to an inn-yard; "but when the youth had carried the Kettle to the Inn-gate (being hooted at all the way by the common spectators), the Innkeeper would not suffer the Kettle to be brought into his yard, and so his man set it out in the middle of the Street."

"The next day, which was the market-day, the Justices understanding how *Battison* was discouraged in his work," and probably feeling that this brass-kettle affair was not a very dignified proceeding, "commanded the officers to break open the doors and levy the distresses. Immediately old *Battison,* with a file of soldiers and the constables, in the middle of Market-time,

* William Foster resided in a house with nine 'hearths' in Well Street Ward, Bedford.

† In 1670, Thomas Battison lived in a three-hearthed house in the Prebend Ward. The Editor possesses a copy of Charles Doe's Folio edition of Bunyan's works which bears the signature—'John Battison bought this book Annoy Dom 1692' (the year of its publication). There is also the name 'Joseph Battison, 1773.' Possibly John was the son of 'old' Battison.

[1] For the source of this and following extracts, see p. 208.

advanced again to the malt-house of *John Bardolfe* (scituate in an Inn-yard in the middle of the Market-place) and breaks open the doors and distreyned fourteen Quarters of Malt."

Still the brethren met for worship as usual next Sunday morning, as if nothing had happened:

"The next day being Lord's day, Fines were doubled upon the Meeters, before the first could be levied; for they assembling again at the same House, according to their custom, Battison with the two Apparitors, by another Warrant from Mr. Foster, entered the Meeting-place about nine of the clock in the morning: but the Meeters refusing to depart before their Exercise was ended (unless forced) Battison sends word of it to Mr. Foster, who returns a Verbal Order that Battison should charge certain Gentlemen of the Town (whose names he had sent by the messengers) to assist him; which Battison did, going to their houses to call them, though there were near a hundred common people spectators in the Streets. . . . About ten of the clock in the morning the Meeters went with Battison and the Apparitors (being constrained so to do) to the Swan in Bedford, where being kept till four of the clock in the afternoon, and their names taken by the Justices, they weer set at liberty."

"Next morning Mr. Foster, the Justice, appears early in the streets, with old Battison and the two Apparitors, a file of soaldiers and some constables, to see the Fines levied upon the Meeters' Goods; charging to his assistance such persons he sees, and sending for others to their houses, but got few or none besides his first company; most of the Tradesmen, Journeymen, Labourers, and Servants having either left the Town or hid themselves to avoid his call. The Town was so thin of people, that it looked more like a Country Village than a Corporation; and the shops being generally shut down, it seemed like a place visited with the Pest, where usually is written upon the Door, Lord have mercy upon us!"

But such assistance as he had Foster now set to work. In the house of Nicholas Hawkins, the cutler, and of Thomas Honylove, the shoemaker, they found the children sick of the small-pox, and naturally made short work of their visit there. At Michael Shepherd's they distrained for five shillings, and at Thomas Cooper's, the heel-maker, for forty, "distreyning three cart-load of Wood, cut especially for his working, which was of more value than any of his household Goods, he being a poor man, and living only upon making Heels and Lasts." Daniel Rich, a tanner and constable of his ward, had his best coat distrained for a fine of five shillings upon his wife, and John Spencer, the grocer, his shop-goods for a fine of forty. After visiting and plundering Jay, the baker, and Isaac, the blacksmith, taking from the latter "Locks, Shovels, and the very Anvil upon which he forgeth his work," they made their way to the parish of St. Cuthbert, to the house of Thomas Arthur, the pipe-maker. This man was somewhat of a celebrity in his time, and now and again tobacco-pipes of his making, with "T. A." upon them, and with exceeding small bowls, as indicating the costliness of the weed in those days, turned up among the ancient *débris* of the town. Arthur's door was locked when Foster arrived, but was opened immediately, and as Foster proceeded to distrain he was asked for what sum demand was made, to which he replied £11.

"Thereupon Thos. Arthur desired to see the Warrant; which being produced, he, seeing himself therein but six pound, told Mr. Foster so; to which Mr. Foster answered that there was five pound more for keeping his door locked. When Thos. Arthur perceived that Mr. Foster would distreyn all his Goods, he said, 'Sir, what shall my Children do? shall they starve?' Mr. Foster replied, that so long as he was a Rebel his Children should starve. And so on Wednesday following, old Battison, the two Apparitors, with a File of Musquetiers and a Cart, carried away what Household Goods they thought fit, and all the Wood, both within doors and without, necessary to his Trade, by three Cart-load, not leaving so much as to suffice for the burning of a Kiln of Pipes, ready set, though earnestly desired by the poor Pipemaker himself, and also by others of Battison's Company."

After distraining Robert Brown, the gardener, for a fine of three pounds—

"They passed into Peter's Parish to the House of Mris. Mary Tilney, Widow, a Gentlewoman, well descended, and of a good Estate, who was fined Twenty pounds; and to make her exemplary in suffering for that offence Mr. Foster himself, being attended by his Publick Notary, will see the fine effectually levied upon her Goods; and indeed the same was effectually done; for (a Cart being provided for that purpose) they distreyned and carried away all the Goods in her House they thought worth their labour, as Tables, Cupboards, Chairs, Irons, Feather-beds, Blankets, the very Hangings of the Room, and Sheets off her Bed, insomuch that the Widow was forced that night to borrow Sheets of her Neighbours to lie on, being not willing to lodge out of her own House, though invited by her friendly Neighbours. As for the value of those Goods taken away, it is supposed to be betwixt forty and fifty pounds. Yet the said Mris. Tilney was more troubled at the crying and sighing of her poor Neighbours about her (who were much affected with her Sufferings, she being very charitable), than for the loss of her Goods, which she took very chearfully. And so the officers left her, having finished this dayes work."

"The next day being Tuesday more Fines were to be levied on the Goods of the rest of the Meeters. About ten of the Clock old Battison, with the Souldiers, and some Constables whom he had warned overnight to be in readiness, marcheth up the High-street, where he levieth the Fine of five pounds upon John Fen, the Haberdasher of Hatts before-mentioned, at whose House the meeting was; taking away all the Hats in his Shop, and the next Day carted away his Household Goods, because there was twenty-nine Hats in the Shop, besides Hat-bands, that they took away. Having thus dealt with this Hatter, he proceeds to deal the same measure to another Hatter, one Samuel Fen, who was also fined five pounds, and dealt with as his Brother before him."

So the work went on from day to day, from one parish to another, and from Bedford to Cotten End, where Sir George Blundell of Cardington joined William Foster in his crusade, clearing out the weaver's loom and the farmer's cows, as the penalty for worshipping with those with whom they felt most in sympathy. At Cotton End

"Thomas Thorowgood's Fine (at whose House* the Meeting was said to be) was Nineteen Pounds, who was by the Officers distreyned, and all that he had, with the Implements of his Trade (he being a Weaver), taken from him, and the said Thorowgood, with his wife, is since departed away from their dwelling and gone."

* Said to be the one standing next to the School.

These particulars, with others, are found in a pamphlet entitled 'A True and Impartial Narrative of some *Illegal* and *Arbitrary* Proceedings by certain Justices of the Peace and others, against several innocent and peacable *Nonconformists* in and near the Town of *Bedford,* upon pretence of putting in execution the late Act against Conventicles. Published for general information. Printed in the year 1670.'

There was no publisher's name to the pamphlet, for to give that would have been to bring down vengeance upon the publisher; but from its appearance we may judge that it was issued from the press of Francis Smith at Temple Bar. The writer, who signs himself—it was not safe to say more—"Your assured Friend," makes a quiet and serious appeal to the public opinion of the time.

"The Narrative," he says, "is true, and will be proved in every part: the Sufferers are chearful and peacable; their immediate Persecutors are the scum of the people, and chiefly the appurtenants of the Commissaries' Court; and the most forward Instrument of that Sort is one that hath openly avowed and declared his Esteem for Popery above other religions."

"This instance of the Execution of the late Act is not thus made publick, as though there were no other of the same kind in other places, but as one of the first whose Tragical Acts have been collected. Nor is the design of publishing hereof to cast any reflection on the Act itself; let it stand or fall in the Providence of God, as it shall be found complyant with, or opposite to, the Honour and Interest of his Majesty, with the Peace, Welfare, and Prosperity of the Kingdomes. Councels for public good are the Province of our Superiours; ready Obedience or peacable Sufferings are the lot of Private Men. There is no intention to meet Violence by Violence; it is the intention of their Enemies to hurry them into a disturbance of the Publick Peace. But all Endeavours of that kind will be in vain, and the hopes of some about it wholly frustrate. It is nothing Else but the Authority of God in their Consciences which imposes a necessity upon them to practise those things in their Christian Profession for which they are made obnoxious to so great Sufferings, and gives them a supportment under them. The disturbance of the Publick Peace would be at once to renounce the Principle of their Actings and to deprive themselves of the Comfort of their Sufferings.

"The Ends, therefore, of publishing this Account are plainly and only these: First, to prepare others for suffering; 2ndly, humbly to demand of our Legislators whether this be the Garment of their Offspring? 3rdly, to give a clear Prospect into the sad Effects of the Prosecution of this Act, showing that there hath been very little regard to Law, Equity, Peace, Love, Humanity, or, indeed, anything that is desirable or useful among Mankind. Whether the Evils inflicted will be recompensed to the Kingdom by the Satisfaction given, Men, wise, peacable, and sober, will in their own minds judge and determine."

The same year there appeared a reply to this narrative, from the pen of Foster himself, of which a single copy survives among the pamphlets in the Bodleian.[1] He makes no attempt, for it would have been useless, to deny the facts of the case. But he seeks to diminish their damaging effect by retort of taunt and sneer and base insinuation. He goes even farther still, and the gross indecencies of his pages cannot, as they need not, be reproduced in our time. It would have been better to have remained silent. This pamphlet of defence is a deepening of the accusation. It is one more proof, if proof were needed, that persecution is a weapon that kills both at the breech and at the muzzle, that, though it may strike and wound those against whom it is directed, it yet more certainly debases and degrades those who use it.

[1] *The Act against Conventicles Executed*: with a Vindication of the Bedfordshire Justices' Proceedings from the Aspersions of a False, Impertinent, and Libellous Pamphlet, entitled *A true and impartial Narrative, &c.* London: Printed by W. G. MDCLXX. (Pressmark 4⁰. H, 32 Art.)

X.

THREE YEARS OF LIBERTY: 1672—1675.

THE months between May, 1670, when constables and musquetiers were making raids upon the Nonconformists of Bedford, and March, 1672, when the Conventicle Act was suspended by the Declaration of Indulgence, may be roughly divided into two parts; the first extending to April, 1671, when Parliament was prorogued, not to be called together again for two years; the second, embracing the following eleven months during which the King, uncontrolled by the House of Commons, did very much as he liked. The first of these periods was, of course, the hardest for the Nonconformists, who usually fared worse under the Cavaliers in Parliament than at the hands of the King. During this time a yet more determined endeavour was made to put an end to all religious services outside the Established Church. The business of detecting and suppressing conventicles was organized into a system under the local magistracy. Some of the worst men in the community found lucrative employment as spies; their pay depending upon the diligence with which they hunted down the peaceable people who frequented these gatherings. They had every inducement to be vigilant, for they received at the rate of £7 or £8, and sometimes even as much as £15 for a single successful conviction.

In special cases the offenders were reported to the central Government. Among the State Papers there is a Spy-book arranged alphabetically, showing how the district between Bedford and Cambridge was at this time placed under surveillance. In reports that one Audey lives at Meldreth, three miles from Royston, "where are concourses of many hundreds both Independents and Baptists," and how he rides into Herts, Cambs, and Beds, to gather concourses of people to their meetings; that Francis Holcroft stops at the house of Widow Hawkes, at Barlyn in Herts, and holds meetings in the neighbourhood, three hundred at a time, and also meets with many hundreds at Cambridge; that Lock, Audey's assistant, "takes turns to ride" to

Hitchin, Paul's Walden, Bedford, and Shefford. The system of espionage had been more or less at work ever since the passing of the Act of Uniformity, but in 1670—1, it was more rigorously carried out than before. This trade, always odious in the eyes of Englishmen, became more odious still because more vigorously plied. In *The Life and Death of Mr. Badman,* Bunyan makes his typical scoundrel turn informer for the sake of harassing his Christian wife, and he also introduces, by the way, the story of W. S., whom the Quaker records enable us to identify as William Swinton, the Sexton of St. Cuthbert's, a man of very wicked life, "who would needs turn informer." He tells how this man would watch of nights, climb trees, and range the woods of days to find out the meeters who, at that time, were forced to gather in the fields. The common people had many stories of the judgments of Heaven which befell these men. It was told how Swinton fell from the bell in the steeplehouse and was picked up besmeared with blood, dying miserably. How, as Bunyan himself narrated, an informer at St. Neot's died from a bite and gangrened wound, his flesh rotting from his bones; and how Fecknam, Swinton's colleague at Bedford, a man who turned to this wretched trade after running through a considerable estate at Turvey, was suddenly smitten at the Visitation at Ampthill, the very month after harassing the meeters in John Fenn's house, and how he died in great pain and anguish of body, now raving against the fanatics and now blaming Mr. Foster for setting him in his office.

Besides those who suffered at the hands of the local magistrates, others of the Bedfordshire Nonconformists were convicted in the Court of Exchequer at Westminster. In 1671, seventy-seven persons from the county were certified by the Lord Treasurer's Remembrancer as having been convicted and fined £20 each; their united fines with the monthly accumulations for persistent refusal to come to Church, amounting to £4,370. Sixteen of these were from Turvey, six from Ampthill, eight from Woburn, four from Westoning, of whom Lawrence Bunnion the joiner was one, eleven from Toddington, the remaining thirty-two being from eleven other villages of the county. The Deputy, in his certificate, raises the question as to the desirability of enforcing payment of the accumulations reckoned at the rate of £20 a month, by which, instead of the £277,090 due from twenty-three counties, there would accrue a sum of four or five millions sterling. "Upon the whole question," says he, "a considerable summe might be raised by putting these laws in execution, but," he cautiously adds, "what disorder it might produce in His Majesty's affairs is worthy consideracion."[1]

The following year the severity was considerably mitigated, and Bunyan had so much liberty allowed him that the Church began to consider the propriety of electing him as their pastor, prisoner though he was. They had never all been reconciled to the necessity of mutual exhortation by the brethren in turn. Brother Whitbread of Cardington, for example, had for some time stayed away from their gatherings, explaining:

"To dismember myself I never intended, as having bene persuaded from Scripture grounds of the consonancy of the Congregationall way with the rule. I waited to see if any doore might be opened for redresse by the choyce of a fit Pastor and the mercy of a spirit of government among us, which since the death of our Pastor hath been greatly wanting."

Eventually his scruples were overcome, and a more settled order provided for, as the following entries show:

"At a Meeting of the Church at Bedford the 9th of the 8th moneth [9th Nov.] (1671) our beloved brother Whitbread was received againe into close Comunion with the Church; he making a gracious acknowledgment of his sorrow and repentance for all those miscarriages of which he had bene admonished before. In his giving up of himself to the Church againe, he did also in the most full manner, without any reservation, commit himself, as also his gifts, in the Lord, to the dispose of the congregation; and did with freenes acknowledge the Eldership that is among us, and commit himself to their care and government. It was also concluded that the 24th day of this moneth being ye 4th day of the week there should be at Hanes a generall assembly of this congregation.

"At a generall Assembly of the Church at Hanes the 24th of the 8th moneth [24th Nov.]. There was received to walke in fellowship with this congregation our brother John Clarke, and Samuell Holcroft and our sister Thorowgood. The improvement also of the gifts of the Church, and their disposall in an orderly way was proposed to consideration, that God might be sought for direction therein. And a time farther to consider and debate thereof was appointed this day sevennight at Evening at Bedford, when the principall brethren were desired for that end to come together at brother John ffenne's; and a Church meeting was appointed to be there that day week. The

[1] *Addl. MSS.*, 20, 739, Co. Beds.

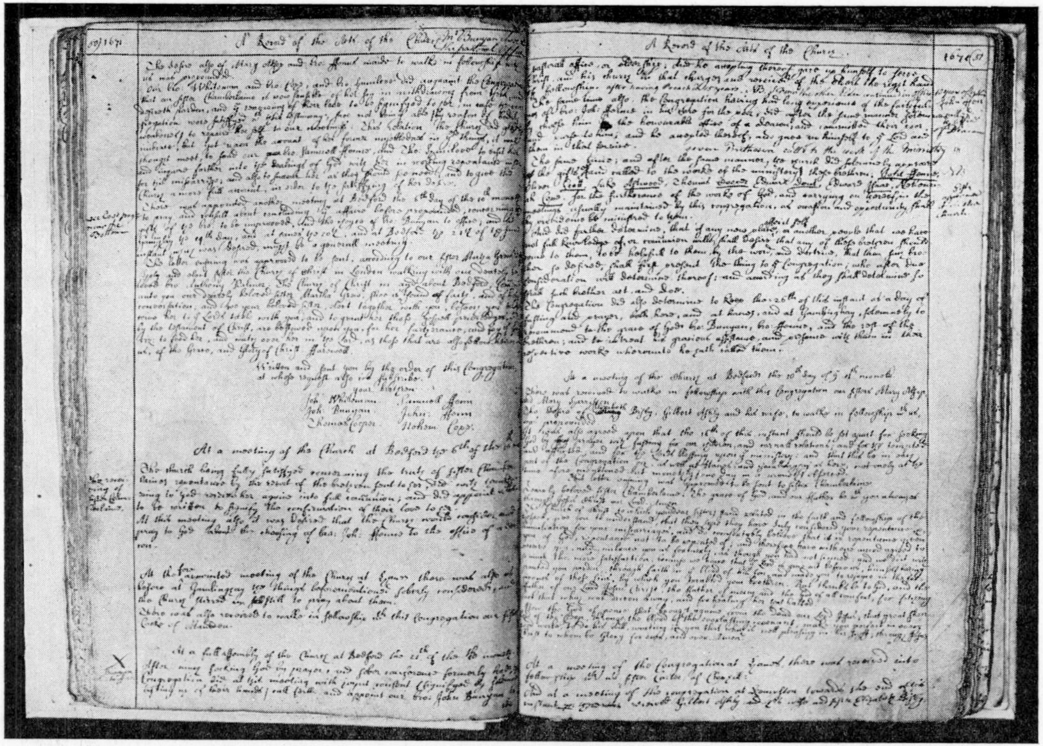

ACT BOOK: BEDFORD CHURCH.
Appointment of John Bunyan as Pastor.
1671.

(Preserved at the Bunyan Meeting Bedford.)
Photo: G. A. Gearey, Bedford.]

Church was also minded to seeke God about the choice of brother Bunyan to the office of an Elder that their way in that respect may be cleared up to them."

The purpose of electing Bunyan to this position had, probably, been for some time taking shape in the minds of the brotherhood. Many things seemed to point to him as the sent of God. Through a long imprisonment he had remained true to his convictions. Mentally as well as spiritually he had grown in grasp and power, as book after book of his, issuing from the press, had borne witness. His *Grace Abounding* especially, by giving them a deeper insight into the workings of his experience, had given him a stronger hold upon their affection and confidence. His influence had grown and his power of service with it. When letters had to be written to their persecuted brethren and sisters, he was the chosen scribe; when anxious conference had to be held with wavering members, he was the appointed messenger. Still more, his power as a preacher commended him to them as the chosen of God to be the shepherd of the flock. But the matter was grave, and demanded frequent conference and prayer, as the following entries show:

"Bedford, the last of ye 9th moneth [31st Dec.]. There was appointed another meeting at Bedford the 6th day of the 10th moneth [6th Jan.] to pray and consult about concluding ye affaire before propounded concerning the gifts of the brethren to be improoved, and the choyce of brother Bunyan to office, and at Gamlinghay the 14th day, and at Hanes the 20th, and at Bedford the 21st of the same instant, which was desired might be a general meeting.

"Bedford, the 6th of the 10th moneth [6th Jan.]. At this Meeting it was desired that the Church would consider and pray to God about the choosing of brother John ffenne to the office of a deacon.

"At the fore-appointed Meeting of the Church at Hanes there was also as before at Gamlinghay the things before-mentioned soberly considered and the Church stirred up still to pray about them.

"At a full Assembly of the Church at Bedford the 21st of the 10th moneth [Jan. 21st, 1672]: After much seeking God by prayer, and sober conference formerly had the Congregation did at this meeting with joynt consent (signifyed by solemne lifting up of their hands) call forth and appoint our brother John Bunyan to the pastorall office or eldership. And he accepting thereof, gave up himself to serve Christ and his Church in that charge; and received of the Elders the right hand of fellowship.

"The same time also, the Congregation having had long experience of the faithfulness of brother John ffenne in his care for the poor, did after the same manner solemnely choose him to the honourable office of a deacon and committed their poor and purse to him, and he accepted thereof, and gave up himself to ye Lord and them in that service.

"The same time and after the same manner the Church did solemnely approve the gifts of and called to the worke of the Ministery these brethren: John ffenne, Oliver Scott, Luke Astwood, Thomas Cooper, Edward Dent, Edward Isaac, Nehemiah Coxe, for the furtherance of the worke of God, and carrying on thereof in the meetings usually maintained by this Congregation as occasion and opportunity shall by providence be ministred to them.

"And did further determine that if any new place offered itself, or another people that we have not full knowledge or communion with, shall desire that any of these brethren should come to them to be helpful to them by the word and doctrine, that then such brother so desired, shall first present the thing to ye Congregation; who after due consideration will determine thereof; and according as they shall determine so shall such brother act and doe.

"The Congregation did also determine to keep the 26th of this instant, as a day of fasting and prayer both here, and at Hanes, and at Gamlinghay solemnely to recommend to the grace of God brother Bunyan, brother ffenne and the rest of the brethren, and to intreat his gracious assistance and presence with them in their respective worke whereunto he hath called them."

Having thus made a more memorable election of a minister than they realised themselves, "God appearing in his glory once more to build up his Zion," by the calling out of seven earnest men as preachers and workers with him in the villages round; the Church began to look out for a settled home as well as a pastor. It was now nearly twelve years since they left the church of St. John on the south side of the river, and during all that time they had been homeless wanderers, meeting now in each other's houses, and now in fields and woods. They dared to hope that they had at last reached the end of the way of the wilderness. For the King's Declaration, which came out within about seven weeks after Bunyan's election to the pastorate, while admitting that it was "Evident by the sad experience of twelve yeares that there is very little fruit of all these forceable Courses" so long persisted in, went on to say:

"That there may be no pretence for any of Our Subjects to continue their illegall Meetings and Conventicles, Wee doe Declare, That wee shall from time to time allow a sufficient number of Places, as they shall bee desired, in all parts of this Our Kingdome, for the use of such as doe not conforme to the Church of England, to meete and assemble in, in Order to theri Publick Worship and Devotion; which Places shall be open and free to all Persons."

The liberty thus granted was, by Bunyan's congregation, speedily accepted. One of their number, Josias Ruffhead, purchased from Justice Crompton of Elstow an orchard in Mill Lane, in which there was a barn. This barn was at once duly licensed as their place of meeting, as the following document shows:

A place for a Teacher in Bedford.

CHARLES, &c. To all Mayors, Bailiffs, Constables, and others, Our Officers and Ministers, Civill and Military, whom it may concerne, Greeting. In pursuance of our Declaracõn of the 15th of March, 167½, Wee have allowed and Wee doe hereby allow of the House of Josias Roughed in Bedford to be a place for the use of such as doe not conforme to the Church of England who are of the Perswasion commonly called Congregationall to meet and assemble in, in order to their Publick Worship and devotion. And all and Singular Our Officers and Ministers, Ecclesiasticall, Civill, and Military, whom it may concerne are to take due notice hereof. And they and every of them are hereby strictly charged and required to hinder any Tumult or Disturbance, and to protect them in their said Meetings and Assemblies. Given at our Court at Whitehall the 9th day of May in the 24th yeare of our Reigne, 1672.

By His Ma$^{tie's}$ command,

ARLINGTON.

The barn thus licensed with the orchard in which it stood were, on payment of a sum of £50, duly conveyed by indenture dated August 20th, 1672, from "Josias Ruffhead to John Bunyan, of the Towne of Bedford, Brasier; John Fenn, Samuel Fenn, of the said Towne, Haberdashers; Thomas Crocker of Kimbolton in the county of Huntingdon, Linen Draper; Thomas Cooper of the Towne of Bedford, Last Maker; and Samuel Hensman of the same towne, Draper." The orchard "with all that Edifice or Barne upon it" thus sold to Bunyan and his friends, was situate on a strip of land between Castle Lane and Mill Lane or School Lane on the south and north, and between a garden held by John Eston, on the east side (with a barn upon it) called Pynners, and a garden with a dove-house upon it on the west side, still held by Josias Ruffhead, and separated by a paling.[1]

[1] *Corporation Records*, List of Hagable Rents, 1681.

This strip of land, probably part of the moat of Bedford Castle, which was dismantled in 1224, was so much lower than the street on the north side that when the barn gave place to a new meeting house in 1707, in the days of Bunyan's successor, Ebenezer Chandler, some wag, descending with him the four or five steps that led to the building, turned to him with the query:

> "If *upward* be the road to bliss,
> Pri'thee, Chandler, where leads this?"

The friend who wrote the continuation of Bunyan's Life to complete the *Grace Abounding* was evidently under the impression that a new building was erected for Bunyan to preach in on this site after his release from prison. He says:

> "Hereupon he gathered his congregation at Bedford, where he mostly lived, and had lived, and had spent the greatest part of his life; and there being no convenient place to be had for the entertainment of so great a confluence of people as followed him upon the account of his teaching, he consulted with them for the building of a meeting house, to which they made their voluntary contributions with all cheerfulness and alacrity, and the first time he appeared there to edify, the place was so thronged that many were constrained to stay without, though the house was very spacious, everyone striving to partake of his instructions, that were of his persuasion, and show their good will towards him by being present at the opening of the place."

This writer, probably one of his London friends, was under a misapprehension when thus stating that a new meeting house was erected for Bunyan; for when the building in which he preached till his death was taken down in 1707 to make way for its successor, it was still described in the deed of transfer of that year as "All that Edifice or Barne." It was probably therefore on the furnishing and opening of this barn that the great interest was shown and the great crowd gathered which this contemporary writer has described for us. The spot thus chosen for Bunyan on his release from prison has been the home of the Church ever since, and for the remaining sixteen years of his life was the centre of his activity, the circumference of his influence reaching to the borders of the adjacent counties and even to London itself. He quickly became the organizing 'bishop' of the whole district. When he applied for his own licence to preach, in May, 1672, and for Josias Ruffhead's barn, he applied also for licences for twenty-five other preachers and for thirty other buildings. Nineteen of these were in Bedford-

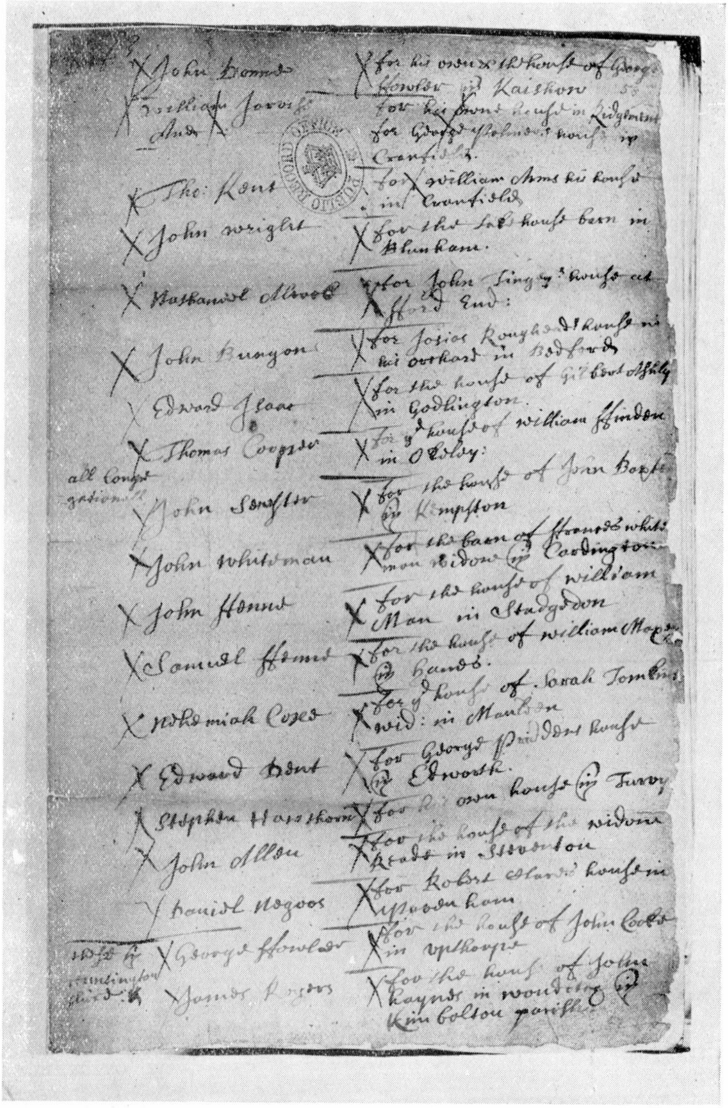
John Donne — for his own & the house of George ffowler in Kaishoe
William Jarvis — for his owne house in Ridgmont
Andr — for George Holmes's house in Cranfield
Tho: Kent — for William Mims his house in Cranfield
John wright — for the said house barn in Blunham
Nathaniel Alcock — for John Singly's house at fford End:
John Bunyon — for Josias Roughed's house in his orchard in Bedford
Edward Isaac — for the house of Gilbert Ashly in Godlington
Thomas Cooper — for ye house of William ffinden in Okley:
all Congregationall
John Sewster — for the house of John Baxter in Kempston
John Whiteman — for the barn of ffrancis Whiteman widow in Cardington
John ffenne — for the house of William Man in Stagsden
Samuel ffenne — for the house of William Hoppe in Haynes
Nehemiah Coxe — for ye house of Sarah Tomkins wid: in Maulden
Edward Dent — for George Pridden's house in Edworth
Stephen Hawthorn — for his own house in Turvy
John Allen — for the house of the widow Reade in Stevington
Daniel Negoos — for Robert Rland's house in Upsoden
Hunt. George ffowler — for the house of John Cook in Upthorpe
James Rogers — for the house of John Rayns in Wooddey in Kimbolton parish

JOHN BUNYAN'S APPLICATION FOR LICENCES TO PREACH
in his own handwriting.

(Preserved at the Public Record Office, London.)
Photo: G. A. Gearey, Bedford.]

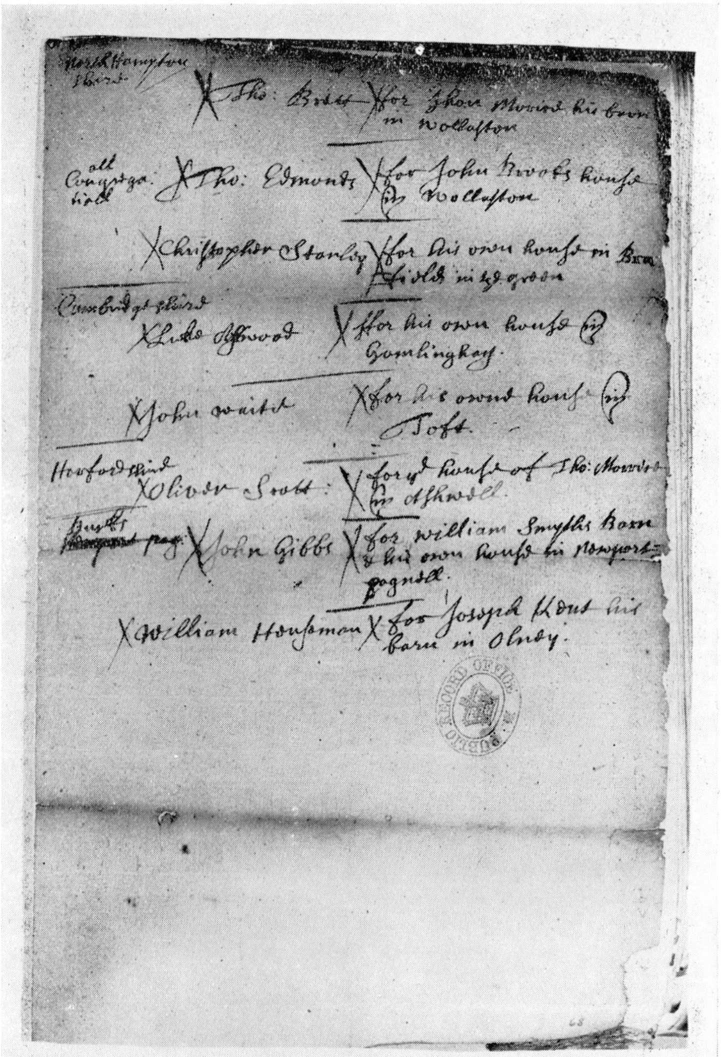

North Hampton shire

X Tho: Brett X for Thom Moore his barn in Wollaston

all Congregationall X Tho: Edmonds X for John Brooks house in Wollaston

X Christopher Stanley X for his own house in Brm field in the green

Cambridge shire

X Luke Astwood X for his own house in Gamlingay.

X John waite X for his owne house in Toft.

Hertford shire

X Oliver Scott X for ye house of Tho: Moore in Ashwell.

Bucks pag. X John Gibbs X for william Smyths Barn & his own house in Newport pagnell.

X William Housman X for Joseph Kent his barn in Olney.

JOHN BUNYAN'S APPLICATION FOR LICENCES TO PREACH
in his own handwriting.

(Preserved at the Public Record Office, London.)
Photo: G. A. Gearey, Bedford.]

shire, three in Northamptonshire, three in Buckinghamshire, two in Cambridgeshire, and one in Hertfordshire. The application, which is in Bunyan's handwriting, is preserved in the Record Office in a bundle containing hundreds of similar applications from all the counties of England. Advantage was taken of the new freedom offered by the king to ask for licences as preaching places for upper rooms, barns, malting floors, gardens, houses, buildings in orchards, halls belonging to public companies, and even chambers in ruined monasteries, and cellars in old castles. The following is the form of application sent in by Bunyan:

Bedf.	John Donne,	for his own and the house of George Fowler in Kaishow.
	William Jarvis,	for his owne house in Ridgemont and for George Palmer's house in Cranfield.
	Thos. Kent,	for William Amis, his house in Cranfield.
	John Wright,	for the Lake-house barn in Blunham.
	Nathaniel Alcock,	for John Tingey's house at Ford End.
	John Bunyon,	for Josias Roughead's house in his orchard in Bedford.
	Edward Isaac,	for the house of Gilbert Ashley in Godlington.
	Thomas Cooper,	for the house of William Findon in Okeley.
All Congregationall.	John Sewster,	for the house of John Baxter in Kempston.
	John Whiteman,	for the house of Frances Whiteman, widow, in Cardington.
	John Fenne,	for the house of William Man in Stadgeden.
	Samuel Fenne,	for the house of William Maxey in Hanes.
	Nehemiah Coxe,	for the house of Sarah Tomkins, widow, in Maulden.
	Edward Dent,	for George Pridden's house in Edworth.
	Stephen Hawthorn,	for his own house in Turvy.
	John Allen,	for the house of the Widow Reade in Steventon.
	Daniel Negoos,	for Robert Chine's house in Pavenham.
These by Huntingtonshire.	George Fowler,	for the house of John Cooke in Upthorpe.
	James Rogers,	for the house of John Haynes in Wonditch in Kimbolton Parish.
Northamptonshire. All Congregationall.	Thos. Brett,	for John Moore, his barn in Wollaston.
	Thos. Edmunds,	for John Brooks' house in Wollaston.
	Christopher Stanley,	for his own house in Brafield-in-the-Green.
Cambridgeshire.	Luke Astwood,	for his own house in Gamblinghay.
	John Waite,	for his own house in Toft.
Herfordshire.		for the house of Thos. Morrise in Ashwell.
	John Gibbs,	for William Smyth's barn and his own house in Newport Pagnell.
Bucks.	William Hensman,	for Joseph Kent, his barn in Olney.

In the autumn of the same year in which he was released* we find Bunyan preaching at Leicester on the 6th of October, which was Sunday. The fact is chronicled in the *Town Records*,† because it was necessary for the preacher to show his licence "to Mr. Overinge the Mayor, Mr. Freeman, and Mr. Browne being present." The old house in which, according to tradition, he preached on that occasion, stood nearly opposite to St. Nicholas' Church, and is the one in which, in the course of the

* The original Pardon of Release, granted by Charles II to about four hundred persons imprisoned under sentence of præmunire, mostly Quakers, (but among the few who were not was John Bunyan), is in the Friends House, Euston Road, London.

† *Vide* addendum.

following century, that other great itinerant preacher, John Wesley, slept for a night when on a Gospel errand to the town. About the time Bunyan was showing his licence to Mr. Mayor at Leicester, there came out a reply to the book he had published in the spring on the *Doctrine of Justification by Faith,* in which he had dealt rather closely and in some respects not altogether fairly with the work on the *Design of Christianity,* by Edward Fowler, rector of Northill. This reply was licensed on the 10th of September, 1672, and had the sort of title which so often graced the pamphlets and heralded the controversies of those days.[1] It professed to be written by a friend on Fowler's behalf. Fowler, himself, however, is credited with the performance, the truth probably being that it was the joint work of himself and his curate. The book has some good qualities, but meeekness and gentleness are not its most conspicuous features. A country rector is accustomed to a good deal of deference from his rural neighbours, and when a book of his has been rudely assailed by a tinker, he naturally feels somewhat impatient. "Among the many successors of the Pharisees in these days, there are none," the writer has "reason to believe, whose breasts are fuller of rancour and malice than is the breast of the man that hath occasioned the publication of this pamphlet, viz., John Bunyan, a person that hath been near these twenty years, or longer, most infamous in the Town and County of Bedford for a very Pestilent Schismatick." This no doubt was the estimate of Bunyan held in the average country rectories and vicarages of Bedfordshire, and it was scarcely likely that Fowler, whose self-complacency had been ruffled by the tinker's criticisms, would take a broader view of the man than his brethren did. Bunyan's book, the writer thinks, is ill-conceived, and has not the merit of originality. "For, first, How should he come by sayings out of Campian? but, secondly (which is more considerable) he hath a company of Terms and Phrases that he was never in a capacity of understanding, as *Commixed, Radicals, Abstract, Replication,* &c., derived from the *Latin.* Again, *Characteristical, Diametrical, Parenthesis, Paragraph,* &c., borrowed from the *Greek* language. And he is up with his *arguing from a thing to a thing, habits and acts,* which smell of one whose name hath had the honour

[1] *Dirt Wip't Off*: or a manifest Discovery of the Gross Ignorance, Erroneousness, and most Unchristian and Wicked Spirit of one John Bunyan, Lay-Preacher in Bedford. London: Richard Royston, Bookseller to His most Sacred Majesty, 1672.

to stand a little while in a Colledge Buttery Book, and that had the luck sometimes to hear his masters chopping logic together." Thus, through seventy pages, he goes on replying to one who, he is perpetually protesting, is not worth replying to at all; and concludes by appealing to the authorities of the time whether this man, John Bunyan, "ought to enjoy any interest in His Majestie's Toleration, and whether the letting such Firebrands and most impudent malicious Schismaticks go unpunish't doth not tend to subversion of all Government? I say, let our Superiors judge of this." Thus this writer vanishes into space, demanding as he goes yet more imprisonment for a man who had just completed twelve years of it already. Happily the dust of oblivion is plentiful, and in the main kindly; and both he and his book are long since peacefully at rest.

Bunyan appears to have made no rejoinder to this attack, for he was by this time engaged in warfare that concerned him more nearly. The book he had published in the early months of 1672, in which he had contended for the reception of saints into church fellowship as saints, independently of water baptism, had been violently assailed by Paul D'Anvers, and William Kiffin, the leader of those London Baptists who held to the principle of strict communion. As Bunyan's attitude on the question of baptism is still of present interest to many, both in this country and in America, it may be well to define it as accurately as we can.*

* *Vide* **Addendum.**

The Church at Bedford, of which he was now the pastor, had from the beginning taken up on this question a position of neutrality. All its earliest members had been brought up in the National Church, and in their infancy baptized into its communion. Most of them, too, before coming together in a separate church, had had their own children baptized at the hands of the clergy. The registers of St. Paul's, in Bedford, mention the baptism of the children of John Eston, John Grew, Anthony Harrington, and of others afterwards in fellowship with them. John Gifford is usually spoken of as a Baptist. As a matter of fact, there is not a single line of evidence one way or the other to show what his personal convictions upon the subject were. He appealed to the brethren from his death-bed not to divide the Church on such questions. "Concerning separation from the Church about baptism," says he, "laying on of hands, anointing with oil, psalms or any externals, I charge every one of you respectively, as you will give an account for it to our Lord Jesus Christ, who shall judge both quick and dead at his coming, that none of you be found guilty of this great evil, which, while some have committed—and that through a zeal for God, yet not according to knoweldge—they have erred from the law of the love of Christ, and have made a rent from the true Church, which is but one." The fact is that baptism was but one of several externals on which there was at that time considerable ferment of opinion. Their neighbour, William Dell, who, as we have seen, had great influence with the brethren at Bedford, rector of a parish and head of a college though he was, was in favour of dispensing with baptism altogether. Indeed so pronounced were his opinions in this direction that he has sometimes been classed as a Quaker, and his books published as Quaker books. He held that there were two baptisms, that of John and that of Christ, the one of water, the other of the Spirit. The baptism of John was the baptism of bodies, the baptism of Christ the baptism of souls. John's water-baptism was to last but till Christ's fire-baptism began, and then the fire should lick up the water, the water-baptism decreasing as the spirit-baptism increased. Christ was baptized of John, just as he was circumcised as a child, to fulfil all righteousness, that is, to meet the last of the requirements of a system under which he was born, but which was vanishing away. Christ, he said, never baptized, neither did Paul care to do so, though he preached the word in a circuit from Jerusalem to Illyricum. And though some of the other Apostles used baptism, they only did so for a time as they used circumcision, for their sakes who were weak. Ceremonies are not easily and suddenly laid down, and it was best to leave circumcision without hands, to put an end by degrees to that made with hands. For ceremonies are best laid down and old customs best laid aside by the efficacy of the Spirit and the power of righteousness.

Such were the advanced opinions of William Dell, which, sustained as they were by his strenuous advocacy, were possibly not without influence among his Bedford neighbours. Be that as it may, they had resolved from the first that character rather than ritual should be the foundation of fellowship, and that on external matters every brother should be left to walk as he believed himself to be led by the Spirit of God. So strongly did they feel on this point that, somewhat inconsistently as it seems to me, they refused to recognise as churches of Christ those communities which held to the strict communion principle. They even refused to transfer their honoured sister, Mrs. Tilney, to a church in London of which her own son-in-law was the pastor, because that Church made baptism by immersion an indispensable condition of membership. In yet another case a similar refusal was given and persisted in. In their own records there is no mention whatever of the baptism of any of their members. Beyond the two cases of refusal just referred to, the mere word 'baptism' only occurs twice between 1650 and 1690. This was in 1656, and the passages are these: "Our sister Linford having upon the account of Baptisme (as shee pretended) wthdrawne from the congregation, was required to be at the meeting to render a reason for her so doing." The following month it was mentioned that Brother Crompe, who had been previously proposed for fellowship, "desires to stay still upon the account of Baptisme." These are literally the only references to the subject in the Act Book of the Church from its foundation to the time of Bunyan's death, and they are, as will be seen, extremely slight, while the scruples of the brother and sister concerned may be interpreted either one way or the other.

It is natural to suppose that Bunyan would be considerably influenced by the feeling of his brethren on this matter. In his work entitled *Differences in Judgment about Water Baptism no Bar to Communion,* he rather implies than plainly states that he is a Baptist.* He defends "the godly in the land who are not of *our* persuasion"; he pleads "not for a despising of baptism, but a bearing with our brother that cannot do it for want of light." He asks, "Because I will not suffer water to carry away Epistles from the Christians, and because I will not let Water Baptism be the rule, the door, the bolt, the bar, the wall of division between the righteous and the righteous, must I therefore be judged to be a man without conscience of the worship of Jesus Christ? The Lord deliver me from superstitions and idolatrous thoughts about any of the ordinances of Christ and of God." In his work entitled *The Heavenly Footman,*† which he left in MS., and which Charles Doe published ten years after his death, he asserts his ecclesiastical position more plainly. In this little book he says

* *Vide* addendum.

† A copy of the Frst Edition (1698) is in the British Museum Library.

to his reader, "Have a care of thy soul, and that thou mayest so do, take this counsel: mistrust thy own strength, keep company with the soundest *Christians* that have most experience of Christ, and be sure that thou have a care of Quakers, Ranters, Freewillers: Also do not have too much company with some Anabaptists, *though I go under that name myself.*" This is plain enough. The only difficulty is how to reconcile his practice with his declaration, for he seems to have had three of his children baptized at church in their infancy, as we gather from the register of the parishes of Elstow and St. Cuthbert's. The following are the extracts in question:

Elstow: "Mary, the daughter of John Bonion, baptized July 20, 1650."

"Elizabeth, the daughter of John Bonyon, was born 14th day of April, 1654."

St. Cuthbert's, Bedford, 1672: "Baptized Joseph Bunyan, y[e] son of John Bunyan, Nov. 16."

There is no difficulty in respect to the first case, that of his blind daughter Mary, inasmuch as her baptism at Elstow Church took place three years before he united himself with the brethren at Bedford. The case is not so clear with respect to Elizabeth, who was baptized at the same place in 1654; for John Bunyan joined John Gifford's church in 1653, and if on his admission he was baptized by immersion, it is difficult to account for the baptism of his infant daughter the following year by sprinkling. It will be pointed out, perhaps, that the register notes that Elizabeth Bunyan was *born* on the 14th of April, and says nothing about her baptism. But it must be remembered that the previous year an Act of Parliament had been passed requiring the date of birth to be inserted in the register instead of that of baptism. There is a curious entry in the parish register of Maid's Moreton, county Bucks, which removes all doubt on the point:

"A.D. 1653. Now came in force a goodly Act made by the Usurper Cromwell's little Parliament, who ordered not the baptism but the birth of children to be recorded in the parish Register. And though the baptism of some be not expressed here, yet these are to certify all whom it may concern, and that on the word of a priest, that there is no person hereafter mentioned by the then registers of the parish but was duly and orderly baptized."[1]

[1] *Parish Registers in England*, by R. E. Chester Waters, 1883, p. 12.

To show further that this Act of 1653 sufficiently accounts for the form of entry in 1654, it may be mentioned that in the Transcript Register from Elstow parish that year the name of Elizabeth Bunyan occurs in a list of twenty-three children, all returned under the head of 'Christenings,' and that the word 'borne,' and not 'baptized,' is used in every case. There can be little doubt, therefore, that the year after John Bunyan joined the Bedford brotherhood his second daughter, like his first, was baptized at Elstow Church. The third case, that of his son Joseph, is the most remarkable of all, for this child according to the register was baptized at St. Cuthbert's Church after Bunyan's twelve years' imprisonment for conscience' sake, and during the time he was conducting the controversy on open communion with D'Anvers and Paul. The fact is curious, and can only be accounted for on the supposition that upon the question of baptism he had no very strong feeling any way. In his reply at this time to D'Anvers and Paul he says:

"You ask me next, How long is it since I was a Baptist? I must tell you I know none to whom that title is so proper as to the disciples of John. And since you would know by what name I would be distinguished from others, I tell you I would be, and hope I am, A CHRISTIAN, and choose, if God should count me worthy, to be called a Christian, a believer, or other such name which is approved by the Holy Ghost. And as for those titles of Anabaptists, Independents, Presbyterians, or the like, I conclude that they came neither from Jerusalem, nor Antioch, but rather from hell and Babylon for they naturally tend to divisions. You may know them by their fruits."

His *Confession of my Faith and a Reason of my Practice*[1] touched upon baptism and the terms of communion, but only in a subordinate way. It was written in the early part of 1672, at the end of his imprisonment, and its main purpose was to vindicate his teaching, and, if possible, to secure his liberty. In his address to the reader, at the outset he says:

"I marvel not that both you and others do think my long imprisonment strange (or, rather, strangely of me for the sake of that), for

[1] *A Confession of my Faith: And a Reason for my Practice* . . . 1672. [Dr. Brown knew of no copy, but copies are now in the Manchester Free Library, and in the M'Alpin Collection of the Union Theological Seminary, New York. In the Bodleian Library is a book with a mulilated title-page—*Some Reflections* on that Part of Mr. Bunion's *Confession of Faith,* Touching . . . Communion with Unbaptized Persons. . . . London, Printed for Francis Smith, 1673. There was also published, at about the same time, Penn's *Truth outweighing Error,* being an Answer to a Treatise of *J. Bunyan's* entituled *A Confession of his Faith.* Printed for F. Smith.]

verily I should also have done it myself had not the Holy Ghost long since forbidden me. . . . I have not hitherto been so sordid as to stand to a doctrine right or wrong, much less when so weighty an argument as above eleven years' imprisonment is continually dogging of me to weigh and pause, and pause again, the grounds and foundation of those principles, for which I thus have suffered; but having not only at my trial asserted them, but also since, even all this tedious tract of time, in cool blood, a thousand times, by the word of God, examined them and found them good, I cannot, I dare not, now revolt or deny the same on pain of eternal damnation."

Faith and holiness are, he says, his professed principles, and his endeavour is to be at peace with all men. Here are his teachings, let his enemies judge for themselves whether there is anything that savours of heresy or rebellion, anything that renders him worthy of almost twelve years' imprisonment, or deserving to be hanged or banished for ever according to their tremendous sentence. He cannot hold communion with the ungodly and openly profane, and he cannot consent that his soul should be governed in any of his approaches to God by the superstitious inventions of this world. With this exception, for which he does not think he ought to be rebuked, spite of slander and falsehood, he shall always show himself a peaceable and obedient subject. "But," he adds finely, "if nothing will do unless I make of my conscience a continual butchery and slaughter-shop, unless putting out my own eyes, I commit me to the blind to lead me, as I doubt not is desired by some, I have determined, the Almighty God being my help and shield, yet to suffer, if frail life might continue so long, even till the moss shall grow on mine eyebrows, rather than thus to violate my faith and principles."

In this Confession of his he sets forth his belief in the main doctrines of Scripture, and it is only towards the end that he touches upon the question of baptism and the terms of communion. It was this latter part which led to the controversy with D'Anvers, and to the appearance in 1673 of Bunyan's reply, entitled *Differences in Judgment about Water Baptism no Bar to Communion,*[1] and of his rejoinder in 1674, under the title, *Peaceable Principles and True.*[2] He had no great liking for

[1] *Differences in Judgment about Water Baptism, no Bar to Communion*: or to Communicate with Saints, as Saints, proved Lawful. By John Bunyan. London: Printed for John Wilkins, and are to be sold at his Shop in Exchange Alley, next door to the Exchange Coffee House, over against the Royal Exchange. 1673.

[2] *Peaceable Principles and True*: or a Brief Answer to Mr. D'Anvers and Mr. Paul's Books against my Confession of Faith, and Differences in Judgment about Baptism no Bar to Communion. Wherein their Scriptureless notions are overthrown, and my Peaceable Principles still maintained. No copy of First Edition known. [Despite diligent search, a first edition has not been discovered.]

controversy, least of all on the subject of baptism. He would not, he says, have set pen to paper upon the question but for those continual assaults which for the last eighteen years the brethren of the rigid way had made not only upon the congregation at Bedford to rend it, but also upon many others about them. He thinks it childish and carnal to divide a church on such mere matters of ritual. "You must know I am still of that mind, and shall be so long as I see the effects that follow, viz., the breach of love, taking off Christians from the more weighty things of God, and to make them quarrel and have heart-burnings one against another." With such words as these he left this dispute and these disputants, never, so far as we know, to return to them again.

It was soon after this war with D'Anvers and Paul that there came into Bunyan's life the painful episode narrated in the experience of Agnes Beaumont, and related by herself.[1] She gives no dates in her story, but the mention of the death of her father enables us by the help of the Edworth register to fix the time as the month of February, 1674. The story is as follows: In those days, and in a farmhouse still pointed out, there lived at Edworth, a village on the Bedfordshire border towards Hertfordshire, a farmer named John Beamont or Beaumont. He was widowed, and his unmarried daughter Agnes, then in her twenty-first year, kept his house, a married son and a married daughter living at adjacent farms in the parish. The whole family had at one time felt the influence of the Nonconformist preachers. Some of them, indeed, had been sufferers for conscience' sake, as we gather from William Foster's Act Book, where it is recorded that John Beaumont the son, with his wife Elizabeth, were presented by the churchwardens of Edworth at the Court of the Archdeaconry held at Bedford in the spring of 1669, for refusing to come to the sacrament at the parish church the previous Easter, and were fined accordingly. John Beaumont, the father, had himself been more than once deeply moved under Bunyan's own preaching. "Some time before," says Agnes, "my father had heard him preach God's word, and heard him with a cry to the Lord in secret as well as I." But by-and-by some Edworth neighbour, who had great ascendancy over him, contrived to turn his mind against the meetings and the preachers,

[1] *Addl. MSS.* 2414. Narrative of the Persecution of Agnes Beaumont. This MS., in the British Museum, if not in the actual handwriting of Agnes, is evidently a contemporary document.

and especially against Bunyan himself. His daughter Agnes had, however, joined the Bedford Church at Gamlingay in December, broken heart, as he had several others, and afterwards would the church book in Bunyan's handwriting after he became pastor, he himself also inscribing her name in the church roll, spelling it thus—Agniss Behemont. In February, 1674, she was anxious to be present at a meeting of the church to be held at Gamlingay. With much reluctance her father gave his consent, she going over in the morning to her brother's house, to join him and others on the journey. Here an unexpected difficulty arose; John Wilson with whom it had been arranged she should ride to Gamlingay, for some reason failed to come; the February roads were impassable on foot, and the only horse that could be spared from the work of the farm was to carry her brother and his wife, pillion-wise, to the meeting. In the midst of this perplexity Bunyan himself unexpectedly rode up on his way thither also, and was asked to take up Agnes behind him. Knowing the elder Beaumont's feeling he hesitated. "Your father will be grievous angry," said he, "if I should." Overcome at length, however, by her entreaties he started, taking her with him. From a distant field the old man saw them together, a sight at which his anger knew no bounds. He was too far away to prevent their going; but on her return Agnes found the door of her home relentlessly bolted against her, her father from within refusing to open till she would promise to break with these people and all their ways. That cold February night, wrapped in her riding-dress, she spent in the barn. Next morning, her father being still inexorable, she crossed the fields to her brother's house, remaining there till the following Sunday, when, after much exercise of mind and in deep anguish of spirit, she yielded to her father's will, and returned to her home. She had only been back two days, when on the Tuesday, as they were alone in the house together, her father was strangely, fatally seized, and suddenly died.

That same day, as she was bending over the dying man, a clergyman named Lane was busy sending forth a scandalous story at Baldock Market concerning Bunyan and herself. This man, though preaching at Edworth, lived at Bedford, and therefore knew them both, and had recognised them riding together "at Gamlingay town-end." His story, and that of John Beaumont's strange and unexpected death, now went forth together.

It was known that there had been bitter difference between father and daughter, followed by tardy and quite recent reconciliation; there needed but one stroke of malignant ingenuity to complete the whole. This was furnished by a neighbouring lawyer named Farrow, who, writhing under the recent rejection of his suit by Agnes, gave forth that she had poisoned her father, and that Bunyan had furnished her with the means of doing it. The whole parish was in commotion, the funeral deferred, and the coroner called. For those most deeply concerned it was a time of painful anxiety. "I did not know," writes Agnes, "how far God might suffer this man and the devil to go. It also troubled me to think that in case I suffered, another as innocent as myself must suffer too," referring, of course, to Bunyan and his implication in the charge; "but the Lord knew our innocency in this affair, both in thought, and word, and deed."

Under official investigation the cruel charge came to nothing. Comparatively rude as was the medical science of those days, it was sufficient to show that though John Beaumont's death was painfully sudden, it was yet simply natural. The innocent, therefore, were acquitted, and their accusers covered with shame. Agnes outlived this anxious time by nearly fifty years, dying at Highgate in 1720. In compliance with her own request she was brought to be buried in the graveyard of the Tilehouse Street Chapel at Hitchin, where an inscription keeps up her memory and the remembrance of her story.

It was probably after this painful incident that Bunyan added to his *Grace Abounding* that passage of vindication not found in the first edition of 1666, but which does occur in a later edition, the sixth, which appeared in 1688—probably also in editions intervening—in which he says:

"It was reported with the boldest confidence that I had my Misses, my Whores, my Bastards, yea, two Wives at once, and the like. My foes have missed their mark in this their shooting at me. I am not the man. I wish that they themselves be guiltless. If all the Fornicators and Adulterers in England were hanged by the neck till they be dead, John Bunyan, the object of their envy, would still be alive and well. I bind these lies and slander to me as an ornament; it belongs to my Christian profession to be vilified, slandered, reproached, and reviled; and since all this is nothing else, as my God and my conscience do bear me witness, I rejoice in reproaches for Christ's sake."

In the year 1675, after publishing his *Peaceable Principles and*

True, he sent forth another work also entitled *Light for them that sit in Darkness.* Between these two, as being about the same time, though without date, Charles Doe places in his Catalogue of Bunyan's writings a work entitled *Reprobation Asserted, or the Doctrine of Eternal Election promiscuously handled.* It professes on the title-page to be "by John Bunyan, of Bedford, a lover of Peace and Truth," and Doe coming across this little quarto accepted it as genuine. In this I venture to think he was mistaken, as he might very well be in reference to a book published several years before his personal acquaintance with Bunyan began. There were certainly four other books passed off falsely in Bunyan's name, for the purpose of trading upon his popularity, it is therefore not incredible that there was a fifth, provided there are sufficiently strong reasons to point to such a conclusion. There seem to be such reasons in the case of this book on Reprobation. For, to take the external evidence first, it was printed in different form from the rest of his works, and the imprint, which is peculiar, is given thus: London: *Printed for G. L., and are to be sold in Turnstile-alley in Holbourn.* The initials were probably intended to suggest the name of George Larkin, but it was this publisher's custom to print his name in full upon each title-page and his place of business was not in Turnstile Alley, but at the sign of the Two Swans, Without Bishopgate.* Further, the book in question did not appear in any of the three collected editions of Bunyan's writings, bearing date 1692, 1736-7, and 1774. It was not till 1780 that Alexander Hogg published it for the first time with the rest of Bunyan's productions as genuine†. This he did in the collection issued by him and edited by Mason and Ryland. Then, when we pass to look at the book itself, to analyse its spirit and substance we feel at once that it is in altogether a different key from what we are accustomed to. It neither begins nor ends in Bunyan's characteristic fashion, nor is there in it a single touch to remind us of his own peculiar vein. Let him write on what subject he may, he writes not long before he either melts with tenderness or glows with fire. This writer never deviates into anything of the kind. He is hard and cold in style, thin in scheme and substance, and he is what Bunyan never was—pitiless in logic, without being truly logical. This book, I think, we may safely leave out of the record, and go on our way.

* The British Museum Catalogue gives the date of this work [1674?]. The second edition, revised and corrected was "printed by *George Larkin, Junior,* for William Marshall at the Bible in Newgate Street . . 1696." W. Marshall published Doe's Folio, in 1692.

† There is a volume in the Bodleian Library, Oxford, with a list of books published by *Joseph* Marshall, at the Bible in Newgate Street, London. Amongst these is—'Quarto. *Bunyan* of Election and Reprobation. The date is 1720. (*Life of John Owen,* by D. Clarkson, B.D.)

It has been already mentioned that a genuine work of Bunyan's, entitled *Light for them that sit in Darkness,*[1] came out in 1675. It is a discourse upon the doctrine of the person, deeds, and sufferings of Christ, it is therefore a discourse into which he put his whole heart. "Reader," says he, "hear me patiently. I have presented thee with that which I have received from God. I know it to be the way of salvation. I have ventured my own soul thereon with gladness; and if all the souls in the world were mine as mine own soul is, I would, through God's grace, venture every one of them there. I have not writ at a venture, nor borrowed my doctrine from libraries. I depend upon the sayings of no man. I found it in the scriptures of truth, among the true sayings of God." The book is the expansion of a sermon preached from the text—"Of this man's seed hath God according to His promise raised unto Israel a Saviour Jesus." It dwells upon the promise which lighted up pre-Christian times, and upon the way the promise was fulfilled in Christ when the hour was ripe. It sets forth how the Saviour addressed Himself to the work of our Redemption, taking upon Him our nature, being made under the law, taking upon Him also our sins, and being made a curse for us. The writer then passes to a series of nine demonstrations conclusively showing that Christ really ransomed the souls of sinners by His great work, and obtained eternal redemption for them. The proof of this great fact is seen in that He was raised from the dead, that He was received up into heaven, that he sent forth the gift of the Holy Spirit, that the preaching of His gospel has from that time to this been a mighty conqueror over all kinds of sinners, that it has brought peace and holiness into the souls of men. Further, our prayers are now accepted of God for the sake of Christ, we are commanded to give thanks in His name, are exhorted to look to His second coming for the full and glorious enjoyment of our redemption, and finally the threatenings of God have gone forth against those who shall refuse to be saved by Him. He then sets forth the practical uses of these great teachings, in discovering to us the glorious attributes of God, and our own weakness and need, and in sustaining the tried and tempted. For indeed

[1] *Light for them that sit in Darkness*: or a Discourse of Jesus Christ: and That he undertook to accomplish by himself the Eternal Redemption of sinners. By John Bunyan. London: Francis Smith, 1675. Copies of the First Edition in the Bodleian, and in the Bunyan Collection at Bedford. [Also in the Guildhall Library, London.]

the tempted have sore need of sustenance. "O, the toil of a truly gracious heart in this combat! If faith be weak he can scarce get higher than his knees; Lord help! Lord save! and then down again, till an arm from heaven takes him up, until Jesus Christ be evidently set forth crucified for him, and cursed for his sin!"

While thus earnestly plying his pen as a writer Bunyan was also earnestly making use of his newly acquired liberty as pastor and preacher. Indeed he seems to have been too busy to keep any records of his busy life. The minutes of the Church's proceedings during the time he was pastor are comparatively scanty. Of the twenty folio pages embracing these sixteen years, only about five were in his own handwriting, three others were left blank to be filled up afterwards which, as a matter of fact, they never were, and the remainder were in the handwriting of other officers of the Church. Some of the proceedings during the time of renewed persecution were evidently entered up from memory afterwards, and irregularly kept. The following are the only entries that need detain us between 1672 and 1675. Three weeks after Bunyan's acceptance of the pastorate, that is, on the 10th of February, 1672,

"It was agreed upon that the 16th of this instant should be set apart for seeking God by prayer with fasting for our children and carnall relations, and for the tempted and afflicted, and for the Lord's blessing upon ye ministery; and that there be in each part of the congregation, viz.: as well at Hanes and Gamlinghay as here, not only at the time aforementioned, but monethly, one day in a moneth observed.

"25th of the 4th moneth [25th July]: It was ordered that a brief confession of faith bee drawne up by the elders and gifted brethren of the congregation against the next meeting, that after the Churches approbation thereof it may be propounded to all that shall hereafter give up themselves to ye Lord and to us by the will of God, and their unfeigned consent thereto required. There was also appointed a meeting for prayer for our children and relations.

"29th of the 6th moneth [29th Sept.], 1672: The matter heretofore propounded concerning ye drawing up of a brief confession of faith, &c., was omitted by reason of brother Bunyan's absence. There was also deputed to go to ye meeting of ye messengers of the adjacent congregations, which was appointed at Stadgeden, the elders, Mr. Waite, Mr. Whitbread, and brother Man."

The following passages are in Bunyan's handwriting, the one relating to John Rush being characteristically vigorous:

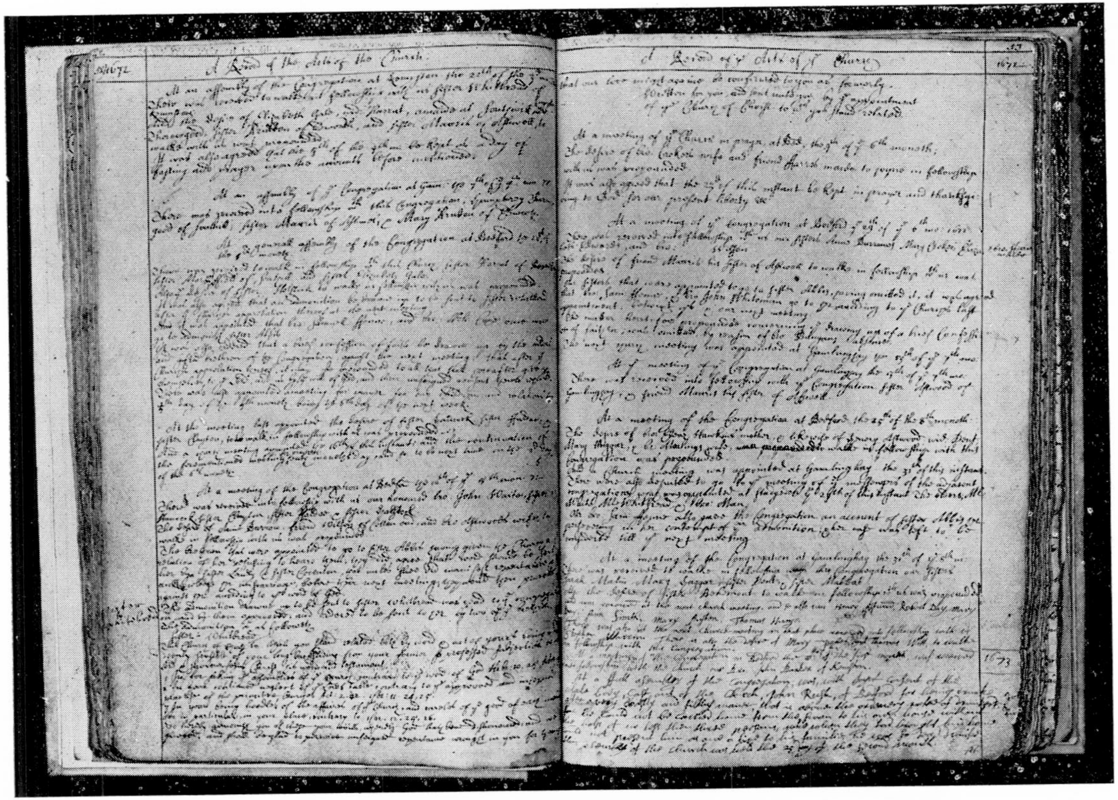

ACT BOOK: BEDFORD CHURCH.
1672.
Pages of John Bunyan's Writing.

(Preserved at Bunyan Meeting, Bedford.)
Photo: G. A. Gearey, Bedford.]

"Gamlinghay, the 31st of the 8th moneth [31st query, 30th? Nov.]: The desire of Sister Behemont to walke in fellowship with us was propounded and [she] was received at the next Church meeting.

"At a full assembly of the Congregation was with joynt consent of the whole body, cast out of the Church, John Rush, of Bedford, for being drunk after a very beastly and filthy maner, that is above the ordenery rate of drunkerds, for he could not be carried home from the Swan to his own house without the help of no less than three persons who, when they had brought him home, could not present him as one alive to his familie he was so dead drunke. This assembly of the Church was held the 25th day of the second month [25th May].

"At the same meeting there was propounded the desire of these friends to joyne in fellowship with us, to witt, Thomas Bunyan, Sister Ward. It was desired by the Church at Hitchin that this congregation would give up to them our brother Nehemiah Cox in order to the exercise of the office of an Elder or pastor with them: the which the congregation concluded to take into consideration.

"At an assembly of the congregation on the 6th of the 4th month [6th July, 1673], was received into the ffellowship our brother Thomas Bunyan and our Sister Wheeler.

"Concluded that the 14th day of this month be kept as a day of humiliation and praire upon several weighty accounts.

"An assembly of this congregation was held at Edworth the 3rd of the 8th month [3rd Nov.].

"At a Church meeting at Gamblinghay the 18th of the 8th month [18th Nov.], was cast out of the Church the wife of our brother Witt, for railling and other wicked practises. Concluded that som dayes be sett appart for humiliation with fasting and prayer to God because of som disorders amongst som in the congregation, specialy for that som have run into debt more than they can satisfie, to the great dishoner of God and scandall of religion.

"1674. A Church meeting was holden at Bedford the 10th of the 2nd month [10th May], to pray to God to bless admonition upon four in the congregation that had transgressed.

"At the same meeting also, the Church was told that our Sister Landy had bin admonished for withdrawing communion againe, for countenancing Card-play, and for deceiving the Church with her former seeming repentance. At the same meeting the Church was told that our Sister Elizabeth Maxey had bin admonished for disobedience to her parents, to witt, for calling her father lier, and for wicked carriages to her mother.

"On the 7th of the 3rd month [7th June] was a meeting of the Congregation holden at Cotten End, wher was a relation made of severall acts of the Church, there also our Brother Nehemiah Coxe did publickly make an acknowledgment of several miscaridges by him committed, and declared his repentance for the same; and because he had been faulty in such things heretofore, therefore it was desired by some of the Brethren: That the form of his submitting should be presented to us in writeing, which it accordingly was, and was as followeth: Whereas several words and practises have bin uttered and performed by me that might justly be construed to have a tendencie to make rents and devisions in the congregation I doe declare myselfe unfeignedly repentant and sorry for the same. Ne. Coxe.

"At the same meeting, singing of Psalmes was propounded to the Congregation,* also that the Congregation at Hitchin intreated that the Church would consent to give up our Brother Wilson to them to be chosen to office by them.

"At a Church meeting holden at Gamblingay the 18th of the 3rd month [18th June] was our Sister Landey withdrawn from. The causes were for that she had withdrawn communion from the saints, had despised gifts in the Church, had taught her children to play at cards, and remained impenitent after several admonitions.

"At a Church meeting holden at Bedford the 29th of the 3rd moneth [29th June] was our sister Eliz. Burntwood openly rebuked for her immodest company keeping with carnal and light young fellows at Elstow.

"Ordered that a letter be sent to that Church of whom Brother Jesse once was pastor, to know whether it be their Church principle still to hold communion with saints as saints, though differing in judgment about watter Baptizm, that we may the better know what to doe to as to our Sister Martha Cumberland as to her joyning with them or not. At the same time, John Overhand was mentioned to be joyned in fellowship with us, but considering that upon several accounts his life of profession hath not bin accompanied with that holyness as becomes the gospel it was concluded on the negative."

* Apparently, at the Bedford Meeting, previously to Mr. Chandler's pastorate (1691), "it was not usual to sing in public worship, nor for the minister to pronounce the blessing at the close of the service." (Rev. S. Hillyard, *Memoir of Rev. E. Chandler*, 1816.)

These entries, made in 1674, are the last in Bunyan's handwriting till we come to the year 1678, important events as we shall see taking place in the interval. From the minutes thus given, and still more from the mere entries of the reception of members, which have been omitted, it would appear that the Church under Bunyan's care was a widespread community of believers, drawing some of its members from Ashwell in Herts, and Gamlingay in Cambridgeshire, as well as from far outlying villages in Bedfordshire on all sides. The oversight of this brotherhood involved much going to and fro on the part of the pastor who preached in towns and villages by the way far and near. 'Bishop' Bunyan, as partly in jest and partly in earnest he came to be called, had a large diocese, and one could have wished that he had kept such a journal of his experiences as his great contemporary, George Fox, kept in that century, or John Wesley in the next, giving vivid pictures of the men he met, of the scenes in which he took part, and of the times that passed over him. Traditions of the man linger in places about which he himself is silent, as silent as he was about most things in his outward life. It is said, for example, that the Congregational Church at John Street, Royston, was founded by William Bedford,* a Cambridge student, who was converted to God through stopping to hear John Bunyan preach at Melbourn near by.[1] At Coleman Green, too, a small hamlet in the parish of Sandridge, near St. Albans, some cottages are pointed out where he is said to have preached, possibly during some of the journeys he made to London. On the old ivy-covered chimney there has been fixed this inscription, "John Bunyan is said by tradition to have preached, and occasionally to have lodged in the cottage of which this chimney was a part."[2] In those days of persecution there was a congregation of Nonconformists at Kensworth, in Hertfordshire, which was central to a wide district extending southward to Hemel Hempstead and St. Albans, northward to Luton, Tilsworth, Houghton Regis, and Dunstable, and eastward to Hitchin and Baldock. In 1675 this church numbered as many as three hundred and eighty members, nineteen of whom were residents in Luton. It was about this date that these Luton brethren separated from the Kensworth Church and formed themselves into an independent community, worshipping secretly in an apartment in the roof of the old house of the Dallow Farm, the trap-door of the apartment being still to be seen. In that secret chamber tradition reports that Bunyan often preached to these early Nonconformists in days when the vigilance of spies necessitated his coming and going in disguise, or under cover of the darkness of night. Eastward, too, in the direction of Hitchin, the tradition of his visits is even stronger still. About three miles from the town stood in those days the country house known as Hunsdon House, and afterwards as Preston Castle, which with its pleasant gardens and shrubberies has long since disappeared. It may be mentioned by the way that some thirty years after Bunyan's time it was in the possession of a certain Captain Hinde, who was a quaint compound of the old soldier and the country gentleman, and who is generally recognised as the original of the character of Uncle Toby in *Tristram Shandy*. This worthy seems to have amused his neighbours, and kept up his own military memories by surrounding his house with fortifica-

* *Vide* Addendum.

[1] Urwick's *Nonconformity in Herts*, p. 814.
[2] *Ibid*, p. 215.

tions, giving it an embattled front, and summoning his labourers from the harvest-field by bugle call.

Within a few hundred yards of the gateway to Preston Castle, and in the midst of a thick wood, which bordered the Castle meadows and is known as Wainwood,* there was a green space forming a sort of natural ampitheatre, which has come to be called Bunyan's Dell. It is capable of holding several hundred people, and here while the loneliness of the wood sheltered them from their enemies, and friendly scouts kept watch on every side, Bunyan often preached to the people the word of life. There were those living near who were in earnest sympathy with him.† We find from the records that the house of Widow Heath, in Preston, Hartfordshire, was licensed for a Congregational meeting-place on the 2nd of May, 1672, and that a licence was granted to Thomas Milway to be congregational teacher there. At Hunsdon House also there were then living six brothers of the name of Foster,‡ staunch and true men, whose descendants likewise have many of them both in that county and in the three counties adjacent, borne honoured names in the annals of Nonconformity. These six brothers were among those who for conscience' sake risked the spoiling of goods and the loss of liberty. In the stormy times passing over them, their house was the asylum of the persecuted, and among the friends from a distance there was no guest more frequent or more welcome at their fireside than Bunyan himself. These dwellers in Preston formed the nucleus of the greater gatherings in Wainwood Dell, to which when Bunyan happened to be the preacher the people came from all the country round. The tradition of those secret assemblies, where because they met at their peril, earnest men sent up their prayers with strong crying and tears and listened to the truth of God as those who hungered for bread, has come down unbroken to our own times. There is a soul of good in things evil, and the memories of those anxious days have appealed to the imagination and sympathy of every generation since, have deepened the love of liberty, and made more precious to thousands the truth their fathers loved so well, and for which they suffered so much.

* *Vide* Vol.I., p. xxxvi. f.n., *Bunyan's Works*, by George Offor.

† There is a cottage near the wood where a bench in the inglenook is shown as 'Bunyan's Seat.'

‡ *Vide* pamphlet, *Brief Outline of the Tilehouse Street Church, Hitchin . . . anecdotes of the Foster family*, by Edward Foster, 1856. Descendants of the "six brothers" still reside near Hitchin. The Editor posesses a volume of Bunyan's *Come and Welcome* (1691 edition), with John Foster, 1691, written on cover.

ADDENDA—Chapter X.

(Page 217). **Bunyan at Leicester, 1672.**

It may interest readers to have the exact entry from the

"Records of the Borough of Leicester. DCCCV. Original Letters, No. 84. John Bunyan's License. (6th Oct. 1672.)

> JOHN BUNNYANS License beares date the ninth day of May 1672 to teach as a congregationall person being of that perswasion in the house of Josias Roughead in the Towne of Bedford, or in any other place roome or house licensed by his Maiestie.

Memorandum the said Bunnyon shewed his license to Mr Maior Mr Overing Mr Freeman, and Mr Browne being there present the vjth day of October 1672 being Sunday."

In *A History of Leicester* (1923), Mr. S. H. Skillington locates the house as having stood in Shambles Lane (now Saint Nicholas' Street), where Bunyan preached on this occasion, and John Wesley a hundred years later. For many years a cast-iron tablet on the front stated, "In this House John Bunyan was once lodged; also John Wesley on his first visit to this place in 1770." The premises of Mr. H. H. Peach now occupy the site. The old house was demolished for city 'improvements' about 1895. *The Leicester Mercury,* for June 30th, 1924, had the following paragraph: "In an interesting letter, Mr. Samuel Russell tells me that he watched the taking down of John Bunyan's house in St. Nicholas Street, and he is fairly sure that no general rebuilding took place. . . . The house had so much history attached to it that it ought to have been removed carefully and re-built."

Of the room in this house in which Bunyan preached, in 1672, the authoress of *Catherine Hutton and Her Friends** quotes from another writer who had said: " . . . it is only three days since I re-visited this singular, antique apartment, over which is the room in which I was born. This said great parlour is wainscoted with carved dark oak, and has a chimney-piece curiously carved by the Huguenot refugees. . . . The date of the house was ancient, and it is believed to have been built of the ruins of Lady Jane Grey's house at Bradgate; it had, when we lived in it, a quadrangular court at the back, along one side of which ran an open gallery."

Fortunately the oak panelling and chimney-piece, together with the iron tablet, have been preserved, and now adorn the dining-

* *Catherine Hutton and Her Friends.* Edited by Mrs. Hutton Beale. Privately printed, 1895.

room of the home of Mr. George Dennis Day, M.A., at Saint Ives, Huntingdonshire.

(Page 221). **Bunyan and Baptism.**

The attitude of John Bunyan respecting baptism has been, and still is, a subject of controversy: Was he or was he not a Baptist? His own writings on the subject are often quoted, but, too frequently, inadequately quoted. In his *Differences in Judgment about Water Baptism* (1673) he leaves the reader, perhaps, somewhat perplexed. However, Bunyan would not tolerate baptism as the condition for Church membership; and in this he differs from his opponents with whom he was forced to wage war. Perhaps it was a matter of Peter and Paul over again. It was a hard fight with Bunyan when the Scriptures were to be the final appeal, for he knew them far too well to be easily defeated. With him Water Baptism—whether by immersion or by sprinkling—was not to "be the rule, the door, the bolt, the bar, the wall of division between the righteous and the righteous." In fact, with Bunyan, no Christian, truly converted, must be debarred from fellowship and communion on the sacred rite. He accepted an unbaptised one, providing that such showed real repentance and acceptance of God's plan of Salvation. His broad vision and large-heartedness could not be narrowed down to denominational teaching. Yet he could say, whole-heartedly, in regard to the Anabaptist, "I go under that name myself." Let it be remembered, however, he did not, and could not, hold with much that the anabaptists said or did. His was no inconsistency, but, rather, love for all true Christians. The heated arguments that have been put forth both in America and in England during past years, might have all been avoided by recognising Bunyan as Bunyan, and not as anyone else! In his days those of his own way of thinking persecuted him through the misunderstanding of the man. His religious convictions were not to be measured by rules and regulations; hence he ran amok of the laws of the land as well as of those of his "denomination." His own children's christening has been cited to prove that he was not a Baptist—that is, an advocate of believer's baptism by immersion. His open mind on the subject made it possible for his first or his second wife to exercise her own conviction, which she undoubtedly did, as the registers of Elstow and Saint Cuthbert's, Bedford, show. Anglicans and other pædo-baptists have endeavoured to embrace Bunyan within the circumference of their own beliefs, and not without some rightful claim, for Bunyan belongs to all. The author of this biography, in an able article contributed to *The British Weekly,* on January 18th, 1889, entitled, "Was John Bunyan a Baptist?" had under review two books, one by Dr. Thomas Armitage (*A History of the Baptists*) and the other, *John Bunyan NOT a Baptist,* by William Urwick, M.A.* Dr. Brown deals very ably with both opinions, and he sums up his conclusions in the words: "Briefly put, the net result of all this seems to be that Bunyan was a Baptist of a very mild type." This then is the decision of a pædo-baptist. On the other hand, the late Canon Thompson, in his *Southwark Cathedral: Its history, etc.,* boldly asserts that "Bunyan was a CHURCHMAN at heart." Bunyan's outspokenness in regard to Anabaptists was directed against the opinions they held or expressed in their books, and not against baptism itself. In short, he upheld Baptism as an ordinance of God, and not as a church ordinance, as the following quotation from his introduction to *A Holy Life the Beauty of Christianity,* published in 1684, fully shows:

> " . . . the hypocrite will give us the slip by betaking himself to exterior matters, as to 'mint and anise and cummin.' . . . But let such know that God never ordained ordinances, such as baptism, the Lord's supper, or the like for the sake of the water, or of bread and wine; nor yet because He takes any delight that we are dipped in water, or eat that bread; but they were ordained to minister to us by the aptness of the elements, through our sincere partaking of them, further knowledge of the death, burial, and resurrection of Christ, and of our death and resurrection by Him to newness of life. Wherefore, he that eateth and believeth not, and he that is baptized, and is not dead to sin, and walketh not in newness of life, neither keepeth these ordinances nor pleaseth God."

Because Bunyan, when applying for licences for himself and others as "Congregationall," many have been led astray by the term which appears to have been used indifferently in describing Independents and Baptists as well; in fact, to such as disclaimed to be either Episcopalian or Presbyterian.

The Rev. John Jukes, in *A Brief History of Bunyan's Church,*

* In *Bible Truths and Church Errors,* Fisher Unwin (now Ernest Benn, Ltd.). 1888.

(published in 1849), mentions that John Burton, like his predecessor, John Gifford, was a Baptist. Infant baptism was not, seemingly, adopted by the Bedford Meeting until Ebenezer Chandler, a pædo-baptist and Bunyan's successor, entered upon office as pastor. In a letter, dated February 23rd, 1691, Chandler wrote: "In pursuance of your request, I have here written an account of what the Church hath agreed for since my coming among them, that if I continue I may have my conscience clear towards God, and peace and comfort in my being with you. . . . *Again,* with respect to baptism, I have my liberty to baptize infants without making it a business to promote it among others; and every member is to have his liberty in regard to believers' baptism, only to forbear discourse and debates on it that may have a tendency to break the peace of the Church. . . . *We do not mean to make baptism, whether of believers or infants, a bar to communion.*"

The policy thus outlined leaves but one impression: that hitherto believers' baptism had been observed when baptism at all was administered.

It is thought advisable to enlarge somewhat upon this vexed question, because so many advocates of pædo-baptism have claimed, and do still claim Bunyan as one of them; but there can be no doubt, whatsoever, that once convinced of the Scriptural injunction for a *believer* to be baptised, John Bunyan passed through the waters of baptism, "upon Confession of Faith," led by his faithful guide, "holy" Mr. Gifford, about the year 1651-3, as Charles Doe relates.†

(Page 233). **William Bedford.**

"A tradition exists . . . at Royston that Mr. Bedford (minister at Royston) was educated at Cambridge, and was one of the students who are reported to have stopped John Bunyan in one of his itinerant excursions, with a determination to hear the tinker preach; and that the result was the conversion of Mr. Bedford, who afterwards joined the non-conformists." (Quoted from the MS. Memoirs of the Rev. J. Geard, minister of the Baptist Church, Hitchin, 1775-1831.)

† *The Struggler,* in Charles Doe's Folio, 1692.

XI.

THE PILGRIM'S PROGRESS.

"As I walked through the wilderness of this world I lighted upon a certain place where was a Den, and I laid me down in that place to sleep; and as I slept I dreamed a dream." These words, which open for us the story of the Pilgrim, suggest to the majority of its readers the culminating point of interest in Bunyan's life. It may be well, therefore, to try to settle, if we can, the place of the den and the time of the dream.

That *The Pilgrim's Progress* was written in prison we have on the highest authority of all, that of Bunyan himself. When the third, which was the first complete, edition of the book appeared in 1679, by the side of the word 'den' in the text he placed the explanatory words 'the Jail' in the margin. This evidence is, of course, conclusive, even if we had not, as we have, contemporary testimony to the effect that the Dream was a prison book. But the inquiry is not without interest as to what gaol it was and to what imprisonment these words refer. As previously mentioned, it has become one of the common-places of literature that the great allegory was written during Bunyan's twelve years' imprisonment. If so, it was written in the county gaol, for, as we have seen, the evidence is conclusive that the writer could not have spent twelve years in the prison on Bedford bridge; yet on the other hand the old tradition, which had come down from most reliable authorities, confidently asserted that Bunyan was confined in the prison on the bridge, and that he there wrote *The Pilgrim's Progress.* Is there any way of reconciling these seeming opposites? I think it will be found there is, and that a careful examination of all the available evidence points to the following conclusions, namely, that three years after his twelve years' imprisonment was over, Bunyan was again in prison during the winter and early spring of 1675-6; that this time he was a prisoner in the town gaol on Bedford bridge; and that it was during this later imprisonment he wrote his memorable dream.

Let us first see what reason there is for supposing that Bunyan was again in gaol three years after his release in 1672, and after he had been for that length of time the pastor of the Bedford Church. That there was a later imprisonment is placed beyond all manner of doubt, though the date of it was not given. The friend who tells us that he paid Bunyan a visit in gaol during his long imprisonment tells us also that that imprisonment was divided into two parts, of six years each, with a brief interval between the parts, and that when the second six years was ended "another short affliction, which was an imprisonment of half a year, fell to his share." To the same purpose Charles Doe relates that "they put him in prison a third time, but that proved but for about half a year." These writers give us no clue to the date of this third imprisonment, but we are not altogether without evidence on the point. This evidence takes a three-fold shape.

In 1675, which, of course, according to Old Style, extended to March, 1676, Bunyan published a little book in Catechetical form, entitled *Instruction for the Ignorant.** Its prefatory dedication runs thus: "To the Church of Christ in and about Bedford, walking in the Faith and Fellowship of the Gospel, your affectionate brother and companion *in the Kingdom and patience of Jesus Christ,* wisheth all grace and mercy by Jesus Christ." He goes on to say that though he has designed this treatise for public and common benefit, yet "by reason of special bonds which the Lord hath laid upon me to you-ward, I could do no less *being driven from you in presence, not in affection,* but first present you with this little book." He signs himself, "yours to serve by my ministry *when I can* to your edification and consolation, John Bunyan." It is difficult to attach any other meaning to these words than that in 1675, when he wrote them, he was once more in prison.

* The only known copy of the first edition, dated 1675, is in the Bodleian Library.

The assumption of a later imprisonment at this time has this in its favour also that it removes a discrepancy which has always been felt to be a difficulty in the story of Bunyan's life. The contemporary writer, to whom reference has been made, tells us that "after this blessed man had suffered twelve years' imprisonment for the testimony of a good conscience, and stopt the mouths of his greatest enemies by his holy, harmless, and inoffensive conversation, it pleased God to stir up the heart of

Dr. Barlow, Bishop of Lincoln, to be a means of his deliverance, which I mention to this bishop's honour." Now we happen to know, from an independent source, that Barlow did actually interfere on Bunyan's behalf, and that it was John Owen, the great Nonconformist divine who, at the instigation of some Bedford neighbour of Bunyan, first moved the bishop on his behalf. Barlow had been Owen's tutor at Queen's College, Oxford, as far back as 1630, and in the Commonwealth days was librarian of the Bodleian and Provost of Queen's when Owen was University Vice-Chancellor.* The story as it relates to Bunyan is told with circumstantial detail by Asty in his *Life of Owen,* he having obtained the particulars from Owen's friend, Sir John Hartopp.

* Thomas Barlow (1607—1691) was librarian at the Bodleian from 1642 to 1660.

He says, "Dr. Barlow, formerly his tutor, then Bishop of Lincoln, upon a special occasion failed him when he might have expected the service of his professed friendship. The case was this: Mr. John Bunyan had been confined to a gaol for twelve years upon an excommunication for Nonconformity; now there was a law that if any two persons will go to the bishop of the diocese and offer a cautionary bond that the prisoner shall conform in half a year, the bishop may release him upon that bond; whereupon a friend of this poor man desired Dr. Owen to give him his letter to the bishop on his behalf, which he readily granted. It was soon after the discovery of the Popish Plot when this letter was carry'd to the Bishop who, having read it, told the person who delivered it That he had a particular kindness for Dr. Owen and would deny him nothing he could legally do. 'Nay,' says he, 'with my service, tell him, I shall strain a point to serve him.' (That was his very expression.) 'But,' says he, 'this being a new thing to me, I desire a little time to consider of it; and if I can do it you may be assured of my readiness.' He was waited upon again about a fortnight after, and his answer was, 'That indeed he was informed he might do it,' but the law providing that in case the Bishop refused, application should be made to the Lord Chancellor, who thereupon should issue forth an order to the Bishop to take the cautionary bond and release the prisoner, 'now,' said he, 'you know what a critical time this is, and I have many enemies; I would desire you to move the Lord Chancellor in the case, and upon his order I will do it'; to which it was replied, 'this method would be chargeable and the man was poor, not able to expend so much money, and being satisfy'd he could do it legally it was hoped his Lordship would remember his promise, there being no straining a point in the case.' But he would do it upon no other terms, which at last was done, and the poor man was released; but little thanks to the Bishop."[1]

In giving this circumstantial account of the matter Asty is evidently wrong as to the time, as he might well be, writing in 1721, or more than forty years afterwards. In no way could 1672, the year of Bunyan's release from his twelve years' imprisonment, be made to coincide with the time of the Popish Plot, which was in 1678. But though he was wrong as to time he evidently was certain as to the fact. Barlow was undoubtedly concerned in Bunyan's release, and concerned not as a friend* but in his official capacity as bishop of the diocese; yet Barlow was not Bishop of Lincoln till 1675. His predecessor in the see, Dr. Fuller, died on the 23rd of April in that year. Dr. Barlow was elected May 14th and consecrated June 27th. In his official capacity, therefore, he could be concerned in no release which took place as early as 1672, but might very well have to do with one effected in 1676.

* In the "Lincoln" Collection of books, bequeathed to the Bodleian Library, Oxford, by Dr. Barlow, there are several volumes of Bunyan's writings, and on the title page of a work bound up with one is apparently Barlow's own signature. Three of these books were published in 1675. This fact seems to suggest that the bishop had, at least, some regard for Bunyan.

Further, it is important to note that 1675 was the year of the ascendancy of the Danby Administration and of that important change in the policy of the government towards the Nonconformists which led to the withdrawal of the licences granted to their preachers and their places of worship under the Declaration of Indulgence. That Declaration had now been in force for three years, but had never been really popular in the country. Even the Nonconformists, while largely availing themselves of the liberty which it gave, looked with cold favour upon that exercise of the royal prerogative by which it was conferred. It was an unconstitutional Act, and there was a shrewd suspicion on all sides that it was mainly intended by the king to benefit the Roman Catholics. That the High Church party should dislike the granting of liberty to the Nonconformists was, of course, only to be expected; but, as we have said, even the Nonconformists themselves accepted that liberty with sore misgiving. It was, they felt, a perilous thing to leave it in the power of the Crown to suspend an Act of Parliament by prerogative. If it might suspend one it might suspend forty, and where then

[1] Asty's *Life of Owen*, folio 1721, p. xxx.

would be the liberties of the country in the hands of a Stuart king? When the Declaration was debated in Parliament in 1673 a conspicuous Nonconformist, then in the House, objecting to it strongly, was met by the remark: "Why, Mr. Love, you are a Dissenter yourself, it is very ungrateful that you who receive the benefit should object against the manner." "I am a Dissenter," he replied, "and thereby unhappily obnoxious to the law, and 'if you catch me in the corn you may put me in the pound.' The law against the Dissenters I should be glad to see repealed by the same authority that made it. But while it is law the king cannot repeal it by proclamation; and I had much rather see the Dissenters suffer by the rigour of the law, though I suffer with them, than see all the laws of England trampled under the foot of the prerogative, as in this example."[1]

These resolute words expressed a feeling widely shared; and, after vehement debate, the House resolved, that penal statutes in matters ecclesiastical cannot be suspended but by Act of Parliament. Four days later this resolution was followed by the voting of an address conveying that information to His Majesty. The result was that very soon the Nonconformists were in a worse plight than before. A new Test Act was passed which, though aimed mainly at the Roman Catholics, bore hardly upon all in the nation who could not conform; the king, with his own hand, tore off the Great Seal from the Declaration of Indulgence; and the ministry was broken up, the reins of power passing into the hands of the Earl of Danby. In matters ecclesiastical, the new minister was simply Clarendon over again, just as resolutely bent as he had been on building up the Church on the lines of the Act of Uniformity, and on stamping out everything in the shape of Dissent. Thus, in 1675, the reign of intolerance had set in again as violently as at any time since the Restoration. The king was prevailed upon to call in all the licences granted to Nonconformist preachers and places of worship. In a sermon of the time before the House of Commons a high church preacher sounded the note of storm. Nonconformity, he said, could only be effectually vanquished by vengeance, and the right thing to do was to set fire to the faggot to teach these obstinate people by scourges or scorpions, and to open their eyes with gall. These preliminary mutterings were soon followed by the outburst of the storm itself. Nathaniel Heywood, a well-known Noncon-

[1] Wilson's *Life of Defoe*, i., 58.

formist minister in Lancashire, tells us that at this time he was met by more bitter opposition in his work, and went through sorer trouble than at any time since his ejectment. Warrants, he says, were shot against him like arrows, and when he and his people tried to meet for worship they found the officers already at the meeting doors. Such being the temper of the time, no wonder if John Bunyan, as well as Nathaniel Heywood, was made to feel the change. For three years he had held a licence from the king which secured him as a preacher from arrest. Now all such licences had been recalled by public proclamation, and, therefore, for the first time since his release in 1672, he was defenceless against informers, and was once more sent to gaol: this time to the town prison on the bridge.* We may say this because there are various indications and traditions pointing in this direction, which leave little room for doubt. We happen to know, for example, that the town gaol was that same year made ready for use again, as though with a view to requirements which were felt to be near. It had lain in dismantled condition ever since the great flood of 1671; but at a council meeting held on the 13th of May, 1675, "it was agreed and ordered That the Prison upon the Bridge shall be rebuilt: And it shall be done with the ould materyalls."[1] In pursuance of this order a committee was appointed to oversee the work which was to be taken in hand forthwith. In the case of a structure so small, and with the materials ready to hand, the prison might very well be ready for use again by August or September at the latest.

*** Familiarly known as The Clink.** *Vide* **Foxe's** ***Acts and Monuments*** **for use of term.**

Then, further, we have these two facts in confirmation of this view—First, the tradition that Bunyan was confined in the prison on Bedford bridge was unbroken from the earliest times, and firmly believed by the oldest inhabitants of the town till the enquiries of Mr. Wyatt, in 1868, raised the question of the county and borough jurisdiction; and, secondly, we have a piece of personal testimony to which considerable importance may be attached. In the year 1814 there died at Newport Pagnel, in his seventy-seventh year, the Rev. William Bull, Congregational minister there, a man of local influence, character, and genius, and the intimate personal friend and correspondent of the poet Cowper. He was often at Bedford, and it was his quaint and characteristic custom when crossing the town bridge, to make solemn pause and do reverent homage to Bunyan's memory,

[1] *Act Book of the Bedford Corporation.* May, 1675.

explaining on one occasion to a friend who crossed the bridge with him and who lived till 1849,[1] that he did so because on that spot Bunyan suffered imprisonment for conscience' sake. Now, Mr. Bull's testimony as to the place of imprisonment is especially trustworthy, for in the year 1758 he was living in the town of Bedford, where he was in business with his uncle. He joined the Bedford Church in 1760, at the time that Bunyan's great grand-daughter, Hannah Bunyan, was a member of the congregation, and ten years before her death. He was the intimate friend of Samuel Sanderson, the minister of the church, by whom he himself was sent into the ministry. Sanderson again was for ten years the colleague, in the pastorate at Bedford, of Ebenezer Chandler, who was Bunyan's immediate successor, and the first editor of his collected works. Not only did Chandler immediately follow Bunyan in the pastorate of the church, of which he was for nearly forty years the minister; but also he was the close personal friend of Bunyan's eldest son, John, who at the time of his father's third imprisonment was a young man of eighteen, and would therefore know very well in which gaol he was last confined. By the time of Chandler and Sanderson, relating to him would be a matter of interest and frequent conversation. The circle into which William Bull was thrown in Bedford, in 1760, and into which he subsequently married,* was therefore in the way of being exceptionally well-informed as to the main facts of Bunyan's life, and would have received his information directly from them. It is needless to say that tradition like this is more than respectable, it is conclusive.

* He married Hannah, daughter of Thomas Palmer, of Bedford, on June 7th, 1768.

This bridge-house, in which Bunyan was confined for six months, served the double purpose of a prison and a toll-house at a time when incoming grain and other products were subject to charges levied by the municipality. The bridge, with its gate-houses, was built in 1224, out of the ruins of the old Bedford castle. With its seven arches spanning the stream of the quietly-flowing Ouse, it was a picturesque object to the eye, and in a peregrination of 1526, is described as one of the "fayre stone bridges" of England. Though 330 feet long it was only 13½ feet wide, and its parapet, which was little more than a yard high, was re-built from the materials of the dismantled church Bunyan's name and fame had steadily grown, and everything

[1] The late Mr Thomas Kilpin of Bedford. [He married Esther Giffard, grand-daughter of Rev. W. Bull.]

of St. Peter Dunstaple, which, till 1545, stood as sister church close to St. Mary's. On each side of the central arch was a tower gateway, that to the north being used as the town gaol, the one to the south as the military magazine and storehouse for the county. The portion of the north tower gateway used as a prison was the upper chamber on the east side, beneath which was a stone staircase, leading to a small island covered with shrubs and greenery, that existed when the water was lower than it is now.

* *Vide* Addendum.

If we are right,* then, in saying that Bunyan was again in gaol in 1675-6, and that the place of his confinement was this prison on Bedford bridge, we come now to ask: Was it then and there that he wrote *The Pilgrim's Progress*? Two considerations seem to give us the answer in the affirmative. First we know for certain that the book was written in prison, and if we suppose that it was written during his twelve years' imprisonment we shall have to account for the long interval of six years between its composition and its publication; for from that imprisonment Bunyan was released in 1672, whereas *The Pilgrim's Progress* was not published till 1678. His own account of the matter seems to suggest a very much more prompt procedure. He tells us that as soon as he had finished the book he was curious to see what reception it would meet with at the hands of his neighbours:

> "When I had put mine ends together,
> I show'd them others that I might see whether
> They would condemn them or them justify;
> And some said let them live; some let them die.
> Some said John print it; others said, not so;
> Some said it might do good; others said no."

His book thus being met by grave looks of dubiety, as well as with bright smiles of appreciation, Bunyan was for a time in as much perplexity as a man usually is who takes counsel of his neighbours. Therefore, in the exercise of his sturdy common sense, he will settle the matter for himself:

> "Since you are thus divided,
> I print it will, and so the case decided."

There is an air of briskness about this which, to say the least, is not suggestive of a six years' interval before publication.

He also tells us something further, which may help to a conclusion. He says that at the time when, all unexpectedly to

THE OLD BRIDGE, BEDFORD.
Showing the Town Prison, in which John Bunyan wrote 'The Pilgrim's Progress.'

himself, there dawned upon him the conception of the Pilgrim story, he was actually engaged in the composition of another book:

> "Thus it was: I writing of the Way
> And Race of Saints in this our Gospel-day,
> Fell suddenly into an Allegory
> About their journey, and the way to glory."

No sooner did the vision dawn upon him, and the fast-coming troop of fancies begin to multiply "like sparks that from the coals of fire do fly," than he began to be afraid lest the new-comer would push aside the more serious and, as he judged then, the more important work on which he was already engaged:

> "Nay then, thought I, if that you breed so fast,
> I'll put you by yourselves, lest you at last
> Should prove *ad infinitum*, and eat out
> The book that I already am about."

As a matter of duty, therefore, he pushed aside the witching fancies that were lighting up his prison cell, and proceeded to finish the work on which he was engaged before they came, a work setting forth, as he says, "the Way and Race of Saints in this our Gospel-day." Now, we find that a book answering to this work, entitled *The Strait Gate*, was published by Bunyan in 1676. No other work published during his long imprisonment, or for years after, at all meets the requirements of the case. But this book does. It is concerned with "the Way and Race of Saints." It was preceded in 1675 by the work entitled *Instruction for the Ignorant*, which was evidently a prison book. It came out in 1676, and it was followed by *The Pilgrim's Progress*, entered at Stationers' Hall in 1677.

The conclusion we have thus reached is that the first part of the memorable dream was written in the prison on Bedford bridge in the early months of 1676.* Whether it was actually finished there may be open to question. There is a curious break in the story which seems almost to suggest that it was not. After describing the parting of Christian and Hopeful with the Shepherds on the Delectable Mountains, Bunyan says, "So I awoke from my dream." Then in the next paragraph, he adds, "And I slept, and dreamed again, and saw the same two Pilgrims going down the mountains along the highway towards the city." This is the only break that occurs in the First Part of the book. It is not artistically required by the plot of the story; indeed it somewhat interferes with it; and the more probable conclusion is

* *Vide* Addendum.

that Bunyan's dream was broken by Bunyan's release from his den, and that the remainder of the story, which amounts to nearly a third of the First Part, was written after he was at large.

The circumstances of the case seem to point to the early summer of 1676 as the time when Bishop Barlow's order of release came from Buckden palace to Bedford gaol, and when Bunyan finally bade farewell to his prison life. If there be any truth in the supposition just made, that nearly one-third of his book was written after his release, it would probably be sometime in 1677 that he set out for London, taking with him the manuscript of the 'Pilgrim' for publication. The publisher fixed upon was Nathaniel Ponder, at the sign of the Peacock, in the Poultry, near Cornhill.* His was a new name on Bunyan's title-pages, but it was one destined frequently to re-appear during the next ten years; and though this was the first time these two had had business relations with each other, Ponder was no stranger to the Nonconformists of Bedfordshire. In 1671, from his shop, which was then in Chancery Lane, he had published a work, entitled *England Saved,* the author of which was Robert Perrot, the ejected minister of Dean, Bedfordshire. In 1672, when a licence was granted to John Whitman, an elder of the Bedford Church, to preach at George Cokayn's house, at Cotten End, it was endorsed, "Pray deliver this to Nathaniel Ponder." There was also this further link of connection: Dr. Owen had recently been concerned in Bunyan's release, and Nathaniel Ponder was Owen's publisher, and indeed at that very time bringing out for him his work entitled *The Reason of Faith.* As, after the interest Owen had recently taken in his release, Bunyan would probably call upon him on his arrival in the city, the talk between them would be likely to determine the Peacock in the Poultry as to the distination of the 'Pilgrim.'

* An interesting article upon the Ponder Family, by F. W. Bull, F.S.A. (a descendant of Rev. W. Bull), appeared in *The Northamptonshire Advertiser,* August 15th, 1924.

The arrival of the MS. proved to be an epoch in the life of the publisher as well as in that of the author; for, as John Dunton tells us, after the success of the famous book he was known among his brother craftsmen of the Stationers' Company sas 'Bunyan Ponder.' He was an agreeable man to have dealings with. "He has," says Dunton, "sweetness and enterprise in his air which plead and anticipate in his favour." Notwithstanding his pleasant manners, however, 'Bunyan Ponder,' like 'Elephant Smith,' had in the previous year found his way to the Gatehouse prison, as may be seen from the Minutes of

THE

Pilgrim's Progress

FROM

THIS WORLD,

TO

That which is to come:

Delivered under the Similitude of a

DREAM

Wherein is Discovered,

The manner of his setting out,

His Dangerous Journey; And safe

Arrival at the Desired Countrey.

I have used Similitudes, Hos. 12. 10.

By *John Bunyan.*

Licensed and Entred according to Order.

LONDON,

Printed for *Nath. Ponder* at the *Peacock* in the *Poultrey* near *Cornhil*, 1678.

Title-Page of the First Edition of
'THE PILGRIM'S PROGRESS.'
1678.

Privy Council, where there is the following record: "1676. At the Court at Whitehall, May 10th (the King present), a warrant was issued to commit Nathaniell Ponder to the Gatehouse, for carrying to the Presse to be printed an unlicensed Pamphlet tending to Sedition and Defamation of the Christian Religion." Ponder's prison experiences, however, proved to be much more brief than those of his friend Bunyan, as his spirit was certainly much less resolute. On the 26th of the same month, on the 10th of which he had been committed, before the same council, "Nathaniel Ponder, Stationer, was discharged upon his humble petition, setting forth his hearty sorrow for his offence and promising never to offend in like manner." He was ordered to pay due fees and to enter into a bond of £500. The year after this experience of his the MS. of *The Pilgrim's Progress* would be in Ponder's hands, for we find the following entry in the register of the Stationers' Company: "22nd December, 1677, Nathaniel Ponder entered then for his Coppy by vertue of a licence under the hand of Mr. Turner, and which is subscribed by Mr. Warden Vere, One Book or Coppy Intituled The Pilgrim's Progress from this world to that which is to come, delivered in y^e^ Similitude of a Dream, by John Bunpan, vj^d^." The sixpence indicated at the end was, of course, the customary fee for registration. Entered thus at Stationers' Hall at the end of December, Bunyan's Dream, we find from a "General Catalogue of Books printed and published at London in Hilary term $167\frac{7}{8}$," was licensed February 18th, 1678, and therefore early in the year was in the hands of that public which so quickly and for so long was to give it hearty welcome. In the catalogue referred to it was announced as "price bound 1s. 6d." It was printed in small octavo on yellowish-grey paper, from apparently new type, and extended to 232 pages in addition to title, author's apology and conclusion.

As in the case of his earlier work, *Grace Abounding, The Pilgrim's Progress* grew under Bunyan's hands after its first publication. Some very characteristic additions were made in the second edition, which came out the same year as the first, and also in the third, which appeared as early as 1679. In the first edition there was no description of Christian breaking his mind to his wife and children,[1] no appearance of Mr. Worldly Wiseman, no second meeting with Evangelist,[2] no account given by

[1] "In this plight . . . what shall I do to be saved?"
[2] "Now as Christian was walking solitary . . . Worldly Wiseman's counsel."

Christian to Goodwill at the wicket-gate of his own turning aside.[1] Christian's discourse with Charity at the Palace Beautiful was added afterwards, as were the four verses on his leaving the palace.[2] The other additions were the third appearance of Evangelist as the Pilgrims were nearing Vanity Fair;[3] the further account of Mr. By-End's rich relations,[4] with the conversation which took place between him and his friends, and between him and the Pilgrims;[5] the sight of Lot's wife turned to a pillar of salt, with the talk it occasioned;[6] the whole account of Diffidence, the wife of Giant Despair;[7] and, finally, the description of the Pilgrims being met on the farther side of the river by the King's trumpeters in white and shining raiment.[8] It may be mentioned further that in the first edition several of the songs were introduced without the sentences which afterwards connected them with the narrative or dialogue.

The first edition of the first part of *The Pilgrim's Progress* was, on the whole, much more roughly spelt than the first edition of the second part, which was published six years later. We have wrong spellings by themselves, and also wrong spellings side by side with right. We have, for instance, Slough of Despond and Slow of Dispond, Pliable and Plyable; lie, lye, ly; die, dye, dy; raiment and rayment; and such forms as morgage, drownded, grievously, travailers, lyons, ai for aye, two wit for to wit, bin for been, thorow for through, tro for trow, bruit for brute, strodled for straddled, anoiance, strook, bewayling, toull, forraign, suddain, stounded, sloath, melancholly, choaked, chaulketh, carkass, and villian. There is nothing remarkable in the doubling of the final consonant in such words as generall, untill, and the like, for this was the seventeenth-century custom; but Bunyan also doubles it in such words as bogg, denn, scarr, ragg, quagg, and wagg; and, what was even more unusual, he doubles the medial in such words as hazzard, steddiness, fellon, eccho, shaddow, widdow. In his entries in the Church Book he often dropped the final 'e,' and in the book before us also, we find wholesom, lightsom, bridg, and knowledg; while he uses this letter to give the old plural form in shooes,

1 "Truly, said Christian, I have said the truth of Pliable . . . cast out."
2 "Then said Charity, Christian . . . from their blood."
3 "Now when they were got . . . faithful Creator."
4 "Almost the whole town . . . by Father's side."
5 "Now I saw in my dream . . . devouring fire."
6 "Now I saw just on the other side . . . remember Lot's wife."
7 "Now Giant Despair had a wife . . . search them in the morning."
8 "There came out also at this time . . . glorious joy be expressed."

braines, decaies, alwaies, paines, rayes, and the like. In this first edition also we have such colloquialisms and irregularities as: catch't up, shewen, brast for burst, maiest, didest, then for to go, I should a been, practick, a little to-side, let's go over, like for likely, afraid on't, ransak't, mist for missed, such as thee and I, you was, we was, two miles off of Honesty, and things prophanes. The second edition had fewer mis-spellings, but more printer's errors. Some very characteristic marginalia which were found in the first edition were, one fails to see why, omitted in subsequent issues. By the side of the narrative there were such racy comments as these: "A man may have company when he sets out for heaven and yet go thither alone"; "A Christian can sing alone when God doth give him the joy of his heart"; "O brave Talkative!"; "Christian snibbeth his fellow"; "Hopeful swaggers"; "Christian roundeth off Demas"; "O good riddance!"; "They are whipp't and sent on their way."

The most important addition made to the second edition, which came out only a few months after the first, was the introduction of Mr. Worldly Wiseman; and to the third edition, which appeared the following year, the characteristic additions to the story of Mr. By-ends. It was to this third edition of 1679 there was first added an illustrative engraving in the shape of a portrait of the author by Robert White. In this portrait Bunyan is represented as sleeping over a den in which there is a lion, while above him Christian, with book in one hand, staff in the other, and burden on his back, is toiling up from the City of Destruction, low-lying, to a city on the heights bathed in sunlight.

The fact that three editions were thus called for within a year, shows that *The Pilgrim's Progress* leaped at a bound to that popularity which it has retained for two and a half centuries. An artist has given us an imaginary sketch of Nathaniel Ponder's shop at the time he first sent forth the book. A scholar is coming out from under the Sign of the Peacock, and a peasant, whip in one hand and money in the other, going in, while near the shop door are a gay gallant and a fair lady, schoolboys, and grave men, all intently reading that story of the 'Pilgrim' they have just purchased over the counter within. The picture is true to the time then and true to the time now. There is the less need therefore to give the story which thus laid hold at once and still keeps hold of minds so diverse. Briefly told it is this:

Walking through the wilderness of this world the writer lights upon a den where he lays him down to sleep. As he sleeps, he dreams, and in his dream he sees a man who is clothed in rags, carrying a heavy burden and in deep anguish of soul. Turning homeward this man tells out his heart-grief to wife and children, who conclude that some frenzy has seized him and hope that sleep will settle his brain. But night brings no rest, the morning no relief, and with the day he wanders forth disconsolate. In this condition he is met by Evangelist, who urges him to flee and tells him whither. Forth he fares at once as his counsellor advises. Wife and children call after him in vain, and two of his neighbours bent on bringing him back by force are so far from succeeding, that one of them, Pliable by name, is prevailed upon to join him in his pilgrimage. These two, talking as they go of the glories of the heavens, are suddenly plunged into the mire of earth. Struggling out in rueful fashion, Pliable will have no more of these fine visions if this be the road to them. To Christian, however, for that was the name of the Pilgrim, the burden on his back is infinitely more grievous than any bedaubing of the Slough, and in the hope of getting rid of that, onward he goes. Turned out of his way by Mr. Worldly Wiseman, he is again set right by Evangelist, and reaches the wicket gate, where Good Will receives him. Directed by this new friend, he reaches the house of Interpreter, where he sees things rare, profitable, things pleasant, dreadful, things to make him stable. On a wall there is the picture of a man who has eyes lift up to heaven, the best of books in his hand, the law of truth upon his lips, a man who stood as if he pleaded with men. This picture a sculptor in our own times has fitly idealised in bronze as a statue for Bunyan himself.* Besides this picture Christian sees also the symbols of Passion and Patience, of the fire not to be put out, of the man who in grim earnest fights his way into the palace, of the despairing soul in the iron cage, and of the man startled by dreams of judgment.

* At Bedford.

Leaving the House of Interpreter, the Pilgrim, to his joy, finds his weary burden fall off at the sight of the Cross, and is saluted by Shining Ones, who pronounce him forgiven, clothe him with new raiment and set a mark upon his forehead. Passing then by Simple, Sloth, and Presumption, and encountering Formalist and Hypocrite, he climbs the Hill Difficulty to the arbour where he loses his roll, passes the lions and reaches a stately palace, the name of which is Beautiful. Here he is welcomed by a grave and beautiful damsel named Discretion, is entertained by Prudence, Piety, and Charity, and ultimately lodged in a large upper chamber named Peace, the window of which opened towards the sun-rising, and where he slept till break of day. Here, also, as in the house of Interpreter, he sees many rarities, and in the armoury is harnessed from head to foot with what was of proof, being then sent on his way.

Glory and gloom alternate, and after these pleasant experiences Christian goes down into the Valley of Humiliation, where he is met by the fierce fiend Apollyon, a devil such as Luther met and Bunyan himself had known. The conflict that followed is one of the most spirit-stirring scenes in the whole book. Dean Stanley, who, at the request of the Duke of Bedford, selected the three subjects for the bas-reliefs on the pedestal on the Bunyan statue, showed his fine instinct in fixing upon this scene as the foremost of the three, the artist showing instinct equally fine in making Christian's form the embodiment of all that is staunchly upright, true and trusty, and that of Apollyon the incarnation of whatever is sinister, sinuous, and gliding. Into these words, which wind up the story, Bunyan has evidently poured the most burning memories of his own life:

> "In this combat no man can imagine, unless he had seen and heard, as I did, what yelling and hideous roaring Apollyon made all the time of the fight, he spake like a dragon; and on the other side what sighs and groans brast from Christian's heart. I never saw him all the while give so much as one pleasant look, till he perceived he had wounded Apollyon, with his two-edged sword, then indeed he did smile, and look upward: but 'twas the dreadfullest sight that ever I saw."

The way of a Pilgrim to the better life is ever an arduous journey. No sooner is Christian past this terrible brush with Apollyon than he finds himself among the fearsome shapes, the doleful voices, and the ominous rushings to and fro of the Valley of the Shadow of Death, fit symbol of "the struggle with what is darkest and dreadest in human experience, all that has in it the least of the lightsomeness of life, most of the chill and darkness and mystery of death, giving to all that in human experience, which before death is worse than death itself, a local habitation and a name."[1] Once out of this grim valley, however, Christian comes up with Faithful, a kindred soul, who for some time at least is to be his companion on the way. Passing the caverns

[1] John Service. [The Scottish theologian: 1833—1884.]

of the two giants Pope and Pagan, the two friends hold good discourse of past experience till they are joined by one Talkative, the son of Saywell, of Prating Row, a man of facile tongue and slippery life. Ready at a moment's notice for what you will, this man can with equal facility and equal emptiness "talk of things heavenly or things earthly; things moral or things evangelical, things sacred or things prophane; things past or things to come; things foreign or things at home; things more essential or things circumstantial." The only condition the wretched windbag stipulates being that all be done to spiritual profit. At first Faithful is somewhat imposed upon by his fair seeming, but Christian, who knows the man to be, in spite of his fine tongue, but a sorry fellow, puts his brother upon his guard. Then Faithful, true to his name, tears away the mask from this piece of hollow pretence, provoking him to the sneer, "You lie at the catch, I perceive," and sending him on his way a shamed if not a wiser man.

Parting with Talkative, they are joined by Evangelist, whom they are right glad to see, but whose words are prophetic of approaching storm. For they are now nearing a town where is kept that fair of ancient standing called Vanity Fair, through which lies the way to the Celestial City. This memorable scene was doubtless suggested to Bunyan by one of the many fairs held in those days which were then of so much importance as means of traffic. Elstow Fair had been a great institution ever since Henry II. had granted a charter to the nuns of the Abbey there. But the one fair of all others likely to suggest and be the historical basis of Vanity Fair, was that held for centuries at Sturbridge, near to Cambridge. Like the great fairs of Frankfort, Leipsic, and Novgorod, it lasted for weeks. It was proclaimed by the Vice-Chancellor of the University, and opened with great state by the mayor and other members of the Corporation of Cambridge. It was of large extent, covering an area of half a square mile, and had its long line of booths named in rows after the forms of traffic there carried on. It had its Great One of the fair, its Court of Justice presided over by the mayor or his deputy, who was attended by his eight Redcoats or Runners. It was a vast emporium of commerce. Mercers from France brough their silks, and Flemings from the Low Countries their woollens; traders from Scotland and from Kendal set forth their pack-horses on the road to be in time for the fair, while barges from London came round by Lynn and brought the merchandise of the city along the Ouse and the Cam. All new discoveries and foreign acquisitions were here first brought to public view; the voyages of Drake and Cavendish and Raleigh furnished their novelties, while products from beyond the East and west of the Atlantic found their way year by year to Sturbridge Fair. When business was over it was succeeded by pleasure. Round the square, in the centre of which rose the great maypole with its vane at the top, there were coffee-houses, taverns, music-halls, buildings for the exhibition of drolls, legerdemain, mountebanks, wild beasts, monsters, dwarfs, giants, rope-dancers, and the like. In 1481 a grotesque masquerade was held personating Louis XI. of France, and in the fifteenth century the Duke of York spent a day there in a tent of cloth of gold, attended by noblemen and ladies and much musical display. As year by year the country gentry for ten or twelve miles round came in with their sons and daughters for the diversions of the place, the sight presented was that of Vanity Fair indeed.[1]

Bunyan, often in the neighbourhood of Cambridge, as we know he was, must several times in his life have looked on this remarkable scene at Sturbridge, a scene which lent itself so readily to the purposes of his allegory. Having such memories in his mind the Dreamer sees Christian and Faithful pass into Vanity Fair, with its rows, its innumerable forms of traffic in houses, lands, trades, places, honours and preferments, titles, pleasures, delights, and what not; with its jugglings, cheats, games, plays, fools, apes, knaves, and that of every kind; with its great one of the fair, its court of justice, and its power of judgment. No wonder the pilgrims found themselves out of sympathy with their surroundings, and that Faithful was sent by way of the persecutors' fires to the martyr's crown.

Christian now has to go alone, but not for long, for Hopeful springs up out of Faithful's fidelity and becomes his successor in the pilgrimage to the city. As, after coming out of the Valley of the Shadow of Death, the Pilgrims met with Talkative, so now, after the sorrows of Vanity Fair, they come up with By-ends of Fair-speech, "a subtle evasive knave," drawn with infinite skill, whose grandfather was a waterman, looking one way and rowing another; and whose distinguishing characteristics are that, in religion, he makes it a point never to go against wind

[1] *Sturbridge Fair*: Nichol's *Bib. Topographica*, vol. v., p. 73 *et seq.*

and tide, and to be the best friend of religion when she goes in silver slippers, walking in the sunshine, and is applauded of the people.

Passing on their way, after scathing this empty worldling, the pilgrims leave Demas and his silver-mine on the one side, and Lot's wife, transformed into a pillar, on the other, till they come to a pleasant river lined with fruitful trees, where they are rested and refreshed. But the shadow follows the sunshine, and before long they are within the grim walls of Doubting Castle and the cruel grasp of Giant Despair. Released therefrom by the key of Promise, they come next on their way to the Delectable Mountains and the kindly Shepherds. Here it would be pleasant to stay, but life tarries not, neither must the pilgrims of life; they are therefore on the road once more. As they go Christian beguiles the tedium of the journey by the story of Little-faith, who was robbed hereabouts. The sturdy rogues who plundered him have been a terror to stronger men than he. They have left scars and cuts even on the face of Great-grace; they made David groan, and moan, and roar; yea, Heman and Hezekiah too, though champions in their day, were forced to bestir themselves when by these assaulted. But who was Heman, asks the poet Southey when, about a century ago, he set forth to edit a new edition of Bunyan's dream? Heman was that Ezrahite with whose renowned wisdom Solomon's was compared (1 Kings 4, 31), and who yet wrote, as the title shows, one of our most plaintive Psalms of sorrowful experience (Psalm 88). It appears, however, that with all his reading, Southey had never read of him, and he concluded that Heman was a misprint for Haman. But even then the difficulty was not over, for Haman was surely a sorry specimen of the champions of faith; so Southey boldly cut the knot and substituted Mordecai for Haman in the text of the 'Pilgrim.'* But this new reference was pointless in its connection, and Bunyan, who knew his Bible better than Southey, had given the better name. It was Heman, and neither Haman nor Mordecai who in spite of strength of wisdom, had, as his sorrowful Psalm testifies, been hardly bested in the battle of life.

* John Murray's edition, 1830, p. 170, Line 5.

Encountering Flatterer with his net, and Atheist with his laugh, Christian and his companion pass over the Enchanted Ground in safety, and reach the Country of Beulah. This was a land of flowers and of the singing of birds, where the air is very sweet and pleasant and the sun shineth night and day, a land where the angels come, for it is on the borders of heaven. Yet, pleasant as it is, not even this land, but the City of God is the destination of the true pilgrim; therefore still they go. But the end is not far distant, and there is now but one trial more. The bridgeless River has to be crossed, the river which men find deeper or shallower as they believe in the King of the place. The crossing of that river and the glorious reception into the city beyond; the celestial escourt that leads the pilgrims to the gate; the joy-bells that ring as they enter; all the glad sights and sounds that made the Dreamer wish himself among them—the description of all this is the crowning effort of his genius, a possession for ever to the literature of man, and no man may give it but Bunyan himself.

The striking and unexpected success of his pilgrim story, surprising no one more than himself, may have had much to do in determining Bunyan to venture upon one of those continuations which are proverbially dangerous experiments. Yet it would almost seem as if, even before the First Part had left his hands, he had some glimmering thought of a Second. In the last two lines of the poetical conclusion to the First Part, he says that if his reader should

> "Cast away all as vain
> I know not but 'twill make me dream again."

His first intention and endeavour was to complete the picture by a contrast. He had given the story of a noble life, of a life whose course was upward to the City of God; his purpose now was to paint in shadow the story of a life steering for the outer darkness, of a soul ever "unmaking itself." Immediately after the third edition of 1679, which was the First Part in its completed form, he set about the book entitled *The Life and Death of Mr. Badman.* In Charles Doe's Catalogue the date of its first appearance is given as 1685, but earlier editions have come to light since then, and we now know that it was actually published in 1680. That he connected this work with his 'Pilgrim' in his own mind, he tells us himself. The preface commences thus: "As I was considering with myself what I had written concerning the Progress of the Pilgrim from this world to glory: and how it had been acceptable to many in this nation: It came again into my mind to write, as then of him that was going to Heaven, so now of the Life and Death of the Ungodly and of their travel from this world to Hell." But whatever Bunyan's intention might be, the popular instinct was in this case truer than his own. The story of Badman's Life only served as a foil to that of Christian and could not be accepted either as its complement or continuation. Indeed, after the appearance of this book, other writers, ignoring it, undertook to complete Bunyan's allegory for him. In 1683 a writer who signs himself T. S. stepped into the field with a book which, in size and type, closely resembled the First Part sent out by Nathaniel Ponder. It was entitled 'The Second Part of *The Pilgrim's Progress,* from this present World of Wickedness and Misery to An Eternity of Holiness and Felicity: Exactly Described under the Similtude of a Dream.' It was printed for Jho. Malthus at the *Sun* in the Poultry and, so far as is known, only one copy has survived the lapse of time, a copy which was formerly in the library of the poet Southey, and is now in that of the Baptist Union.* The writer, whoever he was, had no intention, as in the case of the spurious Third Part of a later time, of palming off his book as Bunyan's own production. With not too much modesty, he merely intended to mend Bunyan's work, to supply what he considered to be missing in the First Part of the story. Pressed by the importunity of others, he had, he said, issued his meditations, "in such a method as might serve as a Supplyment or a Second Part to it, wherein I have endeavoured to supply a fourfold defect which I observe the brevity of that discourse necessitated the Author into." He has endeavoured to be more theological and "to deliver the whole in such serious and spiritual phrases that may prevent that lightness and laughter which the reading of some passages [in Bunyan's book] occasions in some vain and frothy minds." In other words, the original *Pilgrim's Progress* was not doctrinal enough and it was too attractive, charges which no one will think of bringing against his own production, which he hopes will help on a practice recently proposed: "viz., The giving of Books of this nature at Funerals, instead of Rings, Gloves, Wine or Bisket."

* There is a copy in the Henry E. Huntington Library, U.S.A., and another in Scotland.

This, which came out in 1683, was not the only attempt made to improve upon Bunyan. At the beginning of the genuine Second Part, which came out the following year, he says:

> "Some have of late to counterfeit
> My Pilgrim, to their own my title set;
> Yea, others, half my name and title too
> Have stitched to their own book to make them do;
> But yet they by their Features do declare
> Themselves not mine to be whose'er they are."

JOHN BUNYAN.
After the Portrait by Thomas Sadler, in the National Portrait Gallery, London.

This Second Part by Bunyan himself was published early in 1685, or in 1684, Old Style. The title-page was a reproduction and adaptation of the title to the First Part, and this later work, like that, was published by Nathaniel Ponder. Unlike the first edition of the First Part, however, which had no illustrations, this had a frontispiece depicting Christiana and her companions setting forth to the Celestial City; there being a sleeping-portrait of Bunyan at the foot of the picture. Between pages 52 and 53 also, there was a rude engraving of Greatheart carrying a huge sword in front of the pilgrims; and another between pages 162 and 163, in which the pilgrims are seen mirthfully dancing round the uplifted head of Giant Despair. On the reverse of the title there was this note:

"I appoint Mr. Nathaniel Ponder, But no other, to Print this Book.
John Bunyan."
"January 1st, 1684. [1685 N.S.]"

In this Second Part, as in the First, we have such spellings as, gon, lodg, knowledg, dwel, welcom, Samaritane, venome, combate, scarrs, curr, bitt, marr, lillies, eccho, linnen, robbin, shaddow. We have such variations as mercy and mercie, Apollyon and Apollion, sagasity and sagaciety, giant and gyant; such plurals as shoos, hosen, nosegaies, bodys. We have also such forms as suckered, nutriture, awrie, fether, foyled, craul, hault, jocond, surfits, crums. We have stere for steer, bryers for briars, role for roll, and faireth for fareth. We come also upon such colloquialisms as 'above-head' for 'over-head,' 'would a had him,' 'like to a bin,' 'not a bin,' 'I was a dreamed,' 'the highways have a been unoccupied,' 'greatly gladded'; and such expressions as 'she all-to-be-fooled me,' 'most an end,' 'they made pretty good shift to wagg along,' 'to get a thing by root-of-heart,' 'he cried her down at the cross,' 'heart-whole,' 'good-tasted,' and 'a beck'n of farewell.'

After sending forth his First Part, Bunyan's next intention, as we have seen, was to complete the story of a good life by placing side by side with it the contrast of a life that was basely bad. His second conception, which turned out to be more successful, was to supplement the story of Christian's pilgrimage by that of his wife and children; the record of the religious life in man by the story of that same life as it shows itself in woman. That the influence of the spiritual world upon her more susceptible nature had for him a special interest, we gather from the graceful passage he puts into the lips of Gaius, mine host:

"I will say again, that when the Saviour was come, Women rejoyced in him, before either Man or Angel. I read not that ever any man did give unto Christ so much as one Groat, but the Women followed him, and ministred to him of their Substance. 'Twas a Woman that washed his Feet with Tears, and a Woman that anointed his Body to the Burial. They were Women that wept, when he was going to the Cross; And Women that followed him from the Cross, and that sat by his Sepulcher when he was buried. They were Women that was first with him at his Resurrection-morn, and Women that brought Tiding first to his Disciples that he was risen from the Dead. Women therefore are highly favoured, and show by these things that they are sharers with us in the Grace of Life."

He was himself singularly fortunate in the two companions of his home life and pilgrimage. Mr. Lynch[1] acutely suggested that in Christiana, with her vigorous strength of character, Bunyan was idealising his second wife Elizabeth, who in the Swan Chamber so nobly confronted judges and magistrates in his behalf; while in the gentler character of Mercy we have his heart-reminiscence of her who had been the wife of his youth in his far-off Elstow days. Whatever there may be in this, the reference did not extend to his household, for Christiania's children were four sons, while Bunyan's were three sons and three daughters, the youngest child in each household, however, being a Joseph. There was one difficulty in constructing this story of Christiania which must have been felt from the first—the difficulty inherent in sending forth women and children on a hazardous journey like that which Christian had taken before them. This difficulty, however, was overcome by the device, old as the days of mediæval romance, of providing them with an attendant champion, who, as Mr. Greatheart, sees them safely past the perilous places of their pilgrimage and on to their journey's end.

Picturing substantially the same road as the first, this second dream nevertheless opens up to us with some variations of form. It is six years since the pilgrimage of Christian was given to the world, of which interval the writer gives this explanatory word: "Now it hath so happened thorough the multiplicity of business that I have been much hindred and kept back from my

[1] *Mornington Lecture*—Bunyan. [By Thomas T. Lynch. London, 1869.]

wonted travels into those parts whence he went, and so could not now obtain an opportunity to make further enquiry after whom he left behind, that I might give you an account of them. But having had some concerns that way of late, I went down again thitherward. Now having taken up my lodgings in a wood about a mile off the place, as I slept I dreamed again." He is thus no longer in his den, no longer in prison, but in more pleasant surroundings when the second vision comes upon him. In opening up its story also, he has recourse to an expedient he had not used before, an expedient similar to the device of Euripides among the Greek tragedians, who introduces some hero or god in the prologue of the story to tell us what is the present state of affairs, and what has happened up to the time of his speaking. The intervening interpreter in this case is an aged gentleman named Mr Sagacity, who comes up to the dreamer in his vision, and after describing how Christiania was led to go forth on pilgrimage, and carrying on the narrative as far as the scene at the wicket-gate, drops out of the story, to be seen by us no more.

Alike in the case of Christiana as in that of Christian, this setting forth on pilgrimage makes a stir among the neighbours, and while Obstinate and Pliable try to turn Christian from his purpose, Mrs. Timorous and Neighbour Mercy come on the same errand to Christiana. In both cases one of the two remonstrants ends in going with the pilgrim, with this difference, however, that Pliable afterwards turns back, which Mercy does not. The later conference among Pliable's nelghbours has its counterpart also in the lively conversation carried on between Mrs. Timorous and her friends Mrs. Bat's-eyes, Mrs. Inconsiderate, Mrs. Light-mind, and Mrs. Know-nothing. These animated gossips first conclude that if Christiana will go they are well rid of her, for 'twas never a good world since these whimsical fools dwelt in it; they then turn to more congenial themes, listening to Mrs. Light-mind as she tells how yesterday she was at Madam Wanton's, where they were all as merry as the maids. The second part lies along the same main lines as the first. We have the City of Destruction, the Wicket-gate, the House of Interpreter, the Hill Difficulty, the Palace Beautiful, the Valley of Humiliation and that of the Shadow of Death, Vanity Fair, the Delectable Mountains, the Enchanted Ground, the Land of Beulah, and the River without a bridge. We meet with some of the same people along the road or some of their relations, and all through the journey the pilgrims find that every one knows Christiana's husband, and the mere mention of his name proves a passport to hospitality and honour for her and her children.

But while there are many and substantial resemblances between the two parts, there are also additions and important variations. In the House of Interpreter the later pilgrims see in the significant rooms sights which Christian saw not. They are shown the man who could look no way but downward, and who went on raking sticks and straws and dust of the floor, all unmindful of the celestial crown to be seen over his head; 1672, the account of her admission being the first entry made in the spider which, repellent creature as it is, yet finds its way into king's palaces; the hen that has such various calls for her brood; the sheep that yields up its life so uncomplainingly; the robin, pretty of note, colour, and carriages, that yet catches and gobbles up unclean spiders; the tree, fair of leaf but rotten within, fit type of men of plausible exterior whose hearts are yet good for nothing but to be tinder for the devil's tinder-box; and the garden of the Interpreter's House, where was great variety of flowers—flowers diverse in stature, in quality, in colour, and smell and virtue, where some are better than some, and yet there was this to be noted, that where the gardener has set them there they stand and quarrel not one with another. In the Palace Beautiful, again, they were shown additional rarities: one of the apples that Eve did eat of; Jacob's ladder, on which the angels were going up and coming down; the mount on which Abraham offered up his son Isaac. A golden anchor also was given unto them, and they were had into the dining-room, where stood a pair of excellent Virginals, on which Prudence played, turning the sights she had shown them into an excellent song. At a later stage of their journey, too, they were had to some new places on the Delectable Mountains; to Mount Marvel, from which they saw a man at a distance that tumbled the hills about with words; to Mount Innocent, where they could see Prejudice and Ill-will casting dirt upon a man clothed in white, from whom the dirt fell as fast as it was thrown; and to Mount Charity, where they could see a man cutting coats and garments for the poor from a roll of cloth which grew never the less.

In this second part Bunyan shows his many-sided sympathy by unfolding the variety there is in spiritual experience. In this respect it is not a mere repetition. Going through the Slough of Despond Christiana's company looked well to the steps and made a shift to get staggeringly over without being so grievously bemired as Christian was. It was daytime when they went through the Valley of the Shadow of Death; Apollyon appeared to them only as a distant shape, and no sooner approached than he vanished; and Giant Despair, so far from shutting them up in his dungeons, gets Doubting Castle pulled about his ears, and his head struck from his shoulders by Greatheart, Old Honest, and the rest. Few things are more marked in the story than the contrast between the Valley of Humiliation as it presented itself to Christian, and as it presented itself to those who came after him—to the man of high spirit and to the women queenly in their passive meekness. To him it was a scene of awful conflict with Apollyon, to them it was a tranquil dwelling in green pastures and by still waters. To the sweet, contented spirit of Mercy this valley was a place where she loved to be. "Methinks," said she, "one may without much molestation be thinking what he is, whence he comes, and to what the King has called him. Here one may think and break at heart and melt in one's spirit, until one's eyes become like the fish-pools of Heshbon." The gentle nature of Mr. Fearing, too, found in this valley its congenial home. "Here he would lie down, embrace the ground, and kiss the very flowers that grew in this valley. He would now be up every morning by break of day, tracing and walking to and fro in this valley." It is a valley that to the meek and lowly in heart is ever green, and beautified with lilies; many labouring men have got good estates therein, for grace, more grace is given to the humble. Our Lord Himself had his country house in this valley and loved much to be here, loved much to walk these meadows, finding the air to be pleasant. Here a man may be free from the noise and from the hurryings of this life, and here he shall not be so let and hindered in his contemplations as in other places he is apt to be. It was in this valley the pilgrims came upon a shepherd-boy, simply clad, but of a fresh and well-favoured countenance who lives here a merrier life and wears more of that herb called heart's-ease in his bosom than he that is clad in silk and velvet. "Hark! said Mr. Greatheart, to what the shepherd-boy saith." So they hearkened and he said:

"'He that is down, needs fear no fall,
He that is low, no Pride:
He that is humble, ever shall
Have God to be his Guide.

I am content with what I have,
Little be it, or much:
And, Lord, contentment still I crave,
Because thou savest such.'"

In a story especially meant to exhibit the passive, trustful, feminine side of the religious life we might expect what we find—a loving sympathy with the bruised reeds of life, the souls all quivering with sensibility in the midst of a hard world. None of Bunyan's creations ever laid deeper hold of his heart than did Mr. Fearing, who was dejected at every difficulty, and stumbled at every straw, yet curiously enough did not much fear the lions, "for you must know that his trouble was not about such things; his fear was about his acceptance at last." His Lord was very tender to such as he. At the House of Interpreter some of the good bits at the table were sure to be laid upon his trencher; when he went through the Valley of the Shadow of Death it was as quiet as ever was known, before or since; and when he was come at the River where there was no bridge, "I took notice of what was very remarkable: the water of that river was lower at this time than ever I saw it in all my life; so he went over at last not much above wet-shod." Equally tender and sympathetic is Bunyan with Mr. Feeble-mind, Mr. Ready-to-halt, Mr. Despondency, and his daughter, Miss Much-afraid.

Yet, while we have this side of life given with such exquisite tact and insight, and while we are presented with such graceful women of Puritan type as Mercy and Christiana, we have also creations of masculine strength and force such as might have stood in the ranks of Cromwell's Ironsides. We have Great-heart—stout champion of womanly chastity and gentleness; Old Honest, sturdy in greatness of soul; and Valiant-for-Truth wielding a right Jerusalem blade, and leaving marks of his valour on the foes he fought, fighting one against three:

> "Who would true Valour see,
> Let him come hither;
> One here will Constant be,
> Come Wind, come Weather.
> There's no Discouragement,
> Shall make him once Relent
> His first avow'd Intent
> To be a Pilgrim."[1]

Even this hasty glance at its story may serve to show that this Second Part of *The Pilgrim's Progress* is not altogether unworthy of the First. Inferior to that no doubt it is, has more incongruities, is less powerfully sustained, and presents dialogues of mediocre type such as its predecessor does not. Yet, when all deductions have been made, we feel that it carries with it sufficient impress of Bunyan's genius, enough of charm and individuality all its own to entitle Christiana to go hand-in-hand with Christian on his pilgrimage through time. Between these two there is vital relation. They are the creations of the same genial soul, the outcome of the same heaven-kindled fire; and he who brooded over and called into shape this later child of his brain sent it forth with this foreword on its front:

> "Go, now my little Book, to every place,
> Where my first Pilgrim, has but shewn his Face:
> Call at their door . . .
> . . . *ask them yet again*
> If formerly they did not Entertain
> One Christian a Pilgrim; If they say
> They did: And was delighted in his way:
> Then let them know that those related were
> Unto him: Yea, his Wife and Children are."

[1] Bunyan had surely read Shakespeare's *As you like it,* and there met with this song:

> "Who doth ambition shun,
> And loves to live i' the sun,
> Seeking the food he eats,
> And pleased with what he gets.
> Come hither, come hither, come hither:
> Here shall he see
> No enemy,
> But winter and rough weather."

ADDENDA—Chapter XI.

The Warrant for Bunyan's Third Imprisonment.

MUCH of the foregoing chapter might have been omitted from this new edition of Dr. Brown's work, but the arguments brought forward by him so exemplify his close and logical reasoning that their retention seems warranted. They show, too, what immense trouble he took to investigate any point in doubt. The subsequent discovery of the Warrant of Arrest of John Bunyan makes certain what Dr. Brown had surmised, when he says: "I ventured in the first edition to put forth a theory of my own as to the time of Bunyan's later imprisonment, and to express my belief that he was arrested for the third time in 1675. I little thought that this supposition of mine would so soon receive complete confirmation. Yet such is the fact." The original document, written on a half-sheet of foolscap, was bought by Mr. W. G. Thorpe, F.S.A., of the Middle Temple. He tells his own story of it in a pamphlet re-printed from *The Gentleman's Magazine*, 1890. In a letter to *The Times*, in 1887, Mr. Thorpe says: "The document is so little thumbed or soiled that it cannot have been long in a constable's horny palm."

The nonconforming minister of 1662, Ichabod Chauncy, a son of Charles Chauncy, the second President of Harvard College, settled in Bristol as a physician, and at the same time helped the Dissenters, and defended those who were prosecuted under the Acts relating to religion. Mr. Thorpe suggests that Bunyan's friends forwarded the warrant to Chauncy, hoping that some use might be made of the time, a month, between the date of the proclamation—until which there could be no legal offence—and that of the warrant. Upon Bunyan's release, after six months' incarceration, the warrant, Mr. Thorpe thinks, might have been pigeon-holed by the physician, and remained with other papers which passed eventually into the hands of his grandson, Dr. Charles Chauncy, and so to the London sale-room, where it was purchased by Mr. Thorpe for the nominal sum of ten pounds.

In 1904 the warrant again came under the hammer, and Mr. Pierpoint Morgan, of New York, secured the treasure, through Mr. Bernard Quaritch. It was rightly described in the catalogue as "A Document of the greatest interest and value."

Clever facsimiles of the warrant with its seals were produced

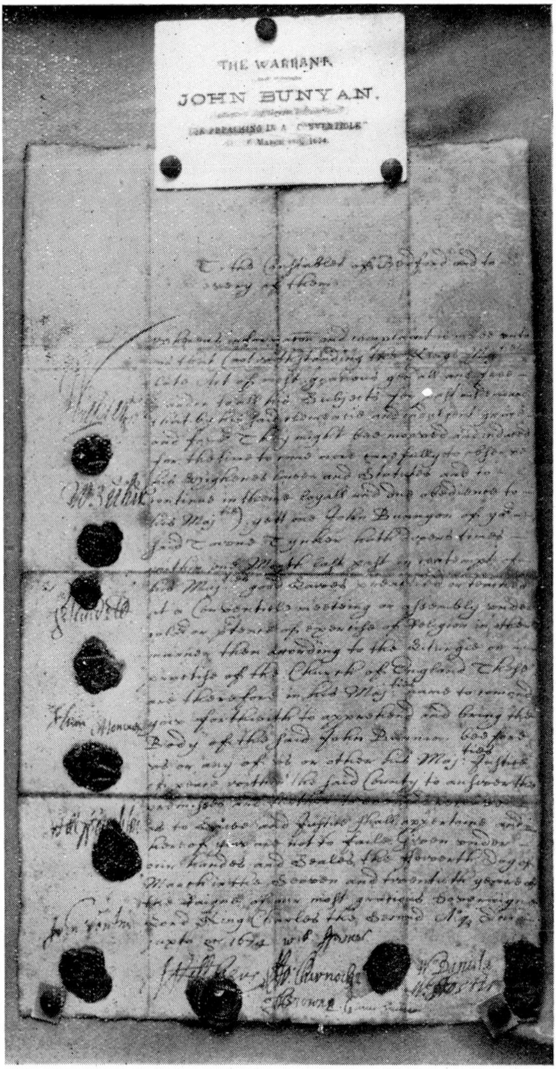

WARRANT

under which John Bunyan was apprehended and imprisoned for six months on Bedford Bridge, where he wrote 'The Pilgrim's Progress.'

(The original warrant is in the possession of the Pierpoint Morgan Library, New York.)

at the time (one being by Van der Wayde), and a copy was accepted by Her Majesty Queen Victoria.

A reproduction of the 'facsimile' warrant is given, and the wording of the document, signed by no less than thirteen justices, here follows:

TO THE CONSTABLES OF BEDFORD AND TO EVERY OF THEM.

Whereas information and complaint is made unto us that (notwithstanding the Kings Maj^{ties} late Act of most gracious generall and free pardon to all his subjects for past misdemeanours, that by his said clemencie and indulgent grace and favour they might bee mooved and induced for the time to come more carefully to observe his Highenes lawes and statutes, and to continue in theire loyall and due obedience to his Maj^{tie}), yett one John Bunnyon of your said towne, Tynker, hath divers times within one month last past in contempt of his Maj^{ties} good laws preached or teached at a Conventicle meeteing or assembly under colour or pretence of exercise of Religion in other manner then according to the Liturgie or Practise of the Church of England. These are therefore in his Maj^{ties} name to com̄and you forthwith to apprehend and bring the Body of the said John Bunnion beefore us or any of us or other his Maj^{ties} Justice of Peace within the said county to answer the premises and further to doe and receave as to Law and Justice shall appertaine, and hereof you are not to faile. Given our handes and seales the ffowerth day of March in the seaven and twentieth yeare of the Raigne of our most gracious Soveraigne Lord King Charles the Second, A^{o} q^{m} D^{ni} juxta gr: 1674. [New Style 1675.]

J. Napier (L.S.)
W. Beecher (L.S.)
(L.S.) G. Blundell
(L.S.) Hum: Monoux
Will: Franklin (L.S.)
John Ventriss (L.S.)

Will: Spencer
Will: Gery St: Jo: Chernocke (L.S.) Wm. Daniell (L.S.)
(L.S.) T. Browne Gaius Squier W. ffoster (L.S.)

Dr. Brown, in his preface to the third edition of this Life of Bunyan, says: "The document is undoubtedly genuine. To those familiar with seventeenth century MSS., the paper and handwriting are evidence sufficient of this. In addition, Mr. E. Maunde Thompson, head of the department of MSS. in the British Museum, has verified several of the seals with the coats of arms of the justices, and I have myself independent evidence bearing on the genuineness of some of the signatures. The magistrates signing were: Sir John Napier of Luton Hoo, Sir William Beecher of Howbury, Sir George Blundell of Cardington, these two being also upon the bench at Bunyan's first conviction in 1661; Sir Humphrey Monoux of Wootton, Sir William Franklin of Bolnhurst, Mr. Ventriss of Campton, Mr. Spencer of Cople, Mr. Gery of Bushmeade, Sir St. John Chernocke of Hulcote, Mr. Daniell of Silsoe, Mr. Browne of Arlesey, Mr. Squier of Eaton Socon, and Dr. Foster of Bedford.[1]

It will thus be seen that there was a formidable and unusual list of names to the warrant, and Bunyan was evidently regarded as an offender to be secured by the strongest exercise of authority. Foster [Francis Wingate's brother-in-law], whom Bunyan had met at the time of his first arrest in 1660, whom he then described as "a right Judas," and who, as this work shows, pursued the Nonconformists with relentless malignity through all the intervening years, was almost certainly the main mover in the matter. The document was evidently prepared beforehand by a professional scrivener, probably one of Foster's own clerks, and was ready to be signed and sealed when the Justices met for Quarter Sessions at Bedford. Foster was in hot haste; for the King's proclamation recalling the preachers' licences was only signed on the 3rd of February. It would be the 4th before it was known in London, and probably the 6th before it reached Bedford. The month therefore mentioned in this warrant signed on the 4th of March, was a short month indeed. Bunyan, as a marked man and an old offender, was probably on his arrest committed for trial, he being held to bail, and the trial coming on at the following Quarter Sessions. Various considerations, such as the date of the publication of *The Pilgrim's Progress;* the tardy and circuitous interference on his behalf by Bishop Barlow, who was not consecrated till the end of June; and the condition of Bedford Gaol in the early months of 1675, all point to the latter half of that year as the time of his six months' imprisonment after conviction. It may be indeed that it was in prospect of such a prisoner as Bunyan that the Borough Council gave that order for the repairing of the prison on the bridge, which was passed on the 13th of May."

'Scenes' of 'The Pilgrim's Progress.'

It is almost superfluous to refer to the controversy that has been carried on for many years in respect to the *locale* of the scenes in Bunyan's immortal dream-story; but as advocates for

[1] "It is noticeable that only five of the magistrates use their own seals, the others availing themselves of their fellows' seals, or that of Paul Cobb, clerk of the peace, who, as in 1660, drew up the warrant: while three did not seal it at all."

the Surrey claim are loth to abandon it, a few words on the subject seem necessary.

In 1871, General Sir Henry James, R.E. (then Colonel James), a director of the Ordnance Survey, set forth the hypothesis that Bunyan, when depicting his scenery, had in mind the Pilgrim Way which passes through Surrey from Winchester to Canterbury. Later on, Mr. H. R. Skipton, F.R.Hist.S., followed up the conjecture.[1] To some this may appear plausible, because the Surrey Hills have been popularly known as the "Delectable Mountains"; and there exists also a Doubting Castle on Walton Heath. But these, surely, prove nothing at all, for country-folk of the neighbourhood would naturally connect their familiar places with Bunyan's descriptions—as well might also people of other counties throughout the land—for Bunyan's book was read everywhere by the "common-folk." However, to follow Mr. Skipton, Christian starts from Shalford (Shallow-ford) Meadows, at the ferry across the Wey leading from Saint Catherine's Hill. Here the Pilgrim meets a Slough of Despond: slough-like even in fine weather. Guildford itself (in its seventeenth-century condition, be it noted) is the City of Destruction that Christian flees from. He enquires at the Chantries (the Wicket Gate), and toils up Saint Martha's Hill "Difficulty." He has seen on the way possibly a Calvary Cross (not very likely to appeal to Bunyan), and near Saint Martha's, or Martyr's Chapel, he seeks refreshment at a rest-house or priest's residence (and now a farm-house), which, by imagination, becomes the Palace Beautiful. From this vantage ground could be seen, no doubt, "most pleasant mountainous country, beautified with woods, springs, and fountains, very Delectable to behold." History, too, aids the mind which reverts to bygone days when Surrey and Sussex had glaring fires from which sparks ascended as iron was melted. Here then Christian was in a veritable Valley of the Shadow of Death with all its horrors and torments. It was here that Bunyan saw his valley "as dark as pitch." Dorking (of that day, but not now) presents all the fascinations of Bunyan's Vanity Fair, and the Pilgrim refreshes himself at the silently flowing river Mole. With sunshine upon it, a chalk-pit "a little off the road," does well for the silver mine on Hill Lucre, and a convenient By-path Meadow (minus the stile) brings Christian into the clutches of Giant Despair;

[1] A Paper read before St. Paul's Ecclesiological Society, January, 1915.

but not for long: the summit of Leith Hill is reached, and he beholds the Celestial City. So the Surrey dream ends.

That Bunyan visited Surrey is well within the range of possibility, but he had little need to go there for the scenes of his story—the setting of which belongs to his own county, where he had more than enough around him of scenery that exactly fits his descriptions. This he must have seen and traversed, on horse and on foot, times innumerable, during the fifty years preceding the writing of *The Pilgrim's Progress.*[1]

As already said, it is deemed advisable to include this topic, because as recently as 1924, the Surrey claim was broadcast by Mr. Kennedy Skipton. To Mr. Skipton's claim the late Mr. Richard Henry Poynter (curator of the Museum and Librarian at the Bunyan Meeting, Bedford) ably replied in a series of articles in *The Bedfordshire Standard.* Unfortunately, too, the legendary accounts of "Bunyan Cottages" in the vicinity of Guildford have to be received with reservation.

[1] *Vide—Bunyan's Country*: Studies in the Bedfordshire Topography of *The Pilgrim's Progress.* By A. J. Foster, M.A. London: Virtue & Co., 1901.

XII.

THE PLACE OF *THE PILGRIM'S PROGRESS* IN LITERATURE.

HAVING looked at the relation the two parts of *The Pilgrim's Progress* sustain to each other, it may be interesting to form some estimate of the book as a whole, and to account for its widespread and various influence. In attempting to do so it would be beside our purpose to compare it with the few kingly books enthroned on the supreme heights of literature, and reigning there by common suffrage of civilised nations and successive centuries. There is no need to demand entrance for it where entrance would not be willingly and universally accorded. This allegory has its distinctive merits and its own distinct place in the short roll-call of really illustrious books.

One of the foremost causes of its success is that with such singular felicity it meets a pre-existing love of metaphor, fable, parable, and allegory, which is deeply rooted in human nature. How congenial this form of literature was to the temperament of the Oriental, no one with the Bible in his hand needs to be told. Nor is the love of it confined to the glowing East or to the Sunny South. Kriloff has shown that even on the snowy steppes of the ungenial North, the Russian peasant finds a new charm for his intellect and a fresh glow for his feeling in mind-pictures based upon the instinctive conviction that the outward world of fact and form stands in vital relation with the inward world of personal experience and abstract truth.

Not that we are to suppose that allegory has been made to minister merely to the pleasures of the imagination. There has usually been serious earnest purpose beneath the charm of the story. It has either set forth the pregnant choice made at fateful moments of human life between folly and wisdom, between pleasure and duty, with the far-reaching consequences resulting from the choice; or, and this perhaps more frequently, it has become a protest under thinly veiled disguise against the oppressor's wrong and the proud man's contumely. The two earliest examples remain still among the best illustrations of the uses to which allegory has ever been put, the one the parable of Jotham concerning the choice of a king by the trees, the other the story told by Nathan to David of that rapacious rich man, who with many flocks and herds of his own, yet robbed the poor man of the one little ewe lamb which lay in his bosom and drank of his cup. The prophet, thus bringing home to the king's conscience his cruel wrong against one of his subjects, was anticipating by centuries the exceeding bitter cry against the evils of the time raised by William Langland, in his *Pier's Plowman's Vision;* by John Gower in his *Vox Clamantis,* and by Sir David Lyndsay in that *Dreme* of his, which was really an appeal to the conscience of the young Scottish Prince to whom it was addressed.

It is not, however, with allegory in general we are now concerned so much as with that special form of it which in various ways has depicted the pilgrimage of life. In 1330, Guillaume de Guileville, a monk of the royal abbey of Chaliz, was reading the *Roman de la Rose,* that memorable mediæval romance begun about 1230 by the *trouvère* Guillaume de Loris, and finished by Jean de Meung. As he read the book there was suggested to him, he says, the conception of his own vision of *Le Pélerinage de l'Homme,* a work of interest to us inasmuch as it has been repeatedly affirmed that to it Bunyan was largely indebted for the idea of his own Pilgrim.[1] Under the title of *The Pilgrimage of the Sowle,* "translated oute of Frenshe into Englyshe," it was printed in 1483 by William Caxton, at his press in Westminster. There is also in manuscript on vellum, another English translation "made by Johan the preeste," which is preserved in the University Library at Cambridge. This copy concludes with the following colophon: "Here endeth the Romance by the monk of the Cisteaux, in France; of the pilgrymage of the lyffe of the manhood, which is made for good pilgrymes y[t] in this world such waye wol holde that would goo to good haven, and that they have heven's Ioye, ymagined after the manner of the Romans of the Roos."[2]

The writer tells us how he had a dream in which there was

[1] The Ancient Poem of Guillaume de Guileville, entitled *Le Péleringe de l'Homme,* compared with the *Pilgrim's Progress* of John Bunyan. Edited from notes collected by the late Mr. Nathaniel Hill; [By Miss Cust]. London: B. M. Pickering, 1858.

[2] J. O. Halliwell's *Rarities of the University of Cambridge,* 1841, p. 166.

JOHN BUNYAN'S CHAIR and WALKING STICK.

(Preserved at Bunyan Meeting, Bedford.)
Photo: G. A. Gearey, Bedford.]

given to him a sight within a mirror large and bright of the fair city of heaven, a sight which stirred his soul to go thither on pilgrimage. He describes what the city was like, and what people he saw there, doctors and prelates, canons, and austin friars, "with other folk full divers both temporal and secular." Setting out on this pilgrimage, with staff and scrip, he meets Grâce Dieu, a lady of great fairness and noblesse, who asks him wherefore he weeps as he goes, to whom he makes reply that he weeps because that he is kept back by the clog of his mortal body from flying upward to the city of his desire. She tells him that she is the helper of pilgrims, bids him keep in view the wicket-gate which none ever entered till they had put off their mortality, and takes him to her house, which he finds he cannot enter without passing through the waters of baptism. The waters passed, he is received into the house, a place right inly fair, where he sees personifications of Reason or Prudence, and Nature, who are attended also by Sapience, Repentance, and Charity. After a long allegorical description of the Eucharist, he is shown the rarities of the place and equipped for his journey. There is given to him a scrip of green silk called Faith, and an imperishable staff of shittim wood called Hope; he is had also to the armoury where are heaulmes and gambesons, gorgerettes, and haubergeons, targes, and whatever else is need for the pilgrim's defence. Grâce Dieu presents him with a gambeson or coat of mail called Patience, telling him that it was wrought by the great armourer above who, without tools, created the sun and starry host; that it is proof against all kinds of tribulation, that it was worn by our Lord and the holy martyrs, and will resist like an anvil the stroke of the foe. She equips him also with the helmet of Temperance, the gorgette of Sobriety, the sword named Justice, and with all other panoply complete. Overweighted, however, with all this equipment, he begs that, like David, he may go without it, which he does, carrying simply the self-same pebbles with which David slew Goliath.

Leaving the house of Grâce Dieu, he comes to where the ways part, on the right sitting Industry and on the left Idleness. Turning to the right, after encountering and escaping from Gluttony and Lust, he meets with Wrath and Tribulation, the latter bidding him lay down his staff and protect himself with the shield and sword his attendant Memory carries. Making his prayer to the Virgin, he finds good and sure refuge, after which he is assailed by Avarice and Necromancy, also by Heresy, Satan, Fortune, Idolatry, Sorcery, and Gladness-of-the-World, with all of whom he holds colloquies. In the distress of this time there comes sailing to him a ship, on the top of the mast of which there is a cross whereon sits a milk-white dove. From the deck of this ship there lands Grâce Dieu, who opens a fountain in the rock, in which the pilgrim is washed and purified. She then offers him choice of monasteries for refuge, he fixing upon that at Cisteaux, to which he is fetched over by the porter, Dread-of-God. Welcomed within this monastery by Charity, he is instructed by Lesson, and shown a wonderful mirror by Hagiography. These teachers are succeeded by Obedience, Discipline, Abstinence, Poverty, Chastity, Prayer, Infirmity, Old Age, and Death. As Death runs him through the body with his scythe, de Guileville awakes with a start, scarcely knowing whether he is dead or alive. To his relief he hears the sound of the Chaliz convent bells, and the crowing of the cocks. Brought back thus to earth and time by the old familiar sounds, he bids his reader retain what of good his story may contain, rejecting the rest. So he draws to a close, commending his work to all good winnowers, skilled in separating reality from error, and truth from falsehood.

That there are several ideas in common between Bunyan and de Guileville will be seen at once; the sight of the city in the heavens acting as an incentive to pilgrimage, the mention of a wicket-gate, the reception into the house of Grâce Dieu, and the equipment of the pilgrim in the armoury. But how far Bunyan was indebted to de Guileville may be matter of question. The looking for the city with eternal foundations and the equipment of the Christian soul with spiritual armour were New Testament ideas equally accessible to both. The wicket-gate of de Guileville was barely referred to in passing, not taking actual shape in the narrative, and signified that gate of death which awaits every man at the end of the way; whereas with Bunyan it was a prominent part of the story, and was the strait gate through which men enter upon a life of faith. Finally, the house of Grâce Dieu and the Palace Beautiful are kindred in conception to that household of faith, the Church of the living

God spoken of by St. Paul and, like the House of Mercy in Spenser's *Faery Queen,* may have been in part suggested by the old houses of entertainment for pilgrims or travellers by the way.

There are many works subsequent to this of the Monk of Chaliz, in which we have the regular introduction of the dream and the allegory. The *Chemin de Vallance* of Jean de Courcy (1426); the *Palace of Honour* by Gawin Douglas, of Dunkeld (1501); the *Golden Terge* of William Dunbar (1508); the *Bowse of Court* of John Skelton (1508); and the *Example of Vertu* (1503) and the *Pastime of Pleasure* (1506) by Stephen Hawes; these being followed by Sir David Lyndsay's *Dreme* of 1528.

Passing from the works of these allegorists we come next upon a series of books relating to pilgrims and pilgrimages, which might seem to be the natural forerunners of Bunyan's dream. The connection, however, is little more than the mere suggestion contained in the titles. Some of these are simply descriptions of literal pilgrimages to literal local shrines, while others are nothing more than religious treatises or books of pious meditation under titles suggestive of an allegorical journey. To this latter class belong the *Pérégrination Spirituelle* of Pascha (1576); the *Viaggio Spirituale* of Bellanda (1578); the *Pilgrimage to Paradise* of Leonard Wright (1591); the *Pilgrim's Journey towards Heaven* of William Webster (1613); the *Pilgrim's Practice* by Robert Bruen (1621); the *Pilgrim's Passe to the New Jerusalem* by M. R. Gent (1659); and the *Spiritual Journey towards the Land of Peace* (1659). *The Pilgrimage of Perfection* by William Bond (1526), like *The Pype or Tonne of the lyfe of Perfection* (1532), is slightly allegorical, but in the main both these books are only a sort of code of direction for monks and nuns. The *Pilgrimage of Dovekin and Willekin to their Beloved in Jerusalem,* the work of the Dutch engraver, Bolswert, though popular once and described to Southey by his friend Bilderdijk, as "one of the delights of his childhood," is nothing more than a weak and foolish story in the allegorical vein. Bernard's *Isle of Man,* again, though wise and witty, is, like Phineas Fletcher's *Purple Island,* more akin to *The Holy War* than to *The Pilgrim's Progress,* and, as Southey says of Bernard's book, alike they want the charm of story and that romantic interest, "which holds children from sleep."

There is one other book on which, as preceding Bunyan's Dream by only about a dozen years, a word or two must be said, namely, Bishop Patrick's *Parable of the Pilgrim.* It appears to have been written in 1663 and published in 1665, during Bunyan's first imprisonment. Beyond the fundamental idea of a godly life as a pilgrimage there is not much in common between the two books. Less than twenty pages out of Patrick's five hundred sufficed for his story, which is of the slightest possible character, a mere framework, indeed, for connecting together lengthy meditations, discourses, and soliloquies. Its main purpose was to show the superiority of the Established Church over the Sectaries outside. A traveller named Theophilus, weary of life's surroundings, sets forth in search of a better land, when he remembers to have heard of Jerusalem, to which he resolves to go. But how shall he get thither? Perplexed by contradictory voices he has recourse to a venerable man—the personification of the Church of England—to whom he resorts for advice. In the form of elaborate discourse and exhortation, this advice is given so plentifully that we find ourselves at the two hundred and eightieth page of a book of five hundred and twenty-seven pages, or more than half-way through, before the pilgrim has so much as set out on his journey. Theophilus then starting for Jerusalem finds rough roads and sinks into low spirits, but is comforted by receiving a letter from his venerable friend. But before long he is again overtaken by sadness of heart, when to his great delight, in a little oratory by the wayside, he again meets with his guide, who remonstrates with and encourages him through some thirty pages more. After this they arrange to travel together, and are overtaken first by a mounted horseman, representing the Church of Rome, to whom the guide says some rather plain things by way of rebuke, then by a second traveller, who represents the Nonconformists, and to whom Theophilus gives even less quarter than his guide gave to the mounted horseman. Leaving these travellers, the pilgrims come to the top of a high hill, where they meet with a knot of excellent persons who are looking at a fair prospect of the heavenly Jerusalem, reminding us of Bunyan's shepherds on the Delectable Mountains. Again they set forth and again have long discourse together on the nature of religion, a chance meeting with a third traveller leading them still farther into an elaborate unfolding of justification by faith. The book concludes with an expression of gratitude from the pilgrim to his guide, and the request that he would always accompany him in his travels.

Besides the dreamers, story tellers, and didactic teachers, several of the poets also, of the seventeenth century, have thrown the charm of their genius round the idea of life's pilgrimage. Whitney in his *Emblems* (1586), George Herbert in his *Temple* (1633), and Francis Quarles in his *Emblems* (1635), has each taken up the conception in verse; as did also Sir Walter Raleigh in lines which somehow always steal into our hearts:

> "Give me my scallop shell of quiet,
> My staff of faith to lean upon,
> My scrip of joy, immortal diet,
> My bottle of salvation,
> My gown of glory, hope's true gage;
> And thus I'll take my pilgrimage."

Often, however, as the conception of the pilgrim life has found utterance, no previous or subsequent writer has given expression to it with the same completeness, unity, force, and beauty, as Bunyan, whose dream stands alone and unrivalled in the literature to which it belongs. Before we ask whether he was indebted to other men for the imagery of his book, we must remember that he was in prison when that book was written. Access, therefore, to the literature of mediæval romance, to such writers as de Guileville and Edmund Spenser would be impossible. And even if he had not been in prison it may be doubted whether a book like that of de Guileville would be likely to come under his notice. It existed in old French and in what even in Bunyan's time had become almost obsolete English, and while one would certainly be unintelligible the other would probably be inaccessible. The only printed English translation of which we have any certain knowledge is that issued by William Caxton, and there is no reason to suppose that even two centuries ago 'Caxtons' were often within the reach of men in Bunyan's walk of life. No doubt the pilgrim idea had often appeared in literature, but libraries of English literature were not then so readily available to mechanics and tinkers as they have come to be since.

Certainly Bunyan had not been intentionally gathering materials beforehand, for, as he tells us, the idea of the book dawned upon him in quite unlooked-for way while he was in prison, and while engaged upon a different line of thought:

> "When at the first I took my Pen in hand,
> Thus for to write; I did not understand
> That I at all should make a little Book
> In such a mode; Nay, I had undertook
> To make another, which when almost done,
> Before I was aware, I this begun."

The crowding fancies came so thick and fast that he felt he must have a care:

> "I'll put you by your selves, lest you at last
> Should prove *ad infinitum*, and eat out
> The Book that I already am about."

On this question of the originality of his famous Dream,* Bunyan himself has a right to be heard, and he has spoken with most unmistakable plainness. Between 1678, when the work in question was published, and 1682, when he sent forth his *Holy War*, it appears that its originality was more than once challenged by the men of his own time, and to their challenge he replied thus in his own vigorous fashion:

> "Some say the *Pilgrims Progress* is not mine,
> Insinuating as if I would shine
> In name and fame by the worth of another."

This suggestion he repels with scorn—"John, such dirt-heap never was since God converted him:"

> "Manner and matter too was all mine own,
> Nor was it unto any mortal known,
> 'Till I had done it. Nor did any then
> By Books, by wits, by tongues, or hand, or pen,
> Add five words to it, or wrote half a line
> Thereof: the whole, and ev'ry whit is mine."

Nothing could be more explicit than this, or coming from a man so conscientious more decisive. Indebtedness there undoubtedly was, such indeed as not even the most exalted genius can free itself from, the unconscious indebtedness which in the current thought of the present inherits the transmitted life of the past. The endeavour to hunt up recondite sources for Bunyan's inspiration has, in truth, been a little overstrained. It is not worth while to go to Sir John Mandeville's *Valley Perilous* for the suggestion of the Valley of the Shadow of Death while we have the twenty-third Psalm; or to the engraving of the Christian Soldier by Jerome Wierix for the arming of the pilgrim while we have the sixth chapter of the Epistle to the Ephesians; or to de Guileville for the wicket-gate while

* The subject is ably discussed in a pamphlet, *Who was the Author of the Pilgrim's Progress* by W. Winters. London, 1874.

we have the strait gate of the Gospels. Neither indeed is it necessary to go back to mediæval chroniclers of whom probably Bunyan never so much as heard, or to de Guileville's *Pilgrimage of Man,* or Spenser's *Faery Queen* for the main conception of life as a warfare and a pilgrimage. The thought of life as a warfare goes at least as far back as Paul's earnest call to Timothy to fight the good fight of faith; and the conception of life as a pilgrimage, common to all the centuries, carries us back even farther still to those first wanderers from the Chaldean plains, who set forth in search of the city which had foundations, whose builder and maker is God. Bunyan was steeped in his Bible, and what indebtedness there was, was mainly to that. The Dreamer in Bedford gaol derived his inspiration from the same source as the great Florentine who preceded him by more than three centuries. *The Pilgrim's Progress* is an English flower, as the *Divina Commedia* is a Tuscan flower, grown on Jewish soil. Dante may accept Virgil's guidance in his mystic pilgrimage through unseen realms, and he may mingle the classic element with the Christian in his visions, but the subject of his great Trilogy—the thought of "the human soul placed for its trial in a fearful and wonderful world, with relations to time and matter, history and nature, good and evil, the beautiful, the intelligible, and the mysterious, sin and grace, the infinite and the eternal"[1]—this came to Dante as it came to Bunyan, from the Sacred Scriptures, the teachers of both.

And if we may digress for a moment, one can scarcely refrain from referring to one or two points of resemblance between these two heaven-kindled souls, their life and work. First their visions open out alike. Bunyan lights upon a den in the First Part, and wanders into a wood in the Second Part, where he dreams his dream. Dante also finds himself in a dark wood and full of sleep when the vision descends upon him. Then both writers treat of invisible things, and lift up to view that ideal of life which the men around, distracted by the interests and passions of the hour, had lost from sight. Alike they are animated by earnest purpose while yet kindling with the glow of imagination, and alike they have the same simple certainty and strength of language, the one wielding the vigorous Tuscan dialect, the other, the picturesque English of the common people round him. Then, too, both these great souls had been schooled

[1] R. W. Church—*Dante*. p. 62.

in that suffering out of which so much of life's noblest work has come. The strong, earnest face of the great Florentine comes up before us from *la valle d'abisso doloroso,* and his visions are born out of years of disappointment and weary wanderings in exile; while the great Englishman in his inward life tarried long at Sinai to see the fire and the cloud and the darkness, and in his outward life longer still amidst the gloom and captivity of his prison days. At first sight Dante's Trilogy and Bunyan's Allegory may seem to move in separate spheres, the one taking us into the world of shades, the other confining us to earth and time; but, as a countryman of Dante's with profound insight has shown, there is an underlying unity between the two. They represent the two parts into which, from the Christian point of view, the history of the human soul must be divided, and thus the conceptions of the one complete those of the other. "In the poem of the Englishman," says Zumbini, "we have the first part, the vicissitudes and condition of the soul while it is on earth, the first life; in the poem of the Italian we have the last part, the state of the soul in the world beyond, the second life. Death is at once the limit which divides, and the bond which unites the two epics. With Bunyan we reach, but do not pass the threshold of heaven and hell: with Dante, no sooner does the pilgrimage begin than the earthly world is left behind. And yet of those two parts of human history, the one could not exist without the other, and therefore each poet, while taking only one part for his theme, founded his conception upon both, showing his profound understanding of the whole ideal history of the Christian soul."[1]

Passing now from the question of the originality of *The Pilgrim's Progress* we come to ask what were the elements of its power, the secret of its success? M. Taine, whose sketch of Bunyan is as like to the Dreamer of Bedford gaol as Roubillac's statue of Shakespeare in its posturing self-consciousness to the great Dramatist himself, has a singularly infelicitous way of accounting for its wide-spread influence. He says: "After the Bible, the book most widely read in England is *The Pilgrim's Progress* by John Bunyan. The reason is, that the basis of Protestantism is the doctrine of salvation by grace, and that no writer has equalled Bunyan in making this doctrine understood."[2] Doubtless Bunyan believed in the doctrine of Justi-

[1] *Saggi Critici,* di Bonaventura Zumbini, Napoli, 1876.

[2] *History of English Literature,* by H. A. Taine, i., p. 398.

fication by Faith, with all his heart and soul, and it lies at the basis, penetrating through and through his conception of the Christian life. But many people have been charmed by this book who do not accept this doctrine, and we must go farther afield for an adequate explanation of the 'Pilgrim's' influence. Foremost among its literary qualities is its perfect spontaneousness. It has all the simple freedom of life. There are no signs of toil, no inartistic traces of elaboration; the vision grows up like a flower, effortless and fair. And this not because art has succeeded in concealing art, but because the artist himself has been taken captive by his own creation. It has that one supreme quality of all true inspiration, that it is not so much the man deliberately taking possession of the subject as it is the subject coming down upon and bearing away the man:

> "And thus it was: I writing of the Way
> And Race of Saints, in this our Gospel-Day,
> Fell suddenly into an Allegory
> About their Journey, and the way to Glory,
> In more than twenty things, which I set down;
> This done, I twenty more had in my Crown,
> And they again began to multiply,
> Like sparks that from the coals of fire do fly."

It has been said that *The Pilgrim's Progress* is the last English book that was written without any thought of a reviewer. It may be said also that it was written without even any thought of a reader:

> " . . . I did not think
> To show to all the world my Pen and Ink
> In such a mode; I only thought to make
> I knew not what; nor did I undertake
> Thereby to please my Neighbour; no not I;
> I did it mine own self to gratifie."

The construction of this book, which was to place him among the Immortals, never became to him the serious business of life, the burden of exacting toil:

> "Neither did I but vacant seasons spend
> In this my Scribble; nor did I intend
> But to divert my self in doing this,
> From worser thoughts which make me do amiss.
> Thus I set Pen to Paper with delight,
> And quickly had my thoughts in black and white.
> For having now my Method by the end,
> Still as I pull'd, it came; and so I penn'd
> It down, until it came at last to be
> For length and breadth the bigness which you see."

This is Bunyan's own account of the production of his own book. He tells us all he knows, but then even he knows not all. Genius is the gift of God, and it is the breath from beyond the instrument that creates the music and gives to it its mystic power of ravishment. That which touches us most deeply is the charm of free life, that indescribable something which lays hold of us wherever we find it, either in the works of genius or the exuberance of sportive childhood, in the jocund gladness of trees and birds and flowers, or in the free wild life of forest and prairie. To get at the secret of that is to get at the mystery of life, that mystery which lies at the fount of being and is wrapped in the shadows which veil it round. Well has it been said that "the work which man has brooded over, and at last created, is the foster-child too of that wisdom which reaches from end to end, strongly and sweetly disposing all things."

The Pilgrim's Progress, while it has thus free spontaneous life, is marked also by a dramatic unity such as is not always possessed by even greater books. The latest, who is perhaps also the profoundest critic of Spenser's great work,[1] *The Faery Queen,* has contrasted for us its characteristic excellences and defects. He points out its quaint stateliness and grandeur, the stateliness of highly artificial conditions of society, the grandeur like that of some great national spectacle. He dwells upon its wonderful sweetness and beauty—sweetness and beauty like that of the most gorgeous of summer gardens, in the glory and brilliancy of its varied blooms, in the wonder of its strange forms of life, in the changefulness of its exquisite and delicious scents. He points out also that while thus lavish of external beauty Spenser has at the same time joined to it the counter-charm of purity, truth, and duty, this too with a music and melody of verse such as none had reached in English poetry before him. At the same time, as an impartial judge, he is bound to say that on the other side there are in this great English work some very grave defects. *The Faery Queen,* he justly says, by its first aspect rather inspires respect than attracts and satisfies, and the reader has therefore to cross the bar and persist in his search before he fairly enters into the spirit of the book. Further, it carries with it no adequate account of its own story, and the poet gives up all attempt to hold the scheme together. Either he exhausts his proper allegory, or he gets tired of it, and the poem becomes a mere receptacle for whatever happens to interest the poet himself. The book has really no unity. As much as *The Arabian Nights* or the *Idylls of the King* it becomes a mere collection of separate tales and alle-

[1] *English Men of Letters*—Spenser, by R. W. Church.

gories. It is simply a wilderness in which the reader is left to wander, and he does not lose his way, because there is no way to lose. The poet once on to his story never knows where to stop. It is like wading among unmown grass. He drowns us in words.

This description of the defects of *The Faery Queen* by Dean Church, as just as it is powerful, may be almost entirely reversed in the case of *The Pilgrim's Progress*. There is no bar to cross before our interest is aroused. From this first sentence, "As I walked through the wilderness of this world I lighted on a certain place where was a Den, and I laid me down in that place to sleep, and as I slept I dreamed a Dream," the reader's interest is arrested and retained. The unity of the story is kept up from point to point. There are incongruities, of course, which could easily be pointed out, as there probably must be in any allegory which is long sustained, and in which this matter-of-fact world blends its scenes and surroundings with those of the spiritual universe. But from the moment we see the man in rags setting out with his burden our interest in his fortunes never flags till he is fairly within the portals of the celestial city. The episodes by the way never draw us so far aside that we forget the main story, but they rather contribute to its effect. There is no unmown grass of weariness to wade through, no wilderness of tedium in which to wander. Bunyan's characters never linger, and therefore never tire us. As soon as they step on to the scene we feel their personality so vividly that we are sure we should know them again. They proceed at once to instruct or amuse or interest, having done which they disappear, leaving us regretful they have vanished so soon.

The Pilgrim's Progress is interesting also not merely for its dramatic unity, but for the rapidity and power with which its characters are drawn. By a few strokes only, sometimes by the mere giving of a name, an abstraction rises up clothed in flesh and blood. We seem at once to know the brisk lad Ignorance, of the county of Conceit; the man Temporary, who lived in a town two miles off of Honesty, and next door to Mr. Turnback; Mr. Anything, Mr. Smoothman, Mr. Facing-both-Ways, Sir Having Greedy, Mr. Highmind, Lady Feigning's daughter, and Mrs. Lechery, who is such a well-bred gentlewoman; Lord Time-server, and Madam Wanton; the young woman whose name was Dull, with her neighbours Slow-pace, Sleepy-head, and Short-wind. How vividly Obstinate stands before us with his dogged pertinacity, Pliable with his feeble vacillation, and Madam Bubble, picture of this vain world—a tall, comely dame, something of a swarthy complexion, who speaks very smoothly, giving you a smile at the end of a sentence, wears a great purse by her side, and has her hand often in it, fingering her money as if that was her heart's delight. The forms moving to and fro in the Palace Beautiful—Innocence, Prudence, Piety, and Discretion—are not mere abstractions, but creations of womanly grace, making the place brighter with their presence. What a living personification we have of despair in the man in the iron cage, of terror in the man awaking from his dream of judgment, of earthly-mindedness in the man with the muck-rake. What a picture is presented to us of the way in which a soul can torment itself by vain regrets and bitter self-reproaches as we read how Giant Despair gets him a grievous crab-tree cudgel, and after rating his prisoners like dogs, falls upon them, and beats them fearfully, in such sort that they were not able to help themselves, or to turn them upon the floor. What a picture, too, we have of the shabbiness of a sham life, where hypocrites are described as going "not uprightly, but all awry with their feet; one shoe goes inward, another outward, and their Hosen out behind; there a Rag and there a Rent, to the disparagement of their Lord."

There is great humanness in the book. We have homely touches about "the dish of milk well-crumbed," brought out for the boys in the house of Gaius, and humorous thrusts about Hopeful's courage when the thieves were at a distance, and at the way in which "Peter would swagger, ay, he would; but who so foiled and run down by villains as he?" We have touches of pathos which, to use a favourite phrase of Bunyan's, make the water to stand in our eyes; and strokes of pleasantry which bring back the smile to our faces. We walk in the King's gardens, into which the children of the land of Beulah go to gather nosegays for the pilgrims, bringing them to them with much affection. Our senses are regaled with the fragrance of camphor, with spikenard, and saffron, calamus, and cinnamon, with trees of frankincense, myrrh, and aloes, with all chief spices; and with these the pilgrims' chambers were perfumed while they stayed there. We hear through the interlacings of green leaves the melodious notes of the country birds, and the sweet sounds of distant bells. Then within doors we have the pleasant music of virginals, the social converse round the cheerful table, where the fruit is spread, and where there is the cracking of nuts, and, to keep Old Honest from nodding, the reading of riddles, such riddles as this:

> "He that will kill, must first be overcome;
> Who live abroad would, first must die at home,"

and this other:

> "A man there was though some did count him mad,
> The more he cast away, the more he had."

At another time we find ourselves joining a party of pilgrims who, with country dance, are making merry out of doors over the downfall of Giant Despair. For "Christiana, if need was, could play upon the Vial, and her daughter Mercy upon the Lute: So, since they were so merry disposed, she plaid them a Lesson, and Ready-to-halt would dance. So he took Dispondencies Daughter, named Much-afraid, by the hand, and to Dancing they went in the Road. True he could not Dance without one Crutch in his Hand, but I promise you, he footed it well: also the Girl was to be commended, for she answered the Musick hansomely."

But with all its homeliness, humour, and humanness the book is never coarse or unclean. Dean Church, in the sketch of Spenser, to which reference has been made, while doing justice to his great poem, its stateliness and grandeur, its exquisite sweetness and beauty, and the music and melody of its verse, feels compelled to refer to one drawback and say, that Spenser does not know what to leave unsaid; that he gives us pictures from which we shrink, and introduces scenes and descriptions which may have been playfully and innocently produced, but which it is certainly not easy to dwell upon innocently now. On the other hand, Professor Masson, treating of the literature of the Restoration period, calls our attention to the fact that the taste of the tinker of Bedford in matters of speech was more fastidious and cleanly than that of a good many of the scholars and men of letters of the time who had been educated at the universities. This cleanness of speech was the outcome of a lofty ideal of soul. The style is the man, and the man had for the keynote of his book high-minded purity, and for the soul of his religion a noble scorn for all that was base and selfish and mean. The manhood within him had too much self-respect, too much godly loyalty to life's ideal, to bedabble itself in the mire.

Bunyan's real humanness also led him to deal with man as man apart from all the social distinctions of life. His book forms a link of transition from Elizbethan to modern times, and, in common with Wordsworth and George Eliot, he possesses this merit, that he sees with profound insight the real greatness of the lowliest life. His characters belong to a commonplace region; they are of the plain burgher type, to be met with every day in an ordinary midland town. Yet what a world of passion glows behind all that quiet exterior! What stern tragedy unfolds itself, what unfathomable depths lie yawning, what delectable heights rise gleaming when the sober grey uplifts itself! The matter-of-fact people met on the road between Bedford town and Elstow village take their place in the great commonwealth of universal thought, and are the revealers of humanity in its grandest aspects and its most sublime relationships. Behind them are the stars, and behind the stars, height over height, are the angels of God. It is this universality of thought that gives to the book its large catholicity of feeling. Once within the charm of its story we are out of the reach of sectarian clamour. He was too much of an Englishman, and too near the days of Queen Mary and the Spanish Armada not to have a fling at the Pope; but with the exception of that passing glance into the cave where the two giants, Pope and Pagan, dwelt in the old time, we have nothing to mark the writer's ecclesiastical whereabouts. Even this Romanists have left out without detriment to his story when they printed his book. That book has been truly described as one of the few which act as a religious bond to the whole of English Christendom, as one which, with perhaps six others, and equally with any one of those six has, after the English Bible, contributed to the common religious culture of the Anglo-Saxon race.[1]

He who is nearest to the Bible is nearest to *The Pilgrim's Progress* in its comprehensive Christ-like spirit. He belongs to that region where men are neither of Paul, nor Apollos, nor Cephas, but of Christ. And as there is no nationality in that Christ who on His human side is the universal man, so he whose work comes nearest to Christ comes nearest to the uni-

[1] Dean Stanley—Address at Bedford, 1874.

versal heart. This is why *The Pilgrim's Progress* has found its way to almost every people under heaven. It is one of the first books translated by the missionary who seeks to give true thoughts of God and life to heathen men, because it is one of the few books that can easily make themselves at home among nations the most diverse. It lends itself so readily to idiomatic thought and dialectic variety, and so livingly touches the universal heart beating under all nationalities that, as has been beautifully said, "it follows the Bible from land to land as the singing of the birds follows the dawn." The reason is not far to seek. More than half a century ago Macaulay pointed out that "*The Pilgrim's Progress* is the only book of its kind that possesses a strong human interest, that while other allegories only amuse the fancy, this has been read by thousands with tears." It not merely gives pleasure to the intellect by its wit and ingenuity, it gets hold of the heart by its life-grip. With deepest pathos it enters into that stern battle so real to all of us, into those heart-experiences which make up for all the discipline of life. It is this especially which has given to it the mighty hold which it has always had upon the toiling poor, and made it the one book above all books, well thumbed and worn to tatters among them.

Nor is this its only heart-power. While written specially for no one class, it has found its way to the affections of every class, and secured the homage of cultured and uncultured alike. Every one knows what a charm it has for children; it has a charm, too, for those who are in the thick of the fight, for those also who have reached the quiet evening of life. This charm is that of an ideal future, ever alluring us with its visions of brightness. In language as truthful as it is eloquent it has been said: "In lonely houses of shepherds and ploughmen it is frequently the only indication of any kind of literature that may be seen. They may be careless of the grandeur of their silent glens, they may not have one responsive chord to the subtle loveliness of nature; but their attachment to such books as this shows that the sublime in human life is even a still more subtle factor in the formation of character than the sublime in nature; and on the other hand, that the love of the beautiful cannot be eradicated even by the most slavish toil and hardship. Such people will spell over *The Pilgrim's Progress* after a hard day's work, by their farthing rushlight, and they will laugh and exult and tremble and sigh with poor Christian when they do not even understand what poor Christian's joy or trouble is; but they all in a measure understand what is meant by the celestial country for which this homely hero with the burden on his shoulder is bound, and without measure they can all dream of the solace and glory of so heavenly a paradise."[1]

ADDENDUM—Chapter XII.

Modern Criticisms of 'The Pilgrim's Progress.'

(These excerpts are given by the kind permission of the respective authors or publishers.)

Although Mr. BERNARD SHAW, in the Epistle Dedicatory to his *Man and Superman,* states that Bunyan expressed himself "in the terms of a tinker's theology," and that the "whole allegory is a consistent attack on morality and respectability, without a word that one can remember against vice and crime," yet, after comparing characters of Shakespear and Dickens, he says:

"Now you cannot say this of the works of the artist-philosophers. You cannot say it, for instance, of 'The Pilgrim's Progress.' Put your Shakespearian hero and coward, Henry V. and Pistoll or Parolles, beside Mr. Valiant and Mr. Fearing, and you have a sudden revelation of the abyss that lies between the fashionable author who could see nothing in the world but personal aims and the tragedy of their disappointment or the comedy of their incongruity, and the field preacher who achieved virtue and courage by identifying himself with the purpose of the world as he understood it. The contrast is enormous: Bunyan's coward stirs your blood more than Shakespear's hero, who actually leaves you cold and secretly hostile. You suddenly see that Shakespear, with all his flashes and divinations, never understood virtue and courage, never conceived how any man who was not a fool could, like Bunyan's hero, look back from the brink of the river of death over the strife and labor of his pilgrimage, and say 'Yet do I not repent me'; or, with the panache of a millionaire, bequeath 'my sword to him that shall succeed me in my pilgrimage and skill to him that can get it.' . . . Your man of letters thinks he can get Bunyan's or Shakespear's style without Bunyan's conviction or Shakespear's apprehension, especially if he takes care not to split his infinitives. . . ."

ROBERT LOUIS STEVENSON'S Introduction to the Bagster edition of *The Pilgrim's Progress** is devoted mainly to an ecstatic eulogy of the little woodcuts by the publisher's daughter, Eunice, to which are added a few by her brother, Jonathan. But whilst

[1] David Sime. (*Vide* Appendix III.)

* London: Samuel Bagster & Sons, Paternoster Row.

enamoured of the pictures by "the best illustrator of Bunyan," Stevenson does not lose sight of the text which inspired the artist.

"The designer," he says, "also has lain down and dreamed a dream, as literal, as quaint, and almost as apposite as Bunyan's; and text and pictures make but two sides of the same homespun yet impassioned story. . . . Bunyan was fervently in earnest; with 'his fingers in his ears, he ran on,' straight for his mark. He tells himself, in the conclusion to the first part, that he did not fear to raise a laugh; indeed, he feared nothing, and said anything; and he was greatly served in this by a certain rustic privilege of his style, which, like the talk of strong uneducated men, when it does not impress by its force, still charms by its simplicity. The mere story and the allegorical design enjoyed perhaps his equal favour. He believed in both by an energy of faith that was capable of removing mountains. And we have to remark in him, not the parts where inspiration fails and is supplied by cold and merely decorative invention, but the parts where faith has grown to incredulity, and his characters become so real to him that he forgets the end of their creation. We can follow him step by step, into the trap which he lays for himself by his own entire good faith and triumphant literality of vision, till the trap closes and shuts him in an inconsistency. . . . In every page the book is stamped with the same energy of vision and the same energy of belief. The quality is equally and indifferently displayed in the spirit of fighting, the tenderness of the pathos, the startling vigour and strangeness of the incidents, the natural strain of the conversations, and the humanity and charm of the characters. Trivial talk over a meal, the dying words of heroes, the delights of Beulah or the Celestial City, Apollyon or my Lord Hate-Good, Great-Heart and Mr. Worldly-Wiseman, all have been imagined with the same clearness, all written of with equal gusto and precision, all created in the same mixed element, of simplicity that is almost comical, and art that, for its purpose, is faultless."

"Criticism of Bunyan's work is beyond me. I might as well try to criticise the Lord's Prayer . . .," writes ROBERT BLATCHFORD in *My Favourite Books,* and adds:

"Bunyan was a man of abnormal imagination. His imagination was vivid, active, flaming, Dantean. It gave light—often lurid light—and heat, and form, and colour to all he saw. It made his thoughts stand out in blazing, sun-bright relief, or sink into seas of gloomy shadow; it gave glory, and sweetness, and celestial tone to all his joys, and put cruel edge and piercing point on all his sorrows. He was a nervous man, too, one whose soul-harp was high-strung, answerable in quivers of pain, and shrieking sharps of repulsion to every jar or discord; and his conscience was a lynx-eyed tyrant, unsleeping and remorseless. . . . What are the chief literary characteristics of John Bunyan's book? Sincerity and imagination. That which he wrote he believed. Had he not lived it? . . . There is not in 'The Pilgrim's Progress' a single speck of the garish colours of romance. To its author the story was not a romance. It was a true story, his own story, told allegorically, but without the smallest attempt at conscious embellishment. Such art or device as the work contains was the direct result of the author's own innate genius. He was a born story-teller, with an imagination so virile and magnificent as to impose upon his own judgment. . . . Bunyan's English is tinker's, and soldier's, and preacher's English. It is the English of the Bible, of the Ironsides, and of the village green."

The introduction to Cassell's "National Library," and "Little Classics" editions of *The Pilgrim's Progress,* contributed by G. K. CHESTERTON, contains, amongst other expressions, the opinion that:

"Nowhere, perhaps, except in Homer, is there such a perfect description by the use of merely plain words. . . . The Elstow tinker produced an original thing, if an original thing was ever produced."

In a prefatory note to Methuen's standard edition of *The Pilgrim's Progress,* the late Sir SIDNEY LEE says:

"Bunyan had no conscious literary aim. His sole object was to bring directly home to masses of men the familiar idea that human life is a pilgrimage through this world to the next, and that the journey of the traveller was inevitably beset by spiritual perils against which the Christian virtues were the only sure preservatives. His ideal of life is that of the Puritan. 'The Pilgrim's Progress' has been justly called the prose epic of English Puritanism. . . . Bunyan's style was mainly founded on the language of the Bible. But he freely used colloquial expressions of the workman and the shopkeeper, and adopted to his allegorical purpose the homeliest experiences of himself and his neighbours. The stirring and sustained human interest of 'The Pilgrim's Progress' renders it the greatest example of allegory in literature . . . and Bunyan deserves to be reckoned, from the point of view of the literary historian, among the founders of the English novel."

In a lengthy but profoundly interesting introduction to the Methuen edition (1898) of *The Pilgrim's Progress,* Sir CHARLES H. FIRTH says:

"'The Pilgrim's Progress' is so closely related to the life of Bunyan that it is impossible to appreciate the one without some knowledge of the other. How was it, one naturally asks, that a man of little education could produce two centuries ago a masterpiece which is still read wherever the English language is spoken, and has been translated into every European tongue? It is not sufficient to answer that the author of the work was a genius: it is necessary to show what the conditions were which enabled his genius to develop itself, led him to find the form of expression which best suited its character, and secured for what it produced both immediate popularity and lasting fame. . . . Bunyan was not merely the first of English allegorists; he is one of the founders of the English novel and the forerunner of Defoe. . . . Bunyan took a familiar idea as the basis of his story, and told it in a language that was simple or elevated, just as the subject required. He put the essence of his own life into the story. . . . That which gives the book a lasting power is the ideal of life which underlies it all—of life as the Puritan conceived it then and conceives it still. . . . Everywhere the seeker after personal holiness or ideal perfection turns his face from his home, and sets forth on the same journey: let others stay by their farm or their merchandise, he must follow the light he sees, or thinks he sees; happy if at last he beholds the shining spires of the city he travels to, glad if he catches by the way only a glimpse of the glory of it. Some may laugh at him as a fool, others may tell him there is no such city: like Bunyan he heeds them not, but dreams his dream and holds it true."

'*The Pilgrim's Progress:* A Lecture delivered at the Royal Institution of Great Britain, March 14, 1924, by J. W. MACKAIL,' (Professor of Poetry, Oxford University, 1906-1911). In the pages of this work, published by Longmans, he adds to the bibliography of Bunyan what is, perhaps, one of the most convincing literary criticisms of the Dream-story yet contributed. Those, who heard Dr. Mackail deliver his lecture on the tinker's book to a fashionable west-end audience, were privileged indeed, for the rhythmical sentences so agreeable to read, fell upon the ear like music. He says:

"Bunyan was more than an artist; and 'The Pilgrim's Progress' is more than a work of art. The 'similitude of a dream' is also the clear vision of one who had probed life to its depths. It is the statement of and appeal to truths which, under whatever form they may be expressed from one age to another, are unchangeable: that there is but one way; that the difference between right and wrong, between good and evil, is fundamental; that the laws of God are inflexible and inevitable; that ignorance, so far from being a venial error, still less a flaunted merit, is a vice and a sin, the root of all other sins and vices. . . . 'The Pilgrim's Progress' may be left to produce its own impression."

The foregoing are but a few opinions culled from the criticisms of modern writers, of varied thought. Others might well be cited, but those given are representative. To quote from the works of theologians would be difficult and, perhaps, inexpedient. To differentiate between shades of religious opinion would be invidious.

XIII.

INTERVAL BETWEEN *THE PILGRIM'S PROGRESS* AND *THE HOLY WAR*, 1676—1682.

BUNYAN wrote the First Part of *The Pilgrim's Progress* when he was forty-seven and the Second Part when he was fifty-five, *The Holy War* coming in between.* What may therefore be regarded as the flowering time of his genius came late in life. In this respect he more nearly resembles his great contemporary, John Milton, while contrasting with that other gifted soul, with whom, otherwise, he had so many points in common—Robert Burns. Bunyan and Burns, alike in their simple ancestry, their original genius and their wonderful heart-power over men in every walk of life, came thus variously to the full development of their powers. Burns had done most of his best work before he was thirty and had passed away before he was forty, while at fifty Bunyan stood scarcely midway between the two parts of his greatest work, Milton bearing him company so far as this that his *Paradise Lost* was not produced till he was fifty-seven. It may be mentioned by the way that while Bunyan's mother died when he was a youth of fifteen, his father, Thomas Bunyan, the old tinker of Elstow, lived on till 1676, being buried according to the parish register on the 7th of February in that year. It would appear, therefore, that he died when his son was in gaol for the last time, and just when the wonderful dream was taking shape. The old man seems always to have kept in the communion of the Church of England. What he thought of his son's career and convictions in later years, whether he was proud of his popularity and influence or disapproved of his perversely resisting the authorities of the times, nothing remains to show. His will has been preserved in the District Registry, and if its language may be taken as the expression of his own religious feeling he was not altogether out of spiritual sympathy with this son who went his diverse way. As giving us some items of information about the Bunyan family at this time, the reader may like to see this will for himself.

* Bunyan wrote also, in 1680, *The Life and Death of Mr. Badman.*

DOOR FROM THE COUNTY GAOL, BEDFORD,
where John Bunyan was imprisoned
1660—1672.

(Preserved at Bunyan Meeting, Bedford.)
Photo: G. A. Gearey, Bedford.]

"In the name of God, Amen, the two and twentieth day of Jany., 1675 [1675-76], according to the computation of the Church of England, I, Thomas Bunyan of Elnestow in the county of Bedford, Braseyer, being of perfit memory and Remembrance, praised bee God Doe make and ordaine this my Last Will and Testament in manner and forme following, viz.: first, I bequeath my soul into the hands of Almighty God my Maker, hoping that throug the meritorious death and passion of Jesus Christ my only Saviour and Redeemer to receive pardon for my sins. And as for my body to bee buried in Christian buriall at the discretion of my Executors hereinafter nominated. Imprimis I give unto my Sonne John Bunyan one shilling. And unto my sonne Thomas I give one shilling. And unto my daughter Mary Bunyan I give one shilling. And unto my daughter Elizabeth Bunyan I give one shilling. All of them to bee paid within a yeare after my death. And all the rest of my goods and all that I have I leave with Anne my wife to doe with what she pleases and to be at her own disposing."[1]

This will, signed with a reversed B as a mark, was attested by Robert Rose, Michael Gilbe, and Samuel Gale. The bequests to his children are not to be supposed to mean that Thomas Bunyan cut off his sons and daughters with the customary shilling of ironical or irate testators. The smallness of his legacies must rather be taken as indicating the scantiness of his means. The returns from Bedfordshire for the Hearth Tax of 1673—4 have been preserved in the Record Office, giving the names of every householder in the county, both those who paid taxes on their chimneys and those who were too poor to pay. Among the latter we find Thomas Bunyan, of the parish of Elstow, who was exempted by legal certificate.[2] The parish register informs us that his widow Ann Bunyan was "buried in Woolen, September 25th, 1680."

Once more, and finally, released from prison, John Bunyan was again at work among the Nonconformists of Bedfordshire, whose numbers seem to have steadily grown in spite of the measures used for their repression. In that year, 1676, Archbishop Sheldon ordered a religious census to be taken of the province of Canterbury. The returns furnished by his own officials have been preserved, and are of interest as furnishing an approximate estimate of the population of the county in that year. They were carefully made, parish by parish, and were brought together in a bound volume, formerly in the possession

[1] *Bedfordshire Wills,* 1675—6, No. 74.

[2] *Subsidies*—Bedfordshire: Hearth Tax, 25 Car. II.—Elstow. [Thomas Bunyan occupied a "one hearthed house" in Elstow, in 1670.]

of the Duke of Sussex and now among the MSS. of the Salt Museum at Stafford. The returns give the number of Conformists, Nonconformists, and Papists in each parish above the age of sixteen. In similar returns made in the reign of William III., the number of those above sixteen is doubled to get at the entire population. As this gives an estimate of five millions, which there is reason to believe was somewhere near the population of the country at the time, we may assume the principle to be approximately correct. If we apply it to Bedfordshire in 1676, we find that the entire population of the county in that year was 50,752, that in the 119 parishes of the six deaneries there were 1,944 Nonconformists above sixteen years of age and 40 Papists, and therefore a total Nonconformist population of between 3,000 and 4,000, a number somewhat remarkable, taking into account the sternly coercive measures brought to bear upon them for a period of now nearly sixteen years. In the town of Bedford there were in the five parishes 121 Nonconformists and one Papist above sixteen, so that the thirty of 1669 had multiplied fourfold after the Declaration of Indulgence, and the number under Bunyan's pastoral care, including those from the villages must have been considerable. In the whole of Lincoln diocese the Nonconformists were 1 in 21 of the population, in the county of Bedford 1 in 12, and in the town of Bedford 1 in 10, a proportion which is somewhat suggestive as to Bunyan's personal influence.

The year after the appearance of the First Part of *The Pilgrim's Progress* was made memorable by the great national scare of the Popish plot and the intense excitement of a general election after the dissolution of a Parliament which had sat for eighteen years. It was rumoured that the Jesuits were in deadly earnest about the conversion of England to the Romish faith, that the King was to be assassinated, the Protestants in London massacred, and the crown offered to that resolute Papist, the Duke of York. The nation felt as if it were once more on the verge of civil war; and Daniel Defoe, who was then a boy, tells us how men polished their blunderbusses again and refurbished their military gear as in the days of strife between Roundhead and Royalist. To the same purpose Bunyan himself says: "Our days indeed had been days of trouble, especially since the discovery of the Popish plot, for then we began to fear cutting of throats, of being burned in our beds, and of seeing our children dashed to pieces before our faces. But looking about us, we found we had a gracious king, brave parliaments, a stout city, good lord-mayors, honest sheriffs, substantial laws against them, and these we made the object of our hope, quite forgetting the direction in this exhortation—Let Israel hope in the Lord."[1] In the midst of all this excitement Parliament was prorogued, and on the 24th of January, 1678—9, dissolved. It will always be memorable for its persecuting spirit and for its venal corruption. With open effrontery, Lord Danby bought the votes of Members of Parliament, increasing the annual grant for this purpose from £12,000 a year to £20,000. In its earliest years this Second Long Parliament had been pitilessly cruel; in its later years it was shamelessly debased.

Naturally the general election which followed was attended with considerable excitement. Electors, who had had no opportunity of recording their votes for nearly twenty years, rode in to the polling booths by thousands, and in the slow process of polling in those days could find no accommodation in inns or houses, and had to sleep in the market-places, lying like sheep round the market crosses. Almost everywhere the country party, as it was called, was victorious, and the court party defeated. Edmund Verney, writing to Sir R. Verney, 24th of February, 1678—9, says: "I hear the Bedfordshire election cost £6,000. They were three days a-polling. But Lord Bruce and his party lost it by five hundred votes, whereat the Earl of Ailesbury his father was extremely angry."[2] In the county Lord Bruce was defeated by Lord William Russell and Sir J. Napier by Sir H. Monoux; while for the borough Sir William Beecher, whom we met on the bench at Bunyan's trial, was supplanted by Sir William Franklyn, along with whom William Paulet St. John was returned as before.

During these politically stirring times Bunyan went on writing his books, and looking out upon the storm, not knowing whether it would blow him to the haven of settled liberty or once more on to the rocks of prison life. Having for convenience' sake already considered together the two parts of *The Pilgrim's Progress* and leaving for future consideration *The Holy War,* we may now briefly glance at the other books which belong to this period of our Author's life.

[1] *Bunyan's Works,* i., 585. [George Offor's Edition. Vide also, Doe's Folio. 1692.]
[2] *MSS. of Sir Harry Verney, Bart.,* 1678—9; Feb. 24.

It has been already mentioned that the little work entitled *Instruction for the Ignorant,*[1] dated 1675, was written in prison. It was published by Bunyan's old friend Francis Smith, the copy of the first edition in the Bodleian being the only one known to be in existence. The book was sent forth, the writer says, as "a salve to cure that great want of knowledge which so much reigns both in young and old." In the form of question and answer it deals with the elementary truths relating to the nature of God, the character and confession of sin, faith in Christ, prayer and self-denial, but has no special value in any way. The same year also there appeared the book entitled *Saved by Grace,*[2] which Charles Doe places between the catechism just referred to and the discourse on *The Strait Gate.* In this work on Salvation by Grace there are one or two foregleams of the greater book by which it was immediately followed. We are reminded of the description of the raptures of the blessed given by Christian to Pliable as we read in the section on completed salvation this:

"The soul will be filled in all the faculties of it with as much bliss and glory as ever it can hold. We shall have perfect and everlasting vision of God; our will and affections shall be ever in burning flame of love; our conscience have that peace and joy that neither tongue nor pen of men or angels can express, and our memory be enlarged to the everlasting ravishment of our hearts. The body too shall be glorified and between soul and body there shall be perfect harmony without jarring. In this world the body oft hangs this way and the soul the quite contrary, but then they shall never jar more; the glory of the body shall so suit with the glory of the soul and both so perfectly suit with the heavenly state that it passeth words and thoughts. Shall I speak of the place? It is a city, a kingdom, paradise, everlasting habitations. Shall I speak of their company? They stand in the presence of God and of the Lamb, they are with an innumerable company of angels, with patriarchs and prophets. Shall I speak of their heavenly raiment? They are clothed with the garment of salvation, they walk in white, they are crowned with righteousness. O sinner, what sayest thou? How dost thou like being saved? Doth not thy mouth water? Doth not thy heart twitter at being saved?"

Here also is a variation of the well-known simile of the oil and the water cast on that fire seen in the House of Interpreter.

[1] *Instruction for the Ignorant:* or a Salve to Cure that great want of knowledge which so much reigns in Old and Young. London: Francis Smith, 1675. *Premiers Principes de Christianisme* expliqués dans un Dialogue Simple et Familier, par Jean Bunyan. Paris, 1827.

[2] *Saved by Grace:* or a discourse of the Grace of God. No copy of the First Edition known to exist. *Cadwedigaeth trwy ras,* &c. Caernarfon, 1824. 12mo.

"O what an enemy is man to his own soul! I am persuaded that God hath visited some of you often with his word, even twice and thrice and you have thrown water as fast as He hath by the word cast fire upon your conscience."

We seem to see the tears welling up to his eyes and to hear his voice, tremulous with emotion, as we read this characteristic passage about the grace of Christ to sinful man:

"Thou Son of the Blessed, what grace was manifest in thy condescension! Grace brought thee down from heaven, grace stripped thee of thy glory, grace made thee poor and despicable, grace made thee bear such burdens of sin, such burdens of sorrow, such burdens of God's curse as are unspeakable. O Son of God! grace was in all thy tears, grace came bubbling out of thy side with thy blood, grace came forth with every word of thy sweet mouth. Grace came out where the whip smote thee, where the thorns pricked thee, where the nails and spear pierced thee. O blessed Son of God! Here is grace indeed! Unsearchable riches of grace! Unthought-of riches of grace! Grace to make angels wonder, grace to make sinners happy, grace to astonish devils. And what will become of them that trample under foot this Son of God?"

This book on Salvation by Grace, having gone from his hand he entered upon that other to which reference has already been made, the book which was probably the expansion of a sermon preached during his three years of liberty, and entitled *The Strait Gate,* or the Great Difficulty of going to Heaven.[1] It is based on the well-known passage Luke xiii., 24. The stress of the book is against an unreal profession of Christian life, against the "many that make Christ's word and his name, and his ways, a stalking-horse to their own worldly advantage." In the searching hour of final judgment those things that these mere professors but not possessors "count sound and good will then shake like a quagmire, even all their naked knowledge, their feigned faith, pretended love, glorious shows of gravity in the face, their holiday words and specious carriages, will stand them in little stead. I call them holiday ones, for I perceive that some professors do with religion just as people do with their best apparel—hang it against the wall all the week and put it on on Sundays. For as some scarce ever put on a suit but when they go to a fair or a market, so little house religion will do with some; they save religion till they go to a meeting, or till they meet a godly chapman. O poor religion! O poor

[1] *The Strait Gate*: or the Great Difficulty of going to Heaven. London: Francis Smith, Cornhill, 1676. Copies of the First Edition in Bodleian and Camb. Univ. Lib. *De Enge Poorte,* obte het groote . . . Werk van ten Hemel in te gaan. Amsterdam, 1727.

professor! What wilt thou do at this day, the day of thy trial and judgment? Cover thyself thou canst not, go for a Christian thou canst not, stand against the Judge thou canst not."

In the application of his theme Bunyan speaks to those who are, as he says, upon the potter's wheel, in whom great thoughts and anxious resolves are stirring, but who are too apt to check a convincing conscience. "Such poor sinners are much like to a wanton boy at the maid's elbow, to blow out her candle as fast as she lights lights it at the fire. Convinced sinner, God lighteth thy candle and thou puttest it out. God lights it again and again thou puttest it out. Take heed lest like the Egyptians you dwell all your days in darkness and never see light more. Give glory to God, and if He awakens thy conscience quench not thy convictions." Having thus for a moment turned aside he returns once more to the unreal professors in the Church and asks leave to set his trumpet to their ears again. He sets them in classes and has a word for each—for the talkative whose religion lies only in his tongue; for the covetous professor who makes a gain of religion and uses it to bring grist to his mill; for the wanton professor, with his feastings and eating without fear, not for health but for gluttony; for the formalist who has lost all of religion but the shell; for the temporising latitudinarian whose religion is like the times, turning this way and that way like the cock on the steeple; and for that professor who is for God and for Baal too, can be anything for any company, can throw stones with both hands, alter his religion as fast as his company; can live in water as out of water, with Christians and away from them. Nothing that is disorderly comes amiss to this man. He will hold with the hare and hold with the hounds, carry fire in one hand and water in the other, is a very anything.

After these three books which belong to 1675—6 came, as we have already seen, the First Part of *The Pilgrim's Progress.* The same year this was published, in addition to the sending forth a second edition, in which Mr. Worldly Wiseman first appears, Bunyan gave to the world his *Come and Welcome to Jesus Christ,* which Offor places in 1681, but which, as we now know, first saw the light in 1678.[1] It was the enlargement of a

[1] *Come and Welcome to Jesus Christ.* London: B. Harris, 1678. *Komst en Welkomst tot Jesus Christus.* Amsterdam: J. Boekholt, 1689. *Die Zarteste Liebe Christi allen Sündern gezeiget,* durst J. Bunian. Hamburg: Gottfried Liebernicknel, 1698. *Tyred a groesaw at Jesu Crist.* Caerfyrddin: 1770. *Thig agus se do bheatha Chum Iosa Criosd.* Edinburgh: 1859. *Jesu Hjerte aabnet for Syndere* (Norsk). Horten: 1882; after an Edition of 1772.

sermon on John vi., 37, the words of whcih—Him that cometh to me I will in nowise cast out—had been like heaven's balm to his own heart-wounds in his days of spiritual struggle. Salvation, he tells us, has its roots in fatherly love: "I myself have often found that when I can say but this word Father, it doth me more good than when I call Him by any other Scripture name." The Father is the giver of those who come, and as to what is the true coming, the four lepers in the Book of Kings were a famous semblance. The famine was sore in the land, these lepers were thrust without the city, and as they sat in the gate, hunger was, as I may say, making his last meal of them; and being therefore half dead already, what do they think of doing? Why, first they display the dismal colours of death before each other's faces and then resolve to go into the city to the Syrians. Die they may if they go in, but die they must if they stop where they are. Here now was necessity at work, and this necessity drove them to go thither for life, whither else they would never have gone for it. Thus it is with them that in truth come to Jesus Christ. Men should warm their hearts by the sweet promise of Christ's acceptance. Discouraging thoughts are like unto cold weather, they benumb the senses and make us go ungainly about our business; but the sweet and warm gleads of promise are like the comfortable beams of the sun which liven and refresh. You see how little the bee and fly do play in the air in winter; why the cold hinders them from doing it; but when the wind and sun is warm, who so busy as they? He that comes to Christ cannot, it is true, always get on as fast as he would. Poor coming soul, thou art like the man that would ride full gallop whose horse will hardly trot. Now the desire of his mind is not to be judged of by the slow pace of the dull jade he rides on, but by the hitching and kicking and spurring as he sits on his back. Thy flesh is like this dull jade, it will not gallop after Christ, it will be backward though thy soul and heaven lie at stake.

The promise is large, Christ will in nowise cast out. Let the best master of arts on earth show me if he can any condition in this text that depends upon any qualification in us. They shall come? Shall they come? Yes, they shall come. But how if they want those things, those graces, power and heart without which they cannot come? Why, *shall come* answereth all this and all things else. And him that cometh shall in nowise be cast out. Let him be as red as blood, let him be as red as crimson. Some men are blood-red sinners, crimson sinners, sinners of a double dye, dipped and dipped again before they come to Jesus Christ. Art thou that readest these lines such an one? Speak out man! Art thou such an one? Fear not! trouble not thyself, coming sinner. If thou seest thy lost condition, if thou seest thy need of the spotless righteousness of Jesus Christ, if thou art willing to be found in Him, take up thy cross and follow, then pray for a fair wind and good weather and come away. Stick no longer in a muse and doubt about things, but come away to Jesus Christ. God hath strewed all the way from the gate of hell, where thou wast, to the gate of heaven, whither thou art going, with flowers out of his own garden. Behold how the promises, invitations, calls, and encouragements like lilies lie round about thee! Take heed that thou dost not tread them under thy foot, sinner. With promises, did I say? Yea he hath mixed all those with his own name, his Son's name, also with the name of mercy, goodness, compassion, love, pity, grace, forgiveness, pardon, and what not, that may encourage thy coming, sinner.

This book, *Come and Welcome,* with its musical title and soul-moving pleas, was published for Bunyan by "B. Harris, at Stationers Arms in Swithings Rents in Cornhil, 1678." His next book, like his 'Pilgrim,' came out under the auspices of Nathaniel Ponder. It was entitled *A Treatise of the Fear of God,* and was published in 1679.[1] It has for a frontispiece a woodcut reproduction of Robert White's engraved sleeping portrait of Bunyan, prefixed to the third edition of *The Pilgrim's Progress,* and at the end there is the following note: "Errata's. Reader, thou art desired to correct these errata's (with some others) which were occasioned by the Printer, by reason of the absence of the Author." The treatise is founded on the words, "Blessed is every one that feareth the Lord." He will not, he says, trouble his reader with a long preamble or "forespeech" to the matter, nor will he so much as meddle with the context, but immediately fall upon the words themselves, which are weighty enough. He shows the difference between a noble fear

[1] *A Treatise of the Fear of God.* By John Bunyan. London: Printed for N. Ponder. 1679. *Verhandelinge van de Waare Vreese Gods*: **Aantoon-Ende Waar in die bestaat.** In't Engels beschreven door Mr. Johannes Bunjan. Dordrecht: **Johannes t' Hooft.** 1727.

and a fear that is ignoble. The noble fear has its roots in reverence of that which is high and majestical. Some men have it not. Even when they seem to come for the worship of God they come only to sleep there, or they come thither to meet with their chapmen or to get into the wicked fellowship of their vain companions. There is an ignoble, ungodly fear, which driveth men away from God, which withers their power of serving him as it did the man with the one talent. For what does he? Why, he takes his talent—the gift that he was to lay out for his master's profit—and, burying it, lies in a lazy manner at to-elbow all his days, not out of, but in, his lord's vineyard. It is this unfilial fear which makes men superstitious before God. It was this that put the Pharisees upon inventing so many traditions, as the washing of cups, and beds, and tables, and basins, with abundance of such other like gear. And how it has racked and tortured the Papists for hundreds of years together! For what but this ungodly fear of God is the cause of their penances, as creeping to the cross, going barefoot on pilgrimage, whipping themselves, wearing of sackcloth, saying so many Paternosters and Ave-marias, making so many confessions to the priest, and giving so much money for pardons? The true, the noble fear is of quite other sort; it is called a grace, that is a sweet and blessed work of the Spirit of Grace. It is called God's treasure, for it is one of his choice jewels, one of the rarities of heaven. Poor vagrants when they come straggling to a lord's house may perhaps obtain some scraps and fragments; they may also obtain old shoes and some sorry cast-off rags, but they get not any of his jewels, they may not touch his choicest treasure, that is kept for the children and those that shall be his heirs. We may say the same also of this blessed grace of fear, which is called here God's treasure.

Be not high-minded, then, but fear. Fear, and that will make you little in your own eyes, keep you humble, put you upon crying to God for protection, and upon lying at his foot for mercy; that will also make you have low thoughts of your own parts, of your own doings, and cause you to prefer your brother before yourself, and so you will walk in humiliation and be continually under the teachings of God and under his conduct in your way. The lowly God teaches, the meek will he guide in judgment. To abound in this fear is a sign of a very princely spirit, and the reason is, when I greatly fear my God I am above the fear of all others. Keep then this grace of fear, and if you would, take heed of a hard heart; take heed of the beginnings of sin. There is more in a little sin to harden than in a great deal of grace to soften. Take heed also of a prayerless heart. The man that prays but little, fears God but little. Prayer is as the pitcher that fetcheth water from the brook therewith to water the herbs; break the pitcher and it will fetch no water, and for want of water the garden withers.

It may vary the line of thought somewhat if we now turn from Bunyan as an author to Bunyan as a pastor during the years with which we are at present concerned, that is, from 1676 to 1682. The only glimpses we get of him during this time are from the Church Records, and these were but scantily kept. Several of the entries are in Bunyan's own handwriting, the rest variously written. It will be seen that he was not without his heart-sorrows in watching over his flock. Disregarding the mere routine entries relating to the admission of members, we come upon such minutes as these:

"At a church meeting at Gamlingay the 14th of the 11th month, 1676 [14th Feb., 1677] Brother Oliver Thodye made acknowledgment of summe miscarages the Church had charged him with as namely, breakeing the Saboth and brawling with neighbours.

"The 7th of the 12th month, 1676 [7th March, 1677]. The Church of Christ in and about Bedford to the Church of Christ in and about Braintree, sendeth greeting. Holy and beloved, we fellow heires with you of the grace of life having considered your request concerneing our honnered and beloved brother Samuel Hensman . . . doe as before God and the Elect Angels grant and give up to you our elect brother to be receaued by you in the Lord, and to be nourished in the church at Braintree with you as one that is dear to the Father and our Lord Jesus Christ. And this we the willinger doe because as we are informed conserneing you beloved, you are not ridged in your principles, but are for communyon with saints as saints; and have been taught by the word to receaue the brotherhood because they are beloued and receaued of the Father and the Sonne to whose grace we commend you with the brother of late a member with us; but now one of you. Grace be with you all. John Bunyan, Sam. ffenn, &c.

"The 29th of the 1st month, 1677 [April 29th]. (The dismission to the church at Hitchin of 'our beloved Bro. John Willson' to be their minister). . . . God haveing bowed the heart of the Church to consent to what you have both longed and as we trust much prayed for, [they have] granted and by these lines doe grant and give up our beloued Brother to fellowshipe with you for your mutuall edification and ioy of faith. We need not as some others to commend him to you, God haueing before prevented that by commending him to you himselfe. Now God and our Father and our Lord Jesus Christ that great Shepherd of the Shepe make this both our and your beloued brother a double blessing unto you both in his ministery to and membershipe among you, and as a watchman ouer you, if God and the Church with you shall call him therto. Amen. John Bunyan, Sam. ffenn, Thomas Woodward, John Bardolph, &c.

"1677. At a meeting of the church in Gamlingay the Congregation withdrew Communyan from Edward Dent of Gamlingay, the matter of fact charged upon him was for being negligent and unfaithfull as to the management of his sisters Imployment which he was intrusted with; and alsoe for contracting many debts which he nether was able to pay nether did he so honestlye and Christianly take care to pay his creditors in due time as he oght, though he had bene often exhorted to it and admonished before by his brethren."

The following is in Bunyan's handwriting:

"1678. At a meeting holden at Bedford the 24th of July, our sister Mary ffosket (after private admonition given her before) was publikly admonished for receiveing and privatly whispering of an horrid scandal (without culler of truth), against our Brother Honylove and for other evils by her committed, all of which she standeth convicted of and so must doe till her repentance for the same (according to the word) is manifest unto the congregation."

The next entries are by another hand:

"Cottenend the 12 month, 1678 [March, 1679], our brother John Stanton was admonished by the Church of his evill in abuseing his wife and beateing hir often for very light maters. Hee promised us reformation and seemed sory for his fault.

"At a Generall Church Meeting at Cottonend the 15th September, 1679, it was taken notise of that the church was much decayed in hir faith and louse and allsoe that the members of the congregation while manie tarried not ther relation to the congregation were too much neglected, it was proposed to the Church that care might be taken to consider of wayes and meanes how we might Joyntly reforme and performe our dutyes one unto another According to what our relation in the fellowship of the gospel calls for.

"At a Generall Church Meeting at Cottonend, the 12 day of November, 1679, the church did sollemnely giue them selves up to the lord and one unto another, and did promise in the strength of Crist to walke more in loue one with another, and to performe the dutyes of ther relation more carfully then formerlie they had done.

"At a Generall Church meteing at Cottonend the 2 day of November, 1680, John Wildman did at that church meteing manage a charge against the congregation which he had drawne up, most of it in wrighting, and sent to us summe time before, in the manageing of which charge he was found extriordinary guilty of a kind of railery and very great passion very much condemned by the whole congregation. Alsoe he was found guilty of slandering the congregation, in perticular our beloued and honnered brother Bunyan, in what he had spoken to Mr. Gibs.

"Alsoe he did desperately charge our brother and pastor, John Bunyan, with calling the sisters to know ther Husbands estates, in order to put a levy opon them wher In he was proued before the whole congregation an abominable lyer and slanderer of our beloved brother Bunyan; ffor those causes with others the congregation did at that meeteing in Christ name with draw church comunyan from him with a poynt consent, not one so much as makeing the least sticke at it. And it was then agreed opon that if the congregation did not perseaue repentance in him at the next church meeting he should be cast out of the church."

The following are all in Bunyan's handwriting:

"1681. A letter sent by the elders to sister Hauthorn by way of reproofe for her unseemly language against Brother Scot and the whole church.

"Sister Hauthorn—It was not a little surprizing to us to behold in what spirit you acted, and with what taunts and reflections you let our your anger when you with with us at Bedford, not only against our beloued Brother Scot, but against the church in general and against the elders in perticuler, of which a perticuler account may be given you when we shall next speak with you when and where we shall expect satisfaction by the proof of your repentance towards God and your unfeigned acknowledgement of your abusinge of your Brethren. Jo. Bunyan, Sam. ffenn. Off which miscariag she soon made humble acknowledgement to satisfaction.

"1681. On the tenth day of November our aged and much honnered Brother John Sewster departed this life; on the twelfth day of the same our honnoured Brother Samuel ffen, one of the elders of this congregation, departed this life.

"Appointed that on the 22 of this month the church doe meet together to humble them-selves before God for the sin that hath provoked God to lay this heavie hand upon us. Also on the 24 day of the same month we had a meeting ta Gamblingay upon the same account.

"At which meetings we also concluded that upon the 12 of December next the brethren com together to pray to God and to consider how to manage the affairs of the church for her further edification. The which was also don, for then at Cottenend was these things concluded:

"1. That the several meetings that are upheld by the congregation to witt; Bedford, Kemston, Malden, Cotten End, Edworth, and Gamblingay be better supplied.

"2. That there be another Deacon chose for the help of our brother John ffen, and our brother John Croker.

"3. That the work of ruleing Elders be considered of and their qualifications in order to the choyce and apointment of som to that work in this congregation.

"4. That the congregation doth make enquiries after those gifts that may be of service in the church, and that a way be found out for there exercise and increas if God will.

"5. That the first in every month be kept in prayr for to beg God's blessing upon the preaching of the word, ffor the conversion of our children and for the mercie and blessing of God upon the king and governors.

"6. That the preachers in the congregation do agree to meet together once in six weeks to conferr and to pray to God for a blessing upon their ministry.

"The Church of Christ in and about Bedford to the Church of Christ walking with our beloved Brother Cockain in London,[1] wisheth abundance of grace by Jesus Christ. Beloved Brethren, we commend unto you our Brother William Breeden, who is one of us, but by reason that his place of habitation is with you in London, and so remote from us; and becaus he desireth that his distance from us might not be a bar as to his Christian communion; and also becaus he desireth to be helped forward in his Christian course by haveing admittance by you into all Christ's ordinances; therefore we pray you in the bowels of Christ to receive him, and to be a nurs to him in the lord. John Bunyan, John ffenn, Anthony Harrington, &c.

"Several meetings for prayer and breaking of bread."

This brings us to the close of 1682. There is one more entry in Bunyan's handwriting, and as it is the last made by him in the Church Book, though he remained pastor five years longer, we may give it here.

"1683. A church meeting at Cotton-end the 20 of April for breaking of bread where there was also a frothy letter of John Wildman's presented to the congregation, wherein he counteth our dealing with him for his correction and amendment scuffling and fooling, and so

[1] The church in Red Cross Street, removed to Hare Court in 1692. *The Story of Hare Court,* by J. B. Marsh. 1871.

desires a corispondence. In answer to which was sent him this following admonition from the same meeting: ffriend Wildman, your letter has bin plainly read before us, and since you have bin withdrawn ffrom by the church ffor lying, railing and scandalizing of the church in generall, and som of the brethren in perticuler: It is expected:

"1. That there be the signes of true repentance found in you for the same.

"2. And also that you bring from the hands of those in the countrey before whom you have abused us som signe of their satisfaction concerning your repentance before we can admitt you again into our communion. Written for you and sent you by order of the congregation—Wittnes, John Bunyan, &c."

From John Wildman to *The Life and Death of Mr. Badman*[1] is only a step. This book of Bunyan's was published through Nathaniel Ponder in 1680, and, as we have seen, was meant to be the companion picture to his 'Pilgrim.' It was thrown into dialogue form after the manner of Arthur Dent's *Plain Man's Pathway to Heaven,* one of the two books Bunyan's first wife brought him in his far-off Elstow days. The resemblance between Dent's work and Bunyan's is too close to be merely accidental. In each the dialogue is supposed to be carried on through one long day. Bunyan's Mr. Wiseman, like Dent's Theologus, holds forth instructive discourse, while the Mr. Attentive of the former, like the Philagathus of the latter, listens and draws on his teacher by friendly questionings. There is not in Bunyan's conference, as there is in Dent's, an Asunetus, who plays the part of an ignorant man, to come out enlightened and convinced at last, or an Antilegon who carps and cavils all the way; and there is not in Dent's book what there is in Bunyan's, a biographical narrative connecting the various parts of the dialogue; but the groundwork of each is the same—a searching manifestation of the nature and evils of pride, uncleanness, swearing, dishonesty, lying, and drunkenness.

Badman is the typical scoundrel whose story is opened up to Attentive by his neighbour Wiseman as together they speak of the passing bell, which yesterday tolled for this man who has gone from life to death. Badman was his name, and he was bad from the first, even as a child, lying and standing to his

[1] *Life and Death of Mr. Badman,* presented to the world in a familiar dialogue between Mr. Wiseman and Mr. Attentive. London: Nathaniel Ponder, 1680. *Leven en Sterven van Meester Quadt.* Amsterdam: 1685. *Mr. Quaats Leben Und Sterben,* Hamburg: 1767. *Bywyd a marwolaeth yr annuwiol dan enw Mr. Drygddyn.* Lerpwl, 1782. 12mo. *Beath agus Bas Mhr Droch-dhuine.* Inverness: 1824. 12mo.

lies, and given to pilfering and profanity. His father, baffled, put him apprentice to a godly master, whose good ways the lad will have none of. This master he first robs, and then runs away from, and so comes to the end of the first stage of his unpromising career. His next master was as bad as himself. They were well met for wickedness, and could young Badman have filled his master's purse by his unprincipled ways, "he had certainly been his whiteboy," but as bad men have no greater liking to have their business neglected, their tills robbed, and their families seduced than good men have, he and his master were at odds. His father next starts him in business, but he is no sooner set up than he is set down again, for he gathers loose companions about him who egg him to the ale-house and make him "jack-pay-for-all," borrow money from him and forget to repay it; so want comes upon him like an armed man. But his audacity hides his condition till by a bold stroke he has retrieved it. Tall and fair, and not without natural parts, he marries an orphan with money, who little dreamed that her peace and comfort, her estate and liberty, were all going to their burial when she was going to her bridal. With the money thus obtained he pays his debts, only that he may run into debt the deeper while seeming to drive a brisk trade. He plays his part according to the company in which he happens to be, chuckling over his craft the while. So he goes on, and after making show of great trade, and getting large credit, makes "hatfuls of money" by breaking, coming out of his bankruptcy a better man than when he shut up shop by several thousands of pounds. No one is surprised to find before long that he is in business again, and as before he defrauded his creditors, now he cheats his customers, keeping weights to buy by and weights to sell by, measures to sell by and measures to buy by. Let customer or chapman watch him ever so closely, he will with sleight of hand get little turns of advantage, and misreckon men's accounts to their detriment, so that in time Badman now grows well-to-do, and though his neighbours have no faith in the man, yet he is prosperous, and prosperity covers over much that is odious. He struts in the sunlight, and is proud and vain, shews great height, and is of a domineering spirit. If you quote the Scriptures against him he will ask you how you know them to be the word of God, and would say that the Scriptures were as a nose of wax, and a man may turn them whithersoever he lists. He is happy if only he can lay hold of some scandal, no matter how false, against a godly man. "O! then he would glory, laugh, and be glad, and lay it upon the whole party, saying, 'Hang them rogues; there is not a barrel better herring of all the holy brotherhood of them. Like to like, quoth the devil to the collier; this is your precise crew.' And then he would send all home with a curse."

Yet even he cannot climb above the clouds which now darken round him. In a drunken fit he comes by a broken leg, and dangerous illness seizes upon him. He is penitent, but for no longer than he is in peril. His fine words when he is ill are followed by no good actions when he is well. After years of trouble his poor broken-hearted wife is laid in the quiet grave, while retribution in kind comes back; for by-and-bye, while in his cups, he is tricked into a marriage with a woman as vile as himself, and as the years went by they sinned all away, and "parted as poor as howlets." He would have his way, and she hers, he his companions and she hers, and so "they brought their noble to ninepence." Thus the story comes to its miserable end, the man dying as he had lived, worthless and impenitent.

Such is an outline of the story of this book, in which there is a good deal of powerful writing, not a little keen insight into character and knowledge of life, but which it is impossible to read without feeling that artistically it is beneath the level of the Pilgrim story which went before it. It would be easy to point out many vividly picturesque and life-like touches in the book, but the book as a whole is weighted, as the 'Pilgrim' is not, by a series of otherwise excellent dissertations on lying, swearing, stealing, impurity, dishonest bankruptcy, pride, and the like, which run on to such length that you lose the thread of the narrative while listening to the moralities of the sermon. Then, too, there are stories introduced by the way which are sometimes clownish, sometimes commonplace, and sometimes simply unbelievable now, though Bunyan evidently believed them then. Yet, with all these deductions, we may assent in the main to Mr. Froude's admirable summing-up of the book when he says, "It is extremely interesting merely as a picture of vulgar English life in a provincial town, such as Bedford was when Bunyan lived there. The drawing is so good, the details so minute, the conception so unexaggerated, that we are disposed to believe that we must have a real history before us. But such a supposition is only a compliment to the skill of the composer. . . . Bunyan conceals nothing, assumes nothing, and exaggerates nothing. He makes his bad man sharp and shrewd. He allows sharpness and shrewdness to bring him the rewards which such qualities in fact command. Badman is successful; he is powerful; he enjoys all the pleasures which money can buy; his bad wife helps him to ruin, but otherwise he is not unhappy, and he dies in peace. Bunyan has made him a brute, because such men do become brutes. It is the real punishment of brutal and selfish habits. There the figure stands: a picture of a man in the ranks of English life with which Bunyan was most familiar, travelling along the primrose path to the everlasting bonfire, as the way to Emmanuel's Land was through the Slough of Despond and the Valley of the Shadow of Death. Pleasures are to be found among the primroses, such pleasures as a brute can be gratified by; yet the reader feels that even if there were no bonfire, he would still prefer to be with Christian."[1]

[1] *English Men of Letters*—Bunyan, pp. 112-113.

XIV.

'MANSOUL' AND THE BEDFORD CORPORATION.

AFTER the appearance of *The Life and Death of Mr. Badman* in 1680, we have nothing further from Bunyan's pen for the next two years. During this time, however, he was engaged upon his second greatest work, *The Holy War*, made by Shaddai upon Diabolus.[1] It was published by Dorman Newman, at the King's Arms in the Poultry in 1682, and Macaulay has said of it that it would have been our greatest religious allegory if *The Pilgrim's Progress* had never been written. Perhaps there would be more discrimination in saying that in the subtlety of its psychological distinctions and the completeness of its details *The Holy War* is superior to *The Pilgrim's Progress*, but that, judged by the standard of epic completeness, and by the power of laying hold of the simple instincts of the heart, it is greatly inferior. The characters in the former work are mere abstractions when compared with those of the latter. Captain Credence and Captain Conviction, for example, are shadowy shapes indeed by the side of Mr. Greatheart in his brave humanness, or Old Honest in his sturdy directness. Both books are alike in this, that while they move in the region of the spiritual and supernatural, they at the same time tread the common earth, their scenes and circumstances being drawn from the writer's actual surroundings.

[1] *The Holy War*, made by Shaddai upon Diabolus for the regaining of the Metropolis of the World; or the Losing and Taking again of the Town of Mansoul. By John Bunyan. London: Printed for *Dorman Newman* at the *Kings Arms* in the *Poultry* and *Benjamin Alsop* at the *Angel* and *Bible* in the *Poultry*, 1682. *Den Heyligen Oorlogh* . . . Uyt 't Engels Vertaalt. Amsterdam, 1685. 12mo. *Der Heilige Krieg* . . . Ins Hochteutsche übersetzet von Johann Lange. London, 1751. 8vo. *Y Rhyfel Ysbrydol*. Caerfyrddin, 1812. 12mo. *La Sainte Guerre*, traduite de l'Anglais. Paris, 1842. *Eachdraidh fhirinneach m 'un Chogadh naemh*. Eadar-theangaichte gu Gaelig le I. Rose. Duneidin, 1846. *The Holy War*, in Oriya. Cuttack, 1851. *As Guerras da famosa Ciudade de Alumana*, 1870. 12mo. *The Holy War*, in Bengali, N.D. *The Holy War*, in Canarese, translated from the Tamil version. Bangalore, 1884. *The Holy War*, in Arabic with 18 cuts. *Den hellige Krig* (Norsk). Bergen: 1878. *Mbuk Edisana Ekön* (Efik). 1836.

[The Second Edition appeared in 1684 with an altered title: *The Holy War* made by Christ upon the Devil for the Regaining of Man: Or, the Losing and Taking Again of the Town of Mansoul. This was also published by Dorman Newman. The next known edition, issued by *Nath. Ponder*, in *London-Yard*, in 1696, and all subsequent editions, bear the original title.]

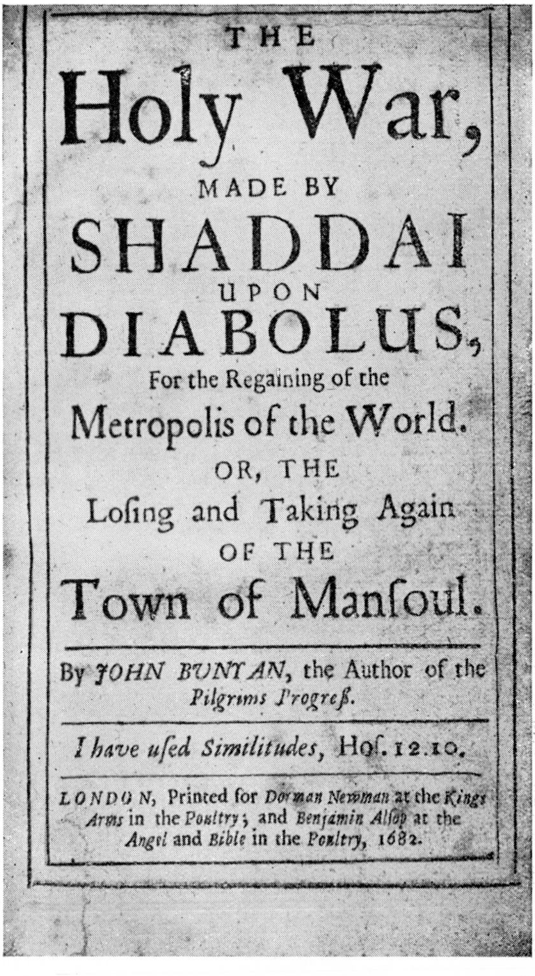

THE

Holy War,

MADE BY

SHADDAI

UPON

DIABOLUS,

For the Regaining of the

Metropolis of the World.

OR, THE

Losing and Taking Again

OF THE

Town of Mansoul.

By *JOHN BUNYAN*, the Author of the *Pilgrims Progress*.

I have used Similitudes, Hos. 12.10.

LONDON, Printed for *Dorman Newman* at the *Kings Arms* in the *Poultry*; and *Benjamin Alsop* at the *Angel* and *Bible* in the *Poultry*, 1682.

Title-Page of the First Edition of
'THE HOLY WAR'
By John Bunyan.
1682.

If it be true, as has been said, that in *The Pilgrim's Progress* "Bunyan's men are not merely life portraits but English portraits, men of the solid, practical, unimpassioned Midland race," it is also true that in *The Holy War* we move in the midst of many of the scenes and surroundings through which Bunyan himself had moved. He may, like Milton, take us down to Pandemonium when Diabolus is in council, or up to the central heaven where the purposes of the Eternal are unfolded; but Mansoul itself, with its walls, gates, strongholds, and sallyport, largely took shape in his mind from the garrison at Newport Pagnell, or the fortifications of the Newarke at Leicester. The army of Shaddai, with its captains clad in armour, its forces marching, counter-marching, opening to the right and to the left, dividing and subdividing, closing, wheeling, making good their front and rear, with their right and left wings, the handling of their arms, the management of their weapons of war, which "were marvellous taking to Mansoul and me," all these were reminiscences of Cromwell's army of the New Model, and of the military manœuvres in which he himself had taken part under Sir Samuel Luke. So again Diabolus new modelling the corporation, changing mayor, recorder, aldermen, and burgesses at pleasure, was simply doing the same thing the king and Lord Ailesbury were doing at Bedford about the time *The Holy War* was written. The taking away of the town charter also and the granting of another which was read to the people of Mansoul in the open market-place, are scenes bearing strong resemblance to those in which Lord Bruce took part before the old Guildhall in Bedford town when Bunyan was living there.

Turning to the book itself, the writer tells us that in his travels he came upon the famous continent of Universe, a large and spacious country lying between the two poles and amidst the four points of the heavens. Its people are many and various, some of them being right and some wrong, even as it happeneth to be in lesser regions. In this country there is a fair and delicate town, a corporation called Mansoul, built by its founder Shaddai for his own delight, a town with walls so firm that it could not be hurt but by the consent of the townsmen themselves.

Its inhabitants being beguiled, Mansoul is taken by Diabolus, after which the image of Shaddai is defaced from the castle gate; there is a new mayor, a new recorder; new aldermen and burgesses are made, and three strongholds are built in the town, the hold of Defiance, Midnight-hold, and Sweet-sin-hold. Thus was Mansoul changed and lost.

Tidings of all this is soon carried to its lawful prince, and in due time the army of Shaddai, forty thousand strong, appears before the town and begins to do execution. That winter was a winter by itself. The rest of Diabolus was broken, the towns-people were distressed, famine stalked into Mansoul, and upon all her pleasant things there was blast and burning instead of beauty. The climax of interest is reached, however, when Prince Emmanuel himself, the son of King Shaddai, appears before the gates of the town and plants his standard. On being summoned to surrender, the town sends one Mr. Loth-to-stoop, a stiff man in his way, who tries to make terms by offering to deliver up one-half of the town if Diabolus may keep the rest. But Emmanuel claims and will be content with nothing less than the whole. Then may Diabolus have some one reserved place in Mansoul? No, not so much as the least corner. May he some-times come for old acquaintance' sake? Nay, for even chance visits from such a guest may cost men their souls. May his friends and kindred have liberty to trade in the town, or letters or passengers keep up old friendship, or love-tokens be left to be looked at when he is gone, or permission be granted for special visits at times?

All concessions being refused, the stress of siege is begun and the town is assaulted and regained. The prince in armour of gold marches in, his standard borne before him, while the Man-soulians are in deadly fear at the fate that may await them. To their infinite joy, however, instead of being punished they are pardoned, instead of being handed over to death they are wel-comed, freed from their fetters and adorned. That night no man in Mansoul could sleep for joy. The prince's pardon was read in the open market-place by the recorder, and order was given to the young men—the lately born desires of the soul—to ring the bells.

Mansoul thus regained was reconstructed. New officers were appointed, a new charter of privilege was granted and was carried to Audience, that is to the market-place, Mr. Recorder reading it there in the presence of all the people; a ministry was provided such as might teach them both law and judgment, statute and commandment, that they might be documented in all good and wholesome things. The two teachers appointed for this were, one from the royal court—the Spirit of Truth, well-skilled in all mysteries—the other a native of Mansoul, Mr. Conscience by name. The town thus new modelled and provided for had this further badge of honour conferred upon it, that the towns-people were clad in white and glistering robes. No place like Mansoul now! It was the very signet upon Emmanuel's right hand, and there was no town, city, or corporation that could compare with it. There was this further thing to be noted, that the town was put under the care of a new officer, and a goodly person he was, Mr. God's-peace by name. So long as all things went as this sweet-natured gentleman would, there were no jars, no chidings, no interferings, no unfaithful doings, in all the town of Mansoul. Every man kept close to his own employ-ment. The gentry, the officers, the soldiers, and all in the place observed their order. And as for the women and children of the town, they followed their business joyfully. They would work and sing, work and sing, from morning till night, so that quite through the town now nothing was to be found but har-mony, quietness, joy, and health. And this lasted all that summer.

Mansoul thus redeemed and reconciled, the Holy War may be said to be at an end. But life in this imperfect world is never a thing of artistic completeness. Even in reconstructed Mansoul there still lurked secret Diabolians whom it was needful to drive out. The rest of the book, therefore, is occupied with two perils which loomed large to Bunyan's thought as besetting the Christian soul—that of being again seduced from the right by the world's blandishments, and that of being forced from it by the world's persecutions. The first peril came upon the town through one Mr. Carnal Security, a very busy man; notable and brisk was he, and one who liked to stand, in his way of standing, with what he took to be the strongest side. Under the influence of this man and the like of him Mansoul began to be corrupted by riches. Being a market town and one that delights in com-merce, there was sent into it Mr. Penny-wise-pound-foolish and Mr. Get-i'-th'-hundred-and-lose-i'-th'-shire, with whom were Mr. Sweet-world and Mr. Present-good. Their great object was to cumber Mansoul with abundance, that the townspeople should be forced to make Heart Castle a warehouse instead of a garrison, for if they can only overcharge the heart with possessions and cares the place is more than half won. This was accounted the very masterpiece of hell, to wit, to choke Mansoul with the fulness of this world and to surfeit her heart with the good things thereof. From this peril Emmanuel saves the town, however, and once more makes joyous entry therein.

Then comes peril from the opposite quarter, from the world's scorn and cruel persecution. An army of Bloodmen, whose land lieth under the Dogstar, and with them another army of Doubters five-and-twenty thousand strong, came against Mansoul and sent in hot as a red-hot iron a summons to yield. The siege this time was long; many a fierce attempt was made, many a shrewd brush met with by the townsmen. At length a charge was made by Emmanuel's men, and the Bloodmen would have fled; for though cruel enough when they feel themselves safe, all Bloodmen are chicken-hearted when they are matched. Captured and taken before Emmanuel, they were found on examination to be of three sorts—those who came out of Blindmanshire, and did ignorantly what they did; those who came out of Blindzealshire, and acted superstitiously; and those who came out of the town of Malice, in the county of Envy, who acted from spite—a threefold division of persecutors not yet obsolete.

Mansoul thus once more rescued, various lurking Diabolonians, both foreign and native, were taken, tried, and executed. One of them, however, Mr. Unbelief, a nimble jack, they could never lay hold of, try as they would, and he is thought to be skulking about still. But the rest being slain, Prince Emmanuel, on a day appointed, came into the market-place in his chariot of state, and an O yes! being called for silence, he addressed the assembled townsmen of Mansoul. After a time, he told them, this famous town of theirs should be transplanted into his own country, and there set up in such strength and glory as it never knew before. Into it should come no more sound of evil tidings or roll of Diabolonian drum. Fears and alarms should be ended, sorrow and grief be no more, and life should last longer than they were even able to desire it here, yet ever be sweet and new. Meanwhile they were to keep white the liveries he gave them, to believe in the constancy of his love, and to hold fast till he came again.

The year 1681, when Bunyan was engaged upon the composition of *The Holy War,* was a year of grave reaction in the government of the country. On the 18th of January, Charles dissolved his fourth Parliament, and shortly after summoned his fifth. This again met one Monday to be dissolved the next, and during the remaining four years of his reign the King summoned no more Parliaments, resolving, like his father before him, to govern without them. But while trampling upon the constitution, he desired to do so with a look of fair seeming. From Whitehall he issued a Declaration explaining why he had dissolved his last two Parliaments. The House, he said, had stood in his way in carrying out the laws against the Nonconformists, and upon it, not upon the Crown, must rest the blame of all unconstitutional proceedings. The document was shrewdly constructed to catch the sympathy of the High Church party, and it succeeded. The Declaration was ordered to be read in all churches and chapels during divine service, and was responded to by loyal addresses sent up by that party from all sides of the country. Not the least obsequious of these was "The Humble Address of the Lieutenant, Deputy-Lieutenant, Justices of the Peace, Military Officers, Clergy, Gentlemen, and Freeholders of the County of Bedford," in which they speak of "His Majestie's Princely goodness, justice, and mercy, and of the benign influence of his most equal and prudent Government."

"But your Majestie's late Gracious declaration as it hath made us the most obliged, so should we be the most ungrateful people in the world if we did not profess (what we here in all humility do) our most hearty and thankful Resentment of the Royal Assurance you are pleased to give us therein to remove all the reasonable fears and causeless jealousies which some ill men (whose attempts we abhor and detest) have endeavoured to insinuate into the people, thus weakening your Majestie's Prerogative (which by law we are bound to support) and defaming the true Sons of the Church of England, which (as now Established) is the best if not the only bulwark against Popery. That your Majesty may see we are not swaid by any such seditious and factious designs, we do assure Your Sacred Majesty That we will (as in duty and conscience bound) stand by You to the utmost hazard of our Lives and Estates in the Preservation of Your Sacred Person, your Heirs and Lawful Successors, and the Government in Church and State, as it is now Established by Law."[1]

This address to the King in June, 1681, when he was engaged

[1] *Bedfordshire Notes and Queries,* pp. 6, 7.

in actual treason against the ancient constitution of the realm, was signed by about two hundred persons in Bedfordshire—not a very heavy representation for the county at large.

* *History of My Own Time.* By Gilbert Burnet, D.D.

These addresses, as Burnet* tells us, were very welcome at Court, and were encouraged to the utmost. The London apprentices were put into the way of sending one, so were the sailors and watermen. Those who brought them were well received, healths were drunk, and the old cavalier swaggerings revived. Encouraged in this way, the King resolved to make a systematic attack upon the municipal charters of the country. The old corporations had great influence in the election of members to Parliament, for if the burgesses determined who the members should be, the corporations determined who the burgesses should be. The King therefore resolved to secure the control of the corporations, and through them of Parliament. London was dealt with first, and afterwards, on one pretence or another, borough after borough was compelled to surrender its ancient privileges and accept a new charter at the hands of the King. As Bedford happens to furnish a good illustration of the way in which corporations were at that time manipulated, charters surrendered, and officials displaced, and as a review of the course of local events will give us a vivid picture of the surroundings of Bunyan's life at a period when he must have been keenly interested in local affairs, it may be well to give the story here for the first time from materials recently come to light.

Charles's last Parliament was dissolved on the 28th of March, 1681, and a few weeks later an Order in Council was made to inquire whether all the officials of the Bedford Corporation had complied with the regulations. It was found that Miles Wale and Andrew Freebody, the chamberlains of the town, had not taken the sacrament at church within twelve months of their being elected; their places thereupon were declared void till they had duly qualified. The following December the Deputy-Recorder of the town, Mr. Robert Audley, was accused at the council at Whitehall of being "an enemy to the Government and to the Church of England, and a great countenancer of conventicles and phanaticks in the town of Bedford. And though there were many other aldermen disaffected, yet he was the great head and pillar of the disaffected party."[1] The Earl of

[1] Dr. Williams' MS.—*Morrice's Entering Book.*

Ailesbury, whose country seat was at Houghton House, near Ampthill, who was Lord-Lieutenant of the county, one of the Privy Council, and also hand-in-glove with the King in his policy, moved thereupon that Mr. Audley and other aldermen should be displaced by virtue of the Corporation Act. The town was troubled at this, and prevailed on the Recorder to appear at the council table on his own behalf and theirs, which he did. In his sturdy English fashion, we are interested in reading, old Mr. Audley told the King that he was Recorder of Bedford, that he was an officer under the King's father throughout the whole war, and that when the war was over he was driven out of the kingdom and his estate sequestered. He went on to say that he was as truly loyal now as he was then; that so far from being a conventicler, he was never at a conventicle in his life, but if the conventiclers preached as well as they were reported to him to do, and churchmen as ill as those did that he had heard of late, he thought it not unlikely that he might go to conventicles yet, but at present his acquaintance lay chiefly with the opposite sort. And so the complaint fell, and Mr. Audley went home again.[1]

We are all the more interested in this because the conventicle preacher for whom the Recorder spoke up was no other than Bunyan himself, and the conventicle referred to was the barn in Mill Lane towards which our thoughts have so often been turned.

But though the old man was for the moment victorious at Whitehall, his enemies soon found other means of working their will. In the minute book of the Bedford Corporation we have this entry: "It is ordained that from henceforth Mr. Audley, ye Deputy Recorder, shall not have any vote in Common Councill or other Assemblies of the Corporacon." Later on, things are still going against him, we find, as we read a private letter from Lord Bruce to the Mayor, who is none other than our old acquaintance of 1661, Paul Cobb, who went to Bunyan in prison and tried to bring him to what he thought a more reasonable state of mind: "Mr. Mayor," says Lord Bruce, "I received your letter, and am glad to find by it that you have made so good a choice in ye room of Mr. Audley. I have taken occasion to applaud your actions since you came in your office where it

[1] *Ibid.*, i. 320.

was well resented." This little episode is strongly suggestive of that passage in *The Holy War* where Diabolus bethinks himself of new-modelling the town of Mansoul, setting up one and putting down another at pleasure, and where he puts Mr. Recorder, whose name was Conscience, out of place and power. "For as for Mr. Recorder, he was a man of courage and faithfulness to speak truth at every occasion, and he had a tongue as bravely hung as he had a head filled with judgment. Now this man Diabolus could by no means abide, because he could not by all wiles, trials, stratagems, and devices that he could use make him wholly his own."

The displacement of Mr. Audley, who was before the Privy Council about the time Bunyan was writing this passage, was a small part of the process of change to be carried out in the Bedford Corporation. In the month of October, 1683, no less than fifty-three persons were at one stroke admitted to the burgessdom of the town, all of them picked men on the King's side. Among these we find the two younger sons of the Earl of Ailesbury, Sir Francis Wingate, William Foster and his son, and many of the surrounding gentry and clergy, whose primary qualification was that they were men on whom Mr. Cobb and his colleagues could rely. The next month, again, twenty-three more were added from the families of the Dyves, the Chesters, and from the sons of safe men already enrolled. Seventy-six new burgesses, on whom reliance could be placed, added to a limited burgess list in the short space of two months made succeeding steps comparatively easy. When all preparations had thus been carefully made, on the 8th of January, 1684, "It is agreed, consented, concluded, and ordeyned unto, by and with the consent of ye Maior, Alldermen, Bayliffes, Burgesses, and Comonalty in this present Councell, That ye Charter of this Corporacon bee surrendered and given up to His Majestie, and that the Maior of this Corporation doe take and carry up the Charter to doe the same: And that His Majestie bee humbly petitioned to grant the town a new one with like privileges as the former was, or such other priviledges as hee shall be pleased to grant."[1]

Thus the municipality of Bedford was at the King's feet to do with it as he liked. Yet even out of those corrupt hands that placed it there it did not pass without a struggle. The Earl of

[1] Minute Book of the Corporation.

Ailesbury, and his son Lord Bruce, found it necessary to play still further the part of tempters to what little virtue there still remained in that debased corporation over which Mr. Cobb presided. Before the surrender was finally agreed upon, an effort was made to retain some part of the privileges of the town, on which Lord Bruce wrote to the Mayor as follows:

"I can give you some perfect assurance that very small fees will be expected as things are ordered, so that you may surrender the wholle charter at a cheaper ratte, then you might doe as you proposed for the surrendering of ye governing part. You should have an Attorney or Sollicitor in town to manage the thing; if you desire it, my Chancery Sollicitor shall take care in it. You had best send me your objections to ye totall surrender. I guesse there is none but ye Lands, which shall be taken care of ye same as those of London were. What else you have to say, insert it in your letter, and I will take care to see all done for the good of your Corporation. I am your most assured Friend, Bruce."[1]

Thus whispering that it would be cheaper to surrender their rights than to keep them, with dulcet words of most assured friendship his lordship led Mr. Mayor and the Corporation down the grassy slopes of subserviency. All being finally arranged, Paul Cobb, with the Town Charter in his valise, takes coach for London. One is tempted to imagine that John Bunyan happened to be near the Old Swan gate at the foot of the bridge that morning, and saw him start, giving his old acquaintance salutation, and thinking of the surrender of Mansoul the while. As for Paul himself, he is in high spirits, and is thinking of quite other things; for he is to be present at a reception by the Earl and his son Lord Bruce, who has told him also that the King has heard good things about him quite lately; he will be in the sunshine of royal smiles; he may even be knighted and come back *Sir* Paul, who knows? In any case he is solicitor as well as mayor, and, as we find from his bill afterwards, he sees certain prospect of substantial honorarium for "my trouble and charges in suing out the new charter."

This new charter was brought down on the 19th of July by the Earl of Ailesbury himself, accompanied by the deputy lieutenants, justices of the peace, and a great number of gentlemen. About two miles from the town, between Wilstead and Elstow, they were met by a deputation from the town itself, the party

[1] Original MSS. in the possession of Mr. W. H. Lloyd, Bedford.

meeting and the party met making up together a company of some five hundred horse. On reaching the High Street, there were great rejoicings before the Guildhall, the new charter being read aloud and an address made to the people afterwards by Lord Ailesbury. His lordship "was pleased to tell them how great His Majesty's grace and favour had been to them (although undeservedly), and how highly they were obliged from thence both to approve themselves eminently loyal, and continue so for ever." It was quarter-sessions at the time, and the new deputy recorder who had stepped into Mr. Audley's place gave a charge to the grand jury, in which he spoke much to the same effect. All this was followed by a sumptuous banquet, for in those days men could not even surrender their privileges without dining and making merry over the performance. "After a splendid entertainment," says a chronicler of the time, "the Mayor, Aldermen, and whole Corporation returned their thanks to his lordship for honouring the town with his presence, and did entreat him with their most humble duty and thanks to assure His Majesty of their steady loyalty for the future. The grand jury likewise waited on his lordship to desire the same on behalf of themselves and the whole town."[1]

After the feast came the reflection, after the riot the reckoning. There was the bill for the "splendid entertainment" and for the "claret, sack, and white wine for the judges"; there was the money for the bell-ringers who had kept the town all day in delirious joy over its good fortune; there were host Lowen's charges for refreshing innumerable people at the Paradine Arms; fees for all sorts of officials in London who had helped the town to change a good charter for a bad one—the Lord Keeper's Secretary, the Clerk of the Hanaper, and Mr. Sambrooke; and there was also "Mr. Mayor's charge for acting as solicitor in the town's behalf";—all these amounting together to a sum it was not pleasant to face. To meet these charges for the charter a tax was to be levied upon all burgesses and freemen, foreigners as well as inhabitants. This tax, however, proved as unproductive as it was unpopular. There was a cloud upon the face of Mr. Mayor, and harmony had so far departed from the council chamber, that it was necessary "to ordayne that no man that is of the Councell shall disclose his fellow's

[1] *Bedfordshire Notes and Queries*, p. 8.

counsell upon any debate whatsoever in the Councell, under a penalty of forty shillings, the like penalty to be visited upon any doorkeeper who should disclose what he had heard, or suffer any one else to listen."

Eventually Mr. Mayor, who was a man of resource, hit upon the happy device of raising a considerable sum by granting a lease in reversion of the charity lands of the town in Holborn to Nicholas Barbon, doctor of physic. In this way not only were all the charges for the new charter met, but there was also a surplus left of £78, which Mr. Cobb divided in the most approved manner between himself and Mr. Christy, a brother lawyer, "to take care of," a trust which Mr. Mayor, at least, so faithfully performed, that six years later it required the threat of an action at law to get the money out of his hands for public use.

This new charter, about which there was so much feasting and financing, gave to the town with one hand the privilege of holding two new fairs yearly, and to the Crown with the other absolute control over the Bedford municipality. Henceforth, by a simple order in council, the King could remove at pleasure any or all the members of the Corporation, whether mayor, aldermen, or councillors, and any officer, from the Lord the Recorder down to the town bailiff. As a matter of fact, this despotic power was not exercised till on the eve of a general election four years later; and the irony of the situation is complete when we remember that, the wheel of circumstance having in the interval "gone full cycle round," the first time it was exercised was to turn out of the Corporation the very men who had given the King the power to do it, and who in giving him that power had betrayed their trust and surrendered the ancient rights and liberties of the town.

The year of this new charter was made painfully memorable in the history of Bedfordshire by the execution of its honoured representative in Parliament, Lord William Russell. On the 21st of July, 1684, two days after the rejoicings at Bedford, Lord William quietly laid his head on the block in Lincoln's Inn Fields.* Like his ancestors and successors, he had strong sympathy with the great cause of constitutional freedom, and felt deeply the encroachments of the King on the liberties of English-

* A stone slab in the garden denotes the spot.

men. That he took counsel, as he had a right to do, with like-minded patriots in the endeavour to resist these encroachments is certain. Equally certain is it that, though he was unfortunate in his associates, he took no actual part in that attempt on the life of the King, for which he was doomed to die. His trial will be for ever memorable as an instance of the way in which the forms of justice may be used against the spirit of justice, and memorable also for his own calmness and for the heroic devotion of Lady Rachel, his wife—

> "That sweet saint who sate by Russell's side,
> Under the judgment seat."

Their tender devotion to each other makes the pain of their parting the night before his execution one of the most pathetic passages in our history. Lord John Russell spoke and wrote some memorable things in his time, but nothing surely more touching than the sentence in which, after telling us that Lady Rachel bade farewell to her husband just before midnight in Newgate, he adds, "Thus they parted, not with sobs and tears, but with a composed silence; the wife wishing to spare the feelings of the husband, and the husband of the wife, they both restrained the expression of a grief too great to be relieved by utterance."[1]

The sorrow felt in 1684 over Lord Russell's death by all who loved the constitutional liberties of England cannot have been unfelt by the great Nonconformist with whom we are mainly concerned. That Bunyan and Lord William were personally and even intimately acquainted is more than probable. The latter, as the representative of the county for six years in Parliament, would certainly be present on many public occasions in the town of Bedford during the time that Bunyan was minister there, and as a statesman who had always striven to mitigate the severities of Churchmen against Nonconformists, he would naturally be looked up to by the great Englishman his neighbour as his champion and friend. His death was more than a personal loss; it was the signal for a national reaction in the direction of renewed persecution. When men like Russell and Sidney were bending their necks to the block, it may easily be supposed that it fared not well with lowlier men. It was not long before the Nonconformists of Bedfordshire were made to feel the fury

[1] *Life of Lord Wm. Russell*, p. 335.

of the returning storm. The instigators of this new crusade were the Earl of Ailesbury and his son, Lord Bruce, whom we have so often met with in the course of our story.[1] Lord Ailesbury lived at Houghton House,* near Ampthill, the house whose dismantled ruins overlook the vale of Bedford. He was *Custos Rotulorum,* and in a somewhat arbitrary manner ordered the General Sessions of the Bedfordshire magistrates of 1684—5 to be held at Ampthill instead of at Bedford as usual. For the first time and the last this was done on the 14th January in that year. At these sessions, over which the Earl presided, the Court resolved:

* Considered by some to be the "original" of The House Beautiful, in *The Pilgrim's Progress.* It was built in 1615, by the Countess Mary, sister of Sir Philip Sidney.

"That all such Laws as had been provided for the reducing all Dissenters to a thorow Conformity shall be forthwith put into a speedy and vigorous execution. We do, therefore, with the concurrence of the Right Rev. Father in God our most worthy, learned, and godly Lord Bishop, desire all ministers and require as well all constables and churchwardens, truly and punctually to present, both at our Quarter Sessions and Monthly Meetings, all such, in their respective Parishes, as shall absent themselves from their own Parish Church; also those who do not come at the beginning of Divine Service, kneeling at all Prayers, and standing up at the Glory, at the Creed, and Hymns. By which means we hope in time the true worship of God will be thoroughly understood and honestly practised by the people of this country, to God's glory and our own Peace and Comfort."

This order, issued by the magistrates, was printed as a broadside, surmounted by the Royal arms, and beneath the order was an address from the bishop of the diocese—that Bishop Barlow who has obtained some reputation by his exceedingly mild interference on Bunyan's behalf. This address of the bishop lays it down that seeing it is a certain truth that subjects are bound to obey their rulers, and since there is such an excellent Liturgy provided:

"The Rejection of this and the Disobedience to the Laws injoyning it render our Dissenters evidently Schismatical in their separation from the communion of our Church. And seeing that our Dissenting Brethren will not conform out of conscience to their duty and obedience to God and their Governours, it is not only convenient but necessary that our good Laws be put in execution for the Preservation of the Public Peace and Unity, and for the good of Dissenters themselves;

[1] It is curious to note that Lady Augusta Stanley [wife of Dr. Stanley, Dean of Westminster], one of the Bruces of Elgin, and therefore the direct representative of these very noblemen who persecuted Bunyan and his people, was the one who in 1874 unveiled the statue to Bunyan's memory erected by the Duke of Bedford.

for Afflictio dat Intellectum and their sufferings by the execution of our Just Laws may (by God's blessing) bring them to a sense of Duty and a Desire to do it. For the attaining of which good ends I require all the Clergy of my Diocese within the County of Bedford to publish this Order the next Sunday after it be tendered to them, and diligently to promote the design of it."[1]

This order thus sent forth on the cynical plea that *afflictio dat intellectum,* or, in plain English, that persecution would bring the Nonconformists to their senses—an assumption which is contradicted by all the facts of history—was read far beyond the borders of Bedfordshire, and brought forth a letter of grave and earnest remonstrance from the great Nonconformist, John Howe. This eminent Englishman, conspicuous alike for eloquence of speech and elevation of mind, said to Bishop Barlow:

"As I must confess myself surprised by your late published directions to your clergy of the County of Bedford, so nor will I dissemble that I did read them with some trouble of mind, which I sincerely profess was more upon your Lordship's account than my own (who for myself am little concerned) or any other particular person's whatsoever . . . I humbly offer to your Lordship's further consideration, whether it be not a supposable thing that some persons sound in the faith, strictly orthodox in all the articles of it taught by our Lord Jesus or his Apostles, resolvedly loyal and subject to the authority of their governors in Church and State, of pious, sober, peaceable, just, charitable dispositions and deportments, may yet have a formed, fixed judgment of the unlawfulness of some or other of the rites and modes of worship enjoined to be observed in this Church? Is there no difference to be put between things essential to our religion and things confessed indifferent on the one hand, and on the other judged unlawful, on both hands but accidental? (though they that think them unlawful dare not allow themselves a liberty of sinning even in accidentals).

"My Lord, your Lordship, well knows the severity of some of those laws which you press for the execution of, is such as, being executed, they must infer the utter ruin of them who observe them not, in their temporal concernments; and not that only, but their deprivation of the comfortable advantages appointed by our blessed Lord, for promoting their spiritual and eternal well-being. I cannot but be well-persuaded not only of the mere sincerity, but eminent sanctity of divers, upon my own knowledge and experience of them, who would sooner die at a stake than I or any man can prevail with them to kneel before the consecrated elements at the Lord's table. Would your Lordship necessitate such perdere substantiam propter accidentia?

[1] *Ashmolean Collection,* Bodl. ii., 23.

What if there be considerable numbers of such in your Lordship's vastly numerous flock; will it be comfortable to you, when an account is demanded of your Lordship by the great Shepherd and Bishop of Souls concerning them, only to be able to say, 'Though, Lord, I did believe the provisions of thine house purchased for them, necessary and highly useful for their salvation, I drove them away as dogs and swine from thy table, and stirred up such other agents as I could influence against them, by whose means I reduced many of them to beggary, ruined many families, banished them into strange countries, where they might (for me) serve other gods; and this not for disobeying any immediate ordinance or law of thine, but because for fear of offending thee, they did not in everything comport with my own appointments, or which I was directed to urge and impose upon them?' Who art thou that judgest thy brother? We shall all stand before the judgment seat of Christ. What if they have appeared conscientious and of a very unblameable conversation in all things else? What if better qualified for Christian communion in all other respects than thousands you admitted?

"But we must, it seems, understand all this rigour your Lordship shows to proceed from love, and that you are for destroying the Dissenters only to mend their understandings, and because afflictio dat intellectum. I hope, indeed, God will sanctify the affliction which you give and procure them, to blessed purposes; and perhaps periissent nisi periissent: but for the purposes your Lordship seems to aim at, I wonder what you can expect. Can you by undoing men change the judgment of their consciences? Or if they should tell you, We do indeed in our consciences judge we shall greatly offend God by complying with your injunctions, but yet to save being undone we will do it: will this qualify them for your communion? . . . I pray God to rectify your error by gentler methods, and by less affliction than you have designed to your brethren: and do not for all this doubt (any more for your part than my own) to meet you there one day, where Luther and Zuinglius are well agreed."[1]

What effect this high-minded appeal produced upon the Bishop there is nothing to show. As we shall see hereafter, he was on the verge of anxious days for himself, when he would find out by a deeper experience the truth of his own saying, that trouble opens men's eyes. Meantime at this point it may be well to go back a little and review the course of Bunyan's literary activity since last we met with anything from his pen. During the three years between the publication of *The Holy War,* in 1682, and the death of the King in the early part of 1685, he sent forth a poetical broadside and five books, one of these being the Second Part of *The Pilgrim's Progress,* which appeared in

[1] *Letter to Dr. Barlow, Bishop of Lincoln.* Howe's Works, iii., 552—555.

1684. *The Barren Fig-tree* was published in 1682, *The Greatness of the Soul* and *A Case of Conscience Resolved* in 1683, while *Seasonable Counsels, A Holy Life the Beauty of Christianity,* and *A Caution to Watch against Sin* came out along with the story of Christiana in 1684.

Of the first of these, *The Barren Fig-tree, or the Doom and Downfall of the Fruitless Professor,*[1] no copy of the first edition is known to exist. The earliest we have is a reprint made immediately after Bunyan's death in 1688, by J. Robinson, of the Golden Lion, St. Paul's Churchyard, and having a broad black border round the title. The work itself is an exposition of our Lord's parable in the thirteenth chapter of St. Luke's Gospel, and is a soul-searching appeal against unreality in the religious life. There is in it the plainest of plain speaking, of which there seems to have been then, as always, an urgent need. There were some in the Churches, he tells us, asking the question, Who had a right to the good things of this life if Christians had not? "And from this conclusion they let go the reins of their inordinate affections after pride, ambition, gluttony; pampering themselves without fear, daubing themselves with the lust-provoking fashions of the times, walking with stretched-out necks, naked breasts, frizzled fore-tops, wanton gestures, in gorgeous apparel, mixed with gold and pearl and costly array." "There are some men that steal into a Christian profession, nobody knows how, and there they abide, lifeless, graceless, careless, and without any good conscience to God at all. Perhaps they came in for the loaves, for trade, for credit, for a blind; or it may be to stifle and choke the checks and grinding pangs of an awakened and disquieted conscience." He would have such cumber-grounds take heed of the axes, such barren fig-trees beware of the fire.

This book was followed in 1683 by the one on *The Greatness of the Soul and the Unspeakableness of the Loss Thereof,*[2] which was originally a sermon preached at Pinners' Hall on one of Bunyan's visits to London, and afterwards "enlarged and published for good," through Benjamin Alsop, at the Angel and

[1] *Y Ffigys-bren Anffrwythlon*: Caerfyrddin, 1768. [1766 in Cardiff Public Library.] 12mo. *Betrachtung über das Gleichniss vom unfruchtbaren Feigenbaun* von Johannes Bunyan, weiland Prediger zu Bedford in England. Hamburg, 1870.

[2] *The Greatness of the Soul* and unspeakableness of the Loss thereof; with the causes of the Losing it. First Preached at Pinners' Hall, and now enlarged and Published for good. London: Printed for Ben. Alsop, 1683.

Bible in the Poultry. In this the preacher shows what the soul is in its powers and properties, what its greatness is, what it is to lose the soul, and for what causes men do this. The text (Mark viii., 37) comes after an appeal from Christ to count the cost of following Him: "For following of me is not like following of some other masters. The wind sits always on my face, and the foaming rage of the sea of this world, and the proud and lofty waves thereof do continually beat upon the sides of the bark or ship that myself, my cause, and my followers are in; he therefore that will not run hazards, and that is afraid to venture a drowning, let him not set foot into this vessel." Speaking in one part of his subject of the loss of the soul, he touches with his own tender pathos upon the saving love of Christ: "Dost thou understand me, sinful soul? He wrestled with justice that thou mightest have rest; He wept and mourned that thou mightest laugh and rejoice; He was betrayed that thou mightest go free, was apprehended that thou mightest be justified, and was killed that thou mightest live; He wore a crown of thorns that thou mightest wear a crown of glory; and was nailed to the cross with His arms wide open, to show with what freeness all His merits shall be bestowed on the coming soul, and how heartily He will receive it into His bosom!" Alas, that it should be true! as true it is, that they are the few that care for the things that are greatest. It is a wanton age—"an age wherein the thoughts of eternal life and the salvation of the soul are with and to many like the Morocco ambassador and his men, men of strange faces, in strange habit, with strange gestures and behaviours, monsters to behold."

The little work entitled *A Case of Conscience Resolved*,[1] which came into the same year, was also published by Benjamin Alsop, and was called forth by the request of some Christian women in London for Bunyan's judgment on the propriety of their meeting separately for prayer, and "without their men." Founding his opinion on what the apostle says about women keeping silence in the churches, he gives judgment against the practice, expressing the fear that it is idleness in the men which is the cause of their putting their good women upon this work. "Surely

[1] *A case of Conscience Resolved*: viz. Whether where a Church of Christ is situate, it is the duty of the Women of that Congregation, Ordinarily or by Appointment, to separate themselves from their brethren and so to Assemble together to perform some parts of Divine Worship, as Prayer, &c., without their men? 1683. 4to.

they that can scarce tie their shoes and their garters before they arrive at the tavern, or get to the coffee-house door in a morning, can scarce spare time to be a while in their closets with God! Morning closet-prayers are now by most London professors thrown away, and what kind of ones they make at night God doth know, and their conscience, when awake, will know. However, I have cause as to this to look at home. And God mend me and all his servants about it, and wherein we else are out."

The following year Bunyan again appealed to Christian men to walk worthy of their calling, in *A Caution to stir up to watch against Sin,*"[1] which appeared in the form of a half-sheet broadside, dated "8 Aprill, 1684," and which Narcissus Luttrell tells us he bought for a penny on that same day. It is a poem in sixteen stanzas, each stanza closing with a variation of a refrain which calls upon the reader to keep sin out of door, lest entrance it may gain and never leave him more. To the same purpose is a treatise Bunyan published through Benjamin Alsop that same year, founded on the words, "Let every one that nameth the name of Christ depart from iniquity," and entitled, *A Holy Life the Beauty of Christianity.*"[2] He would have men take religion as it comes, not picking and choosing the easy things and leaving those in which there is real cross-bearing. "For example, there is reading, praying, hearing of sermons, baptism, breaking of bread, church fellowship, preaching, and the like; and there is mortification of lusts, charity, simplicity, openheartedness, with a liberal hand to the poor, and their like also. Now the unsound faith picks and chooses, and takes and leaves, but the true faith does not so." He has no wish to be austere, "but were wearing of gold, putting on of apparel, dressing up houses, decking of children, learning of compliments, boldness in women, lechery in men, wanton behaviour, lascivious words and tempting carriages, signs of repentance, then I must say, the fruits of repentance swarm in our land; but if these be none of the fruits of repentance, then, O, the multitude of professors that religiously name the name of Christ and do not depart from iniquity." The drift of the book as a whole is to show what it

[1] *A Caution to stir up to watch against Sin.* By J. Bunyan. Broadside on half sheet of copy paper in Luttrell Collection [British Museum]; originally in the Stowe Library. [There is another copy in the Bodleian Library, Oxford.]

[2] *A Holy Life the Beauty of Christianity*: or An Exhortation to Christians to be Holy. By John Bunyan. London: Printed by B. W. for Benj. Alsop, at the Angel and Bible in the Poultry. 1684.

is to depart from iniquity, why it is that some who name the name of Christ do not depart from it, followed by arguments proving that they should, and ending with the applications and uses of the subject.

The only other book which Bunyan sent out in 1684, and which, like so many of his at this period, was published by Benjamin Alsop, was emphatically a book for the times—those times of trial and persecution through which the Church of God was still passing. It is entitled *Seasonable Counsel; or, Advice to Sufferers,*[1] and is worthy of note, first, as containing several sentences almost identical with some found in the letters to the persecuted entered in the Church Book, showing the same hand in both, and next as being a sort of manifesto of Bunyan's loyalty to the Government in spite of the sufferings he had endured at their hands. The magistrate, he says, is God's ordinance, and for conscience sake we must obey him. If there be no conscience, there is no real obedience: "I speak not these things as knowing any that are disaffected to the Government; for I love to be alone, if not with godly men, in things that are convenient. But because I appear thus in public, and know not into whose hands these lines may come, therefore thus I write. I speak it also to show my loyalty to the king, and my love to my fellow-subjects and my desire that all Christians should walk in ways of peace and truth." Elsewhere, also, in words that show the wonderful child-like simplicity of the man, he says, "For my part I have ofttimes stood amazed both at the mercy of God and the favour of the Prince towards us, and can give thanks to God for both; and do make it my prayer to God for the King, and that God will help me with meekness and patience to bear whatever shall befall me for my professed subjection to Christ by men."

There is a foreword to the Christain reader in the book, telling him that since many at that day are exposed to sufferings he gives this word that they may take heed to themselves, and that they that suffer may commit their souls to God as unto a faithful Creator. We have need, says he, of these bitter pills at which we so wince and shuck, and we are but little better as yet, though the physician has had us so long in hand. These times that try us help us to find out what we are, rightly to rectify our judgment

[1] *Seasonable Counsel; or, Advice to Sufferers.* By John Bunyan. London: Printed for Benjamin Alsop MDCLXXXIV.

about ourselves, make us know ourselves, tend to cut off the superfluous sprigs of pride and self-conceit so apt to shoot out. Does the day that bends us, humbles us, and makes us bow before God, do us no good? We could not live without such turnings of the hand of God upon us. We should be overgrown with flesh if we had not our seasonable winters. Remember that in trial God hath one purpose and Satan quite another. It is the soul that Satan is aiming at, the ruin of that he hath bent himself to bring to pass. "'Ware hawk," saith the falconer, when the dogs are near her. But our safety is in God; commit the keeping of your souls unto him. Satan can make a jail look as black as hell, and the loss of a few stools and chairs as bad as the loss of so many bags of gold. But God can make fear flee away and place heavenly confidence in its room. He can bring invisible and eternal things to the eye of thy soul and make thee see that in those things in which thine enemies shall see nothing, that thou shall count worth a thousand lives to enjoy. He can pull such things out of his bosom and can put such things into thy mouth; can make thee choose rather to be gone even though through the flames than to stay and die even in silken sheets. He can make things fearful and terrible to become things delightful and desirable. He can make a jail more beautiful than a palace, restraint more sweet by far than liberty. The three in Babylon saw one like the Son of God walking with them in the fire, and Daniel the hands of the angels that were made muzzles for the mouths of the lions. Was it not worth being in the furnace and in the den to see such things as these?

Thus, then, there was light from the throne of God, water from the eternal fountains, help from the everlasting hills for Bunyan and his brethren in the kingdom and patience of Jesus Christ. They had sore need of it all in 1684, when this 'Seasonable Counsel' saw the light, for, through the pelting of pitiless storm they were still urging their way to the city of God. As the Church records show, they were able to hold scarcely any meetings of the Church between the August of that year and the month of December, 1686. As in 1670, some of them were driven from their homes, ruined by fines, or shut up in gaol. And in these stern experiences they were not alone. In some places matters proceeded to such extremity that at last humane magistrates refused to grant any more convictions, resorting on the bench to all sorts of evasions of the law for the purpose of saving men who were too resolute to save themselves. This leniency, however, was, of course, only partial. In the parish of Hackney, fifty distress warrants, amounting to £1,400, were issued in one month; and two hundred in the town of Uxbridge.[1] In Southwark, Nathaniel Vincent was dragged from his pulpit by the hair of his head, while in the city of London, John Wesley's grandfather, Dr. Annesley, had his house broken into, his meeting-place forced and its fittings destroyed. The Quakers were, however, in this year, as in previous years, the most numerous and the most serious sufferers, and the special mark of the worst forms of the rowdyism of the time. At Leicester, for example, we find the soldiers quartered in the town sending a black drummer into the Quakers' meeting, to mimic the worshippers, while the captain and his company brought in ale and tobacco, and proceeded to smoke and drink and insult the women who were gathered with them.[2] Elsewhere also we find their meetings broken in upon by noisy revellers with drum and fiddle, and their wives and daughters stripped of scarf and hood in rude derision, while seven hundred Friends were that year reported to be shut up in gaol.

In the midst of all this lawlessness came the shadow of death among the persecutors themselves. On the 14th of January, 1685, the Earl of Ailesbury presided at the Ampthill meeting of the Bedfordshire justices, from which went forth that order against the Nonconformists of the county which John Howe branded as unreasonable and unchristian. Within three weeks of that day Lord Ailesbury's son, Thomas, Lord Bruce, was standing with other men of rank in the royal bedchamber, when the King gave a sharp cry, staggered, and fell into his arms insensible and stricken for death.[3] The end of his ignoble reign had come, and before the next Sunday he had been received into the Roman Catholic Church and had gone to his great account. Within that same year also the Earl of Ailesbury himself had finished his life-work, and had vanished from court-house and council-chamber to the regions of the dead. So sud-

[1] *Life of Lord Wm. Russell,* by Lord John Russell, p. 255.

[2] Roger Morrice—*MS. Entering Book.*

[3] Ld. Ailesbury's letter, *Gent. Mag.,* April, 1795.

denly do things turn round in this strange world of ours, and so unexpectedly was constitutional liberty saved at the very moment when despotism seemed to be most sure of its victory.

[Mr. RUDYARD KIPLING wrote a characteristic poem, *The Holy War*, founded on Bunyan's Allegory, but apropos of the Great European War then raging. The poem appeared first in the Christmas number of *Land and Water*, 1917, and subsequently in a volume of the author's works.]

XV.

IN THE REIGN OF JAMES THE SECOND.

On Friday, February 6th, 1685, Charles the Second passed away, and the same day his successor, as James the Second, met his first Privy Council. The advent of the new king saved the liberties of the country, but more through persistent blundering than deliberate intention. He had even less love for constitutional government and religious freedom than his easy-going brother; but these principles were in less danger now than before, for the simple reason that he was more daring in his attempt to subvert them. Happily for the liberties of England, the new monarch was one of those narrow, obstinate men who, when they happen to take up an evil cause, bring it to ruin by the very precipitancy of their haste to serve it. More than anything else in life James II. desired to see the re-establishment of the Roman Catholic religion in England, and, unfortunately for him, that which was nearest to his own heart was the one thing farthest from the hearts of his people. Here was the beginning of that division between the King and the country which was to end in catastrophe for the one and deliverance for the other. The King soon showed the haste he was in. As Duke of York he had hitherto heard Mass with closed doors; now the doors were thrown open. During Lent the palace sermons were preached by Popish divines, and when it was over, Easter was celebrated with unusual splendour. Easter was followed by the coronation, from the ceremonies of which there was the marked absence of the Communion Service and of the customary presentation to the monarch of an English Bible. People generally understood the meaning of the omission, and the situation was expressed with Quaker-like directness by that follower of George Fox who said to the King, "We are told that thou art no more of the persuasion of the Church of England than we are; we hope, therefore, thou wilt grant us the same liberty which thou allowest thyself."

But the fierceness of the struggle was not yet, and meantime the gaiety of the coronation was followed by the excitement of a general election. This came at a time when the Court party and the Tory feeling were supreme. The counties were for the most part safe, and the majority of the boroughs having surrendered their charters and suffered their corporations to be manipulated, were sure to return such men as the King could rely upon. The town of Bedford, the neighbouring squires having been brought into the burgess-lists in troops, returned Sir Anthony Chester, the son of that Justice Chester who had borne hard upon Bunyan's wife in the Swan Chamber, and Thomas Christie, the local lawyer who, with Paul Cobb, had been actively concerned in the surrender of the Town Charter. In the county, the Whig party, who had been represented in the last Parliament by Lord William Russell, made a desperate fight, and carried the show of hands on the nomination day, but were defeated at the poll, the election being in favour of Sir Villiers Chernocke of Hulcote, and William Butler of Biddenham.

The result the country through was as the King would have it. With considerable satisfaction he observed that, with the exception of about forty members, it was just such a House as he would have nominated himself. The Parliament of Scotland had met already, and was also entirely subservient, passing at the King's request a statute framed by his own minister, and enacting that whoever should preach in a conventicle under a roof, or attend, as preacher or hearer, a conventicle in the open air, should suffer confiscation of property and death. The Covenanting shires of Scotland were in consequence handed over to the cruelties of Graham of Claverhouse, and to the licence of his army. It was hoped that the Parliament of England, when it met on the 19th of May, would follow the example set by that of Scotland. Of the five hundred and thirteen members, three hundred and seventy-eight were new to the House, and the Whig party, which before had been in a majority, was now reduced to a minority no greater than a fifteenth part of the whole. But even though thus constituted, this Parliament was not obsequious after the manner of that in the north, but was resolute in maintaining the Test Act and keeping Roman Catholics out of office. Shortly after the session commenced, the House of Commons resolved itself into a Grand Committee of Religion, and in that committee passed two resolutions, one expressing fervent attachment to the Church of England, and the other calling upon the King to publish a proclamation for putting into execution the laws against all dissenters whatsoever from the Church of England. The King very naturally was intensely mortified. He had no objection to harass the Nonconformists, but this resolution called upon him, a Roman Catholic himself, to persecute to the death the teachers of his own faith and the adherents of his own Church. Parliament soon discovered its mistake, and hastened to retrace its steps, reversing in the House the decision adopted in committee, and throwing themselves on the promise the King had given at the first meeting of his Privy Council, to protect the religion established by law.

The course of events was powerfully influenced at this point by the insurrection in Scotland under the Earl of Argyle, and that in the west of England for the purpose of placing on the throne the Duke of Monmouth, a natural son of Charles II. The Duke was at that time living away from his wife and family in Brussels, and in unhallowed relations with Henrietta, the daughter of Lord Wentworth of Toddington, in Bedfordshire. Passionately attached to each other, and with that easy logic which passion employs, they persuaded themselves that they were man and wife in the sight of heaven. But Lady Wentworth was ambitious, and had complete ascendancy over Monmouth. For him she had sacrificed her honour and all the nobler prospects of woman's life; and when she joined the restless exiles around him in urging him to make a descent upon England and claim the crown for himself, he had not the firmness to resist these counsels of ruin. The result of that ill-starred expedition, followed as it was by the Bloody Assize in the West and Monmouth's execution on Tower Hill, belongs rather to the general course of our history than to the local narrative which interests us now. The two, however, touch each other for a moment when the historian, after describing Monmouth's execution and his burial in the Tower, completes the narrative thus:

"Yet a few months, and the quiet village of Toddington in Bedfordshire witnessed a still sadder funeral. Near that village stood an ancient and stately hall, the seat of the Wentworths. The transept of the parish church had long been their burial place. To that burial place, in the spring which followed the death of Monmouth, was borne the coffin of the young Baroness Wentworth, of Nettlestede. Her family reared a sumptuous mausoleum over her remains; but a less costly memorial of her was long contemplated with far deeper interest. Her name, carved by the hand of him who she loved too well, was, a few years ago, still discernible on a tree in the adjoining park."[1]

The autumn which followed Monmouth's failure and death will ever be memorable in the annals of England as the time of the reign of terror under Colonel Kirke and his 'lambs,' and still more under Judge Jeffreys and his Bloody Assize in the West. As the news slowly travelled from shire to shire of the military butchery and judicial murders going on day after day on English soil, a shudder of horror passed over the land, which seems to prolong itself from one generation to another. The cruelty and lawlessness by which a King, who never seems to have known human pity, put down a foolish rebellion, still ran their course long after rebellion was no more. Spent in one form, they next took the shape of such a crusade against religious liberty as not even that century had known till then. It is agreed on all hands that not even in the worst days of Laud had the condition of those who separated from the Church of England been so sorrowful as towards the end of 1685. John Howe left the country because he could not walk the streets of London without insult. Richard Baxter, though an old man now, was shut up in gaol, where he remained for two years more, and where he had innumerable companions in distress. For fresh prisoners were continually being added to the hundreds already deprived of their liberty. With renewed diligence in street and lane, in field and wood, spies and informers plied their odious trade. Magistrates and commissaries, clergy and churchwardens, were once more on the alert. The Ecclesiastical Courts were all day long fining and excommunicating those who refused attendance at church or frequented conventicles elsewhere. The story of meetings broken in upon and worshippers hurried to prison became stale by repetition. The separatists changed the place of gathering from time to time, set their sentinels on the watch, left off singing hymns in their services, and for the sake of greater security worshipped again and again at the dead of night. Ministers were introduced to their pulpits through trap-doors in floor or ceiling, or through doorways extemporised

[1] Macaulay's *Hist. of England*, i., 624.

in walls, or came by quiet paths in gardens and backyards. The poor suffered in their persons and the rich in their purse. At Stoke Newington, distresses were levied for conventicles upon such men as Sir John Hartopp, Mr. Fleetwood, and others of their neighbours to the extent of £7,000.

In some cases the conventiclers, goaded to desperation, stood at bay, and fought like Englishmen. At a prayer-meeting held in a gravel-pit, a company of worshippers rescued their minister, and put to rout the magistrate and constables who had come to arrest him. That autumn-time saw the fiercest but happily the last of the long series of persecutions under the Stuart kings. It has been compared to the last suffered by the early Christians under Diocletian—the last and fiercest on the part of the persecutors, the last and noblest on the part of the sufferers. It is unfortunately but too true that indulgence in cruelty makes men more relentlessly cruel. Happily, on the other hand, the darkest things become the foil of things that are noblest, bring out patient endurance, brave resistance, and firm fidelity to conscience. The harassed Nonconformists of those days still maintained among themselves the faithful and awakening preaching of Christ's evangel; they still kept up that godly family life, that severe morality, which preserved them from the foul corruptions of the time; and still, through all outrage and suffering, the more they were trampled on the more they grew. It was the last systematic religious persecution under the forms of law we have known in England, and from the point of view even of the persecutors themselves, like all that went before it, it proved a failure.

Bunyan's state of mind during these days of trial is clearly revealed by a document which fortunately has come down to us in his own handwriting. It is sometimes popularly spoken of as his will, but is really a deed of gift, by virtue of which he conveys al lhis worldly wealth to his "well-beloved wife, Elizabeth Bunyan." The reason of this unusual step is obvious enough. In the then state of public feeling he might any day be "had home to prison" again, his property confiscated, and his family thrown homeless upon the world. To protect them even if he should be deprived of his liberty, he made over everything in legal form to his wife. It is curious to note that either through skilled intention or, what is more probable, from innocent oversight, his household goods, though conveyed by deed to his wife, really remained under his own trusteeship. For as he failed to appoint another trustee, and the law provides that no trust shall fail for lack of a trustee, he as the husband of Elizabeth Bunyan occupied that position on her behalf.

The deed,* a fac-simile of which we give, is written on one side of a folio page of strong and enduring laid paper, and is as follows:

* The original deed is in the Museum of the Bunyan Meeting at Bedford.

"To all people to whom this present writing shall com, I, John Bunyan, of the parish of St. Cuthbirts, in the towne of Bedford, in the county of Bedford, Brazier, send greeting. Know ye that I, the said John Bunyan, as well for and in consideration of the natural affection and love which I have and bear into my well-beloved wife, Elizabeth Bunyan, as also for divers other good causes and considerations me at this present especially moueing, have given and granted, and by these presents do give, grant and conferm into the said Elizabeth Bunyan, my said wife, all and singuler my goods chattels, debts, ready mony, plate, Rings, household stuffe, Aparrel, utensills, Brass, pewter, Beding, and all other my substance whatsoever moueable and immoueable of what kinde, nature, quality, or condition soever the same arre or be, and in what place or places soever the same be, shall or may be found as well in mine own custodes possession as in the possession hands power and custody of any other person or persons whatsoever, To have and to hold all and singular the said goods, chattels, debts, and all other the aforesaid premises unto the said Elizabeth, my wife, her executors administrators and assigns to her and their proper uses and behoofs freely and quietly without any matter of challinge, claime, or demand of me, the said John Bunyan, or of any other person or persons whatsoever for me, in my name by my means caus or procurement and without any mony or other thing therefore to be yeeilded paid or done unto me, the said John Bunyan, my executors, administrators or assigns.

"And I, the said John Bunyan, all and singular the aforesaid goods, chattels, and premises to the said Elizabeth, my wife, her executors, administrators, and asignes, to the use aforesaid against all people to warrant and for ever defend by these presents. And further know ye that I, the said John Bunyan, haue put the said Elizabeth, my wife, in peaceable and quiet possession of all and singuler the aforesaid premises, by the deliurye unto her at the ensealing hereof one coyned peece of silver commonly called two pence, fixed on the seall of these presents.

"In Wittnes whereof I, the said John Bunyan, have hereunto set my hand and seall this 23d day of December, in the year of the

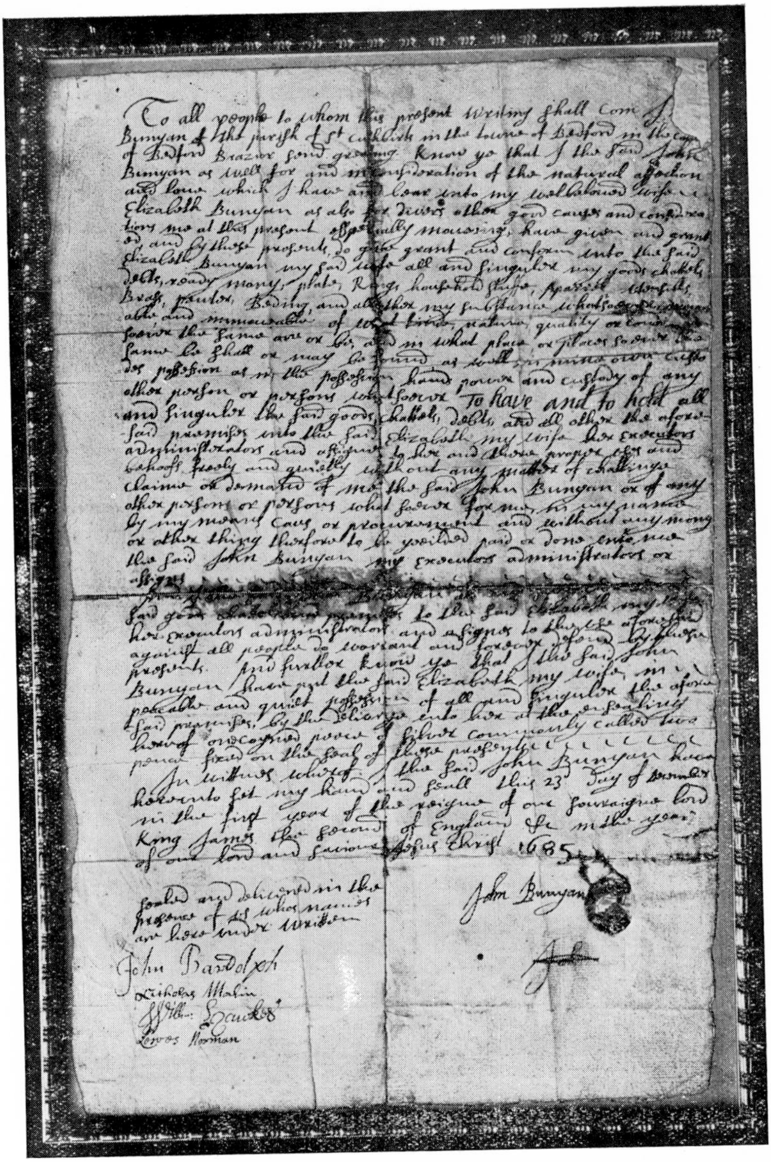
To all people to whom this present Writing shall come I John
Bunyan of the parish of St Cuthberts in the towne of Bedford in the County
of Bedford Brazier send greeting. Know ye that I the said John
Bunyan as well for and in consideration of the natural affection
and love which I have and beare unto my wellbeloved wife
Elizabeth Bunyan as also for divers other good causes and considerations me at this present especially moveing, have given and granted and by these presents do give grant and confirm unto the said
Elizabeth Bunyan my said wife all and singuler my goods chattels,
debts, ready mony, plate, Rings, household stuffe, Apparrell, utensills,
Brass, pewter, Bedding, and all other my substance whatsoever moveable and immoveable of what kind, nature, quality or condition
soever the same are or be, and in what place or places soever the
same be shall or may be found as well in mine own custody or
possession as in the possession hands power and custody of any
other person or persons whatsoever To have and to hold all
and singuler the said goods, chattels, debts and all other the aforesaid premises unto the said Elizabeth my wife her executors
administrators and assignes to her and theire proper use and
behoofe freely and quietly without any matter of challenge
claime or demand of me the said John Bunyan or of any
other person or persons whatsoever for me, in my name
by my means cause or procurement and without any mony
or other thing therefore to be yeilded paid or done unto me
the said John Bunyan my executors administrators or
assignes [illegible]
[illegible] Bunyan [illegible] the
said goods chattels and premises to the said Elizabeth my wife
her executors administrators and assignes to the use aforesaid
against all people do warrant and forever defend by these
presents. And further know ye that I the said John
Bunyan have put the said Elizabeth my wife in
peaceable and quiet possession of all and singuler the aforesaid premises, by the delivery unto her at the ensealing
hereof one coyned peece of silver commonly called two
pence fixed on the seal of these presents.
In witness whereof I the said John Bunyan have
hereunto set my hand and seall this 23 day of December
in the first year of the reigne of our sovereigne lord
King James the second of England &c in the year
of our lord and saviour Jesus Christ 1685

John Bunyan

Sealed and delivered in the
presence of us whose names
are here under written

John Bardolph
Nicholas Malin
Will: Hawkes
Lewes Norman

JOHN BUNYAN'S WILL (DEED OF GIFT).
1685.

(The original is preserved at Bunyan Meeting, Bedford.)
Photo: G. A. Gearey, Bedford.]

reigne of our souraigne lord King James the Second of England, &c., in the year of our Lord and Saviour Jesus Christ, 1685.

"Sealed and delivered in the presence of us whos names are here under written. "John Bunyan (L.S.)"

"John Bardolph.
"Nicholas Malin.
"William Hawkes.
"Lewes Norman.

As the deed itself indicates, there was affixed to the seal a silver twopenny-piece of the period, which has disappeared, while much of the wax remains. The document was attested by four members of the Church under Bunyan's care: John Bardolph the maltster, whose malthouse was besieged by Battison the church-warden, in 1670; Nicholas Malin of Gamlingay; William Hawkes, a deacon of the Church, and the son-in-law of John Gifford; and Lewes Norman. After being duly attested, it was hidden away in a recess of the house in St. Cuthbert's,* where he had lived since his release in 1672, and where his family had probably lived even earlier still. It was hidden away with such perfect safety that even Elizabeth Bunyan herself seems in after years not to have known where it was. For, as we shall see hereafter, on the death of her husband she administered to his estate at the Archdeacon's Court as that of an intestate person; and the deed itself seems not to have come to light till the nineteenth century when it was found, and became the property of the late Mr. George Livius, by whose widow it was afterwards bequeathed to the Bunyan Meeting Trustees.

* Demolished in 1838 when the 'deed' was found. A contemporary water colour drawing of the house is preserved at the Literary Institute Bedford. The site of Bunyan's home is now occupied by Nos. 17 and 19 Cuthbert Street.

From this document it will be seen that, without any pretension and with the utmost simplicity, he still calls himself John Bunyan, *brazier*. This opens up the question as to whether he did or did not still follow at times the brazier's calling side by side with that of his ministry. The writer often quoted by us says that Bunyan "contenting himself with that little God had bestowed upon him, sequestered himself from all secular employments to follow that of his call to the ministry." Yet, as we see thirteen years later, he still describes himself as a brazier. In troublous times there may have been necessity for this calling. His people were for the most part poor; there was not, as in the case of John Gifford and John Burton, the endowment of St. John's church to fall back upon; and it may be that John Bunyan, like a still greater apostle before him, sometimes laboured, working with his hands the thing that was needed. Yet such employment, if followed at all, could only have been occasional. The work of his brain, through tongue and pen, was too incessant to leave much time for the brazier's craft. Besides the nine books he published between 1685 and his death in 1688, he left sixteen unprinted manuscripts behind him, and though two of these were only meant for single-sheet broadsides, one was that of a somewhat lengthy commentary on the first ten chapters of Genesis, and another that of a pocket concordance, which must have taken some time to prepare.

The works he sent forth in 1685 were a discussion on *The Perpetuity of the Seventh-day Sabbath,*[1] and a discourse on the parable of *The Pharisee and the Publican.* The seventh-day Sabbath question is one of very feeble interest to anybody living now. But among the innumerable fancies of that period fertile in crotchets, was one for keeping the Jewish Sabbath as the day of worship and rest. A clergyman of some eminence tried to gather his congregation on Saturdays; and three places of worship endowed for the support of this opinion were continued down to our own times, the worshippers being known as Seventh-day Baptists. Bunyan tells us he was reluctant to enter upon a question of such trifling moment, but he was sorry to see the fictions and factions that were growing among Christian men, each fiction turning itself to a faction, to the loss of that good spirit of love and that oneness that formerly was with good men. For his part, he cannot accept the Jewish Sabbath, nor turn from the day on which his Lord rose from the dead. He cannot believe "that any part of our religion, as we are Christians, stands in not kindling of fires, and not seething of victuals, or in binding of men not to stir out of their places on the seventh day, in which at the dawning thereof they were found. And yet these were ordinances belonging to that seventh-day Sabbath." There are other books on the subject, it is true, but this book of his "being little, may best suit such as have but shallow purses, short memories, and but little time to spare, which usually is the lot of the mean and poorer sort of men."

[1] *Questions about the Nature and Perpetuity of the Seventh-day Sabbath.* And Proof that the First Day of the Week is the True Christian Sabbath. By John Bunyan. London: Printed for Nath. Ponder, 1685.

The Pharisee and the Publican[1] was sent forth by a publisher who appears now for the first time. The previous book was issued by Nathaniel Ponder, while this bears the imprint, "London: Printed for Jo. Harris, at the Harrow, over against the Church in the Poultrey. 1685." This first edition, if indeed it be as Charles Doe gives it in his list the first edition,* is ornamented with an engraved frontispiece, the upper half being a representation of the Temple, with the Pharisee and Publican praying; and the lower half a portrait of Bunyan, with the words underneath, "Vera Effigies Johanis Bunyan, Æt. suæ 57."† He proceeds to contrast these two men:

* No earlier edition has, so far, been discovered.

† *Vide* Addendum, chap. xvii.

"It is strange to see, and yet it is seen, that men cross in their minds, cross in their principles, cross in their apprehensions, yea and cross in their prayers, too, should yet meet in the temple to pray. The Pharisee did carry the bell and did wear the garland for religion, the Publican was counted vile and base and reckoned among the worst of men, even as our informers and bum-bailiffs, are with us at this day. The Publican was a Jew, but he fell in with the heathen and took the advantage of their tyranny to pole, to peel, to rob, and impoverish his brethren. The one was an open outside sinner, the other a filthy inside one. The Pharisee prayed with himself, said Christ. It is at this day wonderful common for men to pray extempore also. To pray by a book, by a premeditated set form, is now out of fashion. He is counted nobody now, that cannot at any moment, at a minute's warning, make a prayer of half an hour long. I am not against extempore prayer, for I believe it to be the best kind of praying; but yet I am jealous that there are a great many such prayers made, especially in pulpits and public meetings, without the breathing of the Holy Ghost in them. For if a Pharisee of old could do so, why may not a Pharisee do the same now? Wit and reason and notion is now screwed up to a very great height; nor do men want words or fancies, or pride, to make them do this thing. Great is the formality of religion this day and little the power thereof. . . . The Pharisee prayed with himself. God and the Pharisee were not altogether, there was only the Pharisee and himself. How many times have I heard ancient men and ancient women at it with themselves, when all alone in some private room or in some solitary path; and in their chat they have been sometimes reasoning, sometimes chiding, sometimes pleading, sometimes praying, and sometimes singing; but yet all has been done by themselves when all alone. So the Pharisee was at it with himself, he and himself performed at this time the duty of prayer. God, saith he, I thank thee that I am not as other men are. I remember that Luther used to say, 'In the name of God begins all mischief.'

[1] *A Discourse upon the Pharisee and the Publican;* wherein several great and weighty things are handled. By John Bunyan, Author of the *Pilgrim's Progress*. London: Printed for Jo. Harris, at the Harrow, over against the Church in the Poultrey, 1685. *Esponiadd ar ddammeg y Pharisead a'r Publican.* Caerfyrddin, 1775. 12mo.

All must be fathered upon God—God, I thank thee, is in the persecutor's lips, is the burden of the heretic's song, is in every man's mouth, and must be entailed to every error, delusion, and damnable doctrine that is in the world.

"But, O thou blind Pharisee, since thou art so confident that thy state is good, prithee when didst thou begin to be righteous? Was it before or after thou hadst been a sinner? What means thy preferring of thine own rules, laws, statutes, ordinances, and appointments before the rules, laws, statutes, and appointments of God? What kind of righteousness shall this be called? What back will such a suit of apparel fit, that is set together just cross and thwart to what it should be? And wilt thou call this thy righteousness; yea, wilt thou stand in this, plead for this, and venture an eternal concern in such a piece of linsey-woolsey as this? O fools and blind! It was partly for the sake of mine own good deeds that I obtained mercy to be in heaven and glory; shall this be the burden of the song of heaven? or is this that which is composed by that glittering heavenly host, and which we have read of in the holy book of God? No, no, that song runs upon other feet, standeth in far better strains, being composed of far higher and truly heavenly matter. Thou hast set thyself against God in a way of contending; thou standest upon thy points and pantables; thou wilt not bate God an ace of what thy righteousness is worth, and wilt also make it worth what thyself shall list. Pharisee, I will assure thee, thou art beside thy saddle; thy state is not good. A man must be good before he can do good, and evil before he can do evil; for a tree must be a sweeting tree before it yields sweetings; and a crab tree before it brings forth crabs.

"And now see how thwart and cross the Pharisee and the Publican did lie in the temple one to another. The Pharisee goes in boldly, the Publican stands behind, a loof off, as one not worthy to approach the divine presence; the Pharisee hath many fine things whereby he strokes himself over the head, and in effect calls himself, and that in his presence, one of God's white boys—but alas! poor Publican, thy guilt stops thy mouth, thou hast not one good thing to say of thyself. What wilt thou do, Publican, what wilt thou do? Make an O yes; let all the world be silent; yea let the angels of God come near and listen; for the Publican is come to have to do with God! 'He smote upon his breast, saying, God be merciful unto me a sinner.' And is this thy way, poor Publican? O cunning sinner! O crafty Publican! thy wisdom has outdone the Pharisee, for it is better to apply ourselves to God's mercy than to trust to ourselves that we are righteous. The Publican did hit the mark—yea, get nearer unto and more into the heart of God and his Son than did the Pharisee."

After the appearance of this book in the early part of 1685, its author sent out only one other work between that year and 1688, an unusual cricumstance for his facile pen, which may possibly be accounted for by the troubles of the stormy intervening years. As number 37 in Charles Doe's list of Bunyan's works we have the following: *A Book for Boys and Girls, or Country Rhimes for Children in verse on seventy-four things,* 1686. It was not reprinted during Bunyan's lifetime, but in 1701, and bearing the title, *A Book for Boys and Girls,* or *Temporal Things Spiritualized,* was issued by R. Tookey, of Threadneedle Street, in strangely altered form. The preface, which was a sort of spelling-book, was left out, the seventy-four meditations were cut down to forty-nine, two staves of music were omitted, and the remaining meditations were subjected to rather ruthless revision. These changes were not suspected till a copy of the original edition, turned up in New York in 1888, was acquired by the British Museum,* and has since been published in facsimile by Mr. Elliot Stock [1889]. This apparently unique copy seems to have belonged to Narcissus Luttrell, from whom it passed to the Dukes of Buckingham, and on the breaking up of the Stowe collection came into the hands of the trade. Somewhere about 1881 it was purchased by an American for forty guineas. In the mutilated edition of 1724 the title was again altered to the form it has kept ever since: *Divine Emblems, or Temporal Things Spiritualized.* In 1707 this book began to be illustrated, and in 1757, E. Dilly, at the Rose and Crown in the Poultry, issued an edition which he called the tenth, with a new series of illustrations and a preface "Addressed to the Great Boys in Folio and the Little Ones in Coats," signed J. D. A later edition was published in 1767, by William Johnston, of Ludgate Hill, and in 1780, the book was brought out by Alexander Hogg, in his Collected Edition, and adorned with copper-plate engravings, the figures represented being all dressed out in the costumes of the days of George III., the men with cocked hats and queues, the women with hooped petticoats and high head-dresses, the clergymen with many tiered wigs, and the housmaids with mob-caps and aprons. A few years ago an edition on fine paper, and with reproductions of the illustrations of 1757, was issued by Messrs. Bickers and Son, with an introduction by Alexander Smith, the Scottish poet.

* Another copy was discovered, and sold by auction in London, December 17, 1926. The two copies vary somewhat, typographically

Bunyan tells us in his characteristic preface that this book is meant for boys and girls, slily adding that he means those of all ages, and of all sorts and degrees, for often "our bearded men do act like beardless boys, our women please themselves with childish toys." To do good to these juveniles of all ages he will come down to meet them:

"Good reader, that I save them may,
I now with them the very dotterel play;
And since at gravity they make a tush,
My very beard I cast behind a bush;
And like a fool stand fingering of their toys,
And all to show them they are girls and boys."

Possibly his book may not be welcome to all, for he who pleases all must rise betimes. He might if he would have taken a higher flight, but to what purpose? The arrow shot out of sight awakes not the sleeper; "it may make children gaze, but 'tis that which hits a man doth him amaze." The book, which is in rhyme, rises here and there to poetry, and everywhere is marked by good sense and wise intent, making up altogether a collection of such similes as were ever coming to the writer's mind like ripples over a stream. There are reflections upon the clouds edged with silver, and upon that which is a comely sight to see, a world of blossoms on an apple-tree. The boy chasing the butterfly, the mole burrowing in the earth, the bush with comely ruddy rose, but bearing also its sharpened thorn, and the child calling to her breast the bird that will not come, all pass before him, and all flash their gleam of light upon the deeper life within. Nothing is too homely for the writer's purpose, not even the whipping of a top, the falling or sputtering of candles, or the cackling of a hen; but there are times when he soars on higher wing. The lark and the fowler set forth the sinner and the tempter; the variety of birds flying in the firmament suggests the variety of individual life in the men who one day shall possess the heavens; the dawn, with its flickerings between light and dark, becomes symbolic of the doubtful soul on which the Sun of Righteousness is beginning to rise; and the swallow soaring on light wing calls up a fancy which might have dropped from George Herbert's pen:

"This pretty bird, O! how she flies and sings,
But could she do so if she had not wings?
Her wings bespeak my faith, her songs my peace;
When I believe and sing my doubtings cease."

A few months after the publication of these *Country Rhimes*, there was politically a strangely altered world in England, and Bunyan's local influence with the Nonconformists made him of sufficient importance to be sought after in the service of the

A

BOOK

FOR

BOYS

AND

GIRLS:

OR,

Country Rhimes

FOR

Children.

By *J. B.*

Licensed and Entred according to Order.

LONDON, Printed for *N. P.* and Sold by the Booksellers in *London* 1686.

Title-Page of the First Edition of
A BOOK FOR BOYS AND GIRLS.
By John Bunyan.
1686.

Government. To understand Bunyan's position at this crisis it is necessary to go back a step or two in the general history of the time.

The King, a Roman Catholic himself, was resolved to give his own religion an equal standing in the country with that of the Established Church. To this the way seemed open; the judges had decided in favour of his dispensing power, and Parliament, so far as he knew, was such as he would have it. He proceeded, therefore, to yet more decisive action. Authority was granted to avowed Romanists among the clergy to remain in their livings; bishoprics as they fell vacant were filled up by sycophants on whom he could rely; and the Court of High Commission, after being long laid aside, was once more set up and invested with absolute control over universities, colleges, cathedrals, and all ecclesiastical corporations whatever, with power of summary excommunication and deprivation of all and sundry who might be disobedient. The result of all this was soon manifest enough. The religious Orders of the Church of Rome began to walk the streets openly, dressed in their peculiar garb; convents rose, and eminent converts were made; the Franciscans found a home in Lincoln's Inn Fields, the Carmelites in the city, the Benedictines at St. James's Palace, and the Jesuits in the Savoy. Bad feeling sprang up between contending parties, and street riots resulted. A mass-house was broken into in Cheapside, the crucifix carried out and fixed on the parish-pump, and when the train-bands were called out to put down the riot, they flatly refused to fight in favour of popery.

The King, who was now rapidly estranging his former friends, sought by a deep stroke of policy to win the Nonconformists to his side. On the 4th of April, 1687, appeared the memorable Declaration of Indulgence, in which, on his own sole authority, he proceeded to annul a long series of statutes, and suspended all penal laws against all classes of Nonconformists. This document went further than the Declaration of 1672, in that it not merely suspended the penal laws, but also dispensed with all religious tests. Constitutionalists and Churchmen grew alarmed, and now they on their part tried to win the Nonconformists over to their side. Thus began what has been called the strangest auction recorded in history, when the Protestant Dissenters, who had lately been the religious outcasts of the country, held the balance of power between the King and the Church. Though both sides were compromised up to the hilt, they each tried to throw on the other the blame of those sufferings which the Nonconformists for so long had endured—the Court on the clergy, and the clergy on the Court. It was a changed world, indeed, when the Court began to treat the once-persecuted sectaries with such deference, and the clergy to speak of them as their dear brethren in the Protestant faith, and both sides with many fair speeches and flattering promises tried to draw the waverers to themselves.

The King, having parted with his former Parliament in anger, found it necessary to call another; but if this were to be of any use to him he felt that it must be manipulated beforehand. Again, therefore, it was resolved to remodel the boroughs, and at the same time to revise the commission of the peace and the lieutenancy of counties, retaining only such persons in the public service as could be relied on to support the policy of the Court. Each lord-lieutenant was immediately to go down to his county, and summoning before him all his deputies and all justices of the peace, put to them a series of questions for the purpose of ascertaining how they would act at a general election. The answers to these questions he was to take down in writing and forward to the Government. He was also to furnish lists of persons suitable for the bench and for the command of the army, to examine into the state of all boroughs in his country, and make his reports. These duties he was to perform personally, and on no account to delegate them to any substitute whatever.

Half the lord-lieutenants of England at once refused to discharge the duty imposed upon them; but among those who consented was that Thomas, Earl of Ailesbury, who had succeeded his father in office in Bedfordshire in 1685. Summoning his deputies and the justices either to the Swan Chamber or to the old chapel of Herne in Bedford, he put to them the three questions which were being put all the country over, viz.—

"(1) If in case you shall be chosen Knight of the Shire or Burgess of a Towne, when the King shall think fitt to call a Parliament, will you be for taking off the Penall Laws and Tests? (2) Will you assist and contribute to the Election of such Members as shall be for takeing off the penall Laws and Tests? and (3) Will you support the King's Declaration for Liberty of Conscience by living friendly with those of all perswasions, as subjects of the same Prince and good Christians ought to do?"

The answers to these questions have been preserved among the Rawlinson MSS. in the Bodleian, and throw curious light on the position of men, many of whom had been harassing their neighbours for years for resisting the law, and now find that they themselves are opposed to the King, in a world strangely turned upside down. To their honour be it said, most of them stood firm to their convictions. From Bedfordshire the answers were as follows: Sir George Blundell "Humbly answers—(1) That as a private person he does not apprehend that he has any legal power to pre-engage himself against Acts of Parliament before they have undergone another parliamentary debate; (2) He submissively answers that occurrences are so variable in future contingencies by the order of Divine providence, that he cannot pretend to a capacity of determining beforehand what his thoughts and actions will be in progress of time in affairs of this nature; (3) Is sincerely willing to live peaceably with such who are of other persuasions, having no animosity to the person of any man for difference of oponion." Clearly, as this third answer shows, Sir George's education had been going forward since he sat on the bench that sent Bunyan to prison in 1660, and since he distrained the cows and looms of the Cotten End Meeters in 1670. Sir John Cotten of Stratton Park, if sent to the House would go with the design of being convinced by the best arguments, and would vote for men of the same sort. So also said Sir Richard Abbot, Sir Edmond Gardiner, and Thomas Dockraw.

Others, such as Benjamin Conquest and Thomas Christie, varied the phrase, but kept their position by saying that they would comply with the king's inclination so far as they could do it with a good conscience. John Osborn "must ingenuously own that he cannot be for the repeal of those laws which he thinks are for the preservation of his King and country, nor assist others to do it." Of the same mind is John Harvey, though he thinks with my Lord Chief Justice Herbert that the king may and ought to dispense with his servants as he thinks best. Sir Anthony Chester cannot consent to the repeal of the penal laws, but is willing to live peaceably with men of other persuasions. Of this mind also were William Butler, the Hon.

Charles Leigh, Sir William Gostwick, Sir Villiers Chernocke, Richard Orlebar, and the Farrers, father and son. Thomas and Ralph Bromsall of Blunham and Northill were for removing the tests so far as they applied to the king himself, but could not consent to repeal the penal laws against phanatiques, to give them too much liberty. John Ventriss would repeal the laws, "if only Roman Catholics were to be eazed by it, for the phanatiques will get too much strength by it, and they are utter enemies to the King's person, crown, and monarchy." There is one other of the Bedfordshire justices whose answer we must not pass by, namely, William Foster, Doctor of Laws and J.P., whom we have so often met since he first held up the candle to Bunyan in the low-roofed hall of Harlington House. The answer opposite to his name is simply this, "He submitts all to His Majestie's Pleasure." That is, though for more than a quarter of a century Foster had been harassing other men for their convictions, he was evidently not overweighted with convictions of his own. It will be remembered that Mr. By-ends, of the town of Fair-speech, had two eminently respectable kinsmen, whose names were Mr. Facing-both-ways and Mr. Anything. Peradventure these worthies were not altogether unknown to Dr. William Foster, nor their principles altogether alien to his spirit. Be that as it may, he was the only man on the Bedfordshire bench in 1687 who was willing to think anything or nothing, as the King might desire, on the great question of the time.[1]

There was small comfort for Lord Ailesbury or his master out of all this, and he proceeded next to regulate—that was the phrase—the Bedford Corporation. But before this, as the following letter from John Eston indicates, he had been feeling his way in the town:

"My Lord. since your Honour spake with me at Bedford I have

[1]*Rawlinson MSS.*—Penal Laws and Test. ff. 134, *et seq.* In the same papers are the following lists of the same date: (1) *Persons proposed to be Justices of the Peace by a Commission of Assistance for the Towne of Bedford*: Wm. Isaac (Intended Mayor), Sir Edmond Gardiner, Wm. Foster, John Eston, Robt. Audley, and Thos. Margetts. (2) *Persons proposed to be Deputy-Lieutenants for the County of Bedford*:—Sir John Napier, Sir Rowland Alston, Sir Wm. Beecher, Sir John Burgoyne, Wm. Foster, Wm. Edmunds of Battlesden, Matthew Dennis of Kempston, Thos. Brown of Arlsey, and Thos. Hillersdon of Elstow. These three names were crossed out—Wm. Foster (reinserted by another hand), Robert Audley of Biggleswade, and John Eston of Bedford. (3) *Persons to be Justices of the Peace besides the above-named*: Sir Jas. Astrey of Harlington, Wm. Boteler of Biddenham, Robert Montague of Sharnbrook, Ralph Bromsall of Blunham, Gaius Squire of Eaton Socon, Samuel Ironsides of Layton Beaudesert, Rich. Orlebar of Harrold, Wm. Whitebred of Cardington, Francis Reynolds of Carlton, Robt. Audley of Biggleswade, John Ventriss, Wm. Daniell, Thos. Bromsall, John Eston of Bedford. It may be presumed that all these gentlemen are named as not opposed to the Declaration of Indulgence. There is the mark of the cross opposite to the names of Ventriss, Daniell, and Thos. Bromsall, possibly as indicating doubt.

conferred with the heads of the Dissenters and particularly with Mr. Margetts and Mr. Bunyon whom your Lordship named to me. The first of these was Judge-Advocate in the Army under the Lord General Monke, when the late King was restored; the other is Pastor of the Dissenting congregation in this Town. I find them all to be unanimous for electing only such Members of Parliament as will certainly vote for repealing all the Tests and Penal Laws touching Religion, and they hope to steere all their friends and followers accordingly; so that if the Lord-Lieutenant will cordially assist with his influence over the Church party there cannot be in human reason any doubt of our electing two such members.

"I nominated to them two such Gentlemen to stand for Burgesses, but (I must confess) they returned upon me with reiterated desires that I would stand for one, and therefore rather than the King shall fail of one to vote for repealing the Tests and Penal Laws I shall be willing to stand. The other they desired to stand with me is Robert Audley, Esq., late Deputy Recorder of our Town, who when in power was very indulgent to all Dissenters. I sent yesterday a letter to him at his howse in Biggleswards, but he was gone into Lincolnshire, and my letter returned. In the next place we had thoughts of Sir Edmond Gardiner, our present Recorder, who we humbly conceive will incline to stand and to vote for repealing, if your Honour be pleased to send for him, and propose it, especially if it be made known that it will be no charge to him and that the Lord Lieutenant's interests shall be conjounct with ours in the Election. Sir Edmond is now in London at Lincoln's Inn.

"My zeal against the Tests and Penal Laws is so fervent that I cannot but strenuously endeavour in my sphere to promote the electing of such Members of Parliament as will certainly damn them, and therefore what further reasonable instruction I shall receive from your Lordshippes to serve my Sovereign in this affair, shall be with all diligence and faithfulnesse observed by, my Lord, Your Honour's most humble and most faithful servant,

"Bedford, November 22, 1687. "JOHN ESTON."[1]

Notwithstanding the hopeful tone of this letter, it would appear that its writer's candidature did not prosper; and it would seem also that it was not possible to obtain the consent of Robert Audley or Sir Edmond Gardiner to stand with him, and that his proposed colleague now was Dr. Foster. The next letter from Eston, a fortnight later, was endorsed, "To the Right Honourable the Earl of Peterborough, at his Lodgings in the Stone

[1] *Rawlinson MSS.* A. 139A. The writer of this letter was the son of that John Eston, one of the founders of the Bedford Church, who died in 1662. [He was high sheriff and justice of the peace for Bedford, and married Grace Stapley, of Twineham, Sussex. He died in 1697.]

Gallery at Whitehall." This nobleman was one of the Mordaunts of Turvey, in Bedfordshire, and though brought up a Protestant, had that same year become a Roman Catholic, and thus reverted to the religion of his ancestors. Macaulay says of him that he had been an active soldier, courtier, and negotiator, but that "now he was broken down by years and infirmities; and those who saw him totter about the galleries of Whitehall, leaning on a stick, and swathed up in flannels and plasters, comforted themselves for his defection by remarking that he had not changed his religion till he had outlived his faculties."[1] To this tottering bulwark of King James and the Papacy, John Eston writes as follows:

"Right Honourable: I most humbly begg your Lordship's pardon for this additional trouble, beseeching that my heartiness for His Majestie's service may expiat for my boldness. The clergy of this Town and several Corporation Officers as well as others, do labour pro aris et focis to oppose both the Doctor and myself, though they understand it to be the King's desire that we should stand. The Dissenters are firm for us, but the Churchmen are implacable against us, and I hear their reasons are, first, because the Doctor and myself are professedly for repealing; secondly, because the King hath nominated us; and for these two reasons they endeavour to expose and ridicule us ever so much that 'tis necessary some measures be taken as shall seem best in his Majestie's princely wisdom to vindicate us and to deter our Adversaries who thrust at him through our sides by their endeavour to abase us for our appearing to stand for his Majestie's service according to our duty and conscience. The cheife of our opposers, the Lord Lieutenant (I presume) can otherwayes influence, if he will heartily endeavour it by his Letters to Mr. Christie, the Mayor and Aldermen, and the Clergy who are the Lieutenant's votaries. I had a prospect at the beginning of my carrying the Election by my own interest in the Town, but now I see it not probable without further countenance from Authority, if it is your Honour's desire we should proceede.

"It is (my Lord) the misery of this kingdom that so much Democracie is mixed in the Government that thereby the exercise of the Soveraign power should be in any manner limited by the suffrages of the common people, whose humours are allwayes fluctuating, and the most part of them guided not by reason, but without deliberation like mere animals. But the circumstances of this nation are much altered from what they were when that democratical alay [alloy] of monarchie was first made; and therefore seeing those circumstances are changed which were the reason of that mixture, 'tis necessary there should be a change of Alay; for otherwise we may be destroyed by that which

[1] *Hist. of England*, ii., 194.

before was our preservation. And I hope this will be considered of next Parliament whether I have the honour to sit there or not. Having represented our case above, I leave it to your Lordship's prudent consideration, resolving whatever the issue be to remain firmly loyal to my Soveraign and to approve myself (my Lord) your Honour's most obliged and most humble servant.[1]

"Bedford, December 6, 1687. "JOHN ESTON."

It would appear that the suggestion of this letter was immediately acted upon, and that the lord-lieutenant wrote down to the Bedford Corporation on behalf of the candidature of Eston and Foster, for in the minutes of that body under date December 19th, we have the following:

"Answer sent to the Right Hon. Thos. Earl of Ailesbury from the Mayor concerning the Election of Burgesses to serve in Parliament. 'In obedience to your Honour's comands, I this day Sumoned a Councill, and did acquaint them with what your Lordship said that my Lord of Peterboro' had acquainted His Majestie that Dr. Foster and Mr. Eston were fit persons to serve; but the Election is not in the Corporation alone, but every Inhabitant (not taking Collections nor being a sojourner and noe freeman) hath a vote, therefore they cannot give assurance how the majority of voices will determine. But all who were in the Councill did declare that when his Majestie shall be pleased to issue writs, they will endeavour the Election of such members as they shall believe to be of undoubted loyalty and that shall be serviceable to the King and Kingdome.'"

It is evident from this reply that the Mayor and Corporation had ideas of their own as to the meaning of undoubted loyalty, and as to the sort of persons who would be really serviceable to the king and kingdom, and did not mean to elect the two candidates proposed to them. This was as clearly understood at Whitehall as in the Bedford Council Chamber. At a meeting of the Privy Council, therefore, held towards the end of January, an order in Council was passed for removing out of the town of Bedford, Thomas Underwood, Mayor, and Aldermen Faldo, sen., William Faldo, jun., and John White; and Councillors John Fenn, John Bundy, Robert Beckett, and Thomas Church; and for electing the king's trusty and well-beloved William Isaack Mayor; Aldermen John Eston, William Beckett, and John Spencer; Councillors John Peck, Andrew Freebody, John Rush, and James Veale. These persons thus substituted were not to take any oaths except for the due execution of their respective

[1] *Rawlinson MSS.* A., 139A, fol. 21.

places, all other tests being dispensed with. The Order in Council was signed by Lord Sunderland, and was accompanied with a Letter Mandatory stating that:

"Whereas by the Charter granted to the Town of Bedford a Power is reserved to His Majesty by His Order in Councill to remove from their Imployments any officers in the said Town, His Majesty in Councill is pleased to order the removal of the persons aforesaid."[1]

A further Order in Council and Letter Mandatory were issued on the 25th of March completing the work begun in January, and displacing "*Paule Cobb,* John Crawley, Ralph Smith, and Robert Faireman, Aldermen; Robert Faireman and Richard Hamont, Councilmen, and nominating the King's trusty and well-beloved William Bamforth, William Nicholls, Thomas Woodward, and William Woodward to be Aldermen; John Bardolph and Henry Clarke, jun., to be Common Councell men." William Hawkes was to be chosen in the place of William Isaak, elected Mayor, and while Paul Cobbe was to be removed from the Council, he was to be continued in his office as Clerk of the Peace. Some six or seven of the men thus brought into the Bedford Corporation by the King's order, were prominent members of Bunyan's congregation; three of them—Thomas Woodward, William Hawkes, and William Nicholls being then or shortly after Deacons of the Church. On the other hand, John Fenn, one of the Councillors displaced, was also one of the Deacons, unless, as is not improbable, this was the son of the John Fenn whom we have known in that capacity and in whose house, as we have seen, the Church held its meetings during the persecution of 1670.

As to Bunyan's personal feeling in reference to the policy of King James, the evidence is somewhat conflicting. The contemporary writer of the continuation of the *Grace Abounding** tells us that against this policy, "Mr. Bunyan expressed his zeal with some weariness, foreseeing the bad consequences that would attend it, and laboured with his congregation to prevent their being imposed on in this kind." On the other hand, John Eston, in the letter just given, states that he had as requested seen the heads of the Dissenters in Bedford, and "particularly Mr. Margetts and Mr. Bunyon, and that he

* "*The Continuation of Mr* Bunyan's *Life; Beginning where he left off, and concluding with the time and manner of his Death and Burial; together with his True Character*, &c." —. . . *Grace Abounding*, the *Seventh* Edition. . . . *London*, Printed for ... *Robert Ponder*, . . . 1692.

[1] Minutes of Privy Council, Jan. 29th and March 25th; Minutes of Bedford Corporation, March 8th and April 16th, 1688.

found them all unanimous for electing only such Members of Parliament as would vote for the repeal of all Tests and Penal Laws touching religion." Possibly the truth lies midway. It would appear that matters had proceeded so far that some place under Government was to be offered to Bunyan to secure his influence. He was not, however, to be worked upon. Yet, while refusing all such overtures and declining even to see the great man who brought them, probably none other than Thomas, Lord Bruce, who had recently succeeded his father as Earl of Ailesbury, we may infer that neither Bunyan nor the leading attendants upon his ministry were averse to accept of the liberty brought by this Declaration of Indulgence, any more than they were to accept of that conferred by the similar Declaration of 1672. The dispensing power might be unconstitutional, and the attempt to repeal the penal laws and tests might have a sinister purpose, still these laws themselves were inhuman and unjust, and ought to be repealed. Beneath the lash of such legislation Bunyan and his people had smarted for now nearly a quarter of a century. It was not wonderful that they should support the policy of repeal and welcome the time of relief without inquiring too curiously into the motives of the men who were trying to bring them about.

Certain it is that for a brief space some of the Nonconformists whom Bunyan had taught and trained came at this time into the Council of the borough, and equally certain that their coming was followed by such a reform of abuses as had not been known for a long time and of which there was urgent need. For example, several previous mayors had for years kept in their own possession moneys belonging to the charitable foundations of the town, and these at once received notice to pay in all such moneys that they might be disposed of according to the will of the donor. The Hagable rent rolls of the corporation required rectification after alienation and unauthorised alterations, and these were put under investigation with a view to restoration at the next Court Baron of the town. For some two or three years past an annual charity of £30, left by a Mrs. Collins for ten poor widows, had been weighted with the assertion "that resorting to church was a qualification required by the will of the person leaving the bequest." The new Mayor and Corporation on the 6th of September entered on their minutes, "the declaration that they had that day seen and read the copie of the said Will and Deed of Settlement, and that the said £30 is given for the maintenance of ten poor widows of the Towne of Bedford yearly for ever without any restriction or lymitation to widdows that resort to Church, and without any other qualification than poverty." So things went on. It was an altered world indeed since the good old times of quiet management with closed doors, and of forty-shilling penalties upon any councilman who should "disclose his fellow's counsell," or upon any doorkeeper of the Chamber who should whisper what he had heard, or suffer curious loiterers to listen. Great must have been the consternation of venerable owls at the letting in of all this daylight and shrill the screeching that followed.

After reconstructing the magistracy of the counties in the way we have seen, and regulating the corporations of the boroughs, the King, on the 27th of April, 1688, put forth a second Declaration of Indulgence in which, after reciting at length that of the previous April, he told his people that his purpose was immutably fixed, and exhorted them to choose such representatives as would assist him in the great work of giving liberty of conscience to the nation. On the 4th of May, an order was issued commanding the clergy to read this Declaration in their parish churches on two successive Sundays during divine service, refusal to be followed within a week by ejection. Great were the searchings of heart which followed in many a rectory and vicarage through the country as the royal command reached parish after parish. Of course it was variously received by those to whom it was sent. Sometimes by misgiving, compliance or stout resistance, and sometimes by clever evasion. In the diocese of Norwich, except in some three or four parishes out of about 1,200, the preacher for the day so contrived to read the document that not one of his parishioners could possibly know what it was about. There is a good story told of one incumbent who informed the people that though he was enjoined to read they were not compelled to listen, and who suggested that they should retire while he read the Declaration to empty benches and mere church walls.[1] Bishop Barlow who, four years ago, laid it down to the Dissenters of Bedfordshire as an irrefragable principle that subjects are bound to obey their rulers

[1] Stoughton's *Church of the Restoration*, ii., 148.

in matters of religion, is now not so clear on that point. One of the clergy of his diocese, in dire perplexity as to what he should do, wrote to the Bishop for counsel, the messenger to wait at Buckden Palace for the reply. He received the following answer which, like the responses from the oracles of antiquity, is not so clear or decisive as it might be:

"Sir,—I received yours, and all that I have time to say (the messenger which brought it making so little stay here) is only this: By His Majesty's command I was required to send that Declaration to all the Churches in my diocese, in obedience whereto I sent them. Now, the same authority which requires me to send them, requires you to read them. But whether you should or should not read them, is a question of that difficulty, in the circumstances we now are, that you can't expect that I should so hastily answer it, especially in writing. The two last Sundays, the Clergy in London were to read it, but, as I am informed, they generally refused. For myself I shall neither persuade nor dissuade you, but leave it to your prudence and conscience, whether you will or will not read it; only this I shall advise, that, if after serious consideration, you find that you cannot read it, but reluctante vel dubitante conscientiâ, in that case, to read it will be your sin, and you to blame for doing it. I shall only add that God Almighty would be so graciously pleased to bless and direct you, so that you may do nothing in this case, which may be justly displeasing to God, or the King, is the prayer of your loving friend and brother:

Thos. Lincoln.[1]

"Buckden, May 29, 1688."

After reading this temporizing deliverance from the Bishop, it is pleasant to listen to a more manly utterance from one of the clergy, an acquaintance by the way of Bunyan's, whom we met with some years earlier in Bedfordshire, Edward Fowler, formerly rector of Northill, but now vicar of St. Giles's, Cripplegate. At the consultation of the London clergy, the feeling at first seemed to be in favour of obeying the Order in Council. As the dispute waxed warm, Fowler rose, and with the clear ring of resolution in his words, he said: "I must be plain. The question is so simple that argument can throw no new light on it, and can only beget heat. Let every man say yes or no. But I cannot consent to be bound by the vote of the majority. I shall be sorry to cause a breach of unity. But this Declaration I cannot in conscience read." This man, who knew his own mind, helped other men to know theirs, and in the end eighty-

[1] Stoughton's *Church of the Restoration*, ii., 150.

five of the city incumbents signed a document pledging themselves not to read the Declaration.

The events which followed—the Trial of the Seven Bishops, and the delirous joy of the nation over their acquittal; the moody vexation of the King at his defeat, and his own steady descent down the steeps of Avernus—all this belongs to the general history of the time rather than to the simpler purpose before us. There is, however, in the back-ground of the story, one ominous figure flitting to and fro between London and the Hague, during the early months of that eventful summer, whom it may be well for us not to overlook. This was Edward Russell, nephew of the Earl of Bedford, and therefore cousin to that Lord William Russell whose untimely fate so many good men deplored. He was a man of courage and capacity, though of turbulent temper, and had seen widely different phases of life. A sailor once and a courtier afterwards, he had been in the royal service both on the high seas and in the palace of Charles. The execution of his cousin had, however, gone to his heart and alienated him for ever from the House of Stuart, and he was now, along with others, carrying on those negotiations with the Prince of Orange which were to end in the great Revolution and a changed England for the generations to come. The same 30th June on which the bells of a hundred steeples were ringing out the joy of the people over the acquittal of the Bishops, Edward Russell's plans had so far succeeded that there was despatched from London to the Hague an instrument, which has been described as scarcely less important to the liberties of England than the Great Charter itself.

BUNYAN'S HOUSE IN ST. CUTHBERT'S, BEDFORD.

From *Old Bedford,* by kind permission of the publisher, Mr. F. R. Hockliffe.]

XVI.

BUNYAN'S LAST DAYS.

DURING the memorable years, over which we have been passing, Bunyan lived on in the parish of St. Cuthbert. This parish, situate on the east side of the town, was very small in extent, having in it only ten families in the reign of Elizabeth, and, according to the Hearth Tax roll of 1673—4, forty-seven families in the time of Bunyan. Even in 1665, the Plague year, when the mortality in some of the Bedford parishes was considerable, the deaths in St. Cuthbert's from all causes were only two. Bunyan's house stood in what was then the common street of the parish, now called St. Cuthbert's Street. It was a plain homely structure, which was unfortunately taken down in 1838 to make way for the two commonplace cottages standing opposite to the house known as The Cedars. The room to the right of the doorway was a narrow apartment, known as John Bunyan's parlour, the fireplace of which had for the upper bar of the grate a steelyard stamped with the letters J. B. On the other side of the entrance was the living room of the family, which was much larger; there was also a small apartment spoken of as the study, and in the garden behind there was an outbuilding which seemed as if it had been used as a workshop.[1]

The only known contemporary reference to Bunyan's residence here is found in the diary of Thomas Hearne, the well-known antiquary, where he says: "I heard Mr. Bagford,* some time before he died, say that he walked once into the country, on

* John Bagford was a bookseller and printer (1650-1715), who collected books on commission for the trade and private buyers. He also made up imperfect copies from title-pages and portions of books he came across: possibly fragments salved from the Great Fire. *Vide* Plomer's *Dictionary of Booksellers and Printers;* and *The Remains of Thomas Hearne,* by Philip Bliss, vol. ii., p. 157.

[1] These particulars were furnished by Mr. William Blower, of Bedford, who as a medical man had known the house for several years.

purpose to see the study of John Bunyan. When he came John received him very civilly and courteously; but his study consisted only of a Bible and a parcel of books, the *Pilgrim's Progress*, chiefly, written by himself, all lying on a shelf or shelves." In a lately published collection of letters addressed to Mr. Hearne, there is one dated 1716, from James Sotheby, from which we gather that Mr. Bagford was then no longer living; and as he attained the age of sixty-five or sixty-six he may well have seen the Dreamer and talked with him in his own house, as he stated to his friend.

It has been already mentioned that Bunyan published nothing after his *Country Rhimes,* in 1686, till 1688, when he made up by increased activity for this unusual interval. Between March 25th, when the year began, and the month of August when he died, he sent out no fewer than five books, while another followed within a month of his death. These six books, thus published almost simultaneously after the second Declaration of Indulgence, were *The Jerusalem Sinner Saved; The Work of Jesus Christ as an Advocate; The House of God; The Water of Life; Solomon's Temple Spiritualised;* and *The Acceptable Sacrifice.* The first of these was on a favourite theme of his, and was the outcome of a favourite sermon. He says, "I have found through God's grace, good success in preaching upon this subject, and perhaps so I may by my writing upon it too." If the circulation of a book may be any test of its usefulness, this hope of his was not altogether frustrated, for before 1728, *The Jerusalem Sinner Saved*[1] had been translated into several languages, and gone through ten editions. The first two editions appeared in successive years—1688 and 1689; and the third edition was issued in 1691, by Elizabeth Smith, at the Hand and Bible, on London Bridge, possibly some kinswoman of Bunyan's former publisher, Francis Smith. The treatise is based upon the command of our Lord to preach His gospel unto all the nations, *beginning at Jerusalem.* The apostle Peter (Acts iii., 25-26) seems

[1] *The Jerusalem Sinner Saved;* or Good News for the Vilest of Men: Being a Help for Despairing Souls. By John Bunyan of Bedford. [There are copies of the First Edition, 1688, in the British Museum Library, and the Pierpoint Morgan Library, New York.]

to imply that because the men of Israel were the children of the prophets and of the covenant, therefore unto them first God having raised up His Son Jesus sent the blessing. Bunyan, however, takes the command to begin with the gospel at Jerusalem as a command to take it to the worst sinners first—because "in a word, Jerusalem was now become the shambles, the very slaughter-shop for saints, the place where the prophets, Christ, and His people were persecuted and put to death. For Christ will show mercy where sins are in number the most, in cry the loudest, in weight the heaviest. It is thus that He gets to Himself a glorious name. . . . Physicians get neither name nor fame by pricking of wheals, or picking out thistles, or by laying of plasters to the scratch of a pin; every old woman can do this. But if they would have a name and a fame, if they will have it quickly, they must, as I said, do some great and desperate cures. Let them fetch one to life that was dead; let them recover one to his wits that was mad; let them make one that was born blind, to see; or let them give ripe wits to a fool; these are notable cures, and he that can do thus, and if he doth thus first, he shall have the name and fame he desires; he may lie a-bed till noon." It is by great deliverances that Christ gets great renown. "Why should he so easily take a denial of the great ones that were the grandeur of the world, and struggle so hard for hedge-creepers and highwaymen, but to show forth the notes of the glory of His grace?" Bunyan says he could on this matter speak from personal experience. He himself had been a great sin-breeder, infecting the youth of the town where he was born.

"Wherefore Christ Jesus took me first; and taking me first, the contagion was much allayed all the town over. When God made me sigh they would hearken and inquiringly say, 'What's the matter with John?' When I went out to seek the bread of life, some of them would follow and the rest be put into a muse at home. Yea, almost the whole town, at first, at times would go out to hear at the place where I found good; yea, young and old for a while had some reformation on them; also some of them perceiving that God had mercy upon me, came crying to him for mercy too."

Let not the Jerusalem sinner despair, for he is, so to speak, called for by name and singled out to come in for mercy.

"Thou man of Jerusalem, hearken to thy call; men do so in courts of judicature, and presently cry out, 'Here, sir'; and then they shoulder and crowd, and say, 'Pray, give way, I am called into the Court.' Why, this is thy case, thou great, thou Jerusalem sinner; be of good cheer, he calleth thee. Why sittest thou still? Arise: why standest thou still? Come, man, thy call should give thee authority to come; wherefore up and shoulder it, man; say, 'Stand away, devil, Christ calls me; stand away, unbelief, Christ calls me; stand away, all ye my discouraging apprehensions, for my Saviour calls me to him to receive of his mercy.' Men will do thus, as I said, in courts below; and why shouldst not thou approach thus to the Court above? Christ pointeth over the heads of thousands as he sits on the throne of grace directly to the man that is the biggest sinner and has the biggest burden, and says, 'Let the Jerusalem sinner that stands there behind come to me.' Wherefore since Christ says 'come' to thee, let the angels make a lane, and let all men give place, that the Jerusalem sinner may come to Jesus Christ for mercy. It is because Christ shows mercy to the vilest that Satan rages so strongly, and as he can do nothing with Christ he assails Christ's people. He holds our hands while the world buffets us; he puts bearskins upon us, and then sets the dogs at us. He bedaubeth us with his own foam, and then tempts us to believe that that debaubing comes from ourselves. Let the tempted think much on Christ's mercy; for the tempted wherever he dwells always thinks himself the biggest sinner. This is Satan's master argument. I say this is his maul, his club, his masterpiece: he doth with this as some do with their most enchanting songs, sing them everywhere. Resist him steadfast in the faith. There is nothing like faith to help at a pinch. Faith must be always in exercise. Only put not in the place thereof presumption. I have observed that as there are herbs and flowers in our gardens, so there are counterfeits in the field; only they are distinguished from the others by the name of wild ones. Why, there is faith, and wild faith; and wild faith is this presumption. I call it wild faith because God never placed it in his garden—his church; 'tis only to be found in his field—the world. I also call it wild faith, because it only grows up and is nourished where other wild notions abound. Wherefore take heed of this and all may be well. But let a true faith be always at work. Faith is the eye, is the mouth, is the hand, and one of these is of use all day long. Faith is to see, to receive, to work, or to eat; and a Christian should be seeing, or receiving, or working, or feeding all day long. Let it rain, let it blow, let it thunder, let it lighten, a Christian must still believe. At what time, said the good man, I am afraid I will trust in thee."

As this on the Jerusalem Sinner was addressed to those outside the Kingdom of God, Bunyan's next book, *The Work of*

Jesus Christ as an Advocate,[1] was addressed to those within. It was published for him by that Dorman Newman at the King's Arms in the Poultry, who six years before had published *The Holy War.* Happening to hear a sermon from an unenlightened scribe, who told the people to see that their cause be good, else Christ will not undertake it, "Lord," thought I, "if this be true, what shall I do, and what will become of all this people, yea and of this preacher too?" At once he set about showing how Christ pleads for those who through their sin have no plea of their own. On other grounds, also, there seemed a needs-be for a timely word. "Christ as Sacrifice, Priest, and King, with the glories in and that flow from him as such, has, God be thanked, in this our day been much discovered by our seers, and as much rejoiced in by those who have believed their words; but as he is an Advocate with the Father for us, the excellency of that doth too much lie hid, and but little of the glory thereof has by writing been in our day communicated." To meet error, therefore, on the one side and glorify truth on the other, he adventures to write of Him that never lost a cause nor a soul for whom He undertook to be an Advocate with God.

The third production of Bunyan's pen, in 1688, was a poetical *Discourse of the Building, Nature, Excellency, and Government of the House of God.* It was first published in a pocket volume of sixty-three pages by George Larkin, and then seems to have dropped altogether out of sight till quite recent years, when a copy was brought to light through the intervention of Mr. Creasy, bookseller, Sleaford. It was then for the first time reprinted, and added to Mr. Offor's edition of Bunyan's Collected Works.[2] Looking at the subject itself, one would have thought that the nature, constitution, and government of a Christian Church would not have furnished a very promising theme for poetry; yet we find that he who pictured the Palace Beautiful

[1] *The Work of Jesus Christ as an Advocate,* Clearly Explained and Largely Improved for Benefit of all Believers. By John Bunyan, Author of the *Pilgrim's Progress.* London: Printed for Dorman Newman, at the King's Arms in the Poultry, 1688. [This work was also issued, in 1688, with another title-page, as *The Advocateship of Jesus Christ,* etc. The text is identically the same. It was, probably, the first of the two. The Epistle to the Reader and Contents are in smaller type than in the other.]

[2] *A Discourse of the Building, Nature, Excellency, and Government of the House of God;* with Counsels and Directions to the Inhabitants thereof. By John Bunyan of Bedford. London: George Larkin, 1688. This only copy of the First Edition was destroyed with the rest of Mr. Offor's Collection. [Three copies are now known: one in the Pierpoint Morgan Library, New York, and two privately owned.]

had not lost the cunning of his right hand when, in this form also, he sets forth the beauty of the Church, its strength and defence, and the delicateness of its situation. It is a fair vision that rises before him. Beneath the very threshold of this house arise goodly springs of lasting grace. Sweet is the air all round, and here are perfumes most pleasant to the sense. The gardens yield richest spice and goodly trees of frankincense, while near are arbours, walks, fountains; standing round are mountains, from which you may see the Holy Land, and in the valleys between are fertile fields adorned with corn and lilies fair:

> "Angels do here go by, turn in and rest,
> The road to Paradise lies by her gate;
> Here pilgrims do themselves accommodate
> With bed and board, and do such stories tell
> As do for truth and profit all excel."

He passes from the governors of the house and its under-officers to the order and manner of government. Love must rule and sympathy share grief; forgiveness is a statute law, watchfulness unto prayer a binding duty. That sincerity which makes heaven smile upon us is enjoined upon the dwellers in this house of the Church; so is Temperance, the mother of Moderation, and that patience which bears all wrongs without resistance:

> "I doubt our pampered Christians will not down
> With what I say, yet I dare pawn my gown,
> Do but compare my notes with sacred story
> And you will find patience the way to glory."

Seeing that idleness gives great occasions to the flesh, the rule of this honourable house is that none dwell here but such as workers be. Fig-trees are here to keep and vines to dress—here's work for all; yet is the toil a pleasure and the labour sweet:

> "The work is short, the wages are for ever;
> The work like we, the wages like the giver."

Almost as if he had an instinctive feeling that for him the time of sundown was near, Bunyan sent forth another book in these closing months of his pilgrimage, on *The Water of Life,*[1] which was published by Nathaniel Ponder. In a preliminary Epistle to the Reader he says we may, if we will, call this book Bunyan's Bill of his Master's Water of Life. He could give accounts of "numberless numbers that have not only been made to live, but to live for ever by drinking of this water; many

[1] *The Water of Life,* or a Discourse showing the Richness and Glory of the Grace and Spirit of the Gospel, as set forth in Scripture by this Term, *The Water of Life.* By John Bunyan. London: Printed for *Nathaniel Ponder,* at the Peacock in the Poultry, 1688. *Uisge na beatha.* Gael. Edinburgh: 1846. 12mo.

of them, indeed, are removed from hence and live where they cannot be spoken with as yet, but abundance of them do still remain here and have their abode yet with men. But be sure to get this life-water from the hand of the Lord Himself, for—

"There are many mountebanks in the world, and every of them pretend that they have this water to sell. Go directly to the Throne thyself, or as thou art bidden, come to the waters. For the price, care not for that, 'tis cheap enough; this is to be had without money or price. But let it not be slighted because it is offered to thee upon terms so full, so free. For thou art sick and sick unto death if thou drinkest not of it. Farewell. The Lord be thy physician."

In the body of the work he speaks of the Spirit and Grace of God signified by the water of life, its great abundance, its source or well-spring under the throne of the Eternal, and its purity and clearness:

"These are the waters that the Doves love to sit by because by the clearness of these streams they see their pretty selves as in a glass. These be the streams where the Doves wash their eyes, and by which they solace themselves and take great content. As in fair waters a man may see the body of the Sun and of the Moon and of the Stars, and the very body of Heaven; so he that stands upon the Bank of this River, and that washeth his Eyes with this water may see the Son of God, the Stars of God, the Glory of God and the habitation that God has prepared for his People. And are not these pleasant sights? Is not this excellent water? has not this River pleasant streams? This River is the running out of God's heart. This is his Heart and Soul; wherefore forbear thy mistrusts, cast off thy slavish fears, hang misgivings as to this upon the Hedge: and believe, thou hast an invitation sufficient thereto, a River is before thy face. As for the dead World that loves to be dead this is nothing to them. They toss their Vanities about as the Boys toss their Shittle-Cocks in the Air, till their Foot slips and themselves descend into the Pit. Let this suffice for this time."

The next book of the series issued by Bunyan in 1688 was the one entitled *Solomon's Temple Spiritualiz'd;*[1] which was published by George Larkin, at the Two Swans. It professes to be an endeavour to show the gospel glory of Solomon's temple.

[1] *Solomon's Temple Spiritualiz'd, or Gospel-Light Fetcht out of the Temple at Jerusalem, to let us more easily into the Glory of New-Testament Truths.* By John Bunyan. London: Printed for and sold by *George Larkin* at the Two Swans, without Bishopsgate, 1688. *Salomon's Temple door het Evangelie light Opgeheldert en Vergeeste-lykt.* Door M. Johan Bunjan Uyt het Engels vertaalt. Te Utrecht, 1731. *Gogoniant y Deml.* Teml Salomon wedi ei hysbrydoli. Aberystwyth: 1810. *Solomon's Temple Spiritualized.* Eleventh Edition. London: Printed for J. Bunyan, above the Monument. [N.D. (? 1770, and issued by *James* Bunyan).]

God had tied up the Church of the Jews to types and figures to be butted and bounded by them in all external parts of worship. Bunyan selects one out of many—the Temple, and in seventy particulars shows the spiritual significance of its symbolism, entering his caveat, by the way, against the manufacture of symbols in later time, sensibly saying that what God provided to be a help to the weakness of his people of old was one thing, and what was invented without his commandment was another.

> "I dare not presume to say," he modestly adds, "that I have hit right to every thing, but this I can say, I have endeavoured so to do. True I have not for these things fished in other men's waters; my Bible and Concordance* are my only library in my writings. Wherefore, courteous reader, if thou findest anything either in word or matter that thou shalt judge doth vary from God's truth let it be counted no man's else but mine. Pray God to pardon it, and do thou lovingly pass it by and receive what thou findest will do thee good."

* The Baptist College at Bristol has a copy of *A New and Useful Concordance to the Holy Bible,* etc. Begun by the industrious Labours of V[avasour] P[owell]. . . . Recommended to the studious Christian, by John Owen, D.D. London: Printed for Francis Smith . . . 1673. On the title-page of this unique copy is written, *John Bunyan, his Book.*

As we might expect in a book on such a subject, there are many Bunyanesque touches. Speaking of the Temple, for example, he says that its porch was large, and so should the charity of the churches be. "O Churches, let your ministers be beautified with your love, that they may beautify you with their love. There are steps up into the temple, for he that entereth into the house of the Lord is an ascending man. The world thinks that it is a going downward to go up to God's house, but that is their grievous mistake. There are steps up—steps of God, steps of faith, steps of truth, steps butted and bounded by a divine rule—these are steps indeed. Then, the hings on which the doors hung were of gold, to signify that they both turned upon motives and motions of love, and also that the openings thereof were rich golden hinges the gate to God doth turn upon. So all the parts and ministries of the temple furnish wise thoughts to a wise heart." Even the very snuffers, it seems, may be turned to edification. "For if our snuffs are our superfluities of naughtiness, our snuffers, then, are those righteous reproofs, rebukes, and admonitions, which Christ has ordained to be in his house for good. As who should say, 'the lights of the temple must be trimmed withal, if they burn not well.' Only, the snuffers must be used wisely. It is not for every fool to handle snuffers at or about the candles, lest, perhaps, instead of mending the light, they put the candle out. And, therefore, Paul bids them that are spiritual do it. Watch, man, watch and let not your snuffs be too long, nor pull them off with your fingers, or carnal reasonings, but with godly admonitions. Use your snuffers graciously, curb vice, nourish virtue, so you will use them well, and so your light will shine to the glory of God." Coming to the singers in the temple, he says, "Let us run a little in the parallel: The songs sung in the temple were new, and answerable to this is the Church to sing now new songs with new hearts for new mercies. New songs are grounded on new matter, new occasions, new mercies, new deliverances, new discoveries of God to the soul, or for new frames of heart; and are such as are most taking, most pleasing and most refreshing to the soul." Here, too, is a characteristic utterance about the temple being but one, on one and the same foundation though divided into the holy and most holy place: "The difference betwixt us and them is, not that we are really two, but one body in Christ, in divers places. True we are below stairs and they above; they in their holiday and we in our working-day clothes; they in harbour, but we in the storm; they at rest, and we in the wilderness; they singing as crowned with joy, we crying as crowned with thorns. But, I say, we are all of one house, one family, and are all children of one Father." Speaking of the symbolism of the temple Ezekiel saw, and calling attention to the fact that in the carved work on the walls palm-trees alternated with cherubim, Bunyan takes a wide sweep of speculation when he suggests that this may be to show us that the elect of God shall fill the vacancies created by the fall of the angels, they for sin cast down from the holy heavens and we by grace caught up thither to complete the ranks.

We have seen already how the political events that were agitating the nation at large keenly affected the municipal life of Bedford, and touched somewhat closely Bunyan himself. Beyond this, and what we learn from the books he sent forth in 1688, we know but little of him during these closing months of his life. There are only some eight lines in the church records referring to this period, and these are merely routine business and by another hand. We catch just one gleam of local Bedford life, and of an event that may have startled him as well as his neighbours, as we read from an old pamphlet of the 17th April of that year, *Strange and Dreadful Newes from the Towne of Bedford,* of two disastrous fires which happened there four days before; one of them in the night, when the bells rang backward to give the alarm; and the other the next morning, at a malthouse close to Bunyan's house on the east side of the town, when "persons were much singed and burnt by the sheets of flame driven in their faces through the fury of the wind."[1] Passing from the month of April, when Bedford was thus lit up with flame by night and day, we come to the beginning of August, when Bunyan took that last journey to London from which for him there was to be no return, taking with him yet one MS. more, the last of his he was personally to place in the printer's hands. This journey was but one of many made through a long series of years to the city where his life was to end. Even in the closing days of the Commonwealth he seems to have had there a considerable circle of friends who looked for his visits with interest. It will be remembered that he tells us how between the two assizes of August, 1661, and January, 1662, he had somewhat more liberty, and "did go to see Christians at London," which his enemies hearing of, were angry with his gaoler. When his long imprisonment was ended, his visits thither became more frequent, and his fame a steadily growing power during the remaining sixteen years of his life. The writer of the Continuation of his Life says that—

> "When he was at leisure from writing and teaching he often came up to London, and there went among the congregations of the Nonconformists, and used his talent to the great good-liking of his hearers; and even some to whom he had been misrepresented, upon the account of his education, were convinced of his worth and knowledge in sacred things, as perceiving him to be a man of sound judgment, delivering himself plainly and powerfully; insomuch that many who came as mere spectators for novelty's sake, rather than to be edified and improved, went away well satisfied with what they heard, and wondered, as the Jews did at the Apostles, viz.: whence this man should have these things."

Among Bunyan's earliest London acquaintances, of course, was his Bedfordshire neighbour of other days, George Cokayn,* the ejected minister of Soper Lane, and now the pastor of the congregation in Red Cross Street. Bunyan was also, as we know, on intimate terms of friendship with Dr. John Owen, who took every opportunity of hearing him preach, telling King Charles that he would willingly exchange his learning for the tinker's power of touching men's hearts. To the pulpits and congrega-

* *Vide* Chap. xi.

[1] Ashmolean Collection. G. 12.

tions of these well-known London preachers, as well as to those of others, he had frequent access during his visits to the city. His sermon on *The Greatness of the Soul,* published in 1683, is described on the title-page as "First preached in Pinners' Hall."* That is in one of those halls of the city companies which were so largely used by the early Nonconformist congregations before they had buildings of their own. Of the Dissenters' Meeting Houses, indeed, Pinners' Hall, Girdlers' Hall, and Salters' Hall ranked among the foremost. The first of these—the one in which Bunyan preached—was situated in Pinners' Hall Court, Old Broad Street, and was a spacious building, having on three sides of the Hall two tiers of galleries. It was here that, as early as 1672, there was established the Merchants' Lecture which, with some migration of place, has come down to our own times, the first six preachers of the Lecture being Bates, Manton, Owen, Baxter, Collins, and Jenkyn, all of them names illustrious in the annals of Nonconformity. The pastor of the regular congregation was Richard Wavel, the son of a Royalist major in the Isle of Wight, and a preacher who, like Bunyan himself, was only too familiar with the inside of gaols and the other rough experiences of those stormy times. It is told of him, that when there came some fresh outburst of persecution, he exhorted his people to constancy, assuring them that, if they would venture their purses, he would venture his person; and when urged to counsels of prudence for his children's sake, he quietly replied, "My children will never want: their Heavenly Father will provide what is necessary; and what is more than necessary is hurtful."

* *Vide* Chap. xvi.

The people formed under a strenuous ministry like this were those who first heard Bunyan's sermon on the greatness of the soul, in Pinners' Hall. It may be, indeed, that it was preached as one of the series of the Merchants' Lecture itself, and in that case the ordinary congregation would be reinforced by many Nonconformist citizens from far and near. For the lecture was already a great institution and a rallying point of the most intelligent of the London Dissenters, helping to create that larger knowledge of the great questions of the religious life which even Bishop Burnet, with commendable candour, tells us was a special characteristic of the Dissenters of his day.

We may well suppose that Bunyan's heart-stirring power as

a preacher, and his growing fame as a writer ever since his 'Pilgrim' surprised and enchanted the world, led to his being lionised not a little in the leading circles of Nonconformist influence in the city. As with the Ayrshire ploughman of a century later, there were men of high social standing, and fair women of gentle birth, who regarded with interest and welcomed with hospitality the wonderful Bedfordshire tinker, whose visions opened a new world to them, and whose preaching came like a fresh breeze from the mountains. In the congregation of his friend John Owen, in White's Alley, Moorfields, to which Bunyan sometimes preached, there were to be found such people as Lord Charles Fleetwood; Sir John Hartop and his lady; Oliver Cromwell's brother-in-law, Colonel Desborough; and the great Protector's granddaughter, Mrs. Bendish, so like him both in face and character. There were also Sir Thomas Overbury, Lady Abney, Lady Vere Wilkinson, and the Countess of Anglesey, besides eminent city merchants and people of consideration living in some of the many 'fair houses' of which Stow tells us as then standing in their own gardens, even in the city itself. Through a misleading reference in *Ellis's Correspondence* the fact also has been preserved that Bunyan stood in some sort of close friendly relation with the Lord Mayor of the time, Sir John Shorter. The passage runs thus: "Few days before died Bunian, his lordship's teacher or chaplain; a man said to be gifted in that way though once a cobler."[1] Of course, the Bedfordshire pastor never was chaplain to the Lord Mayor;* but Sir John may well have attended some one of the Nonconformist places of worship in which Bunyan preached, and a friendship honourable to both have sprung up between them. Some of the few personal relics of the great dreamer which have come down to us through his family were probably the gifts of some of these city friends, possibly even of Sir John Shorter himself—the little cabinet, with curious inlaid work on door and drawers; and the staff of the old pilgrim, a Manilla cane with handsome ivory handle inlaid with silver circlets wrought by the cunning hand of an Indian workman, each alternate circlet having a setting of malachite for its centre. Be that as it may, some of these London hearers seemed disposed to show kindness to Bunyan's children for Bunyan's sake, one of

* *Vide* Addendum.

[1] *Ellis's Correspondence,* ii., 161. Edited by the Hon. G. Agar Ellis. London: 1829. In the MSS. of the Trinity House Corporation, Sir John Shorter is described as a "Merchant and owner of shipping." Nov. 23, 1678.

JOHN BUNYAN'S CABINET.

(Preserved at the Bunyan Meeting, Bedford.)
Photo: G. A. Gearey, Bedford.]

them offering to take his son Joseph to his business, without premium or fee, a kindly offer which, however, was frustrated by Bunyan's own scrupulous feeling, which led him to say that God sent him not to advance his family but to preach the Gospel; an instance of other-worldliness perhaps more consistent with the honour of the father than with the prosperity of the son.

But if Bunyan may have occasionally mingled with some of the great people of the City and had personal friends among them, we may be sure that his heart was even more entirely with the great body of godly people who gathered about him in the various assemblies of the time. As to his reception among these, we have distinct testimony from his friend and admirer, Charles Doe, the comb-maker, whose shop was close to London Bridge on the Southwark side. Doe was a good, earnest, simple soul, who came to know Bunyan during the last three years of his life through hearing him preach, who followed him as Boswell followed Johnson, and did much after his death to preserve his books for the generations to come. Speaking of the storm which burst forth afresh against the Nonconformists in 1685—6, Doe says:

"It was at this time of persecution I heard that Mr. Bunyan came to London sometimes and preached; and because of his fame, and I having read some of his books, I had a mind to hear him. And accordingly I did at Mr. More's meeting in a private house; and his text was, 'The fears of the wicked shall come upon him, but the desires of the righteous shall be granted.[1] But I was offended at the text, because not a New Testament one, for then I was very jealous of being cheated by men's sophisticating of Scripture to serve their turn or opinion, I being then come into New Testament light in the love of God and the promises, having had enough for the present of the historical and doing for favour in the Old Testament. But Mr. Bunyan went on, and preached so New Testament-like that he made me admire, and weep for joy, and give him my affections. And he was the first man that ever I heard preach to my unenlightened understanding and experience, for methought all his sermons were adapted to my condition, and had apt similitudes, being full of the love of God and the manner of its secret working upon the soul, and of the soul under the sense of it, that I could weep for joy most part of his sermons; and so, by a letter, I introduced myself into his acquaintance, and, indeed,

[1] This sermon, expanded for publication, was found among Bunyan's **MSS.** at his death, and included in the folio edition of his works of 1692. It is entitled *The Desires of the Righteous granted.*

I have not since met with a man I have liked so well. I was acquainted with him but about three years before he died, and then missed him sorely."[1]

The days to which Doe thus refers when the meetings were held in a private house were days of stealth, but they were followed by the freer days brought in by King James's Indulgence, with their larger liberty of prophesying and crowds of hearers. It is to these later days of 1687—8 that Doe makes reference when he says:

"When Mr. Bunyan preached in London, if there were but one day's notice given, there would be more people come together to hear him preach than the meeting-house could hold. I have seen to hear him preach, by my computation, about twelve hundred at a morning lecture by seven o'clock on a working day, in the dark winter-time. I also computed about three thousand that came to hear him one Lord's Day at London, at a town's-end meeting-house, so that half were fain to go back again for want of room, and then himself was fain at a back-door to be pulled almost over people to get upstairs to his pulpit."[2]

It has been said that this town's-end meeting-house was the one in Zoar Street, Southwark, on or near the site of the Globe Theatre of Shakespearian fame.* Bunyan may have preached at this place at an occasional service or two, but he could not as frequently have gathered the people here as is sometimes supposed, for the simple reason that this meeting-house was only opened for worship some six months before his death, and that for Presbyterian use.[3]

* *Vide* Addendum.

With all this marvellous influence in the city, which was the centre of his nation's life, it seems remarkable that Bunyan was never prevailed upon to leave the country-town where he had laboured so long for the larger field of service which seemed open to him there. That overtures were made to him to this end is tolerably certain from the hint that Doe throws out that "he was not a man that preached by way of bargain for money, for he hath refused a more plentiful income to keep his station." To all such overtures there was but one reply, that of the Shunamite, "I dwell among mine own people." He was too deeply rooted in the scene of his lifelong labours and sufferings lightly to think of striking his tent, till the command came from the

[1] *Experiences of Charles Doe.* London: 1700.
[2] *The Struggler.* By Charles Doe. 1692.
[3] Wilson's *Dissenting Churches of London,* iv. 188.

Master to come up to the higher service for which he had been ripening so long.

Thus he was no stranger to the city to which he was setting out once more in the month of August, 1688. His route on this occasion was more than usually circuitous. Setting forth on horseback, he first made a journey westward to the town of Reading, where also he seems to have been widely known. There is no mention of his previous connection with the town in his own writings or by his contemporaries, but there are traditions among the townspeople that in the garb of a carter, whip in hand, he came thither, in the days of persecution, to preach. It is said that the place of meeting was in a side lane and that from the back door the people had access to a bridge over a branch of the river Kennett, by the kindly aid of which, on the giving of alarm, they were able to escape.* On this last occasion on which he journeyed thither there was no peril and therefore no need for disguise. His errand this time was two-fold, to preach the gospel, of course, but also and mainly to be a peacemaker, if he might: "For it so falling out, that a young gentleman, a neighbour of Mr. Bunyan, happening into the displeasure of his father and being much troubled in mind upon that account, as also for that he had heard his father proposed to disinherit him, or otherwise deprive him of what he had to leave, he pitched upon Mr. Bunyan as a fit man to make way for his submission and prepare his father's mind to receive him; and he, as willing to do any good office as it could be requested, as readily undertook it." His errand was successfully accomplished: "He used such pressing arguments and reasons against anger and passion, as also for love and reconciliation, that the father was mollified, and his bowels yearned towards his returning son."

* *Vide* Addendum.

Having thus made three hearts glad, his own as well as those of the estranged father and son, Bunyan set forth towards London, carrying with him his MS. on *The Excellency of a Broken Heart*. This journey of some forty miles turned out to be a dreary ride through driving rain, at the end of which he found himself drenched and weary at the house of one who is described by Charles Doe as his very loving friend, John Strudwick. Strudwick was a much younger man than Bunyan, being at this time about thirty-four. He lived in a simple four-storeyed building with gable and overhanging chambers on Snow Hill, there carrying on the business of a grocer under the Sign of the Star.* In an old church roll of Hare Court, whither the congregation of Red Cross Street under George Cokayn had migrated, we find that in 1692, the deacons were Brother John Strudwick and Brother Robert Andrews.[1] It was, no doubt, through this connection of his with the church over which their mutual friend presided that Bunyan and he came to know each other. It would be about the middle of August that he gave welcome to his honoured guest, for on the 19th of that month Bunyan was preaching at Mr. Gamman's meeting,† near Whitechapel, what proved to be his last sermon. It was on the text John i., 13, and was shortly afterwards printed, not from any MS. of the preacher's, but from the notes of some hearer who was present. According to this report there was one passage in this sermon which was indeed the fitting close to the ministry of a man so catholic and large-hearted as we know this preacher was. "Dost thou," said he, "see a soul that has the image of God in him? Love him, love him: say, This man and I must go to heaven one day; serve one another, do good for one another; and if any wrong you, pray to God to right you, and love the brotherhood." If we may trust this report, and there is no reason why we should not, the last words that John Bunyan ever uttered from the pulpit were words that nobly expressed the spirit of his own life. They were these: "Be ye holy in all manner of conversation. Consider that the holy God is your Father, and let this oblige you to live like the children of God, that you may look your Father in the face with comfort another day."

This was twelve days before his death. In the interval between his arrival at John Strudwick's house and the appearance of dangerous symptoms in his disease, he was sending through the press the early sheets of his latest book, *The Acceptable Sacrifice,*‡[2] showing the excellency of a broken heart, and the nature, signs, and proper effects of a contrite spirit. In this discourse upon a verse in David's great penitential Psalm (li., 17), he speaks not from hearsay, but from deepest experience when he says:

"The broken heart is hard to bear, for soul-pain is the sorest pain.

* *Vide* Addendum.

† In the *Lay Subsidies* in the Record Office is an entry: "Stepney: John Gammon, Four Hearths"; and the British Museum Library contains a volume by John Gammon—*Christ and a Christian Life*: A Practical Discourse. 8vo. 2s. 6d. There is an advertisement stating that it was first published in 1691. It seems probable that these both refer to John Bunyan's friend at Whitechapel.

‡ *The Acceptable Sacrifice; Or,* the Excellency of a Broken Heart: shewing the Nature, Signs, and Proper Effects of a Contrite Spirit. (Being the Last Works of that Eminent Preacher, and Faithful Minister of Jesus Christ, Mr. JOHN BUNYAN.) With a preface prefixed thereunto by an eminent Minister of the Gospel in London. (George Cokayn, dated Sept. 21, 1688.) London . . . George Larkin . . . 1689.

[1] *The Story of Hare Court.* By J. B. Marsh. [*Vide* Addendum.]

[2] *Yr Aberth Cymmeradwy.* Caerfyrddin: 1767. 12mo.

With such a man God has wrestled and given him a fall, and now he crouches and cringes and craves for mercy. Like one with a broken limb who so far from hectoring it with a man is afraid lest even a child should touch him, so he begs of God to deal with him with tender hands. Once being at an honest woman's house, I, after some pause, asked her how she did; very badly, was her reply—I am afraid I shall not be saved. Breaking out with heavy heart she said, 'Ah Goodman Bunyan! Christ and a pitcher; if I had Christ though I went and begged my bread with a pitcher, it would be better with me than I think it is now.' This woman had her heart broken, she wanted Christ. This cry of Christ and a pitcher made a melodious noise in the ears of the very angels. At first our pride is laid low. If a man be proud of his strength or manhood, a broken leg will maul him; and if a man be proud of his goodness a broken heart will maul him. Yet a broken heart or a contrite spirit is a heaven-sent blessing. If thou hast it God is giving thee what himself is pleased with; he has given thee a cabinet to hold his grace in, he has given thee a heart that can heartily desire his salvation, an heart after his own heart, that is, such as suits his mind. True it is painful now, sorrowful now, penitent now, grieved now; now it is broken, now it bleeds, now, now it sobs, now it sighs, now it mourns and crieth unto God. Well, very well; all this is because he hath a mind to make thee laugh; he has made thee sorry on earth that thou mightest rejoice in heaven. Covet a broken heart, prize a contrite spirit: I say, covet it now, now the white flag is hung out, now the golden sceptre of grace is held forth to you. It is wounding work, of course, this breaking of the hearts, but without wounding there is no saving. Conversion is not the smooth, easy-going process some men seem to think it, otherwise man's heart would never have been compared to fallow ground and God's word to a plough. The fallow ground must be ploughed and ploughed, and even after that be soundly harrowed, else there will be but slender harvest. To the same purport is that other analogy of grafting, for where there is grafting there is a cutting, the scion must be let in with a wound; to stick on to the outside or to tie it on with a string would be of no use. Heart must be set to heart and back to back, or there will be no sap from root to branch, and this, I say, must be done by a wound. Men are too lofty, too proud, too wild, too devilishly resolved in the ways of their own destruction. Nothing will hinder them from ruining their own precious and immortal souls but the breaking of their hearts."

Thus, as this book shows, there was a firm grip about this man's words to the last. Before the whole of the sheets were through the press, however, he himself was through the gates of the celestial city. Overtaken by heavy rains and drenched to the skin during his recent ride from Reading, he that day received his death-blow. He was no longer in the vigour of life; at any time he was far from strong. In earlier years he was thought to have narrowly escaped consumption, and later his constitution must have suffered from the unnatural conditions of prison life. His friend tells us that though he was only sixty he was worn out with sufferings, age, and often teaching. On the Tuesday after the Sunday he preached in Whitechapel, he was seized with what has been variously described as a violent fever and as the sweating distemper, which ran its course for the next ten days. All that skill and love could do to arrest the mischief at work was doubtless done, but done in vain. This is all we know. Whether Elizabeth Bunyan or any of his children received the news of his illness in time to reach him and receive his beckoning of farewell before departure, we know not. Possibly not. For at first there would be no special alarm; and then, as fears grew graver, it would take two days to send tidings and two days more to reach him. One who was there, probably Strudwick's pastor and Bunyan's friend, George Cokayn, tells us that he bore his sufferings "with much constancy and patience; and expressed himself as if he desired nothing more than to be dissolved and to be with Christ, in that case esteeming death as gain, and life only a tedious delaying of felicity expected; and finding his vital strength decay, having settled his mind and affairs, as well as the shortness of his time and the violence of his disease would admit, with a constant and Christian patience, he resigned his soul into the hands of his most merciful Redeemer, following his pilgrim from the City of Destruction to the New Jerusalem; his better part having been all along there, in holy contemplation, pantings, and breathings after the hidden manna and water of life."

It was on Friday, August 31st, 1688, that Bunyan passed away, and the sorrowful tidings would reach his bereaved Church at Bedford about the time they were gathering for their Sunday services. The following entry in the Church Book throws some light on their feelings at this time of parting:

"Wednesday 4th of September was kept in prayre and humilyation for this Heavy Stroak upon us, ye Death of deare Brother Bunyan. Apoynted also that Wednesday next be kept in praire and humiliation on the same Account."

At this second meeting on the 11th it was determined to spend that day week also in the same sorrowful way:

"Apoynted that all y^e^ Brethren meet together on the 18th of this

HOUSE IN WHICH BUNYAN DIED.
(August 31st, 1688.)

From the original at the Bunyan Museum, Bedford.]

month Sept[r]., to Humble themselves for this Heavy hand of God upon us. And also to pray unto ye Lord for Counsell and Direction what to do in order to seek out for A fitt person to make choyce of for an Elder." "Tuesday ye 18th was the whole congregation mett to Humble themselves before God by ffasting and prayre for his Hevy and Sevear Stroak upon us in takeing away our Honoured Brother Bunyan by death."

The orchard round the place of meeting where Bunyan preached in Bedford, had, since 1681, been used as a place for the burial of their dead. Curiously enough there are the following three entries and no more relating to this place, where we should least expect to find them, in the parish register of St. Paul's Church :[1]

"1681. Buried Elizabeth, dau. of John Herring, at the Meeting Barne, Nov. 11th.

"1681. Buried John Sewster, at the Meeting Barne, Nov. 13.

"Buried Samuel Fenn ye elder, att ye Meeting Barne, Nov. ye 14th."

This last entry relates to Bunyan's predecessor and former colleague in the ministry at Bedford; and, in the ordinary course, Bunyan would probably have been laid beside him; but, dying as he did in London, the removal of his body to the scene of his ministry would, in those days, have entailed a journey too long and too costly to be thought of. Therefore, after, no doubt, many a brotherly reference to his departure, in the

[1] In the same year Bunyan began to keep a record of the deaths of the members of the Church. Only one leaf remains, which contains the names of all who died between November 10th, 1681, and March 21st, 1688. After this another register commenced which seems to have been lost. The entries in Bunyan's handwriting usually record simply name and date, but the fellowing are expressive of special regard:

"Upon the tenth of November, '81, our aged and honoured Brother, John Sewster, departed this life.
"Upon the twelfth of November, '81, our honoured brother, Samuel ffenn, one of the Elders of this Congregation, departed this life.
"Upon the twenty-seventh of November, '81, our sister Bunyan, in the parish of Northill, departed this life.
"1682. Upon the 3rd day of August our honoured sister, Joan Coveington, departed this life."

There are also further entries relating to "our honoured sister Hill," "our much beloved sister Sansom," "our aged brother Edw. Coventon," "our beloved sister Fenn," and, in another hand, to "our Honoured Brother Olyver Scott, one of ye preachers of this congregation," who died April 21, 1687. The sister Bunyan, whose death Bunyan records, was the wife of his brother Thomas. In the register of the parish of Northill, where he lived, there are the following entries relating to Thomas's son John, his wife, and himself. These names occur among the affidavits relating to those buried in Woollen:

"Buried John Bynian, Sept. 3, 1679.
Elizabeth Bynian, Nov. 29, 1681.
Thomas Bunnian, dyed Jan. 5, 1695."

As there are no other entries relating to the Bunyans of Northill, it is probable that by the death of his only son, Thomas Bunyan's family became extinct.

Sunday gatherings of the congregations to whom his face was known so well, all that was mortal of him was, on the Monday, reverently laid in John Strudwick's vault in Bunhill Fields.

Following Southey, many writers have called this place of burial the *Campo Santo* of the Dissenters. This it was; but it was by no means confined to them. Many Roman Catholics were buried here, so were members of the National Church. The site was originally part of a famous fen or moor, described, in early times, as watering the walls of London on the north, Moorfields and Fensbury or Finsbury Fields, preserving the remembrance in the name. In the sixteenth century there appertained to the manor of Finsbury Farm, three great fields known as Bonhill, the Mallow, and the High Field, "where the three windmills stand." The Bonhill field was consecrated as early as 1549, for the purpose of receiving the vast quantities of human remains which were removed that year from the charnel house of St. Paul's. In 1665 it was used as a place of burial for those who died of the Great Plague, and was then, in an inscription placed over the wastern gate, described as a churchyard. After that it was enclosed by a brick wall at the sole charge of the City, and that it was regarded as a consecrated place of sepulture in shown by the fact that two years before Bunyan's death a funeral was celebrated there in which Tillotson, then dean, and Stillingfleet, one of the canons of St. .Paul's, took part; and that subsequently a clergyman of the Church was appointed as chaplain. Still, as being a burial-ground separate from any ecclesiastical building, it was the one most frequently made use of by the Nonconformists. Of these Dr. Thomas Goodwin, who was with Cromwell on his death-bed, and who died in 1679, was the first person of eminence among those buried there; he was followed in 1683 by John Owen, and five years later by John Bunyan. Among other names recorded here and memorable in the annals of Nonconformity are those of Watts and Williams and the mother of the Wesleys, Neal and Morrice and Bradbury, Doolittle and Vincent and Gale, with a long succession of others who did their work and made their mark in the eighteenth century. There are also other names celebrated in other ways—those of Ritson the antiquary, and Blake the painter, of Hardy and Horne Tooke, of Nathaniel Lardner and Abraham Rees. Nor must we pass by that of Thomas Stothard, the painter.* He is, perhaps, most widely

* Born 1755; died 1834. *Vide* Mrs. Bray's *Life of Thomas Stothard.*

known by his picture of the *Canterbury Pilgrims,* but there are not a few who think that some of his best work is to be found in his illustrations to the two most popular of English books, *The Pilgrim's Progress* and *Robinson Crusoe.* It is fitting, therefore, that here he should lie, as he does, side by side with the writers of the books themselves, his dust mingling with that of John Bunyan and Daniel Defoe.

There is no entry in the register of Bunyan's burial, and when Curll published his Bunhill Fields Inscription in 1717, or Strype his edition of Stowe in 1720, there was no record of his name on the grave. In 1737 John Strudwick's son-in-law, the Rev. Robert Bragge, was buried in the same vault, and it was then, probably, that for the first time the names of the dead within were inscribed upon the tablet without. A contributor to *Notes and Queries* for 1864, who signed himself H. J. S., writes: "I have just discovered, in the handwriting of Dr. Richard Rawlinson, LL.D., a copy of the inscription which formerly existed on the tomb in which was interred the author of *The Pilgrim's Progress*:

"Here lyes the body of Mr. John Bunyan, Author of the 'Pilgrim's Progress,' aged 59, who dyed Aug. 17, 1688.

"Here lies the body of Mr. John Strudwick, aged 43 years, who dyed the 15th day of Jan. 1697.

"Also the body of Mrs. Phœbe Bragge, who died the 15th July, 1718.

"Here also lies the body of the Rev. Rob. Bragge, Minister of the Gospel, who departed this life Feb. 12, 1737, Ætatis 72."

It will be seen that the date of Bunyan's death, thus given, is August 17th, while the writer of the continuation of the *Grace Abounding* gives it as August 12th. As Bunyan preached his last sermon on the 19th of August and was seriously ill for ten days before his death, these dates are evidently from memory and manifestly wrong. The date given by Charles Doe is the 31st of August, and as the sorrowful meeting of the Bedford Church was held on the 4th September and would naturally follow immediately upon the receipt of the tidings of his death, this date is undoubtedly correct.

The vault in which Bunyan was laid would appear to have been a new sepulchre at the time it was opened for him, and was then probably first purchased by John Strudwick for his honoured guest. For though eventually eleven persons altogether were buried there, the dates of the burial of the rest were all subsequent to 1688.[1] No writer of the time, not even Charles Doe, who would almost certainly be present, has given us any account of the funeral of the great Englishman who was thus laid to rest in the sepulchre of another, far away from his family and the Church he had served so long. Possessed of more than national fame as author, preacher, and confessor of the truth, he would probably receive more than usual demonstration of respect and affection as he was borne to his resting place, the procession passing from Snow Hill and through the midst of the pleasant gardens which lay between Aldersgate and Bunhill Fields. This would have been in accordance with the custom of the time. Unusual demonstrations were sometimes made at the burial of illustrious Nonconformists even in those days of trial. Men of rank, who had still a secret love for "the good old cause," came forth on such occasions to manifest the regard they felt. When, for instance, John Owen was buried in Bunhill Fields, the procession from St. James's, whither the body had been brought from Ealing, was attended by the carriages of sixty-seven noblemen and gentlemen, besides many mourning coaches and persons on horseback. So, again, in the case of William Jenkyn, another of the lecturers at Pinners' Hall.* Though dying as a prisoner in Newgate in 1685, he was buried with the greatest honours in Bunhill Fields, his remains being followed thither by his friends in a hundred and fifty coaches. And though no demonstration so imposing as this has been recorded of the great Dreamer, yet his literary renown and his great reputation in the City as a preacher would doubtless gather great numbers to the sorrowful scene. As George Cokayn, who, as Bunyan's lifelong friend and John Strudwick's pastor, would almost certainly conduct the funeral service, tells us: "He was removed to the great loss and unspeakable grief of many precious souls." And some of them, no doubt, were there to express their grief and show their regard. But while many were there, one well-known and powerful friend was absent. For that day

* Pinners' Hall in Old Broad Street, was built by the Pin-makers' or Pinners' Company, in 1636. The guild languished, and let the hall (*cir.* 1662) to a Society of Independents. In 1672 the Merchants' Lecture was instituted, when prominent divines preached on Tuesday mornings. The hall was remodelled in 1677, and pulled down in 1692. (*Vide—Lives of British Hymn Writers,* by Thomas Wright, 1914.

[1] The tomb was numbered E. and W. 25, 26—N. and S. 26, 27. The persons buried there were—John Bunyan, John Strudwick, Phœbe Bragge, Robert Bragge, Theophilus Bragge, Anne Jennion, Sarah Poole, Anne Holyhead, Elizabeth Jennings, John Long, Ensign Joseph Jennings Poole.—*Bunhill Memorials.* By T. A. Jones, 1849. [*Vide—Bunhill Fields.* By A. W. Light. London, 1913.]

JOHN BUNYAN'S TOMB
in Bunhill Fields, London.

the Lord Mayor, Sir John Shorter, was himself a dying man. On the previous Thursday he was thrown from his horse, near Newgate, when on his return from proclaiming according to custom Bartholomew Fair, and was picked up, fatally injured, some three minutes' walk from John Strudwick's house, where at that very time Bunyan lay dying. The sad news of this calamity which had overtaken his friend was probably the last piece of intelligence which reached the departing Pilgrim in this world. On the Tuesday after that Friday on which Bunyan went home to be with God, Sir John followed him across the river.*

* *Vide* Addendum.

The loss of two such men at one stroke was great. The times were anxious. During those very days the Nonconformists were eagerly looking for tidings, from across the seas, of the Prince of Orange. It was the 3rd September; on the 21st George Cokayn,† sending forth the unfinished book Bunyan had left in his charge, wrote thus in the preface:

† "One cold winter night, November 21st, 1691," the Rev. George Cokayn, B.D., passed to his rest, aged 72. He was buried at Bunhill Fields.

"Who knows what will become of the ark of God! Therefore it is a seasonable duty with old Eli to sit trembling for it. Do we not also hear the sound of the trumpet, the alarm of wars? Mercy and judgment seem to be struggling in the same womb of Providence, and which will come out first we know not."

Such was the feeling of that eventful time, such the anxieties added to the sorrows of parting. Many of those standing round that open grave in Bunhill Fields had come through rough and stormy experiences of bonds and imprisonment, as had the brother beloved whom they were laying to rest. Even yet they knew not but that the storm might still burst forth afresh as it had so many times before. His deliverance had come—not from the Prince across the seas, but from the King of kings. And theirs—was it near or far off? Nearer than they thought. The sixty eventful years between John Bunyan's birth in 1628 and his death in 1688—that is, between the Petition of Right and the Great Revolution—were reaching their end. A new era was dawning even while they were fearing—an era of liberty. Not many days now, and the last Stuart King would have fled, and religious intolerance, if not dead—for it dies hard—should yet have received such reeling blow as to make the return of such times to England as had been, a thing no bigot need hope for, no lover of freedom need fear.

ADDENDA—Chapter XVI.

(Page 368.)

Sir John Shorter.

In his book, *Southwark Cathedral*: *Its History and Antiquities* (London: Simpkin, Marshall & Co., 1910), Canon Thompson, M.A., D.D., says, p. 229: "Sir John Shorter, Lord Mayor of London, who lies buried in our Ladye Chapel, is said to have so much valued the ministrations of Bunyan, and bestowed so much friendship upon him, that he was looked upon as his lordship's chaplain (unofficially, of course)."

In answer to a question sent to the Mansion House, London, Mr. J. L. Douthwaite, Librarian of the Guildhall (to whom the communication was handed) replied as follows: "There are no official references in support of the statement that Bunyan acted as Chaplain to Sir John Shorter during his mayoralty. The story of the latter's active interest in Nonconformity is recorded in the official journals; I think that if there were any truth in the statement [*i.e.*, from *Ellis's Correspondence*] confirmation of it would be recorded."

There is an entry in the Ancient Church Register of Southwark which states: "Sir John Shorter, Knight, in the Ladye Chapel." He was Sheriff in 1675, and Lord Mayor in 1687, and was a goldsmith.

(Page 370.)

Zoar Street Chapel, Southwark.

"The meeting-house (we learn from Manning and Bray) belonged to Dr. Thomas Barlow, Bishop of Lincoln, who permitted Bunyan, as the friend of his old pupil, Dr. John Owen, to discourse there."—*Vide* Williams, Vol. 2, p. 1047.

Canon Thompson quotes Concannon and Morgan, who say in their record of St. Saviour's (Southwark Cathedral) in 1795, that Barlow had some control over the chapel in Zoar Street; and by his permission Bunyan was allowed to preach there when visiting London. There is no trace of the building left.

"The chapel in Zoar Street, Gravel Lane, Southwark, so usually connected with Bunyan's name, is, in reality, less so than believed. It is stated in *Londini Illustrata,* that the ground on which the chapel was built was not leased out for that purpose until 1687. Bunyan could not, therefore, have preached in it, except on the occasion of his last visit to London."—(*The Hallowed Spots of Ancient London.* By Eliza Meteyard. London, 1862.)

The pulpit, said to have belonged to Zoar Street Chapel, and from which Bunyan preached, belonged for many years to the Sunday School Union, and stood in their premises in the Old Bailey, London. It has been recently handed over to the Bunyan Meeting Trustees, at Bedford.

In *Bygone Southwark* (by Mrs. E. Boger, 1895), it is stated: "Bunyan's connection with the Borough, though slight, must not be passed over. He often preached in Zoar Street, a small alley not far removed from the place where Mr. Spurgeon preached in Park Street, just 30 years ago, and to crowds as vast."

(Page 371.)

Bunyan at Reading.

"Our records are, unfortunately, blank from 1684 to 1692," writes Pastor C. A. Davis,* "and so we miss the record of Bunyan's visit, which would have been of intense interest." Although this portion of the Church Book is lost, it is fortunately known, by apparently well-established tradition, that Bunyan was in Reading on Wednesday and/or Thursday, August 15th and/or 16th, 1688, and that he preached there. At that time the congregation met in a large boat-house on the bank of the river Kennett, "not far from the Bear Inn," near Pigney Lane. The pastor from 1678 to 1695 was John Rance, and the two men must have discussed the subject of Bunyan's visit: the reconciliation of the son at Bedford and his father at Reading.

* *A History of the Baptist Church,* King's Road, Reading. By C. A. Davis, 1891.

(Page 372.)

John Strudwick.

The Trustees of the Bunyan Meeting Museum hold an exceedingly interesting relic of this man, whose name is handed down to posterity with that of John Bunyan. It consists of a part of a bill-head made out, assumably, in Strudwick's handwriting, and reads: "*London. Lord James Radcliffe. Bought of JOHN*

STRUDWICK at the sign of THE STAR, Holborne Bridge, GROCER CHANDLER."

Strudwick's house, the Sign of the Star, is thought to have stood "directly under the eastern pier of the viaduct" at Holborn, on Snow Hill which, in the seventeenth century, was "a circuitous highway between Holborn Bridge and Newgate, very narrow, very steep, and very dangerous. Pink, in his *History of Clerkenwell,* believes that the house in which Bunyan died must have been removed when Skinner Street was formed, in 1802, if it existed so long as that. Skinner Street ran by the south side of St. Sepulchre's Church, but was itself wiped out of existence when Holborn Viaduct was built." (*Vide* Laurence Hutton's *Literary Landmarks of London,* 1889.)

Strudwick survived his friend Bunyan less than ten years, and was buried in the same grave at Bunhill Fields, the inscription over which announced: "Here lyes the Body of John Strudwick, aged 43 years, who dyed the 15th day of Jan. 1697."

From the records of Hare Court Church, of which Strudwick was a deacon, it is gleaned that his name appears for the last time (as a deacon) in September, 1697. From that date he may possibly have been ill, for he was certainly alive in December, 1697, when he paid his quarterly contribution of ten pounds in support of the minister. John Strudwick apparently died between the months of December, 1697, and the end of March, 1698. (*Vide* J. B. Marsh's *The Story of Harecourt*).

Strudwick's name appears in the Hitchin Church Book as a subscriber of five pounds to the fund for the building of Tilehouse Street chapel.

In the *Lay Subsidies* (Record Office, London) there is mentioned, in the year 1686, a "Tho: Stradwicke" of Snow Hill, who was assessed as having "viij hearths." This may, possibly, have been John Strudwick's father. The difference in spelling counts for little at that period.

(Page 379.)

Bunhill Fields Tomb.

"When Bunyan's tomb in Bunhill Fields was restored he (Mr. Spurgeon) also spoke at length in City Road Chapel, the afternoon of May 21, 1862, being too wet for anything but the briefest service at the grave," writes the Rev. W. Y. Fullerton, D.D., in *C. H. Spurgeon: A Biography*, (p. 125), in recording the unveiling of the recumbent figure of the Dreamer, so ably designed and executed by E. C. Papworth.

After sixty years of exposure to weather and other processes of deterioration, the tomb and sculptured form of Bunyan were restored, and the unveiling once more took place, and again in inclement weather.

"The Re-dedication of this tomb after recent repairs will take place on the 10th November, 1922." So ran the preliminary notice of the proceedings which drew a considerable number of lovers of Bunyan to the Wesley Chapel, where the platform was occupied by Mr. Pomeroy, who presided, Rev. Dr. Horton (representing the Congregational Union of England and Wales), who offered prayer; Rev. J. C. Carlile, C.B.E., D.D., of the Baptist Union, who gave an address. The Rev. Leonard Brooks (of the Bunyan Meeting, Bedford) read a portion of Scripture; Mrs. John Brown, the widow of the Rev. Dr. Brown, unveiled the memorial, and the Rev. J. M. Blackwell, who represented the Presbyterians, pronounced the Benediction. Dr. Carlile, in the course of his address, said: "John Bunyan remains one of the few supreme master craftsmen of English speech. He took the common clay of our language and shaped it into a thing of beauty and a joy for ever. His sentences were as clear as crystals, beautiful as pearls, and vital as blood. . . . No anthology of English prose or literature of the world is adequate unless it gives a place to the author of *The Pilgrim's Progress* and *The Holy War*. . . . Tribute has been paid to Bunyan's genius; yet in an age that seldom acknowledges the greatness and grandeur of the past, and too often professes to find nothing in its ancestry but an excuse for the present-day vices, Bunyan may again be reclaimed. He was ever Valiant for the Truth, and never Ready to Halt in the quest for the Palace Beautiful. No Mr. Facing-both-ways was he, but a Greatheart defending the City of Mansoul, a moral leader as well as a master weaver of words; a novelist surprisingly subtle in character study, rich in incident, and prodigal in his plots. In his best work he ranks with the greatest writers the world has known. Bunyan's crown will not tarnish. His fame will not fade." Mrs. John Brown recalled that her husband spent the whole of his leisure for very many years of his life in searching for the materials for Bunyan's biography. "It is fitting," she added, "that there should be a memorial in this busy district of London to remind passers-by that they also may be pilgrims on the way to the Celestial City."

The London daily papers devoted space to record this event, and several of them illustrated the ceremony. A notable report was that of *The Daily Telegraph,* whose tribute to Bunyan, on the following morning, November 11th, may well be included here; for of Bunyan it says: "In the centuries that have elapsed since his death he has 'lit a candle' that gives light and leading to millions of English men and women who still seek to follow his humble teaching. . . . We hear now and then of some modern book with a phenomenal sale, but the sale of the Bible and of *The Pilgrim's Progress* still far and away exceeds them all, not only in numbers, but in the love and influence they have wherever white men build their cities or stake their camps. Bunyan's tomb to-day is one of our national shrines."

XVII.

BUNYAN'S DESCENDANTS AND SUCCESSORS.

BUNYAN was two months short of completing his sixtieth year when he was unexpectedly called away from his life of active service to the Church. He was not an old man, therefore, counting by years, though somewhat worn and beaten by the storms of time. Three contemporary portraits of him, taken in later life, remain to us—an oil picture by Sadler of 1685, the engraving by Sturt of 1692, and the pencil sketch by Robert White, on which were based his engraved portraits of 1679 and 1682.*

* *Vide* **Addendum**

The painting of 1685 by Sadler was, so far as we know, first engraved by Simpson in 1767. This engraving was in the heaviest possible style, and formed the frontispiece to the folio edition of Bunyan's works, published by Johnston, with a preface by George Whitefield. About 1780, also, this portrait was reproduced in mezzotint by Richard Houston, and published by Carington Bowles, the well-known print-seller of St. Paul's Churchyard. Three years later it was admirably engraved in small oval by T. E. Haid, and subsequently also by Spilsbury. On the engraving by Simpson it is stated that the original painting was then in the possession of Henry Stimson, gent. This is probably the portrait of Bunyan sent to the Loan Exhibition at South Kensington in 1866, by the Rev. John Olive, rector of Ayott, and which is now in the National Portrait Gallery.*

* *Vide* **Addendum**

Sturt's engraving, prefixed to the first folio edition of Bunyan's works, published in 1692, was taken from a painting which, if still in existence, is not known. It is somewhat vigorously executed, but harsh and unpleasing. Other copies from the same plate were also prefixed to the later edition of 1736-7. Charles Doe, describing this engraving in 1692, says of it: "His effigies was cut in copper, from an original paint, done to the life, by his very good friend, a Limner." But who this limner was he does not tell us.

The third portrait of Bunyan, to which reference has been made, was the earliest of all, and probably the most life-like, certainly the most expressive of the three. It is simply a pencil sketch on vellum, by Robert White, and was taken thus preliminary to the engraved sleeping portrait prefixed by him to the third edition of *The Pilgrim's Progress,* published in 1679, and which was, indeed, the first of the many illustrations that book has received. The same sketch also formed the basis of the full-length portrait given with the first edition of *The Holy War* in 1682, and in which Bunyan appears as the typical Mansoul, with Shaddai's army on the one side and the forces of Diabolus on the other. Perhaps no artist ever issued more portraits of his eminent contemporaries than did Robert White, who was at work in this way for more than forty years. Vertue collected the names of no less than two hundred and seventy-five portraits by him, all of which are the prizes of the antiquary and the art-collector. As a mere youth he was remarkable for his power of drawing and etching, and was early placed under the instruction of Loggan, whom he rivalled in the delicacy and correctness of his likenesses. He is described as possessing "a wonderful power to take the air of a face." Before engraving a portrait he usually drew a sketch in pencil from the life, which he did with marvellous rapidity and power. Vertue thought some of these pencil sketches even superior to his prints.[1] The one thus taken of Bunyan, on a strip of vellum—about six inches by four—was fortunately preserved, and fell into the possession of the Rev. Clayton M. Cracherode, who died in 1799, bequeathing his splendid collection to the British Museum, where this portrait of Bunyan may now be seen.

We shall get the best idea of the personal appearance of Bunyan if we take this sketch of White's and read side by side with it that other sketch from the pen of the contemporary we have more than once supposed to be George Cokayn:

> "As for his person, he was tall of stature, strong-boned, though not corpulent, somewhat of a ruddy face, with sparkling eyes, wearing his hair on his upper lip, after the old British fashion; his hair reddish, but in his latter days time had sprinkled it with grey; his nose well set, but not declining or bending, and his mouth moderately large; his forehead something high, and his habit always plain and modest."

[1] Dallaway's *Walpole,* Bohn's Edition. 1849, iii., 947.

In addition to this, John Wilson, who had been his companion and fellow-sufferer for many years, tells us that:

"His countenance was grave and sedate, and did so to the life discover the inward frame of his heart, that it was convincing to the beholders and did strike something of awe into them that had nothing of the fear of God."

Passing from the outer to the inner man, George Cokayn tells us also that:

"He appeared in countenance to be of a stern and rough temper, but in his conversation mild and affable, not given to loquacity or much discourse in company, unless some urgent occasion required it; observing never to boast of himself or his parts, but rather seem low in his own eyes and submit himself to the judgment of others; to abhoring lying and swearing, being just in all that lay in his power to his word, not seeming to revenge injuries, loving to reconcile differences, and make friendship with all; he had a sharp, quick eye, accomplished with an excellent discerning of persons, being of good judgment and quick wit."

To the portraiture thus given John Wilson adds this:

"Give us leave to say his natural parts and abilities were not mean, his fancy and invention were very pregnant and fertile; his wit was sharp and quick; his memory tenacious, it being customary with him to commit his sermons to writing after he had preached them. His understanding was large and comprehensive, his judgment sound and deep in the fundamentals of the Gospel. A rich anointing of the Spirit was upon him, yet this great saint was always in his own eyes the chiefest of sinners and the least of saints; esteeming any, where he did believe the Truth of Grace, better than himself. He was not only well furnished with the helps and endowments of nature beyond ordinary, but eminent in the graces and gifts of the Spirit and fruits of holiness. He was a true lover of all that love our Lord Jesus and did often bewail the different and distinguishing appellations that are among the godly, saying, he did believe a time would come when they should be all buried. His carriage was condescending, affable and meek to all; yet bold and couragious for Christ's and the gospel's sake. He was much struck at in the late times of persecution and his sufferings were great, under all which he behaved himself like Christ's soldier, being far from any sinful compliance to save himself, but did chearfully bear the cross of Christ. As a minister of Christ he was laborious in his work of preaching, diligent in his preparation for it and faithful in dispensing the word, not sparing reproof for outward circumstances whether in the pulpit or no, yet ready to succour the tempted; a son of consolation to the broken-hearted, yet a son of thunder to secure and dead sinners.

"He was full of zeal and affection at all times (according to knowledge), more especially at his administration of the Lord's supper, it was observable that tears came from his eyes in abundance, from the sense of the sufferings of Christ, that are in that ordinance shadowed forth. As a pastor, also, he was useful by the accuracy of his knowledge in church-discipline, and readiness to put that in practice in the Church (as occasion offered), which he saw was agreeable to the word of God, whether admonition or excommunication, or making up differences or filling up vacancies or paring off excrescencies. And as he was useful to that Church, so to the whole countrey round and to other churches where he did frequently spend his labours.

"His death was, and is much lamented for that reason; as also because it was somewhat sudden, and he from home at that time. His remembrance is sweet and refreshing to many and so will continue: For the righteous shall be had in everlasting remembrance."[1]

It is needless to say that Bunyan left no great store of worldly wealth behind him. For though his books had so large a sale even in his own lifetime, either they were not productive of much material wealth to their author, or we must accept the explanation given by his friend to the effect that "by reason of the many losses he sustained by imprisonment and spoil, of his chargeable sickness, &c., his earthly treasure swelled not to excess." Certainly the return given in the Book of Administrations[2] shows an estate of very modest proportions indeed. The following is a translation of the document:

"Bedd: 17 Oct. 1688. Administration of the Goods of John Bunyan of the said Town, deceased, was granted to Elizabeth Bunyan, Relict of the said deceased and to Tho. Woodward, of Bedford, Maultster and Wm. Nicholls of the same place, Draper, being under £100. By order of the Commissary of the Court.

"Sum of Inventory £42 19s. 0d."

Upon this and the yearly income from his publications Elizabeth Bunyan lived on at Bedford during the year and a half which was all that she survived her husband. She died in the early part of 1691,[3] "following her faithful pilgrim from this world to the other, whither he was gone before her."

Bunyan had six children; four of these, Mary, Elizabeth, John, and Thomas being born to him by his first wife, the remaining

[1] *Epistle to the Reader.* Works, 1692.

[2] Registry of the Archdeaconry cf Bedford.

[3] The writer of the Continuation of the *Grace Abounding* says that Elizabeth Bunyan died in 1692, but in the folio published in 1692, Charles Doe says, $169^0/^1$; and he was at that time in close correspondence with Bunyan's family, was occasionally down at Bedford between 1688 and 1692, and would therefore be likely to know.

two, Sarah and Joseph, by his second wife. His eldest daughter, Mary, his blind child, died before him, the rest surviving. His eldest son, John, was brought up to the ancestral trade of a brazier, and carried on business in the town till his death in 1728. He appears to have made no open profession of religion during his father's lifetime, but was received to the fellowship of the Church some five years after his father's death, on the 27th of June, 1693. There is no further mention of him in the Church records till seven years later, when we find him sent to visit those who had come under the discipline of the Church. Brother Bunyan was sent, for example, along with Brother Fenn to confer with Brother Butcher, "his sins being drunkenness, card-playing, and light, unbecoming actions about Stool Ball, and the May Pole." On similar service he was sent eight or nine times between 1700 and 1719, after which there is no farther mention of his name. In the records of the Bedford Corporation we find the following entry relating to him: "1705. May 11. It is agreed that John Bunian shall have a lease of a messuage abutting westward upon Duck Lane [a lane no longer in existence, leading from Mill Lane to Lurk Lane],* with backside and appurtenances, late let to Katherine Ridgment, to be for eleven years from Michaelmas next at twelve shillings per ann., with the usual covenants." Again, under date April 20th, 1716, it was ordered that John Bunian's lease be renewed for eleven years. His will, which was written out for him and attested by his father's successor, Ebenezer Chandler, is in existence in the district registry, and seems to indicate that, as he left all he had to his grand-daughter, Hannah Bunyan, and made her sole executrix of his will, neither wife nor child of his survived him. This will, which was dated December 13th, 1728, and proved the following month, is as follows:

* The brackets are Dr. Brown's. Mr. W.Henman, of Bedford, says that Duck Lane was that part of Harpur Street from Silver Street to St. Loyes. Other records give this as the site of the house.

"In the name of God Amen. I John Bunyan of Bedford in the County of Bedford, Brazier, being well in body and of sound mind and memory, Praised be God, do make and ordain my last Will and Testament in manner following. That is to say I give, devise and bequeath to my granddaughter, Hannah Bunyan, whom I have brought up from a child and who now lives with me, my house in the parish of St. Cuthbert's wherein Joseph Simonds the younger now lives, with the outhouses, yard, garden and all the appurtenances thereto belonging, to her and her heirs for ever. Item I give to her my said granddaughter the lease of the House I live in and all the rest of my personal estate, goods and chattels, ready money, debts, household goods and the implements or utensils of trade and all my stock-in-trade, All these I give to my said granddaughter Hannah Bunyan, she paying all my just debts and Funeral expenses. And I constitute and appoint the said Hannah Bunyan whole and sole executrix of this my last Will and Testament."[1]

It would appear from this will that the house in St. Cuthbert's, in which the writer of *The Pilgrim's Progress* had lived, had become his property and passed on to his eldest son; and that so far as this eldest son was concerned, the name and line died out, for, as a tablet in the vestibule of Bunyan Meeting indicates, this Hannah Bunyan to whom John Bunyan the younger left all his possessions died unmarried in 1770 at the age of seventy-six.[2]

With respect to John Bunyan's second son Thomas, a question arises on which a word or two may be said. It will be remembered that on Bunyan becoming the pastor of the Church in 1672, there is mention made in the following year, in his own handwriting, of the reception into fellowship of "our Brother Thomas Bunyan." To this brother there are three other references in the Church Book from one of which it would appear that he was one of those sent forth to preach. In 1692 it is recorded that, "fforasmuch as there has been sum discord for sum time between Brother Sutton and Brother Thomas Bunyan,[3] Brother Pressland and Brother Hunge war apoynted to goe to them And endeavour to make up the differance; but if they could not, then to apoynt a day to com to Bedford, and also to desire the latter to fforbeare preaching till such time as ye differance be made up. And Brother Nicholls, Brother Woodward, Mr. Chandler, Brother Crocker, and Brother Hawkes to hear the matter." The following month "Brother Pressland and Brother Hunge certified ye Church that they had endeavoured to make up the differance between Brother Sutton and Brother Thomas Bunyan, but could not; therefore it is ordered that they apoynt a day themselves sum time next week to come to Bedford, that ye Brethren here may Endeaver Reconsilliation between them." The month after this, again, the Church at their meeting at Gamlingay

[1] *Bedfordshire Wills,* 1729.

[2] The inscription on this tablet is as follows: "In memory of Hannah Bunyan who departed this life 15th Feb., 1770, aged 76 years. N.B. She was great granddaughter to the Reverend and justly celebrated Mr. John Bunyan, who died at London, 31st August, 1688, Aged 60 years, and was buried in Bunhill Fields, where there is a stone erected to his memory. He was a minister of the gospel here 32 years, and during that period suffered 12 years' imprisonment. The Righteous shall be in everlasting remembrance."

[3] They were brothers-in-law, Thos. Bunyan having married Sutton's sister.

received the announcement, "that the differance between Brother Sutton and Brother Thomas Bunyan was Reconsilled."

It has been supposed by former biographers that this Thomas Bunyan was the son of John. A closer examination of the evidence, however, will show that he was not his son but his brother, the Thomas Bunyan mentioned in his father's will, and also in the parish register of Northill, where he died in 1695. For at the time the brother mentioned in the records joined the Bedford Church, Thomas, the son of John, was a mere youth of about sixteen. Then, again, this Thomas Bunyan was evidently living at a distance from Bedford at the time of the difference referred to, for twice over it is arranged that, failing a reconciliation, he is to come to Bedford to meet Sutton, whereas Thomas Bunyan, the son of John, was permanently living there. There is also one other point bearing in the same direction. Thomas Sutton, with whom the difference had arisen, lived at Little Staughton, and therefore, naturally enough, the brother appointed to wait upon him was George Pressland, whose residence was at Eynesbury, in the same neighbourhood. In like manner, the brother appointed to wait on Thomas Bunyan would probably be a neighbour also, and, as a matter of fact, there was sent to him Thomas Hunge, the sturdy Nonconformist carpenter of Northill, who, we happen to know, was four times before Foster's Court in 1668-9 for refusing to come to Northill Church.

If these inferences be correct, there is no reference in the Church Book to Thomas Bunyan, the son of John. There are, however, the following entries relating to his family in the register of St. Cuthbert's parish, where he was living both before and after his father's death:

"1687. Bapt. Steven ye sonn of Tho. Bonnyon, Nov. 14th.
"1689. Departed this Life Frances Bunyan, the wife of Thomas Bunyan on the 4th day of June."

A year or two later he appears to have married again, for in the same register we have the following entry:

"1692. Baptized Elizabeth, daughter of Thos. Bunyan, Jan. ye 29th."

A short time after this there was received to the Church under Ebenezer Chandler, "our sister Katherine Bunyan, who may have been Thomas's second wife. There is also this further entry in the parish register:

"1696. Bapt. Stephen ye son of Thos. Bunyan, Dec. 25,"

from which it would appear that his son Stephen, baptized in 1687, had died in the interval. The following entry is illegible, so far as the Christian names are concerned:

"1711. Bury'd daughter of Bunyan."

Beyond these entries we know nothing of Thomas Bunyan's family, unless the Sarah Bunyan who married John Millard of St. Paul's, in 1767, and the Ann Bunyan who married Samuel Slinn of St. Mary's, in 1768, were grand-daughters of his.

It will thus be seen that if there are any direct descendants of John Bunyan now living and bearing his own name, it must be through his youngest son Joseph, who was born in 1672. All that we know of this son and his Bedford life is derived from the register of St. Paul's parish, in which we find the following entries:

"1694. Dec. married Joseph Bunyan and Mary Charnock. 1695. Oct. 6th. Baptized Chernock ye son of Joseph and Mary Bunyan. 1696. Oct. Baptized Ann, daughter of Joseph and Mary Bunyan. 1696. Nov. Buried Ann, daughter of Joseph and Mary Bunyan."

At this point all further trace of Joseph Bunyan disappears, so far as positive and reliable evidence is concerned. There is a tradition, however, that he removed into Nottinghamshire or Lincolnshire, and conformed to the Church of England. Whether descended from him or not, it is certain that in the eighteenth and nineteenth centuries there were Bunyans both at Lincoln and Nottingham. The last of the name was Robert Bunyan, who died in 1855 at the age of eighty. He combined with his occupation of watchmaker the office of coroner for the city of Lincoln, and seems to have accumulated considerable wealth. He had the place of business opposite St. Peter's-at-Arches, subsequently occupied by Mr. Fisher, the jeweller; and it was said by old tradesmen of the town that his clocks, for the excellence of their workmanship, were famous all the country round. There is a monument to his memory in Lincoln cemetery, expressive of the respect of his fellow-citizens, and stating that he was a descendant of the writer of *The Pilgrim's Progress*. His father, Robert Bunyan, of Bunker's Hill, in the parish of Nettleham, also lived on to the age of eighty, and was buried in 1825 in the churchyard of St. Peter's-at-Arches, his gravestone being close to the street. The father of this man, again, was a Robert Bunyan also, who was born in 1715, and died in 1794. So far all seems clear enough. But at this point arises the difficulty of connecting this Robert Bunyan with Joseph Bunyan, whose eldest son, Chernock, would only be twenty years of age when the Robert in question was born. The family of the Lincoln Bunyans have drawn up a pedigree, which has been kindly furnished to me through Canon Venables. This document is on sure ground as far back as 1715, earlier than that it is confessedly conjectural. It states that "the celebrated John Bunyan married his first wife Mary in 1646, and by her had issue Thomas, the eldest son, born 1646, died 1718; his eldest son, John, was born in 1670, having issue Robert, 1693, who was married in 1713, and was the father of Robert," mentioned above, born in 1715. This pedigree seeems on the face of it to have all its links complete, but unfortunately it is weakest at the point where we could have wished it to be strongest. At the time it states that John Bunyan was married he was, as we now know, only a month or two over seventeen years of age.* His eldest son was not Thomas, but John, and John died in 1728, leaving, as we have seen, only a grand-daughter, who died unmarried in 1770.

* He was still at Newport Pagnell garrison.

If we turn to the Bunyans of Nottingham we come upon a similar difficulty. We can trace them certainly enough as far back as 1754, and then all our information fails. In 1754 George Bunyan was married to Mary Haywood at St. Nicholas' Church, and had eleven children, whose names are given in the register of that Church. The names of George Bunyan, hosier, in Castle Gate, and of his brother, Captain William Bunyan, in Woolpack Lane, are both found in the Nottingham 'Burgess List' of 1774 as voting for the Honourable William Howe at the parliamentary election for that year. In the previous 'Poll List' of 1747, there are no Bunyan names, nor are there any after that of 1774. It is said that George Bunyan suffered in his business in consequence of the part he took in the election referred to; that Lord Howe made him Inspector of Stores in Philadelphia, where he died of fever; and that his brother, Captain William Bunyan, was drowned at sea.[1]

[1] *Notes and Queries*, New Series, Jan., 1860—Note by S. F. Creswell.

This is all that can be said. The registers of the parish churches of Lincoln and Nottingham have been searched, as have also the lists of wills in both Registries of the District Courts of Probate, but without further result. The connection between the Bunyans of Lincoln and Nottingham is tolerably certain; their descent from John Bunyan of Bedford not so certain. It is possible, even probable, but at present not proven.

It has been mentioned that Bunyan had three daughters as well as three sons, and that Mary, his blind daughter, died before him. His second daughter, Elizabeth, was married in 1677 to Gilbert Ashley of the Castle Mill, as we find from the following entry in the register of Goldington Church:

"1677. Matrimonium solemnizatum inter Gilbertum Ashley et Elizabetham Bunyan, April 16°."

This Gilbert Ashley the miller was a man of sufficient local importance to issue copper tokens in his own name, one of which is in the possession of the Archæological Society at Bedford. He was an earnest member of the Church under Bunyan's care; and it will be remembered that, in 1672, Bunyan applied for a licence for Edward Isaac to preach at the house of Gilbert Ashley in Goldington. It is not known whether there were any children of this marriage with Elizabeth Bunyan.

Of the remaining daughter, Sarah Bunyan, we have more positive knowledge; indeed, the only descendants of John Bunyan now living, of whom we are certain, have sprung from her. Her marriage is recorded in the St. Cuthbert's register, at Bedford, as follows: "1686: Maried, William Browne to Sarah Bunyan, Both of this Parish. December 19." Of the immediate children of this Sarah Bunyan we have no knowledge, but her grand-daughter Frances Browne, who was born in 1722, and who afterwards became the wife of Charles Bithrey, a prosperous yeoman at Carlton in Bedfordshire, died as recently as January 7th, 1803. This great-grand-daughter of John Bunyan lived and died at the old Manor House, in Carlton, known as 'The Fishers,' a name probably derived from earlier occupants, there being a Gideon Fisher in the parish in 1672, whose house was licensed for Nonconformist worship under the first Declaration of Indulgence. Frances Bithrey was the second wife of her husband, and survived him nineteen years. She was held in great esteem in the parish, and having about her a certain air of old-world respectability, was familiarly known among the villagers as 'Madam' Bithrey. The youngsters of the place, especially, remembered her from the fact that after her husband's death she gave every year, on his birthday, a penny loaf to every child in the village by way of keeping up his memory among them. Judging from an ivory miniature portrait,* taken in her eightieth year, she had to the last a vigorous face and blue eyes, with light and meaning in them. She was a zealous friend to the Baptist Church in Carlton, of which she was a member, and to its minister, the Rev. Charles Vorley, to whom she presented a house for his residence, which is still in the possession of his family. She died childless, in 1803, after which 'The Fishers' and a cottage close by, together with forty acres of land, came to the children of her nephew, William Brown of Carlton, who died in 1800. To Mr. Vorley, her minister, she bequeathed £200 in the Four per Cents., and various articles of furniture, including "my cedar nest of drawers." This little cabinet, thus described, had come to her as an heirloom of the family, having been the property of her distinguished ancestor, John Bunyan; it is now in the possession of the Bunyan Meeting Trustees. To her old servant, Elizabeth Bishop, 'Madam' Bithrey bequeathed £200 in the Four per Cents., and also "my silver snuff box, silver spoons, and my Scissars Pattern Tea Tongs, and my Bible, and such other of my Books as she shall choose to keep for her own reading (except my three volumes of the late Reverend Mr. Harvey's works) which I give to my Friend, Edward Abraham, of Olney, Gentleman." To the poor of the Dissenting Congregation she left £5, and to the poor of the parish £5. There were bequests also to her nephew, William Brown of Bedford, and to her nephew, Thomas Brown of St. Albans; but the bulk of her property went to the five children of her nephew, William Brown of Carlton.

* In the Museum at the Bunyan Meeting, Bedford.

These Browns, so far as we know with certainty, are the only living descendants of John Bunyan, and sprang, as we have said, from his daughter Sarah. The William Brown mentioned in this will of 'Madam' Bithrey's as her nephew at Bedford is described in a little directory of 1785 as a clothier; and in still later times a descendant of his was the local 'Pickford,' whose waggons, drawn by their six horses each, carried on the heavy traffic with London up to the time when the rail superseded the road. Of the one son and four daughters of William Brown of Carlton we have more precise information owing to the legal disposition of property under 'Madam' Bithrey's will. William Brown, the son, died in 1848, and was represented by his children, George, Richard, John, and Sarah Brown, who lived together unmarried, at Bozeat, in Northamptonshire; Thomas Brown of Wellingborough; Stephen Brown of Guilsborough, in the same county; and Henry Brown of Great Oaks Farm, at Turvey, in Bedfordshire. The four daughters were—Elizabeth, afterwards Norman, who died childless; Sarah, who was married to Stephen Benbrook, and whose family were in America; Frances, who was married to William Johnson, two of whose daughters lived at Newton Blossomville, co. Bucks; and one at Stagsden, in Bedfordshire; and Mary, who was married to William Davison of Turvey, and whose youngest daughter, her only surviving child, lived at Toronto. The different members of this wide-spread family were quite aware of their relationship to Bunyan, one of the four sisters keeping up the memory of the fact in the name of her son, John Bunyan Johnson, a man who in his stalwart strength was famous for being able to run up a ladder with a sack of barley under each arm, each sack weighing some two hundredweight. Beyond the name given to this man of might, however, Bunyan's kinsfolk seemed not to have felt any very lively interest in their kinship. One of them, a man of sixty-five, admitted that though he knew he was descended from its author, he had not read *The Pilgrim's Progress,* explaining this curious literary fact by saying that he "never was much given to books."

Turning from Bunyan's kindred by descent, it may be interesting now to give some brief account of his successors in the ministry of the Church at Bedford. Referring for a moment first to his predecessors, it will be remembered that John Gifford and John Burton were really rectors of the parish of St. John under Cromwell's Established Church. The next two, Samuel Fenn and John Whiteman, were chosen at the beginning of the times of persecution when the Church had no fixed place of meeting, and they still followed their ordinary callings, Samuel Fenn remaining a haberdasher in the High Street, and John Whiteman living on as a yeoman at Cardington. They were therefore not pastors in the sense in which Bunyan was after the Declaration of Indulgence. John Whiteman died in 1672, and

EBENEZER CHANDLER,
Successor to John Bunyan as Pastor at Bedford

though "our honoured brother, Samuel Fenn, one of the Elders of this Congregation," as Bunyan describes him, lived on till 1681, the work of the pastorate really fell upon Bunyan himself, who had been appointed nearly ten years before.

The immediate successor of Bunyan was Ebenezer Chandler, who first came among the Bedford people towards the end of 1689. He was a member of the London Church of which Richard Taylor was pastor, and the brethren of which transferred him "in order to his being separated to office work," and, as they say, "from the prospect of his being eminently serviceable to the common interest of our Lord Jesus Christ, we are brought (although with no small reluctancy) to grant y^{r} Request, and are willing to impoverish ourselves for the enriching of you." The pastor thus sent down to the Bedford Church at their own request, remained with them till his death in 1747, his connection with them thus extending over the long period of fifty-seven years. Till 1707 the Church continued to worship in the barn in which Bunyan had preached since 1672; but in that year a new building was erected for the congregation, which had increased under the larger liberty brought in by the Act of Toleration. While the new building was being erected on the same spot as the old historic barn, another barn was temporarily occupied, notice of its use being given in the following form, the original of which is pinned to a fly-leaf of the 'Book of Caveats' in the registry of the Archdeaconry:

"Bedford, 23 May, 1707:

"In pursuance of an Act of Parliament made in the first year of the Reign of King William and Queen Mary whereby Libertie for Protestant Dissenters to worship God According to their consciences is established; they among other requi^{ts} being required to certifye the place of their worship; We do hereby certifie that we intend to make use of A Barn, now in the occupation of John Randall in the parish of St. Cuthbert, in the town and County of Bedford for the worship of God aforesaid; and desire as the Law directs, it may be recorded. Witness our Hands, Eben. Chandler, Will. Nicholls, Henry Whitbread."

The new building thus erected in 1707 and long known in Bedford as the Old Meeting remained till 1849, and in spite of baldness and even ugliness was dear and venerable to the hearts of many from the sacred associations of a life-time. It took the prevailing shape of the many meeting-houses built after the

Revolution, having three gabled ridges, the roof being supported by two sets of four oaken pillars within. In its pristine simplicity these pillars were at first merely straight oak trees with the bark removed, and it was not till a more refined generation that they were planed into octagon shape. Like the two pillars in Solomon's Temple, that were known by the names of Jachin and Boaz, three of those reaching from floor to roof and standing midway between the pulpit and the front gallery received, in later times, the names of three venerable men in the Church who had long been pillars in the spiritual house. The meeting when finished would accommodate eight hundred people, and cost £400, a price per sitting which would be the despair of modern architects. The long way of the building ran from north to south and on the long side to the east, between two tall windows stood the pulpit, opposite to which and somewhat close upon it was the long front gallery which was completed by two short end galleries. Standing endwise towards the pulpit, in what was called the 'table-pew,' was a massive oaken communion table some thirteen feet long, and round this at the ordinary services sat fourteen or fifteen aged poor men to whom this conspicuous place was accorded as a sort of testimony to their quiet worth and the general esteem in which they were held among the brethren. By virtue of an unwritten law, the usage of generations, no sister ever seems to have sat in that chief place accorded to the poorer brethren. Frequently some deaf brother had a recognised position at the top of the pulpit stairs, and with his ear trumpet and strained attentive face became a marked and familiar object to the congregation. The pulpit itself was of course the prominent feature, with its large book-board, its great cushion of crimson or blue, and its lofty panelled back-board, on which was visible the large brass holder from which was suspended the preacher's hat with its silken band on the then frequent occasions when funeral sermons were preached. The ceiling of the building was low and the windows, with the exception of the one on each side of the pulpit, narrow and small, so that the place with its heavy galleries must have worn a sombre aspect of gloom; yet the old people to whom the venerable place was dearer than the stateliest cathedral could ever be, still maintain that when the pews, all converging towards the preacher's desk, were filled, as they usually were, with earnest faces, it was a grand and noble sight.

In the days of Ebenezer Chandler the services, in winter at least, began at what seems to us an unconscionably early time, when we remember that some of the congregation had come from as far as Gamlingay, nearly fifteen miles away. Under date October, 1697, there is this entry in the Church Book: "The Lord's Supper was deferd for the advantage of light nights till the 2nd Lord's day in Nov. and then to begin our Publick Meeting at nine in the morning and at twelve at noon y^{t} our country members may have time to go home."

If these services, begun thus early, had not many adventitious aids from the architecture of the building in which they were held, neither had they from the inspiring influence of music. It seems strange to us to find that all through Bunyan's time there was not so much as the singing of a hymn at public worship. In this sober order of procedure, however, his people were not so singular as might be supposed; for even in churches the musical element in the services had fallen almost to the point of extinction. The version of the Psalms by Sternhold and Hopkins, men, as Thomas Fuller says, whose piety was better than their poetry, had not yet given place to the new version of Tate and Brady; and Robert Nelson tells us that even serious people excused themselves from taking part in the psalmody because of the bad poetry, which Wesley went so far as to call 'scandalous doggerel.' Much later even than this time we read of that "shameful mode of psalmody almost confined to the wretched solo of a parish clerk, or to a few persons huddled together in one corner of the church, who sung to the praise and glory of themselves for the entertainment and oftener to the wearisomeness of the congregation."[1] The new era of hymnology had not yet dawned, and the loftier strain of song had not yet been awakened even in the services of the National Church.

But it would be a mistake to suppose that it was either the bad poetry of Sternhold and Hopkins or the soul-harrowing music of parish clerks that kept the meeting-house silent from hymns of praise. George Fox had influenced the minds of many outside the Quaker Communion so that they came to think of psalmody as an invention of man in the worship of God, and

[1] T. Hawels' *Carmina Christo.* Preface.

books were written to show that the only Scriptural singing was that from the heart. Something like this was the feeling at Bedford, as the following entry in the Act Book of the Church would seem to indicate: "At a Church meeting at Bedford the 20th day of October, 1690, It was debated and agreed that Publick Singing of Psalms be practised by the Church with a caushion that non others perform it but such as can sing with Grace in there Hearts According to the Command of Christ." In the margin it is noted: "Brethren agreed to it: 18; dissent from it: 2." It would appear, however, that the singing thus agreed upon was confined to the afternoon service, as this extract shows: "June 7th, 1697: Our Brother Chandler did then move that himself and those of his principle might have Lybertie to sing the praises of God in the morning of the Lord's day as well as the Afternoon, and at all times when he preached or those there are willing so to do, there being full Libertie for the practice of it in all other parts of the Church, and after some debate it was consented to by the Church in generall." Even yet, however, the practice seems not to have accorded with the resolution after debate; for at a Church Meeting held about Michaelmas 1700, "'Twas agreed on y^t there should be liberty to sing at every meeting of preaching week dayes as well as Lord's day, and on those dayes morning and afternoon, and also leave was given for the pronouncing the Blessing after prayer."

Besides these changes, which were regarded as doubtful innovations by the more conservative brethren, there appear to have been opinions started and claims put forth which caused concern. In 1726 an English Gnostic, holding that evil was inherent in matter, not in spirit, appeared among them, Brother Samuel Kendall, "asserting the soul was perfect and did not and could not sin, but that sin was only in the body"; he was also "in other instances enthusiastical." By the side of this erring brother was Sister Bar of Blunham, who "pretended to a spirit of prophecy and had predicted several strange unscripturall things as that the Church would suddenly be broke or in her own words that the head and body, meaning Pastor and people should be separated and lye dead." As by the end of two years she was "sensible of her sin, and did much reform, 'twas concluded to exercise patience towards her."

In 1745 a case arose for consideration which, as connected with one of the burning questions of our own time, may be referred to in passing. The Church at Hitchin being troubled and anxious laid before their brethren at Bedford the following case for consideration and counsel: "The Wife of one of our Brethren dying without issue, he has since thought proper to marry her sister, who is likewise a member with us. . . . They have been conversed with since, but can by no means be brought to look upon this action as criminal." They go on to say that upon this vexed question "there are different sentiments among ourselves; some looking on the marriage as incestuous, others viewing it in a more favourable light."*

* The Bill legalising such marriages in England was passed in 1907.

This letter was formally laid before the brethren at Bedford in their Church meeting, where it was discussed and an answer sent to their Hitchin brethren, the gist of which is contained in the following passage:

"We were pretty unanimous in thinking that the Law of God is not clear concerning the Lawfulness or Unlawfulness of such a Marriage, that therefore it were much to be wish'd they who have ventur'd upon it had not done it: especially considering y[t] so many wise and good men esteem it sinful, and y[t] it has occasioned much offence and trouble to some serious Christians; but since they themselves saw no iniquity in it, and it cannot be certainly prov'd there is any, whatever reason there may be to fear it, we were of opinion they should not be excommunicated for what they have done."

Ebenezer Chandler remained pastor at Bedford, from the reign of William and Mary to that of the second George, dying on the 24th of June, 1747. Towards the end of life he was afflicted with blindness, and totally laid aside from public work in the March of 1744. His portrait, presenting him in gown and bands, and with the curled flowing wig of the period surrounding a strong sturdy face, still remains, but as he published nothing during his long public life beyond the preface to the folio edition of Bunyan's works of 1692, and as there are no contemporary references to him, we have scanty means of estimating his character and influence.

His colleague and successor, the Rev. Samuel Sanderson, who first came to Bedford February 26th, 1737, though not destined to so long a service as Chandler, yet remained for the extended period of twenty-nine years. A native of Sheffield and educated at a grammar-school in Hull, he was afterwards trained for the ministry, first under the Rev. Timothy Jollie of Attercliffe, and afterwards by the Rev. John Eames, F.R.S., of Newington Green. Mr. Eames, a man of some eminence in scientific pursuits, was the friend of Sir Isaac Newton, through whose influence he was elected a Fellow of the Royal Society. At a later period John Howard was one of his pupils, and he had among his students at different times Dr. Furneaux, Dr. Savage, Dr. Price, and Thomas Secker, afterwards Archbishop of Canterbury. After completing his studies at Newington Green, Mr. Sanderson resided for some time as chaplain in the house of Justice Birch, Cursitor Baron of the Exchequer, occasionally preaching in and about London. In 1730 we find him settled as minister over the new Independent congregation gathered at Kensington, and he acted also as Assistant Minister of the Weigh House in Eastcheap. He remained at Bedford for the rest of his life. His wife was the grand-daughter of Sir Francis Wingate of Harlington, her mother Frances Wingate having married Thomas Woodward, one of the deacons of the Old Meeting, and it may be remembered that Mrs. Sanderson's sister Ann, also a Wingate, married the Rev. James Belsham, and became the mother of Thomas and William Belsham, men of some literary repute at the end of the eighteenth century.

Mr. Sanderson was a man of solid worth and of great weight of judgment and character. He sent out into the ministry from the Church at Bedford two men of more than ordinary power and influence, Samuel Palmer, one of the successors of Matthew Henry at Hackney, and editor of the *Nonconformist Memorial*, and William Bull, of Newport Pagnel, a man of genius himself and the chosen friend, addressed as 'Charissime Taurorum,' by his neighbour William Cowper, the poet of Olney. Both these men spoke of Samuel Sanderson and of his influence in the formation of their characters with the utmost veneration and affection. Referring to the sermons he heard from him in his earlier days at Bedford, William Bull says: "I seemed to feel the dawnings of the sun of righteousness on my soul. I never before experienced so much pleasure or benefit from hearing."[1] Samuel Palmer, also, when called upon to preach the funeral sermon of this good man, speaks of Samuel Sanderson as "one

[1] *Memorials of the Rev. William Bull,* by his Grandson, the Rev. Josiah Bull, M.A., 1864, p. 18.

with whom I enjoyed a friendship which I esteem one of the greatest felicities of my life, and which I shall think of with pleasure and gratitude to the latest period of it."[1] A man of more than usually vigorous health, Mr. Sanderson died after only a few days' illness, on the 24th of January, 1766. As this illness day by day betrayed more serious symptoms, he sent parting words of loving admonition to the people among whom he had lived so happily for nearly thirty years, blessed God for bringing him among them, and entreating them not to pray too much for his life, but rather that he might have patience to hold out to the end. As the hours went by he continued lifting up his heart in prayer for them, till at last his mind "like sweet bells jangled out of tune" became delirious. Even then the old thoughts and the old love came over him. In his delirium he fancied himself once more in the pulpit where he had loved to be. Once more he gave out his text, a verse from Ecclesiastes, appealing especially to the young, and then proceeded to address this portion of his flock with much of the old orderliness of thought and characteristic warmth of heart. The sermon ended he once more, too, in the old familiar way asked the Great Father to make these words of his to be living words to those to whom he thought he had spoken them. So preaching and praying to the last, he went away upward to the higher service.

His successor at Bedford was Joshua Symonds, the son of an apothecary at Kidderminster, whom Joseph Williams, the Christian merchant of that town, describes as one of those good men for whom "peradventure some would even dare to die." Young Joshua was at first intended for a farming life, but was eventually prevailed on by Mr. Wylde, the minister of Carr's Lane Chapel, Birmingham, to enter the Congregational ministry, for which he was trained by Dr. Conder of Mile End. Sent down to preach at Bedford in March, 1766, he was shortly after invited by the vacant Church to become its pastor, an invitation he accepted, remaining with them till his death, twenty-two years later, in 1788.

During the years of Joshua Symonds' Bedford life he was associated with a little knot of people of more than local celebrity and influence. John Howard had come to his pleasant seat at

[1] *The Appearing of Christ the Chief Shepherd*: a sermon occasioned by the much lamented death of the Rev. Mr. Samuel Sanderson, preached at Bedford, January 29th, 1766. By Samuel Palmer.

Cardington, two miles from Bedford, in 1758, and had connected himself with the congregation at the Old Meeting, subsequently spending his Sundays in a house built by him, close to the three-ridged building where he worshipped. This house, erected on what was originally John Eston's garden, 'The Pynners,' had its west wall towards the burial ground where so many worthies of a past generation lay sleeping. The trelliswork on the east is still covered with a spreading vine, planted by Howard himself, and the sitting-room to the north, with the bedroom over it, were the rooms used by the great philanthropist when staying in the town. While still retaining his membership with the Church at Stoke Newington, he was always a warm friend to the cause of Dissent in the town to the neighbourhood of which he had come. In 1767 he gave a piece of land from his own garden for the enlargement of the burial ground; the same year he subscribed £50 towards the purchase of a house which had first been the private residence of Ebenezer Chandler, and then of Samuel Sanderson, that it might be in perpetuity the manse for the ministers of the Church; and in 1770 he contributed £70 towards the restoration of the quaint old Meeting House, his neighbour, Mr. Samuel Whitbread, contributing also "six score guineas" to the same desirable object. Out of the latter gift the spreading many-lighted brass chandelier so familiar to the worshippers at the Old Meeting, was purchased; while out of Mr. Howard's donation was obtained the old oaken pulpit, which remained the place of exhortation till the erection of a new sanctuary in 1849.[1]

Besides the distinguished man, to whom reference has just been made, there were other people who came ever and again to the Bedford of those days whom it must have been pleasant to meet. The old house in the south-west corner of St. Paul's Square, afterwards removed to extend the grammar-school, was inhabited in the early part of last century by Thomas Woodward, a brewer. His father was the Thomas Woodward who was one of Bunyan's administrators in 1688, and he himself was a deacon of the Church, and had married, as has been said, one of the Nonconformist daughters of Sir Francis Wingate. After him there lived in the old house his nephew, Francis Jennings, the son of the Rev. John Jennings of Kibworth, Doddridge's tutor. He

[1] This brass chandelier is now in the vestry at Cotten End Meeting, while Howard's pulpit is to be seen in the little village chapel at Goldington.

too was a member of the Bedford Church, and a trustee, though it must be owned that his scarlet slippers and his wife's flowing ringlets were regarded by the more sober brethren and sisters as coming perilously near the doubtful ways of an evil world. After Francis Jennings' death, in 1765, the Rev. James Belsham came to live in the house so long associated with the family into which he had married. In his time again it was still the centre of refined intercourse, lighted up by the presence of his wife, a gentlewoman whose letters show how culture and piety may be blended. The circle included also his two sons, Thomas and William Belsham, men of intellectual mark, and his daughter Elizabeth, whom her cousin, Anna Lætitia Aikin, afterwards better known as Mrs. Barbauld, addresses playfully as "Betsy, the joy of the plain," and whom she describes as one who, while "accustomed to mix in the most elegant company, can make herself happy in the plainest, and make them happy by her condescension."

Mrs. Barbauld herself was often a guest in the house, as were her brother, Dr. Aikin, and his daughter Lucy, with their kinsman, Gilbert Wakefield, all of them people of some literary reputation. At an earlier time also Dr. Doddridge had tarried here with the Jenningses, with whom he had been so intimately associated, and it was here, too, as well as at Warrington, that John Howard and John Aikin conferred together and put into shape that book on the *State of Prisons,* by which the great philanthropist roused the conscience both of the Parliament and the people of England. It would seem, indeed, that out of these meetings in St. Paul's Square there might easily have grown a closer tie between the grave philanthropist and the poetical and vivacious Anna Lætitia. It is said by one of her kinsfolk that after the death of his wife Henrietta, Howard made her an offer of marriage, a statement which seems to be borne out by the last letter she wrote before her marriage with Mr. Barbauld to her friend Betsy Belsham (May 22nd, 1774), in which she says: "It was too late, as you say, or I believe I should have been in love with Mr. Howard. Seriously, I looked upon him with that sort of reverence and love which one should have for a guardian angel. God bless him and preserve his health for the health sake of thousands." That year, though returned at the poll, Howard was defeated on an enquiry in committee of the House of Commons as to the validity of certain votes, in the election for the borough, Sir William Wake being returned along with Mr. Whitbread. On this Mrs. Barbauld wrote to her friend: "Truly, I did not know whether I was in charity enough with Bedford to write to you at all. No, never more shall I think of you with patience. If it were in my power I believe I should put your town under a sentence of excommunication. Your worthy Mayor, Mr. Cawne, I see by the newspapers, has acted very wisely, and slipped out of the way, not chusing to have his house pulled over his head. I commend him for it.[1] All I can say to *you* is, that you should shake off the dust of your feet against the town and come to us at Palgrave, where we will drink Mr. Howard's health every day in a glass of lemonade, and wish, not that he should represent his unworthy borough, but that they in some degree may resemble him. As Mr. Whitbread is, however, chosen, I should be glad to know how you disposed of the favour you said you had made up, whether you wore that on one sleeve and a mourning knot on the other, or how you managed?"[2]

While the little provincial town was brightened by such peoples as these—of more than provincial fame—there were other visitors also who, as Joshua Symonds' daughter tells us, looked in at her father's manse, as it stood in its pleasant garden and orchard in Well Street. Lady Austen, the friend of Cowper, and Thomas Scott, the commentator, from Weston Underwood; John Newton, also from Olney, called in on his way to his friend Barham, the retired West India planter, a member of the Moravian Church, who lived on the other side of Foster's Hill. To the manse also Newton sent to his friend Symonds some of those characteristic letters which were afterwards printed in the *Cardiphonia*. Here also came year by year John Thornton the banker, Wilberforce's brother-in-law, his carriage so stacked up with Bibles, Testaments, and other good books for distribution that there was scarcely room for himself, and after leaving £15 or £20 for benevolent purposes went on his way again. Joshua Symonds' daughter, Mrs. Emery, who preserved so many of these

[1] The mayor in order to defeat Mr. Howard, who was regarded as the representative of "Presbyterians, Moravians, and other sectaries," had struck off from the poll, after the election and for the first time, the votes of all recipients of the Harpur Charity.

[2] From unpublished letters from Mrs. Barbauld to Miss Belsham, which were in the possession of Miss Reid, Hampstead, in 1885.

gossiping details for us, was herself a curiosity worthy of mention. She died in the year 1862, at the age of ninety-three, and remembered three generations of her ancestors, and saw four of her descendants. She recalled how, as a child she had been lifted up to the window to see a gentleman carrying an umbrella, as one of the latest novelties; how she rode to London in her uncle's carriage, the postillion avoiding the main streets as they approached the city, because the buildings were on fire from the Gordon Riots, and the rioters were raging; and she could distinctly recollect her great-grandfather, Mr. Ludd, who, born in the year of the Revolution, lived to be ninety, so that these two lives stretched from 1688 to 1862.

Joshua Symonds, like his predecessors Chandler and Sanderson, was a Pædo-baptist on his first coming to Bedford, but six years later he publicly announced his adoption of Baptist views. Conscientious and frankly honest, he wished, he said, to be relieved from the necessity of baptizing infants or adults by aspersion, and promised that if he might have liberty of conscience in the matter he would do nothing to disturb the peace of the Church on the question at issue. This was in February, 1772, and the Church resolved to take a year for deliberation before coming to a final conclusion as to his continuance as their pastor. In the month of July, however, objection was taken by some that he was seeking unduly to spread his views among those already in fellowship. John Howard, who seems to have felt strongly on the matter, addressed a letter to the deacons, while another brother sent one to the Church, in remonstrance and protesting against the continuance of Mr. Symonds. The majority were, however, in favour of his continuance, provided he would make arrangements for the baptism of their children and would refrain from undue proselytism to the views he had embraced. Upon this, John Howard and other members of the congregation withdrew and formed a separate Church, worshipping in what was at first called the Second Meeting and is now known as Howard Chapel. It is pleasant to find from Mr. Symonds' Diary that he and the great philanthropist remained in unbroken friendship even when separated in their fellowship, and that John Howard subsequently subscribed £10 towards the stipend of the minister whose services he had left.

After this separation a new Trust Deed was drawn up in 1774, and the Church at the Old Meeting was, for the first time in its history, defined and described as a "Congregation or Society of Protestants Dissenting from the Church of England, commonly called Independents or Congregationalists, holding mixt communion with those who scrople the Baptizing of Infants, commonly called Baptists." This description has been continued in subsequent deeds.

In 1773, the Senatus Academicus of Rhode Island, now Brown University, United States, conferred upon Mr. Symonds the honorary degree of M.A., a similar distinction being accorded at the same time to Augustus Toplady, John Newton, Robert Robinson, of Cambridge, and others.[1] Mr. Symonds' diploma is still in existence and is one of the latest American documents of the kind, bearing the Colonial Seal of Great Britain with the embossed medallions of King George and Queen Charlotte upon it.

Joshua Symonds died November 23rd, 1788, after a long and trying time of suffering, and was succeeded in his ministry by Samuel Hillyard, who first came to Bedford in December, 1790. Born at Wellingborough, in 1770, he was the son of the Rev. Thomas Hillyard, afterwards of Olney, and was trained for his work in the Institution presided over by the Rev. William Bull of Newport Pagnel. A mere youth of twenty, he came to a position which might well have tried a much older man, for there were discordant elements, the issue of which was another secession and the formation of a separate Baptist Church in the town. But with singular tact and amiability the young minister bore himself so as to pluck up weeds and drain away waters of bitterness. During the nearly forty-nine years he presided over them, the Church and congregation steadily grew in numbers and influence, obtaining a position not reached hitherto in their history. Genial and kindly in the common intercourse of life, and most persuasive as a preacher of Christ's Gospel, Samuel Hillyard, like his distinguished predecessor John Bunyan, was a veritable 'bishop' among the churches of the county and even beyond the county border. Every good cause seemed to awaken the interest and inspire the ardour of this warm-hearted man: the evangelization of the heathen abroad, and the spreading of the Gospel among the villages of Bedfordshire at home; the emancipation of

[1] *Early History of Brown University.* By R. A. Guild, Librarian. Boston, 1864.

the slave, and the enfranchisement of his fellow-countrymen. He worked with all his heart for Bible, Missionary, and Tract Societies, and just as earnestly stood up on the Bedford hustings of 1830, to second the nomination of Lord John Russell as a candidate for the borough, before the bringing in of Reform. Passionately attached to the great principles of civil and religious freedom, and urging his co-religionists to support Lord John and the House of Russell on the principle that your own friends and your father's friends you should forsake not, he held his own position with firmness and yet with such perfect good-temper and gentlemanly feeling, that he seems never to have made an enemy or lost a friend. Staunch dissenter as he was, clergymen, like his neighbours Legh Richmond of Turvey, A. J. Crespin of Renhold, and R. P. Beachcroft of Blunham, were his co-secretaries in working the great religious societies of the time. Among his own brethren, it goes without saying, he held a high place. In the circle of his friends, as frequent visitors at Bedford, were Andrew Fuller and Thomas Toller* of Kettering, and Robert Hall of Leicester. This last distinguished preacher used to say, with a smile, that his friend was the very pine-apple of humanity for sweetness, and that no man loved the Lord Jesus Christ aright who could not love the Rev. Samuel Hillyard of Bedford. It was on one of those friendly ministerial reunions which if not more frequent were more leisurely before railway times than now, that Thomas Toller preached that memorable sermon at the Old Meeting, at Bedford, to which Robert Hall tells us he listened and of which, prince of preachers as he was himself, he said: "The effect of this discourse on the audience was such as I have never witnessed before or since. . . . All other emotions were absorbed in devotional feeling: it seemed to us as though we were permitted for a short space to look into eternity, and every sublunary object vanished before 'the powers of the world to come.'"[1]

* *Joseph* Toller of Kettering published an edition of *The Pilgrim's Progress* in 1843.

Loved by, and loving such friends as these, and loved most of all by the people among whom he spent a public life of nearly half a century, Samuel Hillyard was called to his rest on the 4th of March, 1839. It is therefore now more than forty years since he passed away, and those who remember him are growing few; but with those few his memory is still fragrant, and they

[1] *Hall's Works*, iv., 315. [Robert Hall, 1764-1831.]

rarely speak of him but with some kind word expressive of enduring esteem.

We are close upon our own day when we come to his successor, the Rev. John Jukes, formerly of Yeovil, who settled at Bedford on the first Sunday of 1840. Along with Dr. Vaughan, afterwards president of the Lancashire College, he was placed under the care of the Rev. John Thorp of Bristol, a man of some eminence in his day as a preacher. In many respects a contrast to his predecessor, Mr. Jukes was yet a man of weight and worth, who did good service of a steady solid sort through the more than twenty-six years he was pastor of the Bedford Church. Defective in the quality of humour and in power of imagination, his preaching was yet instructive and impressive, and his conduct in public life, if erring on the side of caution, was marked by firmness and kindliness. Together with his friend and neighbour, the Rev. William Alliott of Howard Chapel, he carried on a missionary college at Bedford, in which were trained very many of those sent out by the London Missionary Society, besides many other young men who were preparing for colleges elsewhere with a view to the ministry at home.

In 1849 the venerable three-ridged Meeting was taken down, the present place of worship being erected on the site and opened in 1850. From 1854 Mr. Jukes had as co-pastor the Rev. J. J. Insull, a man of earnest spirit, who died in the autumn of 1863. The same year in which this colleague died, the senior minister himself sustained a serious shock to his health, and within three years from that time was called to his rest on the 22nd of May, 1866, in the sixty-sixth year of his age. The scene at his funeral was a remarkable manifestation of the esteem in which he was held by the town at large. On the hillside on which the cemetery stands it seemed as if the whole community had come forth to express the widespread feeling that a consistent, honourable, and useful career had come to its close.

The writer of this biography, the next minister, accepted the invitation of the Bedford Church on the 15th of April, 1864.* In 1867 the new school-buildings behind Bunyan Meeting were opened, and in 1876 the Duke of Bedford presented to the congregation the noble bronze doors at the entrance of their place of worship. These doors are the work of Mr. Frederick Thrupp,

* *Vide* Addendum.

and are marked by fine artistic feeling and power, the sense of which grows upon us as we look. There are ten panels in alto-relievo, presenting these ten scenes from *The Pilgrim's Progress*: (1) Christian reproached by his family; (2) Goodwill helping Christian through the gate; (3) Christian met by the Shining Ones; (4) Christian sleeping in the arbour; (5) Christian passing the lions; (6) Simple, Sloth, and Presumption; (7) In the armoury of the Palace Beautiful; (8) Demas in the Silver Mine; (9) The death of Faithful; (10) Crossing the River. Mr. Thrupp was engaged upon this work for more than two years, simply as a labour of love, and without any conception as to its ultimate destination. Eventually, a brother artist Mr. Richmond, struck by the beauty and feeling expressed in these scenes from the 'Pilgrim,' brought them under the notice of the Duke of Bedford, whose generous kindness seized the opportunity of giving to the town of Bedford a noble work of art which would be a possession for ever; and to the artist himself the pleasant satisfaction of feeling that his work would stand where for so many years Bunyan himself had stood as a preacher of the truth.

The sketch thus briefly given is a faithfully told story of one of the Free Churches of this country which is still strong and vigorous after the vicissitudes of more than two centuries. It still carries on its Christian work in the town and in the villages round as in the old days, and may fairly be regarded as a reliable testimony to the worth and enduringness of Christian willinghood. Cradled in the storms of persecution, it has outlived them, and through evil report and good report pursued its beneficent course to this day. It has asked nothing from the State but freedom to work out those convictions of the Christian life received from Christ Himself and unfolded by the Spirit of God. In the long-continued harmony and enduring peace of its fellowship it has seemed as if the benedictions of the sainted confessors of the earlier time still hovered near. What is perhaps unique in the history of a church, all its former ministers, as this narrative has shown, have continued at their post of service till death itself removed them.

And while in previous years and generations there have been honourable and able men in the pulpit, there have also been honourable and devout men and women in the pew, of whom any Christian community might well be proud. From the times of John Eston, Anthony Harrington, and "that reverend man, John Grew"; from the days of those devout women who sat talking in the summer's sunshine of the joys and sorrows of the spiritual life, down to our own times, there has been a long and unbroken succession of Christian men and women, of very many of whom it may indeed be said that they were the excellent of the earth. We glorify God in them. Recalling the long and honourable roll of the sainted dead we but the more magnify their Saviour and ours, that Saviour whose divine beauty, shining through them, made them what they were, and in whose eternal life both they and we find that true unity of the Church which in systems and creeds will ever be sought for in vain.

ADDENDA—Chapter XVII.

(Page 385.)

Portraits of Bunyan.

The portrait, forming the frontispiece of this book, is, as Dr. Brown says, from the pencil-sketch on vellum which came to the nation in the Cracherode Collection in the closing year of the eighteenth century. It is a delightful little picture, and in handling it one realises that Bunyan himself must have also examined it. The original drawing requires no embellishment: its very "sketchiness" is its attraction. Robert White, the artist who executed it, was a personal friend of the Dreamer. White, renowned for his fidelity in portraiture, was commissioned to delineate the features of scores of celebrities of his day, including George Herbert and Thomas Barlow. Bunyan was fifty years of age when he sat for this portrait. The artist also produced other sketches of him, including the famous "sleeping-portrait," which appeared in the first illustrated edition of *The Pilgrim's Progress* (1679), and has since been used with varying success in innumerable editions, especially in those of the eighteenth century; but many of the reproductions are so crude as to be almost unrecognisable. The only full-length figure of Bunyan known to exist, is that of the very scarce folding-plate in the First Edition (1682) of *The Holy War.* This, too, was the work of Robert White. In 1861, Offor possessed a whole-length portrait of Bunyan travelling as a Tinker; also two old indian-ink drawings, inscribed 'Mr. and Mrs. Bunyan.'

Another interesting portrait was included in the engraved frontispiece to *A Discourse upon the Pharisee and Publican,* published by John Harris, in 1685. Around the head of the author are the words, "VERA EFFIGIES JOHANIS BUNYAN ÆTATIS SUÆ 57."

In the same year (1685) Thomas Sadler, a son of John Sadler (1615-1674), Master of Magdalene College, Cambridge, executed an oil-painting of Bunyan. This portrait was acquired for the nation in 1902, and now hangs in the National Portrait Gallery, Room VII., No. 1311. The picture is inscribed "John Bunyon Anº Ætatˢ 56. T. S. pinx"; and on the frame "JOHN BUNYAN / Tinker and Author / of / 'The Pilgrim's Progress' / Painted at the age of 56 by / THOMAS SADLER." It had been bequeathed to Mary, Countess of Cavan, by her father, the Rev. John Olive, who was rector of Ayott St. Lawrence, Hertfordshire, from 1830 to 1874. Mr. Olive had, in 1854, purchased it from Mrs. Sarah Clarke, to whom it had been given by her former employer, Rev. Thomas Capron, a dissenting minister, near Bedford. This portrait of Bunyan has been copied and reproduced many times and in many ways: some are faithful to the original, others are almost unrecognisable; but the fine mezzo-tints of Houston and Spilsbury are much sought after for their value as works of art, as well as relics of Bunyan. That by Jonathan Spilsbury was published about 1763. He signed his plates as 'J.' Spilsbury, and he is sometimes confused with his brother John. After the exhibition of his works at the Royal Institution in 1807, Spilsbury is no more heard of. The mezzo-tint by Houston is a yet finer accomplishment, being softer and more entrancing. This has become very scarce. Born in Dublin in 1721, Richard Houston eventually became a pupil of John Brooks, and was a mezzo-tinter of great promise and talent. He died in 1775. (*Vide* Whitman's *Masters of Mezzo-tint.* London, 1898.)

Charles Doe's Folio Portrait is, as Dr. Brown says, not so pleasant to look upon, but it is less unpleasant than Simpson's engraving of Sadler's in 1767. It is regrettable that Doe fails to name the artist. There is yet one other portrait that might be mentioned: an oil painting in the possession of Mr. John Beagarie of Hitchin: whether an original or a copy it is not possible to say.

In *The Advocateship of Jesus Christ,* published by Dorman Newman, in 1688, is a steel-engraved portrait of John Bunnyon, executed by Van Houe.

In 1902, a London daily paper stated that there was a portrait of Bunyan in Stationers' Hall: a statement based no doubt on a passage in a book by John Gough Nicholls, written about the Company's Hall. On the back of the frame, however, is the name, 'T. Marsden,' and more probably it is his portrait; for the resemblance to Bunyan is too remote to imagine it to be of him.

There is an etched engraving, signed 'J. H. f. 1756,' which presents Bunyan with a fierce countenance and wearing a skull-cap, and a broad collar over his gown; and abundant locks of curly hair flowing over his shoulders. 'JOHN BUNYAN' is imprinted on the plate, otherwise the features have but little or no resemblance to those of his reputed portraits. Another portrait, finely engraved by S. Freeman, "From a Picture in the possession of George Phillips, Esqr.," appeared in Fullarton's edition of *The Pilgrim's Progress* issued from Glasgow. A smaller engraving of the same portrait, dated 1825, shows Bunyan seated, with his left arm on the chair elbow, and his hand resting on an upright Bible. The fingers of his right hand, uplifted, denote movement, whilst his expression is genial but earnest. It would be interesting to know the whereabouts of the original painting. A very beautiful medallion portrait of Bunyan, a stippled engraving with representative figures around him, forms one of that famous set after the designs of Thomas Stothard.

Fortunately, affection for John Bunyan does not depend upon the graven art: the word-portraits by his nearest and dearest friends, together with one's own conception of the Man and his books, suffice.

(Page 410.)

Bunyan's Successors at Bedford.

Dr. John Brown resigned his ministry at the Bunyan Meeting in 1903, at the age of seventy-three. He then removed to London, where he spent his latter days. His immediate successor was the Rev. W. Charter Pigott (1905-1912). In the years following the pastorate has been filled by the Revs. W. J. Coates, B.D. (1912-1917), and Leonard Brooks, B.A. (1918-1924). The present minister is the Rev. C. Bernard Cockett, M.A.

XVIII.

BUNYAN'S POSTHUMOUS PUBLICATIONS.

FOR the preservation of those MSS. of Bunyan which remained unpublished at the time of his death we are indebted to the untiring devotion of his enthusiastic admirer, Charles Doe, who tells us in his own good, simple way how he, a comb-maker, came to take in hand the publishing and selling of books. After narrating how he first became acquainted with Bunyan, as already described, he goes on to say:

"In March, 1686, as I was reading Mr. Bunyan's Book 'Saved by Grace,' I thought certainly this is the best Book that was ever writ or I read except the Bible, and then I remembered I had received a great deal of comfort in all of his Books. Some time after my assurance, and being under the sense of the peculiar Love of God, it came into my mind as I was upon my Stair-head what work I should do for God, and about the middle of the Stairs I reckoned that to sell books was the best I could do, and by that time I came to the bottom I concluded to sell Mr. Bunyan's, and so I began to sell Books and have sold about 3,000 of Mr. Bunyan's, and also have been concerned in printing the following Books: The works of Mr. John Bunyan in folio, and the 'Heavenly Footman' by John Bunyan."

This account is given in a little book entitled '*A Collection of Experience,* by Charles Doe. London: Printed by Charles Doe, a Comb-maker, between the Hospital and London Bridge, 1700.'

It would appear that there had been some scheme projected in the author's lifetime for publishing a Collected Edition of the Works of Bunyan. Doe describes the folio edition of 1692 as "containing ten of his excellent manuscripts prepared for the press before his death, never before printed, and Ten of his Choyce Books formerly printed. Collected and Printed by the Procurement of his Church and Friends, and *by his own Approbation before his Death.*"* Elsewhere also in his *Struggler* he says: "It had succeeded in Mr. Bunyan's lifetime even all his labours in folio; but that an interested Bookseller opposed it."

* *Vide* Appendix I.

Chandler and Wilson add: "The Propriety of several pieces already Printed is lodg'd in Particular Persons' hands who were not willing, to resign up their Rights at reasonable Rates." Probably this refers mainly to Nathaniel Ponder, who, having for some time past discovered that *The Pilgrim's Progress* was a good book in a sense other than the religious one, was unwilling to let go his hold of it even so far as to let it appear in folio form. Possibly also the same difficulty prevented the completion of Doe's design; for while on his title-page he has the words—*the first volume*—no second volume made its appearance till more than forty years afterwards. Soon after Bunyan's death, therefore, Doe set about the preparation of the first volume of the collected works. Many of them in their separate form were growing scarce even then. He had, he says, by great labour secured a single copy of some of them, and that others "are not to be bought; and that I have proved by often trying most London booksellers; and before that, given them about twice the price for a book; and I know not how to get another of those sorts for any price whatsoever." He first issued, in 1691, a circular containing thirty "Reasons why Christian People should Promote by subscription the Printing in folio the labours of Mr. John Bunyan." When the volume appeared he tells us that "notwithstanding the many discouragements I have met with in my struggles in this so great work, we have (and I may believe by the blessing of the Lord) gotten about 400 subscriptions, whereof about thirty are ministers."

It was intended to issue the work to subscribers at about twelve shillings for a book containing 140 sheets, but "by reason of the smallness of the writing of the manuscript it could not be so exactly computed"—as the Church Book shows, Bunyan had two styles of handwriting,* one bolder, and one exceedingly minute—so that the volume ran on to 155 sheets and the price to a shilling more, with which Doe hopes the subscribers will not be displeased.†

* *Vide* Addendum —Chapter VI.

† *Vide* Addendum —Appendix I.

This folio edition of 1692 was prefaced by an epistle to the reader, the joint production of Ebenezer Chandler, Bunyan's successor at Bedford, and John Wilson, the minister at Hitchin, his friend of many years. It was printed and published by William Marshall, at the Bible, in Newgate Street, and had for a frontispiece the engraved portrait of Bunyan by Sturt. It contained also a folded sheet with engraved "map, showing the order and causes of salvation and damnation"; on one half being shown the path of life, and on the other the way of death. This map was originally published as a broadside about the year 1664, and sold for sixpence.*

* The Editor knows of but one original copy of this broadside still existing. It is in a private collection.

The following were the ten new MSS. contained in the volume and prepared for the press by Bunyan himself:

(1) *An Exposition on the Ten first chapters of Genesis and part of the Eleventh.* This work ends abruptly in the midst of an account of the Tower of Babel, and with this note, "☞ This is all Mr. Bunyan hath writ of this *Exposition,* as we perceive by the blank paper following the manuscript." It would seem as if he had intended this fragment at the commencement of a continuous Commentary on the Scriptures. Speaking of the Sabbath of Creation (Gen. ii. 3), he refers to the Sabbath of weeks, the Sabbath of years, and the great jubilee enjoined in Leviticus xxv. 1-13, and adds: "Of all which more in their place if God permit." There is perhaps no great reason to regret that this intention was not fulfilled. Bunyan's special *forte* was not exegesis. What he could do and do admirably was to take accepted views of truth, and make them luminous and living by the radiance of his own genius. What neither his training nor the qualities of his mind fitted him for, was the judicial weighing of evidence, the power of forming a profound estimate of the growth and unity of Revelation, or of following the strict logical sequence of a line of scripture thought. In this exposition of the book of Genesis, as we might expect, he accepts easily the points most controverted now; after the manner of his time, he shines in conceits which have become obsolete, and falls into that spiritualizing of historic fact and circumstance which has so often and so seriously hindered a true spiritual interpretation. This, however, was the vice of his age, and Bunyan has it in far less degree than many of his contemporaries, his strong common sense having saved him. For instance, when he comes to speak of the Ark and its construction, one storey being above another, he sees in this a foreshadowing that in the Church of Christ there would be some higher than some, apostles above pastors; and also degrees of

glory, rank above rank in the Christian life. On the other hand, where he finds mentioned the month and the exact day of the month when the flood came upon the earth, he hesitates whether he ought or ought not to attach spiritual significance to these particulars: "For I dare not say this scribe wrote this in vain, or that it was needless thus to punctilio it; a mystery is in it, but my darkness sees it not: I must speak according to the proportion of faith."

(2) The treatise, *Justification by imputed righteousness,* is in the line of previous writings of his, and is an unfolding and enforcement of the proposition "that there is no other way for sinners to be justified from the curse of the law in the sight of God than by the imputation of that righteousness long ago performed by, and still residing with, the person of Jesus Christ." He bases the relation of Christ and the believer upon the community of nature between Christ and humanity. The Son of God took hold of *us* by taking upon him flesh and blood. He took not on him a *particular* person, though he took to him a human body and soul; but that which he took was, as I may call it, a lump of the common nature of man. Hence he in a mystery became *us* and was counted as *all* the men that were or should be saved. And this is the reason why we are said to *do* when only Jesus Christ did *do*. The defect of Bunyan's position is, that while he sees Christ's federal relation to the race he restricts Christ's atonement to the elect, saying that all the elect did righteousness when Christ wrought and fulfilled the law. Passing from this he shows that by the law we have not salvation but only a deeper knowledge of our own sin. There is the meeting of opposites—the law is spiritual, I am carnal. Strike a steel against a flint and the fire flies about you; strike the law against a carnal heart and sin appears, sin multiplies, sin rageth, sin is strengthened. And conscience is Little-ease if men resist it, whether it be rightly or wrongly informed. Speaking towards the close on the inherent power of faith, he shows that it doth the same against the devil that unbelief doth to God. Doth unbelief count God a liar? Faith counts the devil a liar. Doth unbelief hold the soul from the mercy of God? Faith holds the soul from the malice of the devil. Doth unbelief quench thy graces? Faith kindleth them even into a flame. Doth unbelief fill the soul full of sorrow? Faith fills it full

of the joy of the Holy Ghost. In a word, doth unbelief bind down thy sins upon thee? Why, faith in Jesus Christ releaseth thee of them all.

(3) The next of the MSS., first published in 1692, is entitled *Paul's Departure and Crown,* being an extended sermon on 2 Tim. iv. 6-8. He shows what it is to be offered up and what to be ready to be offered up. Paul sees in death something more than the common fate of men. As a believer's prayers and praises are a sacrifice and an acceptable offering to God, so should his death and martyrdom for the Gospel be both sweet in the nostrils of God and of profit to his Church. To be ready to be offered is to be daily in the posture of fidelity. Both Enoch and Noah walked with God: that is, they kept touch with him, still keeping up to the work and duty that every day required, not doing their duty by fits and starts, but in a fervent spirit they served the Lord. It is said also of Abraham that he died in a good old age, thereby insinuating that he made both ends meet together, the end of his work with the end of his days. It is not thus with all. Religion to most men is but a by-business, with which they use to fill up spare hours; or as a stalking-horse, which is used to catch the game. We should try to get at the real facts of the case between this world and the next. Take, then, heed; Satan is here a mighty artist, and can show us all earthly things in a multiplying glass; but when we look up to things above we see them as through sackcloth of hair. Honours, pleasures, and the like, are, after all, but poor, low, base things, and he that hath the most of them may in the fulness of his sufficiency be in straits. A horse that is loaded with gold and pearls all day may have a foul stable and a galled back at night. And woe be to him that increaseth that which is not his, and that ladeth himself with thick clay. O man of God, throw this bone to the dogs; suck not at it, there is no marrow there. On the other hand, when men are faithful they have peace at their latter end. Ah! when God makes the bed he must needs lie easy that weakness hath cast thereon; a blessed pillow hath that man for his head though to all beholders it is as hard as a stone. I once was told a story of what happened at a good man's death, the which I have often remembered with wonderment and gladness. After he had lain for some time sick his turn came that he must depart, and behold while he lay, as we call it, drawing on, to the amazement of the mourners there was heard about his

bed such blessed and ravishing music as they never heard before; which also continued till his soul departed, and then began to cease, and grow, as to its sound, as if it was departing the house and so seemed to go further and further off till at last they could hear it no longer.

(4) Under the title of *Israel's Hope Encouraged,* Bunyan sets forth from Psalm cxxx. 7, what hope is and how it is distinguished from faith. Faith comes by hearing, hope by experience; faith lays hold of that end of the promise that is next to us, to wit, as it is in the Bible, hope lays hold of that end of the promise that is fastened to the mercy-seat: for the promise is like a mighty cable that is fastened by one end to a ship and by the other to the anchor. Thus faith and hope, getting hold of both ends of the promise they carry it safely all away. Hope saves by prevailing with the soul to suffer all troubles, afflictions, and adversities, betwixt this and the world to come for the sake of Christ. Hope has a thick skin, and will endure many a blow; it will put on patience as a vestment, it will wade through a sea of blood, it will endure all things, if it be of the right kind, for the joy that is set before it. It is for want of hope that so many brisk professors that have so boasted and made brags of their faith, have not been able to endure the drum in the day of alarm and affliction. We have a right to cherish hope, for our best things are yet behind and in reversion. They are things too big as yet to enter into our hearts and things too big if they were there to come out or to be expressed by our mouths. There is heaven itself, the imperial heaven; does anybody know what that is? There is the Mount Zion, the heavenly Jerusalem, and the innumerable company of angels: doth anybody know what all they are? There is immortality and eternal life; and who knows what they are? There are rewards for services and labours of love showed to God's name here; and who knows what they will be? There are mansion-houses, beds of glory, and places to walk in among the angels; and who knows what they are? There will be badges of honour, harps to make merry with, and heavenly songs of triumph; doth any here know what they are? There will then be a knowing, an enjoying, and a solacing of ourselves with prophets, apostles, and martyrs, and all saints; but in what glorious manner we all are ignorant of. There we shall see and know, and be with for ever, all our relations, as wife, husband, child, father, mother, brother, or sister, that have

JOHN BUNYAN'S JUG.

(Preserved at the Bunyan Meeting, Bedford.)
Photo: G. A. Gearey, Bedford.]

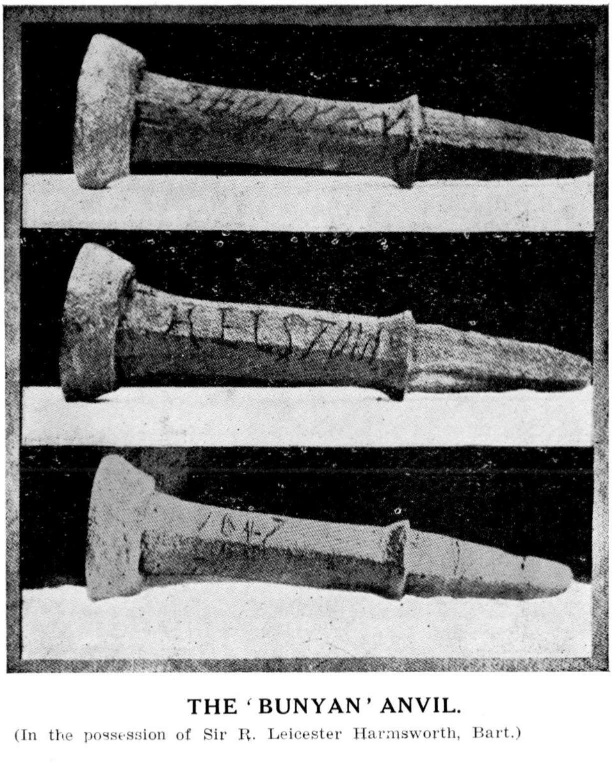

THE 'BUNYAN' ANVIL.

(In the possession of Sir R. Leicester Harmsworth, Bart.)

died in the faith; but how gloriously they will look when we shall see them, and how gloriously we shall love when we are with them it is not for us in this world to know.

Let Israel, therefore, hope in the Lord, and for another reason: for with the Lord there is mercy, tender mercy, great mercy, he is rich in mercy, there is with him a multitude of mercies. And as they are called *a multitude,* so they are called *mercies manifold.* There is no single flower in God's gospel-garden, they are all double and treble; there is a wheel within a wheel, a blessing within a blessing in all the mercies of God. Manifold—a man cannot receive one but he receives many, many folded up, one within another. The very door and inlet into all these mercies is Christ Jesus; therefore, Christian man, look well to thyself, that thou goest no whither, and dost nothing but as thou art in him. Walk in him, speak in him, grow in him, for he is THE ALL. Many there be that count this but a low thing; they desire to soar aloft, to fly into new notions, and to be broaching of new opinions, not counting themselves happy except they can throw some new-found fangle, to be applauded for, among their novel-hearers; but fly thou to Christ for life. And remember humbly thy sins. There be some alive in the world, who, though they count the nature and commission of sin the very evil of evils, yet can say that the remembrance of how vile they are and of what evils they have committed, has been to them a soul-humbling, a Christ-advancing, and a creature-emptying consideration. Hold fast to the great truth of a Mediator. It is with many that begin with this doctrine as it is with boys that go to the Latin school, they learn till they have learned the grounds of their grammar and then go home and forget all. He that will keep water in a sieve must use more than ordinary diligence. Our heart is the leaky vessel, and therefore we ought to give the more earnest heed to the things which we have heard, lest at any time we should let them slip.

(5) It will be remembered that Charles Doe tells us how, having heard of Bunyan's fame, and having read some of his books, during the persecution of 1685-6, he went for the first time to hear him at Mr. More's meeting, in a private house, and that his text was, "The fears of the wicked shall come upon him, but the desires of the righteous shall be granted." This sermon afterwards grew to more, and under the title *The Desires*

of the Righteous Granted was found among Bunyan's MSS. and added to this volume Doe sent forth. After telling us who is the righteous man, he proceeds to speak of his desires. Even in him there are contradictory desires: How may I know to which my soul adheres? Why thus—which wouldst thou have to prevail? What thinkest thou of the grace thou seest in gracious souls who are near thee? Dost thou not cry out, O, I bless them in my heart! O, methinks grace is the greatest beauty in the world! Yea, I could be content to live and die with those people that have the grace of God in their souls. A hundred times and a hundred, when I have been upon my knees before God, I have desired, were it the will of God, that I might be in their condition. Then again, how art thou when thou thinkest that thou thyself hast grace? O then, says the soul, I am as if I could leap out of myself; joy, joy, joy, then is with my heart. It is, methinks, the greatest mercy under heaven to be made a gracious man. Is it thus with thy soul indeed? Happy man! Be of good courage, thou art on the right side.

The full desire of the righteous can only be accomplished in eternity, and the strength of this desire shows itself in this that it is willing to grapple with the king of terrors rather than be detained from that sweet communion that the soul looks for when it comes into the place where the Lord is. I have a desire to depart and to be with Christ. To see Jesus Christ, to see him as he is, to see him as he is in glory, is a sight that is worth going from relations, and out of the body, and through the jaws of death to see; for this is to see him head over all; to see him possessed of heaven for his church; to see him preparing of mansion-houses for those his poor ones that are now by his enemies kicked to and fro, like foot-balls in the world; and is not this a blessed sight? This desire may not always be equally strong upon us. Many times it is with our desires as it is with saffron, it will bloom and blossom, and be ripe, and all in a night. Tell me, dost thou not desire to desire? Yea, dost thou not vehemently desire to desire to depart and to be with Christ? I know if thou art a righteous man thou dost. When God in this life satisfies our desires, we must consider that great grace is reserved for great service. When thy desire cometh thou wilt have occasion for it; new work, new trials, new sufferings, or something that will call for the power and virtue of all the grace thou shalt have to keep thy spirit even and thy feet from slipping, while thou art exercised in new engagements. Assure thyself thy God will not give thee straw, but he will expect brick. Wherefore as thou art busy in desiring more grace, be also desirous that wisdom to manage it with faithfulness may also be granted unto thee. Thou wilt say grace, if I had it, will do all this for me. It will and it will not. It will, if thou watch and be sober; it will not, if thou be foolish and remiss. Men of great grace may grow consumptive in grace, and idleness may turn him that wears a plush jacket into rags.

(6) *The Saint's Privilege and Profit* is a treatise on prayer, based upon the invitation in Hebrews iv., 16, to come boldly unto the throne of grace. Though not published till 1692, it was evidently written even before the work entitled *The Water of Life,* which Bunyan published in 1688, for on page 38 of the first edition of the latter, he says, —" But because I have spoken of this more particularly upon that text [' Let us therefore come boldly to the throne of grace, &c.]. I shall therefore here say no more." He here shows that the place of mercy is a throne, a glorious high throne, with a High Priest standing near, and to it there is to be an orderly coming by the new and living way, and with a true heart in full assurance of faith. Faith, if it be strong, will play the man in the dark, will like a mettled horse, flounce in a bad way, will not be discouraged at trials, at many or strong trials. But even faith must cling to the sacrifice of Christ as well as to the promise of God, for alas! faith is sometimes in a calm, sometimes up, and sometimes down, and sometimes at it with sin, death, and the devil, as we say, blood up to the ears. Faith now has but little time to speak peace to the conscience: it is now struggling for life, it is now fighting with angels, with infernals; all it can do now is to cry, groan, sweat, fear, fight, and gasp for life.

After speaking of the legal and natural qualifications of Christ for his High-priestly office, arising out of his appointment of the Father, and his quick and vivid sympathy with the believer, he proceeds to show that there are times of need when we need to come boldly. Such a time is the beginning of the Christian life. Then the devil has lost a sinner, a captive has broke prison, and hell is awaking from sleep. To want the spirit of prayer now is as much as thy life is worth. You that are broke loose from hell, that do hear the lion roar after you, and that are kept awake with the continual voice of his chinking chain, cry as you fly. This is a needy time. Now thy hedge is low, now thy branch is tender, now thou art but in the bud. Pray that thou beest not marred in the potter's hand. Times of spiritual prosperity ever are times of need, and this through the deceits of our heart. There are snares laid for us in our best things, and he that has great enjoyments and forgets to pray for grace to keep him humble, then, shall quickly be where Peter was after his knowledge of the Lord Jesus by the revelation of the Father. Such a time also is the hour of worldly adversity. Then Satan will say, "It is not a time now to retain a tender conscience, to regard thy word or promise, to pay for what thou buyest, or to stick at pilfering, and filch from thy neighbour." Times of persecution, of changes in our life, of decay, of guilt, of reproach and slander, and desertion also are times of need. Finally, such time also is the day of death, when I am to pack up and be gone from hence, the way of all the earth. Now the greatest trial is come, excepting that of the day of judgment. Now a man is to be stripped of all, but that which cannot be shaken. Now a man grows near the borders of eternity. Now he begins to see into the skirts of the next world. Now death is death, and the grave the grave indeed! Now he begins to see what it is for body and soul to part, and what to go and appear before God. Now the dark entry, and the thought of what is in the way from a death-bed to the gate of the holy heaven, comes nearer to the heart than when health and prosperity do compass a man about. Wherefore this is like to be a trying time, a time of need indeed, while strong death is loosing his silver cord, and breaking his golden bowl!

(7) The next of Bunyan's posthumous works, *Christ a Compleat Saviour,*[1] deals with a subject of which he never wearied, the power which Christ's intercession gives him to save to the uttermost. It is, says he—taking a leaf out of his own experience—struggling work to come to Christ. Evils within will rise and take this man and toss and tumble him like a ball in a large place, so that he is not master of himself, of his thoughts, nor of his passions. Strange, hideous, and amazing blasphemies will fix themselves upon him. These blasphemies are like those

[1] *Crist yn Iachawdwr Cyflawn.* Caerfyrddin. [1820?] 8vo. [Cardiff Public Library has a copy dated 1798.]

frogs that I have heard of that will leap up, and catch hold of, and hang by their claws. Now help, Lord; now, Lord Jesus, what shall I do? Now, Son of David, have mercy upon me! Guilt, too, rises up and breaks the heart with its burden. And Satan has the art of making the uttermost of every sin; he can blow it up, make it swell, make every hair of its head as big as a cedar. It is hard coming to God when a man's own conscience sides with the enemy. Better can a man bear and deal with any objection against himself than with those that himself doth make against himself. They lie close, stick fast, speak aloud, and will be heard; yea, will haunt and hunt him, as the devil doth some in every hole and corner. But come, man, come, for he is able to save to the uttermost.

We need such an intercessor as Christ, for there is in us mistrust and doubting, aptness to errors, and inclination to faint under the Cross. We seek too much to save ourselves, to dissemble the known truth for the obtaining a little favour with men, and to speak things that we ought not that we may sleep in a whole skin. And then how imperfect our prayers are! Where is the man that pursues with all his might what but now he seemed to ask for with all his heart? Prayer is become a shell, a piece of formality, a very empty thing, as to the spirit and life of prayer at this day. I have heard of many that have *played,* but of few that have *prayed,* wrestling with God for mercy in that duty. Then as to the hearing of the Word. Alas! the place of hearing is the place of sleeping with many a fine professor. I have often observed that those that keep shops can briskly attend upon a twopenny customer; but when they come themselves to God's market, they spend their time too much in letting their thoughts to wander from God's commandments, or in a nasty drowsy way. The head, also, and hearts of most hearers are to the Word as the sieve is to water: they can hold no sermons, remember no texts, bring home no proofs, produce none of the sermon to the edification and profit of others.

(8) *The Saints' Knowledge of Christ's Love* is an exposition of Paul's prayer for the Ephesians (iii. 18, 19) that they might be able to comprehend with all saints what is the breadth and length and depth and height, and to know the love of Christ which passeth knowledge. This is a text, he says, made up of words *picked* and *packed* together by the wisdom of God, *picked*

and *packed* together on purpose for the succour and relief of the tempted. Christ's love suits and answers a Christian's condition while in this world, let it be what it will. If his afflictions be broad, here is a breadth; if they be long, here is a length; and if they be deep, here is a depth; and if they be high, here is a height. And this I will say, that while in a state of trial and temptation nothing is more helpful or comforting than to know that there is a *breadth* to answer a *breadth,* a *length* to answer a *length,* a *depth* to answer a *depth,* and a *height* to answer a *height.* The main part of this book is concerned with what knowing of the love that passeth knowledge is possible in this world. It may be known as to its nature in many of its degrees, and, above all, we may know that it passes knowledge. Thus to know that love is to be filled with all the fulness of God, and what a man is he who is filled thus! Such men are at this day wanting in the Churches. These are the men that *sweeten* Churches, and that bring glory to God and to religion.

(9) Bunyan's work, entitled *The House of the Forest of Lebanon,*[1] is a somewhat fanciful, and not very appropriate analogy based upon 1 Kings, vii. 2, which narrates that Solomon, after building the Temple and his own house, built also the house of the forest of Lebanon. He says that as the temple was a figure of the Church under the Gospel as she relateth to worship, so the house of the forest of Lebanon was a figure of the Church as she is assaulted for worship, as she is persecuted for the same. In other words, it is a type of the Church in the wilderness, or as she is in her sackcloth state. The comparison is not a very happy one, for if this house were actually built in the forest of Lebanon, the probability is that it would be a summer palace for the king's enjoyment. But the greater likelihood is that it was simply one of the range of palaces built at Jerusalem, and so called either because it was built of Lebanon cedar or because it displayed a perfect thicket or forest of cedar pillars. But though we cannot go with Bunyan in the main course of his analogy, we can accept an occasional illustration like this: "Let a man and a beast look out at the same window, the same door, the same casement, yet the one will see like a man, and the other but like a beast." We can also feel the force of his power-

[1] *Traethawd am y Ty yn nghoedwig Libanus.* Merthyr. 1835. 16mo. [Cardiff Public Library has a copy dated 1791.]

ful words when, after reminding us that through many tribulations is the very roadway to heaven, he says:

"Let this, then, encourage the saints to hope and to rejoice in hope of the glory of God, notwithstanding present tribulations. This is our seed-time, our winter; afflictions are to try us of what metal we are made; yea, and to shake off worm-eaten fruit, and such as are rotten at core. Troubles for Christ's sake are but like the prick of an awl in the tip of the ear, in order to hang a jewel there. Let this also put the saints upon patience: when we know that a trial will have an end, we are by that knowledge encouraged to exercise patience. I have a bad master, but I have a year to serve under him, and that makes me serve him with patience; I have but a mile to go on this dirty way, and then I shall have my path pleasant and green, and this makes me tread the dirty way with patience. I am now in my rags, but by that quarter of a year is come and gone, two hundred a year comes into my hand, wherefore I will wait, and exercise patience. Thus might I multiply comparisons. Be patient, then, my brethren; but how long? to the coming of the Lord. But when will that be? the coming of the Lord draws nigh."

(10) The last of the works printed for the first time in the folio of 1692 was entitled, *Of Antichrist and his Ruine, and of the Slaying of the Witnesses.* Bunyan begins by showing that Antichrist is the adversary of Christ; an adversary really, a friend pretendedly. Against him in *deed,* for him in *word,* and contrary to him in practice. *Antichrist* first made his appearance in the Church of God. Not that the Church of God did willingly admit him there to sit as such; he had *covered* his cloven foot; he had *plumbs* in his dragon's mouth, and so came in by flatteries. He evidently means by Antichrist the spirit of the priestly system, and gives a description of its crippled condition in his time, which would have to be modified considerably before it would suit ours. "For as concerning his masses, prayers for the dead, images, pilgrimages, monkish vows, sinful fasts, and the beastly single life of their priests, though when the spirit of Antichrist was in them they did bear some sway in the world; yet now of what esteem are they? or who has reverence for them? They are now blown together under hedges, as the dry leaves for the mice and frogs to harbour in." There shall be brave days when Antichrist is utterly dead. The people born in that happy time shall see Antichrist only in its ruins; they shall, like the sparrows, the little robins, and the wren, sit and sing and chirrup one to another,

while their eyes behold this dead hawk. Then shall the differences, the divisions, and debates among the godly cease; for men shall see eye to eye when the Lord shall bring again Zion, yea the watchmen of God's people shall do so; for it is for want of light *in them* that the lambs have so butted one another. He is jubilant over the nearing end. Now, since Antichrist is dying, let us ring her passing-bell; for when she is dead we that live to see it intend to *ring out.* No peal ever rung out of Elstow steeple by him ever went forth with more heart and soul than would this; but the passing-bell of Antichrist was not destined to be rung in his time. Babylon says he shall be an habitation of devils and a cage for every unclean and hateful bird—a cage, not to imprison them in, but for them to sit and sing in, to confer their notes in, to make melodious music in; I mean melodious to their own thinking; for the ass thinks that he sings full favouredly, and the owl endeavours to lift up her voice above all the birds of the wood.

Among the instruments that God will use to compass the ruin of Antichrist, Bunyan trusts mainly to kings. With James II. on the throne, at that very time striving might and main to re-establish that Popery which to Bunyan's mind was Antichrist, one is surprised that he should. Yet so he does, and makes this declaration against Romanism a manifesto of his own loyalty to his Prince:

"I speak the more of this, because (as I have said) I believe that by magistrates and powers we shall be delivered and kept from Antichrist. Let the King have verily a place in your hearts, and with heart and mouth give thanks for him; he is a better saviour of us than we may be aware of. Pray for Kings to the God of heaven, who has the heart of Kings in his hands. Pray for the long life of the King. Pray that God would always give wisdom and judgment to the King. Pray that God would discover all plots and conspiracies against his person and government. Pray also that God would make him able to drive away all evil and all evil men from his presence; and that he may be a greater countenancer than ever of them that are holy and good. I do confess myself one of the old-fashioned professors that covet to fear God and honour the King. I also am for blessing of them that curse me, for doing good to them that hate me, and for praying for them that despitefully use me and persecute me. And have had more peace in the practice of these things than all the world are aware of. I only drop this because I would show my brethren that I also am one of them, and to set them right that have wrong thoughts of me, as to so weighty matters as these."

Such were the ten books by Bunyan first given to the world in the folio of 1692, within four years of his death. There were still four other works of his unprinted: *A Pocket Concordance to the Scriptures; A Christian Dialogue; The Heavenly Footman;* and the *Relation of his Imprisonment.* The first two may have never been printed, but *The Heavenly Footman* was published by Charles Doe in 1698, and the *Account of his Imprisonment* was given to the world in 1765. It is matter for congratulation that this last, one of the most characteristic of his writings, and one of the most interesting in a biographical sense, was not altogether lost during the hundred years between its composition in Bedford gaol and its publication. It is probable that we are indebted to Samuel Palmer, the editor of the *Nonconformist Memorial,* for its preservation. His family at that time lived in Bedford, his native town, where he was a frequent visitor during his ministry at Hackney, and this 'Relation' of Bunyan's imprisonment was published by James Buckland, at the Buck in Paternoster Row, who was also Palmer's publisher. The MS. of this little book had probably remained in the possession of Hannah Bunyan, and was only printed four years before her death. That it was printed at all and not lost, considering the long period it remained in MS., will be felt to be a fortunate circumstance by all who remember that it contains the account of Bunyan's arrest at Harlington, of his trial before Kelynge, and of the memorable interview between his wife and Sir Matthew Hale.

The Heavenly Footman had been in the possession of Charles Doe, in MS., for six years before he gave it to the public in 1698. He was still hoping to send out a second folio volume containing Bunyan's already published writings, to which this might have been added. But publishers' rights still barred the way, and at length he sent forth this little work separately. Three copies of the first edition are in existence, one of which is in the possession of the trustees of Bunyan's Meeting.* The title is as follows: '*The Heavenly Footman;* or, a Description of the Man that gets to Heaven, together with the ways he runs in, the marks he goes by. Also, some Directions how to Run so as to Obtain. Briefly Observed and Published by John Bunyan. London: printed for Charles Doe, Comb-maker, in the Borough, Southwark, near London Bridge, 1698.'[1] To the book itself Doe

* There is a copy in the British Museum, and another in the library of Sir R. Leicester Harmsworth, Bart.

[1] *Casgliad byrr o'r Rhedegwr Ysprydol.* Casgliad. 1766. *An Gille-riuth neamhaidh.* Gael. Edinburgh, 1858.

added a Catalogue of all Bunyan's writings, which appears to have been carefully drawn up and was introduced as follows:

"Running Reader! I that now help you to this Heavenly Footman in Print (being the Person that first moved and procured the Printing in Folio above Twenty of our Author Bunyan's Pieces), have also now given you here a Catalogue of all that great Convert's Works in order of Time, as they succeeded each other in Publication (as near as I can understand), and I do also love them, and would have you do so too, as they are the Experience and Knowledge of a great Convert, which indeed is a great Monument of the mighty power of Grace, and a fit Fellow-Traveller for a Heavenly Foot-man.

"Charles Doe.

"BOROUGH, LONDON, March 26, 1698."

At the end of the Catalogue he says:

"The four Books following were never yet Printed, except this now of the Heavenly Footman, which I bought in 1691, now six years since, of Mr. John Bunyan, the eldest son of our Author; and I have now put it into the World in Print, Word for word as it came from him to me."

The book thus published by Doe is based upon the text, "So run that ye may obtain" (1 Cor. ix. 24), and is prefaced with "An Epistle to all the Slothful and Careless People," calling to the spiritual sluggard as with trumpet tone to awake and arise.

"Time runs, much of your lives are past, and your souls are worth a thousand worlds—do not loiter, for the angels do not and Christ did not. What is before you is worth striving for. As the men of Dan said to their brethren after they had seen the goodness of the land of Canaan, 'Arise, for we have seen the land, and behold it is very good. Be not slothful to go and to enter and possess the land.' Farewell. I wish our souls may meet with comfort at the journey's end.

John Bunyan."

He would have the heavenly runners get into the right way first and so not lose their labour.

"Here is one runs a-quaking, another a-ranting; one again runs after the Baptism, and another after the Independency. Here is one for free-will and another for Presbytery; and yet possibly most of all these sects run quite the wrong way, and yet every one is for his life, his soul, either for heaven or hell."

Get, therefore, into the right way, use a wise thoughtfulness when you are therein, strip yourself of hindrances, beware of bye-paths, do not listen to every man who wishes to talk with you by the way, do not be daunted with difficulties; above all, do not be offended with the Cross, for it is the standing way-mark by which all that would go to glory must pass.

"You know if one ask you the way to such and such a place, you for the better direction, do not only say, this is the way, but then also say, you must go by such a gate, by such a style, such a bush, tree, bridge, or such like. Why, so it is here; art thou enquiring the way to heaven? Why, I tell thee, Christ is the way; into him thou must get, into his righteousness, to be justified; and if thou art in him, thou wilt presently see the cross, thou must go close by it, thou must touch it, nay, thou must take it up, or else thou wilt quickly go out of the way that leads to heaven, and turn up some of those crooked lanes that lead down to the chambers of death."

It is this Cross that is the difficulty with so many. "I am persuaded were it not for the Cross, where we have one professor we should have twenty; but this Cross, that is it which spoileth all." The way to take the bitterness out of the Cross is to keep your eye upon the Crown. Think much of those who have gone before, how really they are in the kingdom, how safe in the arms of Jesus, how unwilling they would be to be here for a thousand worlds, and what they would think of the man who lets his heart fail him in the journey or sin allure him. "O!" they would say, "did he but see what we see, feel what we feel, and taste of the dainties that we taste of!"

"Sometimes when my base heart hath been inclining to this world, and to loiter in my journey towards heaven, the very consideration of the glorious saints and angels in heaven, what they enjoy, and what low thoughts they have of the things of this world together, how they would befool me if they did but know that my heart was drawing back; hath caused me to rush forward, to disdain these poor, low, empty, beggarly things, and to say to my soul, Come, soul, let us not be weary, let us see what this heaven is; let us even venture all for it, and try if that will quit the cost."

Think, too, how many seeming simple ones are wise in this.

"Will it not be a dishonour to thee to see the very boys and girls in the country to have more wit than thyself? It may be the servants of some men, as the horse keeper, ploughman, scullion, &c., are more looking after heaven than their masters. I am apt to think sometimes, that more servants than masters, that more tenants than landlords, will inherit the Kingdom of heaven. But is not this a shame for them that are such? I am persuaded you scorn that your servants should say that they are wiser than you in the things of this world; and yet I am bold to say, that many of them are wiser than you in the things of the world to come, which are of greater concernment."

* *Vide* Addendum. Appendix I.

In the first collected edition, that of the Folio of 1692,* there were published twenty of Bunyan's works, ten of the twenty being then printed for the first time. The intervention of publishers' rights, as we have said, prevented this edition going on to a second volume, and it was not till 1736 that Doe's original idea was able to be carried out. In that year there appeared an edition in two volumes folio, edited by Samuel Wilson, of the Barbican, the grandson of that John Wilson who was Bunyan's friend. This new edition was published by subscription, and contained, in addition to the twenty works of the first folio, twenty-seven others which had been previously published in separate form. In 1767 there appeared a third edition of the Collected Works in two volumes folio, with a preface by George Whitefield—this edition containing three works of Bunyan not included in previous collections, though previously published. Other collected editions have been issued—one in six volumes octavo, published in 1780 by Alexander Hogg; one in 1853, which was revised in 1862, under the editorship of Mr. G. Offor, in three volumes imperial octavo; and one in four volumes imperial octavo, edited in 1859 by the Rev. Henry Stebbing, F.R.S. Mr. Offor gave himself as enthusiastically to the work of editing this his favourite author as did Charles Doe before him, and as possessing greater advantages with more complete success. His notes, like some others, are occasionally a little superfluous, sometimes indeed raising a smile by their very simplicity; his *Life of Bunyan,* too, is confusing by its involved repetitions, and is frequently inaccurate; but he must always receive grateful mention among the lovers of Bunyan for the immense pains he bestowed upon his work, and for his careful bibliographical account of the varied editions of his author's varied works.

The writings of Bunyan which we have sought all the way through to connect chronologically with his life are all that can with certainty be declared to be genuine. Other works, however, have appeared under his name to which passing reference may be made. Immediately after his death—for it was endorsed as "Licensed September 10th, 1688"—there appeared a pamphlet of six or eight small octavo pages, entitled *Mr. John Bunyan's Dying Sayings,* the history of which is a little uncertain. These sayings consist of a series of pious utterances arranged under ten heads—such as Sin, Affliction, Prayer, the Love of the World, and the like. They are most of them such things as Bunyan might have spoken in his sermons, but it is difficult to think of him as saying some of them on his death-bed. It is difficult, for example, to imagine his haranguing the friends or the family of John Strudwick in any such way as this—" O sinner, what a condition wilt thou fall into when thou departest this world," &c., &c. Some of the sayings here collected have a certain force and pungency, as, for example, " When thou prayest, rather let thy heart be without words than thy words without a heart"; " Prayer will make a man cease from sin, or sin will entice a man to cease from prayer." On the whole, however, the probability is that this collection of so-called dying sayings was really a compilation made from various sources, and made in haste for some publisher with a shrewd eye to business, and bent on taking advantage of the feeling stirred by the tidings of Bunyan's death.

In 1688, immediately after his death, and with a black border round the title, there appeared a second edition of *The Barren Fig-tree,* the title saying, 'To which is added his *Exhortation to Peace and Unity.*' This exhortation follows on upon *The Barren Fig-tree* with continuous registration, and with a half-title without any author's name, the two works being reprinted together in the same form in 1692. There is a pretty strong consensus of opinion against accepting this 'Exhortation to Peace and Unity' as genuine. Charles Doe makes no mention of it in either of his catalogues; and though it was included in the collected edition of 1736, subsequent editions include it only under protest. The reasons for doubting its genuineness are—(1) The references and illustrations are of a different character to those usually found in Bunyan's works. For example, the writer refers to Agesilaus and Lacedemon, to Plutarch and his story of Silurus, to Camden's *Britannia,* with its account of Austin's Oak, to the 'learned' Stillingfleet, and his *Irenicon,* to the Gnostics, and to what he terms the *terra incognita* of Scripture. (2) The general style of composition as well as the special references is unlike that of Bunyan. (3) The writer also goes directly counter to the position Bunyan so distinctly took up for himself on the terms of Church Communion, insisting that baptism is indispensable to salvation and to Christian fellowship.

The same year in which this work appeared, there appeared also *The Saints' Triumph; or, the Glory of the Saints with Jesus Christ.* 'Describing the Joys and Comforts a Believer reaps in Heaven, after his painful Pilgrimage and Sufferings on Earth. By J. B.' Beyond these initials, Bunyan's name was not given, but his portrait was on the title. This ingenious way of suggesting without actually affirming authorship was a piece of trade smartness on the part of that publisher of somewhat shady reputation, Joseph Blare, of the Looking Glass, on London Bridge, the publisher, it will be remembered, who sent forth the *Scriptural Poems* as Bunyan's, and who issued also a Latinised edition of *The Pilgrim's Progress,* from which his name was withdrawn.*

* *Vide* footnote, p. 35.

Two other works by other authors have been assigned to Bunyan, the writers themselves being perfectly innocent of any attempt to deceive. George Larkin, like some other eminent publishers, turning author as well as publisher, wrote a book entitled *The World to Come;* 'the Glories of Heaven and the Terrors of Hell lively displayed under the similitude of a Vision; by G. L. London, 1711.' Fourteen years later Edward Midwinter, who had succeeded Blare in the publishing business at the 'Looking Glass,' and also apparently in his doubtful way of carrying on the business, published an exact reprint of this book of Larkin's under the altered title: *The Visions of John Bunyan;* 'being his last remains; recommended by him as necessary to be had in all families.' John Dunton, the well-known bookseller, was in no manner of doubt that his friend George Larkin, the son of the first publisher of that name, and whom he says he had known for twenty years, was the real author of the book.

The story of the other work ascribed to Bunyan, but not really by him, is as follows. In 1690, James Bardwood, the ejected minister of Dartmouth, published a little book entitled, *Heart's Ease in Heart's Trouble;* 'by J. B., a servant of Christ.' The title was taking and somewhat after Bunyan's manner, and in 1762, some enterprising publisher, putting a new construction on the initials, sent forth the book with the same preface, signed 'Thy humble servant, John Bunyan,' instead of 'J. B.,' as Bardwood left it. The original date, March, 1690, however, remained unchanged, and Bunyan was thus made to sign a preface a year and a half after he had been laid in his grave.

Later still in the last century two other publishers, this time in Scotland, ventured to trade upon Bunyan's reputation among the common people. In 1731 there was published in Edinburgh, and a generation later, in Glasgow, a work bearing the title, '*Rest for a Wearied Soul,* being the last legacy of Mr. John Bunyan of Bedfordshire.' The book, as we might expect, is a feeble production, made up of pious platitudes. In 1737 also there was published in Edinburgh a pamphlet entitled '*The Riches of Christ;* or, the glorious treasure of Heavenly Joys. With a devout Prayer. By J. Bunyan.'

Other pamphlets, rather of the nature of squibs than serious performances, were also issued under Bunyan's name, without, of course, any expectation of deceiving any reader thereby. About these nothing need be said, as, indeed, nothing can be said, beyond the fact that a century later they furnished additional illustration of the practice against which, in 1688, Nathaniel Ponder protested, that "Of certain ballad sellers about Newgate and on London Bridge, who have put the two first letters of this Author's name and his effigies to their rhimes and ridiculous books, suggesting to the world as if they were his."

But leaving now all these spurious ventures, and returning for a moment to the genuine and general writings of this seventeenth-century author, it may be worth while to point out, as we have previously done in the case of *The Pilgrim's Progress,* a few of the antiquarian references, unusual or obsolete words, and proverbial or popular expressions they contain. Bunyan speaks of people dying quietly 'like unto chrisom-children,' that is, like unto children who, dying within the month after their baptism, were shrouded in the white cloth, the chrisom put on the head at baptism, and who were supposed to die in special innocency and peace. In *The Holy War,* he speaks of the angels 'riding reformades' when Emmanuel came to deliver Mansoul, that is, coming with him from personal interest in a voluntary rather than an official capacity. He speaks of doing a thing 'without indenting,' that is, without making a bargain; of 'bating God an ace'; or being 'one of God's whiteboys' or specially loved ones; of 'trencher-chaplains'; of 'hedge-creepers,' in the sense of foot-pads; and of 'sensitives,' meaning thereby animals acting from instinct rather than reason.

We have such expressions as 'to learn me'; 'while of late,' meaning till of late; 'most an end,' that is, continually; 'it principles us,' 'to be principled so to do'; 'to grammar and settle the common people'; 'they mattered no words,' that is, paid no attention; 'more groundedly,' that is, with better foundation; 'he told his tale the rightest'; 'he betakes himself to house'; 'he got a haunt,' that is, was marked by the habit.

Scattered here and there are proverbial expressions like these: 'as familiar as the boy with the bird'; 'to turn and twist like an eel on an angle'; 'as poor as howlets'; 'they brought their noble to ninepence'; 'a snowball loses nothing by rolling'; 'as white as a clout'; 'to keep at stave's end'; 'thou standest upon thy points and pantables'; 'a tongue tipt with talk and tattle'; 'to grow lean and look like an anatomy.' We have also such unusual words as *overly* for slightly; *glavering; gravelled;* to *famble,* that is, to falter; to *daff* for to doff; to *slagar* for to slacken; to *scrabble; bickerment; malapertness; dotterel; frusturate; blandation; achare* for ajar; *gleads,* and a *gload* for bright rays; a *flam* or fable; *spaked,* in the sense of defective; *me-hap-soes; thodes,* that is, gusts or blasts of wind; and *runagates.*

Mingling as Bunyan did all his life with the common people, he abounds in such expressions as these: to flatter and cogg, to tick and toy, to shuck and cringe, to shuck and shrink, to winch and shuck, he glavers and flatters, butted and bounded, streaks and smirches, frampered Christians, squabbling frumps and taunts, childish talk and frumpered carriages. We have such expressions as: 'to talk too much at rovers'; 'to run headlong upon a bravado'; 'to lie in a lazy manner at to-elbow'; to be 'snaffled under guilt and terror'; 'to lie grabbing under black thoughts'; 'to perk it and lord it'; 'to punctilio'; 'to make orts,' that is, refuse; 'to pole and peel and rob.'

As a writer of nervous and forcible English of the kind that carries with it the warm glow of its prevailing Saxon element, few have equalled the untrained man whose works we have been considering, his power being native and inherent rather than acquired. The very earliest product of his pen, the book entitled

Some Gospel Truths Opened, which appeared in 1656, and only a few months after he had commenced preaching, was a remarkable production for a working man, whose schooling was a far-off memory, and who was occupied all the week at the handicraft of a tinker. There is an ease of style and a directness of speech, together with logical arrangement and coherence such as we should not have looked for in one so untrained and unpractised as he. In his later works there are signs of growth, of course, but this first book of his, thrown off at a heat, will bear favourable comparison with most of them as to clearness and force. There are in it no affectations of style, there is no aiming at mere fine writing, that bane of beginners. He speaks because he has something he much wishes to say, and he says it in the most direct way he can. With some obvious deductions, what has been said about *The Pilgrim's Progress* will largely apply to his other works:

"The style of Bunyan is delightful to every reader, and invaluable as a study to every person who wishes to obtain a wide command over the English language. The vocabulary is the vocabulary of the common people. There is not an expression, if we except a few technical terms of theology, which would puzzle the rudest peasant. We have observed several pages which do not contain a single word of more than two syllables. Yet no writer has said more exactly what he meant to say. For magnificence, for pathos, for vehement exhortation, for subtle disquisition, for every purpose of the poet, the orator, and the divine, this homely dialect, the dialect of plain working men, was perfectly sufficient. There is no book in our literature on which we would so readily stake the fame of the old unpolluted English language, no book which shows so well how rich that language is in its own proper wealth, and how little it has been improved by all that it has borrowed."[1]

As to the intellectual value of the general writings of Bunyan little need be added to what has been already said upon each work in detail. The secret of his success is not that he was a great theologian profoundly striking to the heart of spiritual truth, and showing it in new relations to meet the needs of the new time. To be a pioneer to unexplored realms of truth was not his function, as indeed it is the function of but few in any

[1] *Macaulay's Essays,* vol. i.; see also Southey's edition of *The Pilgrim's Progress. Studies in the English of John Bunyan.* By J. B. Grier. 1872. 12mo. *Grammatical Notes on the Language of John Bunyan.* By Alexander E. Widholm, Licentiate in Philosophy. With permission of the Philosophical Faculty of Lund [Sweden] to be publicly maintained for the degree of Doctor of Philosophy. Jönköping. 1877. 4to.

generation. The mental difficulties of many men would begin at the point where Bunyan left off. Accepting implicitly the Puritan system of religious thought as he found it, he neither questions nor hesitates. A verse from any part of Scripture has for him equal and decisive authority, settling problems the most complex and profound. To say this is only to say that he was the child of the seventeenth century rather than of the nineteenth. His service to humanity was, therefore, not that of massively grouping great truths into systematic form and opening the way to new realms of light. What he did, and did powerfully, was to make vital with the warm life-blood of his own strong heart truths and systems already in existence around him. With the wealth of his one opulent imagination he places these in vivid and striking light, and in such fervid shape that at once they lay hold of the popular mind and heart. Beautiful images, vivid expressions, forcible arguments all aglow with passion, tender pleadings, solemn warnings, these, all through his writings as through his preaching, make those to whom he speaks all eye, all ear, all soul. To use a phrase which has come to have an equivocal significance, he was a popular preacher and writer, but only in a high and noble sense. He never panders to the mere love of excitement and novelty. His errand is much too serious, and men's need and peril much too urgent, for him to waste time and power in merely playing before them on a pleasant instrument. He would beseeech them with tears, as Paul did, and like him, too, speak with authority as a messenger from heaven. To him the burning pit was a reality, from which he had himself barely escaped, and heaven a substantial verity he could all but see. The master passion of his soul was love to that redeeming Son of God to whom he felt he owed everything, and whose glory it was the joy of his life to unfold to his fellows. These are the special characteristics of the writings of this great Nonconformist preacher, and they are an adequate explanation of the firm hold he has secured upon the hearts of the people to whom he spoke and wrote.

XIX.

EDITIONS, VERSIONS, ILLUSTRATIONS, AND IMITATIONS OF *THE PILGRIM'S PROGRESS.*

THE story of the first creation of *The Pilgrim's Progress* has been told already, the story of its after-circulation is not unworthy to be told also. A book by an English writer, which has been sold by hundreds of thousands in this country, in the British Colonies and in the United States of America; which has been translated into a hundred and twenty languages or dialects of other countries;* and after two and a half centuries is still continually reappearing in new forms and translations, is, leaving the Bible out of account, a fact unique in literature.

* *Vide* Appendix II.

When Southey sent forth a new edition of *The Pilgrim's Progress* in 1830, he mentions that at that time there was no copy of the first edition of the First Part known to be in existence, that there was a second edition in the British Museum, but that the earliest besides which his publishers had been able to obtain for him, either by means of diligent inquiries or the kindness of friends, was the eighth edition of 1682. Since then more copies of the first edition have come to light, there are also other copies of the second and of the third editions. Besides these three editions which show the book in its three stages of growth, there are existing copies of all the editions down to our own times.[1] So that there are sufficient materials for a complete bibliography of the subject.†

† This is in preparation by the Editor.

Of the known copies of the first edition of the First Part of *The Pilgrim's Progress*, the one which came first to light, then in the possession of Mr. R. S. Holford, of Tetbury, Gloucester-

[1] The New York Public Library (Astor, Lenox, and Tilden Foundations) has a complete set of editions, up to and including the 32nd edition (1771), with the exception of the 11th and 17th editions, but including the two ninth editions, 1683 and 1684. After the thirty-second edition (1771) confusion arises in regard to dates of issues by various publishers. The British Museum Library possesses a similar series, but lacks the 1684 "ninth," and also the 17th editions. [The Editor has, after diligent search for the 17th edition, succeeded in discovering a copy (the only known one), in a private collector's library. It is dated 1710, and is in excellent condition.]

shire, and Park Lane, is still the most interesting, inasmuch as it is in perfect preservation, and is in the original sheep-leather binding, the sections also being sewn round strips of leather instead of cord. It was purchased years ago with the rest of the books in Lord Vernon's library, where it had apparently lain undisturbed since its first publication.* A second copy in the Public Library, New York, was, in 1851, purchased by the late Mr. Lenox from Mr. Pickering the publisher. A third copy was the property of Mr. Elliot Stock, by whom it was purchased from Mr. Coombs, a bookseller, of Worcester, who had acquired it with miscellaneous purchases. It is now in the Rylands Library, Manchester. A fourth copy was purchased for the British Museum in 1884 from the Rev. Ernest S. Thies, Wesleyan minister. It had been for many years in the possession of his brother-in-law, Mr. Thorne, of Dalston, to whom it came through a kinsman who was a book-collector. Another copy was brought to light, in February, 1886, through the publication of the first edition of this work. It was the property of Mr. Nash, of Langley, Slough, and is in perfect condition. It appears to have been rebound in calf in the early part of the eighteenth century, and is unique among the known copies of the first edition, in that it has for a frontispiece White's sleeping portrait of Bunyan. This may, however, have been added when the book was rebound. After Mr. Nash's death this copy was sold at Sotheby's in 1901 for £1,475.† It passed from the purchaser after the sale to Messrs. Dodd, Mead and Co., New York. It is now in the Henry Huntington collection, San Marino, California, and is known as the 'Palmer-Nash' copy. [There are, in addition to those already mentioned, first editions in Sir Leicester Harmsworth's collection, in England; and in the Pierpoint Morgan, and Charles W. Clark libraries, in the U.S.A. Second and third editions are in the British Museum, Bodleian, and Sir Leicester Harmsworth's libraries in this country; and, the second edition only, in the Cambridge University library, England, and the Pierpoint Morgan collection, New York. Of the third edition, copies are also in the Bunyan Meeting Museum, at Bedford, and the Henry E. Huntington library, U.S.A.] Of the first edition of the Second Part of the work there are copies in the British Museum, the John Rylands, and Sir Leicester Harmsworth libraries in England, and in the

* This unique copy afterwards became the property of the late Sir George Holford, of Dorchester House, Park Lane, London. It was privately disposed of to an American purchaser in or before 1927.

† *Vide* Addendum. Appendix IV.

New York Public Library, the Henry E. Huntington, and the Pierpoint Morgan* libraries in the States.

After the first three editions of the First Part, when, having received the additions of Worldly Wiseman and By-ends, the book was practically complete, there were only a few unimportant subsequent additions, consisting of Scripture passages and marginal references. The interest of succeeding editions lies therefore mainly in the question of illustrations, and for a century there was in this country nothing in this way really artistic. An ideally perfect *Pilgrim's Progress* would have been the Pilgrim story by Bunyan with illustrations by Albrecht Dürer or Hans Holbein. But this was, of course, impossible, and with the exception of White's 'sleeping' portrait the earliest engravings to the work were of the rudest possible kind. The first and second editions had no illustrations whatever; the third and fourth (1680) had only the 'sleeping' portrait as a frontispiece; the fifth (1680) had an inferior copy of the portrait and one rude engraving (p. 128) of the martyrdom of Faithful, with these lines, evidently from Bunyan's pen, underneath:

> "Brave *Faithful,* bravely done in word and deed:
> Judge, witnesses, and jury, have instead
> Of overcoming thee, but shown their rage.
> When they are dead, thou'lt live from age to age."

On the verso of the frontispiece portrait was the following—"Advertisement: *The Pilgrim's Progress* having found good Acceptation among the People, to the carrying of the Fourth Impression, which had many Additions, more than any preceding: And the Publisher observing that many Persons desired to have it illustrated with Pictures hath endeavoured to gratifie them therein: And besides those that are ordinarily Printed to the Fifth Impression [*i.e.,* portrait and burning of Faithful] hath provided Thirteen Copper Cuts curiously Engraven for such as desire them." These cuts were charged a shilling extra, and were sold either separately or with the book. This probably accounts for the fact that there were two fifth and two sixth editions. No specimens of these copper-plate engravings have been preserved, unless they are the illustrations found in the fifth edition of 1682 in the Lenox Library; but reproduced on wood they were probably those added to the eleventh and twelfth editions.

* This copy is, apparently, dated 1685. In chapter XI. Dr. Brown says: "This Second Part . . . was published early in 1685, or in 1684, Old Style."

The sixth edition (1681) had a better engraved portrait than the fifth and also the same wood engraving of the burning of Faithful. [The seventh (1681) is a much more worthy edition than the last two editions. It has a new but poor portrait, and "cuts." It is "Printed for Nath. Ponder in the Poultry."] The eighth (1682) and the ninth (1684) had the same illustrations as before, with two additional, one a rude engraving of Giant Despair, the other, a better one, representing the Pilgrims soaring through the clouds after crossing the river. In the tenth edition (1685) Giant Despair has disappeared, but the other two remain.

It was in the eleventh edition of 1688, the last which came out in Bunyan's life-time, and the last directly published by Nathaniel Ponder,[1] that the greatest changes were made in the matter of illustration. This, as well as the twelfth edition of 1689, contained, in addition to the three engravings of the tenth edition, twelve others, viz.: (1) Christian meeting with Evangelist; (2) Christian and Worldly Wiseman; (3) At the Wicket-gate; (4) The Burden falling off; (5) In the Arbour; (6) Passing the Lions; (7) Descending into the Valley of Humiliation; (8) The Fight with Apollyon; (9) The Valley of the Shadow of Death; (10) Faithful on his trial; (11) The Pilgrims and the Shepherds; (12) The Pilgrims soaring through the Clouds.

Subsequent changes were made, to a right understanding of which we must now cross over to Amsterdam and see what was taking place there. In 1682 *The Pilgrim's Progress* was translated into Dutch and published by Joannes Boekholt in a well-printed edition bound in vellum.[2] It had a copper-plate frontispiece of Christian at the Wicket-gate, and also eleven small copper-plate engravings (2½ in. by 2 in.) printed on the same pages as the letter press, but, of course, by a separate impression. These plates seem not to have been used again, but in 1685 Boekholt published a superior edition of *The Pilgrim's Progress* in Flemish French for the Walloons.[3] The ordinance

[1] The 12th edition is described as printed for Robert Ponder, and sold by the booksellers of London, 1689; the 13th edition as printed for Robert Ponder, and are to be sold by Nich. Boddington at the Golden Ball in Duck Lane, 1693. With the 14th edition Nathaniel Ponder reappears. It is described as printed for W. P., and are to be sold by Nat. Ponder in London-House Yard, near the west end of St. Paul's, 1695. So that he is no longer at the Peacock in the Poultry; and this is the last time we find his name on the title-page of the Pilgrim. [*Vide* Appendix.]

[2] *Eens Christens Reyse na de Eeuwigheyt.* In't Engels beschreven door Mr. Joannes Bunjan: Leeraar in Bedford. T'Amsterdam: Joannes Boekholt. 1682.

[3] *Voyage d'un Chrestien vers l'Eternité.* Ecrit en Anglois, par Monsieur Bunjan, F. M. en Bedtfort, et nouvellement traduit en François. Avec Figures. Amsterdam, Chez Jean Boekholt, 1685. Avec Privilegie.

of State authorising its publication is prefixed, is in Dutch, and signed by Gasp. Farel, 16 May, 1684. The work was beautifully printed, but its special interest to us just now lies in the fact that it was illustrated by nine copper-plate engravings by the eminent Dutch engraver, Jan Luiken, which have not only been continued in the various Dutch editions down to our own time, but seven out of the nine were reproduced after a rude fashion and added to the English editions also. At first only one of these was imported. In the thirteenth edition (1693), the Dutch engraving representing Christian and Hopeful crossing the river was substituted for the English one where they are seen soaring through the clouds. But, oddly enough, though the print was changed the four lines underneath the old picture remained unchanged, and we see the pilgrims struggling through the river, with this verse as descriptive of the scene :—

> " Now, now look how the holy Pilgrims ride,
> Clouds are their chariots, angels are their guide:
> Who would not here for him all hazards run,
> That thus provides for his when this world's done! "

This absurd mistake was repeated in edition after edition for nearly a century. It may be seen in the one issued by John Rivington and Sons as late as 1786, and possibly there were others even later still.*

* This is so in 'A New Edition' of 1792.

One Dutch picture being thus introduced in the thirteenth edition the process went forward, and in the fourteenth (1695) all but two of Jan Luiken's engravings were added. So from this time seven English and seven Dutch engravings appeared together in all the small editions down to about 1780.[1] Jan Luiken's originals were admirably executed; but the English copies became ruder and coarser by repetition till they were at last almost unrecognisable.

The name of Nicholas Boddington first appears on the title-page of Bunyan's Dream with the thirteenth edition of 1693. It is to this publisher Gay's humorous reference points in his farce of *What-d'ye-call it?* where he represents a man about

[1] The *English* engravings which were dropped were: (1) Worldly Wiseman; (2) At the Wicket Gate; (3) In the Arbour; (4) Descending into the Valley of Humiliation; (5) Apollyon; (6) Valley of the Shadow of Death; (7) Soaring through the Clouds. The *Dutch* pictures inserted were: (1) Christian at Sinai; (2) At the Wicket Gate; (3) Hill Difficulty; (4) Parley with Apollyon; (5) Valley of the Shadow of Death; (6) Vanity Fair; (7) Crossing the River.

to be shot, when a countryman offers him a book to pray by; he takes it and says:

> "I will! I will!
> Lend me thy handkercher [*reads and weeps*]. "The Pilgrim's Pro—
> I cannot see for tears; 'Pro—Progress': Oh!
> 'The Pilgrim's Progress, eighth edi-ti-on:
> London print-ed-for-Ni-cho-las Bod-ding-ton:
> With new ad-di-tions never made before':
> Oh, 'tis so moving, I can read no more!"

This farce was first acted in 1715, and while it proves nothing as to the dates of the editions it proves much as to the popularity of the book. John Dunton tells us of this new publisher, Nicholas Boddington, that "by an industrious management he has gathered a good estate and makes a considerable figure in the Parish where he lives."

The editions of which we have been speaking were those duly authorised; but besides these there were numerous pirated editions about which, as early as 1680, Nathaniel Ponder complained bitterly. In the fourth edition of that year there is the following: "Advertisement from the Bookseller. The *Pilgrim's Progress,* having sold several Impressions, and with good Acceptation among the People (there are some malicious men of our profession, of lewd principles, hating honesty, and coveting other men's rights, and which we call *Land Pirates,* one of this society is *Thomas Bradyl* a Printer, who I found Actually printing my Book for himself, and five more of his Confederates)."[1] One of these pirated editions is before me as I write, and both in type and paper is greatly inferior to those issued by Ponder himself, though it boldly bears his name on the title-page, claims to be licensed, and to be the fifth edition of 1682.* Doe tells us that 100,000 copies of *The Pilgrim's Progress* were sold in Bunyan's life-time, a remarkable fact in an age when the buyers and readers of books were relatively few. As time went on editions multiplied to meet the popular demand, and as they multiplied, the get-up of the book deteriorated, till at last, as Grainger tells us, it was often printed on tobacco

* At Magdalene College, Cambridge, is a copy of what was, probably, a chap-book: *The Pilgrim's Progress* to the Other World: or, A Dialogue between Two Pilgrims in their Way to Paradice . . . By J. B. an unworthy Labourer in Christ's Vineyard. London: Printed by H. Passinger at the three Bibles on London Bridge. 1684. It is 8vo. and consists of nineteen pages, in black-letter.

[1] Over against this testimony by Ponder it is only fair to place that by John Dunton the bookseller, who says: "Mr. Braddyll a firstrate printer. He is religiously true to his word and faithful to the booksellers that employ him. But Mr. Braddyll has met with back enemies. I dealt with him for many years, and have not only found him just, but well accomplished as a printer." *Life and Errors of John Dunton.* London, 1818. [*Vide* Appendix]

Photograph by G. A. Gearey, Bedford.

The Bunyan Memorial Window
Westminster Abbey.

Window Designed by J. N. Comper.

paper, and the illustrations became coarser and more smirchy. There were editions published even by respectable houses like Caddel and Dodsley (1783), John Rivington and Sons (1786), and Osborne and Griffin (1787), having illustrations such as we usually associate only with the name and fame of James Catnach of the Seven Dials. There was an edition also with dreadful woodcuts issued in octavo form in 1768 by D. Bunyan of Fleet Street, who may have been remotely a kinsman of the author—as may also have been that "J. Bunyan above the Monument" who published an edition of *The Heavenly Footman* in 1777.*

* James Bunyan issued *The Water of Life* in 1760.

But though inferior copies like these continued to be produced till the end of the eighteenth century, editions of a more ambitious character began to be sent forth as early as 1728. In that year there appeared in octavo form and on good paper "the two-and-twentieth edition, adorned with twenty-two copper plates engraven by J. Sturt." It was published by J. Clarke, who had succeeded Nicholas Boddington at the 'Golden Ball' in Duck Lane, and in the preface it was stated that being unable to read the poor print of the copies of *The Pilgrim's Progress* usually sold, "some persons of distinction and piety," in order to remedy that inconvenience, had "proposed that it might be sent into the world in the handsome manner it now appears." The writer of this preface goes on to say that after the great care taken in the printing[1] and engraving "it is not in the least doubted but the whole will give such entire satisfaction to the public in general, as well as to those worthy gentlemen in particular who have so handsomely and generously contributed to this beautiful edition, by their large subscriptions, as will fully answer their expectation." The belief thus expressed seems not to have been in vain. In the preface to his folio edition of Bunyan's Works in 1736-7 Samuel Wilson says: "Nor was it a little pleasing to me to see the encouragement which the polite part of mankind lately gave to the new Cloathing of his Pilgrim, a book which has been translated almost into every

[1] Notwithstanding the great care thus said to be taken in the printing of this, which was long reprinted as the standard edition, some extraordinary errors crept in and were repeated for more than thirty years. In Part I., p. 95, "brute" is altered to "Brewer," and it is said of Talkative, "Yea, the Brewer, in his kind, serves God far better than he"; p. 152, a line was left out; p. 180, "one duty" was altered to "one day"; p. 189, "our thoughts" was printed "the thoughts." In Part II., p. 63, "lions" was changed to "lines"; p. 71, in the catechising by Prudence, the answer to the question, "How doth God the Son save us?" was entirely left out, together with the following question; p. 135, a line was left out; p. 163, "stages" was altered to "stables," and the line read, "Behold, how fitly are the Stables set!"

language." Six of these new and larger engravings by Sturt were largely indebted in their conception to the Dutch pictures of 1685. The last engraving to the First Part, for example, gives the forms of Christian and Hopeful crossing the river, angels waiting for them on the farther shore, as in Boekholt's engraving, only that the pilgrims are crossing from left to right instead of from right to left, and again, as in the earlier English editions, there is the old verse underneath about their riding through the clouds on chariots. These engravings, while superior to those previously published in this country, were inferior to the Dutch originals, being some of them badly drawn and grotesque in conception. In one case, for instance, Christian is represented as clothed in figured flowing dressing-gown and in slippers, and as running up the Hill Difficulty at a pace which indicated considerable athletic power on his part and must have considerably astonished the beholders. This edition of 1728 was frequently repeated down to 1800, and the engravings printed together, four on a page, were inserted in the folio editions of 1736-7 and 1767.

In the collected edition of Bunyan's Works published by Alex. Hogg (1780) *The Pilgrim's Progress* with *The Holy War* formed the seventh volume. The whole series was illustrated by plates more or less related to the subject, and the editor stated that as the copper-plates to the old editions had been more a disgrace than an embellishment, he had in this edition employed the most able and renowned artists in the kingdom, so that the illustrations might justly correspond with the dignity and elegance of the works they were intended to embellish. Those to *The Pilgrim's Progress* are thirteen in number, and are of no special merit. They were chiefly drawn and engraved by G. Burder, and are inferior to those given with *The Holy War,* which were drawn by Hamilton and engraved by Grainger, Walker, Goldar and Thornton, and are marked by considerable softness and depth.

In 1786 a few engravings of higher quality were published with Harrison's edition of that year, and in 1792 a series of illustrations of *The Pilgrim's Progress* was issued by C. Sheppard of Doctor's Commons. In 1794 also he sent out a new and larger series in oblong quarto, to be sold separately from the text of the book. These engravings are destitute of the least vestige of imaginative power, are intensely realistic, and to the last degree marked by the matter-of-fact spirit so characteristic of the eighteenth century. The sketch of Vanity Fair, for instance, might be a London scene from one of Hogarth's pictures; and in the illustration of Doubting Castle the very coat, small-clothes, and shoe-buckles of Giant Despair are in the prevailing mode of the days of George III.

This time of deepest bathos, of the apparent extinction of all imagination, was yet, strange to say, the birth-hour also of the new period of higher artistic life, and saw the production of a series of illustrations to *The Pilgrim's Progress* which have never yet been surpassed. In 1788 Mr. Thane of the Haymarket published sixteen designs by Thomas Stothard, R.A., which were engraved in his best style by the antiquarian artist Joseph Strutt during his residence in Hertfordshire. To those who have seen these engravings it is needless to say that they are all marked by fine artistic feeling, and that some of them, that representing the Three Shining Ones by the Cross, for example, are characterised by exquisite softness and grace. They were originally issued separately from the book, but in 1792 were repeated in an edition published by Matthews of the Strand, to which were appended "Notes by a Bachelor of Arts of the University of Oxford." [J. Bradford.] Reduced in size and re-engraved by Stocks, Goodall, R. Graves, Engleheart and others, they were reissued in 1839, with descriptive sonnets by the Rev. George Townsend, Prebendary of Durham, and again the same year as illustrations to an edition of the text in octavo. In 1857 also they were given with an edition published by Henry G. Bohn, and more recently still were reproduced in Autotype by Messrs. Bickers and Son, in connection with a handsome edition of *The Pilgrim's Progress* published by them in 1881.

The edition of Bunyan's Allegory with Stothard's illustrations in their original form, issued in 1792, was followed in 1796 by the well-known edition of T. Heptinstall of Fleet Street. This came out in large octavo and was illustrated by eight new engravings, three of them by Stothard, the remaining five by Woolley and Corbould, the whole being engraved by Neagle, Springsguth, Collier, Saunders, and Rothwell. The same year there were four engravings issued with *The Pilgrim's Progress* forming part of Cooke's Pocket Edition of 'Sacred Classics.' These engravings were of high merit and specially pleasing.

Between the appearance of Heptinstall's edition in 1796 and that edited by Southey for Murray and Major in 1830, there were some twenty octavo editions published in England, besides numerous others in smaller forms. Most of these were well printed, and we may single out for special mention the editions with the admirable illustrations by Isaac Taylor (1805), by the celebrated Thomas Bewick, after Thurston (1806), by L. Clennell, one of Bewick's pupils (1811), and by R. Westall, R.A. (1820). These, with the editions printed by Henry Fisher at the Caxton Press (1824); by George Virtue of Ivy Lane (1830); and the one with an interesting and able Introductory Essay on the 'Genius of Bunyan,' by James Montgomery of Sheffield, all show that valuable copies of *The Pilgrim's Progress* were steadily in demand.

The edition of 1830 by the poet Southey may be said to begin the more modern series reaching down to our own time. It was described by Macaulay in that same year as "an eminently beautiful and splendid edition of a book which well deserves all that the printer and the engraver can do for it."[1] The work was illustrated with wood engravings by Heath, and two steel engravings by John Martin, representing the Valley of the Shadow of Death and the Celestial City. The latter are marked by Martin's peculiar genius, but are certainly open to the damaging criticism brought by Macaulay against his pictures generally, that "those things which are mere accessories in the descriptions become the principal objects in the pictures; and those figures which are most prominent in the descriptions can be detected in the pictures only by a very close scrutiny."[1]

The many years which have elapsed since the appearance of this edition by Southey have, judging by the number and character of the editions by which it has been followed, been marked by a steady increase rather than by any diminution of interest in Bunyan's Dream. The best are the editions published by Fisher and illustrated by J. M. W. Turner, R.A., G. Cruikshank, and others:[2] that edited by Godwin and Pocock, in oblong folio and illustrated by the prize drawings in outline of the Art Union, executed by H. C. Selous;[3] the one edited by George

[1] *Macaulay's Essays*, i. 132.

[2] London and Paris: Fisher, Son, and Co. 8vo.

[3] London: M. M. Holloway, Covent Garden, 1844. Folio.

Offor for the Hanserd Knollys Society;[1] that published by W. Pickering and printed at the Chiswick Press (1849); the two editions issued the same year, the one illustrated by William Harvey,[2] the other by David Scott, R.S.A.;[3] the edition published by Bagster in 1845 and illustrated by his daughter with 270 small engravings, some of which are of great merit;[4] those with the illustrations of Sir John Gilbert, engraved by J. W. Whymper;[5] that with 100 illustrations by Thomas Dalziel,[6] and the one with the coloured plates of H. C. Selous and the wood-engravings of Selous, Priolo, and Friston.[7] An excellent edition was published by Macmillan and Co. in 1862, which was adorned with a charming vignette by W. Holman Hunt, engraved by Jeens. An edition with the *Grace Abounding* appended to it, carefully edited for the Clarendon Press by Canon Venables, was published in 1879; another, called the 'Elstow Edition,' has outline drawings by Gunston and others, and is bound in oak-boards taken from the old timber of Elstow Church at the time the church was restored in 1880.[8] There are also some spirited drawings by Gordon Browne in an edition published by Sampson Low and Co. (1833).

But while there is this embarrassment of riches in really attractive editions of *The Pilgrim's Progress* issued in recent years, none of these just referred to attains to the rank of the four now to be mentioned. These are, the one illustrated by C. H. Bennett* and prefaced by Charles Kingsley;[9] that with 110 designs by J. D. Watson, engraved by the Brothers Dalziel;[10] and the 'Edition de Luxe' published by Strahan and Co. in 1880; and the one illustrated with the admirable etchings of William Strang and published by J. C. Nimmo in 1895. The illustrations by Charles H. Bennett strike out a new line, and are simply sketches of heads as descriptive of character instead of the usual scenes and groupings. The kind, strong face of the Interpreter and the womanly grace of Discretion are strikingly rendered;

* Vide Addendum.

[1] London: Printed for the Society by J. Haddon, 1847. 8vo.
[2] London: D. Bogue, Fleet Street, 1850. 4to.
[3] London, Edinburgh, and Dublin: A. Fullarton and Co., 1850. Large 8vo.
[4] *Byways of Book Illustration*, Magazine of Art, Feb., 1882. [*Vide* Addendum, chapter XII.]
[5] London: James Nisbet and Co.
[6] London: Ward, Lock, and Tyler.
[7] London: Cassell, Petter, and Galpin.
[8] London: John Walker and Co., 1881.
[9] London: Bradbury, Evans, and Co., 1859. 4to.
[10] London: Routledge, Warne, and Routledge, 1860. 4to.

several of the others also are marked by great power and insight into character. The delineations by J. D. Watson are in that eminent artist's best manner, and make the edition which has had the advantage of his pencil one of the most attractive yet issued. The 'Edition de Luxe' with one hundred illustrations by Frederick Barnard, Sir J. D. Linton, and others is a most princely looking copy of the Tinker's Dream. It is printed on special hand-made paper, the proofs of illustrations are on Japanese paper, and though, of course, of varied merit, present some unusually good examples of artistic power. The representations of Great Heart, Valiant-for-Truth, and Old Honest, from the pencil of Sir J. D. Linton, are among the finest things we have. Of this edition there were 500 copies printed, 200 of which were taken by the United States.

* *Vide* Addendum.

Besides these editions, separate illustrations of *The Pilgrim's Progress* were issued by F. J. Shields*[1] and Claude Reignier Conder,[2] the former being of very considerable merit. It may be mentioned also that George Cruikshank left behind him at his death a series of new illustrations to *The Pilgrim's Progress* drawn on wood, ready for the engraver.†

† These belonged to Mr. Edwin Truman, a friend of the artist, and were issued from the Oxford Press by Mr. Henry Frowde in a superbly printed edition of a thousand copies in 1903.

Another edition worthy of mention is the fac-simile copy of the First Edition of 1678, published by Mr. Elliot Stock. In this the First and Second Parts were originally printed together, but subsequently a more literal fac-simile of the First Edition was issued.*

The cheap editions of *The Pilgrim's Progress* issued of recent years have been simply numberless. In 1855 it formed the 330th volume of the Tauchnitz series published at Leipsic. Both the Religious Tract Society and the Book Society for many years sent forth the work in large and small type, and in various attractive forms within the reach of all. The Tract Society, especially, has rendered service it is impossible to over-estimate, not only in issuing these English editions, but in co-operating with missionaries and others in the production of very many of the foreign versions. In some cases they have undertaken the entire publication; in others they have furnished paper and

[1] *Illustrations to Bunyan's 'Pilgrim's Progress,'* by F. J. Shields. Manchester: A. Ireland. 1861.

[2] *Pictorial Scenes from 'Pilgrim's Progress,'* by Claude R. Conder. London: 1869. 4to.

plates* Other publishers also have helped to swell the stream of popular supply. A paper edition in quarto, with 100 illustrations by Thomas Dalziel, was sold by Ward, Lock and Co. for sixpence. Editions have also been published at a penny or twopence.

* A popular edition issued by the Religious Tract Society, first appeared in 1903, with attractive drawings by Harold Copping. In the following year Byam Shaw's clever illustrations added interest to Messrs. Jack's edition.

Besides the editions published in London, there were also in former years many published in the provinces by country printers. In some of the places mentioned there were several successive editions, but the following is the order, so far as we can now ascertain it, of the first appearance of these country issues: Shrewsbury, 1699; Glasgow, 1717; Newcastle-on-Tyne, 1744; Bristol (abrgd.), 1748; Edinburgh, 1759; Nottingham, 1765; Wolverhampton, 1769; Paisley, 1772; Coventry and Gainsborough, 1775; Preston, 1790; Dublin, 1795; Bath, 1796; Manchester, 1799; Berwick, 1801; Leeds, 1802; Bungay, 1805; Taunton (with frontispiece and woodcuts by Thomas Bewick), 1806; Rotherham, 1806; Liverpool, 1807; Durham, 1807; Stourbridge, 1809; Halifax and Burslem, 1810; Buckingham and Wellington (Salop), 1811; Birmingham, 1812; Oxford, 1814; Chelsea, [1815]; Romsey, 1816; Boston, 1817; Plymouth and Uxbridge, 1822; Derby, 1829; Kettering, 1843; Cambridge, 1862; Guildford, 1902; Stirling, 1903.

Passing from our own country it may now be mentioned that in less than three years after its first appearance *The Pilgrim's Progress* was reprinted by the Puritan colony across the Atlantic. On the issue of the Second Part, in 1684, Bunyan could say of the First:

> "'Tis in *New England* under such advance,
> Receives there so much loving Countenance,
> As to be Trim'd, new-Cloth'd, and deck't with Gems,
> That it may show its Features, and its Limbs,
> Yet more; so comely doth my *Pilgrim* walk
> That of him thousands daily sing and talk."

A copy of this first American edition was formerly in the possession of the late George Brinley of Hartford, Connecticut, and according to Mr. Henry Stevens the imprint ran thus: "Boston in New England / Printed by Samuel Green upon As / signment of Samuel Sewall and / are to be sold by John Vsher / of Boston 1681.[1]/ It was hoped that this interesting copy would have been found among Mr. Brinley's books after his death.

[1] *Contributions to a Catalogue of the Lenox Library.* No. IV. Bunyan's *Pilgrim's Progress*, &c. New York: Printed for the Trustees. 1879.

His collection was left in the care of Dr. Trumball, Librarian of the Watkinson Library, Hartford, and I happened during a visit to America, to call upon that gentleman, in May, 1882, just after he had completed his search for this first edition, only to find him sorrowfully regretting that it was nowhere to be found. Subsequent American editions in the Lenox Library were printed at Boston; New York; Philadelphia; Brattleborough, Vt.; and Cleveland, Ohio. In 1898 an edition in folio, with 120 illustrations of a bold and striking character by the Brothers Rhead, and with an introduction by the Rev. H. R. Haweis, was issued by the Century Co., New York. It is not possible, however, in the case of the United States, any more than in that of England, to compute with any approach to accuracy the untold multitude of editions of a book which, along with that of Shakespeare, forms the strongest link in the literary bond binding that country to ours. Everywhere through the States, Bunyan's name is found as a household word and his 'Dream' among the household treasures.

We come next to the interesting question of the many FOREIGN VERSIONS of *The Pilgrim's Progress* that have appeared. The book had, as we know, begun to be translated quite early. With pardonable pride Bunyan himself said in 1684:

> "In France and Flanders, where men kill each other,
> My *Pilgrim* is esteemed a Friend, a Brother.
> In Holland, too, 'tis said (as I am told),
> My *Pilgrim* is with some, worth more than gold."

The Dutch translation mentioned last, and already referred to, was probably the first of the foreign versions in order of appearance, being published, as has been said, by Joannes Boekholt, of Amsterdam, in 1682. The book seems to have been early and for long a favourite with the people of Holland. Numerous editions have appeared both at Amsterdam, Rotterdam, Gröningen, Utrecht, Deventer, Arnhem, and the Hague.

The French version, prepared by Boekholt for the Walloons in 1685, is thought to have been the first sent forth in that language. Bunyan, however, as early as 1684, speaks of his 'Pilgrim' as being already in France; if so, no copy of that earlier edition remains to us. A new French translation made direct from the English and beautifully printed, was published at Rotterdam, in 1728, and described as the Third Edition.[1] The

[1] *Le Voyage du Chrétien vers L'Eternité.* Par Jean Bunian, Ministre du Saint Evangile. Traduit de l'Anglois. A Rotterdam: Chez Abraham Acher, 1728.

reason the writer in his preface gives for this new version is, that Boekholt's was inferior as being in the Walloon *patois.* At the end, there were printed seven 'Cantiques' for various seasons, by B. Pictet, Pastor and Professor at Geneva. A separate French edition was also published at Toulouse, in 1708; 'Avec approbation et permission,' the permission being signed by the Marquis de Villeron and by Monseigneur Dumirail. A copy of this edition, purchased in the shop of G. Klostermann, St. Petersburg, is in the library of the Religious Tract Society, with this inscription on the cover: "This book was picked up by Lord Tyrconnel (who was at the time on a political mission to Russia) on the field of battle, after the Battle of Borodino." Yet another French edition, published at Tours in 1852, is inscribed with the approbation of "Genet, docteur de la maison et Société de Sorbonne," which is dated, Paris, 16 Juillet, 1772, and in which it is said: "Cet ouvrage est orthodoxe, et animé de l'esprit Evangélique." Bunyan's book thus endorsed by a doctor of the Sorbonne, with Giant Pope left out and prayers bound up at the end (with continuous pagination) to be said before the Holy Mass, together with Anthems to the Holy Virgin, would have astonished the Protestant soul of the Bedfordshire Tinker, could he have seen it. Another French edition was also published at Epernay, Lyons, and Paris, by the Society of St. Victor, in 1847, having the approbation of the Bishop of Chalons, who says that he has examined the book, and thinks it will offer to all "une lecture agréable et utile." Yet other French issues have been published at Paris, Rouen, Valence, Plancy, and Basle.

The German version of *The Pilgrim's Progress* was first translated, not from the English, but from the Dutch. Dr. F. H. Ranke tells us that as a young man at Nürnberg, he first met with a German copy on a stall where old Christian writings were offered for sale along with old iron, and just as cheaply. It was a translation of 1703, from Dutch into German, and though the language was so antiquated that he had at times almost to guess the meaning, yet, as he says, the Dream made such an impression on his mind, that in after years he formed classes of young men for the study of the book, and also, in 1832, issued a new edition himself in an abridged form.[1] Many other German

[1] *Des Christen Wallfahrt nach der himmlischen Stadt.* Nach dem Englischen des John Bunyan, von Dr. Friedrich Heinrich Ranke, Consistorialrath zu Ansbach. Mit einer Einleitung von Dr. Gotthelf Heinrich von Schubert, Geheimerath in München. Erlangen, 1845.

editions followed that first rude translation of 1703, and the book worked itself into the German mind. Dr. Gustav Kettner suggests that in two of Schiller's poems, 'Der Pilgrim' and 'Die Sehnsucht,' Bunyan's influence is distinctly traceable. The first of these especially stands, he thinks, among the rest of Schiller's works as a strangeling, expressing not in name only, but in conception and longing the idea of Bunyan's Dream. The book was, we know, early received into the pietistic circles of Germany. Jung-Stilling, in his *Schlüssel zum Heimweh,*[1] in which he has attempted a broad, artistic, but unimpassioned imitation of Bunyan's work, tells us how, in 1748, when in his eighth year, he had read with inexpressible pleasure *The Pilgrim's Progress.* Other German minds also were greatly influenced by it. Crabb Robinson tells us that when dining with the Grand Duchess, at Weimar, in 1805, he there met with the poet Wieland, who was born earlier in the eighteenth century than Schiller. Wieland was very communicative; he spoke of English literature, to which he confessed great obligations, and when Robinson mentioned that the first book he recollected having read was *The Pilgrim's Progress,* "That delights me," said Wieland, "for in that book I learned to read English. English literature had a great influence on me, and your Puritan writings particularly."[2] It is not improbable, therefore, that Schiller, who as a boy at Ludwigsberg and later, read many pietistic works, may have met Bunyan's Dream, and that Dr. Kettner is right in thinking he sees traces of its influence in the Pilgrim thought and ideal longing expressed in 'Der Pilgrim' and 'Die Sehnsucht.'[3]

These three in the Dutch, French, and German languages were the earliest versions, though not the only ones. Though subsequently lost, it would seem as if, even in Bunyan's lifetime, there were versions also in Gaelic and native Irish. After speaking of those in use in France, Flanders, and Holland, he says:

"Highlanders and wild Irish can agree
My *Pilgrim* should familiar with them be."

Welsh versions were published in London, in 1688, and in Shrewsbury, in 1699, a Swedish version at Gotheberg, in 1743,

[1] Jung-Stillings *Sämtliche Werke,* v. 310. Stuttgart, 1841.
[2] *Diary of Henry Crabb Robinson,* i. 113. Third Edition.
[3] *Zeitschrift für Deutsche Philologie.* Zu Schillers Gedichten. Halle, 1885, pp. 109—115.

and a Polish, in 1728. All the rest came later, and were born out of the missionary movement of the nineteenth century. The earliest of these later ones, which was also the most affecting in its history, was that prepared for the native Christians of Madagascar by the Rev. D. Johns, one of the first missionaries who carried the Gospel to that island. This version is said to be strongly idiomatic, and in literary quality to stand deservedly high. The Allegory itself was a great solace to these native Christians during the long and terrible night of persecution by which their faith was tried. It was printed on paper the same size as that of their New Testaments, and was often bound up with them, as *The Shepherd of Hermas* was with the canonical Scriptures of the Early Christians.

The book which thus so soon and so truly made a home for itself in one mission field, gradually spread, and is spreading to others. In some cases the people have themselves taken active part in the production of the versions referred to. The Kaffir was translated by Tiyo Soga, a native of Kaffirland, who was educated in Scotland, in connection with the Free Church Mission; and as far as the manual work was concerned, it was neatly printed and bound by Kaffir lads in the Lovedale Mission Seminary. The Ashanti version, also printed in 1885, was simply a revision by Mr. Christaller of the Basle Missionary Soceity of a translation made many years before by two natives of Akropong. It is interesting also to notice that the Chinese version, in the Canton vernacular, sent forth by the Rev. G. Piercy of the Wesleyan Mission, was illustrated by a series of pictures both drawn and engraved by Chinese artists. In these, Christian appears in Chinese costume, the House Beautiful as a Chinese pagoda, and all the scenes and incidents in a garb familiar to the people for whom the book was intended. Before leaving the subject of these versions, it should be noticed that this book of Bunyan's, which has contributed so largely to the sacred cause of Christian unity, is in its very production a manifestation of the spirit to which it has contributed. It is pleasant to find that it has been translated and published under the auspices of missionaries connected with the Church, London, Baptist, Wesleyan, and United Free Church Presbyterian Missionary Societies; also of those sent forth by the American Board of Foreign Missions, the German Mission, and the Basle Missionary Society. It has also been printed in India by the Christian Knowledge Society and by the Punjab Religious Book Society of Lahore.

Apart from the religious influence exerted by the 'Pilgrim,' the book has become a classic in the general literature of many of the peoples to whom it has been given. Mr. Pearce of Canton said, in 1883, that not only was the copy in the Canton Vernacular regarded by his committee as one of the best books in their depository, a favourite work with the native preachers, and read in Christian families, but it was also taught in the native schools, and he had seen, he said, Chinese who knew or cared little for Christianity poring over *The Pilgrim's Progress* with interest and delight.[1] A Syrian gentleman, also (Antonius Ameuny), writing to an English lady concerning the Arabic version of *The Pilgrim's Progress,* said: "The book has now become a classical one. It is read in all the American schools throughout Syria. Copies of it have gone into Arabia, Mesopotamia, India, Egypt, and the Coast of Barbary." A monk at Beirut, as he called upon him in his cell, said: "I read this book during the long winter evenings, and feel quite delighted to think that your Protestant friends have *at least one good book* to offer us." He climbed up into the bower of one of the watchmen over the vineyards, during the season of grapes, and found among other Arabic books a well-used copy of *The Pilgrim's Progress.* Explaining why the book was so well used, the man Nicola said: "Such a book was never made for you men who live in cities, who are ambitious, rich, and luxurious; but I who live in this tree for three months in the year—I see the sun rise in majesty in the morning, and go down in power in the evening; I see the moon appear in glory, and set in splendour—with ante-Lebanon for my habitation—and Lebanon, Hermon, and Iulan around me—I have need of such a book; I can understand it."[2]

Passing now from Editions, Versions, and Illustrations, we come next to IMITATIONS of *The Pilgrim's Progress.* This brings us to the consideration of the spurious Third Part which continued to be sold till the middle of the nineteenth century with the First and Second. It made its appearance in 1693, and although the title-page does not directly say it was written by

[1] Letter to the author from Rev. J. W. Pearce, Canton, June, 1883.
[2] Appendix to *Le Pélerinage de l'homme,* p. lxii. *et seq.*

Bunyan, the book virtually claimed to be; for it was described as 'The Third Part, to which is added The Life and Death of John Bunyan, Author of the First and Second Part; thus compleating the whole *Progress'*; the preface also was signed J. B., and the book itself begins with these words: "After the two former Dreams concerning Christian and Christiania his wife. . . . I fell asleep again, and the Visions of my Head returned upon me: I dreamed another Dream, &c." It was a piece of sharp practice in which we find once more implicated our old friend J. Blare, of the Looking-glass on London Bridge. The public were the more readily deceived because Bunyan had himself given a sort of half-promise of a Third Part. The concluding words of the Second Part, it will be remembered, are these: "Shall it be my lot to go that way again, I may give those that desire it, an account of what I here am silent about; meantime I bid my Reader Farewell." Indeed, if his publisher may be trusted, Bunyan had got the work under way before his death. He says: "The Third Part now abroad was not done by Bunyan. But *the true copy left by him* will be published by Nat. Ponder." This definite statement was somewhat modified shortly after. On the reverse of the title of the thirteenth edition of the First Part, 1693, there is this advertisement: '*The Pilgrim's Progress*: The Third Part: in a Dream, Printed in 1692, is an Impostor thrust into the world by a nameless author, and would insinuate to the Buyers that 'tis Bunyan's, by adding a false Account of his Life and Death, not compleating the work as is said, &c. The Skeleton of his Design and the main of his Book Done by him as a Third Part remains with Nath. Ponder; which when convenient time serves shall be Published.' If there really were anything like a Third Part written by Bunyan, it seeems never to have seen the light, and the spurious pretender held on its way, having a considerable sale. It was dishonest in its claim to authorship and was evidently intended in an unworthy way to trade upon Bunyan's reputation; otherwise it was not without a certain amount of interest and literary power.[1] It sets forth the adventures of a pilgrim named Tender Conscience, going over much of the ground Bunyan had gone over before.

[1] A striking extract from this book relating to our "endowment with different faculties suitable and proportional to the different objects that engage them," is prefixed by Professors Stewart and Tait to their joint work entitled, *The Unseen Universe*. Macmillan & Co., 1876.

* Other early imitations were: *The Pilgrim's Guide* from his Cradle to his Death-bed. By J. Dunton, 1684; and *The Pilgram's (sic) Guide* From his Cradle to his Death Bed, with his Glorious Passage from thence to the New Jerusalem. Collected by Robert Russell in Sussex. Printed for *J. Blare* at the Looking Glass on London Bridge. [N. D.]. There is a title-page *only* of this work in the British Museum.

† By Francis Bugg. London, 1688.

‡ Also, *The Spiritual Pilgrim*: Or, the Christian's Journey to the New Jerusalem. By Henry Wilson. London, 1710.

This Third Part was followed by many other imitations.* Some of these were put forth for sectarian purposes, and we have '*The Pilgrim's Progress* from Quakerism to Christianity,'† and 'From Methodism to Christianity.' About 1685 there was a burlesque allegory, entitled '*A Hue and Cry after Conscience,* or the *Pilgrim's Progress* by Candle-light.'‡ Some were made the vehicles of political satire, instruction, or warning. '*The Statesman's Progress,* or a Pilgrimage to Greatness,' was aimed at Sir Robert Walpole and his mode of corrupting Parliament by bribes. Under the name of Badman, Walpole is represented as going to Greatness Hall, where grew the Golden Pippins, by aid of which he exercises absolute sway. At the beginning of the nineteenth century, the sister of Sir James Bland Burgess wrote a book of warning against those principles of Reform of which, in the days following upon the French Revolution, conservative people were so timidly afraid. This work was entitled, '*Progress* of the Pilgrim Good-Intent in Jacobinical Times.' It went through several editions, being thought a good and safe book for parish libraries. On the other side, in favour of Reform, we have 'The Political *Pilgrim's Progress,*'[1] in which a Pilgrim sets out from the City of Plunder, with a heavy burden on his back labelled 'Taxes.' He is bent on finding the City of Reform, and his going forth on pilgrimage thither makes great talk among his neighbours; some of them maintaining that there is no such place as Reform, others saying there is, but that it is a long way off, and the way thither is perilous. As he goes he meets with Worldly Wiseman, who reproves him for being discontented, telling him that all people cannot be rich; others try to persuade him that his load is a great benefit to him and that he would be uneasy without it. In the course of his travels two men, named Temporary and Expediency, try to mislead him by short cuts; he has a life and death grapple with the Apollyon of Political Corruption; and he passes through Vanity Fair, where pensions, places, and decorations are offered for the purpose of keeping up the existing system. Eventually, after many a shrewd brush and stern experience, he reaches the City of Reform, the place of his desire, where Taxes are all but unknown and every man breathes the air of freedom.

There have been other imitations, such as '*The Drunkard's*

[1] Newcastle-upon-Tyne; Office of the *Liberator,* 1839.

Progress from Drouth to the Dead Sea,' by John Bunyan, Junr. (1853); '*The Pilgrim's Progress* from the Town of Deceit to the Kingdom of Glory' (1790); '*The Christian Pilgrim,* from the Land of Destruction to the New Jerusalem.' (Worcester, U.S.A., 1798); *The Christian Pilgrim,* by John Allen, London, (1800); *Iter Cœleste* (1721); *The Sailor Pilgrim* (1806); *Zion's Pilgrim* (1809); *The Infant's Progress,* by Mrs. Sherwood (1823); *The Indian Pilgrim,* also by Mrs. Sherwood (1825); '*The Travels of Humanitas* in Search of the Temple of Happiness' (1809); and Benjamin Keach's *Travels of True Godliness* (1684); *A New Pilgrimage to the New Jerusalem,* by W. Shrubsole, is meant to be, under assumed names, a description of the state of religion in England in the times of Whitefield and Wesley. Similar in purpose and with special doctrinal intent, we have '*The Female Pilgrim,* or the Travels of Hephzibah'; '*Pilgrims of the Nineteenth Century;* a continuation of *The Pilgrim's Progress,*' by Joseph Ivimey (1827); '*Magdalena's Voyages and Travels* through the Kingdom of this World into the Kingdom of Grace,' a work illustrated by three curious symbolical maps (1850); '*The Pilgrimage of Theophilus* to the City of God' (1812); and '*The Pilgrim Travellers* to the Land of Peace (1847). There have also been several other works of a similar kind, but they were, for the most part, the outcome of the dullest mediocrity, and it is scarcely necessary to lift them again into the light.

Two later works of more ability and opposite character are '*The Sojourn of a Sceptic in the Land of Darkness and Uncertainty,* between the Land of Original Impressions and the City of Strongholds in the Kingdom of Light';[1] and '*An Agnostic's Progress* from the Known to the Unknown.'[2] In a travesty of *The Pilgrim's Progress,* under the title of '*The Celestial Railroad,*'[3] Nathaniel Hawthorne, some years ago, satirised what he thought the softer fibre of the religious life of our times, as contrasted with the days of Bunyan.* He found, on visiting the City of Destruction, in a dream, that there was now a railroad between that place and the Celestial City, so that a pilgrim's progress was by no means the stern experience it used to be. The Slough of Despond was converted into firm ground; there was

* Another edition based on Hawthorne's, by W. Thomson, appeared in 1910.

[1] By Peter Hately Waddell, Girvan. London: H. K. Lewis, 1847.
[2] London: Williams and Norgate, 1884.
[3] *Masses from an old Manse.* By Nathaniel Hawthorne.

no need of any stopping-place at the House of the Interpreter; the Hill Difficulty had been tunnelled through, and the Valley of Humiliation levelled up. Between the townsmen of Vanity Fair and the pilgrims, too, there was now a very good understanding and considerable traffic. The silver mine of Demas also was worked by them to great advantage, and Doubting Castle was quite an airy-looking edifice, built in the most modern style. There was even a steam ferry-boat over the bridgeless river, to which, however, there was this one drawback, that no one knew whether it ever reached the city on the other side or not. For at this point the Dreamer awoke and had, therefore, no more to relate.

Besides IMITATIONS and BURLESQUES of *The Pilgrim's Progress,* there have also been numerous ABRIDGEMENTS, John Wesley publishing one in 1774; and there were several editions that were supposed to be amended and improved. We naturally expect that Roman Catholics would leave out Giant Pope from the version authorised by them, but it does seem a little superfluous to put forth an edition for the purpose of improving the English of the book. An excellent but mistaken clergyman, Joshua Gilpin, vicar of Wrockwardine, published at Wellington, in 1811, what he calls "a new and corrected edition, in which the phraseology of the author is somewhat improved, some of his obscurities elucidated, and some of his redundancies done away." It is needless to say that the book was not so much improved as weakened, and that it remains an illustration of the degenerate taste of even educated people in the days in which it saw the light. This work of the good vicar of Wrockwardine, who with all his heart believed the truths that Bunyan believed, was harmless and well meant, however, when compared with the treatment *The Pilgrim's Progress* received later at the hands of another clergyman of the English Church, the Rev. J. M. Neale, warden of Sackville College,[1] who set about making Bunyan say what he believes Bunyan would have said, if only he had been as 'enlightened' as he ought to have been. "The Editor," he says, "cannot be called dishonest for making his author speak what he believes, that with more knowledge, that author would have said." In pursuance of this piece of jesuitry, he

[1] *The Pilgrim's Progress of John Bunyan, for the Use of Children in the English Church.* Edited by the Rev. J. M. Neale, M.A., Warden of Sackville College. Oxford: J. H. Parker, 1853.

in the garden at the Wicket Gate, into which Christian dips him- introduces baptism as the means of spiritual life; placing a well self three times, "the which when he had done, he was changed into another man, moreover"—here at the baptismal well, not at the Cross as Bunyan had it—"his burden fell from his back." There are other changes besides: Giant Pope is turned into Giant Mahometan; Worldly Wiseman and Legality are left out; the scene in the House Beautiful is turned into the ceremony of Confirmation and of first Communion; and the dusty room in the House of Interpreter is made the symbol of the heart of a man who was never regenerated by baptism. The statement of the changes thus made in another man's book is the most effective indictment of the man who made them. This attempt to foist upon an author opinions directly contrary to those he was known to hold, caused some stir, and called forth, among others, a remonstrance with the title of '*The Pilgrim*: or John Bunyan's Apparition in the Bedroom of the Rev. J. M. Neale.' There have been other editions of *The Pilgrim's Progress* of a more reputable sort for children and young people, Isaac Taylor, of Ongar, leading the way as early as 1825, with his "Bunyan explained to a Child," illustrated with a hundred engravings. We have *The Child's Bunyan*, '*The Pilgrim's Progress* in words of One Syllable,' *The Pilgrim Children*, and picture-cards and toy-books, with coloured plates illustrative of the work.* There have also been, what seem quite unnecessary, many poetical versions of *The Pilgrim's Progress*. The Dream is a poem as it is, and for such a book to be 'metrically condensed' into cantos, to be 'rendered into blank verse,' or 'into familiar verse,' 'converted into an epic,' or 'done into verse,' is to be dragged down from sublimity into mediocrity or even lower.

Finally, besides thus coming out in versions innumerable, poetical and otherwise, the 'Pilgrim' has once at least taken dramatic form, after the manner of the old mediæval mystery plays. In June, 1877, the poet and novelist, George Macdonald, assisted by his family, gave a series of illustrative scenes from the Second Part of *The Pilgrim's Progress*.†

It has sometimes been thought that Bunyan's cordial reception by the great arbiters of literature is of comparatively recent date;

* *The Pilgrim's Progress* Illustrated, a coloured panorama, 168½ in. by 2½ in., in a coloured pictorial cylinder, was issued by Ralph Hudson, Cheapside, London. [N. D.]

† This was re-issued by the Oxford Press in 1925. Other dramatic versions are those by E. A. Rudd (1912); W. Stephens (1914); *Christiana and Her Children*, by Mrs. D. Pearce (1914); C.R. Haines (1920); *Scenes from the Pilgrim's Progress*, by E. U. Ouless (1923).

that, as Macaulay puts it: "*The Pilgrim's Progress* is, perhaps, the only book about which, after the lapse of a hundred years, the educated minority has come over to the opinion of the common people." Cowper's lines about Bunyan:

> "I name thee not lest so despised a name
> Should move a sneer at thy deserved fame,"

have contributed not a little to this impression. But by a fair amount of evidence on the other side, it is clearly shown that we must not follow Cowper too implicitly in this matter.[1] There were, no doubt, writers like Cox who, in his account of Bedfordshire, complained that Bunyan's books were "too frequently met with in the hands of the common people," and others, later, who thought the Pilgrim 'jejune'—that was the word in those days. It is true also that Dr. Young compared Bunyan's prose with the poetry of the wretched D'Urfey; that Addison said disparagingly, that he never knew an author that had not his admirers, for Bunyan and Quarles pleased as many readers as Dryden and Tillotson; and that Mrs. Montagu, after her manner, following in the wake of Addison, called Bunyan and Quarles, "those classics of the artificers in leather," laughing at them as "forming the particular entertainment of her neighbours, the Kentish squires." But it is also true that there is on the other side the great authority of Dr. Johnson himself, who said that Bunyan's book was one of the three which all their readers wished had been longer. Madame Piozzi also, writing four or five years later than Cowper, classes Bunyan with Correggio, and asks, "Who shall dare say that Lillo, Bunyan, and Antonio Correggio were not *naturally* equal to Johnson, Michael Angelo, and the Archbishop of Cambrai?" Horace Walpole, no mean authority in literary taste, evidently thinks he is paying Edmund Spenser a compliment when he speaks of him as "John Bunyan in rhyme." Hearne, the antiquary, tells us how his friend, Bagford, went down into the country to see Bunyan for himself.* Writers in the *Gentlemen's Magazine* (1741 and 1765) ventured to say that "there never was an allegory better designed or better supported"; that "*The Pilgrim's Progress* is a work of original and uncommon genius"; and even Dean Swift says: "I have been better entertained and more informed by a few pages in *The Pilgrim's Progress* than by a long discussion upon the will and the intellect, and simple or complex ideas."

* *Vide* Chap. xvi.

[1] *Saturday Review*, August, 1880.

It will be seen that Professor De Morgan, in saying "all honour to Granger" for this, was mistaken in supposing that he was the first man of literary standing who spoke of Bunyan appreciatively; but Granger also said that *The Pilgrim's Progress* is "one of the most popular and, I may add, one of the most ingenious books in the English language"; backing up this opinion of his by that of his friend Merrick, who thought Bunyan had not a little of Homer's power, and by that of a similar opinion held by Dr. Roberts, a Fellow of Eton College. This is a considerable consensus of opinion on the part of the intellectual world of last century, and it was sustained, as we have seen, by the two weighty names of Wieland and Schiller. Doubtless, there were in those days learned men ignorant of Bunyan's intellectual claims; but so there have been since Macaulay said that the educated minority has, on this question, come over to the opinion of the common people. Thackeray used to tell, as only he could, how he once went down to Oxford, to give his lectures on the English Humourists, and, in order to prepare the way for the attendance of the undergraduates, waited on the Heads of Colleges. Among others upon whom he called was Dr. Plumptre, Master of University, who it seems had not heard of the great novelist, and therefore asked him who he was and what he had written? By way of furnishing his credentials, Thackeray modestly intimated that he was the author of *Vanity Fair*. Upon this, the Master at once turned round upon him suspiciously with the remark that there must be some mistake somewhere, for that John Bunyan was the author of 'Vanity Fair!' Finding afterwards that people were laughing, Plumptre explained to a friend, from whom I had the story, that he had not read Bunyan's book, "never being a reader of novels."

Over against this story of the Oxford don we must, however, set the fact that Bunyan has nevertheless been duly honoured from the chair of the professor of Ecclesiastical History in that university to which Plumptre belonged. In his Address at the Bunyan Celebration, in Bedford, in 1874, Dean Stanley said:

"When (if I may for a moment speak of myself) in early youth I lighted on the passage where the Pilgrim is taken to the House Beautiful to see 'the pedigree of the Ancient of Days, and the rarities and histories of that place, both ancient and modern,' I determined that if ever the time should arrive when I should become a professor of ecclesiastical history, these should be the opening words in which

I would describe the treasures of that magnificent storehouse. Accordingly when, many years after, it so fell out, I could find no better mode of beginning my course at Oxford than by redeeming that early pledge; and when the course came to an end, and I wished to draw a picture of the prospects yet reserved for the future of Christendom, I found again that the best words I could supply were those in which, on leaving the Beautiful House, Christian was shown in the distance the view of the Delectable Mountains, 'which, they said, would add to his comfort because they were nearer to the desired haven.'"

These words of Dean Stanley were spoken on the memorable occasion when the statue of Bunyan, executed by J. E. Boehm and presented by the Duke of Bedford to Bedford town, was unveiled by Lady Augusta Stanley, in 1874. A recumbent monument, designed and executed by E. C. Papworth, had, by a Committee of which the Earl of Shaftesbury was President, been placed over Bunyan's tomb in Bunhill Fields, in 1861.[1] The statue erected in Bedford, however, was a yet nobler creation of the sculptor's art, and the public celebration connected with its unveiling will long be remembered as an occasion when men in all ranks of life and of all diversities of religious opinion joined together in doing honour to the memory of one who, perhaps, more than any other Englishman, is the representative of all that is most central in the Christian faith. Presided over by the Mayor of the town, the great assembly, gathered on that occasion from all parts of the United Kingdom, and containing representatives from America and the British Colonies, was addressed by Earl Cowper as Lord Lieutenant of the County; by Mr. Whitbread, who was not only the Parliamentary representative of the borough, but also the representative of ancestors who, as we have seen, were personally associated with Bunyan himself; by Dr. Brock and Dr. Allon as standing for the great body of the Nonconformists; and by Dean Stanley as representing the National Church. The Dean, with his wide catholic sympathies, was never more truly himself than when, as on this occasion, seeking to atone by large-minded utterances for the injustice wrought two centuries before by the Church to which he belonged. He himself had, at the request of the donor of the statue, selected the subjects for the bas-reliefs of the pedestal; she,* who was the inspiring influence of his public life, had performed the ceremony of unveiling; and it was he who gave the one distinctive tone

* Lady Augusta Stanley.

[1] Besides this monument in Bunhill Fields and the statue in Bedford, two memorial windows have been placed in the chancel of Elstow Church, the one presenting scenes from *The Pilgrim's Progress*, the other from *The Holy War*. [*Vide* Appendix.]

STATUE OF JOHN BUNYAN: BEDFORD.
Erected in 1874.

to the gathering of the day. He showed how Bunyan was great as the man and the preacher, but greater still as the dear teacher of the childhood of each of us, as the creator of those characters whose names and faces are familiar to the whole world; as the writer of one of the few books which act as a religious bond to the whole of English Christendom. The pilgrimage Bunyan described is, he said, the pilgrimage of every one of us, and the combination of neighbours, friends, and enemies whom he saw in his dream, are the same as we see in our actual lives. We have met, nay, we have ourselves been, the people he describes:

"All of us need to be cheered by the help of Greatheart, and Standfast, and Valiant-for-the-Truth, and good old Honest. Some of us have been in Doubting Castle, some in the Slough of Despond, some have experienced the temptations of Vanity Fair; all of us have to climb the Hill Difficulty, all of us need to be instructed by the Interpreter in the House Beautiful; all of us bear the same burden; all of us need the same armour in our fight with Apollyon; all of us have to pass through the wicket gate, all of us have to pass through the dark river; and for all of us (if God so will) there wait the Shining Ones at the gates of the Celestial City, 'which, when we see, we wish ourselves amongst them.'"[1]

The task we have undertaken draws to its close. There remains but th expression of hope that we may each of us take to his own life the lesson of the life-story we have followed; the lesson that through all opposing force of ill we should each be true to our better selves, true to the light which comes to each man from heaven, and true to the generation in the midst of which it was ordained that our own life-work should be wrought. The history of the past fails of its deepest purpose if it holds up no guiding light to the present. In stirring lines called forth by the Bunyan Celebration of 1874, it may be said that:

[1] It is to these closing words the following touching letter, received by me from the Dean shortly after the death of Lady Augusta, refers:

"DEANERY, WESTMINSTER, *March 12th*, 1876.

"MY DEAR SIR,—I thank you sincerely. That day at Bedford was one of the last public appearances of my dear wife, and will always be cherished amongst my brightest recollections of her. We had been so much occupied before we arrived at Bedford, that I had only time to read to her the concluding part of my address (as I read everything to her) a few minutes before we went to the solemnity; and the last words of it—from awaking a chord of some dear scene of former years—quite overcame her. You will see on turning to them why this should be, and why your letter recalls them to me now with such moving power. Do not let her name be forgotten among your people, for she was indeed worthy of remembrance. Yours sincerely, A. P. STANLEY."

"To deal with the Past is of small concern;
That light for the day's life is each day's need,
That the Tinker-Teacher has sown his seed;
And we want *our* Bunyan to show the way
Through the Sloughs of Despond that are round us to-day,
Our guide for straggling souls to wait,
And lift the latch of the wicket-gate.

"The Churches now debate and wrangle,
Strange doubts theology entangle:
Each sect to the other doth freedom grudge,
Archbishop asks ruling of a judge.
Why comes no pilgrim, with eye of fire,
To tell us where pointeth minster spire,
To show, though critics may sneer and scoff,
The path to 'The Land that is very far off'?
The People are weary of vestment vanities,
Of litigation about inanities,
And fain would listen, O Preacher and Peer,
To a voice like that of this Tinker-Seer;
Who guided the Pilgrim up, beyond
The Valley of Death, and the Slough of Despond,
And Doubting Castle, and Giant Despair,
To those Delectable Mountains fair,
And over the River, and in at the Gate
Where for weary Pilgrims the Angels wait!"

ADDENDA—Chapter XIX.

(Pages 449, 450.)

In 1859, Charles Kingsley was consulted by Charles Henry Bennett, "a man full of genius, then on the staff of *Punch.*" Finding that Bennett was in need, and had a difficulty in getting a publisher for his Illustrated *Pilgrim's Progress,* Charles Kingsley "wrote and gave him a preface for it, upon which Messrs. Longmans accepted it." Kingsley also aided F. J. Shields, of Manchester, in getting his Illustrations to *The Pilgrim's Progress* published. In 1926, an autographed presentation set of these—from the artist to Mrs. Charles Kingsley—was sold. The Editor possesses a set given to a friend, "With John Ruskin's dutiful love. December, 1864." (Vide *Charles Kingsley*: *His Letters,* etc. Edited by his Wife. London: Kegan Paul and Co., 1880).

(Page 450.)

"Fac-simile" of the First Edition.

A close comparison of Elliot Stock's 'fac-simile' with the copy of the 'first' in the British Museum discloses the fact that there is considerable difference between the two. It would, perhaps, be more correct to describe Mr. Elliot Stock's clever production as a 'representation' of the First Edition of *The Pilgrim's Progress.* In the catalogue of the Lenox Library (New York: Printed for the Trustees, 1879), the writer of the introductory Note, remarks: "In 1875 Mr. Elliot Stock, of 62 Paternoster Row, London, published (post 8vo. and large paper 4to.) "The Pilgrim's Progress as Originally published by John Bunyan, Being a Fac-simile Reproduction of the First Edition." . . . In the original the pagination is from 1 to 224; in Stock's "*fac-simile*" the pagination is from 1 to 205. It is true that in the original there is a skip in the paging from 105 to 120, but this error, instead of being corrected, should have been copied in the fac-simile; and so should the variation in the type . . ." etc. Mr. George Offor—to whom all students of Bunyan are so deeply indebted—fell into a similar error, in issuing what he termed "an accurate reprint, not merely verbal, but literal," etc., and then to include matter other than that contained in the original copy of the 'first' edition. An exact reproduction has yet to be issued.

[illegible] York [illegible] introductory [illegible] The [illegible]

APPENDIX I.

CHRONOLOGICAL LIST OF BUNYAN'S WORKS.

PRINTED BY CHARLES DOE IN 1698 AS AN APPENDIX TO The *Heavenly Footman,* AND CORRECTED TO THE PRESENT TIME.

A Catalogue of all MR. BUNYAN'S *Books.*

Running Reader!

I *That now help you to this* Heavenly Foot-Man *in Print, (being the Person that first moved and* procured *the Printing in folio, above Twenty of our Author* Bunyan's *Pieces) have also now given you here, a Catalogue of all that great Convert's Works, in order of Time, as they succeeded each other in Publication (as near as I can understand) and I do also love them, and would have you do so too, as they are the Experience and Knowledge of a great* Convert, *which indeed is a great Monument of the mighty power of Grace, and a fit Fellow-Traveller for a Heavenly Foot-Man.*

Borough, *London,* *Charles Doe.*
March 26, 1698.

This Catalogue, is word for word, as it is in the several Title-Pages, except the Texts.

1. S*ome Gospel-Truths opened* according to the Scriptures, or the *Divine* and *Human Nature of Christ Jesus;* His *coming* into the World; his *Righteousness, Death, Resurrection, Ascention, Intercession,* and *Second Coming* to Judgment, plainly demonstrated and proved; and also Answers to several Questions, with profitable Directions to stand fast in the Doctrin of the *Son* of *Mary* against those blusterous Storms of the Devil's Temptations, which at this day like so many Scorpions break loose from the Bottomless Pit, to bite and torment those that have not tasted the Virtue of Jesus, by the Revelation of the Spirit of God.

Published for the good of God's Chosen Ones, by that Unworthy Servant of Christ *John Bunyan* of *Bedford,* by the Grace of God Preacher of the Gospel of his Dear Son, *Job.* 14.6. *Act* 4.12. *Published* 1656, *in about* 11 *Sheets in* 12^{0}. *and it is now in the* Folio.

2. A *Vindication* of the Book called *Some Gospel-Truths opened* according to the Scriptures; and the opposition made against it by *Edward Borrough* a professed *Quaker,* (but proved an Enemy to the Truth) Examined and Confuted by the Word of God; and also the things that were then laid down, and declared to the World; by me are a second Time born witness to, according to Truth; with the Answer of *Edward Borrough* to the Queries then laid down in my Book reproved; and also a plain Answer to his Queries given in symplicity of Soul; and is now also presented to the World, or who else may read or hear them; to the end, (if God will) that Truth may be discovered thereby.

By *John Bunyan* Preacher of the Gospel of Christ, *Act.* 13. 22, 23, and 29, 30, and 32, 33, and 38, and 39. Published 1657. in about 9 Sheets in 4^{0}.

3. *Sighs* from *Hell;* or, the *Groans* of a *Damned Soul,* discovering from the 16th of *Luke,* the Lamentable state of the Damned; and may fitly serve as a warning-word to *Sinners* both Old and Young, by *Faith* in *Jesus Christ,* to avoid the same place of Torment; with a discovery of the usefulness of the *Scriptures,* as our safe Conduct for the avoiding the Torments of Hell. By *John Bunyan.*

Published in about 7 Sheets, [1658] in 12^{0}. It hath now been Printed 9 times.

4. The Doctrin of the *Law* and *Grace* unfolded, or a Discourse touching the *Law* and *Grace*, the nature of the one, and the nature of the other; shewing what they are, as they are the two Covenants, and likewise who they be, and what their Conditions are that be under either of these two Covenants: Wherein for the better understanding of the Reader, there are several Questions answered touching the *Law* and *Grace*, very easy to be read, and as easy to be understood by those that are the Sons of Wisdom, the Children of the second Covenant; also several Titles set over the several Truths contained in this Book, for thy sooner finding them, which are those following the Epistle.

Published by that Poor Contemptible Creature *John Bunyan* of *Bedford*. *Heb*. 7. 19. *Rom*. 3. 28. *Rom*. 4. 5. In about 23 Sheets, in 8⁰.

[4.* *Profitable Meditations, Fitted to Man's Different Conditions*. In a *Conference* between *Christ* and a *Sinner*. In nine *Particulars*. By *John Bunyan*, Servant to the Lord *Jesus* (1661). This work, unknown to Doe, was discovered by J. C. Hotten. *Vide* p. 171.]

5. *I will Pray with the Spirit and with the Understanding also;* or, a Discourse touching *Prayer*, wherein is briefly discoursed, 1. What Prayer is. 2. What it is to Pray with the Spirit. 3. What it is to Pray with the Spirit, and with the Understanding also.

By *John Bunyan*. *Rom*. 8. 26. Cor. 14. 15.

Published 1663, in about 4 Sheets, in 12⁰. *and is now in the* Folio.

[5* Christian Behaviour, 1663. *Vide* No. 19.]

6. A *Map*, shewing the order and causes of *Salvation* and *Damnation*.

By *John Bunyan*, in a Broadside of a Sheet, Copper Cut, Price 6*d*. *and it is now in the* Folio.

7. The Four last things, *Death* and *Judgment*, *Heaven* and *Hell*.

In about 3 Sheets, in 16⁰. in Verse.

8. Mount *Ebel* and *Gerrizem*, or the Blessings and Cursings.

In about a Sheet, in 16⁰. in Verse.

9. Prison-Meditations, in about half a Sheet, in Verse.

10. The *Holy City*, or the New *Jerusalem*, wherein its goodly Lights, Walls, Gates, Angels, and the manner of their standing are Expounded, also her length and bredth; together with the Golden Measuring-Reed explained, and the *Glory* of *all* unfolded, as also the numerousness of its Inhabitants; and what the Tree, and Water of Life are, by which they are sustained.

By *John Bunyan*, a Servant of Christ. *Psa*. 87. 3. *Ezek*. 38. 33.

Published 1665, in 10 Sheets, *now in the* Folio.

11. The *Resurrection* of the *Dead*, and *Eternal Judgment*, or the Truth of the Resurrection of the Bodies, both of good and bad at the last day, asserted and proved by God's Word; also the manner and order of their coming forth of their Graves, as also with what Bodies they do arise; together with a Discourse of the last Judgment, and the final Conclusion of the whole World.

By *John Bunyan*, a Servant of the Lord's Christ. 1 *Cor*. 15. 51, 52. *Job*. 5. 28, 29.

Published 1665, in about 7 Sheets, in 8⁰. *and it is now in the* Folio.

12. Grace abounding to the chief of *Sinners*, or a brief and faithful Relation of the exceeding Mercy of God in Christ to his poor Servant *John Bunyan; wherein is particularly shewed the manner of his Conversion, his sight and trouble for Sin, his dreadful Temptations, also how he despaired of God's Mercy, and how the Lord at length through Christ, did deliver him from all the Guilt and Terror that lay upon him;* all which was written by his own Hand, and now published for the support of the weak and tempted People of God. *Psa*. 66. 16.

In 8 Sheets, in 12⁰ [1666]. Printed 7 times.

13. A defence of the Doctrin of *Justification* by *Faith* in *Jesus Christ*, shewing true Gospel Holiness flows from thence; or Mr. *Fowler's* pretended Design of

Christianity, proved to be nothing more, than to trample under foot the *Blood* of the *Son* of *God,* and Idolizing of *Man's* own Righteousness; as also while he pretends to be a Minister of the *Church* of *England,* he overthroweth the wholsom Doctrin contained in the 10th, 11th, and 13th of the 39 Articles of the same, and that he falleth in with the Quaker and Romanist against them.

By *John Bunyan.* 1 *Pet.* 2. 4.

Published 1671. In about 16 Sheets in 4⁰.

14. *A Confession of Faith,* and Reason of my Practice; or with who, and who not, I can hold *Church-Fellowship,* or the *Communion of Saints;* shewing by divers Arguments, that tho' I dare not Communicate with the open Profane, yet I can with those visible Saints that differ about *Water-Baptism;* wherein is also discoursed, whether that be the Entering-Ordainance into Fellowship, or no. *Psa.* 116. 10.

Published 1672, in about 6 Sheets in 12⁰.

15. *Difference* in Judgment about *Water-Baptism* no Bar to *Communion,* or to Communicate with *Saints,* as *Saints,* proved Lawful; in answer to a Book written by the *Baptists,* and published by Mr. *T. P.* and *W. K.* entituled, *Some serious Reflections on that part of* Mr. *Bunyan's Confession of Faith, touching Chureh-Communion with Unbaptized Believers*: wherein their Objections and Arguments are answered, and the Doctrine of Communion still asserted and vindicated. Here is also Mr. *Hen. Jesse's* Judgment in the Case, fully declaring the Doctrine I have asserted.

By *John Bunyan,* 1673. in about 8 Sheets in 8⁰.

16. *Peaceable Principles* and *true,* or a brief answer to Mr. *Danver's* and Mr. *Paul's* Books against my *Confession of Faith, and Difference in Judgment about Water-Baptism,* no Bar to Communion; wherein their Scriptureless-Notions are overthrown, and my *Peaceable Principles* still maintained. By *J. Bunyan,* Psal. 58. 1.

Published 1674. in about 2 sheets in 12⁰.

17. Reprobation Asserted, or the Doctrine or Eternal *Election* and *Reprobation* promiscuously handled, in eleven Chapters; wherein the most Material Objections against this Doctrine are Answer'd, several doubts removed, and sundry Cases of Conscience Resolved.

By *John Bunyan,* a lover of Peace and Truth. Rom. 11. 7. In about 6 sheets in 4⁰. [*Vide* p. 244.]

18. *Light* for them that sit in *Darkness,* or a Discourse of *Jesus Christ,* and that he undertook to accomplish by himself the Eternal *Redemption* of Sinners: Also, how the Lord Jesus addrest himself to the Work with undeniable Demonstrations that he performed the same; Objections to the contrary answered.

By *John Bunyan,* Gal. 3. 13. in about 10 sheets, [1675] *and it is now in the Folio.*

19. *Christian Behaviour,* being the Fruits of True Christianity, teaching Husbands, Wives, Parents, Children, Masters, Servants, &c. how to walk so as to please God, with a word of Directions to all *Backsliders.*

By *John Bunyan,* Heb. 6. 7, 8. In 5 sheets in 12⁰, *and it is now in the Folio.*

☞ [This work should stand No. 6, being first published in 1663. *Vide* p.164.]

20. *Instructions* for the *Ignorant,* being a Salve to cure that great want of Knowledge which so much reigns both in Young and Old, prepared and presented to them, in a plain and easy Dialogue, fitted to the Capacity of the Weakest.

By *John Bunyan,* Hos. 4. 6. published 1675, in about 3 sheets in 12⁰, *and it is now in the Folio.*

21. *Saved* by *Grace,* or a Discourse of the *Grace* of *God;* shewing, 1. What it is to be *Saved.* 2. What it is to be saved by *Grace.* 3. Who they are that are saved by Grace. 4. How it appears that they *are* saved by Grace. 5. What should be the *Reason,* that God should chuse to save Sinners by Grace, rather than by any other means.

By *John Bunyan,* Eph. 2. 5. In 5 sheets in 12⁰ [1675], *and it is now in the Folio.*

22. The *Straight Gate,* or, great difficulty of going to Heaven; plainly proving by the Scriptures, that not only the Rude and Profane, but many great Professors will come short of that Kingdom.

By *John Bunyan,* Mat. 7. 13, 14. published 1676. in 5 sheets in 12^{0}, *and it is now in the Folio.*

23. The *Pilgrim's Progress,* from this World to that which is to come, delivered under the similitude of a *Dream;* wherein is discovered the manner of his setting out, his dangerous Journey, and safe arrival at the desired Country.

By *John Bunyan.* Hose. 12. 10.

In about 9 sheets in 12^{0} [1678], Printed 13 times.

24. A Treatise of the *Fear* of *God,* shewing what it is, and how distinguished from that which is not so; also *whence* it comes, who has it, what are the Effects, and what the *Privileges* of those that have it in their Hearts.

By *John Bunyan.* Psal. 128. 1.

Published 1679. in about 15 sheets, in 8^{0}.

25. *Come* and *Welcom* to *Jesus Christ,* or a plain and profitable Discourse on *John* 6. Verse 37 shewing the cause and true manner of the Coming of a *Sinner* to *Jesus Christ,* with his happy Reception, and blessed Entertainment.

By *John Bunyan.* Isa. 27. 13.

In about 9 sheets, in 12^{0}. [1678. This should precede No. 24.]

[Life and Death of Mr. Badman, 1680, should stand No. 26. *Vide* No. 32.]

26. The *Holy War* made by *Shaddai* upon *Diabolus* for the Regaining the Metropolis of the World, or the losing and taking again of the *Town* of *Mansoul.*

By *John Bunyan.* Hos. 12. 10.

Published 1682 in about 26 sheets, in 8^{0}.

27. The *Barren Figtree,* or the Doom and Downfall of the *Fruitless Professor;* shewing that the day of Grace may be past with him long before his Life is ended: the Signs also by which such Miserable Mortals may be known.

By *John Bunyan.* In about 8 sheets, in 12^{0}. [1682.]

28. The greatness of the *Soul,* and unspeakableness of the loss thereof, with the causes of the losing of it; first Preached at *Pinners Hall,* and now enlarged, and published for Good.

By *John Bunyan.* [1683.]

29. A Case of *Conscience* Resolved, viz. *Whether, where a Church of Christ is situate, it is the Duty of the women of that Congregation ordinarily, and by appointment, to separate themselves from their Brethren, and so to assemble together to perform some parts of Divine Worship, as Prayer,* &c. *Without their Men*: And the Arguments made use of for that Practice, examined.

By *John Bunyan,* Pub. 1683. in about 5 sh. in 4^{0}.

[A Holy Life the Beauty of Christianity, 1684, should stand at No. 30. *Vide* No. 33.]

30. Seasonable Counsels, or advice to *Sufferers.*

By *John Bunyan,* Pub. 1684 about 9 sh. in 12^{0}.

31. The *Pilgrim's Progress,* from this *World* to that which is to come, *The second part;* delivered under the similitude of a *Dream;* wherein is set forth the manner of the setting out of *Christian's Wife* and Children, and their dangerous *Journey* & safe arrival at the desired *Country.*

By *John Bunyan,* Hos. 12. 10. In about 9 sh. in 12^{0}. [1684. O.S. 1685 N.S.].

32. The *Life* and *Death* of Mr. *Badman,* presented to the World in a familiar Dialogue between Mr. *Wisman* and Mr. *Attentive.*

By *John Bunyan,* In about 16 sheets in 12^{0}.

[This should stand as No. 26, being first published in 1680.]

33. A *Holy Life* the *Beauty* of *Christianity,* or an Exhortation to *Christians* to be ***Holy.***
By *John Bunyan,* Psal. 93. 5. Pub. 1684. [O.S.] In 9. sh. 12°.

34. A Discourse upon the *Pharisee* and *Publican,* where several great and weighty things are handled: As the nature of Prayer, and of Obedience to the Law; with how far it obliges Christians, and wherein it Consists: Wherein is also shewed the equally deplorable Condition of the *Pharisee* or Hypocritical self-Righteous Man, and of the *Publican* or Sinner, that lives in Sin, and in open Violation of the Divine Laws; together with the Way and Method of God's Free-Grace in Pardoning Penitent Sinners; Proving, that he Justifies them by imputing Christs Righteousness to them.
By *John Bunyan,* Luk. 18. 10. 11, 12, 13. Published 1685. in about 10 sheets in 12°.

35. A *Caution,* to stir up to Watch against *Sin.* [1684. ☞ This should precede No. 34.]

36. Questions about the Nature and perpetuity of the Seventh-day *Sabbath,* and Proof, that the *first* Day of the Week, is the True *Christian Sabbath.* By J. B. Mat. 12. 8. Pub. 1685.

37. A Book for Boys and Girls, or Country Rhymes for Children, in Verse, on 74 things. By J. B. Pub. 1686. In about 6 sheets 12°.

38. The *Jerusalem* Sinner saved, or good News to the *Vilest of Men,* being a help for Despairing Souls; shewing that Jesus Christ would have Mercy offered in the first place to the *biggest Sinners*: The Second Edition, in which is added, an Answer to those Grand Objections that lye in the Way of them that would Believe; for the Comfort of those that fear they have Sinned against the Holy Ghost. By *John Bunyan.* Pub. 1688. In 8 sh. in 12°.

39. The Work of Jesus Christ as an *Advocate,* clearly Explain'd and largly Improved, for the Benefit of all Believers, from 1 Joh. 2. 1.
By *John Bunyan,* Pub. 1688. in about 10 sh. 12°.

40. A Discourse of the *Building, Nature, Excellencies,* and *Government* of the *House* of *God,* with Counsel and Directions to the Inhabitants thereof.
By *John Bunyan,* Psal. 26. 8. Published 1688. in about 5 sheets in 12°.

41. *The Water* of *Life,* or a Discourse, shewing the Riches and Glory of the Grace and Spirit of the Gospel, as set forth in Scripture by this Term, *The Water of Life.*
By *John Bunyan.* Published 1688. In about 5 sheets in 12°.

42. *Solomon's Temple Spiritualized,* or Gospel-light fetcht out of the *Temple* at *Jerusalem,* to let us more easily unto the Glory of *New-Testament Truths.*
By *John Bunyan,* Eze. 43. 10, 11. Published 1688. in about 9 sheets in 12°.

43. The Acceptable Sacrifice, or the Excellency of a *Broken Heart;* shewing the Nature, Signs and proper Effects of a Contrite Spirit.
By *John Bunyan,* Psal. 51. 17. Published 1688. in about 7 sheets in 12°.

44. Mr. *John Bunyan's* last Sermon at *London,* Preached at Mr. *Gammon's* Meeting-House near *White-chappel* Aug. 19 1688. upon John 1. 13. shewing a Resemblance between a Natural and a Spiritual Birth: And how every Man and Woman may try themselves, and know whether they are Born again, or not.
Published 1689. in about 1 sheet in 12°.

The Twelve pieces following were left by Mr. Bunyan *in Manuscript, and were never Printed, but in the Folio* 1692, viz.

45. An *Exposition* on the ten first Chapters of Genesis, &c. in about 19 sheets.

46. Of *Justification* by *Imputed Righteousness;* or, No way to Heaven, but by Jesus Christ.

47. *Pauls Departure and Crown,* or an Exposition upon 2 Tim. 4. 6, 7, 8. In about 5 sheets.

48. Of the *Trinity,* and a Christian.

49. Of the *Law,* and a Christian.

50. *Israel's Hope Encouraged,* or what Hope is, and how Distinguished from Faith, with Encouragement for a hoping People. Psal. 130. 7.

51. The *Desires* of the *Righteous Granted,* or a Discourse of the Righteous Mans Desires, Prov. 11. 23. Prov. 10. 24. In about 6 sheets, in Folio.

52. The *Saints Priviledge* and Profit, Heb. 4. 16.

53. *Christ a Compleat* Saviour, or the Intercession of Christ and who are privileg'd in it, Heb. 7. 25. In about 8 sheets, in Folio.

54. The *Saints Knowledge of Christ Love,* or the unsearchable Riches of Christ, Eph. 3. 18, 19.

55. Of the House of the Forest of *Lebanon.* In about 5 sheets, in Folio.

56. Of *Antichrist,* and his *Ruin;* and the Slaying of the Witness, In about 8 sheets, in Folio.

The four Books following were never yet Printed, except this now of the Heavenly Footman, *which I bought in* 1691, *now six years since, of Mr.* John Bunyan, *the Eldest Son of our Author; and I have now put it into the World in Print, Word for word, as it came from him to me.*

57. A *Christian Dialogue.* [Never printed, so far as is known.—Ed.]

58. The *Heavenly Footman,* &c. [1698.]

59. A *Pocket Concordance.* [Never printed, so far as is known.—Ed.]

60. An *Account of his Imprisonment* [1765].

Here are Sixty Pieces of his Labours, and he was Sixty Years of Age.

[There was another work by Bunyan which seems to have been overlooked by bibliographers. In *The Catalogue of our English Writers on the Old and New Testament,* the second impression, London, 1668, is an entry (page 304), of a book on *Revelation,* 21: v. 10 to v. 5 of chap. 22, by John Bunyan, *duod.* 1665. Apparently no copy of this has survived.—Ed.]

ADDENDUM—Appendix I.

Charles Doe's 'Folio.'

The *Mercurius Reformatus* for June 11th, 1690 (Vol. II., No. 27), contained the following instructive as well as interesting advertisement:

"Mr. John Bunyan, Author of "The Pilgrim's Progress," and many other excellent Books, that have found great acceptance, hath left behind him Ten Manuscripts prepared by himself for the Press before his Death: His Widow is desired to print them (with some other of his Works, which have been already printed, but are at present not to be had), which will make together a book for 10s. in sheets, in Fol. All persons who desire so great and good a work should be performed with speed, are desired to send in 5s. for their first payment to Dorman Newman, at the King's Arms in the Poultrey, London: Who is empower'd to give receipts for the same."

This is the advertisement, no doubt, that caught the eye of Charles Doe, the Combmaker of the Borough, for it is to his enterprise that the Folio became fact. Why the publication was transferred from Newman (who brought out *The Holy War* and other works by Bunyan) to William Marshall, is not known. Doe in his circular, called *The Struggler* (1691), tells of his 'struggle' to bring out this collected edition of his late friend's writings.

"The 'Prospectus' of Charles Doe's Folio is not without interest. Some of the names are familiar, and those of others show the widespread esteem Bunyan enjoyed: "'The Labours of John Bunyan.' Subscription-Money to be paid to—Mr. John Strudwick, Grocer, at the Star at Holborn-bridge; Mr. Charles Dow, at the Boar's-Head in the Borrough in Southwark; Mr. Chandler, Minister, and Mr. William Nichols in Bedford; Mr. Edward Den of Cranfield; Nicholas Mayland of Gamlygay; Mr. Luke Astwood of Potton; Mr. Samuel Hensman of Bantery; Mr. James Collidge in Cambridge; Mr. Pack of Exeter; Mr. John Clark of Gilford; Mr. Masey of Harborough; Mr. William Hensman of Wellingborough; Mr. Sory of Lancashire; Mr. Chandler of Malborough; Mr. Grifeth and Mr. Pool in Lanviling. To the Churches of Brostol and Canterbury. . . . 'Bound in good Calves Leather, for Two Shillings a piece.'"

Doe procured Bunyan's unpublished manuscripts (as he says) from the widow and her son, John. These appeared in 1692—after Elizabeth Bunyan's death — together with some others already issued in smaller volumes. Objections were, however, raised by other publishers to the inclusion of Bunyan's greater works, so the companion Folio did not appear until the second edition, under the editorship of Chandler and Wilson, in 1736-1737. To Charles Doe bibliographists are greatly indebted for having collected, and arranged chronologically (but with certain errors pointed out by Dr. Brown) the 'Sixty Pieces' of John Bunyan.

APPENDIX II.

LANGUAGES AND DIALECTS INTO WHICH *THE PILGRIM'S PROGRESS* HAS BEEN TRANSLATED.

BRITISH ISLES.

Welsh. *Taith y Pererin.* Gan John Bunyan: London, 1688; Shrewsbury, 1699 [1761, 1770; Carmarthen, 1771]. Caerfyddin, 1771; Dinbych, 1854; Wrexham, 1861; Caernarvon, 1862; New York, 1880. [Also, New York, 186——.]

Gaelic *Cuairt an Oilthirick.* Dun-Eudainn, 1812. *Turus a' Chriosduidh.* Glasgow, 1869.

Irish. *Gluaiseachd an Oilithrigh.* Aistrithghe o Mbhearla Eoin Bhunian. Dublin, 1837.

[Dr. Ballinger, of the National Library of Wales, has in preparation a Bibliography of Celtic editions of Bunyan's works.]

NORTHERN EUROPE.

Dutch. *Eens Christens Reyse na de Eeuwigheyt.* Amsterdam, 1682 [1684, 1723, 1738]; Utrecht, 1684; Gröningen, 1740, 1747; S'Gravenhage, 1845; New York, 1851. [The Hague, 1845; The Cape, 1862.]

Danish. *En Pillegrims Fremgang.* Copenhagen, 1862. [New York, 1851, &c.]

Swedish. *En Christens Resa til den Saliga Ewighcten.* *Gotheborg,* 1743 (*Preface* signed Stockholm, 1726.) [New York (1854, 189—), 1884; Chicago, 1891; Stockholm, 1894.]

Norwegian. Peasant Dialect: *Pilegrimsferd or denne Verdi til den Komande.* Bergen, 1868. Literary Dialect: *Pilegrimens Vandring fra denne Verden til den tilkommende.* Bergen, 1874.

Icelandic. *För Pilagrimsins frá Pessum Heime til Hins O'Komna.* London, 1876.

Russian. [1811] Translated by J. D. Gassetzky. Imp. 8vo. With the illustrations of H. C. Selous, Priolo and Friston, St. Petersburg, 1881. [New York (*cir.* 1910.)]

Lithuanian. *Krikkezioniês Kelone i auq iszganytingaji Amzia.* Memel, 1878.

Esthonian. *Ristiinnimesse teekäiminne taewa liñna.* Riga, 1870.

Finnish. Place of publication and date uncertain.

Lettish. Place of publication and date uncertain.

CENTRAL AND EASTERN EUROPE.

German. *Eines Christen Reise nach der seligen Ewigkeit.* Amsterdam, 1703. [Hamburg, 1699, 1720, 1738-39.]

Eines Christen Reise nach der seligen Ewigkeit. In die Hochteutsche Sprache übersetzt. London, 1751. [U.S.A.—Ephrata, 1754; Germantown, 1796; Harrisburg, 1831; Atalanta (1898); New York (1840), (1850), (1878).]

Die Pilgerreise von John Bunyan. Hamburg, 1833, 1865; Güns, 1848; Bremen, 1870; Barmen and Stuttgart, 1864, [1899.] [Frankfort.]

Bohemian. *Testa Pautniku na horn Sion.* Dle Jána Bunyána. Pesth, 1871.

Polish. *Droga Pielgrzymuiacego Chrzescianina do Wiecznosci Blogoslawioney przez Jana Buniana.* Translated by X. Davida, Behra, 1728. Copy in the Bodleian, 1764.

Hungarian. *A Zarándok útja.* Bunyan Jánostól. Pest, 1867.

Servian. 1879.

Bulgarian. Constantinople, 1866.

SOUTHERN EUROPE.

French. *Voyage d'un Chrestien vers l'Eternité.* Amsterdam. Jean Boekholt (Walloons), 1685 [or, possibly earlier. *Vide* p. 467]; Bale, 1717; Rotterdam, 1722; Toulouse, 1788, 1878.
Le Pélerinage d'un nommé Chrétien: Tours, 1852. Appended with continuous pagination: Prières durant la Sainte Messe, Prières après la Sainte Messe et Antiennes à la Sainte Vierge. Other Editions: Publication de la Société de St. Victor: Paris, Lyon, Epernay, 1847. Paris, 1821, 1831, 1855; Rouen, 1821; Lyon, 1825; Valence, 1841; Plancy, 1847; [New York, 1849, 1853]; St. Denis, 1860; Jersey, 1818. "Pilgrim's Progress," in French and English. London, 1876.

Italian. *Il Pellegrinaggio del Christiano.* Printed secretly at Florence, 1851? Other editions: Genova, 1855; Firenze, 1863, 1892; New York, 1858.

Spanish. *El Viador bajo del simil de un sueño.* Por Juan Bunyan. London, 1865; New York, 1851 [1858, 1892].

Portugese. *Peregrinaçao* de hum Christao, ou Viagem para a cidade celeste. 1782. A Viagem do Christao. [*O peregrino, ou a Viagem*—Lisbon, 1883.]

Modern Greek. Translated by S. S. Bilsonos. Malta, 1824, 1831; Athens, 1854 [1877].

ASIA.

Hebrew. Translated by S. Hoga, London, 1844, 1851 [1891].

Arabic. Translated by C. F. Schlienz. Malta, 1834. [Beyrout.]

Armenian. American Mission. 1882.

Armeno-Turkish. For Armenians in S.W. Asia Minor, who speak Turkish, but read it only in Armenian character. Constantinople, 1881.

Greco-Turkish. Turkish, in Greek character for the use of Greeks in S.W. Asia Minor. Constantinople, 1879.

Modern Syriac. Translated by American missionaries at Oroomiah, 1848. In native binding, with Questions on the Work.

Persian. Part I.—Translated by J. L. Potter, Teheran.

Pashtu or Afghani. *Sair us Salikin.* Translated by Qázi Abdur Rahman, Khandári, and the Rev. T. J. L. Mayer of the C.M.S. Dedicated to His Highness the Amir of Cabul. Lahore, 1877. 4to.

Urdu or Hindustani. 1841. Panjab Religious Book Society. Lahore, 1847.

Roman Urdu. *Masihî Musáfir Ká Ahwál.* P.R.B.S. Lahore.

Persian Urdu.

Bengali. Serampore; Translated by Felix, son of Dr. Carey, 1821. Calcutta, 1854; Bhowanipore, 1877.

Uriya or Orissa. Translated by A. Sutton. Baptist Mission Press, Calcutta, 1838; Cuttack, Orissa, 1873. Revised by John Buckley.

Hindi. Benares: Translated from the Bengalee Version and compared with the English. [? 1885.]

Sindhi. Translated for the C.M.S.

Panjabi or Sikh Lodiana; American Mission Press, 1843.

Telugu. Madras: C.K.S. Press, Vepery, 1882.

Canarese. Lithographed Edition. A new Edition edited by the Rev. B. Rice from a Translation by G. Weigle and Dr. Moegling: Mangalore. German Mission Press, 1861. Part II. Wesleyan Mission, 1867.

Tamil. English and Tamil. Mission Offices, Vepery, 1793. 4to. A new translation by the Rev. S. Paul, C.M.S., Madras; Vepery, 1882. Fifth Edition, Madras. American Mission Press, 1848.

Santali. *Isai Jatri rea' Darau Kukmu Lekate hor Rorte.* Translated by F. G. Cole, assisted by Harma & Chaitan, native Santals. Calcutta, 1885 [1848].

Malayalam. Cottayam. Printed at the Church Mission Press, 1847. Revised by Dr. Murdoch, 1885.

Marathi-Balbodh. 4th Edition. Bombay: Tract and Book Society.

Gujarati. Translated by W. Raymond.

Sinhalese. Translated by the Rev. A. Hume. Colombo: Wesleyan Mission Press, 1826. Another Edition, with Notes. Colombo, 1867.

Assamese. Sibsagor, Assam. American Mission, 1856.

Khasi. *Ka Jingleit ka jong uba u Nongleit Rinblei.* Translator, Mrs. Lewis. [1877.]

Burmese. American Mission: Maulmain, 1841. Translated by Sarah B. Judson.

Sgau-Karen. Mission Press: Rangoon, 1863. Translated by J. Wade.

Dyak. *Palisang oloh Kristen Manintu lewn Sorga.* For the Dyaks of Borneo. Bandjermasin, 1879.

Malay. Translated by B. P. Keaseberry, Free Church Mission, 1854.

Japanese. Part I.—Translated by the Rev. W. J. White, Baptist Mission, and illustrated by Japanese artists: Tokio, 1887. [1889, 1895.]

Chinese. *Wenli* or *Classical style*: common to the whole empire. Translated by W. C. Burns. *Wenli* or *Classical style*: Translated by Thomas H. Hudson, Baptist Missionary, Ningpo, 1874.

Mandarin or *Court Dialect*. Translated by W. C. Burns. With Illustrations. Shanghai: American Presbyterian Mission, 1872.

Canton Vernacular. Two vols. With Chinese Illustrations. Translated by the Rev. G. Piercy, of the Wesleyan Mission, 1870-1.

Amoy Dialect. Romanised Colloquial. American Mission, 1865.

AFRICA.

Sechuana. *Loeto loa Mokreseti lo lo Coañ hatsiñ Yenn lo ea Latsiñ ye la tlaô.* Yohane Bunyan. Translated by Robert Moffat. Kuruman Mission Press, 1848. [1879.]

Kafir. *Uhambo lo Mhambi, owesuka Kwe lilizwe waye esinga Kwelo Lizayo.* Translated by Tiyo Sogo, Lovedale Mission Press, 1868.

Sesuto. *Leeto la Mokreste la go thloga fatseng la yuale go éa fnyella go le thla thla.* Printed for the Paris Evangelical Missionary Society, 1877. For Basuto Land, for the Bapeli and other tribes of the Transvaal.

Efik. *Inbuk Asaña Usuñ Heon.* Translated by Dr. Robb, of the U.P. Mission, Old Calabar. Part I., 1868; Part II., 1882.

Otyiherero. *Ouyenda ua Mukriste Kondunda ya Zion.* A language spoken by the Ovaherero and Ovambandern, S.W. Africa. Translated by H. Brincker. Berlin, 1873.

Tshi or Ashanti. *Kristoni Akwantee avase okristoni Kwan,* &c. For natives of Gold Coast, W. Africa. Translated by two natives of Akropong and revised by J. G. Christaller. Basel, printed for Evangelical Missionary Society, 1885.

Duala. For Baptist Missionary Society for the Cameroons.

Yoruba. *Ilo-siwaju ero-mimó lati aiyé yi si eyi ti mbo.* Translated by David Hinderer, a German Missionary of the C.M.S., for the several Yoruba tribes—Yoruba proper, Egba, Ijebu, Ijesa, Effon, Ondo—extending from Dahomey to the tribes on the west bank of the Niger.

ISLANDS OF THE PACIFIC.

Malagasy. *Ny Faudehanany mpivahiny*, &c., 1838. Fourth Edition: Antananarivo. London Mission Press, 1878. Another Edition, 1882. [1915.]

Raratongan. *Te Tere o Te Tintarere, mei Teianei*, &c. Raratonga: L. M. Press, 1846. Translated by A. Buzacott. [1892.]

Tahitian. *Te Tere o Pererina oia hoi o Keresitiano*, &c. O Buniana te Ioa. Translated by Charles Barff, L.M.S., London, 1847.

Maori. *He Moemoea. Otira ko nga korero*, &c. Na Hoani Paniana. Translated under the direction of the Government. Poneke, 1854.

Fijian. *Ai Tukutuku kei Vulagi-Lako.* Translated by Wm. Moore and Mrs. Churchill, and revised by James Calvert. Wesleyan Mission, 1867.

Hawaiian. *Ka Hele Malihini Ana Mai Keia*, &c. American Mission. Honolulu, 1842.

Aneityumese. *Intas va Natga u Kristian, par apan an pece Upene.* London, 1880. This is an abridged edition, and bound up with it there are (1) a First Catechism, (2) a Hymn Book, (3) List of the ordinal numbers, (4) Time of Sunrise and Sunset at Aneityum, (5) Assembly's Shorter Catechism. The book is unusually well printed and bound. The first edition was translated by Mrs. Geddie, and revised by Dr. Geddie; the second edition (1880) was revised by Dr. John Inglis, of the Free Church Mission.

AMERICAN.

Mexican. *El Progresso del Peregrino.* Y Traducido al Castellano por Santiago Pascoe. Ixtapan del Oro. Estado de Mexico, 1880. 4to.

Cree. For the Cree Indians. Translated by Archdeacon Vincent, 1886.

Dakotan. *Mahpiya Ekta oicimani ya.* Translated by S. R. Riggs, American Missionary. Oomahoo, 1858. [New York (1857), 1892.]

[Upon enquiry, Dr. William H. Matthews, of the American Tract Society, New York, says: "We now have *Pilgrim's Progress* in Russian, Italian, Rutherian, and Danish. We have plates for it in Hungarian, Spanish, Bohemian, Umbunda (Africa). As a part of the celebration of the three-hundredth anniversary of Bunyan's birth, we are hoping to increase this number of languages to twenty-five."]

ADDENDUM—Appendix II.

The Pilgrim's Progress has been issued by the Religious Tract Society, London, in all the languages enumerated by Dr. Brown and also in those which follow:

Breton (1886), Eskimo (1901), Norse, Slavonian, Czech or Bohemian, Slovak, Rumanian, Judæo-Spanish, Yiddish, Persian Urdú in Verse; Tulu, Malay, Nias, Siamese, Shanghai Colloquial, Hankow Colloquial, Ningpo Colloquial, Ningpo Romanised Colloquial, Swatow Romanised Colloquial, Formosan Colloquial for the Blind, Formosan Romanised, Hainanese, Korean, Ewé, Mbundu, Benga, Fanti, Gâ, or Accra, Galwa, Amharic, Kongo (1901), Bangi, Kele, Ganda, Tswa, Mongo-Nkundu,

Nyanja, Swahili, Mombasa, Tebele, Bemba, Ronga, Hausa, Ngala, Ngombe, Lunda, Samoan, Gilbertese, Cherokee (1844-45), Umtandu, Sumatra (1905).

In 1919 the Society reduced by careful revision the number of languages and dialects. " Allied dialects or editions which differ only in the character in which the version is printed, have been grouped under a single figure." The Religious Tract Society's reports give year by year the latest versions issued.

The Society for Promoting Christian Knowledge has issued *The Pilgrim's Progress* in two parts, in Luganda vernacular, part one being fully illustrated from photographs taken in Africa; and also in Swahili, and Dhuotuo (abridged), both being illustrated in African style.

APPENDIX III.

[The works here enumerated are selected from the vast amount of literature published on John Bunyan and his writings, and is in no way intended to be a complete bibliography.—Ed.]

POETICAL VERSIONS OF *THE PILGRIM'S PROGRESS.*

The Heavenly Passenger, or, The Pilgrim's Progress into verse, by S. M., Sur, 4to., 1687.

Pilgrim's Passage in Poesie. By Ager Scholae, A.M., 1698. 4to.

The Pilgrim's Progress done into Verse. By Francis Hoffman, 1706.

The Pilgrim's Progress rendered into Blank Verse. By J. S. Dodd, M.D., 1795.

Bunyan's Pilgrim's Progress Versified. By George Burder, 1804.

The Pilgrim's Progress (a broadsheet). Ten verses with rough woodcut. N.D.

The Pilgrim's Progress in sixty-nine verses, with six woodcuts. Printed by T. Bloomer, Birmingham.

Explained in Easy Verse. By B. Cave, 1812.

The Pilgrim's Progress rendered into familiar Verse. By Isaac James, 1815.

Poetic Sketches from Bunyan. By J. B. Drayton, 1821.

A Free Poetic Version of the First Part of the Pilgrim's Progress, in Ten Books. By J. B. Drayton, Cheltenham.

Collection of Hymns, founded on Bunyan. By Victor Purdy, 1823.

Original Hymns illustrative of the Pilgrim's Progress. By Thomas Smith, 1831.

Bunyan's Pilgrim's Progress Metrically Condensed. In six cantos. By T. Dibdin, 1834.

Illustrations of the Pilgrim's Progress with Sonnets. By Canon Townsend, 1840.

The Pilgrim's Progress versified after John Bunyan. By W. E. Hume, 1844.

Bunyan's Pilgrim's Progress converted into an Epic Poem. By C. C. V. G., Parsonstown, 1844.

The Pilgrim's Progress, in Verse. By Mrs. Eberle. New York, 1854.

Poetical Illustrations of that Immortal Work, the Pilgrim's Progress. By an Old Pilgrim, 1865.

Pilgrim Songs from Bunyan. By Lady Linton Foulis. Paisley, 1881.

Scenes from the Pilgrim's Progress. By R. B. Rutter. London: Trübner, 1882.

Rendered into Verse. By H. R., 1890.

In Verse. By G. Kathell, 1926.

EDITIONS OF *THE PILGRIM'S PROGRESS* FOR CHILDREN AND YOUNG PEOPLE.

Bunyan explained to a Child. By Isaac Taylor of Ongar, 1825.

The Pilgrim's Progress for the use of Children of the English Church. Edited by J. M. Neale, 1853.

The Pilgrim's Progress in 64mo.; a miniature abridgement, 1854.

The Story of the Pilgrim's Progress told for Young People, 1858.

Picture Cards: Illustrating the Pilgrim's Progress. R.T.S., 1859.

The Children's Pilgrim's Progress, with Sixteen Illustrations. By Edward Wehnert. London, 1860.

Christiana and her Children. Twelve Illustrations. R.T.S., 1860.

The Little Pilgrim, a small penny book. Birmingham, 1861.

The Child's Bunyan: the Pilgrim's Progress for the young. New York, 1864.

The Pilgrim's Progress, in Words of one Syllable. By M. Godolphin, 1869.

The Pilgrim's Progress, in Words of one Syllable. By S. P. Day, 1872.

Places passed by Pilgrims. By A. L. O. E. Twelve Tales illustrating the Pilgrim's Progress, 1869.

The Young Pilgrim: a Tale illustrative of the Pilgrim's Progress. By A. L. O. E., 1869.

The Pilgrim Children. With Coloured Plates, 1871.

The Pilgrim's Progress. Excelsior Toy Book. Seven Coloured Plates.

Words of Life. Picture Cards in Monotone. By M. Irwin. With passages from the Pilgrim's Progress, 1884.

The Pilgrim's Progress. A Story for Children. By H. L. Taylor, 2 vols., 1889-91.

The Pilgrim's Progress for the Little Ones. By E. A. Walker, 1900.

The Pilgrim's Progress Re-told for the Young. By David Davies, 1901.

The Pilgrim's Progress Told to Children. By M. Macgregor, 1905.

The Wonderful Journey. By Charles Brown, D.D., 1908.

Children on the King's Highway. By Charles Brown, 1909.

The Pilgrim's Progress for Little Folks. By A. G. Herbertson, 1909.

The Pilgrim's Progress in one Syllable. By F. Sherlock, 1909.

The Pilgrim's Progress: Stories from Great Writers. 1910.

The Pilgrim's Progress. By E. Elias, 1910.

The Pilgrim's Progress. Selected for Children. By Hodder Williams, 1911.

The Pilgrim's Progress for the Bairns. By W. T. Stead.

The Pilgrim's Progress for School Children. By J. Baldwin, 1913.

The Pilgrim's Progress for a Child. By H. G. Tunnicliffe, 1915.

The Pilgrim's Progress for Children. By J. M. Matthews, 1921.

The Pilgrim's Progress Told to Children (Macgregor) in Braille.

[Some of these are American publications.]

OTHER VERSIONS.

The Pilgrim's Progress. First Phonetic Edition. By Alex. J. Ellis, 1849.

The Pilgrim's Progress, in the Corresponding Style of Phonography, 1876.

The Pilgrim's Progress, for the Blind, in T. M. Lucas's Embossed Stenographic Characters. Published under the direction of the London Society for Teaching the Blind to Read. Edited by J. W. Gowring, B.A. Two vols., 4to. 1860.

The Pilgrim's Progress is also issued in Braille for the blind, in three vols.; also part one only, 2 vols. In the Moon Series, in five vols.

EDITIONS 'DE LUXE.'

W. Pickering: Exquisitely printed. 8vo. 1849.

Strahan and Co.: Japanese paper. Illustrated by F. Barnard and others. Bound in vellum. 1880.

Golden Treasury Series: Vignette on India paper by Holman Hunt. Large paper. 1891.

John C. Nimmo: Illustrated by W. Strang. 1895.

The Essex House Press: Elegantly printed. Bound in vellum. 1899.

C. Arthur Pearson: Illustrated by the Brothers Rhead. 1902.

Henry Frowde: Illustrated by George Cruikshank. 1903.

Religious Tract Society: Illustrated by H. Copping. 1903.

EXPLANATIONS OF *THE PILGRIM'S PROGRESS*.

A Key to the Pilgrim's Progress, in a Series of Letters. By Andronicus, 1790.

Lectures, illustrative of the Pilgrim's Progress, delivered at Haverfordwest. By Daniel Warr, 1825.

Lectures on the Pilgrim's Progress. By W. Gurney, M.A., Rector of St. Clement Danes, 1833.

Cottage Lectures, or the Pilgrim's Progress practically explained. By C. Overton, Vicar of Cottingham, 1848.

A Short Exposition of the Pilgrim's Progress. By W. J., 1857.

The Pilgrim's Progress, with Expository Lectures. By R. Maguire, 1859.

Lectures on the Pilgrim's Progress. By G. B. Cheever, New York, 1844.

A Key to the Pilgrim's Progress. By E. Davies, 1861.

Evenings with John Bunyan, or the Dream interpreted. By J. Large, 1861.

A Description of the Man in the Iron Cage. By W. Odling, of Foot's Cray, 1862.

The Christian Life: An Exposition of Bunyan's Pilgrim's Progress. By James Black, D.D. Two vols., 1873.

Personal Experience: being Lectures on Bunyan's Pilgrim's Progress. By W. Haslam, M.A., 1877.

Full Salvation as seen in Bunyan's Pilgrim's Progress. By W. Haslam, M.A., 1884.

Twenty Plain Lectures on the Pilgrim's Progress. By Robert Nourse, Springfield, Illinois, 1878.

A Humble Companion to the Pilgrim's Progress: being a series of Discourses on that great Allegory. By S. Burn. Huddersfield, 1884.

The People of the Pilgrimage: An Expository Study of the Pilgrim's Progress as a Book of Character. By J. A. Kerr Bain, 1887.

Half-hours with Bunyan's Pilgrim's Progress. By John Burbidge, 1893.

Bunyan Characters. By Alexander Whyte, 1893.

Aids to the Devout Life (The Pilgrim's Progress). By John Brown, D.D., 1898.

Bunyan's Country: Studies in the Topography of The Pilgrim's Progress. By A. J. Foster, M.A., 1901.

Pictures from Pilgrim's Progress (In the Sword and Trowel). By C. H. Spurgeon, 1902-3.

The Road: A Study of John Bunyan's Pilgrim's Progress. By John Kelman, D.D., 1911.

Stevenson's Text Book of The Pilgrim's Progress.

BIOGRAPHIES, LECTURES, &c.

To the Memory of that Eminent Preacher. [John Bunyan.] An Elegy. Folio. Published by Nat. Ponder, 1688.

Autobiography. Grace Abounding to the Chief of Sinners, 1666, and Continuation, 1692.

Life and Actions of John Bunyan, 1692.

Life of John Bunyan, 1700.

A Relation of the Imprisonment of Mr. John Bunyan, 1765.

The Life of John Bunyan. By a Friend of the Gospel, 1787.

The Political Sentiments of John Bunyan. Republished by John Martin, 1798.

A Life of Mr. John Bunyan. By Joseph Ivimey, 1815.

A Life of John Bunyan. By Robert Southey, LL.D., 1830.

Articles on Southey's Life of Bunyan—(1) Sir Walter Scott, "Quarterly Review," October, 1830; (2) by T. B. Macaulay, "Edinburgh Review," December, 1830.

The Life, Times and Characteristics of John Bunyan. By Robert Philip, 1839.

The Bedfordshire Tinker. By G. E. Sargent, 1848.

Life of Bunyan. By James Hamilton, D.D. Works of Puritan Divines, 1845, and Our Christian Classics, 1856.

A Brief History of Bunyan's Church. By John Jukes, 1849.

John Bunyan: a Biographical Lecture. By C. M. Birrell, 1853.

John Bunyan: a Lecture. By W. M. Punshon, 1857.

Life Studies. John Bunyan. By J. Baillie, 1857.

English Puritanism. John Bunyan. By John Tulloch, D.D., 1861.

John Bunyan. A Biography. By Lord Macaulay, 1853. [Also in Braille.]

Life of John Bunyan. By George Offor, 1862.

Bunyaniana. A series of Papers by W. Blower. Bedford, 1867.

Bunyan, his Character, Genius, and Influence. By W. H. Ibberson, 1871.

Life of John Bunyan. By D. A. Harsha, M.A. Philadelphia, 1871.

Johann Bunyan, ein Lebensbild von Dr. A. Immer, Professor der Theologie in Bern. Basel, 1871.

The Book of the Bunyan Festival. Edited by W. H. Wylie, 1874.

The Hero of Elstow. By James Copner, M.A., Vicar of Elstow, 1874.

Who was the Author of the Pilgrim's Progress? By W. Winters, 1874.

The Literary Genius of Bunyan. A Lecture. By G. J. Holyoake, 1874.

Saggi Critici, di Bonaventura Zumbini—Il Viaggio del Pellegrino, di Giovanni Bunyan. Naples, 1876.

The Pilgrim's Progress. By Dean Howson. St. James' Lectures. Second Series: Companions for the Devout Life, 1876.

The Bunyan Doors and their Associations. A Lecture by John Stoughton, D.D. Delivered at the Celebration Service at Bunyan Meeting, July 5, 1876.

Mary Bunyan, the Dreamer's Blind Daughter. A Tale. By Sallie Rochester Ford. [St. Louis, U.S.A.] N.D.

Bunyan's Pilgrim's Progress and Intoxicating Liquors. Boston, U.S.A., 1877.

John Bunyan. An Autobiography. With Illustrations by E. N. Downard, engraved by Edward Whymper. Religious Tract Society. N.D.

Ned Bratts [a Dramatic Idyl of Bedford Jail in Bunyan's time]. By Robert Browning. Dramatic Idyls, First Series, 1879.

English Men of Letters—Bunyan. By J. A. Froude, 1880. [Also in Braille]

The Literary Charm of the Pilgrim's Progress. By David Sime, M.D., 1880.

Personal Relics and Recent Memorials of John Bunyan: a Paper read at the Meeting of the Royal Archæological Institute in 1881. By John Brown, B.A.

The Home of John Bunyan at Elstow. By Canon Venables, "Saturday Review," Sept. 17, 1881.

John Bunyan. A Visit to Bedford and Elstow. By W. Graham, D.D., 1873.

Was John Bunyan a Gipsy? By James Simson, New York, 1882.

The Evangelical Succession Lectures, 1883. Bunyan. By W. R. Nicoll, M.A.

Baptist Worthies, No. 3. John Bunyan. By William Landels, D.D., 1883.

John Bunyan—Esquisse Biographique et Littéraire. Par J. Alfred Porret, Pasteur à Lausaune. Lausaune, 1884.

John Bunyan et ses derniers Critiques. Par M. Marc-Monnier, "Bibliothèque Universelle," Decembre, 1885.

John Bunyan. A Memoir. By James Copner, M.A., Vicar of Elstow, 1885.

The Appeal to Man's Soul. A Sermon preached in Elstow Parish Church at the Dedication of the Bunyan Memorial Window, Sept. 20th, 1885. By Paul W. Wyatt, M.A.

Biographical Lectures. By George Dawson, M.A. Bunyan, 1885.

Since the last entry of Dr. Brown's there have been innumerable biographies, &c., of Bunyan published: too many for the limited space of this volume. The outstanding ones are as follow:

John Bunyan: His Life, Times, and Works. By John Brown, D.D., 1885 to 1888.

John Bunyan: His Life, Times and Works. By John Brown, D.D. (abridged). 2 Vols., 1902.

John Bunyan. By E. Venables, 1888.

John Bunyan's Home. By John Brown, D.D., 1890.

John Bunyan. By F. W. Farrar, D.D., 1898.

John Bunyan. By the Author of Mark Rutherford (W. H. White), 1905. [Also, Last Pages from a Journal. Reference to The Pilgrim's Progress, 1915.]

John Bunyan. By John Brown, D.D. (Camb.Hist.Eng.Lit., Vol. 7), 1911.

John Bunyan. By Sir C. H. Firth, LL.D. (The English Association Leaflet, No. 19), 1911.

John Bunyan as a Man of Letters. By Clifford K. Wright, 1916.

John Bunyan: a Sketch of His Life. By T. Dunlop, 1917.

The Pilgrim's Progress: a Lecture delivered at the Royal Institution of Great Britain, by J. W. Mackail, 1924.

John Bunyan. By Gwilym O. Griffith, 1927.

John Bunyan. A Commentary and Questionnaire. By F. W. Robinson, M.A., 1927.

John Bunyan. By the Dean of Winchester (in the press), 1928.

APPENDIX IV.

PERSONAL RELICS OF BUNYAN.

I. In the custody of the Trustees of Bunyan Meeting, Bedford, are preserved:

(1) The **Church Book,** containing entries in Bunyan's handwriting.

(2) **Bunyan's Will,** or Deed of Gift, signed by him. [Vide p. 338.]

(3) **Bunyan's Cabinet and Staff**, formerly in the possession of his great-granddaughter, Mrs. Bithrey of Carlton, and acquired by the Trustees of Bunyan Meeting through the widow and family of the Rev. C. Vorley. [Vide p. 368.]

(4) **Bunyan's Jug.**[1] Presented to the Trustees by Mrs. Poore, daughter of the Rev. S. Hillyard of Bedford.

(5) A valuable collection of copies of early and later editions and foreign versions of "The Pilgrim's Progress," and other works by Bunyan.

[(6)] The old **Door** from Elstow Church—through which Bunyan would have passed, was recently transferred to the Trustees of the Bunyan Meeting, and is now in the Museum.

II. At Bunyan Meeting, Bedford, is kept **Bunyan's Chair,**[2] which has been handed on in the vestry from his own times. There is also an interesting relic of Bedford county gaol; this is a **Door** with iron cross-bars in the centre, and made of three layers of oak laid transversely, fastened to gether by iron bolts. It was purchased with other materials at the taking down of the gaol, in 1801, by Mr. Wm. Berrill of Bedford, and after being used for many years as the door of a building on the Fenlake Road, was presented to the Trustees by Mr. T. Gwyn E. Elger, J.P. It was always traditionally spoken of as the door of Bunyan's cell, but was more probably the door of the common day-room of the prisoners. The lintel, posts, and sill also are part of the original doorway.

[When enlarging the premises in 1832—5, comprising the brewery in Lurke Street, Bedford, Nathaniel Small, the original owner, bought various fittings, beams, rafters, and joists which once belonged to the County Gaol, where Bunyan was imprisoned from 1660 to 1672. These portions of the building have been lost sight of, but two **Prison Doors** are still there, "one of which," says Mr. F. C. Fuller, in a communication to the Editor, "is believed to be that of the actual cell in which Bunyan was imprisoned, and the other existed in the outer wall of the prison. It is fitted with an iron grid through which prisoners put their hands to beg of passers-by, as explained to me in 1884 by the late Dr. Brown personally. I have been given to understand that the plan of the prison was a corridor with cells on either side."]

III. **Bunyan's copy,** in three volumes, folio, of Foxe's "Book of Martyrs." [Vide p. 154] at one time the property of the Literary and Scientific Institute, Bedford, is now in the Pierpoint Morgan Library, New York.

[1] In which soup was sent by Elizabeth Bunyan to her husband in the County Gaol.
[2] Of this chair it has been said, "No relic in all Britain has been to me so sacred."

IV. In the Record Office, Fetter Lane, London, in a bundle of papers belonging to the year 1672, is the application, in **Bunyan's handwriting,** for licences to preach, described on p. 217.

V. The **Warrant for Bunyan's Arrest in 1675,** which is described on page 267 of this edition, was formerly in the possession of Mr. W. G. Thorpe, F.S.A., of the Middle Temple, London. It is now in the Pierpoint Morgan Library, New York.

VI. The "**Letter from the People of Bedfordshire** to the Lord General Cromwell and the Council of the Army" (p. 95) bearing the signature 'John Bunyan.' This document is owned by the Society of Antiquaries, London. [Vide Addendum.]

ADDENDA—Appendix IV.

Other Articles Claimed to be Relics of Bunyan.
(Not Mentioned in Previous Editions of this Book.)

An important relic, discovered in recent years, is an **Anvil** on which is rudely cut 'J. BVNYAN H ELSTOWE 1647.' The name Elstow spelt as 'Helstow,' is not easily accounted for. That the aspirate long ago formed the initial letter for place-names is undoubted. Arundel, in Sussex, was once Harundel, Helegh became Elegh, Hersham Ersham. etc. But, so far, there has been found no deed or other document in which the name Elstow occurs with the aspirate, except when, as it is known to have been written, or spoken of, as Helenstowe or Helvestowe. There seems to be no reason why the place-name was not pronounced 'Helstow,' and Bunyan, when he returned to his village from his soldiering in Newport Pagnell, admits that he had lost that little bit of learning he had once acquired. The relic is what is known as a "stake" or brazier's anvil, and has a spear-point to hold it firm in a wooden or metal base. It was discovered by Mr. John Beagarie, of Hitchin. It is without doubt of the seventeenth-century, and confirms the date when Bunyan resumed his trade after military service.

A pair of **Candlesticks,** belonging to a lady in the South of England, is said to have come from a Bunyan pulpit.

John Bunyan's **Pew Door.**—"At a sale of a collection of curios at Battle (Sussex) yesterday an old oak door, stated to be from John Bunyan's pew, at Elstow Church, was bought by Mr. Rochelle Thomas for two guineas."—"The Morning Post," Oct. 25, 1923.

The Editor possesses a "Model of **John Bunyan's Pulpit,** carved out of a piece of the real pulpit, by the Rev. R. Philip." So reads the inscription. The model is four inches high, and the base is three inches square, on the underside of which is written: "Part of John Bunyan's Pulpit. Model of Pulpit. Maberley." It is cleverly executed by Robert Philip, the enthusiastic admirer and sympathetic biographer of Bunyan. "Maberley Chapel," says the Rev. William Pearce, M.A., of Memorial Hall, London, was "situated in Kingsland Balls Pond Road, and was founded in 1825 by Robert Philip. In 1893 the property was sold . . ." From which of Bunyan's pulpits Philip made the model it is now difficult to say, unless his own words in the biography of 1839 (p. 583) are the explanation. Philip remarks: "What I value most in my little Museum, is a piece of Bunyan's original Pulpit. . . ."

In his "Life of Bunyan" Robert Philip mentions other relics which have long since been lost sight of—a small **Table** made from the remains of the original pulpit; "**Bunyan's Cup,**"[1] "of exquisite workmanship," and from the splendour of its colours, and the chasteness of its form and ornaments, seems to have been of foreign manufacture; and, adds

[1] It seems possible that Philip may here refer to the Jug (*vide* p. 487) now in the Bunyan Meeting Collection at Bedford.

Philip, "Tradition says, that Bunyan's broth was brought to chapel in it, for his Sunday's dinner in the vestry."[1]

The **Communion Table** of Bunyan's time was subsequently divided, and one-half is now used in the Committee Room of the Bunyan Meeting at Bedford. "The old table," says Philip, "is an extraordinary piece of furniture, which for size and strength might have been the banquet-table of a baronial hall."

Philip searched diligently though unsuccessfully, but yet with hope, for "some of Bunyan's private Letters." Charles Doe says that they were 'many.' Bunyan's correspondence must have been considerable, and the Editor would say with Philip, "I shall not, therefore, believe soon, that they are all lost. Let others, however, help me in my researches." Perchance, in New England, as well as in the Old Country, some of these priceless treasures may one day be discovered. Two lines (only) of Bunyan's writing are preserved in the Rylands Library, Manchester.

A **Bible,** from which Bunyan is said to have preached, was sold in London in 1814 and bought by Mr. Whitbread.

The **Gold Ring,** with 'I. B.' engraved upon it, was found when the Bridge-prison was demolished, and was afterwards the property of Dr. Bowers, Dean of Manchester.

A **Bible,** printed at Cambridge, 1637, having written on the title-page of the New Testament, 'John Bunyan,' is in the Library at Harvard University, U.S.A.

A **Bible,** with silver corners and clasps, published by John Field, 1653, 12°, and probably once possessed by Bunyan, was sold by auction in London, in 1909. It has engraved on a silver plaque, 'Martha Wethered, 1692.' She was the daughter of G. W. Wethered, of Bedford, who helped Bunyan's family when he was in prison. The Bible is said to have been given to Martha Wethered by John Bunyan's widow.

Bunyan Pulpits and Chairs.

A piece of the **Pulpit,** from which Bunyan preached at Bedford, is inserted in the book-rest of the rostrum in the Independent Chapel at Newport Pagnell. On a brass-plate is inscribed William Cowper's much-discussed couplet—

> "Revere the man whose Pilgrim marks the road,
> And guides the Progress of the soul to God."

The Rev. William Bull, minister at the chapel, was a personal friend of the Olney poet.

"Bunyan's Dell," at Preston, near Hitchin, is a natural amphitheatre where the Tinker preached to vast assemblies—at midnight. Near by is a cottage where, in the inglenook, is what is traditionally known as **"Bunyan's Seat."**

At Beachwood Green, in the schoolroom, is a **Pulpit** claimed to have been used by Bunyan; and beyond, at Tinker's Hall, was a tree beneath which he is said to have worked at his trade.

Near Lambeth Palace, London, an old building (afterwards a coffee-tavern) once contained a pulpit of Bunyan fame.

In a chapel in Jewin Street, London—afterwards the schoolroom of Falcon Square Church, was a pulpit used by Bunyan. It has now disappeared.

In the Chapel at Houghton Regis is also a **Bunyan Chair.**

In Park Street Baptist Church at Luton is a vestry chair, known as **Bunyan's Chair.**

[1] It was a custom amongst some ministers to remain in their chapels in order to be "kept in the Spirit" on the Lord's Day.

There is a treasured relic at Tilehouse Street Chapel, Hitchin: a **Chair** which is said to have been given by Bunyan to his friend, John Wilson, the minister. In his declining days Wilson preached seated in this chair.

ITEMS OF INTEREST IN CONNECTION WITH JOHN BUNYAN.

WAS JOHN BUNYAN A GIPSY?

For the sake of completeness, rather than of importance, mention is made of the statements put forward by advocates—including Sir Walter Scott—that Bunyan was of Gipsy origin.

Dr. Brown evidently did not accept the views of these writers, but those who desire to pursue the study may be referred to the books by James Simson, "The Gipsies as illustrated by John Bunyan" (New York, 1883); "John Bunyan and the Gipsies" (New York, 1882 and 1890); "Was John Bunyan a Gipsy?" discussed in the London "Daily News," etc. (New York, 1882). Not in America only, but also in England the theory has occasionally been promulgated, as well as the claim that Bunyan was of Welsh extraction; but the fact that his family can be traced back in Bedfordshire for some four hundred years makes speculation on these lines unnecessary.

BUNYAN AT OXFORD.

The Rev. C. W. Boase, in his "Oxford" (Historic Town Series, 2nd ed., 1887, published by Longmans), says: "The growth of Puritan feeling in the city of Oxford is shown by the formation of the first Baptist Society, under Vavasour Powell, of Jesus College, in 1618. He made many converts in Wales, and in 1657 we hear of John Bunyan accompanying him to Oxford." Unfortunately, Boase gives credit to Powell, in the first place, for having established the Baptist community in Oxford when he was but one year old; and, secondly, as being a student at the University—of which no record can be found. That Powell knew Bunyan is possible, for they both were intimate with John Owen, at one time the Vice-Chancellor of Oxford University; and Powell's "Concordance to the Holy Bible," a copy of which Bunyan not only possessed[1] but also inscribed his name in, was "Recommended to the studious Christian by John Owen, D.D." Undoubtedly Powell delivered, as Anthony Wood states, a "characteristic diatribe at All Hallows" on the fifteenth of July, 1657. In a privately printed pamphlet (1875), "Earlier and Later Nonconformity in Oxford, the author, James J. Moore, says: "John Bunyan was intimate with Vavasour Powell, whom he accompanied to Oxford in 1657. . . . Bunyan's first visit to Oxford. But it was not his last. In subsequent years he passed through the city on his way to Reading, where he was in the habit of preaching."

The Editor has made close and personal enquiry at Oxford, and elsewhere, endeavouring to confirm these traditions, but without success. The statements are given, however, not for their value as information, but as an incentive to others to pursue the investigation.

MEMORIALS OF BUNYAN.

Westminster Abbey.

In the west side of the north transept is a **Window** to the memory of John Bunyan designed by J. N. Comper, the subject being the first part of 'The Pilgrim's Progress.' It was placed there in the year 1912, and

[1] Bunyan's copy is in the Library of the Baptist College, Bristol. *Vide,* also—*Vavasour Powell*—By David Davies, 1896.

largely through the influence of the late Rev. John Clifford, C.H., D.D., who, at its unveiling, and at the time it was handed over to the Dean and Chapter, said at the dedicatory ceremony: "This window is not only a valuable addition to the art which enriches and distinguishes this temple of fame, it also commemorates one of the most powerful books written by one of the greatest saints. But chiefly this work is a memorial of one of the saints who through 'Grace abounding to the chief of Sinners' still continues his ministry to man, and will from this spot witness to the vital truths of the Gospel to the fundamental facts of Christian experience, and to the growing catholicity of Christian men all over the world."[1]

Southwark Cathedral.

"The Children of the Church delighting in the Great Allegory, 'The Pilgrim's Progress,' dedicate this **Window** in memory of its pious Author." Such is its simple but expressive inscription. The design was carried out by Mr. Kemp, and the memorial window was placed in the Cathedral in 1900, at the instigation of the late Canon Rhodes Bristow, whose lectures had attracted so many of the young people of Southwark, and by their donations the cost was defrayed.

Elstow Church.

Two **Windows,** one depicting scenes from "The Pilgrim's Progress," and the other from "The Holy War," were put in at the east end of the north and south aisles, when the Church was restored in 1880.

In Nelson's "Works of the Puritan Divines" (Vol. ii., 1845), is an engraved frontispiece of a "Design for a Monument to Bunyan." There is no mention of a site, and, obviously, the proposal never materialized.

On page 11 of the Preface to "The Riches of Bunyan," issued by the American Tract Society, in 1851, it is stated that: "When the English Houses of Parliament were recently rebuilt, among the imagery commemorative of the nation's literary glories, a place was voted for the bust of the Bedford pastor [John Bunyan], one so maligned and persecuted." Investigation in 1926, however, elicited the following reply from Mr. J. C. B. Wilson, of the Works Department of the Houses of Parliament: "I suspect, as with so many other projects in regard to the decoration of the building from 1850-60, including the various exhibitions of mural paintings, etc., which were never used, the proposal as regards Bunyan's memorialization never reached the stage of realization and remained only a suggestion."

"In 1860 a movement was set afoot to erect by a shilling subscription a memorial statue of John Bunyan, from the design of Mr. Papworth, in Trafalgar Square." (F. C. Papworth designed the tomb at Bunhill Fields.)

BUNYAN'S "FELLOWS."

An interesting study might be made of the friends of, and those in fellowship with, John Bunyan. Space forbids here, save to mention briefly some of those tradesmen who issued "tokens."[2]

Hugh Holton, a Brazier at Bedford, is said to have befriended Bunyan whilst he was in the county gaol. Holton's token, "His Half Peny," is dated 1666. Nothing is recorded of his religious convictions.

[1] *Life of John Clifford.* By Sir James Marchant.

[2] A hundred and twenty-six Bedfordshire tokens have been recorded. *Vide*: G. C. Williamson's *Trade Tokens of the Seventeenth Century,* 1889.

ROBERT HOLDSTOCK, whose "Half Peny" token has no emblem to notify his trade, resided at Elstow. He joined the Church at Bedford after Bunyan's conversion. Holdstock's name appears in the Church Books of Bedford and Hitchin.

JOHN CLARKE, landlord of the Cross Keys Inn at Bedford, came from a greatly respected family living at Sandy. His son, Robert, was baptized in 1662. The Clarkes were councillors, but never mayors of Bedford. John Clarke, whose token bears no date, may be the one mentioned in the Church Book at Bedford (p. 212).

The Rev. C. F. Farrar, in "Old Bedford" (1926), refers to the omission by biographers as to where John and Elizabeth Bunyan did their shopping! Mr. Farrar quaintly adds: "Creed and shopping have ever gone hand in hand."

MEMORABLE COPIES OF 'THE PILGRIM'S PROGRESS.'

When Dean Farrar said: "More to humanity is a page of the Bedford Tinker's writings than all the banks of the Rothschilds," he spoke a great truth in regard to their spiritual value, and, unwittingly, too, of their market value; for, in July, 1926, a copy of the first edition of 'The Pilgrim's Progress' (1678) when offered at a London auction room brought the phenomenal bid of £6,800, or, nearly sixty pounds per leaf; and, although the offer was afterwards withdrawn on a technical point, the little 'eighteen-penny' book was privately purchased, and is now in the library of Sir R. Leicester Harmsworth, Bart. It is known as the 'Warner' copy, is in excellent preservation, and has its original binding.

In 1923, a defective copy of the first edition (1678) of 'The Pilgrim's Progress' was sold by auction in London for £500. It had originally belonged to Thomas Marsom, one of John Bunyan's fellow prisoners.

Another copy of 'The Pilgrim's Progress' of outstanding interest, although imperfect, is that which has written on its fly-leaf: "This portion of 'The Pilgrim's Progress' was presented by Bunyan himself to his friend Mr. [John] Wilson of Hitchin in Bedfordshire (sic); and it was presented to me by a descendant of the Wilson family, as the best way of preserving it. Robert Philip, Maberly Cottage, Dalston. Feby. 19th, 1848." (Robert Philip was born in 1791, and died in 1858.) This 'John Wilson' copy is in the possession of Sir Leicester Harmsworth, Bart.

'TWO OTHER JOHN BUNYANS.'

In the Memoir to the Elstow Edition of 'The Pilgrim's Progress' (London: John Walker and Co., 1881), the writer says: "Though Elstow is generally credited with the honour of being Bunyan's birthplace, there are two rival claims set up by the villages of Harrowden and Chalgrave. . . . Chalgrave establishes a more formidable claim . . . and to Mr. Cary-Elwes, F.S.A., belongs the credit of first searching its parish registers, through his having become possessed of a parchment deed between Robert Bonyon, yoman, and one, Thomas Andrews, both of that parish. Mr. Cary-Elwes traces the descent thus: William Bonyon, living in the parish, had three children. . . . Robert Bonyon, buried in 1615, was father to nine children. . . . The seventh child was William, baptized April 4, 1585, who had issue . . . **John**, baptized June 17, 1626. . . . This John is supposed to be the author of 'The Pilgrim's Progress' . . ." This quotation is given by the Editor, not in any way to throw suspicion upon the Elstow claim, which is undoubtedly established, but rather to suggest that the Chalgrave 'John Bunyan' may be the one whose signature stands second among those attributed to the Dreamer. The writing is that of a man who had received a better education than that which the son of Thomas Bunyan, the tinker of Elstow, could possibly have had (Vide Addendum—Chapter VI.)

Bunyan has been the subject of Broadcasting in Great Britain on several occasions. From Glasgow, in 1924, excerpts from *The Pilgrim's Progress* were given by Mr. Percival Steed, B.A., and a biographical sketch by Mr. Rosslyn Mitchell; from London, in 1925, *The Pilgrim's Progress*—in altered form—as a miracle-play, with music by Dr. Edgar Stillman Kelley. There was a more recent Talk on Bunyan's Allegory by Professor George Gordon.

ERRATA:

Page 187, read '*Vide* Appendix iv., p. 491.'
,, 219, line 20, read '**Paul, D'Anvers,**' etc.
,, 223, f.n., line 4, for 'mulilated' read 'mutilated.'
,, 249, line 21, read 'John Bunyan.'
,, 275, line 7, read '*Chemin de Vaillance.*'
,, 336, line 5, for 'who' read 'whom.'
,, 364, line 27, for 'hings' read 'hinges.'
,, 367, m.n., for '*Vide* Chap. xvi.' read '*Vide* p. 378.'
,, 462, m.n., read '*Vide* p. 357.'
,, 470, line 15, read '*Vide* p. 161.'
,, 471, line 34, read '*Vide* p. 228.'

INDEX

[The Editor has added very considerably to Dr. Brown's Index, and has included many names of those who formed "THE CHURCH AT BEDFORD." These are marked by an asterisk (*). The publishers of the early editions of John Bunyan's books are indicated by the sign (†). The titles of his works are printed in capitals, with (?) when the authorship is doubted.]

THE HULBERT PUBLISHING CO. LTD.
LONDON: 7 Paternoster Row.
GLASGOW: 130 Renfield Street.
BIRMINGHAM: 95 Snow Hill.